This Is My Life

Genreflecting Advisory Series

Diana Tixier Herald, Series Editor

This Is My Life

A Guide to Realistic Fiction for Teens

Rachel L. Wadham

Genreflecting Advisory Series

Diana Tixier Herald, Series Editor

LIBRARIES UNLIMITED

AN IMPRINT OF ABC-CLIO, LLC
Santa Barbara, California • Denver, Colorado • Oxford, England

Library of Congress Cataloging-in-Publication Data

Wadham, Rachel, 1973-
   This is my life : a guide to realistic fiction for teens / Rachel L. Wadham.
      p. cm. — (Genreflecting advisory series)
   Includes bibliographical references and indexes.
   ISBN 978-1-59158-942-6 (acid-free paper) 1. Young adult fiction, American—Bibliography. 2. Young adult fiction, American—Stories, plots, etc. 3. Teenagers—Fiction—Bibliography. 4. Teenagers—Juvenile fiction—Bibliography. 5. Social problems—Fiction—Bibliography. 6. Social problems—Juvenile fiction—Bibliography. 7. Children's stories, American—Bibliography. 8. Children's stories, American—Stories, plots, etc. 9. Teenagers—Books and reading—United States. I. Title.
Z1231.F4W319 2010
[PS374.Y57]
016.813.009'9283—dc22   2010024074

ISBN: 978-1-59158-942-6

14 13 12 11 10 1 2 3 4 5

This book is also available on the World Wide Web as an eBook.
Visit www.abc-clio.com for details.

Libraries Unlimited
An Imprint of ABC-CLIO, LLC

ABC-CLIO, LLC
130 Cremona Drive, P.O. Box 1911
Santa Barbara, California 93116-1911

This book is printed on acid-free paper ∞
Manufactured in the United States of America

Contents

Part II: Teen Issues

Part III: Teen Life at the Extremes

Acknowledgments

Many expressions of thanks and acknowledgments for assistance are important, for works of this type are almost always a team effort.

First, my sincere appreciation goes to my student Melissa who spent many long hours gathering information and then formatting that information in the correct style. Melissa accomplished her tasks with great speed, and she always did it with a smile. Her service was invaluable to making the work what it is.

Second, my overwhelming thanks goes to Sherry for her support and watchful care as this work was completed. Her services reading the work to make sure my drafts had all the right commas and used the right verb tense, as well as her ability to stand by during times of crisis, made this work better than anything I could have done alone.

Additionally, I would like to thank both my libraries, the Harold B. Lee Library and the Provo City Library, and their outstanding librarians for providing all the resources for me to access the data and books necessary for me to make this the best work possible.

For all the other family, colleagues, and friends who gave their support and helped to cheer me on during the writing of this work, I offer my sincere thanks.

Lastly, I offer thanks to the staff and editors at Libraries Unlimited who took my dream of a book of this type and helped to make it a reality.

Introduction

Every day adolescents ask themselves a variety of questions: "Who am I?" "Who do I want to be?" "Where do I fit in the world?" and "What do I want to be as an adult?" Working toward the answers to each of these questions leads adolescents through the major developmental tasks that help them build their individual identity. Fulfilling these tasks is important for teens so that they can figure out who they are and what they stand for and to provide structure and direction in planning for the future. During adolescence, youth move through the developmental changes required of them by extracting information from a variety of sources including parents, teachers, peers, and often books. Books in particular have a unique ability to allow readers to vicariously experience and learn from situations that they may or may not experience in real life. Through the experience of reading, adolescents are able to gain necessary understanding that can help them to formulate their sense of identity as they work to discover their own place in society.

Although all reading can provide teens with exciting experiences that help them learn and grow, realistic fiction, in particular its subgenre of problem novels, provides teens with just the right formula to explore the problems and issues that they face. Scholar Maria Tatar (2009) notes that children and adolescents use stories as road maps for navigating the real world. This is especially true for young adults, who are very responsive to the world they inhabit and desire to read books that map out the issues that are relevant to their own individual experiences and concerns. This book serves as its own road map for librarians, teachers, and other professionals who work to guide teens though life by introducing them to books that talk about real-life problems and issues. This guide stands as an introduction to the numerous issues covered in modern books that are part of the genre of realistic problem novels.

Defining Realistic Problem Fiction

One important subgenre of realistic fiction is the problem novel. Although all realistic fiction may deal with problems, this subgenre presents a more candid realism by dealing with a variety of social and personal issues. In particular, young adult problem novels tend to focus on the contemporary issues that adolescents face as they move toward adulthood. Problem novels address such fundamental issues as love, family relationships, drugs, suicide, sex, crime, death, violence, and peer pressure. The integral elements of the problem novel are the thematic issues surrounding a problem faced by the book's characters and the plot elements that allow the characters to resolve those problems. Although the problem novel is one of the most often published subgenres of realistic fiction, it is not without its detractors. There are some critics such as Egoff (1981) who see the problem novel as formulaic and most often poorly written and others such as Feinberg (2005) who see them as often overtly sad and depressing. However, Egoff and Feinberg also show that there are finely written examples of the genre. The focus of this book is on those best examples of this genre, and it covers a wide range of modern problem novels that are appropriate for contemporary teens. As with any genre, practitioners who work with youth should never assume that problem novels have an appeal for every adolescent. However, the fact remains that the problem novel has great potential to make strong connections with an individual reader's needs.

The Appeal of Realistic Fiction

The elusive connection that is made between a good book and its reader is difficult if not impossible to articulate. However, when professionals consider the circumstances that will help a reader connect with a book, it is of foremost importance to consider the needs of the reader. Of all a reader's requirements, one of the most pertinent is developmental need. Most adolescents find reading connections with books where the protagonists are encountering the same developmental tasks they are.

Although adolescence can be defined from a variety of perspectives that embrace a number of differences, most would agree that it is a period of life that begins with the onset of the biological changes associated with puberty and ends when persons have fully established themselves as adults. This period most often occurs between the ages of twelve and twenty. During this period, individuals undergo a variety of developmental changes in their physical, emotional, intellectual, and social characteristics and roles. Developmental theorist Erick Erickson (1968) sees that among all these changes, the need to form a sense of one's own personal identity is one of the key developmental tasks teens face. Among the core tasks that teens must engage in as they build this sense of identity are those that help them to build a sense of mastery, autonomy, sexuality, intimacy, and achievement. In facing these complex developmental tasks that help teens form their own identities, adolescents often read because they are looking for the guidance they need to help them realize themselves. Because of this, a reader's choice of reading material is often connected with the emotional and developmental needs of that reader.

All works of literature have the capability to help young adults navigate their way through their development and form their identities, but contemporary realistic problem fiction has a unique ability to do this because of the close connection between the themes these books discuss and the problems and issues that real teens are experiencing. Because problem novels portray realistic adolescents engaging in realistic life events, teens are able to see themselves and their own development reflected in the pages of the books they read. Young adults are drawn to works of realistic problem fiction because it is here that they find the map they need to help them navigate their own realities. As teens read about the issues that are relevant to their own individual experiences and concerns, they engage in vicarious experiences that build their individual identities and ultimately allow them to formulate their own value systems and define their own roles and places within society. With these strong developmental connections, many readers find just what they require in realistic novels, and studies of readers' choices have shown that readers often select problem novels. For example, Hopper (2005), in her study of adolescent reading patterns, found that issue-based realistic fiction was among the most popular of the texts selected by students to read.

A Brief History of the Genre

The history of children's literature, and in particular the genre of realistic fiction, has always shown a strong link to stories that discuss human problems. Beginning in the early 1600s the Puritans determined that stories portraying realistic incidents based in strongly theological morals could be effective in instructing children in the proper methods of dealing with difficulties. Works of this period included such titles as *A Token for Children: Being an Exact Account of the Conversion, Holy and Exemplary Lives and Joyful Deaths of Several Young Children,* published in 1672 by James Janeway, and Abraham Chear's *A Looking Glass for Children,* published in 1673. The highly didactic stories of the Puritans influenced the next three centuries of realistic books with one of the few significant changes beginning in the 1740s when realistic fiction moved from the blatant theological didacticism of the Puritans to the different but equally didactic moralizing of the Victorian era. Published during this era were titles such as *Little Pretty Pocket-Book* by John Newbery in 1744, *The History of Little Goody Two-Shoes* by Oliver Goldsmith in 1765, and *Original Stories from Real Life* by Mary Wollstonecraft in 1788. Far into the nineteenth century, realistic children's books remained one of the most important instruments with which children were morally socialized. Continuing into the modern era, works of realistic fiction still had strong themes stressing moral behavior, but their stories were dull and unnatural. Although groundbreaking books such as Louisa May Alcott's *Little Women* in 1868 showed that realistic fiction could discuss the problems of humanity without moralistic overtones, it was not until the late 1950s that children's books truly broke free from their didactic roots. It was works such as Louise Fitzhugh's 1964 book *Harriet the Spy* that finally opened a new view of the purpose of realistic fiction that still defines the genre today. Freed from the need to convey strongly moralistic themes, novels of realistic fiction are now able to delve deeply into the various unique circumstances, problems, and events that adolescents face. This newfound ability to delve deeply and incorporate real life into books allowed the subgenre of realistic problem fiction to fully emerge and flourish starting in the 1960s. From the classics published in the 1970s such as Judy Blume's *Forever* and Robert Cormier's *The Chocolate War* to today's modern classics such as Laurie Halse Anderson's *Speak,* realistic problem novels have become a staple of adolescent literature.

Purpose and Audience

With the enormous amount of young adult literature being published today, especially in the genre of realistic fiction, this book is designed to help librarians connect with a variety of titles. It describes some 1,300 titles and groups them into categories that reflect popular reading interests within the genre This book then serves as a guide to help professionals with readers' advisory and collection development. For readers' advisory, this book provides information about a wide selection of realistic problem fiction that is perfect for patrons looking for books that connect to their real-life experiences or that provide a deeper understanding of problems they and their peer group face. For collection development, this book provides pertinent information on individual titles that librarians may wish to purchase, and it also shows thematic connections to other books that will add interest and depth to collections.

Although this guide provides information about a wide selection of realistic problem novels, it would be an impossible task to make it comprehensive. This book provides an excellent foundation with which to access the genre, but those who wish more depth should consult other sources in addition to this guide. Some of these sources are listed at the back of the book. The primary audience for this book includes librarians who work in any situation, including public, school, or academic environments. In addition, teachers, booksellers, and all avid readers of this genre will find this work beneficial.

Scope, Selection Criteria, and Methodology

This book endeavors to provide readers with wide exposure to modern realistic problem novels and to place each of these titles into thematic categories that will assist readers not only in finding books they enjoy but also in guiding them to additional books that share similarities. Despite all of the wonderful classics that were published in bygone eras, the aim of this book is to focus on those issues that are of most concern to contemporary teens. With this aim, only books published in the past ten years (from 1999 to 2009) in the United States and Canada are included. Although every effort was made to include titles that are still in print, the uncertainties of the publishing industry make it impossible to ensure that all titles will be available for purchase. However, many libraries' collections will have access to these titles, or readers will be able to access them through interlibrary loan. The focus of this work is on young adult novels, excluding novels published for children or adults as well as short story collections.

Titles for this work were selected for inclusion if they clearly fell within the genre parameters and contained thematic issues that are of interest to the widest possible number of modern teen readers. Within these parameters, books that had any part set in the future or the past and books that contained elements of mystery or adventure were excluded. In addition, titles that dealt with situations that, although realistic, border on the fantastic, such as books with girls who fall in love with princes or books that deal with the exploits of the ultra-wealthy, were also excluded. Lastly, this book focuses on the experiences of teens in English-speaking countries, so only books that portrayed teens in the United States, Canada, the United Kingdom, Australia, and the Pacific were included.

Because teens experience a wide variety of problems and issues, the aim of this work was to include as many of these as possible. Even though the nature of many problem novels often leads to the discussion of controversial topics, no attempt was made to censor books that would contain such things as violence, sexual activity, drug use, or profanity. Because individual readers' needs and community values will vary, professionals should be aware that books listed in this work may not be suitable for all readers. It is impossible to determine which topics certain individuals will find offensive. Although every effort was made to highlight possible controversial elements in the annotations and the grade-level designations reflect those books that are best for mature teens, those consulting this book should use their own professional insight to assist them in selecting the right books for each reader and collection.

Organization

This guide is first divided into three parts. Part I covers titles with thematic issues that are of near universal interest to teens, such as romance, working, and schooling. Part II deals with titles that cover themes that not every teen will deal with but will have great interest to certain teen populations, such as race, sexuality, and physical health. Finally, Part III covers titles that deal with extreme issues some teens may face, such as homelessness, abuse, and death. Within each of these parts, books are divided into thematic categories that put together books with the same issues. Some of these major thematic categories are further divided into more specific subcategories when necessary. In these sections, books that fit generally into the overall category are listed first, and then subcategories are listed. For example, in the major thematic category of romance, the books that deal generally with romantic themes are listed first. Then in addition, books dealing with first love, breaking up, summer love, and online romance are annotated. Within the categories, books are listed alphabetically by author, and, if there is more than one author, the book is listed under the primary author's name. Books in series with one author writing the entire series are listed alphabetically by author and are categorized according to the major thematic element of the first book in the series. Series books with multiple authors are categorized according to the major thematic element of the entire series and are listed under the heading of multiple authors and the series title. All series books are then listed in order of publication because, for most books in a series, this is the order in which they should be read.

Information on the author, title, and publication data for the first edition is given for each title in this work. Only ISBNs for the first hardback and paperback edition are listed. ISBNs for additional formats or editions are not included; however, to alert the reader when audio editions were found the code (aud) has been added. It is important to note that because books will go out of print, professionals should verify all ISBN information when submitting orders. If a book has been awarded a major literary prize, this is also listed. Reading levels, in keeping with those assigned in the other Genreflecting titles focused on teen books, are indicated.

M = middle school, grades 6–8, ages 12–14

J = junior high, grades 7–9, ages 13–16

S = high school, grades 10–12, ages 16–20

These reading levels were assigned according to the author's judgment in consultation with professional reviews. However, these levels are not absolute, and professional judgment should be used to determine which books will be best for each reader.

After a brief annotation of each title, subject headings that cover the range of issues covered in each book are offered. Because of the nature of problem novels, they do not always restrict themselves to addressing one thematic issue. Books have been categorized according to the major issues that they discuss, and then subject headings are listed and indexed to assist readers in finding other titles that may also address the same issues, although in a more minor role. These subject headings are drawn from the authoritative Library of Congress Subject Headings (LCSH) Thesaurus. As much as possible, the subject headings are listed in an order that goes from the one that is most covered to the one that is least covered in the title. In addition, subject headings were collapsed to represent only major themes that were the most common among the body of literature represented, which means that minor themes or issues addressed in the text are not represented, and not every theme or issue has a subject heading. Because the individual categories represented in the parts and chapters of this work are not always noted in the subject heading list, professionals should use the table of contents in conjunction with the subject index to guide readers to the variety of titles that will be of interest to them.

Suggestions for Use

This work can be used for a variety of purposes, including helping professionals keep current, perform readers' advisory, and build collections.

Keeping Current

With the large amounts of fiction being published for adolescents today, it is nearly impossible to keep up with any genre and to stay current with what teens are enjoying. With its focus on currently published titles, this work will serve to help professionals overcome some of the challenges of keeping up. Also, the listing of book awards in Appendix A and the listing of professional resources in Appendix B will also help guide readers to additional sources that will assist them in finding the best new titles in the genre. Appendix B includes a variety of both print and online resources because traditional means of staying current are not always adequate anymore.

Advising the Reader

When it comes to guiding teens to the right realistic problem novels, along with the normal considerations for readers' advisory, there are a few additional issues to consider. As noted, teens often choose reading material that is connected to their own emotional and developmental needs. Savvy professionals realize that chronological age does not always coincide with developmental age. So while some twelve year olds may be ready to deal with intensely emotional topics, some sixteen year olds will be unable to deal with the same topics. Knowing your readers and performing readers' advisory interviews will assist professionals in finding books that discuss topics in a way that is appropriate for the developmental level of each reader. When it comes to realistic problem novels, many feel inclined to use them not only to help teach teens about behavior but also to help them to find support in dealing with their own problems. Using books as a therapeutic tool can be a positive way to use problem novels. However, professionals should be aware that although reading can also be healing, many believe damage can also be done if the wrong text is selected. Although this may not be as significant a problem as some believe, the reality is that often our instincts to help teens may lead us to think they need a certain type of book even though they want nothing of the sort. For example, for a young girl whose father has just died, the instinct may be to recommend books in which girls are dealing with their grief. In reality however, this girl may not want to read books with parents who died and may prefer a comedic romance novel instead. Once again, knowing your readers and performing readers' advisory interviews will assist professionals in finding just the right books to help teens face traumatic issues in their lives.

Building the Collection

This book should help professionals find areas in their collections that lack important materials. In addition, it should help bring understanding to the wide range of problems and issues that teens face so that professionals can select titles that will be of interest to the individual teens in their communities.

However you use this book, it is sure to be a meaningful starting place as you work to find just the right book for your teen readers.

References

Egoff, Sheila A. 1981. *Thursday's child : Trends and patterns in contemporary children's literature*. Chicago: American Library Association.

Erikson, Erik. 1968. *Identity, youth and crisis*. New York: Norton.

Feinberg, Barbara. 2005. Reflections on the "problem novel." *American Educator* (Winter 2004–2005): 1–19.

Hopper, Rosemary. 2005. What are teenagers reading? Adolescent fiction reading habits and reading choices. *Literacy* 39 (November 2001): 113.

Tatar, Maria. 2009. *Enchanted hunters: The power of stories in childhood*. New York: W.W. Norton.

Part I

Contemporary Teen Life

No matter what an adolescent's race, ethnicity, gender, or social class, there are certain experiences that are nearly universal to this stage in life. As teens move through the major developmental tasks necessary for them to develop into their adult identities, they must move through various rites of passage that help them build their social, cognitive, and physical abilities. This part lists books that encompass the universal experiences that build teens' abilities. In these books, teens build social skills as they develop both platonic and romantic relationships with peers. Social skills are also developed as adolescents maintain or develop their family relationships. Cognitive abilities are enhanced as teens participate in schooling, work for pay, or travel outside their normal realms of experience. Books that show teens building their physical abilities through sports are also discussed.

Chapter 1

Making and Keeping Friends

As children transition into adolescence, young people begin building a greater orientation toward peers as they become more sensitive to their age-mates' perceptions and evaluations. In adolescence, building friendships takes on a more significant role when connections with people outside one's family begin to deepen and take on a new quality of intimacy. During the teen years, friendships play an important part in building an adolescent's individual identity. Friends help teens develop their values and morality because they can influence everything from basic ideals to future plans. A friend's influence also extends to other choices such as dress or music, as well as those choices that can lead to negative behaviors such as drinking or having sex. Friends also provide a significant support system for teens as they work out problems or deal with stressful events and circumstances. The books in this chapter show the positive and negative aspects of friendships developed between teens who are the same and also between those who are different. From girls who bond over knitting to teens who can only stay in touch online, these books show friends who help each other grow and learn through all of life's challenges.

Abbott, Tony

Firegirl. New York: Little, Brown, 2006. 145 p. ISBN: 9780316011716; 9780316011709pa; (aud). Teens Top Ten. *M*

> Tom is an overweight seventh grader who goes about his life unnoticed until he befriends Jessica Feeney. Jessica is attending Tom's school while she gets treatments at a local hospital for the severe burns that scar her whole body. When his classmates spread rumors about Jessica and ostracize her, Tom learns that friendship is much more important than popularity.
>
> *Friendship • Burn Victims*

Anderson, Jodi Lynn

<u>Peaches Series</u>. New York: HarperCollins

> Three girls from different backgrounds bond with each other when they are thrown together in a peach orchard in Georgia. Together they deal with life, love, loss, betrayal, and change.
>
> *Friendship • Coming-of-Age*

Peaches: A Novel. 2005. 311 p. ISBN: 9780060733056; 9780060733070pa. *S*

> Three girls, Birdie, Leeda, and Murphy discover an unlikely and supportive friendship when they are thrown together to pick peaches in a Georgia orchard.

The Secrets of Peaches. 2006. 304 p. ISBN: 9780060733087; 9780060733100pa. *S*

> Beginning their senior year, the girls Birdie, Leeda, and Murphy must deal with boyfriends both near and far as well as their families' expectations.

Love and Peaches. 2008. 256 p. ISBN: 9780060733117; 9780060733131pa. *S*

> Returning to Georgia after their freshman year at different universities, Birdie, Leeda, and Murphy must face their past and embrace the future by letting go and growing up.

Bradbury, Jennifer

Shift. New York: Atheneum Books for Young Readers, 2008. 256 p. ISBN: 9781416947325. YALSA Best Books. *S*

> Best friends Chris and Winn decide to take a 3,000-mile bike trip from their home in West Virginia to California before they start college. When Win disappears after they have an argument, Chris is left to face many unanswerable questions thrown at him by Winn's parents and the FBI agent who has been assigned to the case. Looking back on their adventure, Chris realizes what could have happened and returns in search of his friend.
>
> *Friendship • Travel • Missing Persons • Family*

Brashares, Ann

Sisterhood of the Traveling Pants Series. New York: Delacorte Press

> Four girls bond when they find a pair of pants that fits each one of them. Together they face the trials of life and love.
>
> *Friendship • Travel • Boyfriends • Sexuality • Family Relationships*

The Sisterhood of the Traveling Pants. 2001. 294 p. ISBN: 9780385729338; 9780385730587pa; (aud). YALSA Best Books; YALSA Popular Paperbacks. *MJ*

> Facing separation over the summer, four friends, Carmen, Lena, Bridget, and Tibby, find a pair of pants that fits them all and unites them over the summer as they face many individual difficulties.

The Second Summer of the Sisterhood. 2003. 373 p. ISBN: 9780385729345; 9780385731058pa; (aud). Teens Top Ten. *MJ*

> The four friends share the pants for another summer while Bridget tries to connect with her maternal grandmother, Tibby attends a summer program at Williamston College, Lena deals with an on-again, off-again relationship with her boyfriend, and Carmen tries to deal with both her own love life and her mother's.

Girls in Pants: The Third Summer of the Sisterhood. 2005. 352 p. ISBN: 9780385729352; 9780553375930pa; (aud). Teens Top Ten *JS*

> The summer before they go to college, the four friends unite for one final weekend when they deal with family problems and the ups and downs of love.

Forever in Blue: The Fourth Summer of the Sisterhood. 2007. 400 p. ISBN: 9780385729369; 9780385734011pa; (aud). *JS*

> After their first year of college, the friends face new challenges including a pregnancy scare, having a crush on a married man, breaking up with a boyfriend, and how to deal with malicious roommates.

Brashares, Ann

3 Willows: The Sisterhood Grows. New York: Delacorte Press, 2009. 336 p. ISBN: 9780385736763. *MJ*

> Ama, Jo, and Polly are going to be spending the summer apart, learning to face their fears while deepening their friendship.

Friendship • Alcoholism • Boyfriends • Family Relationships

Brugman, Alyssa

Walking Naked. New York: Delacorte Press, 2004. 185 p. ISBN: 9780385731157; 9780440238324pa. *J*

> During detention for being rude to a teacher, popular tenth-grader Megan Tuw meets the school outcast Perdita Wiguiggan. Called "the Freak" by her classmates, Perdita is very different from egocentric Megan. When Megan's friend Candace starts spending more time with a girl Megan does not like to organize a freedom of expression protest for a guy in their school who was caught streaking, Megan is drawn to Perdita. Finding Perdita to be more interesting and intelligent than her other friends, the two girls connect over Perdita's love of poetry, and Megan learns important lessons from her new friend.

Friendship • Cliques • Self-Perception • Suicide • Poetry

Bryant, Annie

Beacon Street Girls Series. Lexington, MA: B*tween Productions; New York: Aladdin Paperbacks

> Five middle school girls in Brookline, Massachusetts, face life as they work together to solve their individual problems.

Best Friends • Friendship • Family Relationships

Worst Enemies, Best Friends. 2005. 212 p. ISBN: 9780974658766pa. *M*

> The new girl Charlotte Ramsey causes an embarrassing scene in the cafeteria when zipping the tablecloth into her pants causes food to be upset everywhere, including on her new lunchmates Avery, Maeve, and Katani. But after the incident, instead of becoming enemies, the girls become friends and form the Beacon Street Girls club.

Good News, Bad News. 2005. 236 p. ISBN: 9780974658704pa *M*

When Charlotte's father wants to move again, things look bleak, but the girls come to her rescue while initiating a new member, Isabel, into the Beacon Street Girls club.

Letters from the Heart. 2005. 224 p. ISBN: 9780974658780pa; (aud). *M*

Maeve is struggling with dyslexia and the breakup of her parents, but with the help of her friends, she learns some important lessons about herself.

Out of Bounds. 2005. 257 p. ISBN: 9780974658797pa. *M*

While the girls are working on their acts for the school talent show, they also struggle to keep the local movie theater from closing.

Promises, Promises. 2005. 212 p. ISBN: 9780975851128pa. *M*

The girls' friendship is endangered when two of the girls run against each other for seventh-grade class president.

Lake Rescue. 2005. 226 p. ISBN: 9780975851135pa. *M*

On the mandatory Abigail Adams Junior High School trip to Lake Rescue, the girls learn a lot about themselves.

Freaked Out. 2006. 226 p. ISBN: 9780975851173pa. *M*

When one of the girls is not invited to Julie Farber's birthday party, the whole group must decide what to do.

Lucky Charm. 2006. 233 p. ISBN: 9780975851197pa. *M*

Saddened when Katani's autistic sister, Kelley, lets Marty, Charlotte's dog, run away, the girls must also face the fact that their favorite place to go, the High Hopes Riding Stable, may close.

Fashion Frenzy. 2006. 240 p. ISBN: 9781933566023pa. *M*

Katani is in a fashion show in New York City.

Just Kidding. 2007. 240 p. ISBN: 9781933566078pa. *M*

The girls learn how pain and chaos can arise when gossip is spread.

Ghost Town. 2007. 317 p. ISBN: 9781933566092pa; *M*

A snowstorm strands Maeve, Avery, and Charlotte in a ghost town while on vacation at a Montana ranch, while Katani and Isabel are back on the ranch with country music stars Nik and Sam.

Time's Up. 2008. 208 p. ISBN: 9781416964223pa; (aud). *M*

Katani is extremely busy with major school projects and twenty scarves to knit, but she still wants to win a contest for young entrepreneurs even though Maeve undermines her efforts by signing up for the tutoring service of the girl with whom Katani is competing.

Green Algae and Bubblegum Wars. 2008. 246 p. ISBN: 9781416964292pa. *M*

Maeve is excited about going to the Sally Ride Science Festival at MIT with her gorgeous tutor, Matt, even though her brother and the other girls are coming along.

Crush Alert. 2008. 256 p. ISBN: 9781416964377pa; (aud). *M*

> Even though they don't look like they're interested, the girls try to attract the boys they like so they can go to the Valentines dance.

The Great Scavenger Hunt. 2009. 304 p. ISBN: 9781416964421pa. *M*

> The girls travel to Cape Cod where they must decipher cryptic clues on a scavenger hunt.

Sweet Thirteen. 2009. 256 p. ISBN: 9781416964384pa. *M*

> When Charlotte gets a visit from a friend from Paris, things go crazy as the girls deal with various problems.

Burton, Rebecca

Leaving Jetty Road. New York: Knopf, 2006. 256 p. ISBN: 9780375834882; 9780553495058pa. *S*

> During their last year of high school, best friends Nat, Lise, and Sofia make a New Year's resolution to become vegetarians. Nat, who has few life goals, gets a part-time job at the Wild Carrot Café, where she develops an obsessive relationship with co-worker Josh, an older boy. On the outside Lise looks focused and secure, but inside she is battling a severe self-loathing that leads to anorexia. Sofia finds true love. Along the way, the girls overcome obsessions and seek to control their lives as they explore options and grow up.
>
> *Friendship • Anorexia • First Love • Vegetarianism • Body Image • Australia • Coming-of-Age*

Carlson, Melody

Carter House Girls Series. Grand Rapids, MI: Zondervan

> Six teenage girls, DJ, Kristi, Rhiannon, Taylor, Casey, and Eliza, live in an old Victorian boarding house with a retired '60s fashion icon, Katherine Carter. Together the girls deal with all kinds of problems, including those relating to dating and high school.
>
> *Friendship • Grandmothers • Romance • Christianity*

Mixed Bags. 2008. 219 p. ISBN: 9780310714880pa. *JS*

> After her mom's death, DJ moves in with her grandmother, the famous '60s fashion model Katherine Carter. Since her grandmother is now running a boarding house for young ladies, DJ finds she has acquired five new "sisters." Despite their differences, the girls soon form a new family as they share clothes and secrets.

Stealing Bradford. 2008. 224 p. ISBN: 9780310714897pa. *JS*

> At Carter House, the girls are beginning to find that boys are hard to understand. Rhiannon is dating popular jock, Bradford; Eliza is seeing Harry; and while DJ was with Conner, he is starting to act funny around her. When Taylor decides that she wants Bradford, things get really complicated, and the girls must figure out not only how to deal with the boys in their lives but with each other.

Homecoming Queen. 2008. 224 p. ISBN: 9780310714903pa. *JS*

> After running away, Taylor has returned, and the girls are able to once again be a family—that is, until DJ finds she has become a local celebrity after saving a child from being run over by a car. Just as DJ is withdrawing from life, Taylor and Eliza compete against each other to become homecoming queen, and once again the girls will have to deal with their problems together.

Viva Vermont. 2008. 224 p. ISBN: 9780310714910pa. *JS*

> Mrs. Carter treats the girls to a trip to a Vermont ski lodge during the Christmas season. Taylor invites some boys to follow them, and DJ, Eliza, Taylor, Kristi, Rhiannon, and Casey find themselves in over their heads when a party gets out of control and must get out of the mess they have created.

Lost in Las Vegas. 2009. 208 p. ISBN: 9780310714927pa. *JS*

> When DJ accepts Taylor's invitation to come to Las Vegas where her mom is performing over Christmas break, she must deal with Taylor's excessive partying and her self-destructive ways.

New York Debut. 2009. 224 p. ISBN: 9780310714934pa. *JS*

> As Mrs. Carter and the girls prepare for the high-stakes Spring Fashion Week in New York City, the girls compete for the best outfits and try to get attention from the guys. As stresses grow, the girls must deal with a variety of challenges.

Spring Breakdown. 2010. 208 p. ISBN: 9780310714941pa. *JS*

> In Florida for spring break with Mrs. Carter, the girls' hope for a simple vacation is shattered when some of their guy friends rent a condo nearby. Clinging to her faith and trying to stay sober is working for Taylor, and it is Eliza instead who spins out of control with her partying.

Craft, Liz, and Sarah Fain

Bass Ackwards and Belly Up. New York: Little, Brown, 2006. 386 p. ISBN: 9780316057936; 9780316057943pa. *S*

> Ashamed of her rejection to NYU, the only school she applied to, Harper tries to cover it by announcing that she has decided to stay home in Colorado and write a great American novel. Inspired by her decision, her three best friends decide to embrace their dreams as well. Sophie flies off to Hollywood to pursue an acting career, Becca chooses to go to Middlebury College so she can ski with a great coach, and Kate defers going to Harvard to travel Europe. Each of the girls embraces her new independence as they face setbacks and even romance as they travel their own roads to discover themselves.

Sequel: ***Footfree and Fancyloose.*** New York: Little, Brown, 2008. 423 p. ISBN: 9780316057950; 9780316057967pa. *S*

> Harper, Kate, Becca, and Sophie are still pursing their dreams, but now these dreams include finding romance. Along the way, each girl learns from the journeys she has undertaken as they grow up and get used to life on their own.

Best Friends • Friendship • Actors and Actresses • Deception • Romance • Coming-of-Age

Danziger, Paula, and Ann M. Martin

P.S. Longer Letter Later. New York: Scholastic Press, 1998. 234 p. ISBN: 9780590213103; 9780590213110pa; (aud). YALSA Quick Picks. *M*

> Twelve-year-old Tara's life and family are finally starting to come together after they move to a new town. At the same time, Tara's friend Elizabeth's life is falling apart. Staying in touch with letters, the two girls support and help each other through the changes they are facing despite the distance and the little misunderstandings that separate them.

<u>Sequel</u>: ***Snail Mail No More.*** New York: Scholastic Press, 2000. 307 p. ISBN: 9780439063357; 9780439063364pa; (aud). YALSA Quick Picks. *M*

> Tara and Elizabeth are now thirteen and are facing new challenges as they continue their correspondence through e-mail. Both girls are uncertain what the future holds. New friends and boyfriends, and at times jealousy, try to draw the friends apart, but their bond stays strong.

> *E-mail • Epistolary Novels • Friendship • Family*

Elliot, Jessie

Girls Dinner Club. New York: HarperCollins, 2005. 256 p. ISBN: 9780060595395; 9780060595418pa. *S*

> Brooklyn high schoolers Junie, Celia, and Danielle form a strong friendship as they begin cooking dinner together. Junie, who has been dumped by her boyfriend after she wasn't ready to have a second sexual encounter, has absent parents who don't bother her much. Celia, who worries she doesn't have a boyfriend, is in conflict with her father over his new girlfriend. Danielle can't seem to move on from her boyfriend, who is a serial cheater. Despite their various backgrounds and problems, the girls help and support each other as they eat and talk through their troubles.

> *Romance • Friendship • Cooking*

Frank, E. R.

Life Is Funny: A Novel. New York: DK, 2000. 263 p. ISBN: 9780789426345; 9780142300831pa. YALSA Outstanding Books for the College Bound; YALSA Quick Picks. *S*

> The story of eleven Brooklyn high school teens over seven years is woven together in a tapestry as complex as each of their lives as they grow up, cope with poor parents, and come to grips with their emotional and physical problems.

> *Interpersonal Relations • Family Problems • Muslims*

Fredericks, Mariah

Head Games. New York: Atheneum Books for Young Readers, 2004. 260 p. ISBN: 9780689855320; 9781416913351pa. *J*

> Ignored by her best friend and constantly afraid after she was attacked when walking alone one night, fifteen-year-old Judith escapes into the

world of online games where she becomes Gareth, an aggressive self-confident teenage boy. When one of her opponents, Irgan, fails to kill her, she sets out to find the gamer's true identity and discovers that he is actually her bad-boy druggie neighbor Jonathan Heitman. Now supported by Jonathan and Katie, a fat, insecure girl she tutors in math, the unexpected friends work to survive high school and deal with complex family issues.

Best Friends • Crime • Mother and Daughter • Misfits

Gauthier, Gail

Happy Kid! New York: G.P. Putnam's Sons, 2006. 192 p. ISBN: 9780399242663. *M*

Infamous for a screwdriver incident in sixth grade that was blown out of proportion, Kyle hopes that in seventh grade, he can shed his undeserved reputation. Having lost all his friends, Kyle has a particularly negative attitude about the year to come. His mother presents him with the book *Happy Kid: A Young Person's Guide to Satisfying Relationships and a Happy and Meaning-filled Life.* Trying to apply the advice he finds when the book falls open at just the right times, Kyle finds that things don't always work out as planned.

Advice • Mothers • Family • Identity • Humor

Goldman, Steven

Two Parties, One Tux, and a Very Short Film about the Grapes of Wrath. New York: Bloomsbury Children's Books, 2008. 228 p. ISBN: 9781599902715; 9781599903934pa. *S*

Seventeen-year-old Mitchell's junior year gets complicated when his friend reveals that he is gay. Dealing with the new ambiguity this adds to their relationship, Mitchell is also struggling with his inexperience as his own relationship with his popular girlfriend heats up. When he turns in a mildly pornographic art film on a book he hasn't read for an English paper, Mitchell is accused of mocking religion, and then when his teacher disappears, Mitchell is forced to reexamine many aspects of his life.

Friendship • Films • Gay Males • Homosexuality • Dating • Girlfriends

Green, John

Paper Towns. New York: Dutton Books, 2008. 352 p. ISBN: 9780525478188; 9780142414934pa; (aud). YALSA Best Books; School Library Journal Best Books; Teens Top Ten. *S*

Unexpectedly popping up late one night at his window, Margo Roth Spiegelman, demands that seventeen-year-old Quentin Jacobsen accompany her on a spree to commit some pranks that will right some wrongs. Having loved neighbor Margo his whole life, Quentin embraces risk in a way that he almost never does and agrees to the quest. Along the way, he soon learns that it is not always possible to know the people around us.

Missing Persons • Revenge • Coming-of-Age

Haft, Erin

Pool Boys. New York Point, 2006. 224 p. ISBN: 9780439835237pa. *J*

At the Silver Oaks Country Club, Brook, Charlotte, and Georgia have always been friends. But when a new girl, Valerie, arrives and not only takes the attentions of the handsome pool boys but steals Charlotte away from the group as well, Brook and Georgia must work through their feelings of betrayal and find a way to fix their friendship.

Romance • Friendship • Best Friends

Howell, Simmone

Notes from the Teenage Underground. New York: Bloomsbury Children's Books, 2007. 250 p. ISBN: 9781582348353; 9781599902319pa. *S*

Trying to navigate the stress of reconnecting with her long-absent father, seventeen-year-old Gem tries to strengthen the relationship with her best friends Lo and Mira. She comes up with a project to embrace '60s counter-culture and make an edgy film in the style of Andy Warhol that they can screen at an upcoming underground party. When Lo rewrites the script and the production gets out of hand, Lo and Mira secretly plan some pranks at school without her. The final straw comes at a debauched party where events conspire to make Gem realize that it may be time to break the ties that hold her to these friends.

Mother and Daughter • Father-Separated Families • Friendship • Parties • Summer • Films Coming-of-Age • Australia

Koja, Kathe

Straydog. New York: Farrar/Frances Foster Books, 2002. 112 p. ISBN: 9780374372781; 9780142400715pa. YALSA Popular Paperbacks. *JS*

Rachel doesn't fit in with any of the students at her high school and doesn't get along well with her parents, preferring to spend her time alone writing and volunteering at the animal shelter. When a savage feral collie, who she names Grrl, is brought in to the shelter, Rachel falls for the dog's fierce wildness, and she begins to write a story from Grrl's perspective. Her teacher encourages her to enter the story in a writing context. When she is partnered with a new classmate, Griffin, he is able to see beyond Rachel's exterior to reveal her talent, and the two from a friendship that helps Rachel grow in understanding.

Dogs • Creativity • Individuality

Lenhard, Elizabeth

Chicks with Sticks Series. New York: Dutton Children's Books

Four girls, Scottie, Amanda, Bella, and Tay, work through problems as they knit together.

Friendship • Grief • Family Relationships

Chicks with Sticks: It's a Purl Thing. 2005. 256 p. ISBN: 9780525476221. YALSA Popular Paperbacks. *MJ*

> Missing her great aunt who taught her to knit and confused about her strained relationship with best friend Amanda, Scottie finds solace in a knitting group at a local shop. Soon joined by Amanda, who is struggling with a learning disability, the two repair their relationship as they also make friends with homeschooled Bella and tattooed and pierced Tay.

Chicks with Sticks: Knit Two Together. 2006. 272 p. ISBN: 9780525477648. *MJ*

> Still knitting, the girls deal with romantic relationships.

Chicks with Sticks: Knitwise. 2007. 260 p. ISBN: 9780525478386. *MJ*

> As the girls prepare to head off for college, each deals with her own unique problems with her family and tries to embrace what the future holds.

Liberty, Anita

The Center of the Universe (Yep, That Would Be Me). New York: Simon Pulse, 2008. 291 p. ISBN: 9781416957898pa. *J*

> In her Manhattan private school, Anita worries about life after she gets dumped by her boyfriend and stresses over taking the SAT. In addition to dealing with her parents, younger sister, and friend, Anita works through the joy and pains of being a teenager as she falls for French exchange students who don't like her back and works on college applications.

> *Interpersonal Relations • Friendship • Exchange Students • Epistolary Novels*

Lubar, David

Dunk. New York: Clarion Books, 2002. 249 p. ISBN: 9780618439096pa; (aud). *JS*

> Fascinated by the clown who taunts people from the dunk tank at the amusement park, Chad believes that it would be the perfect job, giving him the opportunity to blow off some of his anger at his dad, who abandoned him, and his teachers, who think he is a loser. As the summer progresses, Chad gets to know the clown and soon realizes there is a clever art to what he does in picking a mark, reeling him in, and keeping him interested with sarcastic wisecracks. As he uncovers this skill, Chad finds a new understanding of himself, which helps him as he tries to deal with his family problems and the peer pressure around him.

> *Best Friends • Interpersonal Relations • Family Problems • Peer Pressure*

Mass, Wendy

Every Soul a Star. New York: Little, Brown, 2008. 336 p. ISBN: 9780316002561; 9780316002578pa. *MJ*

> When a thousand people from all over the world come to view an Eclipse at her family's wilderness Moon Shadow Campground site, thirteen-year-old Ally meets glamorous Bree, who wants to be a model and is appalled by her physics-scholar parents. When the two discover they will be switching places when Ally's parents sell the camp to Bree's family, neither is excited. Also at the camp is Jack, who loves art and science fiction but failed science and was brought by his

teacher to the event instead of having to attend summer school. Together these young people come to terms with all the changes they face in their lives.

Friendship • Family Problems • Coming-of-Age

Mass, Wendy

Leap Day: A Novel. New York: Little, Brown, 2004. 212 p. ISBN: 9780316537285; 9780316058285pa. *JS*

Born on February 29, Josie Taylor finds herself celebrating her sixteenth year but her "fourth birthday" with many adventures including taking her driver's test, auditioning for the school production of *Romeo and Juliet*, and going on the annual sophomore school scavenger hunt with her best friends. As her day progresses, secrets are revealed, and things go on around her that change her life.

Friendship • Family • Growing Up • Coming-of-Age

McGhee, Alison

Snap. Cambridge, MA: Candlewick Press, 2004. 129 p. ISBN: 9780763620028; 9780763626174pa. *J*

Edwina "Eddie" Beckly wears rubber bands on her arms to help her keep her life in order as she snaps them to remind herself of things, including to cover her mouth when she laughs and not to tip back in chairs. But most important, she uses them to remember to be as brave as her best friend, Sally, whose grandmother Willie is dying from a blood disease. With a mother who is unable to care for her, Eddie fears the stress that is forcing Sally to shut her out and wonders who will care for Sally when Willie passes away. In the end, Eddie must find a way to support her friend and embrace what the future holds.

Best Friends • Grandmothers • Death • Grief

Moore, Peter

Blind Sighted. New York: Viking, 2001. 272 p. ISBN: 9780670035434; 9780142401262pa. *JS*

Sixteen-year-old Kirk Tobak is a shy underachiever who prefers to read about and observe life rather than participate in it. When his smart mouth and poor performance get him demoted to a lower-level English class, he meets musician Beg Glenn. The two find friendship when Glenn realizes that Kirk has an ability to write clever verse that fits with the music he writes. Kirk gets a job reading for Callie, a blind woman; at the same time, he falls for and begins having sex with his new girlfriend. His alcoholic mother starts to get her life together and finally decides to move to California with her boyfriend. Now Kirk must start participating in his life as he is forced to make decisions about his future.

Interpersonal Relations • Disabilities • Alcoholism • Coming-of-Age

Moriarty, Jaclyn

Feeling Sorry for Celia: A Novel. New York: St. Martin's Press, 2001. 276 p. ISBN: 9780312269234; 9780312287368pa. YALSA Best Books. *J*

Fifteen-year-old Elizabeth Clarry has been left alone to cook, clean, and look after herself after her parents divorce. Even when her absent father returns to Australia and tries to reconnect with her, Elizabeth still has few human connections beyond her neurotic friend Celia Buckley, who is constantly running away. When Celia disappears once again and Elizabeth sets out with handsome fellow student Saxon Walker to find her, only to have Saxon fall for Celia, Elizabeth is devastated. Elizabeth has found support from her pen pal Christina, who attends a neighboring school. When the two unexpectedly meet, things begin to get better for Elizabeth.

Father and Daughter • Letters • Australia • Epistolary Novels • Coming-of-Age

Moriarty, Jaclyn

The Year of Secret Assignments. New York: Arthur A. Levine Books, 2004. 352 p. ISBN: 9780439498814; 9780439498821pa. YALSA Best Books. *MJ*

Lydia, Emily, and Cassie have been friends for a very long time, but when a teacher at their private school, Ashbury High, assigns them to be pen pals with three boys at the rough neighboring school, things change. Risk-taker Lydia loves giving her pal, soccer-playing Sebastian, secret covert assignments to carry out. Self-assured Emily connects with her pal Charlie, a sweet boy who has gotten into a few scrapes. As Lydia and Emily's relationship with their pals progresses into clandestine meetings, Cassie's pal Matthew is becoming rude and threatening. The friends realize what is happening to Cassie, who is grieving a loss, and they join together to get their revenge on Matthew and to teach him a little about respect.

Sequel: *The Murder of Bindy MacKenzie.* New York: Arthur A. Levine Books, 2006. 352 p. ISBN: 9780439740517; 9780439740524pa. *MJ*

Also at Ashbury High, gifted student Bindy MacKenzie is frustrated when her classmates, teachers, and even the School Board don't listen to her advice. Bindy is especially frustrated when a group of six of her classmates in her new required course titled Friendship and Development don't realize that she can help them. Soon Bindy is shocked to find that it is actually her that needs the help from her classmates.

Interpersonal Relations • Gifted Teenagers • Peer Pressure • Australia • Epistolary Novels • Diary Novel • High School • Friendship • Romance

Myracle, Lauren

Eleven. New York: Dutton Children's Books, 2004. 208 p. ISBN: 9780525471653; 9780142403464pa; (aud). *M*

In the year before she turns twelve, Winnie Perry struggles when her best friend, Amanda, becomes interested in clothes and boys and leaves her out. But when she connects with Dinah, a girl she once pitied, Winnie is able to find a new friendship that helps her as she deals with her teenage sister, Sandra, her active little brother, Ty, and the excitement of getting her first boyfriend.

Sequel: *Twelve.* New York: Dutton Children's Books, 2007. 208 p. ISBN: 9780525477846; 9780142410912pa; (aud). *M*

> Starting junior high, Winnie must now deal with the rites of passage that come along with puberty, including getting her first bra and starting her period. Despite embarrassments like losing her tampon in the pool, getting rejected by her best friend, and standing up when a classmate abuses a substitute teacher, Winnie learns to deal with life and love.

Sequel: *Thirteen.* New York: Dutton Children's Books, 2008. 224 p. ISBN: 9780525478966; 9780142413708pa. *M*

> With her sister about to leave for college, her mother overwhelmed and pregnant, her six-year-old brother dealing with his friend's battle with leukemia, and her father just trying to keep things together, Winnie's thirteenth year is tumultuous. She finds herself also dealing with changing friendships, first kisses, and breaking up.

> *Friendship • Growing Up • Family*

Myracle, Lauren

Internet Girls Series. New York: Harry N. Abrams; New York: Amulet Books

> Best friends Zoe, Maddie, and Angela deal with the problems of growing up and the complications of love as they progress through high school.

> *Friendship • Dating • Instant Messaging • Romance • Moving • Marijuana • Proms • Sexuality*

Ttyl. 2004. 224 p. ISBN: 9780810948211; 9780810987883pa. YALSA Quick Picks. *J*

> Despite the fact that they have sworn to be best friends for life, at the start of their sophomore year, things start changing for Zoe, Maddie, and Angela. Zoe is developing an unhealthy relationship with her creepy teacher, Maddie dumps her friends when she latches on to popular Jana, and Angela is constantly dealing with boys, but through it all the trio works to maintain their friendship.

TTFN. 2006. 224 p. ISBN: 9780810959712; 9780810992795pa. *J*

> Sixteen-year-old friends, Angela, Zoe, and Maddie deal with new problems in their lives. Maddie is drinking and smoking pot to attract a guy who is already another girl's boyfriend. Zoe worries because she is attracted to a guy Angela once liked, and Angela finds that she must move to California when her father is laid off. Even with all the problems, the girls support and help each other.

L8r, G8r. 2007. 240 p. ISBN: 9780810912663; 9780810970861pa. *JS*

> Zoe, Angela, and Maddie are facing their futures as they decide which college to attend, but in the meantime, they must also deal with present circumstances as Zoe loses her virginity, Angela's pride is crushed by a guy who gives her extravagant presents, and Maddie works to help keep the peace between the friends.

Naylor, Phyllis Reynolds

<u>Alice Series</u>. New York: Atheneum; New York: Aladdin Paperbacks
Alice McKinley faces growing up from sixth grade to high school without the womanly advice of a mother.
Growing Up • Coming-of-Age • Friendship • Family

The Agony of Alice. 1985. 131 p. ISBN: 9780689816727pa; 9781416955337pa. ALA Notable Children's Books. *M*
> Sixth-grader Alice is surrounded by men after her mother dies. She searches for a female role model to help her grow up, which she finds in her teacher Mrs. Plotkin.

Alice in Rapture, Sort of. 1989. 166 p. ISBN: 9780689816871pa. *M*
> Alice has fallen in love with Peter, but even with the help and advice of her best friends Pamela and Elizabeth and her Aunt Sally, the rules of dating and kissing get far too complicated.

Reluctantly Alice. 1991 (reissued 2001), 182 p. ISBN: 9780689816888pa. *M*
> Starting seventh grade, Alice just wants to be liked by her classmates, but when she has a run-in with bully Denise "Mack-Truck" Whitlock and her father and twenty-year-old brother start having problems choosing between the women in their lives, things do not go as planned.

All but Alice. 1992. 151 p. ISBN: 9780689317736; 9780689850448pa. *M*
> In the second half of her seventh-grade year, Alice finally finds that she is part of the popular crowd but also finds that life at the top can be pretty boring. She stands up for her old friends when they are targeted for some nasty pranks.

Alice in April. 1993. 164 p. ISBN: 9780440409441pa; *MJ*
> Turning thirteen, Alice finds that it is hard growing up, especially when your body is changing and you have to be the "Woman of the House" to take care of your father and older brother.

Alice in-Between. 1994. 144 p. ISBN: 9780689318900; 9780440410645pa. *MJ*
> Alice is still trying to figure out how to grow up. She and her sexy-looking friend Pamela and shy friend Elizabeth travel to visit Alice's Aunt Sally at her home in Chicago.

Alice the Brave. 1995. 130 p. ISBN: 9780689800955; 9780689805981pa. *MJ*
> During the summer before the start of eighth grade, Alice tries to overcome her fear of deep water while still trying to figure out the mysteries of kissing and sex.

Alice in Lace. 1996. 139 p. ISBN: 9780689803581; 9780689805974pa. *MJ*
> When Alice's eighth-grade health class starts studying some of life's most difficult problems and choices, Alice and her friends get a taste of what it might be like to be a grown up.

Outrageously Alice. 1997. 133 p. ISBN: 9780689803543; 9780689805967pa. YALSA Best Books. *MJ*

> Alice learns a lot about sex, relationships, and growing up when her boyfriend French-kisses her during a Halloween game of spin-the-bottle and she serves as bridesmaid for one of her brother's former girlfriends.

Achingly Alice. 1998. 121 p. ISBN: 9780689803550; 9780689805950pa. *MJ*

> Obsessed with getting her father to marry the gorgeous teacher he has been dating, Alice decides it is time to plan for the future as she tries to understand how she feels about boyfriend Patrick.

Alice on the Outside. 1999. 169 p. ISBN: 9780689803598; 9780689805943pa. *MJ*

> Once certain that prejudice did not exist at her school, fourteen-year-old Alice is surprised to find that it really does when a lesbian classmate, Lori, asks Alice to be her friend, and Alice is called upon to defend her.

The Grooming of Alice. 2000. 215 p. ISBN: 9780689826337; 9780689846182pa. *J*

> The summer before high school, Alice's friend Elizabeth is becoming anorexic. When her friend Pamela runs away from trouble at home, Alice must decide between revealing her whereabouts or staying loyal to her friend.

Alice Alone. 2001. 229 p. ISBN: 9780689826344; 9780689851896pa. *J*

> When cute girl Penny steals Alice's boyfriend Patrick, Alice relieves the pain by serving others and learns about the horrors of poverty, drugs, and abuse.

Simply Alice. 2002. 222p. ISBN: 9780689826351; 9780689859656pa. *J*

> During her first year of high school, Alice deals with all the different parts of her life, including being on the stage crew and the school newspaper, the threats of hazing, the joys of making new friends, and the mystery of discovering a secret admirer.

Patiently Alice. 2003. 243 p. ISBN: 9780689826368. *J*

> While working as a counselor at a summer camp for poor children, Alice finds out that even small things can make a difference.

Including Alice. 2004. 288 p. ISBN: 9780689826375; 9780689870743pa. *J*

> A sophomore in high school, Alice is excited when the wedding day of her father and longtime girlfriend Sylvia Summers arrives, but as the couple makes plans for changes, Alice begins to feel left out.

Alice on her Way. 2005. 336 p. ISBN: 9780689870903; 9780689870910pa. *JS*

> Nearly sixteen, Alice is looking forward to getting her driver's license, but when she fails the test, things don't look good. On top of it all, her Dad signs her up for a sexuality class at her church, where Alice is surprised to find she learns many things.

Alice in the Know. 2006. 288 p. ISBN: 9780689870927; 9780689870934pa. *JS*

In the summer before her junior year, Alice is struggling with a friend who has leukemia and the breakup of her older brother with his black girlfriend.

Dangerously Alice. 2007. 304 p. ISBN: 9780689870941; 9780689870958pa. *JS*

At the beginning of her junior year, Alice is worried about her image as a good girl and finds herself tempted to have sex with gorgeous senior Tony and to act mean toward a needy student named Amy.

Almost Alice. 2008. 288 p. ISBN: 9780689870965; 9780689870972pa. *JS*

At the end of her junior year, Alice gets back with her old boyfriend Patrick, gets a promotion at the school newspaper, and goes to the prom.

Intensely Alice. 2009. 288 p. ISBN: 9781416975519. *JS*

During the summer before her senior year, Alice volunteers at a homeless shelter and visits boyfriend Patrick at his college dorm with the unrealized hope of having sex with him.

Noel, Alyson

Faking 19. New York: St. Martin's Griffin, 2005. 210 p. ISBN: 9780312336332pa *S*

High school senior Alex is apathetic about everything, including that her father is gone, she probably won't graduate, and she and her best friend, M., spend every weekend pretending to be nineteen so they can party at all the LA clubs. While her friend sinks deeper into the scene, including taking drugs, Alex begins to understand that she cannot drown her life in excess and she must take charge and figure out what she is going to do after high school.

Friendship • Father-Separated Families

Peters, Julie Anne

Define "Normal." Boston, MA: Little, Brown, 2000. 196 p. ISBN: 9780316706315. YALSA Best Books; YALSA Quick Picks. *MJ*

Antonia Dillon, an honors student at Oberon Middle School, is asked to be a peer counselor and is happy to accept so she can have another item to add to her resume. But Antonia is shocked when she is paired with tattooed, pierced, punker Jasmine "Jazz" Luther. In their sessions, the girls begin to develop a friendship as they reveal to each other the secrets about their troubled lives, and the two girls find that their friendship helps them to cope.

Family Problems • Friendship • Parent and Child

Powell, Randy

Three Clams and an Oyster. New York: Farrar, Straus & Giroux, 2002. 216 p. ISBN: 9780374375263; 9780374400071pa. YALSA Best Books. *JS*

Sixteen-year-old captain of his four-man flag-football team, Flint McCallister and his two teammates are unhappy with their unreliable, party-loving fourth player, Cade Savage. As the trio tries to decide whether they should dump Cade, Rachel Summerfield, a self-confident, athletic girl yet inept newcomer who does not shave her legs, arrives on the scene and they realize that they must adapt if they want to win.

Friendship • Sports

Rivers, Karen

The Healing Time of Hickeys. Vancouver, Canada: Polestar, 2004. 304 p. ISBN: 9781551926001 *JS*

Sixteen-year-old hypochondriac Haley Andromeda Harmony, who lives with her marijuana-selling hippie father, chronicles her high hopes for her senior year in her diary. With her best friends, Jules and Kiki, not always being friendly, and her crush, J.T., barely knowing she's alive, things don't look as if they will lead to having the greatest year of her life. When she meets a cute stranger at a party and he givers her chicken pox, things get even worse. Dealing with all kinds of complicated events, Haley is able to cope with humor as she tries to figure out what a great time she really had.

Sequel: *The Cure for Crushes: and Other Deadly Plagues.* Berkeley, CA: Raincoast Books, 2005. 304 p. ISBN: 9781551927794. *JS*

Things are still not great for Haley Andromeda Harmony. Her best friends, Jules and Kiki, keep getting on her nerves, and she is avoiding her really nice boyfriend Brad because she can't get over her crush on J.T., who is now dating Jules. With all kinds of mishaps plaguing her, including broken limbs, horribly dyed hair, and noncooperative horoscopes, Haley has a lot going on that may just prevent her from having the greatest year of her life.

Hippies • Mother-Separated Families • Father and Daughter • Marijuana • Friendship • Romance • Diary Novel

Ryan, P. E.

Saints of Augustine. New York: HarperTeen, 2007. 308 p. ISBN: 9780060858100; 9780060858124pa. *JS*

Seventeen year olds Charlie and Sam have been best friends since they were nine years old, until the summer they just stopped talking to each other. Left alone to deal with his grief following his mother's death from leukemia, Charlie starts smoking pot, a habit that puts him deeply in debt to a threatening dealer, while his father turns to alcohol to drown his own grief. Sam is also dealing with his own changes when his father leaves to live with another man, his mother starts dating a homophobic man, and Sam starts questioning his own sexuality when he is attracted to his new gay friend Justin. When the boys accidentally reconnect one evening, they find that it is only with one another's support that they are going to be able find the courage to face their problems.

Best Friends • Friendship • Homosexuality • Gay Males • Divorce

Shaw, Tucker

The Girls. New York: Amulet Books, 2009. 208 p. ISBN: 9780810983489. *S*

Peggy overhears gossiping snob Sylvia saying that her friend Mary's boyfriend is cheating. After this revelation, numerous other betrayals are revealed. The truth about Sylvia's own two-timing boyfriend and Mary's own cheating comes to light. Watching the devastation that unfolds from the sidelines, Peggy tries to support her friend while hoping to find the balance she needs in her life to achieve her dreams of becoming a chef.

Gossiping and Gossips • Interpersonal Relations • Friendship • Jealousy • Cooking

Sheldon, Dyan

Planet Janet. Cambridge, MA: Candlewick Press, 2003. 223 p. ISBN: 9780763620486; 9780763625566pa. *JS*

Dramatic sixteen-year-old Janet Foley Bandry enters the "dark phase" of her life wearing only black and purple as she explores her creative nature and nurtures her passionate soul. Joined by her best friend Disha, Janet tries yoga, gets her nose pierced, and becomes a vegetarian to attract a boy. While she suffers through the indignities and humiliations of growing up, Janet is oblivious to the chaos around her, until circumstances force her to develop the compassion she needs to confront painful truths.

Sequel: ***Planet Janet in Orbit.*** Cambridge, MA: Candlewick Press, 2005. 304 p. ISBN: 9780763627553. *JS*

Instead of spending the summer in Greece, Janet is forced to get her first job as a waitress. When she meets cute Australian waiter Ethan at work, things look up, but then he falls for her best friend Disha, and the two start spending all their time together. Things continue to go downhill when Janet's divorced mother starts dating an environmental activist, Robert, and she must now vacation with her mother at Robert's cottage in Wales, as well as with his two daughters. As school starts again, Janet must face disastrous driving lessons from her father, but when she lands a job at the school magazine as the anonymous advice columnist, Janet finally finds something that could help turn her life around.

Family Problems • Diary Novel • High School Newspapers • Advice Columnist • Self-Discovery

Shusterman, Neal

The Schwa Was Here. New York: Dutton Children's Books, 2004. 276 p. ISBN: 9780525471820; 9780142405772pa. ALA Notable Children's Books; YALSA Best Books; YALSA Popular Paperbacks. *MJ*

Eighth-grader Anthony "Antsy" Bonano and his friends are amazed at Calvin Schwa's ability to go completely unnoticed, thus essentially making himself invisible, and they come up with the perfect scheme to test his abilities. When the boys take a dare requiring Schwa to enter the house of the town's millionaire, Mr. Crawley, and they are caught, they get out of other punishments by agreeing to walk Crawley's fourteen afghan hounds. After they gain Mr. Crawley's trust, he soon asks the boys to act as companions to his blind granddaughter, Lexie. As they get to know her, they find that their friendship with each other improves not only their own lives, but the lives of others.

Sequel: ***Antsy Does Time.*** New York: Dutton Children's Books, 2008. 256 p. ISBN: 9780525478256; 9780142414873pa; (aud). YALSA Best Books. *MJ*

When his Swedish classmate, Gunnar Ümlaut, reveals that he is dying of a rare disease called pulmonary monoxic systemia, Antsy Bonano assists his doomed friend by signing a formal contract that gives him a month of his own life. As the rest of the school jumps on the bandwagon and everyone starts giving months to Gunnar, Antsy starts to think something is wrong because Gunnar's family largely ignores his imminent death. Working through his attraction to Gunnar's gorgeous older sister, Kjersten, Antsy is also assisting his blind friend Lexie in a plot to kidnap her Grandpa Crawley, all while supporting his father as he struggles to establish the family's new restaurant. All these events help Antsy learn a lot about the true meaning of life.

Death • Interpersonal Relations • Family Problems • Social Acceptance • Self-Perception • Coming-of-Age

Sloan, Brian

Tale of Two Summers. New York: Simon & Schuster Books for Young Readers, 2006. 256 p. ISBN: 9780689874390. *JS*

Fifteen-year-olds straight Chuck and gay Hal have been friends since they were five, and this is the first summer they must spend apart. Keeping in touch through a blog, Chuck is attending a summer theater camp where he will have the lead in a musical play, while Hal stays home. During the summer, the boys traverse the ups and downs of romantic and sexual relationships while they each learn about love and self-respect.

Friendship • Best Friends • Gay Males • Homosexuality • Blogs • Theater • Interpersonal Relations • Summer Camps

Soto, Gary

Mercy on These Teenage Chimps. Orlando: Harcourt, 2007. 160 p. ISBN: 9780152060220; 9780152062156pa. *M*

Even though thirteen-year-old Joey Rios and his friends already feel like monkeys with their gangly bodies and gross smells, Joey is humiliated when his coach calls him a monkey after, in an attempt to impress pretty Jessica by saving her balloon, he climbs up in the rafters. He has now escaped to his tree house. Unable to get his friend out of his tree house exile, thirteen-year-old Ronnie Gonzalez sets out to save his friend's reputation.

Friendship • Bullies and Bullying • Coming-of-Age

Vega, Denise

Click Here (to Find Out How I Survived Seventh Grade): A Novel. New York: Little, Brown, 2005. 211 p. ISBN: 9780316985604. *M*

When Erin Swift begins middle school and finds that she and her best friend Jilly will not have any classes together, the new year gets off to a rough start. Things continue to go downhill when Erin punches mean girl Serena after she insinuates that Erin is Jilly's puppet. Just as Serena's taunts make Erin start to wonder if she really should make some new friends and find her own interests, disaster strikes when the boy she likes starts liking Jilly and then her private Web diary accidently gets posted on the school's Intranet for the whole school to read. Now Erin must truly learn to speak up for herself if she is going to survive the embarrassment of having her private thoughts exposed.

Sequel: *Access Denied (and Other Eighth Grade Error Messages).* New York: Little, Brown, 2009. 288 p. ISBN: 9780316034487. *MJ*

> With a new year ahead of her, Erin Swift is ready for a new start. But eighth grade brings with it its own set of troubles, especially with boys, as Erin gets her first boyfriend and then has her first breakup. Things are bad at home too, with her mother treating her like a child. When a new girl comes to school and takes Erin under her wing, trying to remake her into her own bad-girl image, Erin must make some tough choices about what influence you should have on friends and how much influence friends should have on you.

> *Friendship • Blogs • Diaries*

Wallace, Rich

One Good Punch. New York: Alfred A. Knopf: Distributed by Random House, 2007. 114 p. ISBN: 9780375813528; 9780440422600pa. YALSA Best Books. *S*

> High school senior Michael Kerrigan writes for the local paper and is on the track team. With a determination to be the very best, Michael looks forward to a great year, but when a friend puts four joints in his locker and they are found in a random drug sweep, he faces being expelled. Michael has never been involved in trouble like this, and now, with his future on the team and his plans for college on the line, he tries to decide if he should protect his friend or look out for himself as he deals with the repercussions that his choice will ultimately have.

> *Athletes • Friendship • Marijuana • Drug Use • Ethics*

Williams, Lori Aurelia

Shayla's Double Brown Baby Blues. New York: Simon & Schuster Books for Young Readers, 2001. 300 p. ISBN: 9780689824692; 9780689856709pa; (aud). *MJ*

> Angry when her father and his new wife have a baby whom she thinks will steal what little love he has from her, thirteen-year-old Shayla must also deal with the problems of her best friends Kambia and Lemm. Kambia is now living with foster parents and is undergoing intensive therapy to overcome the years of abuse she has suffered. Lemm is an alcoholic who cannot shed his past, which was filled with abuse. When someone starts sending Shayla creepy anonymous gifts, she finds that she might also be in danger. Shayla begins to realize that there is only so much help you can give, even to those you love.

> *Friendship • African Americans • Alcoholism*

Wilson, Jacqueline

Girls Quartet Series. New York: Delacorte Press

> Three friends—Ellie, Magda, and Nadine—experience the pains of growing up.

> *Friendship • Romance • Body Image • Weight Control • Peer Pressure • Family • Artists • Blended Families • England*

> *Girls in Love.* 2002. 181 p. ISBN: 9780385729741; 9780440229575pa; (aud). YALSA Quick Picks. *J*

> > Worried about her appearance as well as her relationship with her father and stepmother, Ellie finds that the start of ninth grade is harder than she ex-

pected when her two best friends, Magda and Nadine, find boyfriends. Spinning stories that invent a boyfriend for her based on Dan, a geeky guy she knows, things change when he unexpectedly shows up and she finds out that he is not as geeky or awkward as she thought.

Girls Under Pressure. 2002. 214 p. ISBN: 9780385729758; 9780440229582pa; (aud). *J*

Ellie, realizing that she is not the same size as her slim friends Magda and Nadine, begins to fall into anorexia and bulimia. Lying to her parents, hiding food and exercising obsessively, Ellie falls deeper into her problems while her friends deal with their own concerns. Together and with the help of their supportive families, the girls work to deal with the issues they face.

Girls Out Late. 2002. 213 p. ISBN: 9780385729765; 9780440229599pa; (aud). *J*

Thirteen-year-old Ellie thinks she has met the love of her life when she meets Russell, but when she and her friends make plans to meet him at a concert and the plans fall through, the girls end up in a dangerous part of London with boys who want them to drink, do drugs, and make out. The girls barely escape from the negative situation.

Girls in Tears. 2003. 169 p. ISBN: 9780385730822; 9780440238072pa. *J*

With her father and stepmother constantly fighting and her best friends excluding her, things get even worse for Ellie when her boyfriend plagiarizes her cartoons for a drawing contest and then he makes out with her friend Magda at a drunken party. Ellie must deal with the fact that relationships change over time.

Wittlinger, Ellen

What's in a Name. New York: Simon & Schuster Books for Young Readers, 2000. 146 p. ISBN: 9780689825514; 9781416984825pa. YALSA Best Books. *JS*

At suburban Scrub Harbor High School, ten teens deal with many issues as they try to figure out who they really are. Sophomore O'Neill admits that he is gay, leaving his football-star older brother to learn how to deal with the revelation. Nelson, a popular black senior, tries unsuccessfully to connect with Shaquanda, a black girl bused to his school from the city. A Brazilian exchange student deals with a language barrier while making friends with an angry girl, and a transferring senior must deal with the fact that he is not popular anymore.

Friendship • Gay Males • Interpersonal Relations

Wood, Maryrose

My Life, the Musical. New York: Delacorte Press, 2008. 228 p. ISBN: 9780385732789. *JS*

Best friends Emily and Phillip are obsessed with the long-running musical, *Aurora*. Not only have they traveled from Long Island to Broadway every weekend for more than three years to see the show, but they have spent hours in chat rooms with other fans trying to tease out the secret identity of the musical's composer. When the pair find that the show will be closing, Emily lies to her parents and steals money from her grandmother so they can attend all the remaining performances. Soon Emily and Phillip must realize that they have been living in a fantasy world, and it is necessary for them to deal with what is happening in the real world.

Musicals • Theater • Friendship

Wooding, Chris

Crashing. New York: Scholastic Paperpacks, 2003. 160 p. ISBN: 9780439090124pa. *JS*

Sixteen-year-old Jay throws a party as a last hurrah before all his friends drift off in different directions for the summer and to have one last chance to declare his love for Jo, whom he has had a crush on for years. He never imagined that when the drunken boyfriend of an uninvited girl crashes the party, the evening will end in a war between his friends and the party-crashing thugs.

Summer • Parties • Infatuation • Friendship • England

Chapter 2

Falling In and Out of Love

Feelings of love are very real and deeply felt in adolescence, and forming and keeping romantic attachments engages the hearts and minds of most young people. Having romantic feelings for another person is an important part of an adolescent's healthy development and identity formation, as is learning how to deal with these feelings. The books listed in this chapter deal with the intricacies of romance as feelings wax and wane and teens fall in and out of love with their hearts' desire. From the intense and life-changing emotions surrounding one's first love, to the whimsy of a fleeting summer love, to the variety of dating experiences both in person and online, these books look at love in many forms. However, the path to true love does not always run smoothly, and other books discuss the problems with romance. Figuring out what to do when the object of your affection is unobtainable or if, once obtained, the object does not live up to expectations, or even dealing with a broken heart from breaking up, everyone's path to love may not be easy, but usually in the end, everyone lives happily ever after.

General Romance

Abbott, Hailey

Boy Crazy. New York: HarperTeen, 2009. 240 p. ISBN: 9780061253850. *J*
> Cassie and her best friends, Greta and Keagan, make a pact to kiss ten guys before school starts. But when Cassie meets her best friend's ex-boyfriend, he turns out to be the perfect guy, and she realizes that she wants to break the pact.
>
> *Kissing • Best Friends • Ex-Boyfriends*

Abbott, Hailey

Flirting with Boys. New York: HarperTeen, 2009. 256 p. ISBN: 9780152054137pa. *J*
> Celeste Tippen is looking forward to some quality time with her boyfriend, Travis, when he gets a job at her family's resort. But when the son of one of the resort's wealthiest customers, Nick Saunders, begins to flirt with her and she starts hanging out with him, Celeste must decide between the two.
>
> *Jobs • Boyfriends • Rich People*

Abbott, Hailey

Forbidden Boy. New York: HarperTeen, 2008. 256 p. ISBN: 9780061253829. *J*

The next-door neighbors are trying to force Julianne's family from their beach-front home. Julianne is happy for a diversion when she meets Remi at a bonfire party. Things get complicated when Remi turns out be the neighbors' son, and it is up to Julianne to decide if he is an enemy or a friend.

Neighbors • Love

Abbott, Hailey

Getting Lost with Boys. New York: HarperTeen, 2006. 240 p. ISBN: 9780060824327. *J*

Cordelia Packer is surprised when Jacob Stein offers to travel with her from San Diego to her sister's home in Northern California. Faced with Jacob's carefree attitude, Cordelia's perfectly planned itinerary goes out the window, and soon she is learning just how much fun getting lost can be.

Sisters • Travel • Self-Discovery • Love

Abbott, Hailey

The Other Boy. New York: HarperTeen, 2008. 272 p. ISBN: 9780061253836. *J*

Carted off to Napa Valley after she is caught throwing a party, Maddy Sinclare must work in her family's vineyard. Leaving boyfriend Brian is very hard until Maddy meets David, the son of her father's business partner, and must decide if the guy she has is what she wants or if she should try to win the guy who thinks she is a spoiled princess.

Jobs • Punishment • Boyfriends • Rich People

Abbott, Hailey

The Perfect Boy. New York: HarperTeen, 2007. 249 p. ISBN: 9780060824341. *J*

Ciara Simmons is determined to change her reputation as a playgirl this summer. She finds AJ, the perfect boy. This makes things seem easy, but when her friend Heidi puts her sights on him too, things get complicated. Teaming up with friend Kevin, who wants to be Heidi's boyfriend, they both try to attract the right mates.

Vacations • Self-Discovery • Love

Abbott, Hailey

The Secrets of Boys. New York: HarperTeen, 2006. 272 p. ISBN: 9780060824334. *J*

Cassidy is stuck in summer school instead of on the beach, but things heat up when she meets romantic Zach and finds herself attracted to him even though she already has a boyfriend, Eric. Wishing her friend Joe was around to help her figure out what to do, Cassidy must decide whether to stay with what she has or give in to the temptation.

Summer School • Boyfriends • Love

Abbott, Hailey

Waking Up to Boys. New York: HarperTeen, 2007. 256 p. ISBN: 9780060824358. *J*

> Chelsea is focused on winning the Northwest Extreme Watersports Competition and beating out her teacher and longtime crush, fellow wakeboarder Todd. But when Sebastian, a Brazilian tennis player, shows interest in her, Chelsea realizes that it is impossible to force love.
>
> *Sports • Love*

Barkley, Brad, and Heather Hepler

Scrambled Eggs at Midnight. New York: Dutton Children's Books, 2006. 262 p. ISBN: 9780525477600; 9780142408674pa. *J*

> Fifteen-year-old Calliope is tired of the wandering life forced upon her by her mother, who works as a serving wench at Renaissance fairs. At yet another fair in Asheville, North Carolina, Calliope meets Elliot, whose family runs a religious camp for overweight children. Both teens are fed up with their families, and with this in common, together they search for answers to their problems.
>
> *Love • Humor • Family Problems*

Black, Jonah

The Black Book: Diary of a Teenage Stud Series. New York: Avon Books

> The quirky fantasies of high school student Jonah are chronicled as he deals with family, friends, and love.
>
> *Love • Diary Novel • High School • Family Relationships • Sexuality*

Girls, Girls, Girls. 2001. 233 p. ISBN: 9780064407984pa. YALSA Quick Picks. *S*

> Having been expelled from his private school in Pennsylvania, Jonah is now repeating his junior year back home in Florida. With a weird mother who has a talk radio show about sex, an overachieving younger sister, and a father who has remarried, Jonah chronicles his thoughts in his diary. Detailing imaginary conversations and sexual fantasies with an enigmatic girlfriend named Sophie, Jonah watches as his crush and longtime friend, Posie Hoff, falls for the wrong guy.

Stop, Don't Stop. 2001. 233 p. ISBN: 9780064407991pa. YALSA Quick Picks. *S*

> Finally revealing his love for Posie, Jonah discovers that she loves him too, but a series of inopportune events prevent the two from getting together.

Run, Jonah, Run. 2001. 215 p. ISBN: 9780064408004pa. *S*

> Things are finally starting to align, and it is possible that Jonah will be able to have sex with Posie. But when former girlfriend Sophie calls and Jonah makes friends with a mysterious girl on the Internet, things don't go as planned.

Faster, Faster, Faster. 2002. 215 p. ISBN: 9780064408011pa. *S*

> On a road trip with his sister to visit their father, Jonah reconnects with Sophie and finds out the identity of the mysterious girl on the Internet.

Brian, Kate

Megan Meade's Guide to the McGowan Boys. New York: Simon & Schuster, 2005. 272 p. ISBN: 9781416900306; 9781416900313pa. *JS*

> When her parents are stationed in South Korea with the army, sixteen-year-old Megan Meade chooses to stay with the McGowan family so she can remain in the United States and play soccer. But being the only girl in a family of seven boys brings its own set of complications, including being the target of a jealous girl-friend when she is accused of falling for one of the boys.

> *Love • Self-Confidence • Jealousy • Soccer • Asperger's Syndrome*

Cabot, Meg

Pants on Fire. New York: Harper Tempest, 2007. 272 p. ISBN: 9780060880156; 9780060880170pa; (aud). *JS*

> Senior Katie Ellison's life is a lie. She hates the Quahogs her town is famous for but yet is running for the title of Quahog Princess in the hope of using the prize money to pay for the professional camera equipment she wants. She is dating popular football star Seth Turner but spends time making out with actor and singer Eric Flutely. All of this catches up with her when Tommy Sullivan, her best friend from middle school, reappears after four years. Katie betrayed Tommy, and he was ostracized by his classmates and fled to military school to escape harassment after reporting that the high school football players, including Seth's brother, had cheated on their SATs. But the Tommy that has come back is not the skinny brain she once knew, and this confident, gorgeous new Tommy attracts her attention. Trying to keep her attraction secret, she lies yet again, but the pressure of keeping her romantic indiscretions under wraps builds until she realizes that telling the truth is the only way out.

> *Cheating • Dating • Deception • Honesty • Peer Pressure*

Calame, Don

Swim the Fly. Somerville, MA: Candlewick Press, 2009. 368 p. ISBN: 9780763641573. *J*

> Since third grade, fifteen-year-old Matt Gratton and his friends Sean and Coop have always placed just about fifth place in their swim team competitions. This fact does not impress Kelly, the girl of Matt's dreams. Matt takes on the nearly impossible 100-yard butterfly with the hope that it will finally do the trick and impress the girl. The three boys share a summer goal to see a naked girl. Along the way, the boys try various schemes to fulfill their goal, such as sneaking into the girl's locker room, but their attempts always seem to be foiled. While Sean and Coop try to peep at Kelly and her friend Valerie in a dressing room, Matt sneaks into a country-club pool to practice and meets Ulf, a swim instructor who convinces him to take his class. In the end, Coop slices the swimsuit of the major contender in the butterfly competition so that Matt can win. Facing this injustice, Matt must decide what he should do to make things right.

> *Swimming • Infatuation • Best Friends • Dares*

Caletti, Deb

Honey, Baby, Sweetheart. New York: Simon & Schuster Books for Young Readers, 2004. 308 p. ISBN: 9780786273089; 9780689864742pa. School Library Journal Best Books. *S*

Sixteen-year-old Ruby McQueen has lived a quiet life until she meets gorgeous rich-kid Travis Becker, who takes her on motorcycles rides and gives her great jewelry. Being with Travis makes Ruby feel tough and fearless until she learns that he breaks into houses and steals the jewelry he has been giving her. Still, she is drawn farther into Travis's criminal activity. Trying to get her daughter away from Travis's corrupting influence Ann, Ruby's mother and a librarian, puts her on a tight schedule and takes her to a book club that she facilitates for a group of feisty senior citizens called the Casserole Queens. Drawn into the lives of the women, one of whom may have been the lover of a famous author, Ruby soon learns about trust and the true meaning of love.

Self-Perception • Rich People • Crime

Castellucci, Cecil

Boy Proof. Cambridge, MA: Candlewick Press, 2005. 208 p. ISBN: 9780763623333; 9780763627966pa. YALSA Best Books; YALSA Quick Picks. *JS*

Taking on the persona of Egg, the hero of her favorite science fiction movie, *Terminal Earth,* sixteen-year-old Victoria Jurgen shaves her head and wears multiple earrings and an all-white, swirling cloak. Despite the fact that her behavior does not win her any friends at school, Victoria holds a straight-A average and is happy working with her movie special-effects artist dad and bickering with her actor mother. Even though she considers herself immune to the charms of guys, when the gorgeous new student Max Carter arrives, she cannot help falling for him since he shares her love of science fiction. Struggling over her feelings and Max's apparent interest in another girl, Victoria's grades start to fall, and she is called in to see the dean of students at her school. Soon things start to come together, and she learns that there are battles to fight right here on Earth, helping her to become her own person and not a representation of a character.

New Students • Friendship • Love • Alienation • Identity • Films

Cheshire, Simon

Kissing Vanessa. New York: Delacorte Press, 2004. 135 p. ISBN: 9780385732123; 9780440238942pa. *J*

Fifteen-year-old Kevin is clueless when it comes to girls. On the other hand, Kevin's friend Jack knows exactly how to attract the ladies—in fact, he is writing a book about it. Desperate to attract the beautiful new girl, Kevin follows Jack's advice, but this backfires and lands Kevin in many exaggerated and humorous situations.

Love • Advice • Friendship • High School • Humor

Clark, Catherine

Icing on the Lake. New York: HarperTeen, 2005. 368 p. ISBN: 9780060815349pa. *JS*
Kirsten is in the Twin Cities taking care of her sister who has broken her leg while skiing. Kirsten has to fulfill one challenge from her best friends: to find a date for a weekend trip they are all taking in a month. Having earned her nickname "Cursed Kirsten," she believes that things may not go as planned, but when she meets two guys she likes, she has to pick between them.

Dating • Winter • Sisters

Clark, Catherine

Maine Squeeze. New York: Avon Books, 2004. 349 p. ISBN: 9780060567255pa. *S*
When her parents go to Europe on a second honeymoon, Colleen is left behind at their Maine island cottage the summer before she starts college. She is allowed to have a few friends with her if she follows strict rules. Things do not go quite as planned as the responsibilities of taking care of a house get out of hand. While spending time with her boyfriend Ben is great, when her ex-boyfriend Evan shows up, she must decide between the two.

Dating • Boyfriends • Summer • Ex-Boyfriends

Clark, Catherine

Truth or Dairy. New York: Harper Tempest, 2000. 268 p. ISBN: 9780380814435pa. *JS*

Also titled: *Banana Splitsville.* New York: HarperTeen, 2008. 288 p. 9780061367151pa.
Dumped at the beginning of senior year by boyfriend Dave, who is off to college, Courtney Von Dragen Smith vows to continue the rest of the year without a replacement. Things are complicated at home, and her job at an ice cream/health food snack shop has its own problems. Joining student government doesn't help either, and things get really challenging when fellow student Grant's romantic interest finally forces her to take the risk of getting close to another boyfriend.

Sequel: *Wurst Case Scenario.* New York: HarperCollins, 2001. 311 p. ISBN: 9780064472876pa. *JS*

Also titled: *Rocky Road Trip.* New York: HarperTeen, 2008. 336 p. 9780061367168pa.
Attending a small liberal arts school, Cornwall Falls College in Wisconsin, freshman Courtney is dealing with homesickness, the shock of being a vegan in the land of cheese-and-bratwurst, and the trials of having a long-distance relationship with perfect boyfriend Grant. Working for minimum wage at the fast-food chain, The Bagel Finagle, does not make things much better. When her new best friend, Thyme, turns out not to be what she originally thought, Courtney is faced with finding the courage to adjust to her new life.

Jobs • Love • Vegetarianism • Diary Novel

Cohn, Rachel, and David Levithan

Nick and Norah's Infinite Playlist. New York: Knopf, distributed by Random House, 2006. 192 p. ISBN: 9780375835315. YALSA Best Books; YALSA Quick Picks; YALSA Popular Paperbacks. *S*

> Nick is playing a concert with his band when he sees his ex-girlfriend, Tris. He convinces a random girl named Norah to play his girlfriend for five minutes to make Tris jealous. Norah, who is also nursing a broken heart, agrees and even after the plot works, the two stay together and spend the evening roaming New York.

Rock Music • Trust • Love • Girlfriends • Boyfriends • Ex-Girlfriends • Coming-of-Age

Colasanti, Susane

When It Happens. New York: Viking, 2006. 320 p. ISBN: 9780670060290; 9780142411551pa. *S*

> Told in alternating perspectives, two high school seniors, slacker and garage-band member Tobey and brainy and beautiful Sara, navigate the travails of high school. Sara is disappointed in her boyfriend Dave, realizing she has no honest feelings for him besides being attracted to his good looks. Tobey is sure that Sara is the one and enlists the help of her friends to convince her. Soon the two find they have much in common.

Love • Friendship

Cook, Eileen

What Would Emma Do? New York: Simon & Schuster, 2009. 224 p. ISBN: 9781416974321pa. *J*

> Emma Proctor has big dreams of leaving her small town, especially after she messes up and kisses her best friend's boyfriend. When the popular girls begin telling lies about the school outcast's drug poisonings, Emma is one of the people with proof to show they are lying. But Emma is unwilling to risk not only her friendships but also the scholarship that is her way out of town and must decide where her loyalties and priorities lie.

Dating • Jealousy • Faith • Private Schools • Canadian

Davidson, Dana

Jason & Kyra. New York: Jump at the Sun/Hyperion Books for Children, 2004. 336 p. ISBN: 9780786818518; 9780786836536pa. YALSA Quick Picks. *J*

> Paired in English class with brainy outsider Kyra, star basketball player Jason realizes he wants something more than the shallowness of current girlfriend Lisa. Jason is increasingly drawn to Kyra, and they become physically intimate. He finds himself comfortable in her stable home that lets him escape his neglectful father. Jason dumps Lisa, and he and Kyra have to deal with Lisa's plot to exact revenge.

Sexuality • Girlfriends • Father and Son • African Americans

Davidson, Dana

Played. New York: Jump At The Sun/Hyperion, 2005. 240 p. ISBN: 9780786836901; 9780786836918pa. YALSA Quick Picks; YALSA Popular Paperbacks. *S*

> The final hurdle for Ian Striver to complete before he is inducted into Cross High School's elite fraternity, the FBI, is to get plain, unpopular Kylie Winship to fall in love and then have sex with him. Things go as planned, but what Ian had not counted on was falling for Kylie in return. When the plot is revealed in front of the whole school, Ian must deal with why he sacrificed his own integrity before he can win back Kylie's trust.

> *Sexuality • Popularity • Cliques • African Americans*

Davis, Stephie

Boys Series. New York: Dorchester

> Four friends, Blue, Frances, Allie, and Natalie, find unexpected love.

> *Friendship • Love • Camping • Breaking Up • Sports • Boyfriends*

> ***Putting Boys on the Ledge.*** 2004. 208 p. ISBN: 9780843953282pa. *J*
>
> > Blueberry "Blue" Waller and her three best friends, Allie, Frances, and Natalie, have often faced the ledge, that place where you go when you are crushed after a boy dumps you. But when a gorgeous senior, Heath, starts to notice her, Blue begins to wonder if she should put him on the ledge before he can put her there, especially since her family's gardener and farmhand Colin has turned out to be a great kisser.

> ***Studying Boys.*** 2004. 188 p. ISBN: 9780843953824pa. *J*
>
> > Blackmailed by her friends to join a homework club to meet boys because they think she is studying too much, Frances Spinelli faces the threat of her secret crush on Blue's brother Theo being revealed.

> ***Who Needs Boys?*** 2005. 193 p. ISBN: 9780843953978pa. *J*
>
> > Allie's trip to California to visit her father is canceled, so she joins her friends working at a farm stand where she meets brothers Tad and Rand. Tad is Allie's age, but she prefers older brother Rand to Tad's disdainful attitude, and she thinks she has found the perfect guy.

> ***Smart Boys & Fast Girls.*** 2005. 178 p. ISBN: 9780843953985pa. *J*
>
> > Runner Natalie is loved by many boys but only as a buddy. When fellow teammate Matt starts tutoring her so she can stay on the cross-country team, she pretends he is her boyfriend to keep gorgeous Zach Fulton from finding out. But when Zach finally starts noticing her, Natalie begins to question whether it is Matt or Zach who would make the perfect boyfriend.

Delaney, Kaz

My Life as a Snow Bunny. New York: Dorchester, 2003. 240 p. ISBN: 9780843952964pa. *JS*

> Surfing California girl Jo Vincent is forced to spend her winter break with her dad and his girlfriend on a ski trip to Colorado. Soon gorgeous Hans has Jo thinking

that the trip might not be as bad as she expected. When her dad starts pushing jerk Justin as a potential boyfriend and Hans turns out not to be who he says he is, Jo must overcome some real obstacles before she can find true love.

Father and Daughter • Family • Love

Dent, Grace

LBD Series. New York: G.P. Putnam's Sons
The LBD, "Les Bambinos Dangereuse," Fleur, Claude, and Ronnie, rock-and-roll as they have adventures and find love.

Love • Music • Schools • Moving

It's a Girl Thing. 2003. 192 p. ISBN: 9780399241871; 9780142401828pa. *J*
Forbidden to go to the Astlebury Music Festival, the LBD promote their own festival at their school. The project does include finding cute boy bands, and the whole endeavor proves more difficult than anticipated.

Live and Fabulous. 2005. 256 p. ISBN: 9780399241888. *J*
When tickets to the Astlebury Music Festival arrive from rock star Spike Saunders, who remembers the LBD from the previous year's school festival, the girls are finally allowed to go if they consent to be chaperoned by Fleur's older sister.

Friends Forever. 2006. 272 p. ISBN: 9780399241895. *J*
Forced by her mother to move at the end of the summer, the LBDs decide to save Claude from this fate by working as wait staff in an exclusive hotel to earn 10,000 pounds in a modeling contest.

Dessen, Sarah

This Lullaby. New York: Viking, 2002. 345 p. ISBN: 9780670035304; 9780142501559pa; (aud). YALSA Best Books. *JS*
Moving on from a rape and a life of promiscuity, drinking, and drug use, Remy has a strong fear of commitment. Remy's mother is a romance writer who has been married five times and whose current boyfriend is cheating on her. This has confirmed to Remy that every boy will let her down, just like her musician father said, and that love is just too much of a risk—that is, until wild musician Dexter and his sloppy group of band members falls into her life the summer after she graduates from high school.

Love • Dating • Music • Drinking • Drug Use • Rape

Doyle, Larry

I Love You, Beth Cooper. New York: Ecco, 2007. 272 p. ISBN: 9780061236174; 9780061236181pa; (aud). YALSA Best Books. *S*
During his high school valedictory speech, Denis Cooverman blurts out his confession of love for classmate and cheerleader Beth Cooper. That night Denis and his friend Rich are excited when Beth shows up at their solitary

graduation party with two of her girlfriends, Cammy and Treece. But as they try to party with the girls, their fun is cut short by Beth's angry boyfriend Kevin, who shows up intent on killing Denis.

Friendship • High School • Jealousy • Coming-of-Age

Echols, Jennifer

Going Too Far. New York: Simon & Schuster/MTV Books, 2009. 256 p. ISBN: 9781416571735pa. *S*

Meg only wants to get away from her small town and her parents who seem intent on keeping her there. John had the chance to get away and go to college, but he came back to serve as a cop. The two meet when on a dare when Meg and her friends go to the forbidden railroad tracks, where it is rumored that some kids had died. John, who regularly patrols there, catches them. John has nothing but contempt for Meg and her childish actions, and he wants to teach her a lesson by forcing her to ride with him on his nightly patrols. But when Meg pushes back and questions everything he has learned at the police academy, John reacts and the two find themselves falling in love.

Police • Crime • Love

Farrell, Mame

And Sometimes Why. New York: Farrar, Straus & Giroux, 2001. 165 p. ISBN: 9780374322892. *MJ*

Thirteen-year-old artist Jack sees his tomboy best friend, Chris Moffett, turning beautiful, and he's worried about losing her, especially since he thinks he feels more than friendship for her. Jack's parents belong to the country club where they long to be accepted by the popular crowd. While Jack faces his parents' marriage problems at home, he and Chris find themselves spending much of the summer before they start high school at the country club. Facing lots of pressure to keep up and look good, they soon realize that many in this crowd are not what they thought. When Jack finds that his date to the summer formal was just using him, he decides it is time to confess his feelings to Chris.

Friendship • Artists • Peer Pressure • Family Problems • Popularity

Ferraro, Tina

The ABC's of Kissing Boys. New York: Delacorte Press, 2009. 224 p. ISBN: 9780385735827pa. *JS*

Parker Stanhope hopes to land a spot on the varsity soccer team buts finds instead that not only will she still be on junior varsity surrounded by freshmen, the change earns her the animosity of her best friend, Chrissandra, who is the queen bee of the junior class. Sure that she can force the coach to promote her if she earns the most money at the soccer team's kissing booth fundraiser at the annual carnival, Parker convinces her older brother's friend to pay $300 for a kiss. To be sure everything goes off without a hitch, Parker agrees when cute neighbor Tristan offers to give her kissing lessons. When Parker finds herself falling for Tristan, she must decide between her new love or sticking with her plan.

Kissing • Popularity • Soccer

Ferraro, Tina

How to Hook a Hottie. New York: Delacorte Press, 2008. 196 p. ISBN: 9780385734387pa. *S*

> When popular Brandon Callister asks seventeen-year-old Kate, the co-president of the Future Business Leaders of America who plans to be a millionaire by age twenty, to be his date to a sports banquet, she is suddenly skyrocketed to popularity. When all her friends begin asking her for advice, Kate sees a prime business opportunity that will help her fill her end of the bargain with her parents that if she can earn $5,000, they will give her their college savings fund to invest. Motivated to win, Kate launches a matchmaking service with her friend Jason and along the way finds some unintended consequences.

> *Money Making • Advice • Family Problems*

Fredericks, Mariah

In the Cards Trilogy. New York: Atheneum Books for Young Readers

> Declan, Anna, and their friends use tarot cards to find clues about their futures, but the cards don't always lead them down the right path.

> *Friendship • Love • Popularity • Gossiping and Gossips • Jealousy • Actors and Actresses • Family Problems*

> *Love*. 2007. 288 p. ISBN: 9780689876547. *MJ*

> Looking for answers on how to attract her crush, Declan Kelso, who has recently become popular, eighth-grader Anna and her best friends consult a deck of tarot cards that were left to her by an elderly woman. But when dating Declan is not what she expected, they soon learn that there are many ways to interpret the cards.

> *Fame*. 2008. 274 p. ISBN: 9780689876561. *MJ*

> Thirteen-year-old Eve wants to be a star, and when the tarot cards reveal that the school musical could be her big break, Eve auditions. Even though she was cast in a minor role, she perseveres through mean gossip and jealousy with the help of her best friends.

> *Life*. 2008. 272 p. ISBN: 9780689876585. *MJ*

> The summer after eighth grade, the girls use the tarot cards again, but the reading spells out disaster for quiet Sydney as she faces her father's alcoholism while trying to embrace her musical talent. Along the way, Sydney struggles to forgive her dad and become her own independent person.

Fredericks, Mariah

The True Meaning of Cleavage. New York: Atheneum Books for Young Readers, 2003. 224 p. ISBN: 9780689850929; 9780689869587pa. *J*

> High school freshman Jess is frustrated and scared when her best friend Sari falls madly in love with David Cole, a senior at their Manhattan school. Jess is able to see that David, who already has a girlfriend, is just using Sari for sex, but she is so caught up in her belief of their secret romance, she cannot

see the truth until Jess blabs about their relationship. Jess must then learn to develop other friendships as she works to mend fences with Sari.

Friendship • Individuality • Betrayal

Freitas, Donna

The Possibilities of Sainthood. New York: Farrar, Straus & Giroux, 2008. 272 p. ISBN: 9780374360870; (aud). *J*

Fifteen-year-old Antonia Labella is convinced that she can become the first living saint and is constantly petitioning the Vatican with new ideas. While she waits, she must deal with the realities of life, including problems at her Catholic school and dealing with her boisterous and food-loving Italian family as she helps them out at their grocery store. Antonia's other dream is to kiss Andy Rotellini, but when the chance comes along, it is not what she expected.

Family • Catholic Schools • Love

Garfinkle, Debra

Storky: How I Lost My Nickname and Won the Girl. New York: G.P. Putnam's Sons, 2005. 184 p. ISBN: 9780399242847; 9780142407820pa. *J*

Dubbed "Storkey" because of his tall, skinny, birdlike physique, high school freshman Michael Pomerantz is facing many typical challenges. Preoccupied with sex and dealing with his often unwelcome bodily responses, Mike is devastated when his longtime crush, Gina, starts dating a football player. Hoping to win the girls with his sensitive side, Mike keeps a journal that chronicles his parents' divorce, his father's string of girlfriends, and the fact that his mother is dating his dentist. As he makes new friends with a fellow classmate and the Scrabble playing man at the retirement home where he volunteers, Mike is able to find a girl and come to terms with his family situation as he develops confidence in himself.

Divorce • Sexuality • Diary Novel • Dating • Family • Volunteers

Goldblatt, Stacey

Stray. New York: Delacorte Press, 2007. 288 p. ISBN: 9780385734431; 9780385734448pa. *JS*

Sixteen-year-old Natalie has always been good, avoiding the typical pitfalls of adolescence in part due to her veterinarian mother's overprotective attitude and strict rules. Working long hours in her mother's clinic, Natalie meets intern Carver who has come to work and live with them for the summer. With this new influence in her life, Carver opens her eyes to life's possibilities as she begins to experiment, assert herself, and create her own boundaries.

Coming-of-Age • Single Parent • Veterinarians • Friendship • Dogs • Dating • Overprotectiveness

Gould, Peter

Write Naked. New York: Melanie Kroupa Books, 2008. 247 p. ISBN: 9780374384838. *JS*

Escaping to his uncle's cabin in Vermont, sixteen-year-old Victor wants solitude to write on his old typewriter. Testing the adage "you have to be naked to write," Victor works in the buff until he meets fellow writer Rose Anna. A homeschooled free spirit and environmentalist, Rose Anna writes of global warming while Victor writes of his life experiences. Writing brings the two teens together as they learn from each other and the adults around them.

Writing • Identity • Interpersonal Relations

Ha, Thu-Huong

Hail Caesar. New York: Scholastic, 2007. ISBN: 9780439890267. YALSA Popular Paperbacks. *S*

Basketball star and ladies' man John "Caesar" Miller has always gotten the girl—that is until Eva arrives. Obsessed with the girl he cannot have, a chance encounter forces Caesar to let down his guard. Realizing he can care about something other than himself, Caesar opens up and begins to think about his life and what goals he has for the future.

Sports • Coming-of-Age • Romance

Hawthorne, Rachel

Caribbean Cruising. New York: HarperTeen, 2004. 336 p. ISBN: 9780060565077pa. *S*

The summer before she starts college, eighteen-year-old Lindsay Darnell finds herself cruising the Caribbean aboard *The Enchantment,* where her mother is to be married to rich boyfriend, Walter. Finding this the opportunity to shake off her old shy and perfect image, Lindsay vows to be wild for once and plans on finding a guy and losing her virginity, but she hadn't counted on Ryan, Walter's overprotective godson, who won't leave her alone. When, despite all her efforts, Ryan still hangs around, Lindsay finds it hard not to fall for his charms.

Travel • College • Virginity

Hawthorne, Rachel

Love on the Lifts. New York: HarperTeen, 2006. 320 p. ISBN: 9780060815363pa. *JS*

Over winter break, Kate and her two best friends, Leah and Allie, escape Texas to stay at her aunt's condo at a ski resort. But when they arrive, they find that her aunt had also invited Kate's older brother, Sam, and his two friends, Joe and Brad, to stay there, too. Even though the girls are incensed at first, things start to work out when Leah hooks up with a cute ski instructor and Allie and Sam get together. Kate's crush, Brad, won't pay attention to her, so Kate finds herself without anyone—until she discovers that Joe secretly likes her and discovers that she likes him back.

Brothers • Vacations • Friendship • Love

Hawthorne, Rachel

Snowed In. New York: HarperTeen, 2007. 272 p. ISBN: 9780061138362pa. *JS*

Making a clean start after her parents' divorce, Ashleigh and her mom move to a tiny island in the Great Lakes to open a bed and breakfast. On the island, Ashleigh deals not only with adjusting to a new life but also the freezing weather on the island. She makes a friend in Nathalie and discovers that there are lots of hot guys on the island, including Chase and Josh, who is Nathalie's boyfriend. But when Chase seems to be interested in Nathalie, and Ashleigh finds herself interested in Josh, she must deal with the romantic complications that ensue.

Moving • Divorce • Friendship • Boyfriends

Hawthorne, Rachel

Suite Dreams. New York: HarperTeen, 2008. 288 p. ISBN: 9780061688065pa. *JS*

When her boyfriend of one semester, Rick, goes off to Australia and agrees to let an Australian exchange student crash on his couch, Alyssa has to find a place for him when Rick's place is unavailable. When the only place available is the couch in her dorm room, Alyssa finds herself falling for her new gorgeous Australian roommate.

College • Exchange Students • Love

Herrick, Steven

Love, Ghosts, and Facial Hair. New York: Simon Pulse, 2004. 128 p. ISBN: 9780689867101pa. *JS*

Sixteen-year-old Jack is an aspiring poet who is haunted by the persistent grief over the loss of his mother seven years ago. But when Jack falls in love with Annabel and with her finds a powerful cerebral and sexual connection, he is able to grow into his future as he comes to terms with his past.

Sequel: *A Place Like This.* New York: Simon Pulse, 2004. 144 p. ISBN: 9780689867118pa. *S*

Eighteen-year-old Jack and his girlfriend Annabel decide to embark on a post-graduation road trip instead of immediately starting at university. Enjoying the freedom of the road, they are led to work on an apple farm where they befriend Emma, the sixteen-year-old pregnant daughter of the farmer. Despite Jack's hope of spending the time alone with Annabel, the pair become involved in helping Emma survive the challenges of her life.

Poetry • Grief • Sexuality • Travel • Coming-of-Age • Novels in Verse

Hite, Sid

Cecil in Space. New York: Henry Holt, 1999. 150 p. ISBN: 9780805050554. *JS*

Seventeen-year-old Cecil Rowe is stuck in his boring town of historic Bricksburg, Virginia, where he reads anything from Einstein to Freud and philosophizes about time and space. Cecil deals with some typical teenage problems like being attracted to pretty, popular Ariel Crisp. But then he finds out that his best friend Isaac's sixteen-year-old sister, Isabel, is the one he really wants after she accompanies him to visit his aunt, who is in a mental hospital. It's then that he sees Isabel in a new light. But Cecil also deals with some not-so-typical problems when his best friend Isaac is accused of tampering with the town's welcome sign and with grief when his other friend Pauley Harrington's dog disappears. Through it all, Cecil must try to figure out who he really is and just where he fits in.

Vandalism • Friendship • Love

Hogan, Mary

Perfect Girl. New York: Harper Tempest, 2007. 208 p. ISBN: 9780060841089; 9780060841102pa; (aud). *MJ*

> When 14-year-old Ruthie finally realizes that she is interested in her friend Perry, only to have his love stolen away by "the Perfect Girl," the only person she feels she can turn to is her wealthy Aunt Mary, who writes a love column for a magazine. But Ruthie's overprotective single mother forbids her to contact her aunt after a visit to her home in New York three years earlier. When Aunt Mary, in an effort to get away from her own troubles, travels down to help Ruthie in person, Ruthie must deal with the family's strained relationship. As the sisters reconnect, Ruthie finds that her aunt has great advice for her, but when she takes Perry on a date and they kiss, Ruthie finds that there is no spark between them.
>
> *Friendship • Neighbors • New Students • Aunts • Advice • Single Parent*

Hopkins, Cathy

<u>**Mates, Dates Series.**</u> New York: Simon Pulse

> Four high school friends—Lucy, Izzie, T.J. and Nesta—find support from each other as they deal with life and love.
>
> *Love • Friendship • Dating • Body Image • Selfishness • Travel • Boyfriends*

Mates, Dates, and Inflatable Bras. 2003. 176 p. ISBN: 9780689855443pa; (aud). YALSA Quick Picks. *MJ*

> > With her flat chest, fourteen-year-old Lucy feels immature next to her gorgeous friends Izzy and Nesta. When a school assignment asks her to discuss "What makes me 'me,'" Lucy is conflicted until, with the help of her friends, she is able to find confidence with her fashion sense and sewing abilities.

Mates, Dates, and Cosmic Kisses. 2003. 208 p. ISBN: 9780689855450pa; (aud). *MJ*

> > Izzy is obsessed over Mark, a boy she meets selling essential oils at a market. But she comes to realize that Mark is just playing with her heart and she is losing herself in the process. With the support of her friends and mother, she is able to wake up and move on.

Mates, Dates, and Designer Divas. 2003. 208 p. (UK title: *Mates, Dates, and Portobello Princesses.*) ISBN: 9780689855467pa. *MJ*

> > Nesta's family is going through some financial troubles, so when she falls for ultra-rich Simon, she begins pretending to be something she is not to win him and outdo his snobby friend Cressida. When her lies catch up with her, she not only risks losing Simon but her best friends as well, and she must face up to and reveal the truth.

Mates, Dates, and Sleepover Secrets. 2003. 208 p. ISBN: 9780689859915pa. *MJ*

> > Theresa Joanne "T.J." feels alone when her best friend moves away and she must deal with a bullying classmate, Wendy, all by herself. Another problem is the fact that the boys in her life don't seem to notice

she is a girl. When she meets Lucy, she finds the friend she has been wanting, but until she is able to also befriend Nesta and Izzie and be accepted into their group, she will not have the support she needs.

Mates, Dates, and Sole Survivors. 2004. 224 p. ISBN: 9780689859922pa. *MJ*

Everyone seems to be in love except Lucy, especially since her ex-boyfriend Tony has started dating a new girl. But while at a spa with Izzie, Lucy meets a great guy who likes her back. Lucy must decide if this new relationship, in which she starts to feel smothered, is better than being single.

Mates, Dates, and Mad Mistakes. 2004. 224 p. ISBN: 9780689867224pa; (aud). *MJ*

Starting a new year in school, Izzie creates a whole new image for herself including a belly-button ring and a dangerous motorcycle-riding older boyfriend, Josh. Experimenting with drinking and smoking pot, Izzie quarrels with her mother and friends about her new lifestyle. It isn't until she sneaks out of the house for the evening and Josh tries to have sex with her that she realizes bad behavior doesn't make you an adult and it is important to stay true to yourself.

Mates, Dates, and Sequin Smiles. 2004. 208 p. (UK title: *Mates, Dates, and Pulling Power.*) ISBN: 9780689867231pa. *MJ*

Nesta's confidence is shaken when she finds that she must get braces and learns that her friends consider her shallow. She sets out to prove them wrong by getting a guy who is attracted to her brain, not just her body. When she meets cute Luke in an acting class, Nesta regains her confidence and finds that she has more to offer than just beauty on the outside.

Mates, Dates, and Tempting Trouble. 2005. 238 p. ISBN: 9780689870620pa. *MJ*

When Nesta's boyfriend Luke reveals that he really loves T.J., T.J. tries her best to avoid him. But then the two are thrown together when Luke becomes the coordinator of a multi-school project. When the tensions threaten to break up her friendship with her girlfriends and her relationship with her steady boyfriend Steve, T.J. must deal with the situation more directly.

Mates, Dates, and Great Escapes. 2005. 176 p. ISBN: 9780689876950pa. *MJ*

On a school trip to Florence, Lucy discovers a new sophisticated world and a way to distance herself from boyfriend, Tony, who has been pressuring her to have sex. When Lucy meets an American boy, she thinks she might have found someone better than Tony, but she must overcome her insecurities before she can move forward with any relationship.

Mates, Dates, and Chocolate Cheats. 2006. 224 p. ISBN: 9780689876967pa. *MJ*

Over Christmas, Izzie gained some weight, and now she is trying to do anything she can to lose it. As her worries about her weight escalate, she loses confidence in herself and in her friendships until she meets a cute boy at the TV studio where she is participating in a teen panel and finds that the boy likes her just the way she is.

Mates, Dates, and Diamond Destiny. 2006. 272 p. ISBN: 9780689876974pa. *MJ*

Motivated by the fact that she can meet boys, Nesta gets involved in charity work. When the work opens her eyes to the plight of others, she must convince the cute boy, William, that her original selfish motivations have now changed to altruistic ones.

Mates, Dates, and Sizzling Summers. 2006. 160 p. ISBN: 9780689876981pa. *MJ*

T.J. is caught between the attentions of two boys when she finds herself interested in Ollie Axford and then old boyfriend Luke De Biasi returns to town eager to get back together. When a close friend becomes seriously ill, T.J. realizes that there are some things that are more important than deciding between two boys.

Hopkins, Cathy

<u>Truth or Dare Series</u>. New York: Simon Pulse

As they play games of truth or dare, three friends discover truths about themselves and each other.

Romance • Friendship • Dating • Boyfriends • Kissing

White Lies and Barefaced Truths. 2004. 182 p. ISBN: 9780689870033pa. YALSA Quick Picks. *MJ*

Fourteen-year-old Cat can't tell that she was kissed by the new boy Ollie in a game of Truth or Dare because her friend Becca likes Ollie. She also can't tell the truth to her boyfriend that their relationship is over. But Cat must face all her hidden truths, so she finds a way to be assertive and to tell the truth in the way it needs to be told.

The Princess of Pop. 2004. 191 p. (UK title: *Pop Princess*.) ISBN: 9780689870026pa. *MJ*

Becca does not get a part in the school's production of *Grease*. She has a reputation for being a dreamer who cannot see things through, so she takes a dare from boyfriend, Squidge, to audition for the American Idol–type show, *Pop Princess*. Sticking through the tough competition, Becca learns some important lessons about enduring.

Teen Queens and Has-Beens. 2004. 178 p. ISBN: 9780689871290pa. *MJ*

When Lia kisses gorgeous Jonno Appleton during a game of Truth or Dare, she finds herself on the bad side of popular Kaylie O'Hara, who wanted Jonno for herself. When the rumors and bullying get nasty, Lia must find out who her real friends are so she can find the support she needs.

Starstruck. 2005. 196 p. ISBN: 9780689871306pa. *MJ*

Lia's boyfriend gets the opportunity to fulfill his dream and work on a movie. His promise to be honest and totally faithful to her gets tested when he begins to work with the movie's teenage star, Savannah.

Double Dare. 2006. 240 p. ISBN: 9781416906537pa. *MJ*

When Mac accepts a double dare, he finally has the opportunity to live out two of his dreams, to date lots of girls and to find work as a cartoonist. But when his dates are disasters and his work as a magazine cartoonist is difficult, Mac must decide what price he is willing to pay for success.

Midsummer Meltdown. 2006. 224 p. ISBN: 9781416906544pa. *MJ*

Looking forward to a romantic evening with her boyfriend when he joins her family to celebrate her mother's fortieth birthday, Lia is shocked when she finds that her ex-boyfriend has also been invited to the party. Caught between the two boys, she must find a way to handle the situation before it gets out of hand.

Love Lottery. 2007. 240 p. ISBN: 9781416927211pa. *MJ*

When Becca fulfills a dare to kiss the next boy who comes onto the beach, she finds herself attracted to the boy who has just arrived from London for a holiday. As Becca deals with her parents' marriage troubles, she begins to question her own relationships.

All Mates Together. 2007. 240 p. ISBN: 9781416927228pa. *MJ*

Cat's life is changing. Her father is preparing to get married again, and she will move into the newlyweds' new home. She throws one last sleep-over party with her friends. When things start to fall apart and the wedding may be called off, Cat finds that the most important things in life, like friendships, really don't change.

Johnson, Kathleen Jeffrie

Dumb Love. New Milford, CT: Roaring Brook Press, 2005. 163 p. ISBN: 9781596430624. *J*

When she moves to a small mountain town with her mother and her mother's boyfriend, pleasantly plump high-schooler Carlotta develops a crush on Pete, a boy who works at the local garage. An aspiring romance novelist, Carlotta uses all types of literary ploys to win him. But along the way, her aspirations for love and her writing dreams are thwarted.

Dating • Family Problems • Alcoholism • Writing

Kantor, Melissa

Confessions of a Not It Girl. New York: Hyperion, 2004. 247 p. ISBN: 9780786818372; 9780786818082pa. *S*

Jan Miller's senior year is filled with drama, including obsessing about the size of her bottom and the stresses of writing a college application essay. She also longs for romance with her crush, Josh, even though he already has a girlfriend back in Seattle, where he used to live. He is trying to set her up with someone else. Dealing with these stresses, Jan is also worrying as she has to sit by and watch her friend Rebecca seduce an older man by lying about her age, until she finds a way to stop obsessing and make the first move to establish her future and win Josh's heart.

Love • Friendship • Dating • Girlfriends

Kephart, Beth

Undercover. New York: HarperTeen, 2007. 278 p. ISBN: 9780061238932; 9780061238956pa. School Library Journal Best Books. *J*

Following the example of Cyrano de Bergerac, high school sophomore Elisa has created a secret business writing love notes for boys who can't express their feelings. With her father constantly traveling for his own consulting business, her parents' marriage becomes strained, and Elisa often escapes the situation by going to the place she finds inspiration: her favorite pond, the one where she taught herself to ice-skate. Followed to her sanctuary by classmate Theo, who has also been one of her clients as he woos a pretty but cruel girl in their class, Elisa begins to fall for him, and she learns that love can be very complicated.

Loneliness • Poetry • Letters • High School • Family Problems • Ice-Skating

Krovatin, Christopher

Heavy Metal and You. New York: PUSH Books, 2005. 192 p. ISBN: 9780439736480; 9780439743990pa. YALSA Best Books; YALSA Quick Picks. *S*

Metal head Sam Markus wears spiked bracelets and spends his time drinking, smoking, and exchanging vulgar insults with his friends when he is not at his New York prep school. When Sam starts to date straightlaced Melissa, he finds that to please her, he must change by giving up his vices and modifying his behavior. He soon realizes how phony he has become and that true love should mean you don't have to change who you are.

Interpersonal Relations • Loyalty • Music

Limb, Sue

Jess Jordan Series. New York: Delacorte Press

Jess Jordan deals with the pains of growing up, including coming to terms with her body and finding love.

Fathers • Gay Males • Dating • Summer • Secrets • Travel • Automobiles • Friendship • Grandmothers • Mother and Daughter • Body Image • Infatuation • Love • Breaking Up • Best Friends • Exchange Students • England

Girl, 15, Charming but Insane. 2004. 214 p. ISBN: 9780385732147; 9780385732154pa. YALSA Popular Paperbacks. *J*

Fifteen-year-old Jess Jordan wishes she had the perfect body, just like her best friend Flora Barclay, instead of her small breasts, which even her attempts to enhance can't correct. Then maybe she could attract the unattainable Ben Johnson. When Flora admits that she has a crush on Fred, Jess's other friend who is the nerdy class clown, Jess not only covets Flora's physique but her love as well, when she realizes that it is Fred who is her perfect match.

Girl, (Nearly) 16, Absolute Torture. 2005. 216 p. ISBN: 9780385732161; (aud). *J*

Just as Jess is getting used to having Fred as a boyfriend, her mom insists that, along with her grandmother, they all take a family vacation to visit historical landmarks, ending up with a visit to Jess's long-absent dad's beach-side home where her grandmother plans to scatter her grandfather's ashes. While away, Jess worries about whether Fred will be faithful, and she is not surprised when he stays true, but she is surprised in a more personal way.

Girl, Going on 17, Pants on Fire. 2006. 224 p. ISBN: 9780385732185; 9780385732192pa. *JS*
When Fred reveals that he wants to keep their relationship secret once school starts so he does not ruin his reputation as a loner by being part of a couple, Jess is heartbroken. Then when her mother starts dating again, her favorite teacher has been replaced by someone who does not like her, and the annual school comedy show is replaced with a production of a Shakespearian play, Jess must figure out how to deal with all of the changes in her life.

Girl, Barely 15, Flirting for England. 2008. 248 p. ISBN: 9780385735384. *J*
Jess learns that pictures can lie when she falls in love with a picture of a French exchange student, but upon his arrival, she finds that he is a small geeky boy who can't speak English. He gets a crush on her and Jess tries to discourage him by pretending she has a relationship with her best friend Fred, but when another exchange student arrives and he comes on to both Jess and her friend Flora, she must figure out if he is worth fighting for.

Lockhart, E.

Ruby Oliver Series. New York: Delacorte Press
Ruby Oliver deals with the loss of both girlfriends and boyfriends.

Dating • Friendship • Mother and Daughter • Love • Dating • Peer Pressure • Breaking Up • Friendship • Psychotherapy • Panic Disorders

The Boyfriend List: (15 Guys, 11 Shrink Appointments, 4 Ceramic Frogs, and Me, Ruby Oliver). 2005. 229 p. ISBN: 9780385732062; 9780385732079pa; (aud). YALSA Quick Picks. *J*
Fifteen-year-old Ruby Oliver's boyfriend has dumped her, and now he's going out with her best friend. Ruby's tough year gets even worse. Ruby explores her past and tries to make sense of the present. With the help of a boyfriend list she created for her therapist who is helping her with her panic attacks, and despite the setbacks when her ex-boyfriend kisses her and her best friend takes revenge, Ruby finds ways to deal with her problems and find her own self-worth.

The Boy Book: A Study of Habits and Behaviors, Plus Techniques for Taming Them. 2006. 208 p. ISBN: 9780385732086; 9780385732093pa. *J*
At the start of her junior year, Ruby Oliver is dealing with the loss of friends and boyfriends by taking the advice of her therapist to get involved in new activities. She is interning at the local zoo. As she gets involved with new adventures, she meets new challenges, including her ex-boyfriend sending her flirty notes even though he is with a new girl and a great guy her friend likes telling her that he wants to kiss her.

The Treasure Map of Boys. 2009. 256 p. ISBN: 9780385904377; (aud). *J*
Ruby is still receiving mixed signals from her ex-boyfriend while she is trying to navigate a new relationship with a potential boyfriend. Things change when she loses her job and gets a new pet, but with the help of her therapist, Ruby must continue to deal with her panic attacks as she tries to fully understand the painful moments in her life.

Manning, Sarra

Diary of a Crush Series. New York: Puffin.

Edi and Dylan have a tempestuous relationship as they try to stay together through good and bad times.

Moving • Kissing • Dating • Travel • Love • England • Diary Novel

French Kiss. 2006. 224 p. ISBN: 9780142406328pa. *JS*

Feeling alone at her new school, sixteen-year-old English schoolgirl Edie begins sneaking out to exchange secret kisses with Dylan, the nineteen-year-old gorgeous art student who is known for breaking girls' hearts. Dylan ignores her in public, and Edie starts dating another sensitive guy on the side until, on a school trip to Paris, she confronts Dylan, who is finally able to agree to some level of commitment.

Kiss and Make Up. 2006. 272 p. ISBN: 9780142406427pa. *JS*

Constrained by Dylan's many rules that lead to constant fighting, Edie breaks up with him. But when Dylan starts dating Veronique, Edie starts to rethink her decision, even though she can't stop kissing Veronique's brother, Carter.

Sealed with a Kiss. 2006. 288 p. ISBN: 9780142406489pa. *JS*

Finally back together, Edie and Dylan decide to embark on a road trip across America, but they soon find themselves fighting again and must strengthen their relationship through their many adventures.

McCafferty, Megan

Jessica Darling Novels. New York: Crown; New York: Three Rivers Press

Jessica Darling deals with a variety of life's challenges as she enters and graduates from college.

Friendship • Gay Males • Scandals • Coming-of Age • Love • Internships • College

Sloppy Firsts: A Novel. 2001. 280 p. ISBN: 9780609807903pa. YALSA Quick Picks. *MJ*

Jessica Darling is devastated when her best friend moves away. She feels she has lost the only person with whom she feels she can truly communicate. With her intense Type-A personality, Jessica tries to deal with her father's obsession with her track meets, her feelings about Marcus Flutie, and her mother's preoccupation with her sister Bethany's wedding, all on her own.

Second Helpings: A Novel. 2003. 349 p. ISBN: 9780609807910pa. *MJ*

Getting ready to attend college next year, Jessica attends an academic summer camp and meets Professor Samuel MacDougall, a handsome writing teacher, who gets Jessica to imagine a larger world. Returning to school, hot brain Len Levy starts giving her the attention she needs to forget Marcus, and even though she becomes the subject of gossip because she is a virgin, in the end she learns she knows less about her friends and the people around her than she thought.

Charmed Thirds: A Novel. 2006. 368 p. ISBN: 9781400080427; 9781400080434pa; (aud). *MJ*

> Jessica has just finished her freshman year at Columbia and is dividing her summer between home and an internship at *True* magazine. Despite the opportunities, Jessica is unsure about leaving boyfriend Marcus for part of the summer, especially since they go to different schools on different coasts and don't see each other very often. Then she cheats after a drunken night out, an act that finally sends Marcus out of the picture. Jessica is determined to figure out what she wants with her life.

Fourth Comings: A Novel. 2007. 320 p. ISBN: 9780307346506; 9780307346513pa; (aud). *MJ*

> Having graduated from college, Jessica is trying to decide if she should accept the proposal of her on-and-off love, Marcus Flutie. While pondering this decision, she struggles to pay rent and find a job while sharing a Brooklyn basement apartment with best friend Hope and gender-bending high school classmate Manda.

Perfect Fifths: A Novel. 2009. 272 p. ISBN: 9780307346520; 9780307346537pa. *MJ*

> Jessica tries to decide if she should get back with her ex-boyfriend Marcus when she runs into him at the airport where he is returning from building a house in New Orleans and she is there to catch a plane to a friend's wedding.

Morrison, Angela

Taken by Storm. New York: Razorbill, 2009. 320 p. ISBN: 9781595142382. *S*

> After Michael witnesses the death of his parents and friends during a hurricane on a scuba diving expedition, he comes to live with his grandmother and withdraws from the world and his love of the water. When he meets a Mormon girl, Lessie, and falls in love, the pair must deal with their passion within the bounds of Lessie's moral code, and as the couple learn to respect each other. Michael finds a way to heal so he can return to the ocean.

> *Grief • Dating • Love • Personal Conduct • Epistolary Novels*

Ockler, Sarah

Twenty Boy Summer. New York: Little, Brown Books for Young Readers, 2009. 304 p. ISBN: 9780316051590. *J*

> Hiding the secret that her relationship with her best friend Frankie's brother, Matt, had become something more than just friendship days before his death, Anna joins Frankie and her family on a summer vacation. Intent upon enjoying the summer, Frankie convinces Anna that they must meet one boy every day in the hope that by the end of the summer, they will find romance. But Anna's heart is broken, and she is not sure if she can love again.

> *Secrets • Death • Friendship • Love*

Pearson, Mary

Scribbler of Dreams. San Diego: Harcourt, 2001. 223 p. ISBN: 9780152023201; 9780152045692pa. *JS*

Kaitlin Malone's father is in prison serving time for killing Robert Crutchfield, an event that is just one more part of the Malone–Crutchfield feud that has been going on for four generations. Now attending public school under an assumed name, Kaitlin meets and falls in love with Bram, only to discover that he is the son of Robert Crutchfield. Struggling to keep her true identity from him, Kaitlin soon learns that the Crutchfields are not the villains she thought them to be, and when her identity is revealed, the pair must decide if love can conquer all.

Love • Honesty • Murder

Rallison, Janette

Fame, Glory, and Other Things on My To Do List. New York: Walker, 2005. 186 p. ISBN: 9780802789914; 9780802796820pa. *JS*

High school junior Jessica is sure that if she can only convince gorgeous new student Jordan to get his famous movie actor dad to step in, not only will it be the way they can save their school's production of West Side Story, which may be shut down because of lack of funds, but it will also be the break she needs to get her talent noticed. Jordan wants to remain anonymous, and when the truth about his dad's identity is spread throughout the school and everyone else thinks this is their big break too, Jessica must figure out a way to fix the mess she has made so she can save her budding romance with Jordan.

Divorce • Celebrities • Theater • Actors and Actresses • Fame • Competition

Rallison, Janette

It's a Mall World after All. New York: Walker, 2006. 240 p. ISBN: 9780802788535; 9780802797971pa. *JS*

Seeing her best friend Brianna's boyfriend Bryant with another girl, Charlotte begins to try to prove to her that he is cheating. However, each time she tries to catch him, her efforts are foiled by handsome wrestler, Colton, and just serve to make her look like a fool as she sets things on fire and dumps Colton in a pool. Promising that he will use the resources of his rich father to buy Christmas presents for underprivileged kids if Charlotte will stop following Bryant, she must decide if it is more important to be socially conscious or to save her friend from a cad, a decision which could undermine her budding romance with Colton.

Best Friends • Interpersonal Relations • Personal Conduct • Social Classes

Rallison, Janette

Playing the Field. New York: Walker, 2002. 180 p. ISBN: 9780802788047; 9780802776976pa. *MJS*

Thirteen-year-old McKay is faced with the prospect of being pulled off the baseball team if he does not bring up his grade in algebra. His best friend

Tony decides the best way to get him the help he needs is to get straight-A student Serena to like him. Not only will McKay have the help he needs, Tony will have access to flirt with Serena's two best friends. Serena discovers the plot, and the three girls and the boys become enemies. Tony reveals himself as a Casanova, and when McKay realizes that despite the ploy, he really likes Serena, he recognizes that he alone must deal with the problems he has created.

Baseball • Interpersonal Relations

Ray, Claire

Snow in Love. New York: HarperTeen, 2008. 304 p. ISBN: 9780061688058. *JS*

Jessie Whitman is looking forward to spending her school holiday skiing, snowboarding, and hiking in the Alaskan wilderness with her boyfriend Jake. But when Jake does not communicate with her and then brings along a new girl, Evie, Jessie is sure that her perfect evening at the Northern Lights Ball is in jeopardy until she starts noticing snowboarder Will Parker, who may be the guy that can fill Jake's place.

Boyfriends • Vacations • Winter

Rennison, Louise

Confessions of Georgia Nicolson Series. New York: HarperCollins

Fourteen-year-old Georgia faces the ups and downs of teen life as she tries to find true love and deals with family and other problems.

Dating • Diaries • Love • Interpersonal Relations • England • New Zealand • Diary Novel

Angus, Thongs, and Full-Frontal Snogging: Confessions of Georgia Nicolson. 1999. 247 p. ISBN: 9780060288143; 9780064472272pa; (aud). Michael L. Printz Honor Books; YALSA Best Books; YALSA Quick Picks. *MJ*

Fourteen-year-old Georgia Nicolson has fallen in love with seventeen-year-old Robbie, a Sex God, who is currently dating a girl name Lindsay. Winning him away from Lindsay is not her only worry, as Georgia must deal with her bed-wetting three-year-old sister, her dad who has gone to New Zealand in search of a better job, and her pet cat Angus who suddenly goes missing.

On the Bright Side, I'm Now the Girlfriend of a Sex God. 2001. 243 p. ISBN: 9780060288136; 9780064472265pa; (aud). YALSA Quick Picks. *MJ*

When her father finds work in New Zealand, Georgia faces an overseas move, a devastating blow since she has finally won and has started kissing Robbie the Sex God. But when her father calls off the move, things look up, until Robbie decides that Georgia is too young for him and her only option is to use Dave the Laugh as a decoy boyfriend to lure Robbie back into her arms.

Knocked Out by My Nunga-Nungas: Further, Further Confessions of Georgia Nicolson. 2001. 183 p. ISBN: 9780066236568; 9780064473620pa; (aud). YALSA Quick Picks. *MJ*

Dragged off to Scotland for a family vacation, Georgia tries to figure out if she really wants Robbie back now that she finds herself attracted to her decoy boyfriend, Dave the Laugh, who just happens to be the current boyfriend of her friend Ellen.

Dancing in My Nuddy-Pants: Even Further Confessions of Georgia Nicolson.
2003. 224 p. ISBN: 9780060097462; 9780060097486pa; (aud). *J*

Having made her choice of Robby the Sex God over Dave the Laugh, Georgia is happily enjoying their time together kissing, but when Robbie doesn't seem to be around a lot and Dave breaks up with Ellen, Georgia must decide how this will affect her relationship while at the same time working on the school play and dealing with her cat Angus, who has gotten the neighbor's cat pregnant.

Away Laughing on a Fast Camel: Even More Confessions of Georgia Nicolson. 2004. 288 p. ISBN: 9780060589349; 9780060589363pa. *J*

When Robbie goes off to New Zealand to work on an ecological farm, Georgia finds that she is attracted to the new boy in town, Massimo, who just happens to be the half-Italian, half-American lead singer for the Stiff Dylans.

Then He Ate My Boy Entrancers: More Mad, Marvy Confessions of Georgia Nicolson. 2005. 312 p. ISBN: 9780060589370; 9780060589394pa. *J*

On a family vacation in America, Georgia is sad when she cannot connect with her crush Massimo, but when she returns, she is truly devastated when she finds that he is more interested in her nemesis, Wet Lindsay, than in her.

Startled by His Furry Shorts: The Confessions of Georgia Nicolson. 2006. 288 p. ISBN: 9780060853846; 9780060853860pa. *J*

Not only does Georgia have to deal with having a part in the school's production of Macbeth and helping friends Rosie and Sven plan a Viking wedding, but she must also deal with her embarrassing parents, her annoying little sister, and her diabolical cats, while trying to win Massimo's attention.

Love Is a Many Trousered Thing: More Mad, Marvy Confessions of Georgia Nicolson. 2007. 288 p. ISBN: 9780060853877; 9780060853891pa. *J*

Georgia continues to deal with her never-ending romantic woes as she tries to make a decision between the three boys in her life.

Stop in the Name of Pants: The Confessions of Georgia Nicolson. 2008. 256 p. ISBN: 9780061459320. *J*

When Angus the cat is run over and left for dead, Georgia must nurse him back to health, all the while trying to decide between pursuing Dave the Laugh who kisses her at camp or trying to find a way to visit her crush Massimo in Italy.

Are These My Basoomas I See Before Me?: Final Confessions of Georgia Nicolson. 2009. 256 p. ISBN: 9780061459351; 9780061459375pa. *J*

Georgia finally decides which boy she wants as a boyfriend, but when she is cast in a play with the boy she did not choose, it looks as if Georgia's love life is never going to run smoothly.

Ripslinger, Jon

How I Fell in Love and Learned to Shoot Free Throws. Brookfield, CT: Roaring Brook Press, 2003. 170 p. ISBN: 9780761318927. *J*

> When Danny Henderson falls for Angel McPherson, the attractive star of the girl basketball team, he will do anything to get her attention, including letting her beat him doing free throws during a contest while the whole school watches. Excited when the ploy works and Angel agrees to coach him, he is sure that this will bring them closer. As they work together, secrets are revealed about each of their home lives. Angel's mother is a lesbian who lives with her lover, and Danny's mom left the family for another man just before she was killed in an accident. The two must confront the truth if they are to overcome the pressures that surround them and make their relationship work.

> *Single Fathers • Lesbians • Family Secrets • Trust • Basketball*

Ruby, Laura

Play Me. New York: HarperTeen, 2008. 311 p. ISBN: 9780061243271; 9780061243295pa. *S*

> Eighteen-year-old Edward "Eddy" Rochester was raised on movies by his struggling actress mother, who just recently left the family to take a bit part on a formulaic Miami crime show. Now at the end of his senior year, Eddy wants to be a filmmaker and dreams of winning the contest that will get MTV to produce the film, RiotGrrl16, that he and his friends shot. Eddy realizes that he wants more than just the meaningless relationships he has had, but he fails to charm the object of his affections, popular and athletic Lucinda Dulko. He has to realize that he cannot always be in control, and success in life is not instantaneous, realizations that will allow him to reach out to repair his relationship with his mother.

> *Dating • Mother and Son • Videos • Interpersonal Relations • Blended Families • Travel • Automobiles*

Sandoval, Lynda

Who's Your Daddy? New York: Simon Pulse, 2004. 318 p. ISBN: 9780689864407; 9781416954088pa. *S*

> Frustrated in love because of their intimidating fathers, Lila, whose dad is the police chief; Meryl, whose father is vice principal in charge of discipline at their high school; and Caressa, whose dad is a famous blues musician, hold a Celtic ritual of a silent supper that is supposed to help them find their true loves. When the ceremony is interrupted, the girls are not sure if it's fate or just luck when Lila falls for Police Lieutenant Dylan, Meryl is swept off her feet by a Bosnian immigrant who fixes her tire, and Caressa develops a crush on a young musician.

> *Father and Daughter • Friendship • Love*

Scarsbrook, Richard

Cheeseburger Subversive. Saskatoon, Canada: Thistledown Press, 2003. 196 p. ISBN: 9781894345545. *MJ*

> Chronicling the major events in his life from seventh grade to the start of his freshman year of college, Dak Sifter covers events from crashing the lawn mower in his

driveway to all the silly things he does in his endless pursuit of Zoe Perry, only to be dumped by her after a disastrous date to the prom.

Sequel: *Featherless Bipeds.* Saskatoon, Canada: Thistledown Press, 2006. 223 p. ISBN: 9781897235058. *J*

> Now at university, Dak Sifter is seduced by the temptations of the high life when he finds himself impressing the girls as a drummer in a rock band, but fame does not guarantee a smooth life, and Dak must figure out just what kind of person he wants to be.

> *Music • Love • College • Coming-of-Age*

Schreiber, Mark

Starcrossed. Woodbury, MN: Flux, 2007. 305 p. ISBN: 9780738710013. YALSA Quick Picks. *JS*

> Sixteen-year-old horoscope-obsessed Christy Marlow meets eighteen-year-old Ben Penrose in her plastic surgeon's office and discovers he is there to have a tattoo of his ex-girlfriend's name removed just as she is there to remove her ex-boyfriend . The coincidences deepen when they finds their names are Christy and Ben respectively. As the two begin to fall in love, they find that true love does not always run smoothly. Christy's ex-boyfriend returns, and Ben must face the lies he has told about his past.

> *Ex-Boyfriends • Ex-Girlfriends • Parent and Child • Interpersonal Relations*

Scott, Elizabeth

Bloom. New York: Simon Pulse, 2007. 240 p. ISBN: 9781416926832. YALSA Popular Paperbacks. *JS*

> Lauren thought that having a popular boyfriend was all she needed to make her happy. When Evan, the son of her distant father's former live-in girlfriend, suddenly shows up, Lauren soon finds herself lying and finding excuses to avoid her boyfriend and stressed best friend so that she can spend all her time with Evan. Conflicted over her relationships, Lauren tries to decide if her behavior makes her like her mother, who selfishly ran away to pursue her own life, leaving her family behind, as she works to figure out if it's better to play it safe or to embrace the unknown.

> *Father and Daughter • Popularity • Sexuality • Friendship • Secrets • Interpersonal Attraction*

Scott, Elizabeth

Perfect You. New York: Simon Pulse, 2008. 282 p. ISBN: 9781416953555. *JS*

> Kate's life is falling apart now that her father quit his job to unsuccessfully embrace his dream of selling infomercial vitamins in a mall kiosk, her college-graduate brother can't seem to get his act together, and her mother must work two jobs to make ends meet. Abandoned by her friend Anna, who is not talking to her since she lost weight and became popular, the last straw is when her overbearing grandmother moves in with the intent of fixing their family problems. As Kate tries to deal with the chaos, she is ap-

proached by a boy whom she has tried to ignore, and when she now finds herself meeting him to make out, Kate realizes that she has to open herself to the possibilities that his love offers.

Dating • Friendship • Family Problems • Popularity

Scott, Elizabeth

Something, Maybe. New York: Simon Pulse, 2009. 224 p. ISBN: 9781416978657. *S*

In her small town, all seventeen-year-old Hannah Jackson James wants is to blend in, but that is really hard to do when your father is an aging reality TV star with a house full of girlfriends and your mother is a minor actress and former Jackson girlfriend, who now makes her money hosting a webcast skimpily dressed. With all her time taken up trying to stay unnoticed and making sure her mom pays the bills, Hannah has little time left to attract coworker Josh. When her father calls asking for a meeting for the first time in five years, and she goes to see him only to find he was using her for a ratings boost, Hannah finds that love and support come from unexpected places.

Interpersonal Attraction • Mother and Daughter • Father and Daughter

Shull, Megan

Amazing Grace. New York: Hyperion, 2005. 247 p. ISBN: 9780786856909. YALSA Popular Paperbacks. *JS*

Tennis star Grace "Ace" Kincaid can't take the pressure anymore and wants to retire, so with a new haircut, a pierced nose, and a new name, Emily O'Brien, she goes to live in a remote Alaskan cabin with her Aunt Ava, a retired FBI agent. Enjoying the freedom her new lifestyle gives her, Emily falls in love with her surroundings and with gorgeous local boy Teague after he saves her when she gets into a bicycle crash with a moose.

Tennis • Celebrities • Aunts • Cousins • Coming-of-Age

Shulman, Polly

Enthusiasm. New York: G. P. Putnam's Sons, 2006. 198 p. ISBN: 9780399243899; 9780142409350pa. *MJ*

Since elementary school, fifteen-year-old Julia's best friend Ashleigh has thrown herself into one craze after another, and now her latest endeavor is to emulate the times of Jane Austen. Deciding that they need to attend a dance at a local prep school so they can find their true loves, the girls have befriended two boys. Julia has had a secret crush on one of the boys since the day she spotted him in the mall. When Ashleigh sets her sights on Julia's crush, Julia does not know if she can stand another one of her friend's schemes.

Interpersonal Attraction • Musicals • Friendship • Love

Simon Romantic Comedies (multiple authors). New York: Simon Pulse

This series deals with how determined young adults face school, friends, family, and other typical adolescent problems while they traverse humorous circumstances to find love.

Love • Dating • Boyfriends • Ex-Boyfriends • Sexuality

Dokey, Cameron

How Not to Spend Your Senior Year. 2004. 304 p. ISBN: 0689867034. *MJS*
When Jo O'Connor's father insists that they must move quickly, she must fake her own death, and then when she returns to her old school to say goodbye, everyone thinks she is a ghost.

Burnham, Niki

Royally Jacked. 2004. 208 p. ISBN: 9780689866685pa. *MJS*
Fifteen-year-old Valerie is forced to leave her friends behind when she must move with her diplomat father to Europe after her mother reveals that she is gay and moves in with her girlfriend. In Europe things are not all bad, especially when Valerie falls for a handsome prince.

<u>Sequel</u>: *Spin Control.* 2005. 245 p. ISBN: 9780689866692. *MJS*
When the pressures of being the girlfriend of a prince get to be too much, Valerie heads home, but even as she finds romance when she gets back together with an old boyfriend, she finds that she can't stop thinking about the boy she left behind.

<u>Sequel</u>: *Do-Over.* 2006. 240 p. ISBN: 9780689876202. *MJS*
Back in Europe, Valerie hopes that she can get back with her prince, but on a ski trip to the Alps, her romantic plan hits some snags.

Krulik, Nancy

Ripped at the Seams. 2004. 326p. ISBN: 9780689867712pa. *MJS*
Sami is certain that New York is the perfect place to live her dreams of becoming a successful fashion designer until someone steals her ideas and she is blacklisted, preventing her from getting a reputable job.

Weyn, Suzanne, and Diana Gonzalez

South Beach Sizzle. 2005. 272p. ISBN: 9781416900115. *MJS*
When Lula and Jeff get an apartment above the restaurant where they work the summer after high school graduation, they meet a lot of interesting people while they have adventures that lead them to find love.

Krulik, Nancy

She's Got the Beat. 2005. 303p. ISBN: 9781416900207. *MJS*
Miranda reinvents herself when she moves to Austin, Texas, by joining a band as the drummer, but when she falls for the bands gorgeous bass player, she must face complications and jealousy to win his love.

Ostow, Micol

30 Guys in 30 Days. 2005. 304p. ISBN: 9781416902782. *MJS*
When Claudia Clarkson breaks up with her long-term high school boyfriend to pursue new options now that she is in college, she finds that she has forgotten how to flirt, and the only solution is to meet a new guy every day for a month.

Ponti, Jamie

Animal Attraction. 2005. 272p. ISBN: 9781416909873. *MJS*

After living seventeen years without a boyfriend, Jane is sure that this summer she can change that, but when she gets stuck in a furry beaver costume at her job at an amusement park, her plans may be thwarted—it's hard to flirt when you're covered in fur.

Friedman, Aimee

A Novel Idea. 2006. 234p. ISBN: 9781416907855. *MJS*

Norah is excited with the variety of people who show up for the book club she has organized, especially when one of them is a gorgeous guy.

Burnham, Niki

Scary Beautiful. 2005. 272p. ISBN: 9780689876196. *MJS*

Devastated when her boyfriend moves and dumps her because he can't handle a long-distance relationship, Chloe Rand finds that she is treated differently by her friends. When she falls for geeky Billy, she is uncertain if her new relationship will help or hinder her.

McClymer, Kelly

Getting to Third Date. 2006. 304p. ISBN: 9781416914792. *MJS*

Katelyn Spears believes that after two bad dates, no guy should have another chance, that is until the fans of her anonymous advice column find that their guru has never had a third date, and the paper's editor, Tyler, challenges her to give one more date to all the duds and chronicle her adventures in her column.

Downing, Erin

Dancing Queen. 2006. 272p. ISBN: 9781416925101. *MJS*

When Olivia lands an internship at a hot TV music station, she can't seem to stop making a fool of herself in front of all the pop stars she meets. But when one rocker finds her quirks endearing, Olivia finds that she can be in the spotlight.

Echols, Jennifer

Major Crush. 2006. 304p. ISBN: 9781416918301. *MJS*

Quitting the beauty-pageant circuit to become the drum major, Virginia Sauter is disappointed when she has to share the post with gorgeous Drew. When the job is not quite what she expected, Virginia must decide if she's made a big mistake.

Edwards, Johanna

Love Undercover. 2006. 264p. ISBN: 9781439597644. *MJS*

When her federal agent father brings home handsome Blaine, who has entered the Witness Protection Program, and enrolls him in her high school, it is up to Kaitlyn to protect him from the lovelorn girls as well as the guys who want to kill him.

Downing, Erin

Prom Crashers. 2007. 256p. ISBN: 9781416935599. *MJS*

When Emily falls in love at first sight with Ethan, she knows that with the help of her friends she must find him again even though she only knows his first name and has lost his phone number.

Ostow, Micol

Gettin' Lucky. 2007. 240p. ISBN: 9781416935360. *MJS*

When Cass Parker catches her best friend kissing her boyfriend, she decides that it is time to find new friends. She joins the weekly poker night, so she can catch her cheating boyfriend when he cheats at cards.

Echols, Jennifer

The Boys Next Door. 2007. 336p. ISBN: 9781416918318. *MJS*

Lori looks forward to her summers at a lake swimming and spending time with the handsome Vader brothers. When the older brother, Sean, starts to show more than brotherly interest in her, Lori welcomes the attention but wonders what it means for her relationship with younger brother Adam.

Deutsch, Stacia, and Rhody Cohon

In the Stars. 2007. 304p. ISBN: 9781416948759. *MJS*

When Sylvie loses the diamond from her dead mother's wedding ring, her friend Cherise takes it as a sign that she will soon find love. Sylvie does not believe in signs but decides to date the next boy who asks her out and in the process makes some interesting discoveries about love.

Ostow, Micol

Crush du Jour. 2007. 203p. ISBN: 9781416950271. *MJS*

When Laine signs up to teach a cooking class at her community center, she falls for her co-instructor Seth, but when he invites her to come work at his family's restaurant, she must ensure that coworker Callie won't steal her boy.

Ruditis, Paul

Love, Hollywood Style. 2008. 272p. ISBN: 9781416951384. *MJS*

As a tour guide at a real Hollywood studio, Tracy wishes that life could be like the movies, especially when it comes to getting her crush Connor to notice her, so she decides to take her cue from the movies and use everything she has learned on the big screen and transfer it to real life.

Hapka, Catherine

Something Borrowed. 2008. 272p. ISBN: 9781416954415. *MJS*

> When Ava gets dumped by her boyfriend just two weeks before her sister's wedding, she asks to borrow her best friend's boyfriend Jason for the evening, but then things get complicated when she finds herself falling for him.

Lyles, Whitney

Party Games. 2008. 304p. ISBN: 9781416959137. *MJS*

> Sara is caught up in helping her party planner mom create the best sweet sixteen birthday party for spoiled socialite Dakota. While Sara will cater to Dakota's every whim, she draws the line when she wants her to get Sara's crush, Ian, to be her date.

Krulik, Nancy

Puppy Love. 2008. 272p. ISBN: 9781416961529. *MJS*

> When she finds herself complaining to handyman Connor instead of her boyfriend Sammy about the overly pampered pooches she walks, Alana wonders if Connor might be the boy for her until she finds out that he is not who she thought he was.

Hapka, Cathy

The Twelve Dates of Christmas. 2008. 272p. ISBN: 9781416964124. *MJS*

> When the spark goes out of her relationship with boyfriend Cameron, Lexie decides to get him a new girlfriend so she can move on guilt free, but when she sees Cameron in the arms of Jaylene she finds that now she wants Cameron back.

Ponti, Jamie

Sea of Love. 2008. 272p. ISBN: 9781416967910. *MJS*

> Even if she has to help with the Valentine's Day dance, Darby finds that moving from New York to Florida so her family can run a hotel is not that bad, especially after she falls for hot surfer Zach, but when Darby's ex shows up from New York, things get a little too complicated.

Toliver, Wendy

Miss Match. 2009. 304p. ISBN: 9781416964131. *MJS*

> Using her talent for matchmaking, Sasha starts a thriving online business setting up her high school classmates, but when Derek asks her to set him up with her sister Maddie, Sasha has a hard time staying on track when she falls for Derek herself.

Hapka, Catherine

Love on Cue. 2009. 288p. ISBN: 9781416968573. *MJS*

Maggie is excited when it looks like her crush Derek might be her leading man in the school play, but when they change the play to a musical and Maggie realizes she can't sing, both her plans to star in the play and win Derek's heart are in jeopardy.

Downing, Erin

Drive Me Crazy. 2009. 210p. ISBN: 9781416974840. *MJS*

Kate is looking forward to a road trip with her two best friends, Sierra and Alexis, but when she finds out that Alexis's geeky cousin, Adam, is going to come along, Kate is devastated until Adam looks like he just might be the guy for her.

Lyles, Whitney

Love Off Limits. 2009. 304p. ISBN: 9781416975083. *MJS*

Having dated Jeremy since freshman year, Natalie finds that the spark has gone out of their relationship, especially when she is asked to write a romance column for the school newspaper and she finds herself falling for the paper's editor, Matt.

Echols, Jennifer

The Ex Games. 2009. 336p. ISBN: 9781416978466. *MJS*

A battle of the sexes heats up when Hayden's ex-boyfriend Nick challenges Hayden to a head-to-head snowboarding contest.

Rigaud, Debbie

Perfect Shot. 2009. 304p. ISBN: 9781416978350. *MJS*

When London spots Brent, a hot guy, signing up contestants for a beauty contest, she gets in line just to say hello, never thinking she would get picked for the contest. When she does, she finds that she not only wants to win Brent but the contest as well.

Sones, Sonya

What My Mother Doesn't Know. New York: Simon & Schuster Books for Young Readers, 2001. 259 p. ISBN: 9780689841149; 9780689855535pa; (aud). YALSA Best Books; YALSA Quick Picks. *MJ*

Fourteen-year-old Sophie is happy dating handsome Dylan, but when he becomes too clingy, she falls for Chaz, a cyber-boy she communicates with over the Internet. Then, however, Chaz turns out to be very scary. She then falls for her friend from preschool, Zak. Even with the support of best friends Rachel and Grace, Sophie begins to doubt herself as she searches for the perfect boyfriend.

<u>Sequel</u>: *What My Girlfriend Doesn't Know.* New York: Simon & Schuster Books for Young Readers, 2007. 304 p. ISBN: 9780689876028; 9780689876035pa. YALSA Quick Picks. *J*

When school-appointed loser Robin starts dating beautiful Sophie, she becomes an outcast, and Sophie's friends dump her. Feeling responsible for undermining her reputation, Robin is tempted when one of his classmates starts showing an interest in him, and when he is caught kissing her, Robin must do everything he can to not only win Sophie back but to help to repair their reputations by standing up to the bullies.

Popularity • Dating • Girlfriends • Self-Esteem • First Love • Dating • Artists • Novels in Verse

Springer, Kristina

The Espressologist. New York: Farrar, Straus & Giroux, 2009. 184 p. ISBN: 9780374322281. *S*

High school senior and part-time barista Jane Turner finds that she is a natural matchmaker when she sets up two of her customers based on their drink orders. When her boss decides to use her talent to enhance their business, word spreads about her abilities, and people flock to the store in the hopes of finding true love. While Jane is great taking care of others' love lives, she can't see that classmate Cam is really her perfect match and instead sets him up with her newly single best friend, Em. Soon Jane must turn her attentions to herself if she is going to attract her perfect match.

Dating • Interpersonal Relations

Sutherland, Tui T.

This Must Be Love. New York: HarperCollins, 2004. 256 p. ISBN: 9780060564759; 9780060564773pa. *J*

Best friends Helena and Hermia are in love with Dimitri and Alex. When the drama teacher decides that the high school's production of *Romeo and Juliet* will consist of an all-male cast, Hermia's dreams of being the star are dashed. Things get even worse for Hermia when her crush, Alex, invites her to an interactive theater piece called *The Faeries' Quarrel* in New York City, and she sneaks out to attend when her dad refuses to let her go. Dimitri, whom Helena loves, falls for Hermia, and Helena spills her secret plans to go to the play so she can win Dimitri's attention. Things look like they will never be right until the play's fairy queen sets each of the players on the right course to true love.

Best Friends • Interpersonal Relations • Theater • Drama • E-mail • Instant Messaging

Triana, Gaby

Riding the Universe. New York: HarperTeen, 2009. 267 p. ISBN: 9780060885700. *S*

Seventeen-year-old Chlo Rodriguez loves to ride her Harley, which she built with her deceased Uncle Seth and has named Lolita. She finds freedom on the bike as she races her best friend, Rock, down the highways—that is, until her adopted parents threaten to take away her bike and force her to get a tutor to bring up her grades. When she is paired with brainy Gordon Spudinka and finds herself falling for him, and Rock shows that he is interested in her too, Chlo must deal with all the distractions to pass chemistry and keep her bike.

Grief • Dating • Family Relationships • Adoption

Vail, Rachel

If We Kiss. New York: HarperCollins, 2005. 272 p. ISBN: 9780060569143; 9780060569167pa. *MJ*

When ninth-grader Charlotte "Charlie" Collins is maneuvered into French kissing Kevin Lazarus even though she doesn't care for him, she finds herself embroiled in a mess of complications. Not only does Kevin become the boyfriend of her best friend Tess, it looks like he will soon be her stepbrother since Charlie's mother is dating Kevin's father. When the two families take a ski trip and Kevin kisses her again, Charlie finds herself obsessed with wanting to continue the relationship while at the same time feeling extremely guilty about betraying her friend. When the complications of her love triangle result in heartbreak, Charlie must learn the difference between lust and true love.

Dating • Guilt • Kissing • Loyalty • Friendship

Van Draanen, Wendelin

Flipped. New York: Knopf, 2001. 212 p. ISBN: 9780375811746; 9780375825446pa. School Library Journal Best Books. *J*

When Julianna "Juli" Baker first encountered Bryce Loski in her neighborhood six years earlier she fell in love, but at the time Bryce wanted to have nothing to do with her. Times change, and now in eighth grade, it is Bryce who has fallen for Juli, who in turn is now repulsed by his immaturity. Juli fights to save an old tree from being cut down, and Bryce learns some great wisdom from his grandfather when he helps Juli spruce up her family's yard after he makes an unkind remark. Both teens learn that when they must stand up for what they believe in, it is nice to have true friends and family by your side.

Love • Family • Self-Perception

Walker, Melissa

Lovestruck Summer. New York: HarperTeen, 2009. 272 p. ISBN: 9780061715860pa. *JS*

Indie-rock girl Quinn has come to Austin, Texas, for a music internship and finds herself stuck with her sorority-loving cousin "Party Penny" as a roommate. Drawn into Penny's circle of friends, Quinn finds that she can't stop thinking about Penny's cute all-American friend Russ, even though she thinks gorgeous DJ Sebastian, with his great taste in music, would be a better match. Quinn must discover which boy is really right for her.

Internships • Music • Interpersonal Attraction • Friendship • Love

Wizner, Jake

Castration Celebration. New York: Random House Children's Books, 2009. 304 p. ISBN: 9780375852152; 9780375852169pa. *S*

At a summer Yale University arts camp, Olivia writes a musical reworking of *Much Ado about Nothing*, called *Castration Celebration*. As her project, drawing inspiration from the exploits of her fellow campers and her disappointment in men, Olivia satirizes popular culture to make her point and deal with her anger over having found her father cheating on her mother. But when Max tries to catch her attention by accepting the elaborate challenges she gives him, Olivia finds her resolve to stay away from guys challenged as the pair fall in love.

Summer Theater • Sex Role • Drug Use • Musicals

Young, Karen Romano

The Beetle and Me: A Love Story. New York: Greenwillow Books, 1999. 181 p. ISBN: 9780688159221; 9780380732951pa. YALSA Best Books. *J*

Despite the advice of her mechanic father, her uncle, and her aunt, fifteen-year-old Daisy Pandolfi takes on the task of restoring a rusted old 1957 purple Volkswagen Beetle. Even though she has just watched her older sister get dumped, Daisy falls in love with the new boy in town, only to have him fall for her bossy cousin. Daisy then receives a kiss from friend Billy Hatcher, and even though she learns that he has loved her for years, she is not so certain about her feelings. As she spends six months working on the car, she finds out important information about Billy's home life and begins to appreciate him as well as her own family. Before long she is able to take her first drive, and even though things don't go well, Daisy persists and finds that she not only has a car that works but also a new understanding of herself as well.

Automobiles • Self-Discovery • Love

Zeises, Lara M.

The Sweet Life of Stella Madison. New York: Delacorte Press, 2009. 240 p. ISBN: 9780385731461. *JS*

When Stella Madison's parents get her a summer internship to write about the local food scene for the town's newspaper, Stella is a little disappointed because she is not as interested in food as her chef father and restaurateur mother. When Stella meets Jeremy, a gorgeous intern at her mom's restaurant, her topic becomes a lot more exciting, even though her new interest may sabotage her relationship with longtime boyfriend Max.

Internships • Family Problems • Love • Boyfriends

First Love

Beam, Matt

Getting to First Base with Danalda Chase. New York: Dutton Children's Books, 2007. 192 p. ISBN: 9780525475781. *M*

Seventh-grader Darcy Spillman has two obsessions: baseball and getting a date with Danalda Chase. When the new girl, Kamma Singh, offers to give him advice on how to attract Danalda if he will coach her in baseball, Darcy accepts. Dealing with the intense competition to get on the middle school baseball team and with his Grandpa Spillman's Alzheimer's disease makes things even more complicated. But after a date with superficial Danalda, Darcy realizes that it is really Kamma who has stolen his heart.

Love • Baseball • Dating • Grandfathers

Earls, Nick

After Summer. Boston: Graphia, 2005. 226 p. ISBN: 9780618457816pa. *S*

Spending Christmas with his mother on the beach in Australia, Alex Delaney worries about getting into college and the fact that he has never had a girlfriend. When he meets a mysterious girl named Fortuna, he falls in love, and, even more exciting, she seems to like him back. Meeting Fortuna's eccentric family, who make homemade arts and crafts to sell, Alex gets some unique lessons in how to bake bread and how to do nude pottery. Despite the fun he is having, Alex realizes that things can't last, but instead of worrying about the future, Alex learns to live in the moment.

Romance • Girlfriends • Coming-of-Age • Vacations

First Kisses (multiple authors). New York: HarperTeen

This series includes lighthearted young romances in which determined girls find a suitable boy relationship, weather the ups and downs, and get their first kiss.

Kissing • Romance • Love

Hawthorne, Rachel

Trust Me. 2007. 208p. ISBN: 9780061143083. *MJ*

Counselor-in-training Liz is upset when she gets teamed up with troublemaker Sean Reed for their entire program—that is, until she looks into his deep blue eyes.

Davis, Stephie

The Boyfriend Trick. 2007. 240p. ISBN: 9780061143090. *MJ*

Lily cannot find a date for the semiformal dance after her friends tell her that she should go with Rafe, a drummer and fellow student, and she finds out that he is not really that interested in her.

Collins, Jenny

Puppy Love. 2007. 256p. ISBN: 9780061143120. *MJ*

An employee at the Perfect Paws pet grooming salon, Allie is confused as to why she is so jealous that Jack is dating Megan, when she really does not like him that much.

Jordan, Sabrina

It Had to Be You. 2007. 256 p. ISBN: 9780061143137. *MJ*

As the author of the love advice column for her junior high school paper, Emma begins to wonder if she is really qualified to give romantic guidance when she can't get her cute next-door neighbor to ask her out.

Davis, Stephie

The Boyfriend Game (also titled: *Playing the Field*). 2009. 208p. ISBN: 9780061143106. *MJ*

> Tricia finds herself falling for a guy for the first time when she begins to have intense feelings for Graham, a friend who has been helping her prepare for soccer tryouts.

Chandler, Elizabeth

The Real Thing (also titled: *Love at First Click*). 2009. 192p. ISBN: 9780061143113. *MJ*

> Hayley loves to take school newspaper photographs for gorgeous Flynn, but when her sister starts liking him too, Hayley must get her sister out of the picture so she can have him all to herself.

Hogan, Mary

The Serious Kiss. New York: HarperCollins, 2005. 240 p. ISBN: 9780060722067; 9780060722081pa. *J*

> High school freshman Libby Madrigal's dream of having her first serious kiss with popular Zach Nash is impeded by her home life, which consists of her parents' screaming fights and tense family meals. When her alcoholic dad loses his job, he moves the family to Barstow, California, to live next door to Libby's grandmother in a retirement trailer-park community in the middle of the desert. Feeling lost in a school with cruel classmates, Libby finds unexpected support from her grandmother's sage advice. As she makes friends who show her the wonders of her new home, Libby is able to find a direction with both her family, when her parents finally agree to enter counseling, and with her love life, when she meets and kisses her new offbeat boyfriend.

> *Grandmothers • Brothers • Sisters • Family Problems • Alcoholism • Parent and Child*

Soto, Gary

Accidental Love. Orlando, FL: Harcourt, 2006. 179 p. ISBN: 9780525476979; 9780142410981pa. *MJ*

> Fourteen-year-old overweight, angry, tough-talking Marias grabs the wrong cell phone after a fight in which she punches her friend's cheating boyfriend in an elevator. When she returns it to its owner, Rene, a nerdy chess player who attends a school across town, she finds herself attracted to him. As the pair get to know each other and fall in love, Marias sees that she can have a better life. Rene, who is so different from the boys at her rough school, inspires her to turn her life around. When she transfers to Rene's school, the couple face oppositions, especially from her former classmates who don't like her change and from Rene's mother, who opposes their relationship. But through it all, Marias improves her grades, loses weight, and lands a part in the school play.

> *Chess • Hispanic Americans • Romance • Dieting • Weight Control • Love • Popularity • Interpersonal Relations*

Breaking Up

Barnes, Derrick

The Making of Dr. Truelove. New York: Simon Pulse, 2006. 240 p. ISBN: 9781416914396. YALSA Quick Picks; YALSA Popular Paperbacks. *S*

Diego becomes an instant celebrity when he and friend J-Live create the online personality of Dr. Truelove to give advice on love and sex in an attempt to get back with his longtime crush Roxy after his sexual insecurities break them up. When J-Live assumes the persona of the doctor, things begin to get out of control as the teens gain even more popularity, including interest from girls, and it is up to Diego to figure out what is important so he can finally win back Roxy.

African Americans • Romance • Sexuality • Humor

Hoffmann, Kerry Cohen

It's Not You, It's Me. New York: Delacorte Press, 2009. 176 p. ISBN: 9780385736961. *JS*

High school junior Zoe is shocked when Henry, her boyfriend of six months, dumps her saying he wants to focus on his band and not a girlfriend right now. But Zoe knows that he has made a big mistake, and despite her friends' advice to the contrary, she starts a campaign to win him back. As her antics, which include sneaking into Henry's house and snooping in his e-mail, escalate into insanity and it is apparent that they are also futile, Zoe realizes that she was so wrapped up in her relationship with Henry that she lost herself, and instead of getting him back she needs to figure out who she is without him and define her own identity.

Friends • Ex-Boyfriends • Dating

Jones, Carrie

Tips on Having a Gay (Ex) Boyfriend. Woodbury, MN: Flux, 2007. 278 p. ISBN: 9780738710501; 9780738713410pa. *S*

Everyone in town just assumes that high school senior Belle Philbrick and her longtime boyfriend Dylan will get married one day, but when Dylan confesses that he is gay, Belle must deal with her conflicting feelings of still wanting to be there for him and at the same time dealing with her own devastation. Just days after their breakup, Dylan starts a new relationship. Belle knows that being an openly gay student in their small-town school will be hard for him, but what she does not realize is how hard it will be for her until she, too, becomes the target of taunts and gossip. Trying to move on but still salvage her longtime friendship with Dylan, Belle finds support and romance with Tom, a boy who has had a longtime crush on her.

Sequel: *Love (and Other Uses for Duct Tape).* Woodbury, MN: Flux, 2008. 284 p. ISBN: 9780738712574. *S*

> Finishing up her final year in high school, Belle finds that love is in the air all around her with her mother's new romance and her overtly amorous friend Em and her boyfriend. But Belle is not finding her love life to be as smooth as her mother's or Em's, since her new straight boyfriend Tom is reluctant to have sex with her. When Em reveals that she is pregnant, Belle must figure out how to keep her friend's secret as she deals with the problems in her own relationship.
>
> *Dating • Homosexuality • Gay Males • Friendship • Prejudice • Coming Out • Violence • Coming-of-Age*

Kantor, Melissa

The Breakup Bible: A Novel. New York: Hyperion, 2007. 265 p. ISBN: 9780786809622; 9780786809639pa. *JS*

> High school junior Jen Lewis is caught up in working for her school newspaper and in her boyfriend, Max, who is also the paper's editor. When Max dumps her for another girl on the newspaper's staff, Jen feels lost, and she looks for guidance in an old book, Dr. Emory Emerson's The Breakup Bible, which was given to her by her grandmother. As she works on a controversial article with her African American friend about the school's racial divide, Jen is finally able to open up, stand on her own, and see how losing her first love has made her stronger.
>
> *Advice • Friendship • Dating*

Nelson, Blake

The New Rules of High School. New York: Viking/Penguin, 2003. 225 p. ISBN: 9780670036448; 9780142402429pa. *JS*

> Things are good for Max Caldwell. He is a straight-A student, editor-in-chief of the school newspaper, and captain of the debate team. But when one day he inexplicably breaks up with his beautiful girlfriend Cindy, Max can't seem to control anything, especially after a boy-crazy freshman throws herself at him at a party and then joins the newspaper staff. Failing to maintain his closest friendships and drinking too much, Max falls deeper into his confusion as he tries to cope with his family problems and the pressure to get into college until he is finally able to form new bonds and discover who he really is.
>
> *Romance • Drinking • Family Problems • Overachievers • High School Newspapers • Coming-of-Age*

Ziegler, Jennifer

Alpha Dog. New York: Delacorte Press, 2006. 336 p. ISBN: 9780385732857pa. *S*

> Seventeen-year-old Katie is looking forward to her summer college-prep program at the University of Texas where she will be able to get away from her controlling mother and recover from the trauma of having her boyfriend dump her on her birthday. However, with a retro-punk roommate whose boyfriend is constantly camped out on their couch, and a newly adopted homeless dog named Seamus who is out of control, things are not going where Katie had hoped. Enrolling Seamus in an obedience class where she learns that she needs to act like an alpha

dog, Katie soon finds that she is able to take control in all the aspects of her life.

Dogs • Mother and Daughter • Romance • Summer School

Summer Love

Abbott, Hailey

Summer Boys Series. New York: Point/Scholastic
> In alternating points of view, four cousins, Jamie, Ella, Kelsi, and Beth, chase romance during the summer and on holidays.

Romance • Vacations • Boyfriends • Family Relationships • Summer

Summer Boys. 2004. 214 p. ISBN: 9780439540209. YALSA Quick Picks. *J*
> On a summer vacation in Maine, the four cousins find and lose love. Jamie's boyfriend from last summer, Ethan, just wants to be friends, so she tries to take revenge with his friend Scott. Ella is lusting after her sister Kelsi's new boyfriend Peter. Beth is jealous of longtime best friend George's new girlfriend but won't let him know how she really feels.

Next Summer. 2005. 230 p. ISBN: 9780439755405. *J*
> Another summer at their family's beach cottage leads to love and loss. Beth is sad to leave her new boyfriend George but soon starts hanging out with a lifeguard. After her bad breakup last year, Kelsi wants a boyfriend-free summer but finds herself attracted to frat boy Tim. Ella just wants a committed relationship with a nice guy but can't seem to attract that perfect someone. Jamie just wants to focus on her summer writing program.

After Summer. 2006 224 p. ISBN: 9780439863674. *J*
> During thanksgiving break, the girls once again deal with the uncertainties of love. Beth finds that boyfriend George is changing. Ella meets a boy who can flirt just as much as she does. Kelsi's frat boy treats her differently when they are around his friends. Jamie falls for a rich boy at her boarding school.

Last Summer. 2007. 192 p. ISBN: 9780439867252. *J*
> Three of the cousins have their last summer together before they head off to college where everything may change. Beth is no longer with George, but things could change. Kelsi has a new boyfriend, but he just does not make her feel like the old one did. Ella is trying to resist an old ex-boyfriend.

Abbott, Hailey

Summer Girls. New York: HarperTeen, 2009. 224 p. ISBN: 9780545102681. *J*

Three girls on their summer vacation in Maine find and lose love. Greer is attracted to Brady despite his clingy ex-girlfriend. Lara falls for a boy whom she should not and has a hard time dealing with the attraction. Jessica wants to make Liam more than just a friend.

Romance • Vacations • Boyfriends • Ex-Girlfriends • Family Relationships • Summer

Barkley, Brad, and Heather Hepler

Dream Factory. New York: Dutton Books, 2007. 250 p. ISBN: 9780525478027; 9780142412985pa. *JS*

Alternating chapters tell the story of recent high school graduates Ella and Luke. Both performing as costumed characters at Disney World, the pair are attached to one another. Complicating matters are the facts that Luke is dating Cassie and Ella, who is dealing with the death of her brother and her missionary parents moving to Africa, is also attracting "Prince Charming." Even though they are unsure about their futures, the pair work through their uncertain feelings and finds a summer love.

Romance • Jobs • Death • Summer

Clark, Catherine

Picture Perfect. New York: HarperTeen, 2008. 352 p. ISBN: 9780061374975pa. *JS*

Emily is spending an ideal vacation on the Outer Banks with her family where she meets friends she has not seen for more than two years, Heather, Adam, and Spencer. When one of the cute guys in the house next door shows some interest in her, she goes out with him, trying to have the summer fling that her friend Heather recommends as an important step before going off to college. But Emily can't forget the ill-advised confession she made to Spencer of feelings she had for him two years ago. Adam and Spencer get in the way with their overprotective attitudes by showing up at the worst times. In the end, Emily must choose between an old and new flame to find love.

Summer Vacations • Friendship • Summer

Clark, Catherine

So Inn Love. New York: HarperTeen, 2007. 336 p. ISBN: 9780061139048pa. *JS*

At her summer job at Tides Inn, Liza McKenzie wants to do a lot of swimming and make some new friends. Things get complicated when it turns out that she is going to be a chambermaid instead of a reservations clerk, her old friend Caroline is acting like she doesn't know her, and while gorgeous Hayden seems interested in her, it is only when other people are not around.

Romance • Dating • Summer Job • Summer

Friedman, Robin

How I Survived My Summer Vacation and Lived to Write the Story. Chicago: Front Street/Cricket Books, 2000. 173 p. ISBN: 9780812627381. *MJ*

> Thirteen-year-old Jackie Monterey can never get past the first line of nearly anything he writes. But the summer before high school, he is determined to write the next great American novel. He finds himself distracted by his unusual parents and his troublesome friends, Garus and Nick. When he falls in love and then gets dumped, leads his swim team to an outstanding victory, and finds a way to relate to his parents, Jackie finds that he is able to loosen up and focus on writing.
>
> *Writing • Summer • Romance*

Han, Jenny

The Summer I Turned Pretty. New York: Simon & Schuster Books for Young Readers, 2009. 288 p. ISBN: 9781416968238; 9781416968290pa. *J*

> Every year Isabel, "Belly," her older brother Steven, and their mother have shared a beach house with Susannah, Belly's mother's best friend, and her two sons. Every year, Belly has also had a crush on Conrad, Susannah's oldest boy, but just like all the boys, he has always treated her like a younger sister. During the summer she turns fifteen, Belly finds that she has beauty to attract boys, including Jeremiah, Susannah's younger son, and local nice boy, Cam, with whom she has her first date. She still finds Conrad out of her reach until she discovers that Susannah is dying of breast cancer and Belly is able to put her life in focus, realizing that you can't always pick who you end up falling in love with.
>
> *Summer • Romance • Coming-of-Age*

Hawthorne, Rachel

The Boyfriend League. New York: HarperTeen, 2007. 315 p. ISBN: 9780061138379pa. YALSA Popular Paperbacks. *JS*

> Dani is looking forward to playing baseball and also hopes that her summer league will afford her the opportunity to get her first boyfriend. When the league asks for families to help board some of the players, Dani jumps at the opportunity to have the first chance at the best guy. When the hottest guy, Jason, comes to live with them, Dani is in a hard place, since her parents made her promise she would not date the boy in their house.
>
> *Baseball • Summer • Romance*

Hawthorne, Rachel

Island Girls (and Boys). New York: HarperTeen, 2005. 336 p. ISBN: 9780060755461pa. *S*

> In the last summer before college, Jennifer and her two friends Chelsea and Amy are planning on working at a nearby campground and living in her grandparents' house on an island. But things get complicated when Chelsea's boyfriend moves in and Amy keeps bringing home strays, of both

the human and animal variety. When Jennifer meets Dylan, who is camping at their campground, things look up until she finds out that he has not planned to stay on the island for long and is joining the army in the fall. Jennifer must figure out how to make the most of the summer.

Romance • Summer Job • Camping • Summer

Hawthorne, Rachel

Labor of Love. New York: HarperTeen, 2008. 320 p. ISBN: 9780061363849pa. *JS*
When Dawn Delaney discovered her boyfriend Drew cheating on her at the junior prom, she lost her faith in guys and swore to spend a summer without them. She visits a psychic in New Orleans where she and her best friends, Jenna and Amber, have gone to help rebuild houses, and she predicts that Dawn will meet a guy with a red hat and a nice smile. Dawn writes off the prediction until she meets a guy that may be the one who can help her mend her broken heart.

Romance • Summer Job • Summer

Hawthorne, Rachel

Thrill Ride. New York: Avon Books, 2006. 313 p. ISBN: 9780060839543pa. *JS*
To get away from her family, who is planning her sister's wedding, Megan takes a summer job at an amusement park called Thrill Ride. Living with the other teens who are part of the summer program, Megan misses her boyfriend Nick. But when Megan meets gorgeous Parker, the brother of her roommate and finds that being with him is fun and nice, she begins to wonder what the future is for her and Nick and if Parker really is her true love.

Summer Job • Breaking Up • Romance

Herbsman, Cheryl

Breathing. New York: Viking Children's Books, 2009. 272 p. ISBN: 9780670011230. *J*
Fifteen-year-old asthmatic Savannah Brown looks forward to a summer on the Carolina Coast hanging out with friends, working at the library, and studying for the SATs under the eye of her vigilant and strict mother. When handsome eighteen-year-old Jackson Channing comes to town, Savannah is swept off her feet and finds a responsible, loving boyfriend whose very presence seems to keep her asthma at bay. But when Savannah is accepted into a prestigious college program for high school seniors and Jackson leaves for home, Savannah must learn to stand on her own two feet without her mother or boyfriend as she goes for her dreams and gains maturity and independence.

Dating • Romance • Summer

Runyon, Brent

Surface Tension: A Novel in Four Summers. New York: Alfred A. Knopf, 2009. 197 p. ISBN: 9780375844461. *MJ*
Every summer from age thirteen to sixteen, Luke vacations with his parents for two weeks at their cabin on a lake. Through the years, Luke deals with the physical and emotional changes that come with growing up surrounded by a variety of

people, including eccentric neighbors who are obsessed with their lawn and his childhood friend, Claire, who, over the years, turns from being annoying to becoming very interesting.

Vacations • Summer • Family • Coming-of-Age

Wittlinger, Ellen

Heart on My Sleeve. New York: Simon & Schuster Books for Young Readers, 2004. 224 p. ISBN: 9780689849978; 9780689849992pa. *S*

High school senior Chloe thinks she has found love with Julian when they meet while both visiting the college they plan to attend. Back home and maintaining their long-distance relationship over e-mail, they must deal with the problems of family, friends, and other potential romances that complicate their plans to reunite at the end of summer, when they will discover that they don't know each other as well as they thought.

College • Family • Singing • E-mail • Love • Online Romance • Secrets • Proms • Family Relationships • Coming Out • Lesbians • Epistolary Novel • Summer

Online Romance

Draper, Sharon M.

Romiette and Julio. New York: Atheneum, 1999. 236 p. ISBN: 9780689821806; 9780689842092pa. *JS*

Meeting in an Internet chat room, sixteen-year-old Romiette Capelle and sixteen-year-old Julio Montague, who has just recently moved from Texas, have no idea that they go to the same high school. The two, who come from very different backgrounds, soon meet and realize they are meant to be together. When a local gang interferes with their relationship, intent on keeping the African American Romiette away from the Hispanic Julio, and the pairs' parents also have prejudices against the match, the two must overcome great odds to remain together.

Internet • Interracial Persons • Gangs • African Americans • Hispanic Americans

Fraiberg, Jordanna

In Your Room. New York: Razorbill, 2008. 203 p. ISBN: 9781595141934pa. *MJ*

When their families exchange houses, Mountain biker Charlie from Colorado and fashionista Molly from Los Angeles begin a friendship online that soon turns to love. Charlie is bullied because he has two mothers, and Molly is grieving for her father, so together they are able to share their pain. When Molly's gorgeous blond friend, Celeste, tries to steal Charlie and Molly makes friends with his ex-girlfriend Sylvia, the two must deal with a new kind of pain as they try to maintain their long-distance relationship.

Romance • E-mail • Ex-Girlfriends • Stepfathers

Friedman, Robin

The Girlfriend Project. New York: Walker, 2007. 192 p. ISBN: 9780802796240. *S*

Once a nerd, senior Reed Walton's appearance, now with no glasses or braces, has changed, making him very attractive to women. With no experience dating, he needs help to navigate the world of women, so his twin best friends, Lonnie and Ronnie, create a Web site where women can answer surveys to give him advice that will help him along the way. Sorting through the advice and the girls that his new Web popularity brings, Reed must craft his own identity while he works up the courage to tell Ronnie that she is really the girl he wants.

Popularity • Twins • Girlfriends • Dating • Web Sites

Kadefors, Sara

Are U 4 Real? New York: Dial Books, 2009. 311 p. ISBN: 9780803732766. *J*

Shy, awkward Alex is straight even though everyone thinks he is gay because he is a ballet dancer. When he meets Kyla, a party girl from Los Angeles, in an online chat room, he thinks he has found someone to care for as the two open up to each other about their lives. When the two meet in real life, there are just too many conflicts, and the pair does not speak for months. But during that time they realize that they do share something important and that they are willing to deal with the problems that come with a real life relationship.

Internet • Social Isolation • Friendship • Family Problems • Chat Rooms • Ballet

Kilbourne, Christina

Dear Jo: The Story of Losing Leah and Searching for Hope. Montreal: Lobster Press, 2007. 188 p. ISBN: 9781897073513pa. *M*

Twelve-year-old Maxine is dealing with the guilt and anger she feels when her best friend Leah disappears after she goes to meet an online boyfriend face-to-face. Maxine finds strength in her therapist's advice to keep a diary and to help with the police investigation. When she is contacted by her own online boyfriend for a face-to-face meeting, the police suspect that this is the same person who took Leah, and they engage Maxine in a dangerous plan to capture the predator.

Best Friends • Missing Persons • Boyfriends • Internet • Grief Loss • Diary Novel

Papademetriou, Lisa, and Chris Tebbetts

M or F? New York: Razorbill, 2005. 304 p. ISBN: 9781595140340; 9781595140913pa. *MJ*

Best friends Marcus and Frannie each want to find romance. Frannie thinks Jeffrey would be the perfect boyfriend, but she's too shy and insecure to approach him. Marcus, who is gay, knows just what to say to get Jeffrey interested, so he takes over for Frannie, impersonating her in online chats with Jeffrey. But things get problematic when Marcus falls for Jeffrey. When Frannie finds out about what has happened, the two have a fight, but in the end, their friendship wins out as they try to figure out their complex romantic relationships.

Gay Males • Friendship • Chat Rooms • Dating • Internet

Petersen, P. J., and Ivy Ruckman

Rob&sara.com. New York: Delacorte Press, 2004. 224 p. ISBN: 9780385731645; 9780440238737pa. *JS*

A good girl from a military family, sixteen-year-old Sara meets Rob in a chatroom for teen poets, and the two begin an e-mail friendship. As they exchange e-mails, the two get to know each other better, each finding support from the other for their complex lives. Sara is convinced that Rob is the boarding school student he says he is, so she is shocked when she gets an e-mail from Shannon, who says she is a student at Rob's school and she wants Sara to know that Rob is actually Alex, a suicidal boy who suffers from multiple personality disorder. But when Sara is injured in a climbing accident, Rob escapes from school to visit her in the hospital, and the two finally meet and learn the real truth.

E-mail • Interpersonal Relations • Military

Vaught, Susan

Exposed. New York: Bloomsbury U.S.A. Children's Books: Distributed to the trade by Macmillan, 2008. 330 p. ISBN: 9781599901619. *JS*

After being left with a sexually transmitted disease by her ex-boyfriend, sixteen-year-old baton twirling majorette Chan Shealy looks to the impersonal online world to find the perfect guy to whom she can talk without all the complications that real life brings. Despite her parents' rules, Chan meets Paul online, and as the two develop an increasingly steamy online affair, Chan gives Paul all the information he needs to prey on her and her eight-year old sister Lauren, leaving Chan to deal with the consequences of her naive actions.

Sex Crimes • Internet Predators • Sisters

1

2

3

4

5

6

7

8

9

10

11

12

Chapter 3

Living in a Family

From the moment of birth, one of the most fundamental of human relationships is with one's family. Throughout the life span, these relationships change and grow. Many believe that as adolescents work to develop their autonomy, increased emotional distance and conflict occurs in family relationships, especially in the relationships with one's parents. Although this may be true in some cases, the majority of adolescents really do not experience serious family relationship difficulties. That is not to say that the changes in family relations are not stressful, but for the most part they do not undermine the quality of relationships a teen has with his or her family. The books listed in this chapter deal with the close emotional bonds that are developed in families, both with parents and siblings, as well as the transformation these relationships take as adolescents develop their own individuality. In addition, these books include some of the temporary disruptions that add stress to family relationships such as adoption, single parenting, divorce, and the creation of stepfamilies.

Family Relationships

Abbott, Hailey

The Bridesmaid. New York: Delacorte Press, 2005. 266 p. ISBN: 9780385732208; 9780385902496pa. *MJ*

> Having seen firsthand at their parents' business just what brides can become when faced with planning a wedding, Abby and Carol vow not to fall prey to such behavior when they get married. After college graduation, Carol becomes engaged and fifteen-year-old Abby looks on as her sister becomes just what they hate. Abby, who has just gotten her first boyfriend, tries to decide if she should stay behind with him or take up the offer of a soccer scholarship that would take her to Italy, only to find that things don't always turn out like you expect when it comes to love.

> *Sisters • Weddings*

Ackermann, Joan

In the Space Left Behind. New York: Laura Geringer Books, 2007. 394 p. ISBN: 9780060722555. *J*

> Fifteen-year-old Colm loves the family home that his great grandfather built, but when his mother's third marriage threatens the sale of the house, he strikes a bargain with his father who deserted the family fifteen years earlier. Driving with his father from New England to California will earn him the $70,000 he needs to save the house. Along the way, Colm discovers himself as he finds that life can bring some unexpected surprises like a first love and forgiveness for a father.
>
> *Father and Son • Self-Discovery • Coming-of-Age*

Amato, Mary

The Naked Mole-Rat Letters. New York: Holiday House, 2005. 266 p. ISBN: 9780823419272; 9780823420988pa. *M*

> Intercepting an e-mail to her widowed father from a woman named Ayanna, whom he has apparently met and kissed, twelve-year-old Frankie tries to nip the relationship in the bud. Ayanna, however, keeps writing back and Frankie, still grieving for her mother, builds a web of lies that results in the rest of her life spiraling out of control when she ditches school, lies, and shuts out her family and friends. Losing the lead in the school play only adds to Frankie's grief but after help from Ayanna, a family crisis allows her to confront her father and her own feelings of disappointment and anger.
>
> *Family Problems • Grief • Death • Epistolary Novels*

Anderson, Laurie Halse

Catalyst. New York: Viking, 2002. 240 p. ISBN: 9780670035663; 9780142400012pa; (aud). YALSA Best Books. *S*

> Eighteen-year-old Kate Malone's perfect life as a minister's daughter, track star, and excellent student starts to unravel when her rejection letter from the only school she wanted to attend, MIT, arrives. To make matters worse, school bully Teri Litch and toddler Mikey Litch move into the Malone's home when their house nearly burns to the ground. But when Mikey tragically dies and secrets are revealed, Teri and Kate are able to find common ground.
>
> *Self-Discovery • Family Problems • Child Abuse • Coming-of-Age*

Bauer, Joan

Backwater. New York: Putnam, 1999. 185 p. ISBN: 9780399231414; 9780698118652pa. *JS*

> Sixteen-year-old Ivy Breedlove does not want to be a lawyer like the rest of her family; she would rather be a historian. When the task of fully documenting the Breedlove family history is thrust upon her, Ivy discovers a true connection to genealogy. In an effort to document the truth, Ivy tracks down her Aunt Jo, who lives alone in the Adirondacks working as a sculptor. Connecting with her aunt after a harrowing adventure, Ivy also finds that she is not the only one in the family with different ideas about appropriate professions.
>
> *Family Secrets • Aunts • Genealogy*

Bechard, Margaret

If It Doesn't Kill You. New York: Viking, 1999. 156 p. ISBN: 9780670885473. *J*

Football player Ben was happy to be compared to his father, who was also a star athlete, until his father moved out to live with another man. Angry and ashamed by his father's homosexuality, Ben is confused about what it means to be a man. Drawn by peer pressure into the antics of the new girl next door, Chyanna, including body piercing and attending drunken parties, Ben gets into trouble, and it is only when his father's partner is the one to come and rescue him that Ben must finally confront his own prejudices.

Homosexuality • *Father and Son*

Castellucci, Cecil

Beige. Cambridge, MA: Candlewick Press, 2007. 320 p. ISBN: 9780763630669; 9780763642327pa. YALSA Best Books; YALSA Quick Picks. *J*

Fourteen-year-old Katy is forced to leave her home in Montreal to live with her long-absent father in Los Angeles while her mother is off on an archaeological dig in Peru. A drummer for the punk band, Suck, her father, called "the Rat," is a consummate bachelor with a messy apartment and independent lifestyle. Katy is nicknamed Beige for her boring personality by Lake, a girl her father has bribed to befriend her. Katy wants nothing more than to go home until she starts selling T-shirts for Lake's band. Drawn into the punk rock scene, Katy fears the power of the music and the drugs that had once held sway over her parents, but as she befriends Lake and falls for a gorgeous boy, Katy finds new depths of understanding.

Father and Daughter • *Rock Music* • *Self-Perceptions*

Clarke, Judith

One Whole and Perfect Day. Asheville, NC: Front Street, 2007. 248 p. ISBN: 9781932425956; (aud). USBBY Outstanding International Books; Michael L. Printz Honor Books; YALSA Best Books. *S*

Seventeen-year-old Lily has an eccentric family whom she loves even though they are very embarrassing to her. Lily's mother is a psychologist who works in an adult day-care center and is always bringing home the patients to give their caregiver children a little break. Her grandmother Nan has an imaginary friend, and her older brother Lonnie can't seem to get his life together and keeps changing his major at university because he's trying to find himself. When her grandfather threatens Lonnie with an axe if he drops another major, forcing Lonnie to leave home and move into an apartment, Lily begins to have some major misgivings about the upcoming eightieth birthday party for grandfather. Doing the cooking, cleaning, shopping, and all of the other chores, Lily feels like the only responsible, sensible one in the house. But soon events conspire to assist Lily and her family as they come to a new understanding of themselves and make changes in their lives for the better.

Grandparents • *Brother and Sisters* • *Family Problems* • *Australia*

Cohn, Rachel

Cyd Charisse Trilogy. New York: Simon & Schuster Books for Young Readers
Cyd Charisse tries to craft her own identity as she moves between San Francisco and New York and deals with family problems and other complications, including romantic ones.

Boyfriends • Romance • Mother and Daughter • Blended Families • Abortion

Gingerbread. 2002. 172 p. ISBN: 9780689843372; 9780689860201pa. YALSA Best Books; YALSA Quick Picks; School Library Journal Best Books. *JS*
Sixteen-year-old Cyd Charisse has been kicked out of her exclusive boarding school and returned home to San Francisco where she constantly fights with her mother and stepfather. Hiding the fact that she had an abortion, Cyd is able to make friends with an understanding elderly woman, Sugar Pie, and connects with her sexy surfer boyfriend, Shrimp. But when Cyd breaks curfew after being out all night with Shrimp, she is sent to New York to live with her biological father, where she meets and makes friends with her two adult half-siblings and faces some serious questions about her life.

Shrimp. 2005. 272 p. ISBN: 9780689866128; 9780689866135pa. *JS*
Cyd Charisse has returned to San Francisco from New York where she met her biological father. Now her mother wants her to apply to college and her boyfriend Shrimp wants to be "just friends." Even though Shrimp wants to cool things off, Cyd is convinced that they can get back together once he returns from traveling with his parents to Papua New Guinea. Despite her attraction to Alexie the Horrible, the godson of her parents' chauffeur, Cyd tries to get back with Shrimp and confesses to him that she had an abortion. Everyone is affected by the news including her stepfather, and as things change with Shrimp, who wants her to move to New Zealand with him, Cyd must decide what her future will hold.

Cupcake. 2007. 256 p. ISBN: 9781416912170; 9781416912194pa. *S*
Having graduated from high school and rejected a marriage proposal from longtime boyfriend Shrimp, Cyd Charisse moves in with her gay older half-brother, Danny, to help with the cupcake business he runs out of his New York apartment and spends time with her half-sister Lisbeth. Although she is supposed to be attending culinary school, a broken leg and a job as a barista that helps her make new friends distracts her. When Shrimp shows up and the two are drawn back together, things get even more complicated, and Cyd must decide between the man she loves and the life she is trying to build.

Creech, Sharon

Heartbeat. New York: HarperCollins, 2004. 192 p. ISBN: 9780060540227; 9780060540241pa; (aud). School Library Journal Best Books. *M*
Twelve-year-old Annie loves to run but prefers to do it on her own and not on a structured team. When her running mate Max does not understand why she won't join the track team, things become difficult between them. At home Annie is looking forward to her new sibling's arrival, but at the same time, she is very scared because her beloved grandfather's health is failing as he slips further into dementia. When a creative school assignment asks that she draw an apple for 100

days, Annie is able to look inside and find a way to cope with the changes she faces.

Infants • Running • Friendship • Novels in Verse

Cross, Shauna

Derby Girl. New York: Henry Holt, 2007. 234 p. ISBN: 9780805080230. YALSA Best Books; YALSA Quick Picks. *JS*

Sixteen-year-old Bliss Cavendar doesn't fit in at school or at home with her blue hair and her love of punk rock. When her mother forces her to enter the Miss Bluebonnet beauty pageant in their hometown of Bodeen, Texas, Bliss faces her desperation by sneaking out at night to nearby Austin to join a roller-derby league. Lying to the league officials and her parents, Bliss develops a relationship with an exciting older boy, and when her actions are revealed, she is finally able to find a way to connect with her mother.

Mother and Daughter • Beauty Contests • High School

Franklin, Emily

The Other Half of Me. New York: Delacorte Press, 2007. 247 p. ISBN: 9780385734455; 9780385734462pa. *JS*

An artist in a family of athletes, sixteen-year-old Jenny Fitzgerald begins to wonder about the man who donated the sperm by which she was conceived. With the help of Tate Brodeur, a jock who is interested in her, and the Donor Sibling Registry, Jenny discovers she has a half-sister, Alexa, who soon comes for a visit from New York. Looking to find a place to belong in the relationship with Alexa, Jenny discovers that biology is only part of the equation.

Artists • Siblings • Dating • Creativity • Coming-of-Age

Garsee, Jeannine

Say the Word. New York: Bloomsbury Children's Books, 2009. 368 p. ISBN: 9781599903330. *S*

Seventeen-year-old Shawna Gallagher is shocked when she gets a call from her mother's Jewish lesbian partner, Fran, to tell her that her mother, Penny, who left the family ten years earlier, has had a stroke and will soon die. This event throws Shawna's perfect life with her perfectionist physician father into turmoil, as she is drawn to Fran and her two sons, a place where she feels connected to a real family. But when she finds out that one of Fran's sons is actually her blood brother and her father sues for custody, she begins to question her father's rigid ways.

Family Problems • Lesbians • Homosexuality • Grief • Mother-Deserted Children

Hacker, Randi

Life as I Knew It. New York: Simon Pulse, 2006. 240 p. ISBN: 9781416909958pa. *JS*

When her sixty-nine-year old father has a stroke, sixteen-year-old Angelina Rossini's world is thrown into turmoil. After a lengthy hospital stay, he returns home a different man who is unable to speak and is tied to his wheelchair or to his new handicapped-accessible bed and bathroom. Even with the support of her mother and their gay best friends, things are difficult as Angelina refits her life to this new reality.

Father and Daughter • Grief • Gay Males • Family • Friendship

Haddix, Margaret Peterson

Takeoffs and Landings. New York: Simon & Schuster Books for Young Readers, 2001. 201 p. ISBN: 9780689832994; 9780689855436pa. *MJ*

Living on their grandparents' farm for years since their father died, siblings Chuck and Lori have a poor relationship with their mother, a motivational speaker who travels constantly. Hoping to build a better relationship, their mother takes overweight, insecure, thirteen-year-old Chuck and popular, capable fourteen-year-old Lori on a two-week tour with her. Together the family confronts the feelings and secrets that have separated them and begin to work through their grief.

Death • Grief • Mothers • Brother and Sisters

Harmon, Michael B.

The Last Exit to Normal. New York: Alfred A. Knopf, 2008. 275 p. ISBN: 9780375840982. YALSA Best Books. *J*

Ben Campbell has been in a lot of trouble, including smoking pot and getting arrested, since his father revealed he is gay and his mother left. In an effort to curb his destructive path, Ben's father and his partner, Edward, decide to move the family to Edward's hometown in Montana, a town of farmers and ranchers. Ben does not fit in until he meets and falls in love with next-door neighbor Kimberly Johan and helps a kid who is suffering child abuse. These experiences make him want to fit in and be a better person.

Skateboards and Skateboarding • Father and Son • Gay Males • Homosexuality • Coping • Child Abuse • Coming-of-Age

Headley, Justina Chen

Girl Overboard. New York: Little, Brown, 2008. 339 p. ISBN: 9780316011303; 9780316011297pa. *J*

Fifteen-year-old Syrah Cheng is very different from her business-tycoon father, Ethan Cheng, and her half-siblings. At their family gatherings her siblings make formal business presentations, but Syrah's loves are snowboarding and drawing manga. When she wrecks her knee in a snowboarding accident and all hopes of a professional career are ruined, then finds out that the boy she likes only likes her for her money, she feels that her life is shattered. When she learns a friend's younger sister has leukemia, she puts together a snowboarding benefit to raise money for her. The benefit helps Syrah connect with her mother and half-sister, whose shopping and party skills come in handy. As she learns more about her mother's life during the Chinese Cultural Revolution, she is able to find the courage to build her own life and take the next steps toward a new romantic relationship.

Chinese Americans • Rich People • Trust • Accidents

Henkes, Kevin

The Birthday Room. New York: Greenwillow Books, 1999. 152 p. ISBN: 9780688167332; 9780064438285pa; (aud). *M*

On his twelfth birthday, Ben Hunter receives a room he can use as an art studio and an invitation to visit from his Uncle Ian, whom his family blames for an accident that resulted in the loss of Ben's little finger when he was a toddler. Despite his mother's anger and reluctance, they accept the invitation, and the pair travel to Oregon where they meet Ian and his new wife Nina, who is about to have a baby. Dealing with the emotions that surround his past, Ben finds some healing as he makes amends and embraces his family when an accident, for which Ben feels he is partially to blame, hurts the younger brother of his new friend.

Artists • Family • Uncles • Self-Acceptance

Henson, Heather

Here's How I See It—Here's How It Is. New York: Atheneum Books for Young Readers, 2009. 272 p. ISBN: 9781416949015. *M*

Twelve-year-old June "Junebug" Cantrell only feels at home when she is working as a stagehand at the Blue Moon Playhouse, her parents' summer-stock theater. But when Junebug's father Cassius suffers a heart attack and her parents separate because Cassius seems to be having an affair with the lead actress, things fall apart. To further complicate the summer, Trace Waeaver the new intern, arrives, and Junebug finds him to be utterly rude because he won't make eye contact, he stutters, and he needs to have constant order. But when she blows up and says cruel things about him, which he happens to overhear, Junebug learns he suffers from Asperger's syndrome, and soon the two become friends. From him, Junebug learns acceptance, and from her, Trace learns some socializing skills.

Summer Theater • Family Problems • Asperger's Syndrome • Mother-Separated Families

Hill, Kirkpatrick

Do Not Pass Go. New York: Margaret K. McElderry Books, 2007. 240 p. ISBN: 9781416914006. *SJ*

High schooler Deet has always felt out of place in his small Alaskan town since most of his classmates are rich. Things get even worse when he fears that everyone will learn that his stepfather is in prison for possessing the drugs he takes to help him stay alert. While visiting him, Deet gets to know some of the prisoners and gains insight into their lives. When he writes about these prisoners for his English class assignment, he soon forms a friendship with a classmate whose brother is in jail. Deet is finally able to find the courage to face the uncertainties of the future and accept other people's mistakes.

Prisons • Stepfathers • Family • Friendship • Drug Use • Prejudice • Coming-of-Age

Hobbs, Valerie

Tender. New York: Frances Foster Books, 2001. 245 p. ISBN: 9780374373979; 9780142400753pa. *J*

Since her own mother died in the process of giving birth to her, fifteen-year-old Olivia "Liv" Trager has been raised by her eccentric grandmother. When her grandmother passes away, Liv must leave her friends and home in New York City to live in California with her father, a solitary abalone diver she has never met. Feeling alone and grieving the losses she has experienced, Liv finds some solace with her father's girlfriend, Sam, and with Brian, the boy who assists her father on his dives. With this new stability, Liv is able to build a relationship with her father as he teaches her how to dive. Things get worse again when their boat has an unexpected accident, and Sam is diagnosed with cancer. The new little family to a find a way to unite and weather the oncoming storm

Father and Daughter • Moving • Cancer • Family Problems

James, Brian

A Perfect World. New York: Scholastic/Push, 2004. 292 p. ISBN: 9780439673648; 9780439673655pa. *J*

Lacie Johnson is dealing with the aftermath of her father's suicide and trying to please her best friend Jenna. Expecting nothing but the worst, Lacie is convinced to go on a double date with Jenna and her boyfriend, Avery. She is pleasantly surprised to meet Benji, who is dealing with his own pain. As the two get to know one another and fall in love, Benji helps Lacie reconnect with her feelings and gives her the strength to stand up to Jenna. Lacie is devastated when Benji announces that he must move to Portland to escape his alcoholic mother and her sexually abusive boyfriend, and she must learn how to put his needs above her own so she can face the future with courage.

Friendship • Death • Suicide • Father-Deserted Families • Alcoholism

Companion: *Dirty Liar.* New York: PUSH Books, 2006. 285 p. ISBN: 9780439796231; 9780439796538pa. *J*

Benji moved to Portland to live with his controlling father, his stepmother, Janet, and a half-sister to escape from his alcoholic mother and her sexually abusive boyfriend. Spending his days miserably scribbling in notebooks, smoking dope, cursing, and hiding from the world, Benji pines for his former girlfriend Lacie until he meets Rianna, a popular girl from a poor family who works hard to achieve the goals her parents have set for her. He hopes that somehow Rianna will save him from his misery, but when he finds that Rianna has her own problems, Benji realizes he must find a way to heal on his own.

Mother and Son • Family Problems • Father and Son • Stepmothers • Alcoholism • Sexual Abuse • Healing • Depression • Diaries

Kemp, Kristen

I Will Survive. New York: Push, 2002. 160 p. ISBN: 9780439121958pa. *J*

Everyone in Ellen's life is going crazy. With her boyfriend cheating on her with her best friend, her longtime male friend falling in love with her, her beauty queen sister raging, and her mom having an affair with one of her teachers, Ellen decides that the only course of action is to take her revenge, but finds that her actions have unplanned repercussions.

Revenge • Family Problems

Lamba, Marie

What I Meant. New York: Random House Children's Books, 2007. 310 p. ISBN: 9780375840913. *J*

Fifteen-year-old Sangeet "Sang" finds herself defending her reputation and trying to convince her family that she is not bulimic after her bossy aunt from India moves in with her family and starts stealing stuff. Sang tries to fight back, but when, after some misunderstandings, her aunt also ruins her relationship with her best friend and sabotages her secret crush, Sang thinks there is no hope of dealing with her troubles. To top it off, she loses her schedule book, making her grades take a nose-dive until her uncle visits and things begin to change.

East-Indian Americans • Family • Aunts • Dating • Culture Conflict • Best Friends • Bulimia

Lane, Dakota

The Orpheus Obsession. New York: Harper Tempest, 2005. 288 p. ISBN: 9780060741730; 9780060741754pa. *S*

When her older sister, ZZ Moon, introduces her to the music of twenty-one-year-old singer Orpheus, sixteen-year-old Anooshka Stargirl is entranced and spends hours on the Web searching for information about the artist. She feels connected to him by their many intersecting thoughts and interests. A chance meeting at Brighton Beach, where he is doing a photo shoot, allows her to meet Orpheus, and she follows him into his world when he gives her a backstage pass to his next gig. When they hook up and then he drops her, Anooshka has to reevaluate her life.

Singing • Love • Rock Music • Family Problems • Mother and Daughter

Lowry, Brigid

Follow the Blue. New York: Holiday House, 2004. 208 p. ISBN: 9780823418275; 9780312342975pa. *J*

When her father has an emotional breakdown and her parents take an extended trip abroad to help him recover, fifteen-year-old Bec and her younger siblings are left in the charge of a dull housekeeper. Tired of being a good girl, Bec finds this a perfect time to rebel as she colors her hair and gets involved with an older man. But as she deals with gossip at school and peer pressure to do drugs, Bec finds that being a bad girl is not all she thought it might be as she struggles to cope with her life and its problems.

Summer • Interpersonal Relations • Australia

Mackler, Carolyn

Love and Other Four-Letter Words*. New York: Delacorte Press, 2000. 208 p. ISBN: 9780385327435; 9780440228318pa. YALSA Quick Picks. *JS*

Sixteen-year-old Sammie is a hippie chick who plays folk songs on her guitar and has especially large breasts that make her self-conscious about her body. When her parents separate, her mother moves them to New York to a cramped apartment, leaving behind her best friend Kitty, with whom she cannot maintain a long-distance relationship. Coping with the changes, Sammie finds ways to deal with her feelings as she makes new friends.

Interpersonal Relations • Family Problems

Mackler, Carolyn

Vegan Virgin Valentine*. Cambridge, MA: Candlewick Press, 2004. 256 p. ISBN: 9780763621551; 9780763626136pa. YALSA Quick Picks. *S*

Mara Valentine is a good daughter. A straight-A high school senior who has been accepted to Yale, she is trying to beat her ex-boyfriend, Travis Hart, to be valedictorian. When Vivienne "V," the daughter of her thirty-five-year-old sister, comes to live with her family, she brings with her a smoking, drinking, playgirl lifestyle that has her hooking up with Travis. With this new influence, Mara begins to examine her own life, including her relationship with her parents, her feelings for the guy at her job at a local café who is twenty-two and has not gone to college, and also the pressure she puts on herself to succeed as she tries to determine what is the best course for her in life.

Sequel: Guyaholic: A Story of Finding, Flirting, Forgetting . . . and the Boy Who Changes Everything. Cambridge, MA: Candlewick Press, 2007. 176 p. ISBN: 9780763625375; 9780763628017pa. YALSA Quick Picks. *S*

Now a seventeen-year-old high school senior, Vivienne is afraid of commitment and hooks up with lots of different guys, until a hockey puck hits her in the head and she falls into the arms of Sam Almond. Organized, with a direction for his future, and a virgin, Sam is everything V is not. They get together and have sex even though V refuses to call him a boyfriend. Then when her mother Aimme misses graduation, things spiral out of control. V picks a fight with Sam and is caught kissing another guy, forcing Sam to leave her. V soon realizes her mistakes and, intent on finding the root of the problems, she take a road trip to San Antonio to visit her mother. Along the way, she encounters people who help her to discover who she truly is.

Overachievers • Underachievers • Family • Growing up • Aunts • Travel • Emotional Problems

McKay, Hilary

<u>**Casson Family Series.**</u> New York: Margaret K. McElderry Books

Outside London, the Casson family, which includes both natural and adopted children, face the many challenges of life together as a united front.

Bullies and Bullying • Friendship • Dating • Family • Adoption • Shoplifting • Christmas• England

Saffy's Angel. 2002. 152 p. ISBN: 9780689849336; 9780689849343pa; (aud). ALA Notable Children Books; School Library Journal Best Books. *MJ*

> In their ramshackle house outside London, artists Bill and Eve Casson have named their children after colors, which is the clue that lets thirteen-year-old Saffron realize that she is actually an adopted cousin who joined the family when her mother died. With the help of her grandfather and her new friend Sarah Warbeck, Saffy is able to remember her childhood. She stows away with Sarah's family as they travel to Siena, Italy, where Saffy hopes she can claim her inheritance of a statue of a stone angel that she loved during her early childhood. But when the angel continues to elude her, Saffy works to appreciate her adopted family.

Indigo's Star. 2004. 272 p. ISBN: 9780689865633; 9781416914037pa; (aud). ALA Notable Children's Books; School Library Journal Best Books. *MJ*

> Twelve-year-old Indigo Casson is bullied at school. Tom, a lonely American, forms a friendship with Indigo's sister, Rose, and helps Indigo to confront the bullies. With the help of Indigo and Rose, Tom is able to deal with the problems in his own life.

Permanent Rose. 2005. 240 p. ISBN: 9781416903727; 9781416928041pa; (aud). *MJ*

> Dealing with different challenges, the Casson family bonds together as the parents face marital problems, oldest child Caddy faces her new engagement, and Saffy searches for her unknown father. In addition, Rose, pining for Tom who has returned to America, takes up shoplifting. She is consoled by her brother Indigo's stories of King Arthur as well as schoolmate David, who once bullied Indigo, who steps up to help Rose deal with her crimes and helps her track down Tom.

Caddy Ever After. 2006. 224 p. ISBN: 9781416909309; 9781416909316pa. *MJ*

> When oldest sister Caddy is smitten by Alex, the older brother to Saffy's boyfriend Oscar, Rose steps in to help Michael, the man Caddy is engaged to, win back her heart and hopefully save the wedding, while along the way Indigo saves the Valentine's Day dance.

Forever Rose. 2008. 291 p. ISBN: 9781416954866; 9781416954873pa. *MJ*

> The Casson family faces new challenges when friend David is kicked out of his home and comes to stay with the Cassons. Rose deals with her problems by reading at school and worrying about her crazy friend's plans to hide out overnight at the zoo. Their mother becomes sick, their father returns from London where he was living with his

girlfriend, and oldest sister Caddie returns after running away from her wedding.

Penny, Patricia G.

Not Just Proms & Parties Series. Montreal: Lobster Press

Five girls deal with the challenges of complex family relationships while trying to navigate the ups and downs of romantic relationships.

Punishment • Vacations • Camping • Lesbians • Family • Mother and Daughter • Homosexuality • Coming Out • Sex Crimes • Dating

Chelsea's Ride. 2006. 140 p. ISBN: 9781897073445pa. *JS*

Popular Chelsea Davison is struggling to keep her busy social life on track when her parents take away her driving privileges after she has yet another accident. When loser Denny Waddell, who has a huge crush on Chelsea, agrees to be her driver, she takes advantage of the offer. But when Chelsea hooks up with a hot guy and learns what it is like to be used by another person, she finds that Denny may not be the loser she thought.

Rica's Summer. 2006. 140 p. ISBN: 9781897073452pa. *JS*

Rica always feels left out with two tall, gorgeous sisters who always get the guys. While she is on vacation, she faints into the arms of a cute volleyball player, Stefan, and he shows interest in her. Rica is excited until she learns that Stefan is also interested in her sister. Joining to get revenge, the sisters find themselves in an even more frightening situation at a drunken beach party, and the pair must try to regain control of the situation.

Belinda's Obsession. 2007. 134 p. ISBN: 9781897073629pa. *JS*

When she catches her mother having an affair, Belinda struggles to deal with the changes this knowledge brings while trying to figure out how to come out as a lesbian now that she has fallen in love with Candice.

Karin's Dilemma. 2007. 137 p. ISBN: 9781897073636pa. *JS*

Karin has always thought that her mother's new boyfriend was a creep, but when he starts grabbing her and she finds out that he is involved in a criminal case, she knows she has to get away from the situation. Before she can, she must convince her mother that she deserves to have someone better in her life.

Emily's Rebellion. 2008. 140 p. ISBN: 9781897073735pa. *JS*

Despite her mother's objections, Emily can't resist getting a tattoo and dating bad boy Jeremy. When her grandmother asks her to house sit, Emily sees it as the perfect opportunity to throw a party for Jeremy and his buddies. Things go wrong when she finds that her grandmother's jewelry is missing and she must find the identity of the thief to clear Jeremy's name.

Peters, Julie Anne

Between Mom and Jo. New York: Little, Brown, 2006. 232 p. ISBN: 9780316739061; 9780316067102pa. *MJ*

Fourteen-year-old Nicholas "Nick" Nathaniel Thomas Tyler lives with his two mothers, a situation that makes him the target of teasing and discrimination at school. When his biological mother, Erin, is diagnosed with cancer and starts a relationship with another woman, and Erin's partner Jo falls into alcoholism, the pair split, and Nick is left in the middle. Even though Nick wants to live with Jo, she has no rights to be his guardian. Erin refuses to even let him see her until Nick falls into an incapacitating depression and Erin relents, allowing Nick to assert his individuality by making the decision of where to live.

Mother and Son • Lesbians • Homosexuality • Family Problems • Discrimination • Alcoholics • Homophobia • Coming of Age

Pinder, Margaret

But I Don't Want to Be a Movie Star. New York: Dutton Children's Books, 2006. 256 p. ISBN: 9780525476344. *J*

Fifteen-year-old skateboarder Katriona "Kat" thinks her life is over when she is sent to live with her sixty-two-year-old, Oscar-winning grandmother. In a drunken mistake, her grandmother tries to ride Kat's skateboard and breaks her ankle, putting in jeopardy a meeting with a producer that she hopes will restart her career. Soon Kat is pressed into service to impersonate her grandmother in the interview. As she transforms her appearance, she is able to transform her relationship with her grandmother as well.

Grandmothers • Intergenerational Relations • Alcoholism • Skateboards and Skateboarding • Actors and Actresses

Rettig, Liz

My Desperate Love Diary. New York: Holiday House, 2007. 313 p. ISBN: 9780823420339. *J*

Fifteen-year-old Kelly Ann is in love with G. and she writes about her obsession daily in her diary. In real life, Kelly Ann is dealing with all kinds of problems, including her unmarried sister's pregnancy, the breakup of her parents' marriage after her mother has an affair, and her father's escape into alcohol, not to mention the normal teenage problems, including acne and a flat chest. Amid her problems, her two best friends, Liz and Stephanie, try to get Kelly Ann to see the truth that G. is a loser, but Kelly Ann must work through her problems before she can see the truth.

Love • Family Problems • Diaries • Diary Novel

Sachs, Marilyn

First Impressions. New Milford, CT: Roaring Brook Press, 2006. 128 p. ISBN: 9781596431171. *J*

Fifteen-year-old overshadowed middle child Alice has always been a straight-A student until she receives a C+ on an English paper she wrote about *Pride and Prejudice*. Because she misinterprets the novel by connecting to Mary Bennett, the forgotten daughter, and writes her paper from that character's point-of-view, her teacher feels she does not understand the novel and gives her an opportunity to reread the novel over Christmas break. As she does, Alice is able to gain new insight, with the help of Austen and her characters, into her Catholic family, her love life, and her friendship with another overshadowed girl, Jenny.

Books and Reading • Love • Dating • Family

Saenz, Benjamin Alire

He Forgot to Say Good-Bye. New York: Simon & Schuster Books for Young Readers, 2008. 321 p. ISBN: 9781416949633. *S*

In El Paso, Texas, two boys from different social classes work to grow up without the guidance of their fathers. Ramiro Lopez acts as head of household for his single mother and brother, while Jake Upthegrove lives with his materialistic mother and stepfather. When Ramiro's brother ends up brain dead after a heroin overdose and Jake catches his stepfather in an affair, both teens must figure out how to deal with the challenges they face.

Father-Separated Families • Emotional Problems • Friendship • Mexican Americans

Savage, Deborah

Kotuku. Boston: Houghton Mifflin, 2002. 291p. ISBN: 9780618047567. YALSA Best Books. *S*

Seventeen-year-old Wim lives in Cape Cod. She is happiest when she is at her job at a stable working with horses and studying nature. After the death of her anorexic friend, Wim has had recurring visions of a man with a tattooed face. The meaning of her visions becomes clearer when her eccentric Great Aunt Kim arrives and Wim is forced to care for her. With the help of David Te Makara, a professor from New Zealand, and his niece Tangi, who have arrived in town to search for their ancestors, Win gains self-understanding as she learns about her Maori heritage and builds a romantic relationship with David.

Family Secrets • Grief • Intergenerational Relations • New Zealand • Coming-of-Age

Scott, Kieran

Jingle Boy. New York: Delacorte Press, 2003. 230 p. ISBN: 9780385731133; 9780440238317pa. *JS*

Paul Nicholas and his family are devoted to Christmas, and Paul even gets to play Santa this year. When his new girlfriend dumps him, his dad nearly electrocutes himself while decorating the house, and his mom gets fired, Paul decides that because he has lost his lucky Santa hat, Christmas is now cursed. Joined by his best friend Holly and a few other friends, Paul begins an anti-Christmas campaign and takes his revenge on the holiday. After his plots land him in jail, it takes the intervention of St. Nick to get Paul back into the Christmas spirit.

Family • Christmas • Fires

Shanahan, Lisa

The Sweet, Terrible, Glorious Year I Truly, Completely Lost It. New York: Delacorte Press, 2007. 304 p. ISBN: 9780385735162; 9780440240549pa. *MJ*

Fourteen-year-old Gemma Stone has always kept a tight reign on her emotions in her overly emotional family. When her sister gets engaged to a man whose family is obsessed with military discipline, her family life is turned upside down as her sister becomes a crazed bride. To escape it all, and despite her fear of speaking in public, Gemma auditions for a part in her school play so she can be close to her crush, Nick. When it is not Nick but bad-boy Raven with whom she must act, Gemma must work out her complicated feelings of love and shame before she loses control.

Theater • Drama • Weddings • Sisters • Australia • Coming-of-Age

Sheinmel, Courtney

My So-Called Family. New York: Simon & Schuster Books for Young Readers, 2008. 194 p. ISBN: 9781416957850; 9781416979425pa. *MJ*

Thirteen-year-old Leah has always been curious about her father, an anonymous sperm donor, even though she now has a stepfather and five-year-old half-brother. After a fight with her mother, Leah decides to satisfy her curiosity, and using the Internet she discovers she has four half siblings with the same donor father. One of them is a girl her age, Samantha, who is able to connect Leah into a newly discovered family group. Afraid to tell her mother that she making long-distance calls to her new sibling and she wants to meet face-to-face, Leah has to learn how to stop obsessing about other opinions as she comes to accept her unique family and the circumstances of her birth.

Blended Families • Friendship

Smith, Sherri L.

Sparrow. New York: Delacorte Press, 2006. 192 p. ISBN: 9780385733243; 9780440239451pa. *S*

Raised since the age of five by her grandmother after her parents and little brother where killed in a car crash, seventeen-year-old Kendall is left alone after her grandmother's death. Even though she knows little about her, Kendall sets out from Chicago to New Orleans to find her only living relative, her Aunt Janet. Unable to find her aunt, Kendall is taken in by Clare, a woman who needs someone to help care for her disabled teenage daughter, Evie. As Kendall and Evie become friends, they help each other through their loneliness and Kendall is able to find the support she needs to remake her life.

African Americans • Grandmothers • Death • Friendship • Interracial Friendships • Family

Underdahl, S. T.

Remember This. Woodbury, MN: Flux, 2008. 288 p. ISBN: 9780738714011pa. *JS*

Summer looks great for Lucy Kellogg as she tries out for the cheerleading squad with her best friend Sukie and gets a visit from her beloved grandmother Nan Lucy. But when a humiliating accident during tryouts threatens her cheerleading and a boy from the girls' past shows up and puts a wedge between them, things don't look good. Nan Lucy arrives, but she is not quite the same. She forgets things, confuses reality and fantasy, and gets lost. With everything changing, Lucy must find the strength to face her worst fears.

Friendship • Grandmothers

Vega, Denise

Fact of Life #31. New York: Alfred A. Knopf, 2008. 375 p. ISBN: 9780375848193; 9780375843099pa. *J*

Free-spirited yoga Girl Kat is an outsider who realizes that despite her admiration for him, she is no match for jock Manny Cruz. But when Manny starts talking to her and a friendship forms that soon turns to romance, Kat is confused since Manny is distant toward her at school. Maintaining the difference between their private and public life, Kat struggles, especially since she has a hard time getting along with her mother, Abra, a midwife who is always making her feel as if she has done something wrong. As Kat helps her mother in her birthing center and is able to help deliver the baby of one of her classmates, Kat is able to see her mother through the eyes of her clients. As she finds this new perspective, she is able to really discover who she is and redefine her own relationships.

Pregnancy • Mother and Daughter • Self-Discovery • Coming-of-Age

Volponi, Paul

Hurricane Song. New York: Viking Juvenile, 2008. 144 p. ISBN: 9780670061600; 9780142414187pa; (aud). *JS*

After his mother's remarriage, sixteen-year-old Miles moves to New Orleans to live with his musician father, whom he has always resented. Miles tries to focus on making his new school's football team, but when Hurricane Katrina arrives and Miles, his father, and his uncle Roy try to flee, their car breaks down, and they are stranded in the Superdome with all the other refugees. With too little food and other basic services, the environment in the Superdome collapses into one fueled by fear and violence. When the storm ends and Miles and his dad avoid being put on busses to Houston and head back into town, they are able to stop looters from stealing the piano at a jazz club. Through this experience, they are able to find some common ground on which to build their future relationship.

Hurricanes • Uncles • Musicians • Divorce

Wyatt, Melissa

Funny How Things Change. New York: Farrar, Straus & Giroux, 2009. 208 p. ISBN: 9780374302337. *S*

Upon graduating from high school, Remy Walker decides to follow his girlfriend Lisa to college, leaving the mountain house that has been his family's home for more than 150 years. But when the only way he can realize his dream is for his father to sell their land to a mining company, Remy realizes that he cannot deny his strong connection to the land as he gets to know artist Dana, who is in town painting murals on her summer break from college.

Country Life • Small Towns • Artists • Girlfriends

Zevin, Gabrielle

Memoirs of a Teenage Amnesiac. New York: Farrar, Straus, & Giroux, 2007. 288 p. ISBN: 9780374349462; 9780312561284pa; (aud). YALSA Best Books. *JS*

> When high-school junior Naomi Porter falls and hits her head, she finds that she can't remember anything that has happened since sixth grade. Facing the realities of her life, including her parents divorce and the tennis-player boyfriend she may or may not have had sex with, without the benefit of memories from her past, Naomi finds that she has to redefine herself. With the help of her friend and yearbook co-editor Will, Naomi starts filling in the blanks as she falls for handsome James, who is dealing with his brother's death, and she reconnects with her mother and learns to like her dad's fiancée.

> *Accidents • Friendship • Identity*

Adoption

Alvarez, Julia

Finding Miracles. New York: Knopf, 2004. 272 p. ISBN: 9780375827600; 9780553494068pa; (aud). YALSA Popular Paperbacks. *JS*

> Mildred "Milly" Milagros Kaufman must face the fact that she is adopted when Pablo Bolivar arrives at her school and recognizes her as someone from his country. Soon the Bolivar's travel home, and Milly accompanies them on a quest for her birth parents and her heritage. Facing the frighteningly beautiful war-torn country and finding several possible sets of birth parents, Milly discovers new love for her adopted family, obtains a boyfriend in Pablo, and embraces her new identity.

> *Family • Hispanic Americans • Coming-of-Age*

Dalton, Annie, and Maria Dalton

Invisible Threads. New York: Delacorte Press, 2006. 200 p. ISBN: 9780385732864. *S*

> At odds with her adopted family, sixteen-year-old Carrie-Ann sets out to find her birth mother, Naomi. In alternating chapters, Carrie-Ann relates her rebellion and fears and Naomi relates the consequences of her first sexual encounter and her decision to give up the baby.

> *Pregnancy • Birthparents • Family*

Harrar, George

Parents Wanted. Minneapolis, MN: Milkweed Editions, 2001. 239 p. ISBN: 9781571316325; 9781571316332pa. *M*

> With attention-deficit disorder, twelve-year-old Andy Fleck has a problem with impulse control, but even though his dad is in jail and he is in foster care, he is able to keep out of really big trouble until his foster parents Laurie and Jeff Sizeracy want to adopt him. Andy loses control and starts lying,

getting in trouble at school, and stealing money. When he accuses Jeff of molesting him, Andy realizes that things have gone too far, and he must deal with the consequences of his actions to earn back the trust of his potential parents.

Foster Parents • Attention-Deficit Disorder • Trust

Hite, Sid

The King of Slippery Falls. New York: Scholastic Press, 2004. 217 p. ISBN: 9780439342575; (aud). *JS*

Sixteen-year-old Lewis Hinton's one big dream is to catch the giant white trout that lives behind Slippery Falls. When a mysterious letter arrives, Lewis, who was adopted at birth, discovers he might be a descendent of French royalty. Revealing the mystery to his best friend and crush Amanda Dot, Lewis finds himself the inadvertent topic of gossip when Amanda shares his heritage. Lewis's eighty-eight-year-old neighbor, Maple, believes that this is just another extravagant fish tale that people are prone to tell. But when Lewis delves deeper into the past, he makes discoveries about his place in the present.

Family • Friends • Eccentricities

Nelson, R. A.

Breathe My Name. New York: Razorbill, 2007. 320 p. ISBN: 9781595140944; 9781595141866pa. *S*

Eighteen-year-old Francine Jelks is haunted by her past. Eleven years ago, her mother murdered her three younger sisters and attempted to murder her. Francine now goes by the name of Frances Robinson and is completely shattered when a lawyer shows up telling her that her mother is out of jail and wants to see her. Leaving her loving adoptive family, Frances plans a road trip with her best friend, Ann, and boyfriend, Nix, to confront her mother. She hopes to find some answers as well as forgiveness for her family.

Family Relationships • Mental Illness • Murder

Reinhardt, Dana

A Brief Chapter in My Impossible Life. New York: Wendy Lamb Books, 2006. 228 p. ISBN: 9780385746984; 9780375846915pa; (aud). YALSA Best Books; YALSA Popular Paperbacks. *JS*

With her olive skin and dark eyes, sixteen-year-old Simone Turner-Bloom looks nothing like her adopted family, with whom she shares a close relationship—especially with her younger brother. But things change when Rivika, her birth mother, a thirty-three-year-old Orthodox Jew who is dying of ovarian cancer, wants to meet her, and Simone must come to terms with where she fits in.

Jewish Americans • Adoption • Birth Parents • Terminal Illness • Faith • Friendship • Coming-of-Age

Underdahl, S. T.

The Other Sister. Woodbury, MN: Flux, 2007. 256 p. ISBN: 9780738709338pa. *J*

When fifteen-year-old Josey Muller discovers she has a twenty-five-year-old sister, Audrey, whom her parents had given up for adoption when she was a baby, she is devastated. Giving up her place as the only daughter, Josey is not comforted by her brothers or her two best friends. Finding out that her sister is working on a PhD in psychology, which is what she wants to do when she grows up, makes her dislike her new sister even more as she struggles to deal with her friends, the crush she has on a boy, and keeping up her grades in school.

Birth Parents • Gifted Teenagers • Friendship • Sibling Rivalry • Jealousy

Single-Parent Families

Acheson, Alison

Mud Girl. Regina: Coteau Books, 2007. 319 p. ISBN: 9781550503548. *JS*

Sixteen-year-old Aba "Abi" Zytka Jones has been abandoned by her mother. Dealing with a father who has given up on life, Abi is burdened by many responsibilities. These responsibilities just increase when she gets a summer job cleaning houses, and she must decide if she is ready to care for boyfriend Jude's toddler son, Dyl, who can no longer be cared for by his deathly ill grandmother. Supported by a woman from the Big Sister program, who also has her own past to deal with, Abi soon begins to learn what is truly important in life.

Divorce • Mother-Deserted Children • Dating • Coming-of-Age

Cassidy, Cathy

Dizzy. New York: Viking, 2004. 256 p. ISBN: 9780670059362; 9780142404744pa. YALSA Popular Paperbacks. *MJ*

Dizzy and her father were abandoned by her carefree, hippy mother, "Storm," when Dizzy was just four years old. Now she only hears from her on her birthday, until she is turning twelve and her mother unexpectedly shows up in person and takes Dizzy off to a solstice festival in Scotland without her father's permission. There she meets fourteen-year-old Flinn, the son of her mother's friend, and the two become close and befriend and care for seven-year-old Mouse, whom Dizzy loves like the brother she never had. While she finds some of her mother's bohemian ways fun, Dizzy doesn't like the bad food, going without hot water, and the constant threat of arrest. Soon Dizzy realizes that Storm will never be the person she wants her to be and learns to appreciate the care and trust her father has given her.

Mother and Daughter • Summer • Friendship • Abandonment • Dishonesty

1

2

3

4

5

6

7

8

9

10

11

12

Conway, Celeste

The Melting Season. New York: Delacorte Press, 2006. 288 p. ISBN: 9780385733397; 9780440239536pa. *JS*

Little has changed for sixteen-year-old Giselle since her father, a dancer and choreographer, died ten years earlier. Her mother, a former ballerina, who works with her at the New York City arts high school where she studies ballet, has moved on and is dating a man whom Giselle despises. Giselle isolates herself to wallow in her memories of the past even though her friend Magda tries to get her to come out of her shell. One spring Giselle meets handsome Will, and things begin to change as Giselle loses her vulnerability and confronts memories of incidents of abuse. She decides it's time to move forward on a path of her own choosing.

Celebrities • First Love • Ballet • Mother and Daughter • Coming-of-Age

Dee, Barbara

Just Another Day in My Insanely Real Life. New York: Margaret K. McElderry Books, 2006. 256 p. ISBN: 9781416908616; 9781416947394pa. *M*

Twelve-year-old Cassie escapes into writing fantasy in her journal when she is overwhelmed by the fights with her older sister and caring for her younger brother while her single mother works long hours. Despite dealing with her grammar-obsessed English teacher, who objects to her writing fantasy, and being dumped by her friends because of her family's declining social status, Cassie seeks to find the strength to deal with her problems and finds a new friend in overweight outsider Bess, who shares her love of fantasy.

Single Mothers • Siblings • Writing • Self-Esteem

Fogelin, Adrian

The Real Question. Atlanta: Peachtree, 2006. 234 p. ISBN: 9781561453832; 9781561455010pa. *JS*

Fuelled by his compulsive guidance-counselor father who leaves pointers on index cards around his room, sixteen-year-old Fisher "Fish" Brown is stressed out about his future. When he meets Lonny Traynor, Fish is introduced to a whole new world of dropouts who travel the world and get tattoos. With his father out of town, Fish embraces an opportunity for adventure as he hops a bus to visit Lonny, who is doing a roofing job for his ex-girlfriend and mother of his son, Charlie. Soon he finds himself helping the family financially, and he becomes a role model for Charlie. He gets help from a librarian and his best friend so he can get back home and return to school, where he must face his unexcused absences. He finds that he has a new view of himself and the world around him.

Overachievers • Father and Son • Friendship • SAT • Work • Coming-of-Age

Jones, Kimberly K.

Sand Dollar Summer. New York: Margaret K. McElderry Books, 2006. 206 p. ISBN: 9781416903628; 9781416958345pa. *M*

When their single mother is injured in a car accident and relocates the family to her childhood home in Fiddle Island, Maine, so that she can recover, twelve-year-old Annalise "Lise" and her five-year-old brother, Free, see the ocean for the first time. Lise resents their move and finds that she is terrified by the furious wide-open ocean. Even more resentful when her mother's former boyfriend and local doctor, Michael, comes into their lives, Lise clings even harder to her happy brother who never speaks. Making a new friend in Ben, an elderly Passamaquoddy Indian who lives nearby, Lise finally finds someone in whom she can confide. But it is not until Hurricane Fern hits that she is able to begin dealing with her fear of the sea and with the changes in her life.

Single Mothers • Mother and Daughter • Native Americans • Hurricanes • Summer • Coming-of-Age

Jonsberg, Barry

Am I Right or Am I Right? New York: Alfred A. Knopf, 2007. 256 p. ISBN: 9780375836374; 9780375843518pa. *JS*

Things are going great for sixteen-year-old Calma Harrison who has a job at their neighborhood grocery store Crazy Cheep so she can work on attracting her gorgeous coworker Jason. She has also finally found an English teacher who recognizes her writing talent. But Calma's life gets complicated when her father, who left her mother and her years ago, comes back and tries to get in touch with her. When her mother starts skipping work and sneaking around at night, Calma suspects she may have a boyfriend who may or may not be her father. When she discovers that her friend Vanessa is being abused at home, she realizes that she can't solve everyone's problems and that she must accept her life.

Father and Daughter • Child Abuse • Teachers • Books and Reading • Creativity • Coming-of-Age

Stein, Tammar

High Dive. New York: Alfred A. Knopf, 2008. 201 p. ISBN: 9780375830242. *S*

On her way to Sardinia to close and sell her family's cherished vacation home after her father's death in a car accident and her mother's deployment to Iraq as an Army nurse, nineteen-year-old Arden meets three female college students who are going to Europe on a fun-filled sight-seeing tour. Unable to face her task, Arden joins them but finds that with only limited contact with her mother and the girls' constant partying, she feels even more isolated. Finding her courage, Arden travels alone to the house, and as she packs it up, she begins to understand that it is OK to show vulnerability as you open your heart to others.

College • Single Mothers • Iraq • Friendship • Military • Travel

Wolff, Virginia Euwer

Make Lemonade. New York: Henry Holt, 1993. 200 p. ISBN: 9780805022285; 9780590481410pa; (aud). ALA Notable Children Books. *J*

Fourteen-year-old LaVaughn wants to go to college so much, she works to earn money by babysitting the two small children of single parent, seventeen-year-old Jolly. Understanding Jolly's life, because she lives with her own single mother, LaVaughn is able to help Jolly when she gets fired from her job by a boss who is harassing her and as she works to get back on her feet by attending school. Along the way, LaVaughn is able to clarify her own values and find a way to escape her poverty by fully embracing her own dreams of going to college.

Work • Teenage Mothers • Pregnancy • Inner City • Street Life • Novels in Verse

Sequel: ***True Believer.*** New York: Atheneum Books for Young Readers, 2001. 264 p. ISBN: 9780689828270; 9780689852886pa; (aud). Michael L. Printz Honor Books; National Book Award for Young People's Literature; YALSA Best Books; ALA Notable Childrens Books; School Library Journal Best Books. *JS*

Fifteen-year-old LaVaughn is facing challenges as she drifts apart from her best friends Myrtle and Annie when they join a virginity club and her mother begins to date for the first time since her father died. With her goal to get to college to escape the poverty and violence of her neighborhood, she must deal with the pressures of school. When she falls in love, but then sees her crush kiss another boy, LaVaughn must find a way to deal with all of the conflicting emotions she feels as she finds a way to succeed in achieving her dreams.

Best Friends • Mother and Daughter • Inner City • Homosexuality • Gay Males • Novels in Verse

Sequel: ***This Full House.*** New York: HarperTeen, 2009. 496 p. ISBN: 9780061583049; (aud). *JS*

Seventeen-year-old LaVaughn wins a scholarship to a prestigious after-school science program for underprivileged girls where she meets Dr. Moore, the program's founder, who becomes her mentor as she rediscovers her love for science and embraces her plans to enter the medical profession. But all at once, she finds out that her friend Annie is pregnant, her friend Jolly was abandoned in infancy, she realizes that she has hurt her friend Patrick, and she discovers Dr. Moore's dark secret. LaVaughn must learn how to forgive even in situations where the acts may be unforgivable.

Secrets • Friendship • Street Life • Novels in Verse

Divorce and Stepfamilies

Archer, Lily

The Poison Apples. New York: Feiwel and Friends, 2007. 288 p. ISBN: 9780312367626; 9780312535964pa. *J*

At their Massachusetts boarding school, Molly, Reena, and Alice all find they have been abandoned at the school because of their new stepmothers. Together they form the society of the Poison Apples, a group intent on seeking revenge on the women who they see as ruining their lives. As the girls work to destroy their parents' marriages, they also deal with their own romantic trials and find lasting friendship.

Family • Friendship • Boarding School • Stepmothers

Birdsall, Olivia

Notes on a Near-Life Experience. New York: Delacorte Press, 2006. 224 p. ISBN: 9780385733700. *J*

> When her parents decide to divorce, fifteen-year-old Mia Day finds her life turned upside down. With her father dating a new woman, her mother working too much to be at home for her, and her sister Keatie and her brother Allen developing drinking problems, the only bright spot in her life is that her brother's friend Julian finally seems to be noticing her. With her new love and her new driver's license, things begin to look up as Mia works to deal with her emotions.

Family Problems • Father and Daughter • Drinking • Dating

Caletti, Deb

Wild Roses. New York: Simon & Schuster Books for Young Readers, 2005. 296 p. ISBN: 9780689867668; 9780689864759pa. *S*

> Seventeen-year-old amateur astronomer Cassie Morgan is the stepdaughter of the arrogant violin virtuoso Dino Cavalli, who is mentally ill but controls his delusions with medication—that is, until his much anticipated comeback concert approaches and he stops taking his prescriptions. As much as Cassie wants her life to be normal, living with Dino is difficult, as he becomes more paranoid and bullies her. When Ian Waters, a promising but poor young violinist, shows up for lessons with Dino so he can prepare for an audition, Cassie falls in love at first sight. Even though Dino demands that the two stay away from one another to avoid compromising Ian's focus, it is impossible for the two to part. As Dino's concert and Ian's scholarship audition draw closer, even Cassie's loving mother can't protect her from Dino's paranoid behavior.

Stepdaughters • Mother and Daughter • Mental Illness • Love • Stepfathers • Remarriage • Violinists

Caseley, Judith

The Kissing Diary. New York: Farrar, Straus & Giroux, 2007. 199 p. ISBN: 9780374363468. *M*

> Twelve-year-old Rosie Goldglitt's life is complicated after her parents' divorce. Insulted and ignored by her crush Robbie Romano and suspended after punching bully Mary Katz in the face after she could just not stand her taunting any more, things come to a head when Rosie's friends seem to desert her. At home, Rosie's mom is dating again, and her grandfather is suffering from dementia. With all these problems, it is up to Rosie to learn from her trials and develop courage and confidence in herself.

Bullies and Bullying • Mothers • Grandfathers • Diary Novel

Cassidy, Cathy

Scarlett. New York: Viking, 2006. 272 p. ISBN: 9780670060689. *J*

After having been kicked out of five schools, twelve-year-old Scarlett Flynn gets into trouble once again by starting a food "demonstration" in the cafeteria. Her mother is fed up with the situation and sends her off to Ireland to live with her father, his new pregnant wife, and their nine-year-old daughter. With her pierced tongue, black fingernails, and bright red hair, Scarlett is appalled by her new rural home and school and angry at the whole situation. Meeting mysterious gypsy boy Kian and his horse, Midnight, provides Scarlett with a friendship that helps her understand her situation.

Family Problems • Remarriage • Anger

Cohn, Rachel

The Steps. New York: Simon & Schuster Books for Young Readers, 2003. 144 p. ISBN: 9780689845499; 9780689874147pa; (aud). YALSA Popular Paperbacks. *MJ*

Annabel has a complicated family. She and her mother, Angelina, live in New York, where Angelina is dating a man she soon plans to marry. Jack, Annabel's father, has moved to Australia with his wife, Penny; Penny's children from another marriage, Lucy and Angus; and Jack and Penny's baby, Beatrice. Annabel is not very happy when she heads to Sydney over Christmas break to meet her new family, and she is determined to get her dad to come back. But when she and Lucy run away to Melbourne to see Lucy's grandmother and her friends, the two girls bond, and Annabel begins to learn about what it means to love someone.

Sequel: *Two Steps Forward*. New York: Simon & Schuster Books for Young Readers, 2006. 240 p. ISBN: 9780689866142; 9780689866159pa. *MJ*

Annabel and Lucy's life continues to be complicated with four blended families combined. Fourteen-year-old Annabel is looking forward to her summer in Los Angeles where she can see her extended family and her biological father. But at the same time she is worried her mother is running away from her marriage problems in New York City, and she will not be able to see her crush Ben, who is her stepsister Lucy's stepbrother. Lucy knows that Ben is coming for a visit and is concerned that she does not return the feelings of Wheaties, Annabel's stepbrother, who has a crush on her. Dealing with complex relationships, the girls and their families must learn how to compromise and make things work.

Blended Families • Remarriage • Stepsisters • Dating • Friendship • Jealousy

Conrad, Liza

The Poker Diaries. New York: NAL Jam, 2007. 211 p. ISBN: 9780451220240pa. *S*

Lulu is a blend of uptown and downtown, living with her mother on New York's Central Park West and spending weekends with a gambler father in Hell's Kitchen. Capitalizing on her downtown instincts, Lulu plays poker in secret. With an ability to read people and trust her instincts, she often wins. Things go very wrong when she gambles to get her friend's watch back and the event is filmed. The footage is used to blackmail her. Lulu knows that if the film gets out, it will end her mother's engagement to the mayor. To solve the problem Lulu must learn to trust her soon-to-be stepfather and find a blend between both of her worlds.

Stepfathers • Gambling • Scandals • Self-Discovery

Cooney, Caroline B.

A Friend at Midnight. New York: Delacorte Press, 2006. 192 p. ISBN: 9780385733267; 9780385733274pa. *J*

When their negligent father abandons her eight-year-old brother, Michael Rosetti, at a Baltimore airport by himself, fifteen-year-old Lily makes a secret journey to rescue him before their mother and stepfather get back from taking their older sister, Reb, to college. Lily must then work through the effects that her father's cruelty has had on her as she deals with her feelings of hate and resentment that have forced her to question her Christian faith. When Reb wants her father to walk her down the aisle at her wedding, the truth comes out, and Lily strives to make peace with her father.

Remarriage • Faith • Forgiveness • Family Problems

Cooney, Caroline B.

Tune in Anytime. New York: Delacorte Press, 1999. 186 p. ISBN: 9780385326490; 9780440227984pa. *MJ*

Sophie Olivette's life turns into a nightmare when her father divorces her mother to marry her older sister's college roommate and then sells their home so he and his new wife can travel the world. Sophie's mother refuses to deal with the situation, instead focusing on connecting with spiritual matters so she can get in touch with her inner self. With no adults to support her, Sophie turns to classmate Ted, who agrees to help her stop her father. With Ted's help, she hopes to work through her world of chaos and survive.

Stepmothers • Family Problems

Friend, Natasha

Bounce. New York: Scholastic Press, 2007. 192 p. ISBN: 9780439853507; 9780439853538pa. *J*

When thirteen-year-old Evyn's father marries Eleni Gartos, a woman with six children, she and her fifteen-year-old brother are forced to leave their home in Maine and move to Boston. In the bursting and chaotic household, Evyn finds her only peace is in imagining conversations with her dead mother, who councils her to let bad things bounce off. Having a hard time adjusting to her new all-girls school and the mean girls who inhabit it and struggling to accept her stepmother's pregnancy, it is only with her father's never failing love, a deeper understanding of Eleni who also lost her mother, and accepting her step-siblings, that Evyn finds a way to accept her life and embrace the possibilities for the future.

Blended Families • Remarriage • Popularity • Moving

Friesen, Gayle

Losing Forever. Toronto, ON: Kids Can Press, 2002. 247 p. ISBN: 9781553370314; 9781553370321pa. *J*

Ninth-grader Jes Miner-Cooper's parents' marriage failed after her little sister, Alberta, died. Jes is forced into a new reality in which her mother plans to remarry and her father spends all his time fishing and reading Russian novels. When her best friend, Dell, gets a boyfriend, and her other friend, Sam, wants to be more than a friend, things look even worse. But the last straw is when Pamela, the daughter of her mother's fiancée, moves in four weeks before the wedding and takes Jes's friends and her room. When Jes is accused of shoplifting, she is sure things will never be right again. She must learn how to accept change and move on with her life.

Blended Families • *Family Secrets* • *Remarriage* • *Jealousy* • *Canada* • *Coming-of-Age*

Sequel: *For Now.* Tonawanda, NY: Kids Can Press, 2007. 247 p. ISBN: 9781554531325; 9781554531332pa. YALSA Best Books. *J*

Dealing with her new perfect stepsister and eager stepdad, as well as her mother's pregnancy, Jes turns to her psychology class assignment to write a "life resume" and asks her friend Sam for help. When she and Sam start to date, things don't go well, and Jes must learn to embrace her confidence as she tries to help friend Dell work through her own trauma, while she works to accept her father's new girlfriend and decide how she really feels about Sam.

Blended Families • *Family Secrets* • *Remarriage* • *Jealousy* • *School Projects* • *Pregnancy* • *Canada* • *Coming-of-Age*

Goldschmidt, Judy

Raisin Rodriguez Series. New York: Razorbill, 2005. 208 p.

Raisin Rodriguez deals with moving to a new town, growing up, and finding love.

Blended Families • *Friendship* • *Popularity* • *Kissing* • *First Love* • *Blogs* • *Family*

The Secret Blog of Raisin Rodriguez. 2005. 208 p. ISBN: 9781595140180; 9781595140715pa. YALSA Popular Paperbacks. *MJ*

Blogging to her two best friends in Berkeley after she moves to Philadelphia when her mother remarries, thirteen-year-old Raisin Rodriguez tires to fit in as the new kid at school while at the same time dealing with her developing body. But when her blog is printed for the whole school to read after she fails to log out of a computer, Raisin must deal with the embarrassment.

Raisin Rodriguez & the Big-Time Smooch. 2005. 192 p. ISBN: 9781595140579pa. *MJ*

Still blogging to her girlfriends in Berkeley, Raisin finds herself infatuated with CJ Mullen and throws herself into a scheme to get him to kiss her.

Will the Real Raisin Rodriguez Please Stand Up?: A Novel. 2007. 208 p. ISBN: 9781595140586. *MJ*

While Raisin finds kissing CJ to be nice, she finds that it is impossible to have a conversation with him. Back in Berkeley to visit her father, Raisin finds that things have changed, and her old best friends have moved on. When romance beckons, Raisin must decide whether to stay with CJ.

Graham, Rosemary

My Not-So-Terrible Time at the Hippie Hotel. New York: Viking, 2003. 214 p. ISBN: 9780670036110; 9780142403037pa. *MJ*

Dragged off on vacation with her divorced father, brother, and younger sister to a retreat for single-parent families on Cape Cod at the "Hippie Hotel," fourteen-year-old Tracy feels awkward and uncertain. Up to now, Tracy has been dealing with the pain of her parents' divorce by avoiding the music she loves and eating instead. Meeting Sharon, the tie-dyed hippie who runs the house, private school punk Becka and California girl Kelsey, and two other girls who are at the retreat with their families, Tracy is finally able to cope with her parents' divorce.

<u>Sequel:</u> *Thou Shalt Not Dump the Skater Dude and Other Commandments I Have Broken.* New York: Viking, 2005. 288 p. ISBN: 9780670060177; 9780142408360pa. *MJ*

When Kelsey starts dating popular skate-boarding champion C.J. Logan, things look great until she realizes that C.J.'s ego is an unwelcome third wheel in their relationship, and she dumps him. When C.J. rants on his blog that it was he who dumped her because she was a "sex fiend," Kelsey must rebuild her reputation by joining the school newspaper and confronting C.J. She learns that she is an individual who does not need a boyfriend to define her.

Single Parent • Vacations • Ex-Boyfriends • Blogs • Skateboards and Skateboarding • Romance • Coming-of-Age

Jukes, Mavis

Cinderella 2000: Looking Back. New York: Yearling, 2001. 208 p. ISBN: 9780440228660pa. *MJ*

Fourteen-year-old Ashley Ella Toral, who lives with her clueless stepmother, Phyllis, and her younger twin stepsisters, has received an invitation to a posh New Year's Eve party where her crush Trevor will be in attendance. But along with worrying about the right outfit and transportation, Ashley is worried that her stepmother's answer to not having a babysitter for her sisters is to get them invited to the party as well. Ashley thinks her night is ruined until Phyllis's Grammie steps in, saving her evening.

Romance • Stepsisters • Stepmother

Kantor, Melissa

If I Have a Wicked Stepmother, Where's My Prince? New York: Hyperion, 2005. 290 p. ISBN: 9780786809608; 9780786809615pa. YALSA Popular Paperbacks; Teens Top Ten. *JS*

When her father remarries, Lucy Norton has to move from San Francisco to Long Island and finds herself being left almost entirely alone with her stepmother, Mara, and her twin stepsisters, since her father still works and lives on the West Coast during the week. Passionate about basketball and art, Lucy finds an escape from the tensions of high school by eating lunch in the art room, where she meets rude artist Sam. When she displays keen insights into sports, she catches the attentions of Connor, the handsome basketball star, but she also comes under the scrutiny of her stepsisters. This adds to the difficulties of her life at home, where she is treated like a maid and she can't get on the same page with her dad. However, as Lucy enjoys her new popularity and receives an invitation to the prom, she begins to realize that things don't always turn out as expected.

Blended Families • Family Relationships • Popularity • Basketball • Coming-of-Age

Mack, Tracy

Drawing Lessons. New York: Scholastic Press, 2000. 168 p. ISBN: 9780439112024; 9780439112031pa; (aud). *MJ*

When eleventh-grader Aurora "Rory" catches her artist father with one of his models, she is devastated and can no longer create her own artwork, even though she has been painting since she was five years old. As her parents separate, Rory draws further inside herself and away from friend Nicky and her school art teacher. Soon she realizes that she must come to terms with the situation and build her own identity.

Father and Daughter • Artists

McNeal, Laura and Tom

Zipped. New York: Alfred A. Knopf, 2003. 192 p. ISBN: 9780375814914; 9780375830983pa. *J*

When fifteen-year-old Mick Nichols opens one of his stepmother Nora's e-mails by mistake and finds that she is having an affair, he is unable to figure out what to do. Searching for clues to the identity of Nora's lover, Mick gets to know beautiful classmate Lisa Doyle better, and the two begin a romance despite Lisa's interest in another boy. Soon Mick learns that relationships are very complicated, and he must deal with his relationship with Lisa and his friendship with Myra Vidal, a college sophomore and former beauty queen who is very attentive.

Blended Families • Interpersonal Relations • Family Relationships • Stepmothers

Paratore, Coleen Murtagh

The Wedding Planner's Daughter Series. New York: Simon & Schuster Books for Young Readers

Willafred "Willa" Havisham deals with the complexities of life and love as she faces the changes that come with growing up.

Single Parent • Weddings • Blended Families • Books and Reading • Pregnancy • Jealousy

The Wedding Planner's Daughter. 2005. 200 p. ISBN: 9780689873409; 9781416918547pa. *MJ*

Willafred "Willa" Havisham hopes her wedding planner mother, Stella, will stay in one place for longer than their normal two years, now that she has found a home with Willa's grandmother, who runs a candy store. Willa has made a friend in local bookseller Mr. Tweed, who supports her ferocious reading habit. Thinking that the best way to keep her mother in one place is to find her a husband, Willa thinks new neighbor Sam will fit the bill, but first she must convince her mother that it is possible to fall in love again.

The Cupid Chronicles. 2006. 224 p. ISBN: 9781416908678; 9781416954842pa. *J*

With her mother happily married and her stability secured, high school freshman Willa leads a campaign to help save her town's local library while trying to keep friend Ruby from stealing away Joseph, her prospective boyfriend.

Willa by Heart. 2008. 228 p. ISBN: 9781416940760; 9781416974703pa. *J*

This summer is not going as Willa had planned since her mother announces that she is pregnant and a new girl, Mariel, moves in. When Mariel takes the lead role in the town's play away from Willa and then tries to steal her boyfriend as well, Willa must decide how she is going to deal with all the changes in her life.

Forget Me Not. 2009. 178 p. ISBN: 9780545094016. *J*

When her best friend Tina becomes friends with popular Ruby and her boyfriend leaves for Florida for a month, Willa is left alone to deal with planning her Aunt Ruthie's wedding and joining the fight over the creation of an endangered bird habitat.

Parkinson, Siobhan

Blue Like Friday. New York: Roaring Brook Press, 2008. 160 p. ISBN: 9781596433403. *J*

Missing his father, Hal wants to make his mother break off her engagement to her boyfriend, Alec, who will never replace what he has lost. So he and his best friend, Olivia, come up with a plan to get rid of Alec. The plan backfires, and Hal's mother leaves him alone with Alec for five days. Now Hal must learn how to get along with his new stepfather and come to terms with his father's death.

Stepfathers • Friendship • Interpersonal Relations • Missing Persons

Prosek, James

The Day My Mother Left. New York: Simon & Schuster Books for Young Readers, 2007. 304 p. ISBN: 9781416907701; 9781416907718pa; (aud). *J*

For the three years after his mother left her husband and family for another man, Jeremy Vrabec has had many problems that are only complicated when his father marries Susan, who tries to be nice but just does not fill the void. To cope with the hurt and anger he always feels, Jeremy spends time walking in the woods, drawing the birds he sees and spending time at his best friend's house or fishing with his uncle who treats him like a son. However, as Jeremy gets closer to Susan, he is able to realize how self-absorbed his mother has been and come to terms with his life.

Stepmother • Mother-Deserted Children • Family Relationships

Reinhardt, Dana

How to Build a House. New York: Random House Children's Books, 2008. 240 p. ISBN: 9780375844539; 9780375844546pa; (aud). YALSA Best Books. *S*

> Anxious to get away from her indifferent boyfriend Gabriel and her house, which seems empty since her stepmother divorced her father and left with her beloved stepsisters, seventeen-year-old Harper Evans signs up with Homes from the Heart, volunteering to build houses for tornado victims in Bailey, Tennessee, over the summer. Harper has never built anything in her life, but as the summer progresses, she not only builds confidence in her construction abilities, she also begins to rebuild her life as she makes new friends and finds love.

> *Romance • Father and Daughter • Volunteers*

Schroeder, Lisa

Far from You. New York: Simon Pulse, 2009. 384 p. ISBN: 9781416975069; 9781416975076pa. *JS*

> Since her mother died years earlier, sixteen-year-old Alice has lived a topsy-turvy life. Unable to accept her new stepmother and baby sister and finding no support from her emotionally distanced father, Alice clings to her friend Claire, with whom she shares a love of music, and her boyfriend Blaze. Even more out of sorts after a fight with Clarie over her gloomy musical lyrics, and dealing with confusion over whether she should sleep with Blaze, Alice leaves for Thanksgiving with her stepmother's parents. When a blizzard suddenly comes up on their journey home, Alice finds herself trapped with her stepmother and sister, an event that allows her to take stock of her life as she develops a new appreciation for her family and friends.

> *Blended Families • Stepmothers • Grief • Faith • Novels in Verse*

Smith, Kirsten

The Geography of Girlhood. New York: Little, Brown, 2006. 184 p. ISBN: 9780316160216; 9780316017350pa. *MJ*

> Left by her mother when she was six, Penny longs for her as she faces the tribulations of high school. Her father remarried a younger woman, and Penny has a wild older sister and a younger stepbrother whom she must protect. Then her best friend slips into a depression, and her first boyfriend accidentally dies. Penny can't deal with her life anymore. Running from her problems, Penny tries to embrace a wilder life when she leaves with her sister's ex-boyfriend, but quickly realizing her mistake, she is forced to grow up.

> *Mother-Separated Families • Loss • Love • Desire • Death • Blended Families • Coming-of-Age • Novels in Verse*

Sonnenblick, Jordan

Notes from the Midnight Driver. New York: Scholastic Press, 2006. 272 p. ISBN: 9780439757799; 9780439757812pa. YALSA Best Books. *JS*

> Getting drunk one night while his mother is on a date, sixteen-year-old Alex Gregory decides to get revenge for his parents' split by catching his father with his girlfriend, who happens to be Alex's third-grade teacher, and takes his mother's car to

transport himself. When he wrecks the car and is brought up on a drunk-driving charge, Alex must serve 100 hours of community service. His assignment is to visit Solomon Lewis, the meanest resident at the Egbert P. Johnson Memorial Home for the Aged. As he gets to know Solomon, a famous former guitarist, Alex is able not only to improve his own guitar playing but learn something about respect and taking responsibility for his actions.

Friendship • Intergenerational Relations • Musicians • Family Problems • Drunk Driving • Community Service

Vivian, Siobhan

A Little Friendly Advice. New York: Push, 2008. 248 p. ISBN: 9780545004046; 9780545004053pa. *JS*

Beth was the person who helped Ruby pick up the pieces after her dad walked out on the family several years earlier. Now on her sixteenth birthday, Beth is the first one to call her. Later, when Ruby is about to blow out her candles and her dad unexpectedly walks through the door, Beth is there by her side. Despite all the good advice she has given her, Ruby discovers that Beth has been lying to her and has been hiding a letter to her from her father. Her trust in her friend is shattered, and Ruby must decide if their friendship can survive both the lies she has told and the truth that is revealed.

Photography • Friendship • Secrets • Father and Daughter • Father-Separated Families

Weaver, Will

Claws: A Novel. New York: HarperCollins, 2003. 232 p. ISBN: 9780060094737; 9780060094751pa. *JS*

Sixteen-year-old Jed Berg seems to have a great life. He has a close relationship with his parents, his grades are good, and he has a beautiful girlfriend and a place on the varsity tennis team. But when he gets an e-mail picture of his father kissing another woman, sent by the woman's teenage daughter Laura, things spin out of control. Jed's turmoil over the situation and his parents' subsequent breakup spills over into his life, and Jed makes some bad decisions that lead to his being suspended. As Jed gets closer to Laura and helps her, he comes to realize that his life is out of control, and he is able to confront the changes his father's actions have created in his life.

Family Problems • Love • Accidents • Coming-of-Age

Weeks, Sarah

Guy Strang Series. New York: Laura Geringer Book

Guy deals with the challenges of growing up, especially after his parents divorce and remarry.

Eccentricities • Friendship • Mother and Son • Remarriage • Divorce • Interpersonal Relations • Parent and Child

Regular Guy. 1999. 120 p. ISBN: 978006283674; 9780064407823pa. *M*

Eleven-year-old Guy Strang's hippy parents are so crazy that he is sure he must have been switched at birth. With the help of his best friend, he searches the school records and finds that he has the same birthday and was born at the same hospital as the class nerd, Robert "Bob-o" Smith, and he arranges to trade places with him for the weekend on the pretense of a school project. Guy finds that having normal parents who don't have any time for their son is even worse than what he already has.

Guy Time. 2000. 165 p. ISBN: 9780060283650; 9780064407830pa. *M*

Thirteen-year-old Guy's life gets complicated when his parents separate after his father develops a successful piece of software and moves to California and his mother starts dating the geekiest guys she can. When Autumn, a girl he really likes, asks him on a date, he can't tell his best friend Buzz but instead denies his interest and hurts her feelings. Autumn's tough friend, Lana, targets him for revenge, and things go from bad to worse. Guy tries to get his parents back together by posing as his mother and writing to his father, but when things don't turn out like he planned, he works to resolve things with his friends.

My Guy. 2001. 186 p. ISBN: 9780060283698; 9780064407816pa. *M*

When his mother decides to get remarried and becomes engaged to Jerry Zuckerman, a professional clown and the father of Guy's enemy, Lana, the two teens, along with Guy's friend Buzz, decide to break up the romance. But when their scheme succeeds, leaving Guy's mom heartbroken, Guy realizes that he must tell the truth.

Guy Wire. 2002. ISBN: 9780060294922. *M*

When his friend Buzz is injured after being hit by a car in a bike accident and Guy finds himself waiting in the hospital for news of him, he looks back on the time when they became friends in second grade after Buzz arrived from Kentucky.

Zeises, Lara M.

Anyone but You: A Novel in Two Voices. New York: Delacorte Press, 2005. 245 p. ISBN: 9780385731454; 9780440238584pa. YALSA Popular Paperbacks. *S*

When fifteen-year-old skateboarder Seattle's father disappeared, her father's girlfriend, Layla, took her in. Layla's son, seventeen-year-old Critter, is Seattle's best friend and like a brother to her, but when Critter falls in love with a preppy girl, Seattle finds that she is jealous. Critter is also conflicted about his feelings for Seattle as she gets involved with an older skateboarder, Scott, and he finds that he is also jealous and wants to protect her. But when Seattle's father returns, claiming to have been a horrible father, and then suddenly disappears again, the two must decide how to define their relationship as they develop their own identities.

Blended Families • Family Problems • Depression • Jealousy • Sexuality • Friendship

Siblings

Cadnum, Michael

Rundown. New York: Viking, 1999. 168 p. ISBN: 9780670883776; 9780141310879pa. YALSA Quick Picks. *S*

>Sixteen-year-old Jennifer Thayer was lying when she said someone tried to rape her while she was jogging near the U.C. Berkley campus. Building off the reports of a serial rapist who has been attacking women in the area, Jennifer knew that everyone would believe her, and so she would be able to take all the attention away from her older sister, Cassandra. Self-centered Cassandra, who is planning her wedding, has always had the attention from their entrepreneur father and their industrial-psychologist mother. Driven by jealousy, Jennifer saw this as the only way to get what she wants. All the while terrified of being found out, Jennifer is increasingly unable to deal with her deception and makes a mistake that causes the detective on the case to suspect that Jennifer's mother has been abusing her. As events unfold, Jennifer realizes she must face the realities of her life.
>
>*Sisters • Sibling Rivalry • Guilt • Rape*

Charlton-Trujillo, e. E.

Feels Like Home. New York: Delacorte Press, 2007. 224 p. ISBN: 9780385733328; 9780440239499pa. *J*

>Mickey has never forgiven her brother Danny for taking off after his best friend and the town football hero, Roland, died six years ago. But when their abusive father dies, Danny shows up again, and Mickey is resentful that he is meddling in her life, especially now that she is just about to graduate and leave their small Texas town. Danny blames himself for Roland's death, and when Mickey rejects him, he starts exhibiting the same behaviors he despised in his father. Despite their differences, they share a love of the novel *The Outsiders*, a common bond that helps them overcome the obstacles in their relationship.
>
>*Alcoholics • Brothers • Sisters • Death • Fathers • Hispanic Americans • Race Relations • Secrets • Grief*

Corrigan, Eireann

Ordinary Ghosts. New York: Scholastic, 2007. 380 p. ISBN: 9780439832434; 9780439832441pa. *JS*

>After his mother dies, sixteen-year-old Emil is alone with his militaristic father and older brother, Ethan. When Ethan suddenly disappears, Emil searches for clues and finds that his brother holds the master key to their elite private school. Each year the tradition is that one senior pulls off a major prank and then passes the key on to another student, who will commit the prank next year. Emil realizes that he has to step into his brother's shoes and goes into the school to find a worthy prank. There he meets eighteen-year-old Jade, a girl who is secretly working in the art studio. They de-

velop a relationship, and it is Jade who helps Emil cope when he discovers shocking secrets about his mother's terminal illness that led to her suicide and Ethan's role in her death.

Misfits • Family Problems • Brothers • Sisters • Grief • Single Parent

DeVillers, Julia, and Jennifer Roy

Trading Faces. New York: Aladdin Paperbacks, 2009. 304 p. ISBN: 9781416975311; 9781416961680pa. *M*

Twins Emma and Payton Mills have been attending an all-girls school, but now they are starting seventh grade at a public middle school where Payton dreams of joining the "popular" group. She is saved from disaster when brainy Emma switches places with her to avoid an embarrassing situation. Both girls are out of their comfort zones, and they struggle with the problem. They find that there are lots of things about the other girl's life that they really like and find it hard to switch back.

Twins • Sisters • Family

Hughes, Mark Peter

I Am the Wallpaper. New York: Delacorte Press, 2005. 240 p. ISBN: 9780385732413; 9780440420460pa. *MJ*

Feeling overshadowed by her vivacious sister Lillian, who is soon to be married, thirteen-year-old Floey Packer decides to take on a bolder, more interesting persona by dying her hair purple and donning a black fedora. Her endeavor to remake herself is complicated when her life is laid bare by her bratty cousin, who posts her diary and an embarrassing photograph of her online. Now an Internet star, Floey breaks out of her shell, but with her secrets revealed to the world, she wonders if being overlooked is not better after all, as she must deal with the strain her revelations put on her relationship with her crush and her best friend, Azra.

Cousins • Sisters • Family • Sibling Rivalry • Love • Diaries

Levithan, David

Are We There Yet? New York: Knopf, 2005. 215 p. ISBN: 9780375828461; 9780375839566pa. YALSA Best Books; YALSA Popular Paperbacks. *S*

Elijah and Danny are brothers who have grown apart because of their very different lives. Seventeen-year-old Elijah is mellow and likes to live in the moment without a plan. Twenty-three-year old Danny has complete control over his life as an up-and-comer in the corporate world. When their parents trick them into taking a vacation to Italy to help the boys reconnect, things go wrong when they meet Julia, a college dropout, and both boys fall for her. They have to decide if she holds the power to break them apart for good as they look back on their past together and make decisions about the future.

Family Relationships • Brothers • Alienation • Vacations

Lord, Cynthia

Rules. New York: Scholastic Press, 2006. 200 p. ISBN: 9780786295593; 9780439443838pa. ALA Notable Children's Books; Newberry Honor Books. *M*

Twelve-year-old Catherine makes up and records rules of life for her autistic younger brother, David, to help him understand the world. Even though she loves him and is trying to help him, she is still embarrassed by him and feels neglected by her parents and burdened with the responsibilities she has for him. One day, while waiting at her brother's therapy clinic, she meets fourteen-year-old paraplegic Jason, who talks using picture cards in a communication notebook. As Catherine builds a friendship with Jason, she is able to find greater acceptance for differences and strengthen her own identity.

Autism • Interpersonal Relations • Brothers • Sisters

Myracle, Lauren

Peace, Love and Baby Ducks. New York: Dutton Children's Books, 2009. 192 p. ISBN: 9780525477433. *J*

When fifteen-year-old Carly went away to a nature camp, she gained a new belief system that is contrary to her family's wealth and lifestyle. Upon her return, she finds that her sister, Anna, has gained some very big boobs. Jealous of her sister and trying to reconcile her old life with her new ideas, Carly is also dealing with a crush who doesn't notice her but does notice Anna. There is trouble in her parents' marriage and a rivalry between her two best friends. As she grows, she must overcome her negative feelings for Anna and learn who she truly is.

Sisters • Friendship • Peer Pressure • Jealousy

Rallison, Janette

Just One Wish. New York: G.P. Putnam's Sons, 2009. 272 p. ISBN: 9780399246180. *JS*

Seventeen-year-old Annika invents a genie who can grant wishes to comfort her brother, who is about to undergo surgery for cancer, and he wishes that his favorite TV character, Teen Robin Hood, would come and teach him archery. To fulfill the wish, Annika must drive hours to the show's set, break in, and convince the star, Steve, to come with her, and deal with the paparazzi.

Brothers • Sisters • Cancer • Actors and Actresses

Rushton, Rosie

The Dashwood Sisters' Secrets of Love. New York: Hyperion, 2005. 325 p. ISBN: 9780786851362; 9780786851379pa. *J*

After their parents' divorce, the three Dashwood sisters' father marries the shrill health-nut Pandora, a situation that the girls are not happy with. When their father suddenly dies and they find that he has not only left enormous debts and no inheritance but that his will gives their family's ancestral home, Holly House, to Pandora, the girls face another unhappy situation. Forced to leave their home and school to live in a small rent-free cottage in the country, the sisters Ellie, Abby, and Georgie each deal with their predicament in different ways as they also deal with untangling their own romantic relationships.

Sisters • Death • Divorce • Father-Deserted Families • England

Spinelli, Jerry

Smiles to Go. New York: Joanna Cotler Books, 2008. 256 p. ISBN: 9780060281335; 9780064471978pa; (aud). *J*

Learning that scientists have recorded the first proof of proton decay, scientifically minded high school freshman Will Tuppence starts pondering all ramifications of this discovery. Dealing with his kindergarten sister, Tabby, who does nothing but pester him, Will is also trying to sort out his feelings for classmate and fellow scientist Mi-Su, when he catches her kissing their friend B.T. When Tabby tries to catch Will's attention by taking a skateboard ride down Dead Man's Hill and ends up seriously injured, Will finally learns to embrace the unpredictability of things as he learns that not everything in life can be controlled.

Brothers • Sisters • Friendship • Family • Coming-of-Age

Stone, Heather Duffy

This Is What I Want to Tell You. Woodbury, MN: Flux, 2009. 192 p. ISBN: 9780738714509. *J*

Nadio and Noelle, fifteen-year-old twins, find their lives changing when Noelle's best friend Keeley returns from a summer in Europe. Noelle is resentful for all the opportunities her beautiful, rich friend has, and Nadio finds that he has feelings for Keeley. The pair starts dating in secret. Noelle is keeping her own relationship with older bad-boy Parker, a cook whom she meets at a party, a secret as well. While Nadio deals with his feelings of lust for Keeley, realizing they could lead him down the same path as the boy who sexually assaulted Keeley in England, the twins' secrets are revealed, and the pair must deal with the poor decisions they have made as they discover the redemptive power of love.

Best Friends • Interpersonal Relations • Secrets • Friendship • Brothers • Sisters • Twins

Voorhees, Coert

The Brothers Torres. New York: Hyperion, 2008. 316 p. ISBN: 9781423103042; 9781423103066pa. YALSA Best Books. *JS*

By picking up the slack at their family's restaurant, sixteen-year-old Frankie Torres Towers is able to cover up for his older brother, Steve, when he stays out all night and gets into fights. But when Frankie tires to win the attention of Rebecca Sanchez so he can ask her to the homecoming dance and instead gets beaten up by soccer jock John Dalton, Steve is forced to step in and defend him. When Frankie discovers that his parents are thinking of selling their restaurant to John's parents, Frankie thinks it is time for revenge and is drawn into the conflict. But he soon finds that Steve and John are willing to risk too much in the name of honor.

Dating • Hispanic Americans • Interracial Persons • Brothers • Gangs • Rich People • Revenge

Wallace, Rich

Perpetual Check. New York: Alfred A. Knopf, 2009. 176 p. ISBN: 9780375840586. *S*

High school senior Zeke and his brother, freshman Randy, are physical and emotional opposites. The brothers deal with their angry and shallow father in different ways. Hyper-competitive Zeke seems just like his Dad, who pushes aggression as a solution for his boys, which Zeke shows in playing soccer, tennis, and chess. Randy also excels at chess, but he is less competitive and faces challenges with a relaxed attitude. When the boys face off in Scranton for the Northeast Regional of the Pennsylvania High School Chess Championships, the process brings the boys closer, and Zeke gradually realizes that emulating his father is not the best way to succeed in chess or in life.

Brothers • Chess • Sibling Rivalry • Father and Son • Family Relationships

Williams, Suzanne

Bull Rider. New York: Margaret K. McElderry Books, 2009. 256 p. ISBN: 9781416961307. *MJ*

All fourteen-year-old Cam O'Mara has ever wanted to be is a skateboarder, despite his family's heritage as champion bull riders. But when his older brother, Ben, comes home from Iraq severely injured and depressed, Cam returns to the family tradition and starts riding bulls in the hope that he can secretly ride a champion bull to win the prize money so his brother can start his own breeding business, an endeavor Cam hopes will help Ben to rebuild his life.

Bull Riding • Brothers • Skateboards and Skateboarding • Depression • Iraq

Wilson, Martin

What They Always Tell Us. New York: Delacorte Press, 2008. 293 p. ISBN: 9780385735070; 9780385735087pa. *S*

Despite his fears for the future, popular, smart high school senior James seems to have his life on track, unlike his younger brother, Alex, a junior, who is just trying to get his life back after a suicide attempt when he swallowed Pine-Sol at a party. When James's friend, Nathen, gets Alex involved in the cross-country team, Alex is able to see that there is really something worth living for when he falls for Nathen and his feelings are returned. James worries about what will happen if colleges don't accept him, and Alex worries about how people will accept his relationship. But the brothers find support as they get closer when they make friends with a lonely neighbor boy and help him with his problems.

Brothers • Gay Males • Coming Out • Suicide • Popularity • Coming-of-Age

Zusak, Markus

Fighting Ruben Wolfe. New York: Arthur A. Levine Books, 2001, 2000. 219 p. ISBN: 9780439241885; 9780439241878pa. YALSA Best Books. *S*

Hoping to help their unemployed father and their mother who works extra jobs to make ends meet with the money they would earn from winning,

Ruben Wolfe and his younger brother Cameron sign up to compete in boxing matches that are staged between untrained youths. Ruben is a winner, and even though Cameron loses, he fights with gusto and wins the admiration of many fans, who give him money. Then, when the brothers must fight each other, they have to decide how they will deal with the situation as they struggle with their pride and as Cameron works to develop his own identity.

Sequel: *Getting the Girl.* New York: Arthur A. Levine Books, 2003. 261 p. ISBN: 9780439389495; 9780439389501pa. *S*

While Ruben continues to box and get involved with numerous girls, Cameron is distancing himself from his brother, and although he wants a girlfriend and sex, the only girl he is attracted to treats him badly. Then Cameron discovers that he has a passion for writing, and beautiful Octavia, who has been dumped by Ruben, shows some interest in him. Cameron struggles to contain Ruben's violence over the situation as he works to find out who he truly is.

Boxing • Family Problems • Sibling Rivalry • Girlfriends • Australia

Chapter 4

Going to School

School plays a significant part in adolescents' lives, and it serves as a place where they learn both academic and nonacademic subjects. Along with family and peer relationships, interactions and experiences with schooling allow teens to develop the best possible personal and interpersonal attributes that will give them the abilities they need to contribute to society as an adult. The books listed in this chapter deal with the variety of issues that adolescents face in a school environment as they interact with adult school personnel as well as with peer groups Whether it is a student moving from homeschooling to public school or students dealing with the challenges inherent in a boarding or private school, each schooling context offers teens a chance to grow and learn. Participating in school activities such as student government or the prom offer many different experiences that allow teens to build their abilities and talents. Building an ethical outlook is also an important part of schooling as teens face challenges such as deciding whether cheating on tests or college applications is an option. School also provides a context for social interactions and relationship development, especially as teens work to earn their social status among the numerous cliques and popularity contests that are inherent in peer interactions.

General Schooling

Atkins, Catherine

Alt Ed. New York: G.P. Putnam's Sons, 2003. 224 p. ISBN: 9780399238543; 9780142402351pa. *S*

As an alternative to expulsion, six high school students who have committed serious infractions join an after-school alternative education class. The overweight outcast Susan Callaway narrates, relating the experiences in the sessions that include bully Kale, gay Brenden, jock Randy, cheerleader Tracee, and "slut" Amber. Brought together, this unlikely group builds respect for one another, and each finds a greater sense of belonging.

High School • Body Image • Homosexuality • Friendship • Belonging

Beam, Matt

Can You Spell Revolution? New York: Dutton Children's Books, 2008. 208 p. ISBN: 9780525479987. *M*

> Inspired by historical figures and events, new student Clouds McFadden devises a plan to revolutionize the boring work and strict rules of Laverton Middle School by wresting power from Principal Dorfman. Gathering together a group of eighth graders, including Chris Stren, Clouds begins to enact his elaborate plan. But soon Cloud's tyrannical behavior has Chris working to give peace a chance to enact the change they desire.

> *Middle School • Political Activists*

Bradley, Alex

Hot Lunch. New York: Dutton Children's Books, 2007. 272 p. ISBN: 9780525478300; 9780142412992pa. *MJ*

> Molly and Cassie are forced to work together on a class assignment. Their hostility toward one another explodes during a food fight in the cafeteria, which causes the school lunch lady to quit. As punishment, the two must replace her by planning and preparing lunch every day until the student body decides they like what they have prepared. Even with their personalities clashing and their inability to cook, the two finally come to a consensus and develop a new friendship.

> *High School • Punishment • Cooking*

Cohen, Tish

<u>**Zoe Lama Series.**</u> New York: Dutton Children's Books

> Seventh-grader Zoe loves dispensing advice for everything from fashion to art, but sometimes her advice goes wrong.

> *Middle School • Family • Advice*

> ***The Invisible Rules of the Zoe Lama.*** 2007. 247 p. ISBN: 9780525478102; 9780142414002pa. *M*

> > Zoe is juggling a lot, including being the chair of the winter dance committee, helping out a new student Maisie, keeping her Grandmother with Alzheimer's out of a nursing home, finding her mother a new husband, and connecting with her own crush Riley. When Zoe's well-meaning advice backfires, she must soon learn that sometimes letting people be themselves is the best advice of all.

> ***The One and Only Zoe Lama.*** 2008. 256 p. ISBN: 9780525478911. *M*

> > Returning to school after a bout of chicken pox, Zoe finds that Devon Sweeney has taken her place as resident advice giver. Ready to take her down and regain her title, Zoe soon realizes that sometimes compassion dictates that you step aside.

Ehrenhaft, Daniel

Tell It to Naomi. New York: Delacorte Press, 2004. 200 p. ISBN: 9780385731294pa. *J*

Sensitive fifteen-year-old Dave Rosen finds himself authoring "Dear Naomi," the school newspaper's advice column, and hopes it may help him capture the attention of his crush. But when the column is a hit, Dave struggles to keep his job a secret and finds he is growing apart from his best friend. And he is still unable to attract his crush. Revealing his identity requires him to make amends for a betrayal and forge ahead with a new identity.

Advice • Brothers • Sisters • Friendship • High School

Grunwell, Jeanne Marie

Mind Games. Boston: Houghton Mifflin, 2003. 133 p. ISBN: 9780618176724; 9780618689477pa. *M*

Six students in the science club at Clearview Middle School find friendship as they work together on a science fair project about ESP. The group includes honors student Claire and her twin Kathleen, who is in special education; Ji Eun Oh, the twins' friend; Marina, a Russian immigrant; Brandon, who is grieving his mother's death; and Ben, a science geek who is dealing with his parents' divorce.

Friendship • Middle School • Death • Divorce

Juby, Susan

Alice MacLeod Diaries. New York: Harper Tempest

In her diary and through other creative outlets, Alice chronicles her life in a small town in British Columbia.

Misfits • Small Towns • Self-Perception • High School • Diary Novel

Alice, I Think. 2003. 290 p. ISBN: 9780060515430; 9780060515454pa; (aud). YALSA Best Books. *J*

Having been homeschooled by her hippie parents, fifteen-year-old Alice starts attending an alternative public high school where she tries to make friends, attract boys, avoid the bully, and prove to her counselor that he has helped her to progress.

Miss Smithers. 2004. 336 p. ISBN: 9780060515461; 9780060515485pa. *J*

Against the wishes of her feminist mother, sixteen-year-old Alice enters the town beauty pageant as a representative of the Smithers Rod and Gun Club to take advantage of the $400 they give the contestants for clothing. Along the way, Alice explores becoming a born-again Christian, gets drunk, and tries to have sex with her boyfriend for the first time.

Alice MacLeod, Realist at Last. 2005. 320 p. ISBN: 9780060515492; 9780060515522pa. *J*

Now seventeen, Alice is dealing with a lot of complications. The tragedy of breaking up with her boyfriend and trying to find a new boyfriend who is just right is compounded by her inability to get a job, her mother being put in jail after a protest march, and having to deal with a new counselor.

Korman, Gordon

No More Dead Dogs. New York: Hyperion Books for Children, 2000. 180 p. ISBN: 9780786805310; 9780786816019pa. YALSA Popular Paperbacks. *MJ*

Eighth-grade football hero Wallace Wallace is placed in detention and removed from the team when he expresses his true views on the book his class is reading for English. But his detention is held in the auditorium where his English teacher is directing a theatrical version of the very same book, and Wallace makes a few suggestions. To the delight of some and the outrage of others, the production turns into a spectacular rock musical. As the football team starts losing and someone is trying to sabotage the play, Wallace must deal with the complications, especially the ones that arise when he realizes he's falling for drama club president Rachel.

Football • Schools • Romance

Korman, Gordon

Schooled. New York: Hyperion, 2007. 224 p. ISBN: 9780786856923; 9781423105169pa. *MJ*

Thirteen-year-old Capricorn "Cap" Anderson has always lived with his grandmother, Rain, on an isolated farm commune where he has never watched TV or used a telephone. But when Rain is hospitalized after falling from a tree while picking plums, Cap is forced to go to live with a social worker and must attend public school for the first time. Inexperienced in the ways of the world, Cap soon becomes the butt of jokes, culminating in the class's traditional joke to elect their strangest classmate as class president. When he does not react the way the pranksters expect, Cap comes to win the respect and understanding of those around him.

Homeschooling • Hippies • Grandmothers • Belonging • Individuality

Lubar, David

Sleeping Freshmen Never Lie. New York: Dutton Children's Books, 2005. 279 p. ISBN: 9780525473114; 9780142407806pa; (aud). YALSA Best Books. *J*

When his mother reveals that she is pregnant, high school freshman Scott Hudson begins writing letters to his new sibling providing insights into life. He faces a tumultuous year in which he joins the school newspaper, deals with all-night homework sessions, works to get close to the girl he likes by acting as stage manager for the school play, tries to help a fellow classmate who attempts suicide, faces down bullies, and attends the spring dance. Through it all, Scott is finally able to find a place for himself in the complex world of high school.

High School • Brothers • Self-Confidence • Interpersonal Relations • Writing

Oates, Joyce Carol

Big Mouth & Ugly Girl. New York: Harper Tempest, 2002. 266 p. ISBN: 9780066237565; 9780064473477pa; (aud). YALSA Best Books; School Library Journal Best Books. *J*

When witnesses report that Matt Donaghy threatened to bomb the school if his play was not part of their Spring Arts Festival, he is suspended for three days. Matt's comment was just a joke, and things have been blown completely out of proportion. When his friends who heard the comments distance themselves from him and the situation, the only one who has the courage to defend him is Ursula "Ugly Girl" Rigg. Soon the two form a friendship, and Ursula is able to convince the principal to rethink his punishment. Far from the end of the situation, rumors continue to circulate. Matt's parents threaten to sue the school for slander, and the two new friends must face the consequences of a rash action together.

Friendship • High School • Romance

O'Keefe, Susan Heyboer

Death by Eggplant. Brookfield, CT: Roaring Brook Press, 2004. 134 p. ISBN: 9781596430112. *MJ*

Eighth-grader Bertie Hook dreams about attending the Culinary Institute of America even though his mother wants him to be a dream analyst and his father wants him to be an insurance actuary. But before he can even think about living his dream, he must get his grades up by fulfilling his teacher's extra-credit assignment to care for a flour-sack baby for ten days. His mother dubs the flour-sack "Cleopatra." Despite his enemy Nick Dekker's best attempts to sabotage the project by kidnapping the baby, with the help of his parents, Bertie is able to get her back by taking Nick's own mother hostage. Through the conflict, Bertie is able to find his own identity.

Cooking • Family • School Projects

Smith, Greg Leitich

Ninjas, Piranhas, and Galileo. Boston: Little, Brown, 2003. 179 p. ISBN: 9780316778541; 9780316011815pa. *M*

If life isn't complicated enough for seventh-grade friends Elias, Shohei, and Honoria, they now have to face this year's science fair. Honoria is determined to win by teaching her piranhas to be vegetarians. Partners Elias and Shohei decide to recreate Elias's brother's award-winning project that proved classical music helps plants grow. When the project disproves the original findings, Elias's ethics are called into question, and he is sent to Student Court where Honoria acts as his lawyer and Shohei must decide if he should admit his role in the project.

Japanese Americans • Middle School • Friendship • Family • Diary Novel

Fitting In and Popularity

Anderson, Laurie Halse

Twisted. New York: Viking, 2007. 256 p. ISBN: 9780670061013; 9780142411841pa; (aud). YALSA Best Books; YALSA Quick Picks; Teens Top Ten. *S*

> After a summer sentenced to physical labor to atone for spraying graffiti as a prank, Tyler Miller has gained a new physique and a new level of popularity. When his new muscles attract his longtime crush Bethany Millbury while infuriating his tormentor Chip, Tyler begins to struggle with balancing his love life, schoolwork, and dealing with his father's hostility. Things fall completely apart when Tyler is implicated in the appearance of indecent photos of Bethany that appear on the Internet after a wild, drunken party. Overcoming his deep despair, Tyler takes power from the struggles around him by claiming personal responsibility and defining his own identity.
>
> *Social Acceptance • High School • Punishment • Internet • Coming-of-Age*

Barnholdt, Lauren

The Secret Identity of Devon Delaney. New York: Aladdin Paperbacks, 2007. 263 p. ISBN: 9781416935032. *M*

> Spending the summer at her grandmother's house, Devon Delaney re-creates herself into a trendy and popular girl through the lies she tells her new friend Lexi. But when the summer is over and Lexi shows up in her class at school, Devon tells even more lies to keep Lexi from finding out the truth. When her lies alienate all her friends, Devon must learn from her mistakes and come clean to fix her life and repair her friendships.
>
> *Social Acceptance • Dishonesty*

Cabot, Meg

How to Be Popular. New York: Harper Tempest, 2006. 304 p. ISBN: 9780060880125; 9780060880149pa; (aud). *JS*

> Steph Landry has been unpopular since the sixth grade when she spilled a red Super Big Gulp on a popular girl's white skirt. Now starting eleventh grade, Steph has had enough and is determined to join the popular crowd. When she discovers an old book titled *How to Be Popular*, she takes its advice, buys a new wardrobe, and takes on the organization of a school fundraiser. Longtime best friend and next-door neighbor Jason is uncertain of the change. Along the way, their relationship is strained, until Steph realizes that popularity is not all it is cracked up to be.
>
> *Best Friends • High School • Romance • Conformity*

Castellucci, Cecil

The Queen of Cool. Cambridge, MA: Candlewick Press, 2006. 176 p. ISBN: 9780763627201; 9780763634131pa. *JS*

> After years of being popular, which includes partying, sex, and drinking with her friends, sixteen-year-old Libby Brin finds the life she is leading has become very

boring. On an impulse, she gets an internship at the Los Angeles Zoo, and although her friends mock her because she has been partnered with the nerdy overweight Sheldon and Tina "Tiny" Carpentieri, a Little Person, Libby finds that she really likes her work and her two new friends. This outlook changes Libby in important ways, and she is able to embrace a passion for life as she finds out what really matters.

Misfits • *Cliques* • *Zoos* • *Internships* • *Teasing* • *Friendship*

Choldenko, Gennifer

If a Tree Falls at Lunch Period. Orlando, FL: Harcourt, 2007. 224 p. ISBN: 9780152057534; 9780152066444pa; (aud). *MJ*

Seventh-grader Kirsten faces a tough year—she is overweight and has parents who are constantly arguing and are now hardly speaking to each other. She doesn't even have any friends since her best friend, Rory, is now hanging out with the popular girls. At the same exclusive private school that Kirsten attends is Walker, "Walk," who has moved from his inner-city school and is now the only black student. When they are both late to the first day of school and must attend Saturday detention, the two strike up a friendship, and Walk is the only one to defend Kirsten when she is framed by mean girl Brianna for stealing a teacher's wallet. Together the two must face their families' long-held secrets and the prejudice and racism that surround them to find their own self-esteem and strength.

Rich People • *Overweight* • *Misfits* • *Interracial Friendships* • *Race Relations* • *Schools* • *Secrets*

DeVillers, Julia

How My Private, Personal Journal Became a Bestseller: A Novel. New York: Dutton Children's Books, 2004. 212 p. ISBN: 9780525472834pa. *MJ*

Insecure fourteen-year-old Jamie works out her frustrations with catty classmates and the media's images of physically perfect girls in her journal where she has created alterego Isabella "IS" who is able to deal with all these things with superpowers. Things change when she mistakenly turns in the journal instead of an assignment. Her teacher sends it to an agent, and Jamie becomes a published author and an instant celebrity. Fame, however, is not all it is cracked up to be, and Jamie finds that false friends and a jerk boyfriend are no substitute for her best friends and sweet potential boyfriend Connor.

High School • *Diaries* • *Cliques* • *Fame*

Frankel, Valerie

<u>**Fringe Girl Series.**</u> New York: NAL Jam

Dora Benet faces unique challenges in life with the support of her friends.

Interpersonal Relations • *Veterinarians* • *Friendship* • *Summer*

Fringe Girl. 2006. 256 p. IBSN: 9780451217721pa. *JS*

Placed on the fringe of the social classes at her high school, Adora "Dora" Benet decides to stage a political uprising to oust the popular students and place a new regime, which she would lead, in power.

Fringe Girl in Love. 2007. 272 p. ISBN: 9780451220462pa. *JS*

Dora and Noel, Liza and Stanley, Eli and Eric, Joya and Ben, and Mr. and Mrs. Benet are all in love, but the course of true love does not always run smoothly, and soon family and friends are causing problems for the couples.

American Fringe. 2008. 272 p. ISBN: 9780451222923pa. *JS*

Dora is the new teen advice columnist for the local paper. When one of her columns persuades a senator to run for president, Dora and her writing suddenly become popular. Just as things are heating up, Dora is introduced to charming Toby, who is making her rethink her relationship with boyfriend Nate.

Fringe Benefits. 2008. 263 p. ISBN: 9780451224965pa. *JS*

Facing a boring summer without her best friends and boyfriend, Dora's parents force her to get a job. In the end, she lands two jobs, and at the animal shelter where she is an assistant, she meets a cute veterinarian and befriends an abandoned cat. At the exclusive Brooklyn club where she is a waitress, she meets party-girl Stella, who soon becomes her friend. Dora joins her partying ways until she is able to face her problems and learns that life is more than just one big party.

Haworth-Attard, Barbara

My Life from Air Bras to Zits. New York: Flux, 2009. 288 p. ISBN: 9780738714837pa. *JS*

As she starts tenth grade, Teresa Tolliver is unsure about herself and wants nothing more than to improve her social status so that she can attract the attention of "Achingly Adorable Adam (AAA)." When her older sister buys her an air-bra that enhances her bustline, Teresa finds her confidence enhanced even though at home she is dealing with her sister's upcoming wedding, an antisocial father, a mother who is pregnant, and her suddenly popular brother. But when Teresa ignores her friends to try and impress the popular crowd and finally gets a boyfriend, she soon finds out that popularity and romance can't solve the really important problems in life.

Romance • Body Image • Family Problems • Friendship

Howe, James

The Misfits. New York: Atheneum Books for Young Readers, 2001. 274 p. ISBN: 9780689839559; 9780689839566pa; (aud). *MJ*

Four friends are fed up with being called names at school, so seventh-graders Bob "Fatso," Joe "Faggot," Addie "Know-It-All," and Skeezie "Ree-Tard" join together to change the system by running under the alternative platform of their newly created "No-Name-Party" for the popularity-contest student council elections. Facing off against their fellow classmates as well as the school administration, the friends try to convince everyone of the damage that is caused by name-calling. But when Addie's rabble-rousing speeches start offending everyone, it is up to the soft-spoken Bobby to speak his heart so they can find success for their agenda. Along the way, the friends learn about love, loss, and the true meaning of diversity.

Sequel: *Totally Joe.* New York: Atheneum Books for Young Readers, 2005. 208 p. ISBN: 9780689839573; 9780689839580pa. ALA Notable Children's Books. *MJ*

Twelve-year-old Joe Bunch has come to grips with his sexuality, but when he falls for Colin who is less secure, and erroneous gossip begins to surface that the two have been kissing, Colin ends their friendship. Supported by his three friends, Joe is able to overcome bullying and prejudice as he deals with other issues such as trying to relate to his athletic brother and the pain over missing his much-loved Aunt Pam, who was the one who helped him come out to his family when she moved to New York.

Student Elections • Success • Gay Males • Friendship • Homosexuality • Coming-of-Age

Juby, Susan

Getting the Girl: A Guide to Private Investigation, Surveillance, and Cookery. New York: HarperTeen, 2008. 352 p. ISBN: 9780060765255; 9780060765286pa. *J*

At Harewood Technical High School someone is defiling girls by posting their photos in the school bathroom with a circled letter D marked on them. This mark ensures that the defiled girl is ostracized by all the students. When artistic girl Dini appears to be the next one to be defiled, Sherman Mack takes up the cause to find out who is harassing the girls to help prevent another victim and to win the admiration of friend Vanessa, who is also at risk for being defiled.

Peer Pressure • Social Acceptance • Secrets

Korman, Gordon

Jake, Reinvented. New York: Hyperion, 2003. 214 p. ISBN: 9780786819577pa. YALSA Best Books. *JS*

New student Jake Garrett easily won a place in the popular crowd with his athletic ability and the massive keg parties he throws at his house. But when Todd Buckley suspects that Jake has been pursuing his girlfriend, Didi, and he reveals Jake's secret past as a math tutor nerd, Jake's popularity plummets. It is only with the help of Rick Paradis, a member of the popular crowd who does not quite fit in, and the remarkable Dipsy that he is able to understand that high school is a small part of life and the future is much more important.

Peer Pressure • Social Acceptance • Personal Conduct

Koss, Amy Goldman

The Girls. New York: Dial Books for Young Readers, 2000. 121 p. ISBN: 9780786229116; (aud). YALSA Best Books; YALSA Quick Picks. *MJ*

Middle-schooler Maya is devastated when she is shunned, with no explanation, by her group of five popular girls. Members of the group Brianna,

Rene, and Darcy, are not sure what the reasons are for dumping Maya either. They each just follow the direction of the group leader, intimidating Candace. Soon the tensions in the group have everyone turning against each other, and the girls must decide if they are going to let Candace's peer pressure continue to influence them.

Cliques • Peer Pressure

Krulik, Nancy

How I Survived Middle School Series. New York: Scholastic
Constantly thwarted by the popular clique headed by Addie and Dana, Jenny Mcafee, with the support of her friends Chloe, Josh, Liza, Marc, and the twins Marylin and Carolyn, deals with the ups and downs of middle school.

Friendship • Middle School • Cliques • Best Friends

Can You Get an F in Lunch? 2006. 101 p. ISBN: 9780439025553pa. *MJ*
Finding that she is wearing all the wrong clothes, getting caught in a trick played on her by some eighth graders, and losing her best friend, Addie, to the popular crowd, Jenny has a rough start to middle school. After finding a new group of friends, Jenny is able to discover a way to survive what middle school throws at her.

Madame President. 2006. 104 p. ISBN: 9780439900904pa; 9780439025560pa. *MJ*
When Jenny finds out that her former friend is running unopposed for class president, her friends convince her that she has the leadership abilities to run and to win the election.

I Heard a Rumor. 2007. 112 p. ISBN: 9780439025577pa. *MJ*
The new gossip columnist for the school newspaper, Madame X, starts reporting on secrets only Jenny and her friends know. Jenny realizes that the elusive writer could only be a member of her group.

Cheat Sheet. 2008. 112 p. ISBN: 9780545013048pa. *MJ*
Two of Jenny's friends are finalists for top scores on the statewide history test challenge, but they are accused of cheating to get there. Jenny must decide what is the right thing to do.

P.S. I Really Like You. 2008. 112 p. ISBN: 9780545019422pa. *MJ*
While two of her friends are quarreling over an incident during a basketball game, Jenny is trying to figure out the identity of the secret admirer who has been sending her gifts and cards.

Who's Got Spirit. 2008. 112 p. ISBN: 9780545052573pa. *MJ*
When the popular crowd forms their own pep squad, Jenny and her friends decide to fight back by forming their own group, but when a costumed lion mascot shows up, nobody knows which team he belongs to.

Caught in the Web. 2009. 128 p. ISBN: 9780545092739pa. *MJ*
Jenny and her friends create a hit webcast, and the popular girls decide they must do one too, forcing the two shows to compete for the best ratings.

How the Pops Stole Christmas. 2009. 192 p. ISBN: 9780545197601pa. *MJ*

> Jenny's holidays don't look so happy and bright. She picks popular Dana for her secret Santa, she finds out her friend Sam won't be around for the holidays, and her friend Mark does not invite her to his New Year's Eve party.

Into the Woods. 2009. 128 p. ISBN: 9780545092753pa. *MJ*

> When Jenny and her friends Chloe and Sam are forced to share a cabin with the popular girls Addie and Dana at a science camp, Jenny and her friends must find a way to survive their time in the woods.

It's All Downhill from Here. 2009. 128 p. ISBN: 9780545052597pa. *MJ*

> Forced to hang out with popular Addie when Addie has to stay at Jenny's house during a major snowstorm, Jenny must find a way to make the best of a bad situation.

Wish Upon A Star. 2009. 112 p. ISBN: 9780545132701pa. *MJ*

> Popular Addie says she can get superstar pop singer Cody Tucker to perform at the school dance, and ticket sales go through the roof. When it is revealed that Addie was lying, it is up to Jenny to save the day.

Mechling, Lauren, and Laura Moser

<u>**Social Climber Series.**</u> Boston: Houghton Mifflin

> Mimi Shulman finds that popularity is not all she thought it was.

> *Best Friends • Cliques • Secrets • Rich People • Social Acceptance • Friendship*

The Rise and Fall of a Tenth-Grade Social Climber. 2005. 304 p. ISBN: 9780618555192pa. *S*

> When Mimi Shulman returns to New York to live with her dad after her parents separate, she makes a bet with her friend Sam that she can get the coolest girls in the tenth grade at the exclusive Baldwin School to accept her, which they do. Mimi soon finds that she really likes the girls, who are facing their own problems, even though she records the girls' secrets and keeps unflattering pictures of them in her diary. Shocked one day to find her musings published on the Internet, Mimi is humiliated and must make amends to all her friends.

All Q, No A: More Tales of a 10th-Grade Social Climber. 2006. 288 p. ISBN: 9780618663781pa. *S*

> Trying to make up to her friends after her diary was published on the Internet, Mimi Shulman is dealing with a crush on popular Max Roth, who does not notice her, and her divorced parents, who are moving on to new relationships. When her job on the school newspaper gets her an assignment to interview local artist Serge Ziff, Mimi is able to write a revealing article with the help of her friends. When the headmaster kills the story, Mimi must figure out how to deal with school politics and still maintain her tenuous social position.

Foreign Exposure: The Social Climber Abroad. 2007. 312 p. ISBN: 9780618663798pa. *S*

Visiting her mother in Berlin, sixteen-year-old Mimi finds herself burdened with a horrible baby-sitting job and a lack of understanding from her mother, so she heads off to London to be with her best friend Lily. There, Mimi finds an internship with a tabloid magazine and is launched into a world of late-night parties and gossip. Everything does not go as planned, and Mimi must deal with a variety of unusual situations to make it through the summer.

Morris, Taylor

Class Favorite. New York: Aladdin Paperbacks, 2007. 304 p. ISBN: 9781416935988pa. *MJ*

Eighth-grader Sara Thurman just wants to be popular. But when she becomes the brunt of endless jokes because it is revealed that she has started her period, she wears the same outfit as one of her teachers, and then destroys the cherished basketball from the school's only state championship win, things don't look so promising. Adjusting to her parents' separation, having a crush on a guy who is out of her league, and realizing her relationship with her best friend Arlene is on the rocks because she is sure it was she who told about her period, things look even worse. When Sara is given a great surprise at the end of the year, she learns it is loyalty and forgiveness that are important.

Growing Up • Friendship • Loyalty • Forgiveness • Betrayal • Coming-of-Age

Myracle, Lauren

The Fashion Disaster That Changed My Life. New York: Dutton Children's Books, 2005. 135 p. ISBN: 9780525472223; 9780142407172pa. *M*

When twelve-year-old Allison arrives at school not realizing her mother's underwear is clinging to her pant leg and the undesirable guy Jeremy won't let her forget it, Allison finds that she gains some of the recognition she has wanted when popular girl Rachel defends her. Her friend Katy, who stuck by her in the past, has now told cruel stories about her. Feeling that she is ditching her for the popular crowd, Allison must decide where she belongs as she deals with her own insecurities and feelings.

Social Acceptance • Friendship • Family • Diary Novel

Noel, Alyson

Art Geeks and Prom Queens. New York: St. Martin's Griffin, 2005. 226 p. ISBN: 9780312336363pa. *JS*

Having just moved from New York to Southern California, sixteen-year-old Rio has started making new friends in her AP art class. When cheerleader Kristi takes an interest in her, she dumps her other friends, and much to the delight of her former-model mother, she gets a designer makeover at the hands of her new friends. But soon Rio finds that she is becoming more popular than Kristi, and when things go terribly wrong in the sex-and-drugs scene of the popular crowd, she must learn how to be true to herself as she learns the true meaning of friendship.

Friendship • Cheerleaders • Private Schools • Trust • Revenge

Noel, Alyson

Kiss and Blog. New York: St. Martin's Griffin, 2007. 240 p. ISBN: 9780312355098pa. *JS*
> Winter and Sloane have worked all summer to become part of the popular crowd, but then Sloane becomes part of the group and quickly dumps her longtime friend. To get revenge, Winter blogs about the betrayal, but as she finds a new friend in sixteen-year-old Rey, the new waiter at her mother's '60s-themed restaurant, and takes a trip to New York to see her father and falls for an intern at an art gallery, Winter is able to grow up and find herself with a new group of friends.
>
> *Social Acceptance • Blogs • Revenge • Mother and Daughter*

Padian, Maria

Brett McCarthy: Work in Progress. New York: Alfred A. Knopf, 2008. 276 p. ISBN: 9780375846755. YALSA Best Books. *MJ*
> Fourteen-year-old soccer player Brett McCarthy faces changes when in eighth grade her best friend Diane gets interested in cheerleading and becomes friends with snotty Jeanne-Anne. When a telephone prank backfires and Jeanne-Anne blames everything on Brett, even though four girls were involved, Brett loses her temper and hits Jeanne-Anne. Suspended from school for her actions, Brett finds that she has lost all her social status and all hope of attracting hottie Bob Levesque. Things get even worse when Brett learns that her grandmother, Nonna, is battling pancreatic cancer. Brett must now find a way to redefine herself and learn how to deal with her problematic life.
>
> *Cancer • Loss • Friendship • Coming-of-Age*

Palmer, Robin

Geek Charming. New York: Speak, 2009. 338 p. ISBN: 9780142411223pa. *JS*
> Popular Dylan drops her expensive purse in the mall's fountain. She is sure that anyone would be happy to help her and is shocked to find that geeky Josh will only help her if she helps him. Making a documentary about popularity that he hopes will get him a much-needed scholarship to film school, Josh wants Dylan to be his star. As the two form a friendship, it is Josh who comes to her aid when her ex-boyfriend and her friends recognize her bad traits, sabotaging her popularity, and it is Dylan who learns what true friendship really is.
>
> *Films • Interpersonal Relations • High School*

Perez, Marlene

The Comeback. New York: Point, 2009. 208 p. ISBN: 9780545088077pa. *JS*
> Popular Sophie Donnelly is shocked when new girl Angie Vogel shows up stealing not only Sophie's starring role in her school's production of Shake-

speare's *The Taming of the Shrew* but her boyfriend as well. With her popularity in jeopardy, Sophie will do anything she must to get back the life that Angie has taken from her.

Social Acceptance • Romance

Rallison, Janette

Revenge of the Cheerleaders. New York: Walker, 2007. 247 p. ISBN: 9780802789990. *JS*
Seventeen-year-old cheerleader Chelsea has just been dumped by her foot-ball-player boyfriend, and the last thing she wants to deal with is her fif-teen-year-old Goth sister, Adrian, and her heavy-metal musician boyfriend, Rick, who decide to wage a war on Chelsea's popularity. When Rick fills his music with anti-popularity lyrics and forces one of her cheerleading routines to fail in front of the whole school, Chelsea decides that she can get her revenge out-performing Rick on the High School Idol show that will be televised from their town. But when Chelsea finds herself falling for a mysterious college student she meets at one of Rick's concerts, she soon finds that revenge is not always what you want it to be.

Dating • Cheerleaders • Revenge • Brothers • Sisters • Social Acceptance • Goth Culture

Roberts, Laura Peyton

The Queen of Second Place. New York: Delacorte Press, 2005. 256 p. ISBN: 9780385731621; 9780440238713pa. *J*
When she falls in love at first sight, Cassie Howard makes a plan to attract gor-geous Kevin Matthews when he transfers into her school. But first she must thwart her nemesis, Sterling Carter, who has plans to take Kevin to the school's Snow Ball Dance. Concocting a plan that involves plagiarism, lies, driving with-out a license, and running for the title of Snow Queen, Cassie's scheme backfires.

Sequel: *Queen B.* New York: Delacorte Press, 2006. 361 p. ISBN: 9780385731638; 9780440238720pa. *J*
Now that she was chosen as runner-up for the title of Snow Queen at the winter formal and she has a truly popular new boyfriend, fifteen-year-old Cassie Howard is certain that the popular girls will finally allow her into their elite social circle. But Sterling Carter, who is the leader of the popular girls, is determined to keep Cassie out, and having a brother who embarrasses her at parties isn't helping either. When the faculty adviser for the school's first talent show, a fund-raiser for cancer research, takes a leave of absence to care for her husband who is fighting cancer himself, Cassie is left in charge to bring things together. Through the pro-cess, Cassie is able to learn important lessons about herself.

Competition • Cliques • Dating • Anxiety • Interpersonal Relations • Friendship • Family

Ruditis, Paul

Drama Series. New York: Simon Pulse
Dedicated actor Bryan Stark and his friends face challenges while dealing with the problems and joys of being on the stage.

Gay Males • Actors and Actresses • Friendship • Drama • Musicals • Cliques • Secrets

The Four Dorothys. 2007. 256 p. ISBN: 9781416933915. *JS*

> Closeted gay student Bryan Stark chronicles the happenings of the week before opening night of the Orion Academy's production of the *Wizard of Oz*, which has an over-full cast with at least two actors for each role because of the interference of wealthy, influential parents. When the four students cast as the play's Dorothy start dropping out because of life-threatening allergic reactions, scandalous photos, and suspicious accidents, the remaining players must figure out just who is sabotaging the production.

Everyone's a Critic. 2007. 243 p. ISBN: 9781416933922. *JS*

> Gay teen Bryan Stark chronicles the two weeks during which he and his friends prepare monologues and scenes so they can compete for a coveted spot in the Hartley Blackstone Acting School at their summer drama camp, all the while dealing with personal and family problems as well as the unfair favoritism that the children of the rich and famous enjoy.

Show, Don't Tell. 2008. 232 p. ISBN: 9781416959052. *JS*

> When a Renaissance faire arrives in Malibu, Bryan Stark accepts the opportunity to act in their production, but as he gets involved, he begins to worry that the secret of his homosexuality has been discovered.

Entrances and Exits. 2008. 242 p. ISBN: 9781416959069. *JS*

> Hope has written a play for the fall One-Act Festival and is looking forward to producing it with her friends, until they start dealing with romantic problems that threaten to undermine the performance.

Scott, Kieran

Geek Magnet: A Novel in Five Acts. New York: G.P. Putnam's Sons, 2008. 308 p. ISBN: 9780399247606; 9780142414170pa. *JS*

> Junior K.J. Miller loves being the stage manager for her high school's theater production, even though it only seems to help her attract the wrong sort of geeky guys like All Hands Glen, who is always mentioning her large breasts, and dependable neighbor Fred. Wanting to get cute jock Cameron to notice her, K.J. is excited when popular Tama becomes her friend and promises to help K.J. get close to him. But when events show her that Tama and Cameron are not what she thought, K.J. is forced to figure out what matters most.

Dating • Social Acceptance • Musicals • Theater • Alcoholism

Scott, Kieran

I Was a Non-Blonde Cheerleader Series. New York: G.P. Putnam's Sons

> Nontypical cheerleader Annisa tries to be true to herself as she navigates the pitfalls of high school while trying to maintain complex friendships.

Cheerleaders • Social Acceptance • Friendship • Moving • Interpersonal Relations • Teamwork • Individuality • Sex Roles

I Was a Non-Blonde Cheerleader. 2005. 256 p. ISBN: 9780399242793; 9780142406410pa. YALSA Popular Paperbacks. *JS*

> When she falls for a popular girl's boyfriend, makes friends with a punk rebel, and breaks the cheerleading captain's nose when she hits her with a door, sophomore Annisa Gobrowski fails to make a good impression at her new school. Despite the cheerleaders' dislike for her, Annisa tries out for the cheerleading team. After she makes the team, things don't look good, since everyone else is blond and she is the only dark-haired girl. As she deals with pranks, unsupervised parties, and other crises, Annisa must learn about courage and friendship as she discovers how important it is to be true to oneself.

Brunettes Strike Back. 2006. 256 p. ISBN: 9780399244933; 9780142407783pa. *JS*

> Still not quite accepted by her teammates, Annisa is upset when they ask her to color her hair to match theirs. As she works to show her team just how dedicated she is to cheerleading and they all get ready for a national competition, Annisa must also deal with her affection for a boy whose ex-girlfriend is also on the squad.

A Non-Blonde Cheerleader in Love. 2007. 256 p. ISBN: 9780399244940; 9780142411865pa. *JS*

> When the squad decides to allow boys on their team, Annisa is excited for the opportunity to do more challenging stunts and for the chance to work with her boyfriend, Daniel. Then the girls find themselves pitted against the boys in a battle of the sexes, as each side pulls pranks on the other. Before the hijinks break up not only the team but Annisa's and Daniel's relationship, the team must learn how to work together.

Sheldon, Dyan

Confessions of a Teenage Drama Queen. Cambridge, MA: Candlewick Press, 1999. 272 p. ISBN: 9780763618483pa; (aud). YALSA Quick Picks. *J*

> Mary "Lola" Elizabeth Cep is devastated when her divorced mother forces the family to move from New York City to New Jersey. Facing the ups and downs of high school life, she embellishes her dramatic stories in an attempt to be accepted. When Lola challenges Carla Santini for the lead in the school play and wins the role, she finds herself locked in a power struggle with Carla as the two do everything they can to outdo each other. When Lola drags her quiet friend Ella Gerard to New York for the last concert of her favorite rock group, the girls trek through rough neighborhoods and have a run-in with the police before they end up at the exclusive after-party for the drunken rock group. Feeling triumphant over their success, the girls must now convince Carla and her friends that Lola has finally topped anything that Carla could do.

<u>Sequel:</u> *My Perfect Life.* Cambridge, MA: Candlewick Press, 2002. 201 p. ISBN: 9780763618391; 9780763624361pa. *JS*

> When Carla Santini decides to run for student council president, Lola Cep can't let her win and launches a campaign with her best friend Ella as the candidate to beat. For Ella, the idea of giving speeches and being in the spotlight makes her sick, but when Carla's political strategy gets nasty and she spreads rumors that Ella's mother is an alcoholic, Ella can't take it anymore. She must overcome her timidity to stand up for what is right.

Sequel: *Confessions of a Hollywood Star.* Cambridge, MA: Candlewick Press, 2006. 208 p. ISBN: 9780763630751; 9780763634087pa. *S*

The summer after high school graduation, Lola Cep learns that a major movie is going to be filmed in her New Jersey suburb, and she plans to win a part, boasting that she has already been cast. When her nemesis Carla Santini learns of her supposed part, she, too, gets in on the act and convinces her father to house the stars of the movie, an act that not only gets her onto the set but wins her a part. With Carla having taken away her part, Lola now must not only win a role in the movie but earn something that is better than what Carla has.

Interpersonal Relations • High School • Competition • Success • Actors and Actresses • Films

Spinelli, Jerry

Stargirl. New York: Alfred A. Knopf, 2000. 176 p. ISBN: 9780679886372; 9780375822339pa; (aud). YALSA Best Books. *JS*

Susan "Stargirl" Caraway takes Mica High School in Arizona by storm with her unusual clothing choices and her even more unusual behavior, including carrying around her pet rat and serenading kids with her ukulele on their birthdays right in the middle of the cafeteria. When she single-handedly stirs up school spirit, Stargirl attracts a following. Among this group is sixteen-year-old Leo, who is attracted to her and the good works she does. Soon the two get together, but Stargirl's popularity is short-lived. She is shunned, and Leo's social standing falls along with hers. Confused and unable to handle being an outcast, Leo turns his back on Stargirl, an act he only fully comes to understand as he looks back in time.

Sequel: *Love, Stargirl.* New York: Alfred A. Knopf, 2007. 288 p. ISBN: 9780375813757; 9780375856440pa; (aud). *JS*

After boyfriend Leo Borlock dumps her, fifteen-year-old Susan "Stargirl" Caraway is trying to make a place for herself when she leaves Arizona and moves to Pennsylvania. Striving to stay true to herself and overcome her loneliness, Stargirl makes new friends, including talkative five-year-old Dootsies, angry Alvina, agoraphobic divorceé Betty Lou, and developmentally disabled Arnold. When a new boy, amiable thief Perry Delloplane, enters her life, Stargirl finds that she is able to move beyond the sadness she feels.

Homeschooling • Eccentricities • Diaries • Diary Novel • Love • Friendship • Individuality • Social Acceptance

Steele, J. M.

The Market. New York: Hyperion, 2008. 328 p. ISBN: 9781423100133; 9781423100164pa. *S*

High school senior Kate Winthrop finds that she is ranked number 71 out of 140 in the stock market game that ranks the school's female seniors, allowing insiders to buy and sell investments in the girls with the number one girl winning $25,000 at the end of the year. Becoming addicted to the game, Kate, with the help of her friends Dev and Carrie, decides to invest $500 and then remake her image so she can claim the prize. As she transforms, wearing short skirts and dying her hair blond, Kate loses her friends and gets enmeshed in a love triangle, trying to choose between hottie Will and introverted guitar player Jack. However, Kate soon discovers that being popular is not all it's cracked up to be and finds that being part of the in-crowd is not what is important in life.

Social Acceptance • *Social Status* • *Friendship*

Vail, Rachel

You, Maybe: The Profound Asymmetry of Love in High School. New York: Harper Collins, 2006. 208 p. ISBN: 9780060569174; 9780060569198pa. *J*

Self-confident sophomore Josie, who works as a clown at children's parties, follows a careful policy of not getting too involved with any one boy by hooking up with neighbor and longtime friend Michael and popular boy Carson at the same time. Carson shows more than casual interest, and Josie finds herself falling for his charms. She begins to take a new interest in her appearance and finds herself dressing to impress despite the advice of her friends, who are trying to discourage her because of Carson's reputation as a player. Encouraged by her mother, Josie joins the popular crowd on a weekend trip where she finally is able to rediscover her true self.

Friendship • *Cliques* • *Social Acceptance* • *First Love* • *Peer Pressure*

Walde, Christine

The Candy Darlings. Boston: Graphia, 2006. 310 p. ISBN: 9780618589692pa. *JS*

Moving to a new private school after her terminally ill mother passes away, an unnamed teen girl finds that she is now an outcast from the popular crowd and finds her only friend in Megan Chalmers, a girl who eats nothing but candy. Joining with Megan against their school's ruling mean girls, the teen finds an outlet in Megan's outrageously bizarre stories. But when the mean girls ramp up their bullying and Megan begins to disappear for days at a time, the girl must find a way to cope with her life as she develops her own identity.

Moving • *Private Schools* • *Bullies and Bullying* • *Friendship* • *Mother-Separated Families* • *Father and Daughter*

Walsh, Marissa

A Field Guide to High School. New York: Delacorte Press, 2007. 144 p. ISBN: 9780385734103; 9780385734110pa. *J*

High school freshman Andie discovers a book, left for her by her perfect sister Claire, who has recently left for college. It is filled with wisdom on how to navigate the treacherous landscape of her private high school. Claire's personal stories of her four years at school shed light on topics such as the school's physical facilities, personal fashion choices, and the ins and outs of various cliques. The book gives Andie a better understanding of her sister and allows her, and her best friend Bess, to face their anxieties and fears about high school.

Sisters • *Friendship* • *Cliques* • *Private Schools* • *Advice*

Ziegler, Jennifer

How Not to Be Popular. New York: Delacorte Press, 2008. 339 p. ISBN: 9780385734653. *S*

> Seventeen-year-old Sugar Magnolia "Maggie" Dempsey is tired of her hippie parents' nomadic ways, which have resulted in her never living in a place for more than eight months. Maggie is especially tired of the pain of leaving behind the people she has gotten close to, and so on this new move to Austin, Texas, she vows to get close to no one and avoid friendships and love connections at all costs. But when her bizarre outfits and good works designed to make her unpopular actually attract a group of school nerds as well as a potential boyfriend, Maggie must decide how to deal with the friendships her actions have created.

Moving • Peer Pressure • Hippies • Social Acceptance

Student Elections

Morris, Taylor

Total Knockout: Tale of an Ex-Class President. New York: Aladdin Mix, 2008. 265 p. ISBN: 9781416935995pa. *MJ*

> Lucia Latham has been class president for the past two years. At the start of eighth grade, she is ready for a third term and asks her friend Melanie to run for president against her. Knowing that she will lose, Lucia plans to convince the student council to appoint Melanie as vice president, and then with their friend Cooper, who is running uncontested in the position of secretary, certain to win, she can create the perfect presidency. When the school newspaper runs an article revealing her scheme to purchase new vending machines and asks for her resignation, Lucia must face the shame and watch as Melanie becomes president. With her parents stressed over financial considerations at home, Lucia finds things further complicated when she starts having feelings for Cooper, but he seems to be interested in Melanie. Lucia must finally face her insecurities and embrace her newly strengthened self-confidence.

Student Elections • Middle School • Friendship

Rallison, Janette

All's Fair in Love, War, and High School. New York: Walker, 2003. 183 p. ISBN: 9780802788740; 9780802777256pa. *JS*

> After she fails the SATs, cheerleader Samantha's college prospects are dismal, so she comes up with a plan to run for student government to make her applications look better. Her fellow cheerleaders are behind her, but she knows she must also enlist the help of others. She turns to her eighth-grade friend Logan, but he only agrees to help if she can go for two weeks without insulting someone. As she tries to curb her tongue, Samantha must also deal with the dirty politics that the campaign brings, but in the end, she is able to make new friends and learn important truths about herself.

Cheerleaders • SAT • Bets • Friendship • High School • Proms

Rallison, Janette

How to Take the Ex Out of Ex-Boyfriend. New York: G. P. Putnam's Sons, 2007. 272 p. ISBN: 9780399246173; 9780142412695pa. *JS*

Even though she does not really like his snotty friends, sixteen-year-old Giovanna knows she is lucky to have popular Jesse as a boyfriend, especially since she has a criminal record for stealing the dead frogs they were supposed to use in biology class. Her twin brother, Dante, decides to represent the average guy and run against the popular Wilson for student body president, and Giovanna is devastated when Jesse agrees to be Wilson's campaign manager. Seeing themselves so clearly on different sides, she decides that the only solution is to break up with Jesse and throw her hat in with Dante's efforts. When she realizes what a mistake she has made, she needs to campaign not only to get her brother elected but to win Jesse back as well.

Dating • Popularity • Brothers • Sisters • High School

Cheating

Cappo, Nan Willard

Cheating Lessons. New York: Atheneum Books for Young Readers, 2002. 234 p. ISBN: 9780786253258; 9780689860188pa. *JS*

Training for the Classics Bowl state championships, high school junior Bernadette is looking forward to facing their main rival, a team from Pinehurst Academy, a private school. Training the Wickham High School team for the knowledge quizzes and debates they will face is their British teacher, Mr. Malory, who along with the rest of the team understands how important winning is because doing so means status for their small working-class school and a $10,000 college scholarship for each member of the team. Soon, however, Bernadette realizes that someone has been leaking the questions and fixing the scores, and she is shocked to realize that Mr. Malory is the culprit. Wrestling with her conscience, Bernadette must decide if she can go along with the deception or must tell the truth.

Ethics • High School

Cheva, Cherry

She's So Money. New York: HarperTeen, 2008. 290 p. ISBN: 9780061288555; 9780061288531pa. *S*

Left in charge of her family's Thai restaurant when her parents leave for five days, seventeen-year-old Maya lands in a great deal of trouble when the restaurant is fined for health hazards. Needing to earn lots of money fast, Maya plots with bad boy Camden King to do his homework for him. When their idea becomes a thriving business and more and more students become involved, things blow up in their faces.

High School • Ethics • Money Making • Honesty • Family • Coming-of-Age

Fredericks, Mariah

Crunch Time. New York: Atheneum Books for Young Readers, 2006. 317 p. ISBN: 9780689869389. *S*

Juniors at a private Manhattan high school, Leo, Max, Daisy, and Jane, form a private study group to help them prepare for the SAT. From different social groups and backgrounds, they all share the pressure of doing well on the test and getting into college. As they study, they form friendships and deal with romantic entanglements. When they learn that a high-scoring student was paid by someone else to take the exam and will not reveal the cheater's name, everyone suspects the group, and the teens must deal with rumors as they try to withstand the demands of the college admissions process.

Friendship • SAT • Competition • Basketball • Ethics

Koss, Amy Goldman

The Cheat. New York: Dial Books, 2003. 176 p. ISBN: 9780803727946; 9780142401286pa. *JS*

When unpopular Jake tries to impress popular Sarah by giving her a copy of the answers from last year's geography midterm from his sister's files, Sarah, Dan, and Robb use them to cheat. The students realize too late that the exam has changed, and when the teacher figures out they tried to cheat with a previous exam, the three students land in big trouble. Along with their troubles at home, the trio must decide if they will tattle on their friends as they deal with all of the unintended consequences of their actions.

High Schools • Ethics

Lichtman, Wendy

Do the Math: Secrets, Lies, and Algebra. New York: Greenwillow Books, 2007. 183 p. ISBN: 9780061229572pa. *MJ*

Tess has always believed that math can help you understand everything in life, but when she enters the eighth grade and a cheating scandal surfaces, she finds that both math and life are more complicated than she thought.

Sequel: *The Writing on the Wall.* New York: Greenwillow Books, 2008. 216 p. ISBN: 9780061229589. *MJ*

When numeric graffiti appears on a wall near her school, eighth-grader Tess, along with the help of her friends Sammy and Miranda, uses her mathematical skills to figure out how it may be connected to a recent classroom fire while revealing secrets about a classmate and dealing with a bullying classmate.

Self-Discovery • Honesty • Gossiping and Gossips • Friendship • Best Friends • Secrets • Middle School

Steele, J. M.

The Taker. New York: Hyperion Books, 2006. 352 p. ISBN: 9780786849307; 9780786849314pa. *JS*

Driven by her parents' high expectations, Carly Biels plans to go to Princeton just like her father, but when her SAT scores fall short, the Ivy League looks out of her reach. When a mysterious message arrives promising to fix her score when she takes the test again, Carly accepts the offer and its conditions that she study hard so as not to raise suspicions and perform a favor at a later date to pay for the service. Engaging the services of geeky neighbor, Ronald Gross, to tutor her, Carly's skills improve through legitimate means, and she beings to be haunted by her choice to cheat. When her best friend and editor of the school's newspaper begins to report on rumors of a cheating ring, Carly must decide what is the right thing to do.

SAT • High School • Ethics • Tutoring • Honesty • Eccentricities

Wasserman, Robin

Hacking Harvard. New York: Simon Pulse, 2007. 320 p. ISBN: 9781416936336pa. *S*

When their Harvard freshman friend Schwarz bets high school seniors Max and Eric that they can't find a person who Harvard would never consider and then to get him admitted without accessing the university's computer system, the boys find pot-smoking bully Clay Porter and change his academic records to make him into a brilliant artist. But when other hackers begin to bet on the outcome of the plan, the boys find themselves in way over their heads when they blackmail an admissions counselor and find that someone is trying to sabotage them so they will be caught.

College • Bets • High School • Friendship

Prom Night

Anderson, Laurie Halse

Prom. New York: Viking, 2005. 224 p. ISBN: 9780670059744; 9780142405703pa. *S*

High school senior Ashley is ambivalent about lots of things, including her family, her high school dropout boyfriend, her lack of college prospects, and her job, which requires her to serve pizza in a rat costume. But the thing Ashley is most ambivalent about is the prom—that is, until a math teacher steals all the money set aside for the dance and she finds herself joining in to save the prom because it means a lot to her best friend Natalia. Soon finding out that she really does care about the cause she has been working for, Ashley discovers that her commitment to her life and her future has also changed through the process.

Dating • High School • Friendship

Bradley, Alex

24 Girls in 7 Days. New York: Dutton, 2005. 265 p. ISBN: 9780525473695; 9780142405437pa. YALSA Quick Picks. *S*

> Rejected by the love of his life and without a date two weeks before the prom, Jack Grammar is drawn into a scheme by his two best friends, Natalie and Percy, to find him a girl by posting an online personal ad in the school's newspaper. In seven days, Jack dates and rejects many possible prom dates, but it is his mysterious online pen pal who intrigues him the most.

Dating • Friendship • High School

Brian, Kate

Fake Boyfriend. New York: Simon & Schuster Books for Young Readers, 2007. 262 p. ISBN: 9781416913672; 9781416913689pa. *JS*

> After Isabelle is dumped once again by her cheating boyfriend Shawn right before the prom, her two friends Vivi and Lane enact an elaborate plan to ensure that "Izzy" moves on with her life. Creating a MySpace page for dreamy imaginary boy Brandon and convincing Vivi's brother Marshall to act as the man behind the online persona, things seem to be heading in the right direction until Izzy actually wants to meet Brandon. The girls find Jonathan, who agrees to be the fake boyfriend, but when Vivi finds herself falling for him, the whole scheme blows up, and the friends have to find a way to fix everything.

Dating • Boyfriends • High School

Dower, Laura

Rewind. New York: Scholastic, 2006. 243p. ISBN: 9780439703406. *S*

> When high school senior Cady Sanchez sees Lucas, the guy she likes, slap his date Hope on prom night, she begins to delve into what happened before this event to the guy she likes and the girl who used to be her friend. As secrets are revealed, the complex events and choices that lead to one fateful event truly affect all of the participants.

Musicians • Dating • High School • Secrets • Betrayal

Ferraro, Tina

Top Ten Uses for an Unworn Prom Dress. New York: Delacorte Press, 2007. 240 p. ISBN: 9780385733687pa. *JS*

> After Rod "Rascal" Pasqual invites sophomore Nicolette Antonovich to the junior prom, she finds the perfect dress. But when Rascal's girlfriend comes back to town, Nicolette finds herself dateless with no way to use the dress. As her family's financial situation worsens and Nicoletee contemplates what to do to help, she finds that her best friend's older brother, Jared, cannot only help her to manage their money but might be the answer to her romantic problems as well.

Friendship • Family Problems • Dating • High School • Coming-of-Age

Kemp, Kristen

The Dating Diaries. New York: Push, 2004. 266 p. ISBN: 9780439622981pa. *JS*

Just before prom, her boyfriend of five years, Paul, dumps her, and Katie James resolves to date ten guys in five weeks to make up for the time she lost with Paul. Plans don't go as expected, however, and Katie soon learns that she can be a complete person without a boyfriend.

Dating • Breaking Up • Romance

Koja, Kathe

Kissing the Bee. New York: Farrar, Straus & Giroux, 2007. 128 p. ISBN: 9780374399382; (aud). *JS*

As she prepares her senior science project on the life cycle of bees, Dana Parsons is also dealing with her self-absorbed best friend, Avra. As their masquerade prom approaches, Dana tries to help Avra prepare costumes for her and her boyfriend Emil. However, when Emil reveals that it is really Dana that he loves, she must finally deal with the long-repressed feelings she has held for him as she tries to figure out what these changes mean for their group dynamics.

Friendship • Romance • First Love

Le Ny, Jeanine

Once upon a Prom Series. New York: Point

Best friends Jordan, Tara, and Nisha prepare to attend their senior prom, but along the way, they face challenges with friends, family, and romantic relationships.

Best Friends • Popularity

Dream. 2008. 230 p. ISBN: 9780545028158pa. *S*

Best friends Jordan, Tara, and Nisha are looking forward to their senior prom. Jordan is up for prom queen, Tara is on the prom planning committee, and Nisha is looking forward to spending the evening with her wonderful boyfriend. Things do not go as smoothly as planned when Jordan realizes it is time to focus more on grades than fun, Tara can't find a date, and Nisha's old-fashioned Indian parents prevent her from going. The girls must work out their problems if they are to have the best night of their lives.

Dress. 2008. 240 p. ISBN: 9780545031813pa. *S*

One week before prom, Tara may have found a date, but she must make geeky school mascot, Victor, into the perfect boy before everything can be just right. Jordan is struggling with her conflicting emotions between the boy she has just begun to notice, Shane, and her longtime boyfriend, Nate. Nisha is caught when her parents set her up with Raj, a good Indian boy whom they approve of, and she can't figure out a way to go to prom with Brian, the boy she loves. With the clock ticking down, the girls must work through their problems if they are going to have the dates and the prom they have dreamed of.

Date. 2008. 240 p. ISBN: 9780545031820pa. *S*

Time is ticking down before the Prom, and Nisha still can't tell her parents she would rather go with Brian, all the while dealing with Brian's pressure to come and meet his parents. Tara's relationship with Victor is progressing, but with Jordan no longer speaking to her boyfriend Nate, and with the two girls fighting, Jordan decides that she will just forgo the prom. Despite the complications, the girls' strong friendship is able to overcome all the problems they have been facing, and they have a wonderful and surprising prom night.

Nelson, Blake

Prom Anonymous. New York: Viking, 2006. 272 p. ISBN: 9780670059454; 9780142407455pa. *JS*

Convinced that she should attend prom with her two oldest girlfriends, Jace and Chloe, Laura jumps into planning the perfect night. Chloe has little interest in finding a dress or even a date, so Laura takes it upon herself to set her up. Jace wants to get a date with the cute new tennis player but can't find the guts to ask him. In the meantime, Laura's sexually active relationship with her boyfriend is falling apart. In the end, the girls find out that prom night is about more than just dates as they all experience an evening that helps them each to figure out who they are.

Dating • Drinking • Coming-of-Age

Palmer, Robin

Cindy Ella. New York: Speak, 2008. 264 p. ISBN: 9780142403921pa. *J*

Fed up with the constant coverage of the prom, sophomore Cindy sends an anti-prom letter to the school newspaper. The students, including her twin stepsisters Ashley and Britney, are appalled. With only her best friends India and Malcolm standing by her, Cindy is dismayed to find out that even they will be attending the prom. It is not until her instant-messaging friend's identity is revealed that she finds that going to prom might not be so bad after all.

Popularity • Blended Families • Peer Pressure

Sloan, Brian

A Really Nice Prom Mess. New York: Simon & Schuster Books, 2005. 266 p. ISBN: 9780689874383; 9781416953890pa. YALSA Quick Picks; YALSA Popular Paperbacks. *S*

If he has to go, Cameron would rather attend the prom with his football-star boyfriend, Shane Wilson, but since Shane wants to keep their relationship a secret, he is going with gorgeous Virginia instead. When Virginia figures out that Cameron is gay and throws up at Shane's pre-prom party after she drowns her sorrows in alcohol, things spiral out of control. When Cameron gets caught kissing Shane's female date, Shane socks him in the stomach, and Cameron runs off to a gay bar where he teams up with a drug-dealing waiter. By the morning after the prom, Cameron has had lots of adventures and has learned a lot about himself.

Gay Males • Homosexuality • Coming Out • Interpersonal Relations • Dating • Romance

Boarding and Private Schools

Barnholdt, Lauren

Four Truths and a Lie. New York: Aladdin Mix, 2008. 265 p. ISBN: 9781416935049. *MJ*

Hiding a secret, eighth-grader Scarlett is sent to an all-girl boarding school where she fears that everyone will find out what she is concealing. When her pen pal from a neighboring boys school begins a game where he will send statements of four truths and one lie, it is up to Scarlett to figure out what the lie is or risk the revelation of her secret to the entire school.

Secrets • Divorce

Baskin, Nora Raleigh

In the Company of Crazies. New York: HarperCollins, 2006. 176 p. ISBN: 9780060596071. *MJ*

Asked to keep a journal by her teacher at Mountain Laurel, an alternative boarding school in a old country farm house, thirteen-year-old Mia Singer records her experiences. Sent to the school after she withdrew from her friends and family, was caught shoplifting, and lied to her former school's secretary, Mia must deal with six boys with various problems who also reside at the school. Working through the trauma caused by the death of a former classmate and her complicated relationship with her own mother, Mia learns through her experiences to deal with the challenges life brings.

Shoplifting • Alienation • Diary Novel

Bathurst, Bella

Special. Boston: Houghton Mifflin, 2002. 309 p. ISBN: 9780618263271. *MJ*

On a school field trip to the English countryside, thirteen-year-old Jules and her boarding-school classmates are forced into the fresh air with pointless activities and exercise by two teachers whom the girls dislike. All the girls are dealing with their own troubles, including anorexia and addiction, and they are jealous of one another and bitter about life. Sneaking out at night, they find a group of guys to hang out with, and their destructive behavior winds up compounding the already tragic lives of each girl.

Anorexia • Addiction • Friendship • Coming-of-Age

Flinn, Alex

Breaking Point. New York: Harper Tempest, 2002. 241 p. ISBN: 9780066238470; 9780064473712pa. YALSA Quick Picks. *J*

When his mother gets a job as a secretary at an elite private school, Paul Richmond enrolls there but finds that he is not accepted by the rich kids. Rejected by and unable to contact his estranged military father, Paul finds that his mother relies on him for a lot of emotional support. When Charlie Goode, one of the most popular kids, seems to want to be his friend, Paul is flattered and joins in his adventures despite Charlie and his groups' abuse. When Charlie's escapades become more and more illegal and dangerous, Paul is set up as the scapegoat and is sent to prison because of his involvement.

Friendship • High School • Rich People • Social Acceptance • Military

Franklin, Emily

Principles of Love Series. New York: New American Library

Love Bukowski deals with life, love, and family during her time at the private boarding school Hadley Hall and during a semester abroad in London.

Music • Romance • Travel • Coming-of-Age

Principles of Love. 2005. 256 p. ISBN: 9780451215178pa. *JS*

On her first day at her new private school where her father is the new principal, Love Bukowski falls for gorgeous Robinson "Rob" Hall. But he already has a serious girlfriend, Lila, who soon becomes Love's good friend. When the two break up, Love must decide if she should take a chance with Rob, or if the anonymous musician, DrakeFan, whom she e-mails, or the sweet and talented Josh, with whom she spends so much time, would be the match for her.

Piece, Love, & Happiness. 2005. 214 p. ISBN: 9780451216663pa. *JS*

Distracted by the boys she met over summer, Love must face a new school year with her Aunt Mable and her dad acting preoccupied, her former friends forming fast friendships with the evil Lindsay Parrish, all the while playing host to the new exchange student from London, Arabella Piece.

Love from London. 2006. 244 p. ISBN: 9780451217738pa. *JS*

Now studying at the London Academy of Drama and Music, Love is attracted to an unattainable boy. Dealing with the regular problems related to love and school, she must also deal with the problems of her father's new girlfriend and the revelation of her Aunt Mable's breast cancer.

All You Need Is Love. 2006. 256 p. ISBN: 9780451219619pa. *JS*

Now back at boarding school, Love is missing London and dealing with the lack of communication from her British boyfriend as she tries to help her Aunt Mable fight cancer.

Summer of Love. 2007. 256 p. ISBN: 9780451220400pa. *JS*

Ready for a summer on Martha's Vineyard running her Aunt Mable's cafe with her best friend Arabella, Love is trying to decide about her future while following some mysterious clues that will reveal secrets about her mother's identity and her hidden family history.

Labor of Love. 2007. 256 p. ISBN: 9780451222114pa. *JS*

Finding that her mother, who has kept her identity a secret, is on Martha's Vineyard, Love must return from Los Angeles where she met with her half-sister. But at home she does not find what she expected, and she also must decide between her ex-boyfriend who has suddenly returned and current boyfriend Charlie, who is struggling to please his own parents.

Lessons in Love. 2008. 272 p. ISBN: 9780451223098pa. *JS*

During her senior year at Hadley Hall, Love must deal with evil Lindsay Parrish's rules as head monitor while trying to sort out her feeling for her mom; her boyfriend Charlie, who has gone back to Harvard; and her ex-boyfriend Jacob, who will only give her the cold shoulder.

Lockhart, E.

The Disreputable History of Frankie Landau-Banks. New York: Hyperion, 2008. 352 p. ISBN: 9781410414397; 9780786838196pa; (aud). School Library Journal Best Books; Michael L. Printz Honor Books; YALSA Best Books; Teens Top Ten. *J*

When sheltered outsider Frankie Landau-Banks catches the eye of senior Matthew Livingston at the beginning of her sophomore year, she is excited to learn that he is the leader of an all-male secret society in their school called the Loyal Order of the Basset Hounds, just like her father once was. When Frankie realizes that no matter how much time she spends with Matt she will never really be part of the group, she wrests control of it from Matt as she sends the boys on a series of school pranks through e-mails and letters. When her involvement in the pranks is revealed and Matt and his friends are angry, Frankie learns that it is important to be true to oneself.

Social Classes • Friendship • Loyalty • Betrayal • Dating • Coming-of-Age

Marchetta, Melina

Jellicoe Road. New York: HarperTeen, 2008. 432 p. ISBN: 9780061431838; 9781742143651 pa; (aud). Michael L. Printz Award; YALSA Best Books. *J*

Abandoned by her mother when she was eleven, Taylor Markham is now the leader of an underground community of three school gangs that engage in mock war games to control a constantly changing territory. When Taylor finds herself attracted to Jonah Griggs, rival leader of the Cadets gang, and when her housemother Hannah disappears, she begins a quest that leads her to discover a book that reveals the history of the gang rivalry as well as some important secrets about her past.

Abandonment • Gangs • Secrets • Australia

Marchetta, Melina

Looking for Alibrandi. New York: Orchard Books, 1999. 250 p. ISBN: 9780531301425; 9781876584009pa; (aud). YALSA Best Books. *S*

Seventeen-year-old Josephine "Josie" Alibrandi is torn between the norms, traditions, and experiences that make up her life. At her Catholic girls school, she feels out of place among her rich classmates, and within her traditional Italian community, she faces prejudice since she is the illegitimate child of an unwed mother. During her senior year, her absent father returns, and Josie must work out her feelings for him while also dealing with her feelings for the two boys in her life, respectable but unhappy John Barton and wild and uninhibited Jacob Coote.

Enduring tragedy, defining relationships, and unearthing family secrets helps Josie to see herself in new ways as she learns to take charge of her life

Catholic Schools • *Family* • *Father and Daughter* • *Australia*

Zindel, Lizabeth

The Secret Rites of Social Butterflies. New York: Viking Children's Books, 2008. 287 p. ISBN: 9780670062171; 9780142413890pa. *S*

Forced to move to Manhattan when her parents separate, Maggie Wishnick begins her senior year at an all-girl private school, Berkley Prep, where she soon becomes initiated into a group of wealthy, popular girls who call themselves the Revelers. The group's goal is to collect gossip about their classmates and record it on the walls of their secret room. Maggie begins to have second thoughts about the group's purpose, but she betrays a friend with a piece of gossip that prevents her from winning an important academic prize. Then the room is discovered, and Maggie learns some important lessons about trust, honesty, and friendship.

Gossiping and Gossips • *Cliques* • *Rich People* • *Family Problems*

1

2

3

4

5

6

7

8

9

10

11

12

Chapter 5

Getting a Job

Working for a paycheck is often one of the fundamental aspects of an adolescent's daily life. Employment can provide an important basis for the development of teens' expectations of responsibility and independence that shapes their ability to engage in future adult roles. Working also allows adolescents to develop interpersonal and communication skills as they encounter a variety of people and learn the importance of teamwork. The books listed in this chapter deal with the complexities of working life. Working for an eccentric boss, for your own family, or even owning your own business are all jobs that are open to adolescents. While babysitting may not be as glamorous as having an internship for a celebrity, there is always work to be done, and chances are there are adolescents available to do it.

Bauer, Joan

Rules of the Road. New York: G. P. Putnam's Sons, 1998. 201 p. ISBN: 9780399231407; 9780698118287pa. YALSA 100 Best Books; YALSA Best Books; YALSA Quick Picks; ALA Notable Children's Books; School Library Journal Best Books; YALSA Popular Paperbacks. *JS*

> Jenna Boller, at five foot eleven, is a social outsider. She loves selling shoes at one of the Gladstones' shoe stores, a place where she truly belongs. When her alcoholic father shows up, she snaps up the opportunity to drive the seventy-three-year-old owner of the chain, Mrs. Gladstone, from Chicago to Texas for a stockholders' meeting. Visiting stores along the way, Jenna discovers that Mrs. Gladstone's son is engineering a takeover, and it falls to Jenna to stop him.

Sequel: ***Best Foot Forward.*** New York: G. P. Putnam's Sons, 2005. 208 p. ISBN: 9780399234743; 9780142406908pa. *JS*

> Jenna Boller's life is complicated. Assisting Mrs. Gladstone with the merger between Gladstone Shoes and Shoe Warehouse, Jenna is also trying to train former juvenile delinquent Tanner Cobb to sell shoes. With all this going on, she is also trying to work out her feelings toward her father at Al-Anon meetings and working to get a date with Charlie Duran. Failing to notice that Mrs. Gladstone's son is embezzling and cutting costs by outsourcing labor overseas and thus creating a vastly inferior product, things get even more complicated as Jenna works to restore honor to the Gladstone name.

Alcoholism • Travel • Business • Shoplifting • Employment • Honesty • Father and Daughter

Beaudoin, Sean

Going Nowhere Faster. New York: Little, Brown, 2007. 240 p. ISBN: 9780316014151; 9780316014168pa. *S*

> Former child prodigy chess champion Stan Smith is now seventeen years old and is working as an underpaid video store clerk. Enabled by his hippie parents, Stan is unable to take control of any of the school or social responsibilities in his life. Writing film treatments and yearning to get together with Ellen Rigby distracts Stan from his pathetic life. But when Stan is held under suspicion for some vandalism to the video store, he must grow up and take control of his life.
>
> *Eccentricities* • *Employment* • *Chess* • *Coming-of-Age*

Bowers, Laura

Beauty Shop for Rent: . . . Fully Equipped, Inquire Within. Orlando, FL: Harcourt, 2007. 336 p. ISBN: 9780152057640. *JS*

> Abbey is determined to be absolutely self-sufficient and become a millionaire by age thirty-five. Being raised by her grandmother, who owns a beauty parlor in rural Maryland, Abbey has learned a lot about life from the clients and is determined to make her own way and avoid all the romantic mistakes that seemingly every female in her family made. But when Gena takes over the parlor and transforms it into a retro-spa and her longtime friendship with Mitch threatens to become romantic, Abbey must deal with changes as she embraces the opportunity to learn new things and resolve her own conflicted emotions over her mother's abandonment and lies.
>
> *Grandmothers* • *Abandonment* • *Ambition* • *Beauty Shops* • *Employment*

Caletti, Deb

The Fortunes of Indigo Skye. New York: Simon & Schuster Books for Young Readers, 2008. 298 p. ISBN: 9781410409461; 9781416910084pa. YALSA Best Books. *S*

> High school senior Indigo Skye works mornings at Carrera's diner in Seattle where she gets to know the group of quirky regulars and likes to judge what people are like by what they eat for breakfast. Things change when a well-dressed stranger comes into the restaurant, orders a cup of coffee, and then gives her $2.5 million as a tip. The pressure of the money becomes too much as Indigo changes, turning her back on her longtime boyfriend, her family, and her friends at the diner. Realizing the perils of wealth, Indigo tracks down the man and goes to Hawaii to return the money, and on the trip Skye experiences unexpected changes and growth.
>
> *Wealth* • *Waitresses* • *Single Parent* • *Employment*

Clark, Catherine

Frozen Rodeo: Or a Summer on Ice. New York: HarperCollins, 2002. 304 p. ISBN: 9780060090708; 9780064473859pa. *S*

Also titled: *Better Latte than Never.* New York: HarperTeen, 2008. 320 p. ISBN: 9780061367144pa. *S*

Daughter of a former figure skater, seventeen-year-old Peggy Fleming is facing a boring summer since she destroyed her family's car and must work selling coffee at a gas station to pay back her parents for the damage. In addition, summer school French lessons where the regular teacher goes missing and babysitting her three younger siblings, Dorothy, Torvill, and Dean, create a bleak outlook. In her little free time, Peggy rollerblades in a local parking-lot hangout and checks out the boys with her friend Charlotte. But Peggy does have some excitement when she is able to foil a robbery caper and things change at home.

High School • Brothers • Sisters • Ice Skating • Dating • Employment

Corbet, Robert

Shelf Life. New York: Walker, 2005. 184 p. ISBN: 9780802789594. *JS*

The lives of employees of a grocery store all intertwine as their home and school lives are affected by their work life and they all try to reach their dreams. Employee-of the-month Louisa wants to be a nurse but struggles with her dysfunctional home life. Dropout Adam, who wanted to get fired the first day, is now trying to shape up his life so he can attract Louisa. Best friends Jared and Dylan just goof off and play lots of practical jokes. Dealing with customers and their managers, the teens become a team as they build loyalty and friendship with one another.

Employment • Family Problems • Romance • Australia

Esckilsen, Erik E.

The Last Mall Rat. Boston: Houghton Mifflin, 2003. 182 p. ISBN: 9780618234172; 9780618608966pa. *J*

Too young to get a job officially, fifteen-year-old Mitch Grant finds a unique way to make money when a shoe salesman at the mall hires him to harass and intimidate rude customers. When the idea catches on with other mall employees, Mitch creates a thriving business and hires his friends. The scare tactics they use are hands off until Mitch's friend Jimmy punches a customer, and the adults and authorities want to stop them. Supported by his political activist father, Mitch must deal with the chaos his endeavor has created.

Making Money • Father and Son • Ethics

Gauthier, Gail

Saving the Planet & Stuff. New York: G.P. Putnam's Sons, 2003. 232 p. ISBN: 9780399237614. *JS*

After losing his summer job, sixteen-year-old Michael snaps up the opportunity to live with and work for old friends of his grandparents', Walt and

Nora, who run an environmental magazine. Throwbacks to the 1960s, Walt and Nora are obsessed with doing everything to save the planet. Out of his element, Michael is sure he has made a mistake until he finds his talent for business and gets involved with the politics of small businesses as he uncovers a scheme to undermine the magazine's reputation.

Employment • Responsibility • Uncles • Environmentalism

Greenwald, Lisa

My Life in Pink and Green. New York: Amulet Books, 2009. 272 p. ISBN: 9780810983526. *M*

When a large chain store opens in their small Connecticut town, twelve-year-old Lucy Desberg's family pharmacy is threatened. When her grandmother and mother can't decide what to do, Lucy takes it upon herself to save the business. When her advice fixes the homecoming queen's hair disaster just before the big dance, the answer is clear. Her talents with makeup and hair care become popular, and she applies for the towns "going green" grant that helps her to remake the business with a new image by adding an eco-spa with environmentally friendly products to their offerings.

Business • Environmentalism • Creativity

Griffin, Adele

My Almost Epic Summer. New York: G. P. Putnam's Sons, 2006. 192 p. ISBN: 9780399237843pa. *MJ*

Dreaming of opening her own salon one day, fourteen-year-old Irene puts all her passion into drawing the hairdos of literary heroines in her sketchbook. When she is fired after three weeks as a shampoo girl in her mother's beauty parlor, she is forced to take a job as a babysitter. Intrigued by beautiful lifeguard Starla Malloy, who works where she takes the kids to swim, Irene builds a tentative friendship and starts reading her blog, where she witnesses Starla's revenge on her ex-boyfriend D, who dumped her. Things get complicated for Irene when her mother's boyfriend leaves and D starts showing interest in her. Soon she is able to find confidence in her own beauty and build her own identity.

Work • Summer • Employment • Friendship • Blogs • Beauty Shops

Haft, Erin

Meet Me at the Boardwalk. New York: Point, 2008. 208 p. ISBN: 9780545042130pa. *J*

Friends Jade, Megan, and Miles spend their summers working in the resorts of their hometown, Seashell Point, where they make fun of the tourists and spend their free time hanging out on the boardwalk. But even though this summer is shaping up to be a good one with lots of parties since Jade's parents are out of town, Miles falls for a new girl and Megan, who is in love with him, can't handle it. Then a stranger comes to town and wants to tear down the boardwalk, and the three friends must learn to fight for the things they love.

Summer Job • Employment • Romance

Hartinger, Brent

Project Sweet Life. New York: HarperTeen, 2009. 288 p. ISBN: 9780060824112. *JS*

Dave, Victor, and Curtis are forced by their fathers to get summer jobs. Trying to figure out a way to make money without actually working, the boys try out a variety of schemes including staking out banks and scuba diving. But when the schemes fail to make money but instead rack up a lot of debt, the boys try one last scheme to find some stolen gold that should be located in the China Tunnels far below Tacoma, Washington.

Friendship • Family Relationships • Money Making

Johnson, Maureen

Suite Scarlett. New York: Point, 2008. 353 p. ISBN: 9780439899277; 9780545096324pa; (aud). YALSA Best Books. *J*

Starting from their fifteenth birthdays, each child in the Martin family is assigned a suite in their family's small rundown Manhattan hotel to take care of. On her birthday, Scarlett starts to take care of her suite and its newly installed occupant, demanding and charming out–of–work actress Amy Amberson. Scarlett, despite her reservations, soon becomes Amy's overworked personal assistant as she helps with her projects that come and go on a whim. Because she is providing much-needed money for their small business, Scarlett plays along as Amy becomes the patron of her brother's theatre group as they try to stage a production of *Hamlet.* But when Scarlett falls for one of the actors in the play and Amy withdraws her financial support to focus on a plot to get revenge on another actress, it falls on Scarlett to see the production through and determine if she wants to continue with her new romance.

Theater • Business • Brothers • Revenge • Actors and Actresses

Joseph, Danielle

Shrinking Violet. New York: MTV Books, 2009. 320 p. ISBN: 9781416596967pa. *JS*

High school senior Teresa "Tere" Adams is painfully shy and avoids speaking to anyone, but in the privacy of her bedroom, she is free to act with abandon as she acts as an imaginary DJ for the FM radio station owned by her stepfather. When an accident gets Tere into the station and a DJ slot opens up, she releases her alter ego, becoming the station's hottest new DJ "Sweet T." But when another DJ announces a song-writing contest, the winner of which will get a prom date with Sweet T, Tere must come out of her shell as she deals with the publicity as well as her feelings for Gavin, the only guy in school whom she dares to talk to.

Shyness • Work • Prom

Kemp, Kristen

Breakfast at Bloomingdale's. New York: Scholastic Press, 2007. 299 p. ISBN: 9780439809870; 9780439809887pa. *S*

When seventeen-year-old Cat Zappe's grandmother dies, she embraces the dream she shared with her to create a fashion line and runs away to New York to embrace her passion. When things don't go as planned, Kat must find the determination to live her dreams by overcoming the obstacles placed before her.

Grandmothers • Runaways • Psychotherapy • Ambition

Klam, Cheryl

Learning to Swim. New York: Delacorte Press, 2007. 224 p. ISBN: 9780385733724pa. *S*

Seventeen-year-old Steffie is spending the summer working at a country club while trying to ignore her mom's constant relationship crises with a variety of married men that always seem to end up with Steffie and her mom moving. With her only friend, a sixty-year-old coworker named Alice, Steffie is just fine until she nearly drowns and is saved by gorgeous lifeguard Keith McKnight, who then offers to give her swimming lessons. As their relationship progresses, Steffie worries that she is doomed to only have relationships like her mother's, and even if she can move beyond that, it is certain that her mother will force them to leave soon anyway, so Steffie must decide if love is worth working for.

Single Parent • Friendship • Intergenerational Relations • Swimming • Summer Job

Korman, Gordon

Born to Rock. New York: Hyperion Books for Children, 2006. 272 p. ISBN: 9780786809202; 9780786809219pa; (aud). YALSA Quick Picks; YALSA Popular Paperbacks. *S*

Discovering that his biological father is the millionaire lead singer of a punk rock band, Harvard-bound Young Republican Leo Caraway takes a job as the band's roadie. He hopes to earn the money he needs for college tuition after an unfortunate incident led him to be accused of cheating which resulted in the loss of his college scholarship. Assaulted by the band's drug habits and their unscrupulous agents, Leo tries to hold on to his traditional values, but it is not until he learns the truth about his dad that he starts to question everything he has ever learned and finds that his experiences have fundamentally changed him.

Birthparents • Bands • Summer Job • Social Acceptance

Kraut, Julie

Hot Mess: Summer in the City. New York: Delacorte Books for Young Readers, 2008. 352 p. ISBN: 9780385735063pa. *S*

During the summer, Emma Freeman is looking forward to spending time in the glamorous big city with a fabulous internship and lots of social opportunities. When Emma finds that the reality of little money, a boy-crazy roommate, and spending eight hours a day working for a tough boss is not leading to the exciting life she thought, Emma must deal with the lies she has told the cute guy at work in order to keep the summer from turning into a big mess.

Summer Job • Romance

Leitch, Will

Catch. New York: Razorbill, 2005. 304 p. ISBN: 9781595140692pa. *S*

The summer before college, Tim Temples is working in a packaging plant hauling boxes where he is caught in his affair with an older woman. When his golden-boy brother Doug returns home for no apparent reason and starts degenerating socially and physically, Tim looks around him and realizes how quickly his high school friends are fading into their lackluster lives, and he knows that he wants to make something of himself by embracing the prospects that lie within him and getting an education outside his hometown.

Employment • Family Relationships • Coming-of-Age

Lynch, Chris

The Big Game of Everything. New York: HarperTeen, 2008. 275 p. ISBN: 9780060740344. *JS*

Working with his younger brother Egon at their grandfather's golf course, things change for Jock when two of his grandfather's old Marine buddies show up and throw their money around buying whatever they want. Seeing Gramps in a new light when he realizes that the old man is measuring his self-worth on how much money he has, Jock learns about the meaning of success.

Summer Job • Family • Brothers • Bullies and Bullying • Sports • Intergenerational Relations

McDonald, Janet

Twists and Turns. New York: F. Foster Books, 2003. 135 p. ISBN: 9780374399559; 9780374400064pa. YALSA Quick Picks. *JS*

Sisters Keeba and Teesha Washington have avoided many of the pitfalls of their inner-city neighborhood, including pregnancy and gangs, and have both finished high school. With the support of their neighbor and friend, Skye March, now the two start their own hair salon to support themselves. When business is too slow and a new movement is trying to push out the poor residents by privatizing their housing projects, the sisters must face these challenges. When vandals destroy their shop, the girls find the strength to rebuild their dreams.

African Americans • Sisters • Beauty Shops

Parker, Jade

<u>**Making a Splash Series.**</u> New York: Point

Three friends, Robyn, Caitlin, and Whitney, are excited for their summer prospects for work and romance.

Romance • Friendship • Summer Job

Robyn. 2008. 256 p. ISBN: 9780545045407pa. *J*

Robyn is excited that she gets to spend the summer working at the local water park with her best friend Caitlin. Robyn is assigned to work helping the little kids down the slides, but she would rather be with Caitlin, hanging out where the hot guys swim. She thinks her chances for a summer romance are gone. However, things change when Robyn starts to fall for her supervisor, who just happens to be Caitlin's older brother, Sean, but before things can work out, she must keep him away from coworker Whitney.

Caitlin. 2008. 240 p. ISBN: 9780545045414pa. *J*

Caitlin has been disappointed in love before and this summer she is going to keep herself safe by staying away from boys. When she sees Romeo at the water park where she works, she knows she shouldn't show interest, but Romeo is hard to ignore and Caitlin has to decide if he is worth risking her heart.

Whitney. 2008. 240 p. ISBN: 9780545045421pa. *J*

Whitney has been enjoying working at the water park, especially since she has made friends with Robyn and Caitlin, and she has developed a crush on cute ice cream boy, Jake. When Whitney finds out that her ex-best friend, Marci, will be renting the entire park for her sweet sixteen party, she is afraid that everything will be ruined when her friends find out that she is really the daughter of a wealthy businessman.

Savage, Deborah

Summer Hawk. Boston: Houghton Mifflin, 1999. 298p ISBN: 9780395911631; 9780141312200pa. YALSA Best Books. *J*

Fifteen-year-old Melissa Taylor Armstrong-Brown, who wants to be a reporter, is looking forward to her summer job with "Hawk Lady" Rhiannon Jefferies at the Raptor Rehabilitation Center, so she can write a research paper about her experiences that will allow her to enter the honors writing program at the same boarding school her mother attended. When Taylor finds that she has to work alongside Rail Bogart, the only other local smart kid, the summer does not look like it will go well. Then when she catches her father and Rhiannon having an affair, things get even worse. Through the stress, and as Taylor and Rail become closer when they rescue a young hawk, Taylor is able to deal with the changes in her life and finds out the importance of family.

Summer Job • Country Life • Writing

Thomson, Sarah L.

The Manny. New York: Dutton Children's Books, 2005. 181 p. ISBN: 9780525474135; 9780142408032pa. *JS*

Despite the derision of his friends, Jeremy finds the perfect summer job babysitting for rich families in the Hamptons. Making good money and living at an exclusive resort are only two perks of the job. The other is that Jeremy has lots of time to impress the girls that surround him, but soon Jeremy learns that love is closer than he thought.

Summer Job • Rich People • Dating • Vacations

Uhlig, Richard

Last Dance at the Frosty Queen. New York: Knopf, 2007. 357 p. ISBN: 9780375839672; 9780440239840pa. *S*

Eighteen-year-old Arthur "Arty" Flood just wants to leave his small Kansas town after graduation. However, there are a few problems he has to work out first. He is owed over $1,000 in wages by the owner of Stiles' Styles, the dog-clothing company where he is a design assistant, he is having an affair with a teacher, and the sheriff has blackmailed him into dating his daughter, who is desperate to lose her virginity. And there's more—his family's business, a funeral home, is already failing when an arsonist's attack further threatens it. Vanessa, a girl from California, arrives, and she is able to help Arty see his hometown in a new light as he decides what he really wants out of life.

Family Problems • *Business* • *Alcoholics* • *Small Towns* • *Coming-of-Age* • *Arson*

Wallace, Rich

Dishes. New York: Viking Childrens Books, 2008. 160 p. ISBN: 9780670011391. *S*

It is summer and straight-boy Danny has left his New Jersey home. He is now washing dishes at a gay bar in Maine to get to know his estranged father, Jack, who owns the restaurant. Sharing an apartment with his father, Danny finds that his father has not grown up much from the time he fathered Danny at age seventeen and that they have little in common. Getting to know his coworkers and the bar's customers, as well as a girl he meets while he is out for his daily run, Danny finds the support he needs to face the problems he left at home and to develop an understanding relationship with his father.

Father and Son • *Dating* • *Homosexuality* • *Gay Males* • *Summer Job* • *Waitresses*

Zindel, Lizabeth

Girl of the Moment. New York: Viking Childrens Books, 2007. 288 p. ISBN: 9780670062102; 9780142411049pa. *S*

During the summer before her senior year, Lily Miles gets an internship to be the assistant to sixteen-year-old teen celebrity Sabrina Snow and hopes that the experience will help her get into a good university. But when she finds that Sabrina is manipulative and demanding and when Sabrina's boyfriend shows up and decides he prefers Lily, she must work out the complications while maintaining her commitment to Sabrina and at the same time staying true to herself.

Internships • *Rich People* • *Celebrities* • *Eating Disorders* • *Self-Discovery*

Chapter **6**

Seeing the World

Opportunities for travel allow adolescents to get outside their normal realms of experience, expanding their view of the world and the variety of people in it. Travel also provides experiences that help teens develop their sense of independence and strengthen their individual identities. The books listed in this chapter deal with the various ways teens gain new experiences through the wonders of travel. From taking a cross-country road trip with family or friends to moving to a whole new town, travel can help teens find that with a change of scenery, you can change your outlook on life. Sometimes travel experiences happen only in the summer as teens go off to partake of the wonders of a camp where they can swim or put on a play. Many teens have the chance to travel far from home and experience new cultures and peoples in foreign lands as they learn to embrace new experiences that help them figure out where they personally fit into a complex world.

Road Trips

Barnholdt, Lauren

Two-Way Street. New York: Simon Pulse, 2007. 288 p. ISBN: 9781416913184. YALSA Popular Paperbacks. *S*

> When her boyfriend Jordan breaks up with her just before their long-planned road trip to Boston University, Courtney McSweeney is stunned. Forced by her parents to continue through with the plan, Courtney does not know that Jordan is really trying to protect her from the fact that he caught his mom and her dad in a compromising situation. During the trip, Jordan acts unexpectedly kind, and despite some fights, the two ultimately discover the truth behind the deception.
>
> *Travel • Automobiles • College • Dating • Breaking Up*

Caletti, Deb

The Secret Life of Prince Charming. New York: Simon & Schuster Books for Young Readers, 2009. 336 p. ISBN: 9781416959403; (aud). *S*

> Seventeen-year-old Quinn Hunt has had very few positive examples of good relationships since her mother, aunt, and grandmother have had many bad relationships and have even gone as far as posting the warning signs of doomed love on

the refrigerator. Quinn thinks she has not fallen for their fates with her "safe" boy-friend, but when she finds that he has been cheating on her and that her estranged, selfish, womanizing father has stolen a treasured object of emotional importance from each of his ex-wives and ex-girlfriends, things fall apart. Escaping and trying to make amends, she teams up with younger sister Sprout and older half-sister Frances Lee, whom she had never met, to go on a road trip and return these objects to the women. On the trip, Quinn finds a new understanding of her father as well as an unexpected love.

Divorce • Family Problems • Sisters • Travel • Automobiles

Clark, Catherine

Wish You Where Here. New York: HarperTeen, 2008. 212 p. ISBN: 9780060559830; 9780060559854pa. *JS*

On a two-week trip with her mother, sister, and some of her mother's relatives touring America on a bus crowded with senior citizens, sixteen-year-old Ariel is certain it will not be a great summer. Further cut off from her cell phone, e-mail, and iPod because of her mother's desire to have quality time so they can bond, Ariel is forced to keep in touch with her boyfriend Dylan and others back home by writing postcards. Things get complicated when she meets an attractive fellow traveler, Andre. But as she deals with the breakup of her parents' marriage be-cause of her father's gambling addiction that lost her college fund and the family's social standing, as well as the prospect of moving to a new town, she soon realizes that Dylan is not what she once thought and that running away is never a good answer.

Travel • Automobiles • Divorce • Mother and Daughter • Addiction • Intergenerational Relations

Cooney, Caroline B.

Hit the Road. New York: Delacorte Press, 2005. 176 p. ISBN: 9780385729444; 9780440229292pa. YALSA Popular Paperbacks. *JS*

With her parents off on a cruise, sixteen-year-old Brit is sent to stay with her eighty-six-year-old grandmother Nannie. Brit soon finds out that Nannie and her old college roommates Florence and Aurelia are determined to go to their sixty-fifth col-lege reunion and that she is going to drive them even though she has only had her li-cense for two weeks. Forced into her grandmother's plans, Brit helps kidnap Aurelia from her nursing home and then drives the three women from Long Island to Massa-chusetts all the while hiding the trip from her parents. Along the way, Brit connects with her longtime crush, Cooper, who had been acting distant but now calls her fre-quently for support. Brit also learns about the fragility and audacity that comes with age as she comes to understand and love the older women she is helping.

Grandmothers • Kidnapping • Friendship • Travel • Automobiles • Coming-of-Age

DuPrau, Jeanne

Car Trouble. New York: Greenwillow Books, 2005. 288 p. ISBN: 9780060736729; 9780060736750pa. *S*

Beginning with a cross-country road trip from Virginia to California, recent high school grad and seventeen-year-old computer whiz Duff Pringle is ready to start his new life with a job as a games programmer for "Incredibility, Inc." On the road, Duff encounters some problems when his old car breaks down, but he soon finds a replacement by volunteering to drive a car that someone needs to be taken to St. Louis. On his way again, he picks up Stu, a wildly dressed hitchhiker and loses his wallet in a biker bar. But then he meets Bonnie, the teenage daughter of the man who owns the car he is driving and a professional Internet scam artist, and she joins him and Stu for the rest of their trip. That's when good things start to happen, and Duff matures as he begins a relationship with her.

Travel • Automobiles • Interpersonal Relations

Green, John

An Abundance of Katherines. New York: Dutton Books, 2006. 256 p. ISBN: 9780525476887; 9780142410707pa; (aud). Michael L. Printz Honor Book; YALSA Best Book; YALSA Popular Paperback. *S*

Despondent after being dumped by his latest girlfriend, who like all the others was named Katherine, and sure that he will never live up the reputation he once built as a child prodigy, Colin Singleton and his friend Hassan set out on a road trip. Colin is working on a mathematical formula that will predict the length of romantic relationships, and he hopes this will leave his mark on the world. In Gutshot, Tennessee, Colin meets Lindsey. With her help, he is able to perfect his theorem, revive his love life, and learn that even a person's smallest contribution can change the world.

Gifted Teenagers • Travel • Automobiles • Girlfriends • Dating • Self-Perception • Coming-of-Age

Hite, Sid

I'm Exploding Now. New York: Hyperion Books for Children, 2007. 192 p. ISBN: 9780786837571; 9780786837588pa. *JS*

Sixteen-year-old Max Whooten is frustrated and angry with his life. His friend Trevor has just been released from a mental hospital, and Max is dealing with an unrequited crush on his childhood friend Leila, as well as with his annoying parents and younger sister. Max is sure that things will only get worse from here. When the aged family cat, Crappy, dies and Max must travel from his Manhattan home to his aunt's country home to put the now-frozen cat in his final resting place, Max realizes that things just got worse. But when he arrives at his New Age, yoga-instructor Aunt Ginny's home in a converted barn near Woodstock and meets an artistic girl who might actually like him back, Max finds that a positive attitude just might give purpose and meaning to life.

Pets • Summer • Aunts • Travel • Automobiles • Diary Novel • Humor

Hobbs, Valerie

Anything but Ordinary. New York: Farrar, Straus & Giroux, 2007. 176 p. ISBN: 9780374303747. *S*

Winifred Owens and Bernie Federman have been best friends since they met in eighth grade. Growing up together and then finding themselves dating, the couple always believed they would go off to college together. Then Bernie's mother dies from cancer and he decides to forgo college to stay home and work in his dad's repair shop, and Winifred chooses to attend a university in California, changing their lifelong plans. Away at college, other things begin to change. Winifred sheds her geeky image by drastically changing her look, moving her major from nanoscience to communications, and spending her days chasing boys and shopping. Driving cross-country to see her again, Bernie is awestruck by Winifred's change, and he finds himself trying to find a place to fit in as he sleeps in the library, sits in on lectures, and is almost seduced by a graduate student. Now on a different path, Bernie must decide what he is going to do with his life as he and Winifred try to decide what will become of their relationship.

College • Mothers • Death • Travel • Automobiles • Romance • Coming-of-Age

Lieberg, Carolyn S.

West with Hopeless. New York: Dutton Children's Books, 2004. 180 p. ISBN: 9780525471943. *MJ*

Thirteen-year-old Carin is not looking forward to the road trip from her house in Iowa to the home of her father in Nevada with her older half-sister, Hope, who is going to Nevada for a job interview. Along the way, Carin must deal with strange people, cheap motels, and car problems, but as the trip progresses, she is able to find a new appreciation for her sibling as she experiences her great capacity for forgiveness and understanding when Carin involves them in a near disaster.

Divorce • Family • Travel • Automobiles • Divorce • Father and Daughter

Pearson, Mary E.

Miles Between. New York: Henry Holt, 2009. 288 p. ISBN: 9780805088281; (aud). *S*

Having been in and out of various boarding schools for nine years, seventeen-year-old Destiny "Des" Faraday has never become attached to anyone. One day she and three friends find a pink convertible with the key in the ignition in front of the school, and the four classmates grab it and set out on a road trip. Finding a bundle of cash in the glove box to fund their trip, the group bonds as they travel, sharing the coincidences that make up their adventures. Along the way, secrets are revealed, and Des is finally able to come to terms with the reasons why her family abandoned her.

Travel • Automobiles • Secrets • Friendship • Boarding Schools

Resau, Laura

Red Glass. New York: Delacorte Press, 2007. 304 p. ISBN: 9780385734660; 9780440240259pa; (aud). School Library Journal Best Books; YALSA Best Books. *JS*

Sixteen-year-old Sophie is timid and fearful of nearly everything from death to developing relationships with others. Then she rescues a Mexican five-year-old named Pablo. Pablo was orphaned after his parents attempted to illegally cross the border and died, so Sophie opens herself up to the silent little boy and finally gets him to tell her the name of his Mexican village. Building her courage, Sophie decides to take Pablo back home. With her Bosnian great-aunt, Dika; Mr. Lorenzo, a Guatemalan friend of her great aunt; and Angel, Mr. Lorenzo's handsome son, she travels across the border. This trip helps Sophie to change and develop her own identity as she helps Pablo decide if he should remain in Mexico or find a new home in Arizona and then as she supports Angel as he works through his painful past.

Anxiety • Travel • Automobiles • Orphans • Family • Immigrants

Smith, Jennifer E.

You Are Here. New York: Simon & Schuster Books for Young Readers, 2009. 251 p. ISBN: 9781416967996. *JS*

Sixteen-year-old Emma is happy to be alone and has always felt disconnected from her family filled with brilliant people. When she discovers she had a twin brother who died soon after they were born, Emma wants to know more and sets out on a road trip from New York to North Carolina to find her brother's grave. Unexpectedly joined on her journey by her neighbor Peter, Emma reconciles her issues with her family as she opens her heart to a stray dog as well as to Peter, when she finds he has greater depth than she once thought.

Travel • Automobiles • Friendship • Interpersonal Relations • Death • Twins • Family • Dogs • Coming-of-Age

Weeks, Sarah

So B. It: A Novel. New York: Laura Geringer Books, 2004. 256 p. ISBN: 9780066236223; 9780064410472pa; (aud). ALA Notable Children's Books; YALSA Best Books; YALSA Popular Paperbacks. *MJ*

After arriving on her doorstep thirteen years ago, Heidi, now thirteen, and her developmentally disabled mother So B. It, who can only speak twenty-three words, are cared for by their agoraphobic neighbor, Bernie. Bernie was never able to figure out where they come from or if they have any family, but when Heidi discovers an old camera and the developed film shows a picture of her mother at the Hilltop Home for the Disabled in Liberty, New York, she sets off on a cross-country bus trip to discover her family's origins.

Mother and Daughter • Mental Illness • Travel • Automobiles • Developmentally Disabled

Wittlinger, Ellen

Zigzag. New York: Simon & Schuster Books for Young Readers, 2003. 264 p. ISBN: 9780689849961; 978068984998pa; YALSA Best Books; YALSA Popular Paperbacks. *JS*

High school junior Robin's boyfriend, Chris, has chosen to study abroad in Rome instead of spending the summer with her in Iowa. Robin decides to join her Aunt Dory, who was recently widowed, and Dory's two children, thirteen-year-old Iris and ten-year-old Marshall, on a cross-country road trip to California. Robin is able to help her cousins work through their problems as she reconnects with her absent father. Through the process, she is able to find her own strength and redefine her identity.

Cousins • Aunts • Family • Travel • Automobiles • Vacations

Summer Camp

Calonita, Jen

Sleepaway Girls. New York: Little, Brown, 2009. 304 p. ISBN: 9780316017176. *MJ*

Fifteen-year-old Samantha Montgomery's best friend is so caught up in her new relationship that Samantha feels like a third wheel. So she decides to spend the summer as a volunteer counselor-in-training at Whispering Pines summer camp. Samantha has never been to camp before and feels out of place until the popular campers realize she is the girl who appeared in a commercial for the Dial and Dash Phone. Despite her fame, she can't help becoming an enemy of the leader of the popular girls, Ashley, when she proves to be a natural leader and acquires the attention of two boys, perfectly gorgeous Hunter and easygoing Cole. But Hunter is not all he seems to be, and Ashley and Hunter soon make Sam's life difficult until, with the help of her true camp friends, Samantha is able to realize that good guys make the best boyfriends.

Friendship • Summer • Popularity • Romance

Kraut, Julie

Slept Away. New York: Delacorte Press, 2009. 305 p. ISBN: 9780385737371pa. *J*

When fifteen-year-old Laney meets slightly overweight Sylvie at summer camp, she decides that she must get a boyfriend for her. But when Laney finds she is falling for Ryan, a guy who is not popular at her school back home but who, here at camp, has turned into the hottest guy around, Laney learns from her new friends that popularity is really not what she thought it was.

Friendship • Interpersonal Relations • Summer

Lockhart, E.

Dramarama. New York: Hyperion Books for Children, 2007. 320 p. ISBN: 9780786838158; 9780786838172pa; (aud). YALSA Best Books; YALSA Popular Paperbacks. *J*

Big-boned Sarah "Sayde" and her best friend Douglas "Demi," who is black and gay, share a passion for musical theater, and they are ecstatic when they get to spend the summer at a theater camp together. As Sayde discovers that she is not as talented as she thought she was, and Demi becomes the star and finds it more exciting to hang out with his new boyfriends, Sayde must decide about the power of their friendship. When they are caught drinking on the campus rooftop, Sayde decides to take the fall so that Demi can remain at the camp.

Actors and Actresses • Dating • Theater • Friendship • Summer

Roter, Jordan

Camp Rules. New York: Dutton Books, 2007. 272 p. ISBN: 9780525478034. *JS*

For her sixteenth birthday, Penny's parents give her an unwanted eight-week trip to a girls' camp in Maine. Sure that she is going to be unhappy, Penny makes a deal with her parents that if things don't work out after one month, she can come home. In her first days at camp, Penny finds that not only is her arch-enemy from school, Logan Worthe, at the same camp, but that she is an outsider with mean bunkmates who have known each other for years. Deciding that she will work to get sent home even earlier than the agreed-upon one month, Penny comes up with a plan that soon backfires. Along the way, she is able to win the respect of the other campers and find a place for herself in their midst.

Friendship • Popularity • Competition • Interpersonal Relations • Summer

Vivian, Siobhan

Same Difference. New York: Push, 2009. 256 p. ISBN: 9780545004077; 9780545004084pa. *JS*

When Emily enrolls in a summer arts program in Philadelphia, she finds a very different world awaits her. Leaving behind her strip-mall filled suburban life and her best friend with whom she is very comfortable, Emily immerses herself in a new big city life and makes edgy new friends like Fiona, who always draws shadows. As time moves on, Emily finds that the drama and petty cliques she experienced at home are the same even in this new environment. As she tries to understand the forbidden relationship she is having with her teaching assistant, Yates, Emily is able to redefine herself in a way that encompasses all of her old and new experiences.

Best Friends • Artists • Summer • Self-Confidence

Moving

Bauer, Joan

Hope Was Here. New York: Putnam, 2000. 192 p. ISBN: 9780399231421; 9780698119512pa; (aud). YALSA Best Books; ALA Notable Children's Books; Newberry Honor Books; School Library Journal Best Books. *JS*

Sixteen-year-old Hope is once again forced to move with her Aunt Addie, a diner cook, and finds herself in Mulhoney, Wisconsin. When Addie starts work as a cook and Hope as a waitress at their new diner, they find the owner, G.T. Stoop, is facing two battles: one with leukemia and the other with the town's corrupt politicians. Joining with fellow employee Braverman in the cause to get G.T. elected mayor, Ivy finds lots of excitement and friendship as she establishes roots in a new community and finds the love and acceptance she has been longing for.

Cooking • Cancer • Friendship

Ehrenberg, Pamela

Ethan, Suspended. Grand Rapids, MI: Eerdmans, 2007. 256 p. ISBN: 9780802853240; 9780802853172pa. *M*

Suspended from his junior high in the suburbs of Philadelphia, Ethan is sent by his mother to live with his Jewish grandparents in inner-city Washington, D.C. With his parents divorcing and his sister starting college in California,

Ethan finds himself alone, especially since his is the only white kid in an almost entirely black and Latino school. But he soon learns to fit in as he redefines his own identity by joining the jazz band, working on a civil rights project, and falling in love with beautiful Kameka.

Race Relations • *Jewish Americans* • *Social Classes* • *Romance*

Friedman, Aimee

The Year My Sister Got Lucky. New York: Scholastic, 2008. 384 p. ISBN: 9780439922272; 9780439922296pa. *J*

Sisters Katya "Katie" and Michaela Wilder are tried-and-true city girls who attend the New York City Anna Pavola School of Ballet. But when the pair are uprooted by their parents to move to Fir Lake, a town in rural upstate New York, things change. Michaela finds new adventures and friendships, but Katie can only wish for her old friends and desperately misses dancing. Filled with jealousy when Michaela gets a gorgeous boyfriend and becomes homecoming queen, nothing looks right until Katie is able to find a friend of her own, Autumn, and is helped to find a way to fit into her new circumstances.

Friendship • *Jealousy* • *Ballet*

Grab, Daphne

Alive and Well in Prague, New York. New York: Laura Geringer Books, 2008. 247 p. ISBN: 9780061256707. *JS*

Forced to move from New York City to rural Prague, New York, because of her dad's Parkinson's disease, Matisse Osgood is struggling to fit in. Embarrassed by her father and finding the students at her new school boring, Matisse withdraws and becomes disconnected. She is able to deal with the changes she faces as she meets radical girl Violet, falls for farmer boy Hal, and takes on the vicious rumors spread by the ruling cheerleaders as she remakes her identity.

Father and Daughter • *Family Relationships* • *Country Life*

Hepler, Heather

The Cupcake Queen. New York: Dutton, 2009. 242 p. ISBN: 9780525421573; 9780142416686pa. *M*

After her parents' separation, thirteen-year-old Penny moves with her mother from New York to a small seaside community and finds it easier to help out in her mother's bakery and hide than to make new friends. Starting school Penny is finally able to find some unexpected friends and develops a crush on cute boy Marcus. With her new support, Penny is finally able to deal with the school's mean girls and find some peace with her new life.

Family Problems • *Divorce* • *Schools*

Noel, Alyson

Laguna Cove. New York: St. Martin's Griffin, 2006. 224 p. ISBN: 9780312348694pa. *JS*

When her parents divorce, Anne moves from Connecticut to Laguna Beach, California, where she feels decidedly out of place until she makes friends with wild

Lola and free-spirit Jade. The only one she can't make friends with is competitive Ellie, who seems to hate her even more when Anne becomes close to the gorgeous guy Chris, who is teaching her how to surf. When Anne enters the Surf Fest competition, she must compete against Ellie and come to terms with why she is disliked so much.

Divorce • Self-Discovery

O'Connell, Jenny

The Book of Luke. New York: Pocket Books/MTV Books, 2007. 291 p. ISBN: 9781416520405pa. *S*

Emily's parents decide to move from Chicago to Boston in the middle of her senior year. As she loses her shot at being class valedictorian, a position that could have gotten her into an Ivy League college, and then when her father stays behind in Chicago and her boyfriend, Sean, dumps her on the day she moves, things look bleak. But in Boston with friends Josie and Lucy, Emily realizes that she is not the only one who has been ill-used, and the trio decides to create a reference book for guys of the future so they will know how to treat girls. Knowing they need to test their theories, the girls make Luke Preston, Josie's ex-boyfriend, the subject, but when Emily starts falling for Luke, it appears that things will not turn out as planned.

Dating • Revenge • Schools

Purtill, C. Leigh

Love Meg. New York: Razorbill, 2007. 297 p. ISBN: 9781595141163; 9781595141477pa. *MJ*

Every time they have a small problem, fifteen-year-old Meg Shanley's sister and guardian, Lucie, moves them to a new town pursuing new jobs and boyfriends, but Meg is tired of living like a gypsy and wants a chance to make real friends. When a strange man arrives and tells her the truth that Lucie is really her mother and she has a grandmother and an uncle who live in New York, Meg heads off on a cross-country trip to find them. Harboring the hope she will be able to meet and be accepted by her father and the family she has never known, Meg's struggles lead her to the happiness she has been looking for.

Family Problems • Family Secrets • Epistolary Novels

Rosen, Michael J.

ChaseR. Cambridge, MA: Candlewick Press, 2002. 152 p. ISBN: 9780763615383. *MJ*

Fourteen-year-old Chase Riley gets a big dose of culture shock when his family moves from Columbus, Ohio, to a very rural area. Keeping in touch with his sister who is at college and his friends in Columbus by e-mail, Chase recounts the differences in his new life, including tractor pulls, the ridiculous local news, and the plague of cicadas. When one of Chase's dogs is wounded while running in the nearby woods that are overrun with deer hunters, Chase becomes an animal rights activist, but when he discovers that the impoverished farmers hunt for desperately needed meat, Chase must reconcile his beliefs with the needs of the people in his new home.

Dogs • Animal Rights • E-mail • Epistolary Novels

Stevenson, Robin

Out of Order. Custer, WA: Orca Book Publishers, 2007. 221 p. ISBN: 9781551436937. *JS*
Sophie struggles to shed the memories of her past that had her struggling as an overweight girl who was constantly bullied. Now at a new school and with her new slimmed-down body, she thinks she will be able to find the acceptance she so desperately wants. Finding a new friend in Zelia, Sophie eagerly joins her in her reckless behavior, including drinking and smoking. Even though Sophie begins to have some reservations about her friend, it is not until Zelia attempts suicide that Sophie is able, with the help of her gay friend Max, to find ways to accept not only her own insecurities but those of her friend as well.

School • Friendship • Interpersonal Relations • Identity • Honesty • Canada

Weber, Lori

If You Live Like Me. Montreal: Lobster Press, 2009. 336 p. ISBN: 9781897550120pa. *S*
Following along with her anthropologist father as he studies dying cultures, Cheryl "Cher" now finds herself in a small village in Newfoundland. Separated from her friends in Montreal, Cher retreats into herself and her music until she meets next-door neighbor Jim, who also feels out of place since he was sent to live with his aunt so he could finish high school. When Jim is seriously injured on the cliffs near their home and his family rallies around him, Cher finds security amongst them. But when her mother decides to leave the seaside village because of her rheumatism, Cher must decide if she still wants to go home or if she has found the place she really wants to be.

Small Towns • Music • Neighbors

Wittlinger, Ellen

Razzle. New York: Simon & Schuster Books for Young Readers, 2001. 247 p. ISBN: 9780689835650; 9780689856006pa. YALSA Best Books. *JS*
Moving from Boston to help his parents restore their newly purchased resort cottages in Cape Cod the summer before his junior year, Kenyon Baker makes friends with Razzle, a thin girl with a buzz cut who loves discarded junk. While his friendship with Razzle helps him figure out who he really is and discover his passion for photography, when Kenyon betrays Razzle in an attempt to impress glamorous Harley, he must try to reconcile with her while she is trying to deal with her alcoholic mother, her eccentric grandmother, and revelations about who her father really is.

Photography • Friendship • Alcoholism

Americans Abroad

Brian, Kate

Lucky T. New York: Simon & Schuster Books for Young Readers, 2005. 291 p. ISBN: 9780689873515; 9781416935452pa. *J*

> When her favorite T-shirt that is one of the few links she has to her always-absent divorced father, is accidentally sent to a women's shelter in India, fifteen-year-old Carrie tags along with her once friend Darlene and her mother on the pretense that she is going to help them build houses. While on the search for her shirt, Carrie meets older student Dee, who works at a local orphanage. Trying to attract Dee, Carrie also goes to work at the orphanage where, in addition to getting the guy, she learns to love the children and sheds some of her selfish, materialistic tendencies.

> *Travel • Coming-of-Age*

Coman, Carolyn

Many Stones. Asheville, NC: Front Street, 2000. 158 p. ISBN: 9781886910553; 9780142301487pa; (aud). Michael L. Printz Honor Books; YALSA Best Books; School Library Journal Best Books. *J*

> Berry is reluctant to leave her divorced mother and her boyfriend in Washington, D.C., to travel with her father to South Africa on a ten-day trip. Berry finally agrees to the trip because her father wants her there when he presents the money for a memorial swim-athon to honor her sister Laura, who was murdered in the country a year earlier. Together father and daughter face the turmoil of a country trying to rebuild after the many crimes perpetrated during Apartheid and the turmoil and grief in their own lives as they learn to cope with loss and reconcile with one another.

> *Travel • Divorce • Sisters • Death*

Cornwell, Autumn

Carpe Diem. New York: Feiwel and Friends, 2007. 360 p. ISBN: 9780312367923; 9780312561291pa. *JS*

> Sixteen-year-old Vassar has her life planned out to the last detail until one day the family receives a call from her estranged grandmother, Gertrude. Artist Gertrude is in Southeast Asia completing a found-object sculpture and blackmails Vassar into joining her. Backpacking through the jungles, Vassar deals with many challenges as she uncovers the family's secrets, falls in love with a handsome Malaysian cowboy, and ultimately learns how to seize the day.

> *Travel • Grandmothers • Secrets • Summer*

Harrington, Jane

Four Things My Geeky-Jock-of-a-Best-Friend Must Do in Europe. Plain City, OH: Darby Creek, 2006. 160 p. ISBN: 9781581960419. *J*

> On a cruise with her mother in the Mediterranean, Brady writes back home to her friend Delia about her adventures, including her travails as she wears her bikini in public and her attempts to find a hot European boy.

Sequel: *My Best Friend, the Atlantic Ocean, and Other Great Bodies Standing between Me and My Life with Giulio.* Plain City, OH: Darby Creek, 2008. 174 p. ISBN: 9781581960709. *J*

> While waiting for her best friend, Brady, to end her relationship with the hot Italian exchange student in the thirty-four days the Internet promises most teenage relationships last, so that she can have him, Delia keeps score for the football team and writes in her poetry journal. But when she starts to attract some not-so-intelligent football players because of her pushup bra, Delia's plot to wait out Brady does not go as planned, and she realizes that the boy she thought she had wanted is really not the one for her.

> *Mother and Daughter • Travel • Self-Discovery • Epistolary Novels • Jealousy • Best Friends • Exchange Students • Diaries*

Johnson, Maureen

Girl at Sea. New York: HarperTeen, 2007. 336 p. ISBN: 9780060541446; 9780060541460pa. YALSA Popular Paperbacks. *S*

> When her mother gets a fellowship that will take her to Kansas, seventeen-year-old Clio finds she will be spending the summer cruising the Mediterranean with her father, despite the fact that it will prevent her from taking her dream job at an art store and delay her plans to make her crush into her boyfriend. She'll also be trapped with her immature and selfish dad and his new archeologist girlfriend. She will also be forced to share a cabin with Elsa, the girlfriend's daughter, and will be cut off from the world with no Internet or cell phone. But when Clio discovers that the trip really is all about uncovering an important undersea archeological treasure and she finds herself attracted to her father's cute young research assistant Aidan, Clio is able to embrace the adventure.

> *Father and Daughter • Artists • Divorce • Travel*

Johnson, Maureen

13 Little Blue Envelopes. New York: HarperCollins, 2005. 336 p. ISBN: 9780060541415; 9780060541439pa. YALSA Best Books; YALSA Popular Paperbacks; Teens Top Ten. *S*

> When seventeen-year-old Ginny's free-spirit artist Aunt Peg dies of brain cancer, Ginny finds that her aunt had planned a journey for her with several European destinations. Given a plane ticket to London, four rules, and the instruction to open one of thirteen little blue envelopes and complete the task given to her upon her arrival at each place, Ginny heads off, staying with her aunt's friends or in hostels as she uncovers her aunt's past and learns more about her life. Along the way, she finds her own courage and adventuring spirit as she learns important lessons about family and making human connections.

> *Aunts • Artists • Travel • Letters • Grief*

McDonald, Abby

Sophomore Switch. Somerville, MA: Candlewick Press, 2009. 304 p. ISBN: 9780763639365. *J*

> In California, Tasha wants to escape the publicity after a hot-tub incident with a TV star. In England, Emily wants to escape the pain of being dumped by boyfriend Sebastian. The two college sophomores flee their troubles on an international college exchange. Now in California, Emily tries to loosen up and in England Tasha tries to shed her party-girl image and stick to her studying. As both girls face challenges and humiliations, they help each other through e-mails and both gain self-awareness as they discover new aspects of themselves.

College • Self-Discovery • Exchange Students • Belonging

Noel, Alyson

Cruel Summer. New York: St. Martin's Griffin, 2008. 229 p. ISBN: 9780312355111pa. *JS*

> Seventeen-year-old Colby Cavendish is forced to abandon her hot boyfriend Levi Bonham and her new cool best friend Amanda when her parents insist that she spend her summer vacation on a Greek Island with her crazy Aunt Tally. Finding things to be even worse when she realizes she is completely cut off from cell phones and the Internet, it is not until Colby meets Yannis that she discovers things might not be so bad after all. As her relationship with Yannis progresses, even though her feelings for him complicate her relationship with Levi, Colby is able to find joy and a new sense of self in her summer adventures.

Summer • Cliques • Aunts • Travel • Epistolary Novels • Diaries

Perkins, Mitali

Monsoon Summer. New York: Delacorte Press, 2004. 272 p. ISBN: 9780385731232; 9780440238409pa. YALSA Popular Paperbacks. *J*

> Fifteen-year-old Jasmine "Jazz" Gardner is not looking forward to spending the summer in Pune, India, with her mother who has received a grant to do charity work at the orphanage where she lived as a child. Jazz would rather be home in California, with her best friend Steve, whom she secretly loves, building their business selling photographic postcards to tourists. Finding a friend in fifteen-year-old Danita, an orphan who wants to be a businesswomen but who may be forced to marry an older man so she can care for her sisters, Jazz is able to explore her Indian heritage, and she is able to discover that she is truly beautiful with her own strong identity as she helps Danita escape her arranged marriage.

Friendship • Summer • Business • Culture Conflict • Unrequited love • Travel

Resau, Laura

What the Moon Saw. New York: Delacorte Press, 2006. 272 p. ISBN: 9780385733434; 9780440239574pa. YALSA Best books. *MJ*

Living in suburban Maryland with her American mother and Mexican father, who crossed the border illegally many years ago, fourteen-year-old Clara begins to explore a new world when out of the blue her Mexican grandparents invite her to spend the summer with them. Finding herself living in huts in remote mountains, Clara experiences aspects of her father's previous life and in the process discovers new things about herself as she gets to know her grandmother, who is a healer, and falls in love with a young goat herder named Pedro.

Immigrants • Grandparents • Travel • Interracial Persons • Self-discovery

Students across the Seven Seas Series (multiple authors). New York: Speak Press

Capturing the opportunity to travel abroad, a variety of teens from various social classes and cultures experience new and exciting adventures.

Romance • Interpersonal Relations • Travel • High School • Family • Fashion • Moving

Ostow, Micol

Westminster Abbey. 2005. 192 p. ISBN: 9780142404133pa. *JS*

Abby is sent to London as punishment for lying to her parents about being with James, but when she finds that she enjoys the trip, she sees that things might be ruined when James shows up in England.

Strauss, Peggy Guthart

Getting the Boot. 2005. 224 p. ISBN: 9780142404140pa. *JS*

Kelly finds that living abroad is not everything she thought it would be when she finds herself living in a dorm with three roommates and sharing a bathroom with an entire floor, but when she gets involved with bad-boy Joe and gets into trouble, Kelly finds that she wants nothing more than to stay.

Jellen, Michelle

Spain or Shine. 2005. 224 p. ISBN: 9780142403686pa. *JS*

Shy Elena finds that when she goes to Spain for a semester, she is able to come out of her shell, especially after she meets good-looking local Miguel.

Hapka, Cathy

Pardon My French. 2005. 224 p. ISBN: 9780142404591pa. *JS*

Nicole spent most of her childhood moving, so she just wants to stay where she is. But when her parents force her to study abroad in Paris, Nicole finds that getting away from home can be exciting.

Nelson, Suzanne Marie

The Sound of Munich. 2006. 224 p. ISBN: 9780142405765pa. *JS*

Siena is looking forward to her semester in Germany, especially since it will allow her to fulfill the only task on her dead father's wish list that he was never able to accomplish.

Gerber, Linda

Now and Zen. 2006. 224 p. ISBN: 9780142406571pa. *JS*

Japanese American Nori is fed up with being mistaken for a native during her semester in Japan, especially when gorgeous German student Erik begins to treat her like a personal tour guide.

Nelson, Suzanne Marie

Heat and Salsa. 2006. 224 p. ISBN: 9780142406472pa. *JS*

Cat is shocked when she finds that her friend Sabrina's boyfriend will be accompanying them on their semester abroad to Mexico, but when she meets cute Aiden, things look like they have taken a positive turn.

Apelgyist, Eva

Swede Dreams. 224 p. ISBN: 9780142407462pa. *JS*

Calista finds Sweden a welcome escape from her driven twin sister Suzanne, but when her boyfriend, who she thought would also be there, fails to show, Calista wonders if the experience will be worth it.

Ferris, Aimee

Girl Overboard. 2007. 224 p. ISBN: 9780142407998pa. *JS*

Marina is looking forward to her hands-on experience with marine biology aboard a great yacht in the Caribbean, but when she is distracted by the cute Australian aboard, she must decide just exactly where her passions lie.

Gerber, Linda

The Finnish Line. 2007. 224 p. ISBN: 9780142409169pa. *JS*

Ski-jumper Maureen is looking forward to spending time in Finland, but when she finds that balancing practice and classes is overwhelming, she can't resist the offer of a gorgeous boy to help her train.

Supplee, Suzanne

When Irish Guys Are Smiling. 2008. 224 p. ISBN: 9780142410165pa. *JS*

Delk is looking forward to escaping her problems at home to study abroad, but even when she starts to fall in love with a handsome Irishman, Delk is not sure if he will be able to heal her broken heart.

Hapka, Cathy

French Kissmas. 2008. 208 p. ISBN: 9780142411339pa. *JS*

Nicole looks forward to returning to Paris to spend Christmas, but things get difficult when her friend Mike expresses that he wants to be more than just friends.

Liu, Cynthea

The Great Call of China. 2009. 224 p. ISBN: 9780142411346pa. *JS*

When adopted Chinese American Cece gets the chance to study in China, she jumps at the chance to explore her roots, but when she gets close to finding her birthparents, Cece is not sure what answers she wants to find.

Sheldon, Dyan

Sophie Pitt-Turnbull Discovers America. Cambridge, MA: Candlewick Press, 2005. 185 p. ISBN: 9780763627409; 9780763632953pa. *J*

Sophie leaves London when her mother arranges for her to trade places with the daughter of one of her school friends rather than spending the summer in her family's villa in France. Finding herself in a run-down house in Brooklyn, Sophie must deal with the family's odd pets, including a pig and an iguana, while she endures eating tofu and taking care of the family's small children. Taking on her beliefs, stereotypes, and prejudices about nationality, race, and class, Sophie must learn how to change her attitude if she is going to enjoy her stay in America.

Sequel: *I Conquer Britain.* Cambridge, MA: Candlewick Press, 2007. 201 p. ISBN: 9780763633004. *J*

When a lack of finances prevents Cherokee Salamanca from taking a school trip to London, her mother arranges for Cherokee to exchange places with the daughter of one of her old schoolmates. Overwhelmed by the customs and propriety of English society, Cherokee learns that even English families have problems. As she begins to adapt and have fun, she helps her host family by convincing them to adopt some of her free-thinking ways.

Friendship • Interpersonal Relations • Summer • Vacations • Eccentricities • Travel • Family Problems

Silag, Lucy

Beautiful Americans. New York: Razorbill, 2009. 304 p. ISBN: 9781595142221; 9781595142276pa. *S*

Living with host families on a study-abroad program in Paris, four exchange students go wild—partying, having sex, drinking, and smoking—as they try to deal with other problems. Wealthy Alex, who loves nothing more than shopping, is destitute after her mother cuts off her funds. Ballet dancer Olivia is determined to stay despite the fact that her parents want her back home to help with her autistic brother when she is given a position in a local dance troupe. Gay Zach faces disappointment when he can't attract a boyfriend. Blonde beauty P.J. is left at the mercy of her conniving host family when her parents are arrested on drug charges until she is forced to run away.

Travel • Exchange Students • Ballet • Secrets • Missing Persons

Wallach, Diana Rodriguez

Amor and Summer Secrets. New York: Kensington, 2008. 288 p. ISBN: 9780758225535pa. *J*

When her father ships her off to stay in a tiny mountain town in Puerto Rico with her family whom she has never met, fifteen-year-old Mariana Ruiz must deal with the oppressive heat, the spicy food, and having only one cousin, Lilly, who speaks

English. But as Mariana gets involved in the preparations for Lilly's Quinceñera, where family secrets are revealed, she finds joy in her cultural heritage as she makes new friends and finds her first love.

Sequel: *Amigas and School Scandals.* New York: Kensington, 2008. 288 p. ISBN: 9780758225559pa. *J*

Returning home to Philadelphia, Mariana is bringing with her a new understanding of her family and heritage, but she is also bringing her cousin Lilly Sanchez, who will go to school with her. When Mariana's friends don't relate to Lilly and Mariana finds herself developing a crush on Bobby, with whom she shares a locker, she must navigate the challenges as her relationships take on new meanings at her sweet-sixteen party.

Sequel: *Adios to All the Drama.* New York: Kensington, 2009. 224 p. ISBN: 9780758225573pa. *J*

When her summer love from Puerto Rico unexpectedly arrives, Mariana must decide between him and the feelings she has for her locker buddy Bobby. With her best friends, Emily and Madison, dealing with their own boy and family problems, Mariana finds unexpected support from her estranged Aunt Teresa, who is having Mariana and Lilly as bridesmaids in her upcoming wedding on New Year's Day.

Quinceañera • *Romance* • *Summer* • *Puerto Ricans* • *Travel*

Chapter 7

Engaging in Athletic Activities

Sports are a natural part of adolescence. They provide a powerful outlet for many teens and help them discover how they feel about themselves and the world. Participating in sports gives teens a meaningful environment that allows them to enhance their physical abilities and deal with the changes their bodies are undergoing. Sports also provide a context for learning and instilling important values that will form significant parts of their adult identities, such as fair play, teamwork, and putting forth our best efforts even if one doesn't win. The books listed in this chapter deal with a variety of sports, including basketball, baseball, football, ballet, and automobile racing. There is a wide variety of books about sports activities that will spark the interest of any sports fanatic.

Averett, Edward

The Rhyming Season. New York: Clarion Books, 2005. 214 p. ISBN:9780618469482. *MJS*

> In a small town dying due to a lack of jobs, high school senior Brenda is struggling with her own changes. Facing a new basketball coach who makes the team recite poetry as they shoot while also dealing with the tragic death of her older brother Benny and her parents' subsequent separation, she is trying to hang tough. Finding strength inside herself and connecting to the poetry that her coach has "inflicted" on them, Brenda is able to transform her life while assisting her team in making it to the state championship.

> *Basketball • Death • Coming-of-Age*

De La Pena, Matt

Mexican White Boy. New York: Delacorte Press, 2008. 249 p. ISBN: 9780385733106. YALSA Best Books. *S*

> Staying the summer with his Mexican father's family, Danny Lopez deals with his biracial heritage. Feeling that he is the outsider both at home and at his mostly white school, he isolates himself. Danny finds salvation in baseball, and as he perfects his game, he not only develops friendships with his cousins and scheming pitcher Uno but begins to feel love for Mexican immigrant liberty. Through these experiences, Danny is finally able to develop his own sense of identity.

> *Baseball • Interracial Persons • Mexican Americans*

Deuker, Carl

Night Hoops. Boston: Houghton Mifflin, 2000. 212 p. ISBN: 9780395979365; 9780064472753pa. YALSA Best Books. *JS*

When his brother Scott gives up basketball to spend more time on his music, all of their manipulative father's attention is focused on getting Nick to develop his basketball skills. His talent develops further when, against the advice of his father and despite his friends' disapproval, he starts playing nightly one-on-one games with troubled neighbor and fellow teammate Trent Dawson. As Nick deals with his parents' divorce and Trent with the disappearance of his brother Zach, who has committed a murder, the two boys are able to deal with their lives.

Basketball • Divorce • Friendship

Esckilsen, Erik E.

The Outside Groove. Boston: Houghton Mifflin, 2006. 224 p. ISBN: 9780618668540. *S*

Seventeen-year-old Casey LaPlante feels invisible next to her stock-car-racing older brother Wade. Casey wants to study conservation in college but realizes that with all her family's financial resources put into her brother's racing, she will probably not be able to live her dream. Then Casey decides she wants to drive, and, enlisting the help of her uncle Harvey, she is the first female to enter the race. On the track, Casey not only learns how to race, she discovers herself and learns important things about her family.

Automobile Racing • Sex Role • Sibling Rivalry

Fitzgerald, Dawn

Getting in the Game. Brookfield, CT: Roaring Brook Press, 2005. 144 p. ISBN: 9781596430440; 9780312377533pa. *M*

As the only girl on the middle-school hockey team, Joanna Giordano faces ridicule that becomes even worse when her best friend Ben aligns himself with the rest of the team and falls for her enemy, cruel Valerie. At home Jo must deal with her parents' separation and her grandfather's failing health as he is sent to a nursing home. But even though on the ice Jo is able to help carry the team to victory, she must work through her problems so she can stand up for herself.

Hockey • Sexism • Discrimination • Prejudice • Bullies and Bullying

Grover, Lorie Ann

On Pointe. New York: Margaret K. McElderry Books, 2004. 320 p. ISBN: 9780689865251; 9781416978268pa. *MJ*

Clare studies ballet and wants nothing more than to be accepted to the prestigious City Ballet program where she believes she will finally become a real dancer. Her grandfather, whom she lives with so she can take lessons, tries to show Clare there is more to dancing than she envisions. She can't believe him until she is denied entrance to the program for being too tall. When her grandfather has a stroke, Clare is finally forced into the realization that she must find joy in her talent no matter what others may tell her.

Ballet • Grandfathers • Ambition • Family Relationships • Novels in Verse

Harkrader, L. D.

Airball: My Life in Briefs. New Milford, CT: Roaring Brook Press, 2005. 208 p. ISBN: 9781596430600; 9780312373825pa. *M*

Seventh-grader Kirby Nickel believes Brett McGrew, hometown hero and NBA basketball star, is his father, so he joins his school's untalented basketball team to meet him. Everyone in his small Kansas town, including his grandmother who raised him, is mad about basketball, and when the school board refuses to let the team meet Brett unless they start winning games, Kirby's dream is threatened. When in an effort to improve the players' concentration the coach has the boys practice in their underwear, Kirby and his teammates improve, but only when they are not wearing uniforms. Kirby convinces them all to play every game in their underwear, a strategy that puts them on a much-needed winning streak. Kirby is able to realize his dream of finding his father even if in the end he turns out not to be the person he thought it was.

Fathers • Basketball

Hazuka, Tom

Last Chance for First. Weston, CT: Brown Barn Books, 2008. 289 p. ISBN: 9780979882401pa. *JS*

When Jim, Robby Fielder's best friend and co-captain of the varsity soccer team, is taken off the team for drinking after he totals his car, and Robby starts hanging out with Pet, an outspoken outcast with bleached hair and a nose ring, the soccer team's cohesiveness falls apart. As he grows closer to Pet and she reveals dark secrets about her past, Robby must decide if he will fall under his parents' pressure to succeed and get a scholarship like his football-star older brother. He must also choose whether to stick by his coach when his abusive coaching methods are videotaped or to remain loyal to Pet, who was the one who taped the coach, and still lead his team to victory.

Soccer • Secrets • High School • Friendship

Heldring, Thatcher

Toby Wheeler: Eighth-Grade Benchwarmer. New York: Delacorte Press, 2007. 213 p. ISBN: 9780385733908; 9780440421832pa. *M*

Eighth-grader Toby Wheeler decides to join the basketball team when the new coach asks him to try out. Hoping to get back with his best friend JJ who has been ignoring him, things don't turn out as expected when he becomes nothing more than a benchwarmer. Even worse, he finds out that the coach is the father of Megan, the girl he likes, and his parents are at odds since his father works for a lumber company and his mother is a conservationist. With the coach's help, Toby grows as he learns to be a team player.

Basketball • Friendship • Teamwork • Sports

Hughes, Pat

Open Ice. New York: Wendy Lamb Books, 2005. 271 p. ISBN: 9780385746755; 9780553494440pa. YALSA Popular Paperbacks. *S*

> Sixteen-year-old hockey player Nick Taglio always seems to be getting blind-sided on the ice, and after his fourth concussion, his doctor and parents forbid him to play again. Without hockey, Nick loses the support on which he has built his life. When his girlfriend dumps him, things spin out of control, and he begins to blow off school and fight with his parents. When he endangers his baby brother, Nick has to search his soul and figure out his complicated emotions to regain control of his life as he finds new purpose in his schoolwork and reestablishes his bond with his family.

> *Hockey • Brain Injury • Sports • Interpersonal Relations*

Jenkins, A. M.

Out of Order. New York: HarperCollins, 2003. 247 p. ISBN: 9780066239682; 9780064473743pa. YALSA Best Books. *J*

> Sophomore Colt Trammel, wise guy and popular baseball player, is at the top of his high school's social ladder even though his undiagnosed learning disability makes him appear not to be very smart. Covering up his shortcoming by relying on his rebellious comments and cocky pranks, things fall apart when his girlfriend Grace dumps him, causing his grades to fall so low that his ability to play baseball is threatened. Turning to social outsider Corrine to tutor him in English, Colt finds someone who looks beyond his tough exterior, and the two form a friendship even though it threatens his social status.

> *Baseball • Friendship • Girlfriends*

Johnson, Scott

Safe at Second. New York: Philomel Books, 1999. 245 p. ISBN: 9780698118775pa. YALSA Best Books; YALSA Quick Picks; School Library Journal Best Books. *J*

> Star pitcher on his high school baseball team Todd Bannister and baseball trivia and stats guru Paulie Lockwood have been best friends since grade school. When Todd is hit in a game and loses an eye, Paulie is lost without the acclaim and interest that once surrounded Todd—and by default, him as well. Trying desperately to get his friend back into the game, the boy's efforts are thwarted when Todd can't control his pitches and falls apart when he hits a batter. As Todd comes to accept his new way of life, Paulie must also find his own new place.

> *Baseball • Friendship*

King, Donna

Double Twist. Boston: Kingfisher, 2007. 132 p. ISBN: 9780753460238pa. *M*

> Twelve-year-old Laura Lee is devastated when Patrick, her Junior Pair's ice-skating partner, is injured just before the Junior Grand Prix in Montreal where they were likely to have taken the gold medal. Spotting a talented skater, Scott, at a local rink, Laura believes she has found the perfect new partner as she takes on the challenge of training him for competition in just one month.

> *Ice-Skating • Jealousy • Competition*

King, Donna

Game, Set, Match. Boston: Kingfisher, 2007. 136 p. ISBN: 9780753460221pa. *M*

Twelve-year-old Carrie has been pushed with such vigor by her parents to excel in tennis that she now feels she wants to quit so she can have more time to spend on other things like her friends. But when she wins a scholarship to a tennis camp in Florida, Carrie rediscovers her love for the game as she connects with two younger boys at the camp. Upon her return home, she is finally able to confront her parents and help them realize that she is playing not only to please them but for the joy of the sport itself.

Tennis • Competition

King, Donna

Kickoff. Boston: Kingfisher, 2007. 168 p. ISBN: 9780753460825pa. *M*

Forced to move from Florida to an army base in England when her father is reassigned, Tyra Fraser is instantly targeted by her new school's most popular girl, Alicia, as a threat to her since they share the same passion, soccer. On the field, Alicia continues to fight for dominance and the team subsequently loses its cohesion. When they start facing really good opponents, however, it is apparent that the team must work together, and Tyra and Alicia must find a way to work out their differences so they can win and convince the school that girls' soccer is just as important as the boys team.

Soccer • Sexism • Bullies and Bullying • Moving • Teamwork • Military

King, Donna

Slam Dunk. Boston: Kingfisher, 2007. 145 p. ISBN: 9780753461556pa. *M*

Basketball player Ashlee Caron's mother disdains the sport because of the pain she still feels over being abandoned by Ashlee's father, who was a professional basketball player. Ashlee has worked hard to win a place on the junior national team, but her mother thinks she should focus on grades and exams to get ahead. Ashlee has to go to her father for the help she needs to fulfill her dream and convince her mother of her passion for the game.

Basketball • Mother and Daughter • Single Parent • Competition

Lipsyte, Robert

Yellow Flag. New York: HarperTeen, 2007. 234 p. ISBN: 9780060557072; 9780060557096pa. *S*

Seventeen-year-old Kyle Hildebrand comes from a family of famous race car drivers, but playing his trumpet, not driving, is what makes Kyle happiest. When his older brother Kris's injuries prevent him from driving, it is up to Kyle to take his place so their family can get the sponsors they need to keep racing. Finding that he is a skilled driver, Kyle wins the sponsor and the family begins to talk of acquiring a second car so Kyle can race alongside his brother, forcing Kyle to decide if he should give up his music to pursue racing.

Automobile Racing • Music • Brothers

Lupica, Mike

Heat. New York: Philomel Books, 2006. 324 p. ISBN: 9780399243011; 9780142405031pa; (aud). YALSA Popular Paperbacks; ALA Notable Children's Books. *M*

Twelve-year-old Cuban American Michael Arroyo dreams of pitching in the Little League World Series, but to do this, his team needs to beat the best New York team in their regional championship. At home Michael and his seventeen-year-old brother, Carlos, are afraid that they will be separated if anyone finds out that they are hiding the fact that their father died of a heart attack several months ago by telling everyone he is visiting relatives in Miami. Struggling on their own, the boys reveal the truth to their kindly neighbor, Mrs. Cora, and Michael's best friend, Manny Cabrera. Things get bad when a rumor circulates that Michael is too old to play in the league and must produce a birth certificate or be taken off the team. Michael is finally able to find the courage he needs when he develops a friendship with a beautiful girl who turns out to be the daughter of a Yankee's pitcher.

Baseball • Cuban Americans • Brothers • Father-Deserted Families • Foster Care • Coming-of-Age

Lupica, Mike

Travel Team. New York: Philomel Books, 2004. 288 p. ISBN: 9780786274154; 9780142404621pa; (aud). *MJ*

Even though he is told he is too short to be on the seventh-grade basketball team, Danny Walker suspects that the real reason is that his former NBA star father, Richie Walker, whose career was ended by a car accident, overshadowed the coach, Mr. Ross, during their own school days. When Danny's father decides to fight back by starting his own team, his alcoholism and another car accident conspire to take them down. Danny steps in to coach, and the team, joined by defectors from Mr. Ross's team, faces their rivals with a winning attitude.

Sequel: *Summer Ball.* New York: Philomel Books, 2007. 256 p. ISBN: 9780399244872; 9780142411537pa. *MJ*

At a summer basketball camp, Danny Walker once again finds his short stature working against him when he is placed in the younger boys' cabin and he spends a lot of time on the bench. Missing his friends and trying to deal with the fight he had with his girlfriend before he left, Danny suffers at the hands of the coach and his fellow players until he finally makes friends with a younger boy, Zach, and is able to prove his ability on the court.

Basketball • Divorce • Father and Son • Bullies and Bullying • Sports • Competition • Summer Camps • Coming-of-Age

Martino, Alfred C.

Pinned. Orlando, FL: Harcourt Children's Books/Harcourt, 2005. 320 p. ISBN: 9780152053550; 9780152056315pa; (aud). *S*

Ivan Korske's mother is deceased, and with an old-school Polish father, he is an outcast on his wrestling team even though he is an intimidating force on the mat. Ivan hates his coach and hopes for a scholarship to take him away from his blue-collar town even though he is devoted to girl-next-door Shelly. At the other end of the area is Bobby Zen, whose dad is a lawyer and his mom a real-estate agent. In an affluent school with a good coach, Bobby becomes smooth, quick, and strong as a wrestler. When Bobby gets his girlfriend pregnant and his parents' marriage breaks up, he is challenged to deal with the additional stresses on his already-overtaxed body. Both boys face physical and mental challenges in their sport and deal with their personal problems as they work to reach that final match and ultimately confront each other in the finals at the New Jersey State Wrestling Championships.

Wrestling • High School • Polish Americans • Competition • Social Classes • Girlfriends

Murdock, Catherine Gilbert

Dairy Queen: A Novel. Boston: Houghton Mifflin, 2006. 278 p. ISBN: 9780618683079; 9780618863358pa; (aud). YALSA Best Books; YALSA Popular Paperbacks; School Library Journal Best Books. *MJ*

Since her father has broken his hip, her mother is consumed by filling in for the absent principal of the local middle school, and her two older brothers have left for college, most of the heavy work of running their family's dairy farm has fallen on fifteen-year-old D.J. Schwenk. All the extra work has forced D.J. to quit the basketball team. She is overwhelmed and missing her sports involvement, so when she is asked by her father's close friend to train Brian Nelson, the starting quarterback on a rival team, she agrees. But Brian is lazy, and as D.J. whips him into shape, she finds herself not only developing a passion for football, but falling for Brian. Things get complicated when D.J. decides to try out for her football team. Now facing her potential boyfriend as rivals on the field, D.J. must deal with a lot of issues as she works through her family, friendship, and romantic dilemmas to finally discover who she truly is.

Sequel: *The Off Season.* Boston: Houghton Mifflin, 2007. 288 p. ISBN: 9780618686957; 9780618934935pa; (aud). YALSA Best Books. *MJ*

At the start of her junior year, things look great for D.J. Schwenk. On the football field, she seems finally to have been accepted by her male teammates, and despite the tensions, Brian Nelson still seems to be interested in her, even though he never wants to take her out in public. As her gay best friend runs away with an older girlfriend and her family's farm gets into serious financial trouble, D.J. is forced to decide if she should return fully to basketball when her body struggles with the pressures of football. Then, when her brother Winn is hospitalized after a rough college football game, D.J. is finally able to get the perspective she needs to look at her life with new eyes and make decisions about her future.

Sequel: *Front and Center.* Boston: Houghton Mifflin, 2009. 272 p. ISBN: 9780618959822. *MJ*

After two years of being in the spotlight, D.J. Schwenk is looking forward to just blending in and returning to play basketball. But her wish to fade into the background doesn't work out. Her friend Beaner publicly declares that he is interested in her, everyone keeps wanting to know about her brother, and college basketball coaches are scouting her. As D.J. faces her challenges at home and school, she is finally able to build her self-confidence and find the strength to create the future that she desires.

Athletes •Country Life • Football • Sports • Romance • Bullies and Bullying • Lesbians

Oaks, J. Adams

Why I Fight: A Novel. New York: Atheneum Books for Young Readers, 2009. 228 p. ISBN: 9781416911777. *JS*

For six years, Wyatt has lived in his Uncle Spade's car as they travel from town to town. Dealing with his nomadic life and his uncle's "lady friends" and "business associates," Wyatt starts bare-knuckle fighting for money at his uncle's insistence. Tall and strong, Wyatt wins many fights, but as things begin to deteriorate, he must find himself and the love he so desperately wants.

Boxing • Criminals • Travel • Automobiles • Coming-of-Age

Rallison, Janette

Life, Love and the Pursuit of Free Throws. New York: Walker, 2004. 185 p. ISBN: 9780802789273; 9780802788986pa. *JS*

High school freshman basketball players Josie and Cami both like Ethan, but when he starts calling her, Cami feels guilty when she flirts back since it was Josie who liked him first. In addition, both girls are competing to win the honor to play WNBA star Rebecca Lobo at an upcoming game, and while the game comes naturally to Josie, Cami has to work twice as hard. Tensions mount as the girls compete for love and status, and both girls have to work to overcome the jealousy that threatens to undermine their friendship.

Friendship • Basketball • Competition • High School

Ritter, John H.

The Boy Who Saved Baseball. New York: Philomel Books, 2003. 216 p. ISBN: 9780399236228; 9780142402863pa. *M*

Twelve-year-old Tom sets out to save the 320 acres of prime real estate, part of which makes up the Dillontown baseball field, from being sold to developers when he bets the land's owner that the local summer team can beat the all-star team down the road. Trying to achieve the impossible dream, things look up when mysterious boy Cruz de la Cruz appears, and the boys enlist the help of a former Major League player Dante del Gato to be the team's trainer. In the final game, Tom and his team find they are playing better than ever, but when Cruz de la Cruz disappears at the crucial moment, it is up to Tom to deliver the winning run.

Baseball • Summer

Ritter, John H.

Over the Wall. New York: Philomel Books, 2000. 312 p. ISBN: 9780399234897; 9780698119314pa; (aud). *MJ*

Escaping his withdrawn father who has never been the same since he accidentally ran over and killed his daughter ten years ago, fourteen-year-old Tyler Waltern goes to live with his aunt, uncle, and cousins in New York so he can play in a local baseball league. Tyler's explosive temper, which often flares up, looks like it will undermine his dreams of baseball success, until his coach, a Vietnam veteran who understands destructive anger, helps him to heal.

Anger • Violence • Baseball • Cousins

Roberts, Kristi

My Thirteenth Season. New York: Henry Holt, 2005. 154 p. ISBN: 9780805074956; 9780312602420pa. *MJ*

> After her mother's death a year before, which caused her dad to emotionally withdraw, thirteen-year-old Fran has found solace in playing baseball, but when she moves to a new town, the coach there dislikes having a girl on his team. Contention rises as Fran retaliates against the coach's unfair rules and then the coach tries to injure her by bombarding her with hard-pitched balls, an act that gets him removed from his position. Even with the coach gone, the stress leaves Fran shaken, and for a while, she gives up the game. It is not until her one friend, Steven, and her other teammates insist she play in an important game and her dad signs on as a coach that Fran is able to return to her beloved sport.
>
> *Mother-Separated Families • Baseball • Sex Role • Prejudice • Father and Daughter • Grief*

Saldana, Rene

The Whole Sky Full of Stars. New York: Wendy Lamb Books, 2007. 144 p. ISBN: 9780385730532. *S*

> Trained by his now-deceased father as a boxer, Mexican American Barry Esquivel is convinced by his friend, Alby Alonzo, to enter a boxing competition as a way to earn some much-needed money to support his family. But even after he wins, Barry refuses to take his cut of the winnings when he finds out that Alby earned most of it by betting on the match and intended to use his half to pay off his old gambling debts. Without the money, Barry is now forced to sell his father's beloved 1964 Ford to make ends meet, but things work out when Alby's father finds a way to help both his son and his friend.
>
> *Boxing • Gambling • Friendship • Father and Son • Single Parent*

Sweeney, Joyce

Players. Delray Beach, FL: Winslow Press, 2000. 222 p. ISBN: 9781890817541; 9780761452362pa. YALSA Quick Picks. *S*

> As the captain of the basketball team, high school senior Corey Brennan tries to accept newcomer Noah Travers on the team. When mysterious things start happening that rob the team of its best players, Corey is loath to implicate Noah, until Corey's best friend is arrested for having a gun. Now knowing that Noah will stop at nothing to make the starting squad where he can be the star, Corey must trick him into admitting his guilt before the championship game.
>
> *Deception • Basketball*

Tharp, Tim

Knights of the Hill Country. New York: Alfred A. Knopf, 2006. 240 p. ISBN: 9780375836534; 9780553495133pa. YALSA Best Books; YALSA Popular Paperbacks. *S*

> In a town where football rules, the star linebacker, Hampton "Hamp" Green, is burdened by the pressure of taking his high school team through

to their fifth state championship. Dealing with his single mother, who always has a different guy in her life, and his controlling best friend Blaine, makes Hamp's life quite complicated. When Blaine tries to convince Hamp to date the "right kind of girl" despite his interest in intelligent but not stylish Sarah, and then draws him into an altercation with an opposing team in which guns are involved, Hamp must conquer his own insecurities and do what is right.

Football • Single Parent • Competition • Ethics

Wallace, Rich

Playing without the Ball. New York: Alfred A. Knopf, 2000. 213 p. ISBN: 9780786235223; 9780440229728pa. YALSA Best Books; YALSA Quick Picks. *S*

Senior Jay McLeod's life revolves around school, his work as a short-order cook in the bar below the one bedroom apartment where he lives, working out his relationships with the opposite sex, and basketball. His mother left years ago, and now his dad has moved to California to make a new life, but Jay decided to stay behind so he could play on his high school basketball team. Then when the coach cuts him from the squad to make room for some promising sophomores, Jay fills the void by joining a YMCA church league where he takes his team to the championship game. With his new-found team's support, Jay is able to move toward adulthood as he plans for the future and finds his identity by gaining self acceptance.

Basketball • Family Problems • Divorce

Weaver, Will

Saturday Night Dirt. New York: Farrar, Straus & Giroux, 2008. 163 p. ISBN: 9780374350604; 9780312561314pa. YALSA Quick Picks. *J*

United by a love of cars and racing, people from all walks of life come together on a small dirt racetrack in rural Minnesota on one Saturday where they try to solve many problems before a storm hits and ruins their day of racing.

Automobile Racing • Competition

Sequel: *Super Stock Rookie.* New York: Farrar, Straus & Giroux, 2009. 208 p. ISBN: 9780374350611. *J*

Overcoming his reservations that his new corporate sponsor is more interested in looks than ability, stock-car racer Trace Bonham signs on with a lucrative contract that includes a new custom-built car. At his first race, he is accused of having an illegal vehicle, and after he is exonerated by an inspection, his crew discourages him from delving too deep into the issue. With his parents' marriage disintegrating and his new contract forcing him to leave his friends and the girl he likes, Trace must decide on his own what he is able to sacrifice for the fortune and fame the sponsorship offers.

Automobile Racing • Competition

Part II

Teen Issues

For certain teens, some important aspects of their identities and personalities make them unique. The journey of growing up requires that these teens explore the possibilities of each of their special facets and then integrate them into their overall identity. Although these individual characteristics and features may be shared with others, no two teens will go through the exact same process of integrating their individual needs into a complete sense of self. This part lists books with serious, hard-hitting tones that deal with the unique aspects of teens' identities and the journeys they take as they explore these parts of themselves. Explorations of one's ethnic, racial, cultural, spiritual, and sexual identities are fundamental to many teens' experiences. Other teens deal with physical realities, such as health issues, illnesses, body image problems, or disabilities, that make them different from their peers. Still other adolescents deal with things in the world around them that have an impact on their lives, such as differences in social classes, living in the inner city, poverty, dysfunctional families, or the need to engage in political action. Dealing with each of these diverse issues helps adolescents grow into complete individuals with a strong sense of who they are and how they fit into the world in which they live.

Chapter 8

Belonging to an Ethnic, Racial, or Cultural Group

Many adolescents derive personal characteristics from their membership in a particular ethnic, racial, or cultural group. As a part of a given group, they identify commonalities with others. These can include feelings, attitudes, language, interaction style, values, traditions, skin color, religious practices, food preferences, holiday celebrations, or shared histories. As adolescents develop, it is common for them to begin to explore their ethnic identity as it relates to their sense of self and also how it relates to their ability to fit in with other groups. Although some teens find the process easy, for others, such as minority groups or immigrants, the process is more difficult. The books listed in this section deal with the development of a strong ethnic, racial, or cultural identity, a process that is important for many teens to help them feel comfortable in their own skin and gain a feeling of belonging among their peers. Although some books depict this process as an easy one, many books in this section discuss the difficulties that come when teens feel forced to choose between two ways of life or when they must confront a cultural identity to which they previously had not related. These teens must explore and experiment with their identities as they build a sense of completeness by figuring out which attitudes, ideas, and feelings to retain and which to reject.

Ethnicity, Race, and Cultural Identity

Alegria, Malin

Estrella's Quinceañera. New York: Simon & Schuster Books for Young Readers, 2006. 272 p. ISBN: 9780689878091. *MJ*

Estrella is mortified when her mother begins to plan her Quinceañera celebration. Having formed new ties with the wealthy girls at her private school, Estrella fears a gaudy and tacky party. She is ashamed of her mother and family and disliked by her old friends. Forbidden to see Speedy, the boy from the barrio whom she is attracted to, Estrella continues to alienate herself from her family and friends with deceptions and lies. Even as things near complete disaster, Estrella plans the party she wants and finally embraces her heritage as part of her independent identity.

Family • Mexican Americans • Prejudice • Coming-of-Age

Alegria, Malin

Sofi Mendoza's Guide to Getting Lost in Mexico. New York: Simon & Schuster Books for Young Readers, 2007. 304 p. ISBN: 9780689878114. *S*

> Hoping to hook up with her crush, seventeen-year-old Sofi Mendoza attends a friend's house party in Tijuana against her parents' wishes. When her romantic dreams fail in the face of drunken make-out sessions and bad behavior, Sofi only wants to go home. Things get much worse when at the border, her papers are found to be false. Taking refuge with a Mexican aunt she has never known while her parents fight a legal battle, Sofi learns to appreciate the sacrifices her parents have made for her and embraces her heritage.

> *Family • Mexican Americans • Prejudice • Coming-of-Age*

Alexie, Sherman

The Absolutely True Diary of a Part-Time Indian. New York: Little, Brown, 2007. 240 p. ISBN: 9780316013680; 9780316013697pa. National Book Award; YALSA Best Books. *JS*

> Fourteen-year-old budding cartoonist and hydrocephalic Arnold Spirit Jr. faces racism both at home on his Spokane Indian reservation and at his new school. He has been rejected by his best friend Rowdy, and all around him he is faced with rampant alcoholism that leads mostly to death. Even though he loves his family and respects his tribe, Junior realizes that to preserve his own identity, he must escape the reservation's poverty and the destructive behaviors of some.

> *Native Americans • Coming-of-Age*

Bruchac, Joseph

The Warriors. Plain City, OH: Darby Creek: Distributed by Lerner, 2003. 117 p. ISBN: 9781581960020; 9781581960228pa. *MJ*

> Jake Forrest plays lacrosse on the Algonquin Indian reservation where he lives. After leaving the reservation, Jake goes to live with his mother, who has gotten a job as an attorney in Maryland. She enrolls Jake in a boarding school in Washington, D.C., where he struggles with the changes his new situation brings. Jake becomes the star of the lacrosse team even as he deals with his offensive nickname, "Chief," and the biased presentations of events in his history class. In addition, his coach cannot understand the way lacrosse ties into his heritage and his people's view of the world. However, when the coach is killed in a tragic shooting, Jake organizes a game as a prayer of healing that helps everyone to see how he views the spiritual aspects of both the sport and his heritage.

> *Native Americans • Single Parent • Private Schools*

Canales, Viola

The Tequila Worm. New York: Wendy Lamb Books, 2005. 199 p. ISBN: 9780385746748; 9780375840890pa; Pura Belpre Award; ALA Notable Children's. *MJ*

> Fourteen-year-old Sofia lives in McAllen, Texas, in a close-knit barrio community where she dreams of becoming strong and connected to her family, just like the much admired *Comadres*, or confidants, of her family. Sofia receives a scholarship to attend an exclusive boarding school, where she is tormented and called names

by her fellow students. She decides to fight back by getting better grades and being a better soccer player than the girl who is the main bully. Along the way, Sofia finds a natural gift for storytelling. It is through the telling of tales that she is able to stay close to her family and heritage while she is away as it gives her a way to find the courage to stand up for who she is.

Hispanic-Americans • Family • Catholics • Boarding Schools

Carlson, Melody

Diary of a Teenage Girl: Kim Series. Sisters, OR: Multnomah
Korean American Kim Peterson deals with many challenges as she holds strong to her Christian faith.

Korean Americans • Christianity • Romance • Advice • Diary Novel

Just Ask! 2005. 256 p. ISBN: 9781590523216pa. *JS*
Kim Peterson has been asked to write an advice column for teens in her dad's newspaper to win back her driving privileges. She finds that the letters she answers are pretty normal until one of her classmates is killed. Kim finds herself dealing with questions about life and death, and she wonders whether the answers lie with the Christian faith of her adoptive family or the Buddhist faith of her Korean heritage.

Meant to Be. 2005. 272 p. ISBN: 9781590523223pa. *JS*
When Kim's mom is diagnosed with cancer, her true friend Natalie gets hundreds of people to pray for her, and her health begins to improve. Kim starts dating Matthew, a non-Christian. Kim and Natalie's relationship becomes strained when Natalie advises her to end the relationship. When Kim finds that she is tempted to have sex with Matthew, she realizes how good Natalie's advice really was.

Falling Up. 2006. 272 p. ISBN: 9781590523247pa. *JS*
Having lost her mother to cancer wasn't enough. Kim's life turns upside down again when her dad loses his job, and she finds out that her best friend Natalie has lost her virginity to Benjamin O'Conner and is now pregnant.

That Was Then. 2006. 272 p. ISBN: 9781590524251pa. *JS*
Now starting her senior year, Kim is helping her pregnant friend Natalie deal with the fact that the baby's father sees it as his duty to marry her even though he does not love her. At the same time, she receives a letter from her birth mother in Korea and must decide how she feels about her while she tries to welcome her biracial cousin Maya into the family.

Carvell, Marlene

Who Will Tell My Brother? New York: Hyperion Books for Children, 2002. 150 p. ISBN: 9780786808274; 9780786816576pa; International Reading Association Children's Book Award. *JS*
When Evan Hill, who is a Mohawk Indian like his father, takes up the crusade started by his brother to protest against his school's use of an Indian

mascot, he faces humiliation and severe bullying as he struggles to get the school board, the principal, and his classmates to realize how disrespectful their mascot is. When the bullies kill his beloved dog and the school board ignores him, things look bleak, but at graduation when the mascot banner is raised, he is able to see the fruits of his perseverance and courage.

Native Americans • *High School* • *Novels in Verse*

Desai Hidier, Tanuja

Born Confused. New York: Scholastic Press, 2002. 413 p. ISBN: 9780439357623; 9780439510110pa; (aud). YALSA Best Books. *S*

Caught between two worlds, seventeen-year-old Indian American Dimple Lala has never really been certain about her identity. When her parents introduce her to Karsh Kapoor, an Indian boy they deem suitable, things become even more complicated. Wanting only to pursue her photography, Dimple encourages blonde best friend Gwyn's interest in Karsh, only to find that she is interested in him herself.

East Indian Americans • *Immigrants* • *Friendship*

Dhami, Narrinder

Bindi Babes. New York: Delacorte Press, 2004. 192 p. ISBN: 9780385731775; 9780440420194pa. *MJ*

With their indulgent father often absent, fourteen-year-old Geena, twelve-year-old Amber, and eleven-year-old Jazvinder "Jazz" drown their grief over their mother's death a year earlier in shopping and working hard at school. When their aunt arrives from India, at the request of their father, she tries to get him to be more strict and thwarts many of the girls' plans, including their attempt to get Jazz's ears pierced. The girls finagle a meeting with Amber's gorgeous teacher, Mr. Arora, in the hopes that a husband will take their aunt away from them. When their plans don't work out, the girls learn an important lesson about the value of family.

Sequel: *Bollywood Babes.* New York: Delacorte Press, 2005. 213p. ISBN: 9780385731782; 9780440420200pa; (aud). YALSA Popular Paperbacks. *MJ*

Still trying to get their aunt and Mr. Arora together, the girls support their efforts for a Bollywood-themed fundraiser at their school by asking Molly Mahal, a former Bollywood actress, to attend. The star, whose career ended in scandal, has fallen on hard times. In an effort to help, the sisters invite her to live with them and find themselves waiting on her hand and foot. When Molly starts attracting the attention of all the men around her, including the girls' father and Mr. Arora, the girls and their aunt find themselves scheming to get rid of her.

Sequel: *Bhangra Babes.* New York: Delacorte Press, 2005. 185 p. ISBN: 9780285733182; 9780440421061pa. *MJ*

With their aunt finally set to wed Mr. Arora, things are looking up for the sisters until the seemingly talented musician and cute new boy, Rocky, has the girls competing for his attention. In addition, Mr. Arora uses his new status to persuade Amber to help the school bully, Kiran. When Amber discovers that Kiran's problems stem from the death of her father, she convinces Rocky that he also needs to be her friend. When Rocky develops a relationship with Kiran and they find that he does not have the talent that they thought he did, the girls are able to come together and support their aunt through her wedding.

East Indian Americans • Family • Sisters

Elkeles, Simone

How to Ruin My Summer Vacation. Woodbury, MN: Flux, 2006. 240 p. ISBN: 9780738709611pa. Teens Top Ten. *JS*

Typical American teen Amy Nelson-Barak is shocked when her long-absent father asks her to spend her summer with him in Israel so that she can meet her grandmother, who is very ill. Dealing with a cousin who hates her because she is a spoiled American and falling for an older guy, Avi, who will soon enter the military for his mandatory service, Amy learns much about her cultural and religious heritage.

Sequel: ***How to Ruin My Teenage Life.*** Woodbury, MN: Flux, 2007. 281 p. ISBN: 9780738710198pa. *JS*

Back in America and living in Chicago with her father, seventeen-year-old Amy is pining for her Israeli boyfriend, Avi. Worrying about her father's love life as well, she signs him up for an online Jewish dating service without his knowledge. Also worried about her new stepfather and her mother's pregnancy, things get even more complicated when she is attracted to and kisses geeky boy-next-door Nathan and is caught by Avi, who has shown up for a surprise visit.

Culture Conflict • Family Relationships • Romance • Jewish Americans • Military

Esckilsen, Erik E.

Offsides: A Novel. Boston: Houghton Mifflin, 2004. 176 p. ISBN: 9780618462841. *JS*

Star soccer player Tin River moves off the reservation to attend a new school after his father's death. Despite his ability, he does not join the soccer team because he feels uncomfortable with the school's stereotypical Indian mascot. Forming his own team of geeks, freaks, and misfits, Tin River bets the coach of the high school team that his team can beat them with the hopes that a win will change the school's image.

Soccer • Native Americans • Culture Conflict • Bets

Ferrer, Caridad

Adios to My Old Life. New York: MTV Books: Pocket Books, 2006. 256 p. ISBN: 9781416524731pa. YALSA Popular Paperbacks. *S*

A talented singer and guitarist, seventeen-year-old Ali Montero has been raised by her overprotective music-professor father to be a good Cuban American girl, and he is not pleased when she makes the finals of a reality TV show to find the next Latin American superstar. Finding herself wrapped up in the show's whirlwind of fashion, publicity, and crazy staff and contestants, Ali falls for cute Jaime Lozano, a college intern working on the show, as she tries to win not only the competition but her father's respect.

Hispanic Americans • Friendship • Competition • Fame

Friedman, Robin

The Importance of Wings. Watertown, MA: Charlesbridge, 2009. 170 p. ISBN: 9781580893305. *MJ*

Wanting to be fully American, Israeli eighth-grader Ravit has changed her name to Roxanne. Living a bleak life with her nine-year-old sister and cab-driving father as they wait for their mother to return from Israel where she is caring for a sick relative, things change when Liat moves in next door. It's then that Roxanne is forced to confront her beliefs and find confidence in and acceptance for both of her cultures.

Culture Conflict • Friendship • Sisters

Grimes, Nikki

Bronx Masquerade. New York: Dial Books, 2002. 167 p. ISBN: 9780803725690; 9780142501894pa. Coretta Scott King Award; YALSA Best Books; YALSA Quick Picks; YALSA Popular Paperbacks. *JS*

Tyrone Bittings, who just lives for the present; Lupe, who longs to become a mother; Janelle, who is struggling with her body image; and Raul, a Puerto Rican artist, find that in English class, their teacher's open-mike poetry night allows the four friends to express some of their fears and problems as they connect with and support each other.

Poetry • Body Image • African Americans • Novels in Verse

Halpin, Brendan

How Ya Like Me Now. New York: Farrar, Straus & Giroux, 2007. 208 p. ISBN: 9780374334956. *J*

With his father dead and his widowed mom checking into rehab, fifteen-year-old Eddie finds himself in the big city of Boston staying with his Aunt Lily, her husband, and their son, Alex. Thrown into an experimental alternative high school with the popular but underachieving Alex, Eddie finds the students are expected to act and dress like business leaders and achieve high academic success. Eddie must navigate his new surroundings that are filled with nonwhite classmates and some pretty hot girls. Eddie is able to deal with the good and the bad, as well as with his feelings about his mother.

New Students • Mother and Son • Drug Abuse • Friendship • Family Problems • Race Relations • Success • Coming-of-Age

Headley, Justina Chen

Nothing but the Truth, and a Few White Lies. New York: Little, Brown, 2006. 256 p. ISBN: 9780316011280. YALSA Popular Paperbacks. *J*

Half-Taiwanese and half-white, fifteen-year-old Patty Ho is stuck between two worlds and doesn't feel comfortable in either of them. When her "Belly-Button

Grandmother" divines the future, predicting her future husband will be a white man, her domineering Taiwanese mother is devastated, so she sends Patty to a Stanford University math camp. With the help of her Asian roommate and a counselor, Patty is able to embrace her new freedom and find adventure and love. With her open-minded aunt who lives nearby, she is also able to redefine herself as she finds new respect for her mother and her family's heritage.

Culture Conflict • College • Family • Summer Camps • Single Parent • Prejudice

Herrera, Juan Felipe

CrashBoomLove: A Novel in Verse. Albuquerque: University of New Mexico Press, 1999. 155 p. ISBN: 9780826321138; 9780826321145pa. YALSA Quick Picks. *JS*

Struggling to support his mother when his migrant-worker father returns to Denver to live with and support his second family, sixteen-year-old Mexican teen Cesar Garcia also struggles to deal with the realities of the culture of his American high school in Fowlerville, California. Alienated by his language and cultural differences, Cesar does not fit in, and although he wants something more out of life, he gets involved in petty crimes, violence, and drugs. But when he faces tragedy, he is able to find the help he needs to develop a way to deal with his problems as he embraces a better future.

Mexican Americans • Teachers • Hope

Kent, Rose

Kimchi & Calamari. New York: HarperCollins, 2007. 240 p. ISBN: 9780060837693. *MJ*

Fourteen-year-old Joseph Calderaro is dealing with the typical troubles of girls and school until he creates a completely fictitious award-winning essay claiming that Olympic marathoner Sohn Kee Chung was his grandfather. When his lie is revealed, Joseph begins a real search for his Korean birth parents, adding to his troubles. Trying to reconcile his ethnicity with his love for his adopted Italian American family because his quest complicates his relationship with his younger twin sisters and his father, Joseph finally discovers a young girl who may be his cousin and is able to reconcile with his parents, who are finally able to accept his search for identity and work with him to embrace his new culture.

Adoption • Korean Americans • Culture Conflict • Friendship • Family Relationships

McDonald, Janet

Off-Color. New York: Farrar, Straus & Giroux, 2007. 163 p. ISBN: 9780374371968. *J*

Fifteen-year-old Cameron is forced to leave her working-class white Brooklyn neighborhood when her single white mother gets a job in the projects. She discovers that her father, who disappeared before she was born, was African American. Cameron must come to terms with this new aspect of her identity as she learns about culture and what it means to be interracial from the multicultural neighbors, teachers, and new friends.

Interracial Persons • Mother and Daughter • Single Parent • Family Secrets

Meminger, Neesha

Shine, Coconut Moon. New York: Margaret K. McElderry Books, 2009. 253 p. ISBN: 9781416954958. *S*

> Seventeen-year-old Indian American Samar blends in at school, and because her mother cut ties with her extended family, she has never known them and has had no experience with their religion and culture. When her Uncle Sandeep arrives in a turban four days after the terrorist attacks of September 11, Samar realizes what she has been missing and begins a quest to embrace her culture. Facing racism and violence along the way, Samar must learn how to accept herself as she redefines her relationship with her white best friend and boyfriend and develops her own sense of self-awareness.

> *East-Indian Americas • Single Parent • Mother and Daughter • Family • Prejudice*

Na, An

The Fold. New York: G.P. Putnam's Sons, 2008. 192 p. ISBN: 9780399242762. *JS*

> When her Aunt Gomo wins the lottery and offers to pay for the plastic surgery that would make sixteen-year-old Joyce Park's Asian eyelids appear more Western with beautiful double eyelid folds, Joyce faces an agonizing decision. Never having felt like she fits in as only one of the few Asian Americans at her posh Los Angeles high school and obsessing about attracting gorgeous classmate John Ford Kang, Joyce just wants to be like her beautiful, perfect, older sister, Helen, and is increasingly convinced that "the fold" is the ideal of female beauty. Helen, who is outraged about the possibility of the surgery, a classmate who has already had the surgery, and Aunt Gomo who has had numerous surgeries, all make the decision harder, until Joyce finds within herself a self-respect that allows her to see the beauty in everyone's differences.

> *Korean Americans • Infatuation • Peer Pressure • Plastic Surgery*

Na, An

Wait for Me. New York: Putnam, 2006. 240 p. ISBN: 9780399242755; 9780142409183pa; (aud). YALSA Best Books. *S*

> High school senior Mina has created a complex web of lies that includes tales of her being the president of the honor society with straight A's. Feeling forced to satisfy her overbearing mother, Uhmma, who sees Harvard in Mina's future, she hides the truth of her average grades as she struggles to care for her hearing-impaired younger sister, Suna, who is neglected by their mother. To further her plot, Mina uses her brilliant friend, Jonathan Kim, and because he thinks she loves him, he forges report cards and backs up her stories. Soon the lies begin to unravel after Jonathan rapes her. Then when Ysrael, a Mexican immigrant comes to work in their family's dry-cleaning business, Mina finds herself falling in love with him, and she is forced to choose between family responsibility or her own dreams.

> *Korean Americans • Sisters • Deaf Persons • Ex-Boyfriends • Rape • Coming-of-Age*

Namioka, Lensey

Mismatch: A Novel. New York: Delacorte Press, 2006. 217 p. ISBN: 9780385731836. *J*

In a suburb of Seattle, fifteen-year-old Chinese-American Suzanne "Sue" Hua, a talented viola player, meets Japanese American violinist Andy Suzuki in their high school orchestra. While their classmates think they will make a good couple because they are both Asian, their relationship seems doomed because Suzanne's grandmother can't forget the brutality she suffered at the hands of the Japanese during World War II and Andy's father is prejudiced about the Chinese. Visiting Tokyo while on tour with their orchestra, Andy searches for his cultural roots, finding that he is more American than he thought. Sue observes bigotry and discrimination while living with a Korean host family. In the end, Andy and Sue find a way to respect their cultures by accepting the past and identifying themselves as individuals.

Asian Americans • Dating • Culture Conflict • Prejudice • Discrimination • Violinists

Osa, Nancy

Cuba 15. New York: Delacorte Press, 2003. 277 p. ISBN: 9780385730211; 9780385732338pa; YALSA Best Books; ALA Notable Children's Books; Pura Belpre Award. *J*

Violet Paz's dad never acknowledged their Cuban heritage until her grandmother insists that Violet have a big Quinceañera to celebrate her coming-of-age. But Violet wants nothing to do with it. She is an American who looks like her Polish American mother, and she does not want to wear a fluffy dress and tiara. As she, her grandmother, and their two cultures collide, Violet finds that she wants to learn more about the roots of her eclectic family, whose antics are fodder for her comedic speech team's addresses. As the big party moves forward, Violet finds a dress and a boyfriend, and in the end she is able to develop a greater understanding of where she came from and who she is.

Cuban Americans • Immigrants • Coming-of-Age

Ostow, Micol

Emily Goldberg Learns to Salsa. New York : Razorbill, 2006. 288 p. ISBN: 9781595140814; 9781595141446pa. *S*

High school senior Emily Goldberg meets her mother's family for the first time when she leaves her home in New York to attend her grandmother's funeral in Puerto Rico. There she discovers a whole new world as she gets used to foreign customs and language and explores food, music, the landscape, and museums. Getting over her dislike for her cousin Lucy, who thinks she is a spoiled brat, and meeting a gorgeous guy help Lucy to fit in as she finds some connection to her heritage and comes to understand why her mother stayed in New York after college and married Emily's Jewish father.

Hispanic Americans • Jewish Men • Interracial Families • Puerto Ricans

Rosten, Carrie

Chloe Leiberman (Sometimes Wong): A Novel. New York: Delacorte Press, 2005. 210 p. ISBN: 9780385732475; 9780385732482pa. *JS*

Half-Chinese, half-Jewish high school senior Chloe Wong Leiberman has not applied for any college or even taken her SATs, thinking only about fashion to the extent that she mentally remakes the clothing faux pas of her friends and family. Chloe wants to attend a prestigious fashion academy in London, but her disconnected wealthy parents don't understand her ambition. After a mix-up at school, Chloe hopes to finally live her dream with the support of her neighbor, La Contessa.

Jews • Chinese Americans • Ambition • Interracial Persons • Family • Friendship • Interracial Families

Saldana, Rene

The Jumping Tree: A Novel. New York: Delacorte Press, 2001. 181 p. ISBN: 9780385327251. *M*

As he moves through the years from sixth to eighth grade, Rey Castanada learns what it means to be a man as he grows and reconciles his dual Chicano and American heritage. He is influenced by events such as breaking his wrist on a dare; learning about civil disobedience; watching his father, uncle, and cousins as they travel back and forth from Mexico; and losing his friends to drugs and violence. Through all of this, Rey works to build a good life and craft a positive future.

Mexican-Americans • Coming-of-Age

Schorr, Melissa

Goy Crazy. New York: Hyperion, 2006. 352 p. ISBN: 9780786838523; 9780786838530pa. *J*

Knowing her parents would not approve of a non-Jewish boyfriend, fifteen-year-old Rachel Lowenstein develops a plan to use unsuspecting Jewish neighbor Howard Goldstein as a ruse so that she can date basketball star Luke Christensen. Unfortunately, she must act dumb to be cool enough for Luke, he pressures her to get a tattoo, and he and his buddies make rude jokes. Then she almost gets caught when she runs into her parents' friends at a deli. As her relationship with Luke moves forward, Rachel soon discovers that blonde hair and blue eyes are not the best way to determine whom your boyfriend should be.

Jewish Americans • Dating • Secrets • Peer Pressure

Serros, Michele

Honey Blonde Chica. New York: Simon Pulse, 2006. 304 p. ISBN: 9781416915911. *J*

Sophomore Evie Gomez hangs out with her own crowd of Mexican American students, refusing to join the popular clique of Mexican girls who also attend her prep school. Things change when her best friend, Dee Dee, returns from a long visit to Mexico and joins the popular group. Evie must decide if she should abandon her friends, including Raquel and surfer boy Alex, and join Dee Dee in the popular crowd.

Sequel: *Scandalosa!: A Honey Blonde Chica Novel.* New York: Simon Pulse, 2007. 316 p. ISBN: 9781416915935. *JS*

> Facing the cancelation of her fabulous sweet sixteen party if her grades don't improve, Evie Gomez must also deal with a boyfriend who seems to be losing interest in her and the problems of her two girlfriends, one who is battling a drinking problem and the other who wants to move back to Mexico.
>
> *Mexican Americans • Identity • Cliques • Popularity • Friendship*

Sitomer, Alan Lawrence

The Secret Story of Sonia Rodriguez. New York: Hyperion Books for Children, 2008. 320 p. ISBN: 9781423110729. YALSA Quick Picks. *JS*

> Born in the United States to illegal-immigrant parents who crossed the border to escape the poverty around them, sixteen-year-old Sonia is determined to graduate from high school despite the prejudice she faces. She also struggles with having to stay up past midnight to complete her homework because her mother treats her like a servant, expecting her to cook, clean, and care for her younger siblings. Sonia's only support is her father, who works three jobs. After her drunken uncle makes inappropriate advances, Sonia can't stand it anymore and rebels against her mother. As punishment, she is sent to visit her grandmother in Mexico. But while there, she is able to gain a new respect for her roots and find a place for herself in the world.
>
> *Mexican Americans • Family Problems • Grandmothers*

Smith, Sherri L.

Hot, Sour, Salty, Sweet. New York: Delacorte Press, 2008. 167 p. ISBN: 9780385734172. *M*

> Ana Shen wants a conflict-free dinner after her junior high school graduation. That looks impossible, however, when her Chinese and African American grandmothers begin competing for attention and her grandfathers sequester themselves in different parts of the house. Ana is unsure if she can ever get them to come to terms. While dealing with her family problems, Ana must also try to do everything she can to prepare herself to attract her crush, Jamie, who will attend graduation with his parents, especially when her rival for his affections, Amanda, shows up as well.
>
> *Interracial Persons • Middle School • Parties • Interpersonal Relations • Grandparents • African Americans • Chinese Americans • Family Problems*

Triana, Gaby

Cubanita. New York: Rayo, 2005. 208 p. ISBN: 9780060560201; 9780060560225pa. YALSA Popular Paperbacks. *S*

> During the summer before college, seventeen-year-old Cuban American Isabel Diaz is looking forward to working at a summer camp where she can avoid her overprotective mother who knows just how to make her feel guilty. When sexy older man Andrew comes along, Isabel's mother thinks he is trouble, but Isabel overlooks his sleazy ways. As she begins to embrace

her cultural heritage and come to terms with her mother, Isabel finds that she can be her own person.

Cuban Americans • Mother and Daughter • Coming-of-Age

Wong, Joyce Lee

Seeing Emily. New York: Amulet Books, 2005. 280 p. ISBN: 9780810957572; 9780810992580pa. *JS*

Trying to figure out where she belongs, sixteen-year-old artist Emily Wu tries to assert her independence from the heritage of her Chinese immigrant parents. Her best friends, Nina and Liz, encourage her to experiment with makeup, because her first boyfriend, Nick, wants her to look more exotic. But when her parents decide to send her on a visit to her aunt in Taiwan, Emily is finally able to realize that her world is richer because of the combination of her Chinese and American heritages.

Chinese Americans • Family • Artists • Friendship • Immigrants • Novels in Verse • Coming-of-Age

Wright, Bill

When the Black Girl Sings. New York: Simon & Schuster Books for Young Readers, 2008. 266 p. ISBN: 9781416939955; 9781416940036pa. *J*

Fourteen-year-old Lahni Schuler has always felt out of place as the only African American in her private girls' school. She is even more uncertain about her place when a white boy begins harassing her, and then her adoptive white parents break up when her dad leaves to be with another woman. When Lahni's mother takes her to a multiracial church and she starts singing with the gospel choir, Lahni discovers her own unique voice as she is inspired by the music. With the help of the choir director, she finds the courage to enter the school's singing competition and face her harasser.

African Americans • Divorce • Loneliness • Singing

Yee, Lisa

Millicent Min, Girl Genius. New York: Arthur A. Levine Books, 2003. 248 p. ISBN: 9780439425193; 9780439771313pa; (aud). *M*

Eleven-year-old Millicent "Millie" Min, who has a genius IQ, is going to start twelfth grade next year, but in the meantime her parents have enrolled her in summer volleyball and have agreed to let her take a college poetry class. Millie soon finds that college kids are often just as dumb and lazy as one of the boys at school, Stanford, whom she has been pressed into tutoring. Millie has never been very good at making friends because she is always willing to express how much she knows on any given topic, so she is trying to hide her abilities from Emily, the first real friend she has ever had. Millie is shocked when Emily gets together with Stanford. Then Emily finds out about her abilities and is angry that she did not trust her. Through these experiences, Millie learns that being a genius doesn't make you know how to be a good friend.

Companion: *Stanford Wong Flunks Big-Time.* New York: Arthur A. Levine Books, 2005. 304 p. ISBN: 9780439622479; 9780439622486pa. ALA Notable Children's Books. *M*

> Forced to stay home from basketball camp and be tutored by Millicent Min because he flunked sixth-grade English, Stanford Wong is upset. But over the course of the summer, he discovers that he and Millie have quite a few things in common as he worries about his parents' constant fighting, his father's increasingly long work hours, and his grandmother, who has been placed in a nursing home. Through it all Stanford is able to grow as he learns about life off the basketball court. After falling in love and working through his academic issues, he is able to get the acceptance and love he craves from his father.

Companion: *So Totally Emily Ebers*. New York: Arthur A. Levine Books, 2007. 304 p. ISBN: 9780439838474. *M*

> After her parents' divorce, Emily Ebers's mother forces her to move from New Jersey to California. She is not happy and expresses her discontent in a journal addressed to her absent father, who is touring with his old rock band. But soon Emily finds a friend in Millicent Min, when the two meet at their girls summer volleyball league and they are the two worst players. She also meets and falls in love with Stanford, whom she assumes is tutoring Millie. When the truth comes out that it is Millie who is doing the tutoring, she is crushed that her new friends have misled her. As she comes to forgive her friends, Emily learns important lessons about change and along the way she is able to forgive her mother as well.

> *Chinese Americans • Friendship • Basketball • Trust • Mother and Daughter • Divorce Letters • Diary Novel • Epistolary Novels*

Yoo, David

Girls for Breakfast. New York: Delacorte Press, 2005. 294 p. ISBN: 9780385731928; 9780440238836pa. *S*

> Korean American Nick Park is the only Asian in his all-white suburban Connecticut high school. After graduation and a prom-night disaster, Nick tries to figure out what went wrong as he looks back at all the experiences he has had from elementary school on, including his lack of popularity, dates, and sex, despite all the things he did to try to gain attention. As he reminisces, Nick must come to grips with his identity and embrace his cultural heritage.

> *Korean Americans • Asian Americans • Popularity • Racism • Mother and Son • Coming-of-Age*

Yoo, David

Stop Me If You've Heard This One Before. New York: Hyperion, 2008. 374 p. ISBN: 9781423109075. *JS*

> Sixteen-year-old Korean American Albert Kim has cultivated his persona as a loser and further cements it by taking a cleaning job at an inn instead of going to an academic summer camp. On the job, he meets popular Mia, who has just broken up with her gorgeous lacrosse team star boyfriend, Ryan.

Even though Albert and Mia don't get along at first, when their boss makes passes at Mia and tries to fire her, the two find friendship and then love. Back at school, they are challenged by their different social statuses and the fact that Ryan has been diagnosed with Hodgkin's disease. Mia wants to support Ryan, and this puts strain on her relationship with Albert. The two must weather the storm to find out if their relationship will last.

Korean Americans • Cancer • Misfits • Popularity

Yoo, Paula

Good Enough. New York: HarperTeen, 2008. 322 p. ISBN: 9780060790851. *S*

Senior and class valedictorian Patti Yoon struggles with the decision of whether she should fulfill the expectations of her Korean parents and go to Harvard, Yale, or Princeton, or if she should try to get into Julliard as her violin teacher advises. Having always done what her parents expect, Pattie is distracted when she finds herself attracted to a new trumpet player at school. As their friendship develops, Patti learns how she can shape her own identity and embrace her future.

Korean Americans • Violinists • Gifted Teenagers • Musicians • Parent and Child

Immigration

Budhos, Marina

Ask Me No Questions. New York: Atheneum Books for Young Readers, 2006. 176 p. ISBN: 9781416903512; 9781416949206pa. ALA Notable Children's Books; YALSA Best Books. *JS*

Having lived for years as illegal immigrants in the United States with fake social security numbers, the Hossain family, who are originally from Bangladesh, are caught when the government cracks down on immigration after 9/11. Trying to seek asylum in Canada from the routine harassment the family must endure, fourteen-year-old Nadira's father is detained in prison because he does not have a valid passport. While their mother stays nearby, Nadira and eighteen-year-old Aisha, who dreams of studying to be a doctor, must return to Queens. After Aisha breaks down, it is entirely up to Nadira to get her father out of detention and prevent the family's deportation by putting together the documentation to make a case that will help the judges see them as individuals rather than terror suspects.

Family • Muslims

First Person Fiction (multiple authors). New York: Orchard Books

This series focuses on recent immigration experiences.

Cuban Americans • Korean Americans • Diary Novel

Danticat, Edwidge

Behind the Mountains. 2002. 176p. ISBN: 9780439372992; 9780439373005pa. *J*

After Papa leaves for New York, Celiane Esperance keeps a journal of her family's experiences in the Haitian mountains and their immigration to the United States.

Son, John

Finding My Hat. 2003. 192p. ISBN: 9780439435383; 9780439435390pa. *J*

Jin-Han Park, the son of Korean immigrants, has lived all over the United States. He tries to find his place between the culture of his parents and the American culture that surrounds him. We follow Jin-Han from age two through his high school years, as he experiences humorous moments, challenges, and pain.

Ho, Minfong

The Stone Goddess. 2003. 208p. ISBN: 9780439381970. *J*

Fleeing the Phnom Penh when the Khmer Rouge takes over Cambodia, thirteen-year-old Nakri ends up in a brutal labor camp. A trained classical dancer, it is her love of dance that helps her survive and ultimately immigrate to the United States.

Veciana-Suarez, Ana

The Flight to Freedom. 2002. 208p. ISBN: 9780439381994. *J*

Thirteen-year-old Yara keeps a diary in late 1960 during her flight with her family from Cuba to their new life in Miami.

Hobbs, Will

Crossing the Wire. New York: HarperCollins, 2006. 216 p. ISBN: 9780060741389; 9780060741402pa. *M*

After his father dies, fifteen-year-old Victor Flores is unable to support his family with the corn he grows in his tiny Mexican village, so he decides to cross the border into the United States. Without a guide, Victor attempts the dangerous crossing multiple times, but when he unknowingly becomes involved with drug traffickers, he has more to worry about than facing hunger and thirst, or even the border patrol.

Immigrants • Violence • Drug Dealers • Best Friends

Jaamillo, Ann

La Linea. New Milford, CT: Roaring Brook Press, 2006. 144 p. ISBN: 9781596431546. YALSA Best Books. *J*

On his fifteenth birthday, Miguel receives a note from his father telling him that it is time for him to leave Mexico, cross the border, and join his family in California. When his thirteen-year-old sister, Elena, secretly disguises herself and follows him, the two must stick together to brave a harrowing trip through the desert and across the border. During the trek, they are robbed and threatened.

Mexican Americans • Brothers • Sisters

Na, An

A Step from Heaven. Asheville, NC: Front Street, 2000. 156 p. ISBN: 9780786241262; 9780142500279pa; (aud). Michael L. Printz Award; YALSA Best Books; ALA Notable Children's Books; School Library Journal Best Books. *JS*

Young Ju and her family moved from Korea to California in hope of achieving the American dream. From her first struggles as a first-grader trying to learn a new language and understand the culture, to becoming a straight-A student preparing for college, Young Ju faces many challenges. As she grows up, her strict father's alcoholism and abuse increases, and although Young Ju is ashamed of him and their run-down home, she is able to feel some of his pain as they deal with the grief of losing the people and culture they left behind.

Alcoholism • Korean Americans • Moving

Chapter 9

Discovering Spirituality

Spiritual development is a facet central to many teens' identities. Developing a spiritual outlook involves more than adhering to a single organized religion; it encompass understanding one's motivations, building an ethical value system, and actively seeking new ideas that shape one's understanding of the world. Developing a personal relationship with things above and beyond oneself and joining in the search for the sacred elements in one's life are important parts of adolescents' spiritual development. The books listed in this chapter deal with the variety of experiences that teens have as they explore and develop their spiritual lives. Finding a place in an organized religion, such as Christianity, Judaism, or Islam, is the path that many teens take to discover where their beliefs lie. For others, there is a need to break out of the standards of mainstream religion to create their own understanding of spirituality.

Abdel-Fattah, Randa

Does My Head Look Big in This? New York: Orchard Books, 2007. 368 p. ISBN: 9780439919470; (aud). *JS*

> Amal is an Australian-born Palestinian Muslim who is beginning her junior year of high school. She decides she will wear the hijab, the Muslim head covering, full time as a mark of her deeply held faith. While Amal finds support for her decision among family and friends, she also faces intolerance from classmates and potential employers. Falling in love with a non-Muslim classmate tests her faith, but with humor and strength Amal finds a new beginning has unfolded because of her choice.

Muslims • Identity

Abdel-Fattah, Randa

Ten Things I Hate about Me. New York: Orchard Books, 2009. 304 p. ISBN: 9780545050555. *JS*

> At school she is blonde-haired, blue-eyed Jamie. At home she is Jamilah, the Lebanese Muslim daughter of a widowed and very strict father. Desperate to fit in, Jamilah keeps her two lives separate, despite the inconveniences, until they unexpectedly collide when the band she plays with at her Madrassa, or Islamic religious study school, is invited to perform at the tenth-grade formal. With the help of her online friend, John, Jamilah is able to reconcile her two identities.

Muslims • Identity

Baskin, Nora Raleigh

The Truth about My Bat Mitzvah. New York: Simon & Schuster Books for Young Readers, 2008. 138 p. ISBN: 9781416935582; 9781416974697pa; (aud). *M*

When her grandmother dies, twelve-year-old Caroline inherits a Star of David necklace. Raised by her Jewish mom and Christian dad, Caroline has not thought much of religion, but with the gift and the fact that her best friend Rachel is preparing for her bat mitzvah, Caroline begins to wonder about her religious heritage. Struggling with all the realities of normal life such as boys and school, Caroline also struggles with what it means to be Jewish until she finds some resolution to her own religious identity.

Judaism • Family • Prejudice • Grief

Bradley, Kimberly Brubaker

Leap of Faith. New York: Dial Books for Young Readers, 2007. 192 p. ISBN: 9780803731271. *JS*

To stop him from sexually harassing her, Abigail stabs the principal's son, popular Brett McAvery, with a pocketknife. Because nobody believes the motive for her actions, she is expelled from school. With no other alternatives, her parents enroll her in a private Catholic school. Trying to infuriate her nonreligious parents, Abigail starts to pretend she is interested in Catholicism, but soon her interest turns into something more real, as she begins to open herself to new ideas and learns the meaning of forgiveness.

Catholic Schools • Parent and Child • Faith • Violence

Brande, Robin

Evolution, Me, and Other Freaks of Nature. New York: Alfred A. Knopf, 2007. 272 p. ISBN: 9780375843495; (aud). YALSA Best Books. *MJ*

When her church becomes embroiled in a lawsuit because she wrote a letter revealing how some of the church's teens had harassed a supposedly gay schoolmate, eighth-grader Mena Reece is ostracized by her friends and, to some extent, by her family. At school, there is further controversy when a science teacher begins a unit on evolution, which begins a standoff between her former friends and the teacher she admires. When Mena's friendship with her nerdy lab partner, Casy Connor, turns into love, she finds new strength to speak her mind and stand up for her beliefs, even against the odds, as she reconciles her faith and the truths of science.

Faith • Christianity • High School

Carlson, Melody

Diary of a Teenage Girl: Caitlin Series. Sisters, OR: Multnomah

Caitlin O'Conner deals with the problems of family and school as she tries to keep her faith and stay strong in her commitments.

Christianity • High School • Self-Perception • Peer Pressure • Best Friends • Race Relations • Interracial Persons • Dating • College • Diary Novel

Becoming Me. 2000. 248 p. ISBN: 9781576737354pa. *JS*

> Sixteen-year-old Caitlin O'Conner must deal with the pressures of teenage life, including her longing to have a boyfriend, as she struggles to understand the plan that God has for her life.

It's My Life. 2001. 245 p. ISBN: 9781576737729pa. *JS*

> Facing a variety of problems, including her parents's marriage difficulties, a friend drug problems, and other complicated people in her life, seventeen-year-old Caitlin uses her diary and prayer to deal with everything.

Who I Am. 2002. 254 p. ISBN: 9781576738900pa. *JS*

> Now a senior, Caitlin must decide about what she should do with the rest of her life. Her parents want her to attend college, while she wants to help orphans in Mexico. As her relationship with Josh gets serious and friend Beanie begins dating an African American, Caitlin must find strength in the commitments she has made not to date.

On My Own. 2002. 263 p. ISBN: 9781590520178pa. *JS*

> Now at college with a bold new roommate named Liz, Caitlin must deal with her own beliefs regarding dating, kissing, and friendship as she and her old friend Josh enter a pre-engagement covenant that will lead them to marriage.

I Do! 2004. 263 p. ISBN: 9781590523209pa. *JS*

> At twenty-one, Caitlin has accepted Josh's proposal, and they are now planning a wedding. Old friends and in-law troubles get in the way, but Caitlin clings to her faith and manages to make it through the one day that will change the rest of her life.

Carlson, Melody

Diary of a Teenage Girl: Chloe Series. Sisters, OR: Multnomah

> After embracing a new faith, Chloe forms a Christian rock band, and she and her bandmates must face the problems that come with celebrity.

> *Christianity • Rock Music • Identity • Bullies and Bullying • Friendship • Family • Diary Novel*

My Name Is Chloe. 2002. 279 p. ISBN: 9781590520185pa. *JS*

> High school freshman Chloe develops a strong faith and expresses her love of God through the all-girl band she forms.

Sold Out. 2003. 284 p. ISBN: 9781590521410pa. *JS*

> When their band becomes a local hit, Chloe Miller and her fellow band members must sort out lots of problems, including figuring out who their real friends are and dealing with conflicts that arise when a Nashville talent scout discovers the group.

1

2

3

4

5

6

7

8

9

10

11

12

Road Trip. 2004. 292 p. ISBN: 9781590521427pa. YALSA Popular Paperbacks. *JS*

Chloe and her band sign a recording contract with a major company, and the band starts its concert tour. Things become stressful and overwhelming as Chloe must confront her bandmate about the signs she has been showing of a drug addiction.

Face the Music. 2004. 278 p. ISBN: 9781590522417pa. *J*

With their albums now on the best-seller chart, Chloe and the band are looking forward to some downtime to focus on their regular high school lives, including grades, boys, and friends.

Cooper, Ilene

Sam I Am. New York: Scholastic Press, 2004. 252 p. ISBN: 9780439439671; 9780439439688pa. YALSA Popular Paperbacks. *M*

When twelve-year-old Sam Goodman's dog knocks over the family's "Hannukah Bush/Christmas Tree," Sam's parents begin to rethink their decision to bring their children up without a religion. However, Dad is Jewish and Mom is Episcopalian, and the pair can't agree on which religion it should be. The controversy is fueled by Sam's two grandmothers, who don't get along. Things escalate when her class begins a unit on the Holocaust, and Sam begins asking her own questions.

Family • Religion • Christmas • Christianity • Judaism

Erskine, Kathryn

Quaking. New York: Philomel Books, 2007. 272 p. ISBN: 9780399247743. YALSA Quick Picks. *JS*

Matilda "Matt" is intrigued by the Quaker religion of her new foster parents, Sam and Jessica Fox. Attending Friends meetings with them, Matt learns of their commitment to peace and their stand against the war in the Middle East. At home Matt has conflicts with the Foxs' other child, Rory, and their severely disabled son. At school she faces conflicts with a bully and her world civics teacher. When violent vandals target the Quakers, Matt embraces the peaceful values of her new family and takes a strong stance to resolve her own conflicts peacefully, both at home and at school.

Bullies and Bullying • Foster Parents

Hautman, Pete

Godless. New York: Simon & Schuster Books for Young Readers, 2004. 208 p. ISBN: 9780689862786; 9781416908166pa. National Book Award; YALSA Best Books; YALSA Popular Paperbacks. *JS*

Inventing a new religion, "Chutengodianism," that sanctifies water, the source of all life, with their god being their town's ten-legged water tower, fifteen-year-old agnostic Jason Black is rebelling against his Catholic father's demands. His new religion easily attracts converts, including his friend Shin, who writes the group's bible, and Henry, who changes his bullying ways as he is named a high priest of the new group. When the boys break into the water tower on an impromptu pilgrimage, things go awry, and Henry is severely injured. Now the group members must face new trials as they try to decide what is right.

Religion • Catholics • Friendship • Ethics

Howell, Simmone

Everything Beautiful. New York: Bloomsbury Children's Books: Distributed to the trade by Macmillan, 2008. 320 p. ISBN: 9781599900421. *JS*

> Overweight sixteen-year-old Riley is forced by her dad and stepmom to go to a Christian camp in the hope that it will curb her rebellious, promiscuous nature, which resulted from the grief she carries after the death of her mother. Riley does not change as she works hard to rebel against all the Bible-based activities and seduce a gorgeous counselor. Finding a soul mate in fellow camper Dylan, who was recently disabled, the pair begins sneaking smokes, racing around in a stolen dune buggy, and planning a secret vision quest into the nearby desert. As Riley and Dylan fall in love, the experience opens her to the concepts of spirituality, and she begins to see that there is love and meaning in the most unexpected of places.
>
> *Religion • Christianity • Camps • Wheelchairs • Friendship*

Koja, Kathe

Buddha Boy. New York: Frances Foster Books, 2003. 117 p. ISBN: 9780374309985; 9780142402092pa; (aud). YALSA Best Books; YALSA Popular Paperbacks. *MJ*

> When Michael Martin arrives at school dressed like a monk and spends his lunch hour begging, it is Justin who stands up for him when the school's bullies target him. When a teacher pairs them for a project, Justin gets to know Michael, who was a criminal until his parents died and a Buddhist art teacher showed him the beauty in both art and religion. As the friends learn from and support each other, Justin is there to help Michael regain his own balance when two of his prized art projects are vandalized.
>
> *Peer Pressure • Buddhism • Orphans • Bullies and Bullying*

Levitin, Sonia

Strange Relations. New York: Alfred A. Knopf, 2007. 304 p. ISBN: 9780375837517; 9780440239635pa. *J*

> Fifteen-year-old Marne is looking forward to spending the summer in Hawaii with her relatives while her parents are in Paris on a work assignment. Embracing the chance to escape the constant grief her family feels over her younger sister's disappearance some years ago, Marne's dreams of long days on the beach don't materialize when she arrives in the chaotic household of her Aunt Chaya and her husband, Yitz, a Hasidic rabbi. Confronted by the family's religious commitment, which she has never experienced with her secular Jewish parents, Marne is able to gain a new perspective on her heritage and build a sense of her own commitment to her faith.
>
> *Jewish Americans • Cousins • Aunts • Religion • Family Relationships • Ethics • Values • Faith • Summer • Vacations*

Nolan, Han

When We Were Saints. Orlando, FL: Harcourt, 2003. 291 p. ISBN: 9780152163716; 9780152053222pa. YALSA Popular Paperbacks. *MJ*

> Archie's grandfather dubs his fourteen-year-old grandson a saint. When his grandfather dies, Archie begins a spiritual quest, which leads him to befriend Clare Simpson, a strange girl who professes that they are the spiritual manifestations of the original Saint Frances and Clare. Enchanted by Clare and guilty over his grandfather's death, Archie is drawn into Clare's increasingly complex schemes, which involve praying continually, giving up his personal property, and finally going on a pilgrimage to the Cloisters Museum in New York City by stealing and illegally driving his grandfather's truck. Growing more wary of Clare over time, Archie struggles to understand his personal relationship with God as he comes to accept his friend's mental instability.

> *Christianity • Emotional Problems • Death*

Rosenbloom, Fiona

You Are So Not Invited to My Bat Mitzvah! New York: Hyperion, 2005. 190 p. ISBN: 9780786856169; 9780786838912pa. *M*

> Twelve-year-old Stacy Friedman is looking forward to her Bat Mitzvah, but she's dealing with having to sing a portion of the Torah and a party dress that makes her look like an American Girl doll. In addition, she must cope with the consequences when she rescinds the invitation to her Bat Mitzvah to her friend Lydia after she catches her kissing Andy Goldfarb, the boy Stacy has a crush on. When Rabbi Sherwin asks Stacy to perform three good deeds before the ceremony, she finds a new attitude about giving to others as she completes the task.

> **Sequel:** ***We Are So Crashing Your Bar Mitzvah!*** New York: Hyperion, 2007. 224 p. ISBN: 9780786838905. *M*

> Over the summer, thirteen-year-old Stacy Friedman and her best friend Lydia think they have become very cool, but the popular girls don't agree with them, and it is their other friend, Kelly, who the popular girls accept. Kelly wins a coveted invitation to popular-boy Eben's Bar Mitzvah. Anxious to be included, Stacy and Lydia decide to crash the Bar Mitzvah, where they make fools of themselves but also learn that real friendship is better than popularity.

> *Jewish Americans • Cliques • Friendship • Interpersonal Relations • Betrayal • Popularity*

Roth, Matthue

Never Mind the Goldbergs. New York: PUSH/Scholastic, 2005. 368 p. ISBN: 9780439691888; 9780439691895pa. YALSA Popular Paperbacks. *S*

> After a successful run in a local play, seventeen-year-old punk and Orthodox Jew Hava Aaronson is offered a leading role in a television sitcom about a Jewish family and heads off to Hollywood. Thrust into a make-believe world filled with sex, alcohol, and out-of-control Hollywood parties, Hava must now figure out what is real, especially when she and Charles, her television father, share an off-camera kiss. Grounded through it all by her two friends, confidant Ian, who is gay, and

Moishe, who makes offbeat films, Hava is able to figure out what her religion means to her and find a place for both the religious and secular cultures of which she is a part.

Jewish Americans • Friendship • Identity • Religion • Actors and Actresses

Sonnenblick, Jordan

Zen and the Art of Faking It. New York: Scholastic Press, 2007. 264 p. ISBN: 9780439837071. *MJ*

Adopted Chinese-American San Lee is entering a new school in Pennsylvania when he and his mother move there after his father is sent to jail for fraud. San decides to reinvent himself into an eighth-grade Zen master after he finds that his social studies class is learning about Buddhism. Enmeshed in the charade, San continues on with the scheme, especially when he finds that his cute classmate Woody is impressed by his knowledge. Even as he helps Woody with a school project about Zen, volunteers at a soup kitchen, and helps the second-string basketball team take on the starters using Zen strategies, San is caught in his lies and must find a way to be himself and deal with the anger he has toward his father.

Chinese Americans • Identity • Moving • Schools • Buddhism • Volunteers

Weinheimer, Beckie

Converting Kate. New York: Viking Children's Books, 2007. 288 p. ISBN: 9780670061525; YALSA Best Books. *JS*

Sixteen-year-old Kate Anderson is living with her mother at her Great-Aunt Katherine's bed and breakfast, where she finds herself questioning the beliefs of the Holy Divine Church after her estranged father's death. Even though her mother still firmly believes, Kate finds that her parents' divorce and her mother's refusal to have a funeral for her father have further eroded everything she has ever learned. She begins exploring things that were once forbidden. With the help of those around her, including her Aunt Katherine; her friends Will, Jamie, and Richard; and a new church youth group led by young Pastor Browning, Kate is able to develop the courage to find her own beliefs.

Faith • Fathers • Death • New Students • Athletes • Aunts • Family Problems • Grief • Moving • Coming-of-Age

Wittlinger, Ellen

Blind Faith. New York: Simon & Schuster Books for Young Readers, 2006. 288 p. ISBN: 9781416902737; 9781416949060pa. YALSA Best Books. *JS*

Fifteen-year-old Elizabeth "Liz" Scattergood has always felt left out of the close relationship that her artistic mother shared with her grandmother, Bunny. When Bunny passes away, Liz is even more shut out, as her mother is consumed by grief. It is only through visits to a spiritualist church that claims to channel the dead that her mom feels happy. Her atheist dad, who is against his wife's religious interests, soon leaves them. This increases the tension in her family, and it is not until Liz finds romance with her new six-teen-year-old neighbor, who is dealing with the imminent death of his own mother from leukemia, that she is able to deal with her complex feelings and face her problems.

Death • *Cancer* • *Mother and Daughter* • *Dysfunctional Families* • *Faith* • *Grief*

Chapter 10

Facing Economic Challenges

Many adolescents find their lives constrained by their socioeconomic status or the place they live. Having or lacking certain economic opportunities creates different challenges in their daily lives, and teens are very aware of this fact. The books listed in this chapter deal with the constraints that differences in social classes put on teens' lives. Many adolescents find that dealing with the divisions created by social classes may make developing certain friendships or romantic relationships more difficult. Inner-city and urban youth in particular face many challenges. Surrounded by the violence, drugs, alcohol, gangs, and poverty that often typify urban living, teens in these circumstances must find ways to keep their situations from defining the trajectory of their entire lives. Living in poverty or low-income situations leaves many adolescents in situations where the basics of clothing, housing, health care, or effective schooling cannot be provided. Without the chances that others have, teens who live in the inner city or those living in poverty must work harder to develop their complete identities and craft a positive adult life.

Social Classes

Dent, Grace

Diary of a Chav. New York: Little, Brown, 2008. 240 p. ISBN: 9780316034838. *JS*

Fifteen-year-old Shiraz Baily Wood is fed up with her mother and sisters' fights and hurt after being abandoned by her best friend Carrie, who has a new boyfriend. Spouting off to her diary, Shiraz works hard to deny the labels that mark her as working-class, or a "Chav-girl," but it is not until a tough new English teacher arrives at school that her thinking starts to change. She realizes that earning money is not everything as she resolves to work harder at school.

Sequel: *Posh and Prejudice.* New York, Little, Brown, 2009. 224 p. ISBN: 9780316034845pa. *JS*

Excited to find out she is really smart after passing her school exams, Shiraz enters the new school year with great enthusiasm to gain more knowledge. Shiraz quits her dead-end job and begins hanging out with other intellectuals, including handsome Joshua. When her family and some of her friends are not too happy with the changes she's making, Shiraz must look deep into herself to discover what really matters.

Identity • Self-Discovery • England • Diary Novel

Elkeles, Simone

Perfect Chemistry. New York: Walker, Distributed to the trade by Macmillan, 2009, 432 p. ISBN: 9780802798237; 9780802798220pa. *S*

> Popular cheerleader Brittany is paired with gang member Alex Fuentes in chemistry class, and they are both unhappy. When Alex bets his friends he can get Brittany to have sex with him, things start to change. As the two get to know each other, they find they are both dealing with complex home lives, and the two soon fall in love. When Alex gets involved in a violent gang altercation that results in the death of his friend, the two are separated until Alex decides whether he can deny his gang heritage and join Brittany at college.

> *Gangs • Hispanic Americans • Cheerleaders • Bets • High School • Romance*

Koja, Kathe

Headlong. New York: Farrar, Straus & Giroux, 2008. 195 p. ISBN: 9780374329129. *J*

> When punk-rock orphan Hazel Tobias transfers to her preppy high school, sophomore Lily Noble is drawn to her, and the two form an unlikely friendship. Searching for herself, Lily is able to see her school, her family, and her friends in a new way, and with the help of Hazel, she is able to push back against the conventional expectations of her privileged life.

> *Identity • Friendship • Orphans*

Simmons, Michael

Pool Boy. Brookfield, CT: Roaring Brook Press, 2003. 164 p. ISBN: 9780761318859; 9780385731966pa; (aud). *JS*

> Fifteen-year-old spoiled-brat Brett's life is stunningly altered when he, along with his mother and sister, are suddenly forced to move into his Great-Aunt Mary's humble two-story home on the other side of the tracks after his stockbroker dad is put in jail for insider trading and laundering money. Angry with his dad for bringing their family so low, Brett is forced to take a job assisting Alfie, an eccentric pool cleaner. As the two develop a friendship, Alfie gets Brett to try new foods and prepare for his driver's test, but it is not until Brett suffers a real loss that he learns true lessons about life and forgiveness.

> *Criminals • Father and Son • Responsibility • Wealth*

Whitney, Kim Ablon

The Perfect Distance. New York: Alfred A. Knopf, 2005. 246 p. ISBN: 9780375832437; 9780553494679pa. *S*

> Seventeen-year-old Francie Martinez pays for her riding lessons at the prestigious West Hills Stables, where her Mexican immigrant father works as a barn manager, by helping out as a groomer. Surrounded by the privileged riders who are being trained to win, Francie is determined to win in the teen's equitation circuit in the year she has remaining, with the hope that she can join the Olympic team. When she becomes distracted by conflicts with her father, a trainer who does not pay her any attention, social pressures around her, and a new romance, she must face seri-

ous competition as she tries to find her place and a way to make ethical decisions that allow her not to compromise on her dreams.

Horses • *Competition* • *Coming-of-Age*

Inner-City Life and Poverty

Blueford High Series (multiple authors). West Berlin, NJ: Townsend Press
This series chronicles the lives and problems of various students at Blueford High School.

African Americans • *Betrayal* • *Trust* • *School* • *Family Problems* • *Street Life*

Schraff, Anne E.

Lost and Found. 2002. 133p. ISBN: 9780944210024; 9780439898393pa. YALSA Popular Paperbacks. *JS*
> Darcy Wills must work to save her missing sister when she realizes she is being followed by a mysterious stranger and a threatening note is left on her desk at Blueford High School.

Schraff, Anne E.

A Matter of Trust. 2001. 125p. ISBN: 9780944210031; 9780439865470pa. *JS*
> As Darcy Wills tries to build a future for her and her family, she must also deal with the conflict she is experiencing with her old friend, Brisanan, and try to maintain her relationship with Hakeem.

Schraff, Anne E.

Secrets in the Shadows. 2001. 126p ISBN: 9780944210055; 9780439904858pa. *JS*
> While he is trying to impress a new girl in his history class, Roylin Bailey is threatened and caught in a web of lies when one of his friends disappears.

Schraff, Anne E.

Someone to Love Me. 2002. 162p ISBN: 9780944210062; 9780439904865pa. *JS*
> When her new boyfriend, Bobby Wallace, starts acting strangely, Cindy Gibson finds herself involved in a great deal of violent trouble.

Langan, Paul

The Bully. 2002. 190p. ISBN: 9780944210000; 9780439865463pa. *JS*
> When he and his mother move from Philadelphia to California in the middle of the school year, ninth-grader Darrell Mercer becomes the new target for the class bully, Tyray Hobbs.

Langan, Paul

The Gun. 2001. 123p ISBN: 9780944210048. *JS*
When he is publicly humiliated by Darrell Mercer at school, bully Tyray Hobbs will do anything to regain the respect he lost and get revenge.

Schraff, Anne E.

Until We Meet Again. 2001. 144p ISBN: 9780944210079; 9780439904889pa. *JS*
With her grandmother's health declining, Darcy Wills is devastated to learn that her boyfriend Hakeem is going to be moving out of state, until she finds support when a mysterious new person comes into her life.

Langan, Paul

Blood Is Thicker. 2004. 156 p. ISBN: 9781591940166; 9780439904896pa. *JS*
Because of his father's illness, Hakeem and his family have moved to Detroit to live with his uncle. Hakeem has a hard time adjusting when he is forced to share a room with his cousin Savon.

Langan, Paul

Brothers in Arms. 2004. 152p. ISBN: 9781591940173; 9780439904902pa. *JS*
Martin Luna must decide if it is best to stay out of trouble or get revenge after his little brother is shot and killed.

Langan, Paul

Summer of Secrets. 2004. 142p ISBN: 9781591940180; 9780439904919pa. *JS*
When Darcy reaches out to her friends for support during a frightening ordeal, she discovers that one of them is hiding an even bigger secret.

Langan, Paul

The Fallen. 2006. 144p. ISBN: 9781591940661. *JS*
Martin Luna works to get his life back on track after the death of his little brother, but he only seems to get in trouble, both at school and at home.

Langan, Paul

Shattered. 2007. 128 p. ISBN: 9781591940692. *JS*
Trying to redevelop her relationship with Hakeem, Darcy Wills once again discovers that her best friends are keeping secrets from her.

Langan, John

Search for Safety. 2006. 128p. ISBN: 9781591940708. *JS*
New student Ben McKee does everything he can to hide the bruises that cover his body from his teachers and friends.

Kern, Peggy

No Way Out. 2009. 140p. ISBN: 9781591941767. YALSA Quick Picks. *JS*

> Facing placement in a foster home and unable to pay the bills to care for his sick grandmother, freshman Harold Davis agrees to work for Londell James, the local drug dealer.

Langan, Paul

Schooled. 2008. 140p. ISBN: 9781591941774. *JS*

> All Lionel Shephard wants to do is play basketball so he can live his dream of playing for the NBA, but to play, he must face the opposition that surrounds him.

Flake, Sharon G.

Money Hungry. New York: Jump at the Sun/Hyperion Books for Children, 2001. 187 p. ISBN: 9780786805488; 9780786815036pa. Coretta Scott King Honor Books. *MJ*

> Thirteen-year-old Raspberry Hill and her mother have lived on the streets and with friends after they left Raspberry's drug-addicted father. Now they find themselves in the projects. With her mother working two jobs, Raspberry goes to school and tries to do whatever she can to earn extra money. She is supported by her three friends: biracial Mai Kim; Ja'ae, who lives with her grandparents but longs to be with her mother; and Zora, whose father seems to be attracted to Raspberry's mother. Struggling with many challenges, such as drug-dealing neighbors and having everything stolen from their apartment, her mother's ingenuity and the support of generous neighbors enable them to better their situation.

Sequel: *Begging for Change*. New York: Jump at the Sun/Hyperion Books for Children, 2003. 235 p. ISBN: 9780786806010; 9780786814053pa. YALSA Quick Picks. *J*

> With her mother in the hospital after being attacked with a metal pipe by a local teenager, Raspberry Hill's drug-addicted and homeless father returns. Terrified that the circumstances will make them homeless again, Raspberry works two jobs. When her father takes the money she has saved, she steals money from her wealthy friends and must deal with the consequences of having broken their trust.

> *African Americans • Stealing • Mother and Daughter • Street Life*

Garsee, Jeannine

Before, After, and Somebody in Between. New York: Bloomsbury Children's Books, distributed to the trade by Holtzbrinck Publishers, 2007. 352 p. ISBN: 9781599900223; 9781599902920pa. *MJ*

> Fourteen-year-old Martha Kowalski lives a difficult life with her alcoholic mother's string of boyfriends. Living in a dangerous neighborhood and faced with constant poverty, Martha finds solace in playing her cello. In a high school rife with violence, Martha makes some bad choices, such as having sex with a stranger and getting involved in a knife fight that ends up

killing friend Jerome's infant brother. Put into foster care and living with a wealthy lawyer who has his own set of problems, Martha tries to remake herself with a new name and identity, but soon she ends up back with her mother and is forced to adapt to the challenges life has thrust upon her.

Alcoholism • Mothers • Violence • Bullies and Bullying • Drug Abuse • Family Problems • Foster Care

Jones, Traci L.

Standing against the Wind. New York: Farrar, Straus & Giroux, 2006. 192 p. ISBN: 9780374371746; 9780312622930pa; Coretta Scott King Award. *MJ*

Having never known her dad and with her mom in jail, eighth-grader Patrice lives with her aunt in a rough Chicago inner-city neighborhood. When her principal presents her with the opportunity to get a scholarship to a private school in Mississippi, Patrice sees a way to beat the odds. The pressures at home and the harsh realities of inner-city life, where boys taunt her and try to fondle her and many of her classmates are promiscuous and pregnant, threaten to stop her dream. But it is Monty, a gang leader, who steps up to protect Patrice, and with his support and love, she is able to find the courage to be different.

Family Problems • African Americans • Gangs • Dysfunctional Families • Gangs • Social Classes

McDonald, Janet

Brother Hood. New York: Farrar, Straus & Giroux, 2004. 165 p. ISBN: 9780374309954. *JS*

Sixteen-year-old Nate Whitely lives in two different worlds, switching his language, clothing, and behavior between the prestigious prep school that he attends on scholarship and his home in inner-city Harlem. Although he has found a way to fit into both worlds, he lives with conflict and faces many stereotypes. The two worlds collide when a classmate he loves comes to Harlem with his drug-dealing brother. He then visits her snobbish black family, and in the end he must make choices about the moral responsibilities his life entails.

Gifted Teenagers • African Americans • Private Schools • Jewish Men • Friendship • Loyalty • Betrayal • Gangs

Myers, Walter Dean

Love Story (Amiri & Odette). New York: Scholastic Press, 2009. 40 p. ISBN: 9780590680417. *S*

Even though Odette, a drug addict, is under the control of the local drug lord, Big Red, she falls in love with Amiri, a basketball player. The two must face the challenges of life on the streets. While Amiri tries to save Odette from the clutches of her addiction, he must stand up to Big Red when he encounters him armed with a knife and gun.

Drug Abuse • Street Life • Novels in Verse

Myers, Walter Dean

Street Love. New York: Amistad, 2006. 144 p. ISBN: 9780060280796; 9780786296293; 9780064407328pa. YALSA Best Books; YALSA Quick Picks. *S*

Seventeen-year-old Damien Battle is a basketball star who has been accepted to Brown University, but when he falls in love with sixteen-year-old Junice Ambers, despite his parents' encouragement to date middle-class girls, Damien risks his future. Junice is struggling to care for her younger sister and grandmother after her mother is sent to prison for drug dealing, and as the pair struggles to keep it together, they must decide what their future holds and if true love can really conquer all.

Love • Gangs • Romance • Social Classes • Single Parent • African Americans • Novels in Verse

Woodson, Jacqueline

Miracle's Boys. New York: G. P. Putnam's Sons, 2000. 133 p. ISBN: 9780399231131; 9780142406021pa; (aud). Coretta Scott King Award; YALSA Best Books; YALSA Popular Paperbacks. *MJ*

Thirteen-year-old Lafayette's older brother Ty'ree gave up college to take care of him and their brother Charlie, who has just returned home after two years in a correctional facility after he robbed a local candy store. Trying to deal with Charlie's anger as he gets involved in gang fights, the boys also cope with the guilt and sorrow they feel over their mother's death as they struggle to stay together and survive.

African Americans • Secrets • Poor People • Brothers • Family Problems • Orphans • Interracial Persons

1

2

3

4

5

6

7

8

9

10

11

12

Chapter 11

Engaging in Political Action

Many adolescents get involved in political action. Broader than just electing officials, political action involves any type of participation that relates to the concerns and rights of society as a whole and contributes to social change. As adolescents participate in such actions, they often make their communities better while finding direction for their own lives. The books listed in this chapter deal with the many political activities in which teens engage. Environmentalism, animal rights, school funding issues, and anti-consumerism are all causes that engage adolescents' passions and give them the power to make a difference in the world.

Collard, Sneed B.

Flash Point. Atlanta: Peachtree, 2006. 214 p. ISBN: 9781561453856. *JS*

Ex-football player and high school sophomore Luther begins to work for a veterinarian, Kay, who cares for falcons. Through this job, Luther discovers a passion for environmentalism and decides to create a student group dedicated to saving the local forests. This new movement and belief is contrary to the values of his logger stepfather and most of his classmates, who ostracize him when a fire starts to blaze near their home in Heartwood, Montana. Although Luther believes the issues around the fire are complex, the locals lay blame firmly with the government, which has restricted logging in the national forests. When a falcon in Luther's care is shot while flying, tensions mount. Luther believes his former friend Warren Juddson is responsible for the bird's death, and both boys are suspended after a fight. When the fires come close, Luther saves Kay's house and the birds. While he recovers from the injuries he sustained, he is able to come to terms with all the issues in his life.

Veterinarians • Fires • Ethics • Environmentalism

Fitzgerald, Dawn

Soccer Chicks Rule. New Milford, CT: Roaring Brook Press, 2006. 160 p. ISBN: 9781596431379; 9780312376628pa. YALSA Popular Paperbacks. *MJ*

Thirteen-year-old Tess Munro is passionate about soccer, but if the school tax levy fails, she won't have a team anymore because all the sports programs will be cut. Getting involved for the first time in something besides sports, Tess puts all her energies into getting the levy to pass. But some of her efforts go wrong, including making an enemy of classmate Jillian when she accidently hits the boy she likes with a soccer ball. Then the levy doesn't pass, and Tess works on fundraising for the team, thus finding a way to make friends with Jillian again.

Soccer • Friendship • Teamwork

Hiaasen, Carl

Flush. New York: Alfred A. Knopf: Distributed by Random House, 2005. 272 p. ISBN: 9780375821820; 9780375841859pa; (aud). YALSA Best Books; YALSA Quick Picks; ALA Notable Children's Books. *M*

Indignation over the misuse of Florida's natural resources has gotten Noah Underwood's father in trouble once again when he sunk the *Coral Queen,* a floating casino, and then could not prove that the owner had been dumping sewage into the water. With their father in prison, Noah and his younger sister, Abbey, set out to find the truth. Along the way, they face the casino owner's bullying son as they gather the proof they need to put the casino out of business and save their father.

Environmentalism • Gambling • Brothers • Sisters

Hiaasen, Carl

Hoot. New York: Alfred A. Knopf, 2002. 227 p. ISBN: 9780375821813; 9780375829161pa; (aud). YALSA Best Books; ALA Notable Children's Books; Newbery Honor Book. *M*

When twelve-year-old Roy Eberhardt moves to Coconut Cove, Florida, he becomes the target of a bully who tries to strangle him on the school bus. He also befriends a runaway boy, nicknamed Mullet Fingers, and his sister, Beatrice Leep, who have been vandalizing the construction site where a new Mother Paula's All-American Pancake House is being planned. Joining in the fight to save the tiny burrowing owls that live on the site, Roy and all his classmates eventually join the protest.

Environmentalism • Bullies and Bullying • Friendship • Vandalism

Howe, Norma

The Adventures of Blue Avenger: A Novel. New York: Henry Holt, 1999. 230 p. ISBN: 9780805060621; 9780064472258pa; (aud). YALSA Best Books. *JS*

On his sixteenth birthday, David Schumacher changes his name to adopt the persona of the "Blue Avenger," a superhero alter ego he began drawing three years earlier to deal with the grief of his father's death. He finds that there is much for a champion of truth and justice to do, starting with rescuing his school principal from an attack of killer bees, then saving the funding for the school newspaper when its editors try to use tabloid illustrations in their article on condom use. The Blue Avenger moves on to ultimately effecting an end to handgun violence, all the while contemplating the question of fate vs. free will and trying to discover the illusive recipe for a weep-less lemon meringue pie.

Sequel: *The Blue Avenger Cracks the Code.* New York: Henry Holt, 2000. 296 p. ISBN: 9780805063721; 9780064473729pa; (aud). *JS*

> When his attempts to get his girlfriend Omaha back together with her father results in an unhappy reunion, causing her to withdraw into her own dark mood, Blue, bored and depressed, pours his energies into a new mystery. While in Venice with friends, he discovers evidence to support the belief that not Shakespeare but Edward de Vere, the 17th Earl of Oxford, was the real author of Shakespeare's famous plays.

Sequel: *Blue Avenger and the Theory of Everything.* Peterborough, NH: Cricket Books, 2002. 225 p. ISBN: 9780812626544. *JS*

> Millionaire Tractor Nishimura is ready to get his revenge, fifteen years after his graduation speech at San Pablo High was canceled when a girl turned him in after she discovered he was going to begin by saying "Tigers suck!" Tractor approaches Blue to come up with a code that will hide the word "suck" on a license plate well enough to get it past the scrutiny of the same girl who turned him in, since she now works as a license plate censor. With this challenge, Blue must decide if the reward he offers is worth it, even though it could save his girlfriend, Omaha, from getting evicted.

> *Work • Ethics • Death • Free Will • Social Responsibility • Travel*

Hughes, Mark Peter

Lemonade Mouth. New York: Delacorte Press, 2007. 352 p. ISBN: 9780385733922; 9780385735117pa. *J*

> When five freshmen find themselves in detention together and form an impromptu band that plays nontypical instruments and performs quirky tunes inspired by things like dying cats, they are unprepared for the fame they soon find in their Rhode Island town. Calling themselves Lemonade Mouth, in homage to the students' fight to save the school's organic frozen-lemonade machine, the band empowers the school against the soda company, which was instrumental in having the machine removed. Even though the ensuing riot lands them back in detention, they find that the best way to face their problems is together.

> *Musicians • Rock Music • Romance • Diary Novel*

Konigsburg, E. L.

The Outcasts of 19 Schuyler Place. New York: Atheneum Books for Young Readers, 2004. 304 p. ISBN: 9780786264834; 9780689866371pa; (aud). ALA Notable Children's Books; YALSA Best Books; School Library Journal Best Books. *M*

> Sent to a summer camp while her parents are traveling in Peru, twelve-year-old Margaret Rose Kane refuses to participate with her cliquish cabin mates and infuriates the rigid camp director. Rescued by her two elderly Hungarian American Jewish uncles, Margaret finds herself looking forward to spending the summer helping maintain their large garden sculptures that have been standing for forty-five years. Margaret is shocked when she learns that the city is working to get the art removed because it is considered to be a blight on the now-historic area. Joined by some

like-minded adults, Margaret creates a plan, informed by her understanding of civil disobedience, that will help to save her uncles' work.

Jewish Men • *Cliques* • *Social Responsibility* • *Individuality* • *Uncles* • *Summer Camps*

Lyga, Barry

Hero Type. Boston: Houghton Mifflin Harcourt, 2008. 304 p. ISBN: 9780547076638; 9780547248776pa. *JS*

When acne-prone outcast Kevin Ross saves a classmate from being killed, the town lauds him as a hero, even though he doesn't feel like one, knowing he was simply in the right place at the right time. But the public is fickle, and they soon turn against him when a picture is published of him throwing away some Support the Troops ribbons. Ostracized by his classmates and questioning his relationship with his estranged mother, Kevin must face his unpopular opinions about the relevance of the Pledge of Allegiance and what it really means to support the troops.

Heroes and Heroines • *Celebrities* • *Self-Esteem* • *Single Parent*

Lynch, Janet Nichols

Peace Is a Four-Letter Word. Berkeley, CA: Heyday Books, 2005. 168 p. ISBN: 9781597140140pa. *J*

Emily Rankin is inspired by her history teacher, Connell McKenzie, to join a peace demonstration on the eve of the Persian Gulf War. She finds herself at odds with everyone in her conservative community, including the other members of the cheerleading squad and her basketball-star boyfriend. When Ms. McKenzie is fired as a teacher because of her political views, Emily is concerned but knows she must find the strength to form her own opinions and stand up for what she believes.

Popularity • *Values* • *Protests*

Nye, Naomi Shihab

Going Going. New York: Greenwillow Books, 2005. 232 p. ISBN: 9780688161859. *JS*

When big chain stores start destroying the historic San Antonio neighborhoods she loves and pushing small businesses out of the market, sixteen-year-old Florrie is outraged and steps up to organize protests and boycotts. With support from family, friends, and local businesses—including her Lebanese Mexican mom's Mexican diner, El Viento—things start well. But soon interest and support wane. When she falls for Ramsey, the handsome son of the manager of a large hotel, and her brother and mother just want her to bring peace to the family instead of fighting for the buildings, Florrie must decide whether one person can make a difference as she continues her fight to preserve the past and small business competition.

Business • *Protests* • *Romance*

Ostow, Micol

Popular Vote. New York: Point, 2008. 224 p. ISBN: 9780545075213pa. *JS*

The daughter of her town's mayor, Erin Bright finds herself involved in a political controversy when she decides to run for student council president against her boyfriend, who has held the post for the past two years. Running changes not only her relationship with her boyfriend but also that with her dad, as she fights to save the open field next to their school from becoming a gas station and finds that the company involved has contributed to her dad's reelection campaign. Erin must stand up for what she believes in and find out if one person really can make a difference.

Father and Daughter • Student Elections • Environmentalism

Tashjian, Janet

The Gospel According to Larry. New York: Henry Holt, 2001. 227 p. ISBN: 9780805063783; 9780440237921pa; (aud). YALSA Best Books. *JS*

Under the pseudonym Larry, Josh Swensen starts posting anti-consumerism rants on the Web, where his alter ego soon becomes famous, attracting the notice of celebrities as well as Josh's best friend and crush, Beth. Soon his identity is revealed, and things get out of hand as Josh alienates his stepfather, Peter, whose job at an ad agency provided much of the fodder for Larry. When the only answer seems to be faking his own death, Josh must deal with the unintended consequences of his idealistic outlook.

Sequel: *Vote for Larry.* New York: Henry Holt, 2004. 224 p. ISBN: 9780805072013; 9780312384463pa; (aud). *S*

When Beth finds eighteen-year-old Josh, she convinces him to run for office. Too young to be elected president, Josh plans to get young people involved in the political process while saving the planet. Soon there is support for a constitutional amendment to lower the age for presidential candidates, and Josh finds himself in a whole new arena. Along the way, Josh must decide if he likes Beth or the new girl in his life, while at the same time battling the women who revealed he was Larry, as well as the moles in his political camp that are bent on sabotage.

Sequel: *Larry and the Meaning of Life.* New York: Henry Holt, 2008. 224 p. ISBN: 9780805077353; (aud). *S*

Despite all his activities, Josh feels he has accomplished little and finds himself depressed until he meets a guru named Gus. As Josh and his old girlfriend are drawn further into Gus's cult, Josh must decide if Gus has the answer to the meaning of life or if he and what he stands for are all a great hoax. All the while, he works to discover the identity of his long-lost father and save his beloved Walden Pond from demolition.

Spirituality • Web Sites • Fame • Environmentalism • Coming-of-Age

1

2

3

4

5

6

7

8

9

10

11

12

Timberlake, Amy

That Girl Lucy Moon. New York: Hyperion Books for Children, 2006. 304 p. ISBN: 9780786852987; 9780786852994pa. *S*

> Lucy Moon faces the stresses of junior high without her photographer mother, who has left on an extended trip. With annoying boys and no one who understands her passion for political causes, including animal rights, things get even worse when rich Miss Wiggins fences off the town's favorite sledding hill. While many students rally to her cause to "Free Wiggins Hill," the campaign soon causes trouble that lands Lucy in detention, forcing her to grow up as she redefines herself and her relationships.

> *Mother-Separated Families • Father and Daughter • Animal Rights • Photography • Ethics • Coming-of-Age*

Chapter 12

Exploring Sexuality

One of the most significant developments that adolescents undergo is sexual maturation. As teens enter puberty they must deal with the physical changes that increase interest in sexual activity. In addition, they must also deal with the emotional aspects of sexuality, including recognizing one's own and others' feelings and interpreting them correctly, as well as the obligation to make responsible decisions. The pressures placed on both genders regarding sexuality result in many new and overwhelming experiences that teens must navigate to develop a healthy sexual identity. The books listed in this chapter consider how teens deal with their developing sexuality and cultivate control over sexual situations. Trying to experience the pleasures of sexual activity for the first time, dealing with pressures from others to engage in sexual acts, or even overcoming regrets after poor choices were made, teens must work through a variety of concerns as they mature sexually. In addition, some teens struggle with their biological gender identity as they try to redefine who they are on the outside with how they feel on the inside. For others who are trying to embrace their homosexuality, there are other concerns to face, including dealing with feeling compelled to deny their sexuality or facing bias and prejudice.

General Sexuality

Baldini, Michelle, and Lynn Biederman; poems by Gabrielle Biederman

Unraveling. New York: Delacorte Press, 2008. 230 p. ISBN: 9780385735407; 9780385905213. *S*

Unable to please her nit-picking mother, fifteen-year-old Amanda Himmelfarb is pressured into have oral sex with Paul, and then she agrees to have sex with senior Rick Hayes in exchange for a date to a dance. Devastated by her choices, Amanda finds comfort from an unlikely source.

Family • Mother and Daughter • Self-Discovery • Oral Sex

Burgess, Melvin

Doing It. New York: Henry Holt, 2004. 326 p. ISBN: 9780805075656; 9780805080797pa; (aud). YALSA Best Books; YALSA Popular Paperbacks. *S*

Three teenage boys work through the perils of growing up as they deal with various issues relating to their sexuality. Ben is secretly sleeping with his twenty-something obsessive drama teacher. Although he likes it at first and realizes the things they do together should be every boy's dream, he has come to realize he is on a destructive path and formulates a plan to escape. Jonathon, "Jon," is worried that he might have testicular cancer and faces ridicule when he finds himself attracted to an overweight girl named Deborah. Dino wants to have sex with Jackie, who allows all kinds of sexual liberties but can never bring herself to actually sleep with him. Dino finds another a girl he can have sex with, but soon realizes she is not what he first believed. As he deals with this, Dino also catches his mother with another man and watches his parents' marriage fall apart.

Self-Discovery • England • Family Problems

Chbosky, Stephen

The Perks of Being a Wallflower. New York: Pocket Books: MTV Books, 1999. 213 p. ISBN: 9780671027346pa; (aud). YALSA Best Books; YALSA Quick Picks. *JS*

Fifteen-year-old outsider Charlie reveals in letters his innermost thoughts during his freshman year of high school. After dealing with the suicide of his best friend during the previous school year, Charlie is trying to figure out who he is and what the future holds. With a new set of bohemian senior friends, Charlie has his first date and sexual encounter, and he tries drugs while enjoying other things like participating in screenings of the *Rocky Horror Picture Show*. Eventually he learns what the true meaning of friendship is and connects with others in his life, including his family, as he faces the sexual abuse he has experienced.

Sexual Abuse • High School • Death • Drug Use • Friendship • Epistolary Novels • Diary Novel • Coming-of-Age

De Oliveira, Eddie

Lucky. New York: Scholastic, 2004. 239 p. ISBN: 9780439546553pa. *S*

Introduced to London's gay scene by fellow soccer player Toby, nineteen-year-old Sam Smith begins to examine his own sexual identity. Concerned by how his friends will respond, Sam must come to terms with his feelings when he finds himself attracted to both boys and girls.

Bisexuality • Coming-of-Age

Hoffmann, Kerry Cohen

Easy. New York: Simon & Schuster Children's Publishing, 2006. 176 p. ISBN: 9781416914259; 9781416914266pa. YALSA Quick Picks. *JS*

When her parents divorce, fourteen-year-old Jessica feels alone and abandoned when her father moves in with his girlfriend and her mother is lost in her self-absorbed grief and feelings of rejection. But soon Jessica realizes the power her body and sexuality hold, and these urges overtake her life, eclipsing even her passion for photography. Becoming absorbed by her sexual activity, even her friends and a concerned art teacher can't help her realize that while she sees the destructive nature of her mother's neediness and her former friend's promiscuity, she cannot see that she is following the same path and is slowly losing her self-respect.

Divorce • Friendship • Family Problems • Coming-of-Age

Kizer, Amber

Gert Garibaldi's Rants and Raves: One Butt Cheek at a Time. New York: Delacorte Press, 2007. 295 p. ISBN: 9780385734301. *J*

When her friendship with her gay best friend, Adam, is overshadowed by his relationship with his partner, Tim, brainy fifteen-year-old Gert Garibaldi does not know how to handle life without him, especially when she is dealing with crazy teachers, unconnected parents, and a crush on Tim's twin brother. When the cool health teacher begins their sex education unit that not only warns the girls about sexually transmitted diseases and the use of condoms but also encourages educational exploration of the female genitalia, Gert's new awareness of her body helps her to feel better about herself and her place in the world as she finds she is not dependent on Adam. She can make new friends and get a boyfriend of her own.

High School • Infatuation • Coming-of-Age

Levithan, David

The Realm of Possibility. New York: Knopf: Distributed by Random House, 2004. 210 p. ISBN: 9780375828454; 9780375836572pa. YALSA Best Books. *S*

Twenty students who go to the same school, including a gay couple who have been together for one year, a girl who is dealing with her mother's cancer, and an outcast who loves to draw, have lives that interconnect as they deal with the heartaches and joys of being a teenager.

Popularity • Self-Esteem • First Love • Gay Males • Lesbians • Drug Use • Novels in Verse

Mackall, Dandi Daley

Crazy in Love. New York: Dutton, 2007. 192 p. ISBN: 9780525477808; 9780142411575pa. *S*

Seventeen-year-old Mary Jane goes to get soda for a party with her crush, Jackson. Subsequently, her friends begin to ignore her, and lots of boys start asking her out. It seems that Star Simon, Jackson's girlfriend, has been spreading rumors that she's easy. When Star and Jackson break up, Mary Jane and Jackson get together. Things are great until Jackson wants to have sex, and she decides she wants to wait until she finds the man she will marry. Even though Jackson is seemingly supportive of her decision, Mary Jane is uncertain what the future of their relationship will be, and she must decide if she can live with the decision she's made.

Decision Making • Disabilities • Love

12

Nelson, Blake

Rock Star, Superstar. New York: Viking, 2004. 224 p. ISBN: 9780670059331pa. YALSA Best Books; YALSA Quick Picks. *JS*

> When sixteen-year-old bass guitarist, Pete, gets into a new band called the Tiny Masters of Today, he is just ecstatic about the chance to play on stage. Life looks great, especially when he falls for sweet Margaret. When fame and fortune come knocking in the form of a recording contract and Margaret's parents are angry when they find out that the couple is having sex, Pete gets a firsthand lesson in just how tough life and the music business can be.

Bands • Musicians • Rock Music • Fame • Coming-of-Age

Ruby, Laura

Good Girls. New York: Harper Tempest, 2006. 288 p. ISBN: 9780060882235; 9780060882259pa. YALSA Quick Picks. *JS*

> When someone uses a camera phone and takes a picture of her performing oral sex on popular Luke DeSalvio at a party and then e-mails it all around, Audrey is branded a slut. Not only does she have to deal with the ogling and harassment at school, but she loses her friends, her relationship with her father becomes strained when he also sees the picture, and then Luke starts ignoring her. To deal with the trauma, Audrey throws herself into her schoolwork, and as she makes new friends, Audrey rediscovers her self-esteem as her friends help her understand the connection between love and sex and she comes to terms with the double-standard that made her a slut but just made Luke more popular.

Oral Sex • Photography • Parent and Child • Interpersonal Relations • Values

Snadowsky, Daria

Anatomy of a Boyfriend. New York: Delacorte Press, 2007. 272 p. ISBN: 9780385733205; 9780440239444pa. *S*

> High school senior Dominique "Dom" Baylor, who wants to become a doctor someday, has not had a boyfriend until she meets shy Wesley "Wes" Gershwin at a football game. The two fall in love after months of e-mailing each other. Dealing with the physical realities of masturbation, oral sex, and orgasms that Dom had only experienced in anatomical texts, the pair both lose their virginity on prom night, but soon find that not all relationships are lasting.

Dating • Virginity • Romance • Coming-of-Age

Winston, Sherri

Acting: A Novel. New York: Marshall Cavendish, 2004. 253 p. ISBN: 9780761451730. *JS*

> All sixteen-year-old Eve Belinda wants is to escape from her depressed Michigan town, but when her identical twin, Al, gets pregnant and won't tell who the father is, Eve finds herself trapped in a family crisis. Feeling forced to be good to make up for her twin's mistake, Eve tries to decide if she should have sex with her boyfriend. As Al helps her to understand that the decision to have intercourse is much more complicated than she may think, Eve has to make decisions about her own relationship.

Sisters • Twins • African Americans • Pregnancy • Romance • Mother and Daughter

Wittlinger, Ellen

Sandpiper. New York: Simon & Schuster Books for Young Readers, 2005. 240 p. ISBN: 9780689868023; 9781416936510pa. YALSA Best Books. *JS*

> With her mother caught up in her plans to remarry, sixteen-year-old Sandpiper Hollow Ragsdale has no one to turn to when Derek, one of her hook-ups, returns in a rage and starts harassing her about her reputation as a slut who will have oral sex with anyone. Wanting only to leave her past behind, she makes friends with "the Walker," a mysterious young man who does not go to school or seem to have any family. As they share their secrets, the pair find healing and safety.

> *Divorce • Friendship • Sexual Ethics • Dating • Weddings • Oral Sex • Remarriage*

Wizner, Jake

Spanking Shakespeare. New York: Random House Children's Books, 2007. 287 p. ISBN: 9780375840852; 9780375840869pa. YALSA Best Books. *S*

> Writing his memoir in his final year of high school, Shakespeare Shapiro records the various embarrassing moments throughout his life, including drunken mistakes and disastrous dates. He deals with his hippie alcoholic parents and his best friend's obsession with bowel movements and tries to figure out a way to have sex for the first time.

> *Brothers • Eccentricities • Social Acceptance • Writing*

Zarr, Sara

Story of a Girl: A Novel. New York: Little, Brown, 2007. 208 p. ISBN: 9780316014533; 9780316014540pa; (aud). YALSA Best Books; YALSA Quick Picks. *JS*

> Three years after being caught by her father having sex with seventeen-year-old Tommy in the back of his car, sixteen-year-old Deanna is still branded as the school slut and completely ignored by her father. Hoping to escape and make her own life with her brother Darren, his girlfriend, and their baby, Deanna works to earn money to rent an apartment so they can all escape from their family home. When Deanna encounters Tommy again, things get even more complicated. She must learn from her mistakes and find confidence in herself as she heals her relationships with her family and friends.

> *Self-Esteem • Family Problems*

Zeises, Lara M.

Contents Under Pressure. New York: Delacorte Press, 2004. 244 p. ISBN: 9780385730471; 9780440237877pa. *J*

> High school freshman Lucy Doyle finds that she has been left behind now that all her girlfriends have discovered boys, but when junior Tobin Scacheri catches her interest, Lucy starts to wonder about the complexities of dating and just how far a girl should go when it comes to sex. Looking for answers, Lucy finds some help with her friends but finds the most support

from her brother Jack's girlfriend, Hannah, who is pregnant. As she struggles with Jack's inability to be a parent and learns to set boundaries with Tobin, Lucy begins to understand and come to grips with the complexities of relationships.

Pregnancy • Family Problems • Brothers • Sisters

Virginity and First Sexual Experiences

Behrens, Andy

***All the Way* (also titled *Sex Drive*).** New York: Dutton Books, 2006. 256 p. ISBN: 9780525477617: 9780142408339pa. YALSA Popular Paperbacks. *S*

While his friends, Felicia and Lance, were off having fabulous experiences on their summer vacations, seventeen-year-old Ian was stuck in a Chicago mall working at Dunkin' Donuts. With one last weekend before school starts, Ian is determined to salvage the summer by driving to Charleston, South Carolina, to meet face-to-face with a co-ed he met online, hoping to have sex with her. Not willing to be left out, Felicia and Lance tag along, and after many disasters along the way, Ian realizes that the girl he loves was not in another state but sitting right next to him the entire time.

Sexuality • Summer • Work • Travel • Automobiles

Brian, Kate

***The V Club*.** New York: Simon & Schuster Books for Young Readers, 2004. 280 p. ISBN: 9780689867644. YALSA Popular Paperbacks. *S*

All vying for a scholarship that demands the candidates must be pure in body and soul, a group of senior girls, Eva, Kai, Debbie, and Mandy, create the Virginity Club, or V Club, a service organization that promotes chastity to help them proclaim to the world that they are pure. The truth is that Kai has already lost her virginity and everyone thinks Debbie must have because she uses her sexuality to hide her brains. Mandy and her boyfriend have plans to have sex after her birthday, and Eva is just finding love. The girls must find a way to be true to themselves as they learn about self-respect, honesty, and the ramifications of sexual decisions.

Virginity • Sexuality • High School

Hantz, Sara

***The Second Virginity of Suzy Green*.** Woodbury, MN: Flux, 2007. 258 p.; ISBN: 9780738711393pa. *JS*

Sixteen-year-old Suzy Green is the rebellious sibling who drinks alcohol and has been caught by the police, but when her sister Rosie is killed, Suzy is determined to change her ways. Moving to a new town—Adelaide, Australia—assists her in remaking her identity, as she joins a group of nerds and their Virginity Club, even though she isn't one. Suzy's new reputation is threatened, however, when old boyfriend Ryan shows up, and Suzy must learn that you can't pretend to be something you are not.

Australia • Ex-Boyfriends • Family • Moving • Dating

Jahn-Clough, Lisa

Me Penelope. Boston: Houghton Mifflin, 2007. 208 p. ISBN: 9780618773664; 9780547076324pa. *JS*

> Sixteen-year-old Penelope "Lopi" Yeage has enough credits to graduate early and plans to leave town to escape her mother, Viv, who is dating a guy years younger than herself. Before she leaves she wants to find her true love and lose her virginity. After three attempts to attract the right guy, she finds that childhood friend, Toad, is the right one. He becomes her boyfriend, and they have sex. When Viv is in an auto accident, she finds help in therapy, and she and Lopi begin to talk to one another.
>
> *Single Parent • Sexuality • Dating • Coming-of-Age • Guilt*

Johnson, R. M.

Stacie & Cole. New York: Hyperion Books for Children, 2007. 288 p. ISBN: 9781423105985pa. *JS*

> Having dated since their freshman year, sixteen-year-old Stacie and Cole find themselves trying to decide if it is time to take the next step in their relationship. While football star Cole is ready for sex, his problems at home with his mom's new boyfriend and the anger he feels toward his father, who has been absent for three years but has now shown up at a local homeless shelter, distract him. Stacie is uncertain about what she wants to do because she watched her now-overprotective father kick her older sister out of the house when she became pregnant. When Stacie's best friend, Doncsha, tries to take advantage of Cole's distraction to seduce him, the pair must try to figure out their relationship as they make their own decisions and find the courage to deal with the consequences.
>
> *Love • Dating • Sexuality • Peer Pressure*

McVoy, Terra Elan

Pure. New York: Simon Pulse, 2009. 330 p. ISBN: 9781416978725. *J*

> Along with five other Christian girls, Tabitha vowed to remain a virgin until marriage, but now that she is in high school and dating a boy she really likes, things are getting complicated. When one of the other girls breaks her promise, Tabitha stands by her, thus losing her other friends, but the event allows Tabitha to grow as she builds closer relationships with other girls and is surprised to find that her boyfriend respects her choices.
>
> *Friendship • Christianity • Dating • Betrayal*

Robar, Serena

Giving up the V. New York: Simon Pulse, 2009. 242 p. ISBN: 9781416975588. *S*

> Even though her mother takes her for her first gynecological exam and gets her a prescription for birth control pills on her sixteenth birthday, Spencer Davis has no interest in losing her virginity, unlike her best friend Alyssa, who wants to lose hers soon, or like her other friends, Goth-girl Morgan and rich bad-boy Ryan, who are very sexually active. When gorgeous Ben

moves into town and starts showing interest in her, Spencer changes her mind, thinking he might just be the one she could have sex with for the first time.

Dating • Romance

Stone, Tanya Lee

A Bad Boy Can Be Good for a Girl. New York: Wendy Lamb, 2006. 228 p. ISBN: 9780385747028; 9780553495096pa. YALSA Quick Picks. *S*

Three girls are left heartbroken when a sexy jock uses and then dumps each of them. Freshman Josie thinks she has found true love but is devastated to find he only wants her for sex. In a desperate attempt to help other girls, she pens a warning on the back pages of Judy Blume's *Forever*. Junior Nicolette believes that sex is all about power, and as long as she is the one in control, everything is fine, but she soon realizes that in this situation, he holds all the cards. Senior Aviva succumbs to his great charms and loses her virginity to him, even though her friends warn her that he is just playing her.

Sexuality • Peer Pressure

Tracy, Kristen

Lost It. New York: Simon Pulse, 2007. 288 p. ISBN: 9781416934752pa. *J*

Left alone with her grandmother after her parents leave to attend a survival camp in the desert, Tess Whistle has to face her phobias, including one of the out-of-doors, where she certainly could be eaten by wolves. But when best friend Zena starts reacting to her parents' marital problems by threatening to blow up a poodle and gorgeous Benjamin Easter transfers to her school, things are turned upside down. Even though she thought she would wait until marriage, Tess finds herself losing her virginity to Benjamin in the very feared out-of-doors. When all these life events combine, Tess is able to find some control in her life, and she comes to terms with how unexpected life can be.

First Love • Dating • Friendship

Wallington, Aury

Pop! New York: Razorbill, 2006. ISBN: 9781595140920pa. YALSA Popular Paperbacks. *S*

Seventeen-year-old Marit gets cold feet every time things get physical in her relationships, but now she is determined to lose her virginity. At a suggestion from her sister and supported by her best friend, Caroline, Marit decides that her friend Jamie is just the one to help her. Jamie reveals his love for her, but their sexual relationship becomes awkward when a new guy, Noah, enters the scene. It is difficult to maintain her friendship with Jamie, but in the end, Marit finds both friendship and love.

Sexuality • Dating

Gender Identity

Blacker, Terence

Boy2Girl. New York: Farrar, Straus & Giroux, 2005. 296 p. ISBN: 9780374309268; 9780312371463pa. *M*

To initiate him into their group, thirteen-year-old rebellious and tough American Sam Lopez, an American, is dared by his English cousin to go to the first day in his new school dressed as a girl. Escaping his violent father who only wants his inheritance after his mother's death, Sam is eager to find a place with his cousin and his friends, but when the prank continues for several weeks, Sam finds a new sense of himself and acceptance with the boys as well as with the group of girls. When the prank is finally revealed, it is not only Sam who is changed but also those with whom he has come in contact.

Death • Moving • Dares • Family Relationships

Brothers, Meagan

Debbie Harry Sings in French. New York: Henry Holt, 2008. 240 p. ISBN: 9780805080803. YALSA Best Books. *JS*

Just a week after Johnny's thirteenth birthday, his father was killed in an accident. Now sixteen, Johnny finds himself getting out of the hospital after heavy drinking led to an accidental overdose. Taking with him his passion for '80s punk rock, and especially the band Blondie and their lead singer Debbie Harry, Johnny is sent to live with his Uncle Sam in South Carolina. There Johnny finds himself bullied because the guys think he is gay, even though his relationship with Goth chick Maria, who shares his tastes in music, proves otherwise. Supported by Maria and eventually by his uncle, Johnny begins to explore his need to cross-dress and enters a drag contest at a club in Atlanta as Debbie Harry. Along the way, he learns to accept who he is as he learns truths about his father that he never knew.

Alcoholism • Transvestites • Goth Culture • Sex Role • Rock Music • Depression • Coming-of-Age

Katcher, Brian

Almost Perfect. New York: Delacorte Books for Young Readers, 2009. 368 p. ISBN: 9780385736640. *S*

High school senior Logan Witherspoon has spent three years trying to get over his breakup with his old girlfriend and is stunned when, after their first kiss, he finds out that Sage Hendricks is biologically a boy, even though he lives as a girl. Confronting his conflicted feelings, Logan tries to decide if he can ignore the deeply ingrained beliefs of his rural community to be with Sage. Sage is also struggling with the fear of her secret being found out and trying to balance her life as a normal girl, but as they work together, they gain a better understanding of themselves and the world around them.

Transsexuals • Sex Role • Romance

Peters, Julie Anne

Luna. New York: Little, Brown, 2003. 256 p. ISBN: 9780316733694; 9780316011273pa. YALSA Best Books. *S*

> Sacrificing her own needs, Regan has always protected her transgender brother Liam, who also lives as a young woman named Luna. She worries what her family's reaction will be if his secret life is ever discovered. When Liam begins to seriously consider making a permanent change and starts dressing like a girl in public, Regan is unsure if he can handle this change, especially when a new boy starts acting as if he really likes her. Realizing he must free himself to live his true identity, Liam moves to Seattle for sex-reassignment surgery, leaving Regan to focus on her own life as she and her family work to truly accept Luna.

> *Transsexuals • Brothers • Sisters • Sex Role • Family Problems*

St. James, James

Freak Show. New York: Dutton Children's Books, 2007. 224 p. ISBN: 9780525477990; 9780142412312pa. School Library Journal Best Books; YALSA Best Books; YALSA Quick Picks; YALSA Popular Paperbacks. *S*

> Seventeen-year-old drag queen Billy Bloom has moved to live with his wealthy and distant father, and he is glaringly out of place at his new, highly conservative high school. Enduring verbal and physical abuse that escalates until he is brutally attacked, Billy decides that instead of accepting his status as a bullied outcast, he will take a stand by running for homecoming queen. His cause attracts media attention, and, supported by his only ally, gorgeous and popular football player Flip Kelly, Billy's campaign helps him to find the acceptance he so desperately wants while also striking a blow against the wrongs of the world.

> *Bullies and Bullying • Prejudice*

Wittlinger, Ellen

Parrotfish. New York: Simon & Schuster Books for Young Readers, 2007. 304 p. ISBN: 9781416916222. *JS*

> Although she looks like a girl to the rest of the world, Angela McNair knows she is a boy. So when she cuts her hair short, changes her clothing, and announces her name is now Grady, she faces many challenges. With the help of his family and his female gym teacher, Grady is able to face the bullies at school, as well as the challenges of losing his best friend and falling in love with a gorgeous biracial girl at school.

> *Transsexuals • Peer Pressure • Sexuality • Sex Role • Family Problems • Dating • Coming-of-Age*

Homosexuality

Benduhn, Tea

Gravel Queen. New York: Simon & Schuster Books for Young Readers, 2003. 152 p. ISBN: 9780689849947. *S*

> In the summer before her senior year, aspiring filmmaker Aurin has two friends attracted to the same boy. Fred, who is gay, and Aurin's girlfriend Kenney are both interested in handsome, athletic Grant. Aurin finds that she is attracted to another girl—Grant's cousin, Neila. Having never really thought about her sexuality before, Aurin begins to define her identity as she becomes intimately involved with Neila. But when her status as best friend is threatened, Kenney becomes jealous, and Aurin must deal not only with embracing her lesbianism but redefining her relationships with her friends as well.

> *First Love • Lesbians • Gay Males • Friendship*

Boock, Paula

Dare Truth or Promise. Boston, MA: Houghton Mifflin, 1999. 176 p. ISBN: 9780395971178; 9780547076171pa. *S*

> In New Zealand, two high school girls, Willa and Louie, meet working at a fast-food restaurant and fall in love. Louie is an excellent student and wants to be a lawyer, while Willa just wants to make it out of school to become a chef. Their family and friends cannot accept their lesbian relationship, but after a tragic accident, the pair find acceptance and love.

> *Lesbians • New Zealand*

Cohn, Rachel, and David Levithan

Naomi and Ely's No Kiss List. New York: Alfred A. Knopf, 2007. 240 p. ISBN: 9780375844409; 9780375844416pa. *JS*

> Best friends and New York University freshmen, straight Naomi and gay Ely have weathered many challenges, including when Naomi's dad had an affair with one of Ely's mothers. But a rift forms between the two when Naomi's romantic feelings for Ely come out after Ely kisses Naomi's boyfriend Bruce, and the boys decide they want to be together. Naomi and Ely—and all of their friends—are forced to choose sides, but soon Naomi realizes that things will never turn out like she fantasizes, and they both realize that the best things in life, including friendship, must be worked for.

> *Gay Males • Dating • College • Friendship*

Davis, Will

My Side of the Story. New York: Bloomsbury, 2007. 256 p. ISBN: 9781596912946pa. *S*

> Jazz's life is full of complications. He is forced into family therapy when he is caught sneaking out to gay bars. Things continue to spiral out of control

1
2
3
4
5
6
7
8
9
10
11
12

when his grandma has a stroke and his parents' marriage starts to fall apart. After inadvertently outing himself at school and then dealing with the bullying there, he falls for a twenty-two-year-old man who does not want to get involved with a teenager. Through all these experiences, Jazz learns that running away is not the answer to his problems.

Gay Males • Family Problems • Bullies and Bullying

Dole, Mayra Lazara

Down to the Bone. New York: HarperTeen, 2008. 367 p. ISBN: 9780060843106. *S*

Seventeen-year-old Laura "Lauri" Amores is expelled from her Catholic school and thrown out of her Cuban mom's house for being a lesbian. Getting a job and finding a home with her straight black friend, Soli, she wonders if she can ever be with a guy, like her beloved partner Marlena, who left her after she gave in to her family's pressure and married a man. Wanting to regain her family and the acceptance she has lost, Lauri struggles to find her own identity as a gay teen, working to live amid the prejudices around her.

Lesbians • Cuban Americans • Friendship • Self-Acceptance • Coming-of-Age

Earls, Nick

48 Shades of Brown. Boston: Graphia, 2004. 288 p. ISBN: 9780618452958pa; (aud). Children's Book Council of Australia Children's Book of the Year. *S*

When his parents move to Switzerland, high school senior Dan chooses to stay in Australia to finish school. He moves in with his twenty-two-year-old aunt, Jacq, and her roommate Naomi, who are both university students. Even while dealing with the differences between his former suburban lifestyle and his aunt's chaotic house where beer flows freely, Dan falls for Naomi, who has never had much luck when it comes to men. Dan does everything he can to try and impress Naomi, but in the end he is not what she wants and Dan grows a little as he has learned a lot about life, women, and relationships.

Family Relationships • Coming-of-Age

Ferguson, Drew

The Screwed Up Life of Charlie the Second. New York: Kensington, 2008. 320 p. ISBN: 9780758227089pa. *S*

Gay high school senior Charles "Charlie" James Stewart II, faces stress at school with his new-age English teacher, Mrs. Bailey. And then there's fellow student Kyle Weir, who harasses him. Charlie falls for new student, Rob, and is excited to find that his love for him is returned, and the two get together. Things are complicated, however, because both boys are facing family problems. Charlie's parents are probably going to get a divorce, and Rob's mother is dying of Lou Gehrig's disease. When Rob's father is accused of assisted suicide after his mother dies, the boys must learn how to deal with the situation and find support with each other.

Gay Males • Family Problems • Divorce • Death • Coming-of-Age

Ferris, Jean

Eight Seconds. San Diego, CA: Harcourt, 2000. 186 p. ISBN: 9780152023676; 9780142301210pa. YALSA Best Books. *S*

> When cowboy Jon Ritchie attends a week-long rodeo camp the summer before his senior year, he not only discovers how much he enjoys bull riding but also finds a friendship with handsome younger boy Kit. When on his return home, Jon finds out that Kit is gay, and he must not only face bullies and rumors but his true feelings about his friend.

> *Bull Riding • Bullies and Bullying • Gay Males • Prejudice*

Freymann-Weyr, Garret

My Heartbeat. Boston: Houghton Mifflin Co., 2002. 154 p. ISBN: 9780618141814; 9780142400661pa; (aud). YALSA Best Books; Michael L. Printz Honor Books; School Library Journal Best Books. *S*

> Fourteen-year-old Ellen loves James, her older brother Link's best friend, and is shocked to find he is gay. In fact, many believe that he and Link are a couple. Confronting the pair, Link refuses to talk about it, and soon he becomes involved with a girl and drops out of a college prep math program to pursue a career in music. Suddenly finding that she has James all to herself, Ellen learns that while he loves and has had sex with men, he also loves her, and soon the two have sex. Throughout it all, Ellen must untangle her complex feelings of love and find new ways to relate to her parents and to Link.

> *Brothers • Sisters • Gay Males*

Goobie, Beth

Hello, Groin. Custer, WA: Orca Book Publishers, 2006. 271 p. ISBN: 9781551434599. *JS*

> Trying to force herself to have sexual feelings for her boyfriend, Cam, sixteen-year-old Dylan Kowolski hides her homosexuality. Sharing a kiss with Sheila, a girl at a school dance, and dealing with the censorship of a library book display she created, helps Dylan to tell her family and friends she is a lesbian. While everyone around her is accepting, Sheila's family is not and so she must move on without their support.

> *Lesbians • Identity • Sexuality • Peer Pressure • Self-Discovery • Canada*

Hartinger, Brent

Geography Club Series. New York: HarperCollins
> Gay teen Russell navigates the trials and intolerance found in high school.

> *Lesbians • Gay Males • High School • Peer Pressure*

Geography Club. 2002. 240 p. ISBN: 9780060012212; 9780060012236pa. *S*
> Having kept his sexuality a secret, Russell is ecstatic to find out that there are others like him in his small-town high school. Seven gay, lesbian, and bisexual teens, including Russell's friend Min, her lover, and popular athlete Kevin, form a secret support group that they dub the

Geography Club. Russell and Kevin get together and have sex, and things are great until Russell refuses to have sex with a girl, and the truth comes out.

The Order of the Poison Oak. 2005. 240 p. ISBN: 9780060567309; 9780060567323pa. *S*

Escaping his intolerant classmates as a counselor at a children's summer camp for burn survivors, things don't turn out as planned for Russell when he and his bisexual friend Min fall for the same guy, who tries to have unprotected sex with both of them.

Split Screen. 2007. 304 p. ISBN: 9780060824082. *S*

When Russell and Min answer the casting call for extras in a horror film, things get complicated. An old boyfriend of Russell's shows up, and then Min cannot decide if she wants to have a relationship with Leah, who will not come out because she fears losing her friends.

Hines, Sue

Out of the Shadows. New York: Avon Books, 2000. 153 p. ISBN: 9780380811922pa; (aud). *J*

Fifteen-year-old Rowanna has just come to terms with her mother's sexuality. Then her mother is killed by a drunk driver, and Rowanna finds herself living with her mother's lesbian partner and is supported only by best friend Mark, who is dealing with family problems of his own—including an alcoholic father and a neglectful mother. Then Rowanna finds a new friend when gorgeous Jodie comes to school. But Jodie is hiding her own secret: she is a closet lesbian and has developed a crush on Rowanna. Complications ensue when Mark develops a crush on Jodie, but the trio is able to work through their problems as they support each other and stand up to the abuse they face at school.

Lesbians • Romance • Australia • Coming-Out

Jahn-Clough, Lisa

Country Girl, City Girl. Boston: Houghton Mifflin, 2004. 185 p. ISBN: 9780618447916; 9780547223223pa. *MJ*

Thirteen-year-old Phoebe lives in Maine on a small farm with her father and brother, where she loves to take photographs and care for her farm animals. Without her mother, who died when she was two, growing up can be confusing. It gets more complicated when fourteen-year-old cosmopolitan and stylish Melita comes to stay the summer with Phoebe's family while her mother—Phoebe's mother's best friend—goes into a clinic to address her psychological troubles. At first overwhelmed by Melita's sophistication, Phoebe finds a new friend as the two plan an imaginative fashion show and Phoebe learns how to apply makeup and kiss on the lips. But soon Phoebe realizes that their kiss meant more to her than it did to Melita. When Melita returns to New York, Phoebe visits her and sees that Melita has a crush on a boy, and Phoebe must then come to terms with her own feelings.

Interpersonal Relations • Sexuality • Grief • Country Life

Johnson, Maureen

The Bermudez Triangle. New York: Razorbill, 2004. 368 p. ISBN: 9781595140197; 9781595140333pa. *S*

> The summer before her senior year, Nina attends a leadership institute at Stanford where she initially has trouble adjusting but soon finds a place as she falls for eco-warrior Steve, who was brought up on a West Coast commune in an environment that is significantly different from Nina's own upbringing. When she returns, Nina realizes that things have changed and that her longtime friends Mel and Avery are keeping secrets. It turns out that in her absence, Mel and Avery have realized that their feelings for each other go deeper than friendship, and they have become lovers. While both Mel and Avery are coming to understand their sexuality and their new relationship, Nina, who just wants them to be happy, also feels lonely, hurt, and frustrated about being left out. As all the girls come to grips with the changes, they find new friends and redefine their own identities and values.

Lesbians • Sexuality • Coming Out • Family

Juby, Susan

Another Kind of Cowboy. New York: HarperTeen, 2007. 344 p. ISBN: 9780060765170. YALSA Best Books. *J*

> Alex loves horses and has participated in Western riding competitions with his faithful horse Turnip for many years, but his real dream is to compete in the sport of dressage. When a woman who is smitten with his father offers to let him use a dressage horse to take lessons, Alex jumps at the chance. At the stable, Alex meets Cleo, a rich girl with a rebellious streak, who is also being trained in dressage. The two teens develop a friendship as Cleo works through her own family problems and Alex struggles as he tries to reveal to his family and friends that he is gay.

Horses • Gay Males • Coming Out • Loneliness • Family

Kluger, Steve

My Most Excellent Year: A Novel of Love, Mary Poppins, & Fenway Park. New York: Dial Books, 2008. 403 p. ISBN: 9780803732278; 9780142413432pa. *J*

> Best friends Anthony Conigliaro "T.C." Keller and Augie Hwong act as if they are brothers. In their freshman year of high school, the twosome are joined by Alejandra "Ale" Perez, who has just moved from Washington, D.C. In their tumultuous year, musical-theater-loving Augie realizes he is gay and finds love and Ale finally confronts her disapproving parents with her own love for theater. Along with baseball-loving T.C., they mount a fashion show, launch a grassroots political movement, and help a foster child who is deaf achieve his greatest dream.

Friendship • Gay Males • Coming Out • Fashion Shows • Baseball • First Love • Musicals

12

Koertge, Ron

Boy Girl Boy. Orlando, FL: Harcourt Children's Books, 2005. 176 p. ISBN: 9780152053253; 9780152058654pa. *S*

With graduation approaching, best friends Elliot, Teresa, and Larry decide that it is time to flee their small town and overbearing parents and live in California. But as the time to execute the plan approaches, each one begins to discover problems that threaten to pull things off track. Obsessed runner Teresa struggles with an eating disorder and realizes she wants more than just friendship from Elliot. Film buff Larry realizes that his homosexuality will draw him away from his friends someday. Basketball star Elliot begins to realize, with the help of new friend Mary Ann, that his two friends overshadow him. When Elliot faces a homophobic jock on the court and Larry has a near-death experience, each of the friends must find their own identity to discover what the future holds.

Sexuality • Gay Males • Friendship • Interpersonal Relations • Coming-of-Age

Koja, Kathe

Talk. New York: Frances Foster Books, 2005. 133 p. ISBN: 9780786288113; 9780312376055pa. *JS*

When closeted gay teen Kit Webster lands the lead in the school play after he auditions on a dare from his best friend, Carma, and he finds himself cast with popular drama queen Lindsay Walsh, things get complicated when she falls for him and dumps her boyfriend. As the play—a drama about political repression—excites attempts at censorship from the parents and draws the whole town into the controversy, Kit must deal with his own problems, as well as the chaos erupting around him.

Gay Males • Coming Out • Homophobia • Theater • Interpersonal Relations

Konigsberg, Bill

Out of the Pocket. New York: Dutton Children's Books, 2008. 256 p. ISBN: 9780525479963. *S*

Finally finding the confidence to reveal to his best friend that he is gay, high-school senior quarterback Bobby Framingham is shocked when his sexuality is revealed to the whole school in the school newspaper by an unscrupulous reporter. With the revelation turning away his best girl friend and making his teammates and coach furious at him, Bobby is also trying to deal with his father's recently diagnosed cancer. It is not until the team comes together for their championship game that Bobby is able to find acceptance.

Gay Males • Football • Coming Out • Secrets • Sports

LaRochelle, David

Absolutely, Positively Not. New York: Arthur A. Levine Books, 2005. 224 p. ISBN: 9780439591096; 9780439591102pa. YALSA Best Books. *JS*

Sixteen-year-old Steven DeNarski does everything he can to deny he is gay. Following the advice he finds in an ancient teen sexuality handbook for dealing with deviant desires, he tries hanging out with jocks, buying *Playboy* magazines, hanging posters of women in lingerie, and dating and kissing girls. When he finally accepts his sexuality and tells his friend Rachel that he is gay, she announces the fact to her family and everyone in school, urging him to form a gay-straight alliance. He must then deal with both the positive and negative responses to his revelation.

Gay Males • Coming Out • Dating • Friendship • Coming-of-Age

Lecesne, James

Absolute Brightness. New York: HarperTeen, 2008. 472 p. ISBN: 9780061256271. *MJ*

Arriving in Neptune, New Jersey, with his crazy flashy clothes and pierced ears, fourteen-year-old Leonard Pelkey moves in with his cousins, the Hertle family. Resenting his intrusion, fifteen-year-old Phoebe is annoyed when he joins the high school drama crowd and starts giving makeovers at her mother's beauty parlor. When tragedy strikes, Phoebe knows that she has misjudged Leonard and also realizes how much he touched the people around him.

Gay Males • Homophobia • Murder • Hate Crimes • Coming-of-Age • Beauty Shops • Makeovers

Levithan, David

Boy Meets Boy. New York: Alfred A. Knopf, 2003. 185 p. ISBN: 9780375824005; 9780375832994pa; (aud). YALSA Best Books; YALSA Quick Picks. *JS*

High school sophomore Paul has known he was gay since kindergarten, and he fits very well in a town where differences are completely acceptable. In a school where the Gay-Straight Alliance is packed with members, the homecoming queen is the football team's cross-dressing star quarterback, and the cheerleaders ride motorcycles, Paul meets artistic Noah, who is new to town, and the boy falls in love. But when Paul kisses his old boyfriend, who insists he wants Paul back, Paul must find a way to get Noah back and prove that he is serious about their relationship.

Gay Males • First Love • Coming-of-Age

Lieberman, Leanne

Gravity. Custer, WA: Orca Book Publishers, 2008. 245 p. ISBN: 9781554690497pa. *J*

Fifteen-year-old Ellisheva "Ellie" Gold spends the summer with her liberal, unreligious grandmother and falls in love with neighbor Lindsay. Upon her return home to her Orthodox Jewish family, Ellie must figure out a way to adapt to a religion that does not truly accept her homosexuality.

Lesbians • Jewish Men • Faith • Coming-Out • Canada

Manning, Sarra

Pretty Things. New York: Dutton Children's Books, 2005. 256 p. ISBN: 9780525475224; 9780142405390pa. *S*

> Romantic complications ensue when four teens interact while working at a drama workshop staging *The Taming of the Shrew.* Shallow Brie, who knows she is straight, is in a relationship with a sexually demanding boyfriend who tries to rape her, but she loves her gay best friend Charlie, whom she often invites to sleep over in her bed. Charlie, however, is crushing on promiscuous, straight Walker, but he is attracted to politically active lesbian, Daisy, who soon learns that she likes sex with Walker as much as with her girlfriend Claire. Together the four work through their own issues as they discover who they are and establish their sexual identities.
>
> *Gay Males • Lesbians • Sexuality • Alcohol Use • Romance • England*

Medina, Nico

The Straight Road to Kylie. New York: Simon Pulse, 2007. 295 p. ISBN: 9781416936008pa. YALSA Popular Paperbacks. *S*

> When gay seventeen-year-old Jonathan Parish has sex with his virgin best girl friend at a drunken party, rumors abound, and he is approached by gorgeous Laura Schulberg, who offers to take him to London to see his favorite pop star, Kyle Minogue, perform if he will pretend to be her boyfriend so she can raise her popularity. Denying his homosexuality, Jonathan alienates his friends, and he must soon decide if getting what he wants is worth the price.
>
> *Gay Males • Dating • Travel • Deception • Friendship • Coming Out*

Myracle, Lauren

Kissing Kate. New York: Dutton's Children's Books, 2003. 198 p. ISBN: 9780525469179; 9780142408698pa. YALSA Best Books. *JS*

> Sixteen-year-old Lissa has been friends with Kate since seventh grade, but when Kate gets drunk at a party and the pair kiss, things change drastically. Lissa wants to talk about what happened, but Kate is acting cold and trying to pretend that nothing happened. Lissa and her younger sister have lived with their uncle since their parents' death, and Lissa has always felt different from other girls, with no mother to talk to. She tries to date guys as she figures out how she feels. With the help of her new free-spirited friend Ariel and some experiments with dream therapy, Lissa is able to establish her own identity as she confronts Kate and comes to terms with her own sexuality.
>
> *Best Friends • Lesbians*

Peck, Dale

Sprout. New York: Bloomsbury Children's Books, Distributed to the trade by Holtzbrinck Publishers, 2009. 277 p. ISBN: 9781599901602. *JS*

> Sixteen-year-old Daniel, nicknamed "Sprout," sports bright green hair and lives in a trailer park in Kansas with his alcoholic father. Unsure about his homosexuality, it is only with the support of his English teacher, Mrs. Miller, and his friend

Ruthie that Sprout is able to prepare for an important essay contest while dealing with his purely sexual relationship with school hunk Ian and the arrival of a new boy, Ty.

Gay Males • Alcoholism • Family Problems • Coming-of-Age

Peters, Julie Anne

Far from Xanadu. New York: Little, Brown, 2005. 282 p. ISBN: 9780316158817; 9780316159715pa. *JS*

Softball-playing lesbian Mike Szabo has dealt with lots of problems in her life. Then her alcoholic father commits suicide, leaving her obese mother unable to cope with life, and her brother runs the family's business into the ground. When Mike meets a new girl, Xanadu, things seem to be looking up. Mike must deal with more problems when it turns out Xanadu is straight. Mike must find ways to cope. She realizes she will need to use her athletic talent as a way to leave her small town and make her own life.

Alcoholism • Lesbians • Family Problems • Grief • Suicide • Coming-of-Age

Peters, Julie Anne

Keeping You a Secret. New York: Little, Brown, 2003. 250 p. ISBN: 9780316702751; 9780316009850pa. *S*

High school senior Holland Jaeger has a great boyfriend, is student council president, and plans to go to an Ivy League college, but when she meets lesbian Cece Goddard, everything changes. As the pair fall in love, Holland loses all her friends, deals with discrimination, and loses her home when her mother throws her out. With the support of a Gay Resource Center, Holland is able to put her life back together as she makes plans for her future.

Lesbians • Blended Families • Discrimination

Ryan, P. E.

In Mike We Trust. New York: HarperTeen, 2009. 321 p. ISBN: 9780060858131. *J*

When his father is killed in an accident, fifteen-year-old Garth is comforted by his father's twin brother, Mike, who shows up to offer the family financial and emotional support. With Mike's support and help, he begins dating classmate Adam, and Garth is also able to come out of the closet, despite his mother's wish that he keep his sexuality a secret. When Mike convinces Garth to quit his job so he can help him to collect money for "charities," trouble arises. As Garth gets entangled in his uncle's shady past, it takes all his courage to face reality and get help from his friends and his mother.

Coming Out • Gay Males • Uncles • Secrets • Coming-of-Age

Ryan, Sara

Empress of the World. New York: Viking, 2001. 213 p. ISBN: 9780670896882; 9780142500590pa. YALSA Best Books. *J*

At a summer program for gifted teens where she is studying archaeology, fifteen-year-old Nicola, "Nic," becomes friends with outspoken Katrina and spacey music student Kevin. There she discovers that there are other people out there like her who don't really fit in. Along with this discovery, Nic, who has liked boys in the past, is surprised when she falls in love with a dancer named Battle. Battle also falls for Nic, but when Nic's feelings get too intense for Battle, they break up, and Battle runs into the arms of a guy. Dealing with a broken heart, Nic must come to accept her own identity and come to terms with who she is.

Sequel: *The Rules for Hearts.* New York: Viking, 2007. 224 p. ISBN: 9780670059065; 9780142412374pa. *J*

> Striking out on her own, Battle, who has just graduated from high school and is still hurting after her breakup with girlfriend Nicola, moves to Portland, Oregon, to attend college. Battle chose Portland because she wanted to reconnect with her estranged older brother, Nick. For the summer before school begins, she decides to live with him in the house he shares with the members of a theater group. In her new home, Battle learns how to navigate complicated relationships when she begins a new romance with manipulative female housemate Meryl and realizes that Nick is not worthy of her admiration.
>
> *Lesbians • Bisexuality • Actors and Actresses • Drama • Sexuality • Interpersonal Relations • Friendship • Summer • Coming-of-Age*

Sanchez, Alex

Getting It. New York: Simon & Schuster Books for Young Readers, 2006. 224 p. ISBN: 9781416908968; 9781416908982pa. *J*

> Wishing to attract gorgeous Roxy Rodriguez, fifteen-year-old acne-prone and overweight Carlos Amoroso gets openly gay classmate Sal to give him a makeover, like on the popular TV show *Queer Eye for the Straight Guy.* Sal agrees to help on the condition Carlos will help him form a gay-straight alliance at their school. Despite his fears that others will think he is gay, Carlos joins in, and with Sal he learns how to dress and talk to girls. More important, Carlos learns that beauty can only be skin deep as he finds the courage to stand up not only for himself, but for his new gay friends.
>
> *Friendship • Gay Males • Friendship • Makeovers • Coming-of-Age*

Sanchez, Alex

The God Box. New York: Simon & Schuster Books for Young Readers, 2007. 272 p. ISBN: 9781416908999; 9781416909002pa. *S*

> Praying to overcome his attraction to boys, Hispanic high school senior Paul lives a traditional conservative Christian life and dutifully dates girlfriend Angie. When openly gay Manuel arrives to debate scriptural passages in Paul's after-school Bible study group, Paul finds himself attracted to Manuel, forcing him to deal with his feelings and learn to accept who he is.
>
> *Gay Males • Friendship • Christianity*

Sanchez, Alex

Rainbow Boys Series. New York: Simon & Schuster Books for Young Readers

> Three gay friends—Jason, Kyle, and Nelson—discover their identities as they move from high school into their adult futures.

Gay Males • Best Friends • HIV • Homosexuality • College • Betrayal • Alcoholism • Interpersonal Relations • Coming-of-Age • Bisexuality • Vacations • Friendship • Homophobia • Travel • Automobiles

Rainbow Boys. 2001. 224 p. ISBN: 9780689841002; 9780689857706pa. YALSA Best Books. *S*

> As they come out, three gay high school seniors—Jason, Kyle, and Nelson—deal with many issues, including homophobia, AIDS, and stereotyping as they learn lessons about self-acceptance and love.

Rainbow High. 2003. 247 p. ISBN: 9780689854774; 9780689854781pa. *S*

> As graduation and their future approaches, Nelson begins a relationship with HIV-positive Jeremy, Jason loses his college athletic scholarship after he publicly comes out and gains media attention, and Kyle is being pressured by his parents to attend Princeton, a school that would require him to leave Jason behind.

Rainbow Road. 2005. 256 p. ISBN: 9780689865657; 9781416911913pa. YALSA Popular Paperbacks. *S*

> On a road trip from Virginia to Los Angeles, Jason, Kyle, and Nelson learn much about who they are and what it means to be gay in America as they meet and interact with a variety of gay, straight, and transgendered people.

Sanchez, Alex

So Hard to Say. New York: Simon & Schuster Books for Young Readers, 2004. 230 p. ISBN: 9780689865640; 9781416911890pa. *MJ*

> When eighth-grader Frederick moves from California, he meets thirteen-year-old Latina Maria "Xio" Xiomara Iris Juarez Hidalgo, who is immediately attracted to him. Frederick cannot return her affections because he is unsure about his own sexuality. But Frederick is included in Xio's group of girlfriends, and he soon finds a place on the soccer team, where he meets handsome Victor. When Xio catches him in a closet for a kissing game, and it's not her but Victor he imagines kissing, Frederick is forced to face his identity and work to understand the nature of his friendship with Xio.

Mexican Americans • Gay Males • Coming Out • New Students • Friendship • Soccer

Shaw, Tucker

The Hookup Artist. New York: HarperCollins, 2005. 197 p. ISBN: 9780060756208; 9780060756222pa. *JS*

> Gay Lucas, who can't seem to find a steady boyfriend of his own, has always played matchmaker successfully for his two friends Sonya and Cate. When Cate gets dumped, Lucas sees gorgeous new boy Derek as the perfect partner for her, but as he tries to get the pair together, he finds himself attracted to Derek. It's up the friends to figure out which one of them Derek really likes.

Gay Males • Dating • Interpersonal Relations

Taylor, William

The Blue Lawn. Los Angeles, CA: Alyson Books, 1999. 122 p. ISBN: 9781555834937. *J*

When the arrival of new and older rebel-kid Theo Meyer forces fifteen-year old good-kid David Mason to admit to his homosexuality, the two form a friendship that starts to progress into something more. Spending time with Theo's grandmother, Gretel Meyer, who survived the Holocaust, David and Theo come to terms with their sexuality. But when Gretel finds the boys together, she ends their friendship by sending Theo back to live with his mother. Although devastated, David is able to continue his growth alone.

Gay Males • New Zealand

Wittlinger, Ellen

Hard Love. New York: Simon & Schuster Books for Young Readers, 1999. 224 p. ISBN: 9780689821349; 9780689841545pa; (aud). YALSA Best Books; YALSA Quick Picks; School Library Journal Best Books; Michael L. Printz Honor Books. *S*

Splitting his time between his playboy father and his emotionally hardened mother, high school junior John pours out his loneliness and confusion in his 'zine, *Bananafish*. When he finds a kindred spirit in senior Marisol, who also writes a 'zine, *Escape Velocity,* John thinks he has found someone who will save him from being alone, and he falls in love with her. Sadly, Marisol is a lesbian and cannot return his love. But despite the barriers, the two develop a close friendship and together they discover truths about their individual identities.

Sequel: ***Love and Lies: Marisol's Story***. New York: Simon & Schuster Books for Young Readers, 2008. 256 p. ISBN: 9781416916239; 9781416979142pa. *S*

Eighteen-year-old Marisol has decided to defer going to college so she can focus on writing a novel. Working as a waitress at a local coffee shop, she meets Lee, a lesbian teen who is estranged from her family. Taking a novel-writing course through the Cambridge Center for Adult Education, Marisol falls for her beautiful teacher, Olivia Frost, and the pair enter into a sexual relationship. Marisol reconnects with old friends and, with the help of Lee and other new friends, she is able to realize how inconsiderate and manipulative Olivia really is.

Writing • Lesbians • Divorce • Honesty

Wyeth, Sharon Dennis

Orphea Proud. New York: Delacorte Press, 2004. 208 p. ISBN: 9780385324977; 9780440227069pa. *S*

Orphea Proud, a seventeen-year-old African American orphan, takes the stage in a New York poetry club to explain her grief. When she falls in love with her childhood best friend, Lissa, the pair are caught in bed together by her homophobic half-brother, who has been her guardian since her parents' death, and he beats Orphea severely. Lissa and Orphea run away, only to be involved in a car accident that kills Lissa. Coming to terms with her loss and her sexuality, Orphea is able to reconnect with long-lost family.

Poetry • Lesbians • Artists • Interracial Persons • Family • Aunts • Prejudice

Chapter 13

Evaluating Your Body

The way adolescents feel about their bodies changes dramatically as they face extreme physical changes while progressing through puberty. Most teens usually have some negative feelings about these bodily changes, but some experience increased feelings of self-consciousness that lead to a persistently poor body image. The books listed in this chapter deal with the variety of issues that teens face as they evaluate and come to accept their bodies. For example, adolescents with a disfiguring birthmark, or even a larger than normal body part must face a variety of challenges as they come to accept themselves and learn to interact with the world. Teens, especially in the United States, find it difficult to have a positive perception of their bodies when their shape does not match the idealized societal perceptions.

Body Image

Bingham, Kelly

Shark Girl. Cambridge, MA: Candlewick Press, 2007. 288 p. ISBN: 9780763632076. *J*

Artistic fifteen-year-old Jane Arrowood's life changes when she loses her arm after surviving a shark attack. Dealing with the phantom pain and the loss of her dreams of being an artist, Jane is angry and sometimes wishes that she had not survived. But slowly, with the support of her family and friends, Jane finds the strength to remake her life into something that is pleasantly new.

Amputees • Self-Acceptance • Diary Novel

Cirrone, Dorian

Dancing in Red Shoes Will Kill You. New York: HarperCollins, 2005. 213 p. ISBN: 9780060557010; 9780060557034pa. YALSA Popular Paperbacks. *J*

Losing the lead part in her arts high school's ballet production because of her Double D bust measurement, sixteen-year old dancer Kayla is advised to get breast reduction surgery. When the whole school weighs in on the issue, Kayla is supported by her gay best friend Joey and her feminist big sister, but in the end Kayla must make her own decision. Complicating matters, mysterious red ballet shoes keep appearing in the school with cryptic notes. Sleuthing out the mystery and dealing with her own body issues, Kayla learns a lot about gender issues and the feminine ideal.

High School • Conformity • Ballet

Franklin, Emily

At Face Value. New York: Flux, 2008. 264 p. ISBN: 9780738713076pa. *J*

Tennis star, straight-A student, and editor of the school paper, Cyrie Bergerac's big nose is the object of teasing from the school bullies. Her only means to fight back is with her words. When Cyrie's crush, Eddie "Rox" Roxanninoff, begins e-mailing her best friend, Leyla, Cyrie is pulled in to compose the romantic words that Leyla can't. When the truth is revealed, Rox falls for Cyrie despite her physical features.

Romance • Friendship • Tennis

Headley, Justina Chen

North of Beautiful. New York: Little, Brown, 2009. 384 p. ISBN: 9780316025058; 9780316025065pa. *JS*

Terra is beautiful except for the birthmark on her left cheek, which no surgery has been able to remove. In her last semester of high school, she is looking forward to getting away from her verbally abusive father, who belittles her artistic creations. When she and her mother are in a car accident over the Christmas holiday, she meets Jacob, a Goth Chinese boy with a cleft lip and unconventional ideas. As Terra and Jacob grow close, so do her mother and Jacob's adoptive mother. When Terra's brother sends tickets for her and her mother to visit him in Shanghai, Jacob and his mother also go on the trip in the hope of locating Jacobs's birth mother. The trip affects all the travelers but especially Terra, who learns from her past and finds new courage to face her future with a new understanding of the true meaning of beauty.

Family Problems • Asian Americans • Interracial Friendships • Goth Culture • Travel

Margolis, Leslie

Fix. New York: Simon Pulse, 2006. 256 p. ISBN: 9781416924562pa. *S*

Eighteen-year-old Cameron, who inherited a big nose, had it fixed several years ago, a move that finally allowed her to become part of the popular crowd at her prep school. She is now considering more surgery. Her sister, fifteen-year-old Allie, who also inherited a big nose, has always been confident in her appearance, but now her ex-model and former movie star mother insists that it is time for Allie to have surgery even though Allie is uncertain and the timing will force her to miss soccer camp. Finding a friend in an elderly former Hollywood starlet, whom she meets at the senior citizens' home where she volunteers, Allie is able to come to terms with her mother's expectations and stand up for herself.

Sisters • Mother and Daughter • Fashion • Intergenerational Relations • Popularity • Plastic Surgery • Volunteers

Perez, Marlene

Unexpected Development. Brookfield, CT: Roaring Brook Press, 2004. 163 p. ISBN: 9781596430068. YALSA Quick Picks. *S*

For years, seventeen-year-old Megan has fought off the rude stares and comments and endured almost every male she meets trying to grope her because of her double-D-sized breasts. Despairing that she will never find a boyfriend who will like her for more than her bra size, Megan is optimistic when her crush Jake separates from his girlfriend, and he asks her out. As Jake gains her trust and they begin having sex, Megan must decide if she would consider breast reduction surgery or if she can come to terms with her body as it is.

Friendship • Dating • Sexuality • Sexual Harassment • School Projects

Salter, Sydney

My Big Nose and Other Natural Disasters. Boston: Graphia, 2009. 345 p. ISBN: 9780152066437. *S*

Cursed with a big nose, Jory Michaels is sure she will die a virgin unless, in the summer before her senior year, she can earn enough money delivering cakes to pay for cosmetic surgery. At work she meets brown-eyed Gideon, who also has a big nose, and despite her crush on hot Tyler Briggs and the fact that dating Gideon will not raise her social status, Jory finds herself falling for him. Dealing with her mother's fad diets that are part of her quest to be thin and finding her best friend Megan is attracting Tyler's attention, Jory must finally learn to accept herself as she realizes that nobody is perfect.

Body Image • Friendship • Summer Job • Summer • Self-Esteem

Overweight

Beck, Nina

This Book Isn't Fat, It's Fabulous. New York: Point, 2008. 256 p. ISBN: 9780545017046pa. *JS*

Despite her confidence in her size twelve body and her popularity with boys, sixteen-year-old Riley Swain is sent to New Horizons, a residential camp for girls with body-image issues. Knowing this is just a ploy by her soon-to-be stepmother to get her out of the house, Riley is not too happy about the prospect, especially when it means being away from "D," with whom she has just shared a first kiss. Afraid D and her friends will find out about the fat camp, Riley stages elaborate lies to cover up everything. When she starts to develop feelings for the camp director's son, Eric, things begin to look up. Soon her lies catch up with her, however, and she must risk losing Eric and revealing everything to her friends.

Weight Loss • Boarding Schools • Self-Esteem

Brescia, Leigh

One Wish. Lodi, NJ: WestSide Books, 2009. 312 p. ISBN: 9781934813058. *J*

Because of her vocal talent, overweight Wrenn Scoot lands the leading role in her high school musical. Hoping this will help her get a hot boyfriend, she gets some risky dieting tips from a new friend in the show and begins to shed the pounds. But when Wrenn meets geeky stage manager Steven who has a crush on her, and when on opening night she faces a crisis caused by her risky behavior, she begins to realize that there are things much more important than weight and popularity.

Weight Loss • Body Image • Dating

Dessen, Sarah

Keeping the Moon. New York: Viking Juvenile, 1999. 228 p. ISBN: 9780670885497; 9780142401767pa; (aud). YALSA Best Books; YALSA Quick Picks; School Library Journal Best Books. *JS*

After slimming down, former fat girl Colie Sparks is sent to live with her Aunt Mira in the small town of Colby, North Carolina, while her mother is off to Europe to spread her fitness empire. Unable to accept her new body and still holding her negative self-image, Colie is soon made the victim of slanderous rumors. But her job at a restaurant provides a strong friendship with waitresses Isabel and Morgan, who teach Colie about life and love. Soon Colie falls for artistic, shy Norman, and she begins to transform, realizing that she can accept herself inside and out.

Body Image • Weight Control • Waitresses

Dionne, Erin

Models Don't Eat Chocolate Cookies. New York: Dial Books for Young Readers, 2009. 243 p. ISBN:9780803732964; 9780803734357. *MJ*

Overweight thirteen-year-old Celeste is humiliated when the hideous bridesmaid dress she is supposed to wear for her cousin's wedding doesn't fit. Things continue to get worse when her aunt enters her in the Husky Peach modeling competition. Hoping to sabotage her chances at being a plus-sized model, Celeste focuses on losing weight. Lacking confidence because her school friend Sandra has dumped her to hang out with the skinny popular girls, Celeste focuses on making the best of the competition. Her small weight loss and the great makeovers she gets from the competition staff help Celeste find she can be strong and confident in her body.

Beauty Contests • Weight Control • Friendship • Self-Confidence • Makeovers

Edwards, Jo

Go Figure. New York: Simon Pulse, 2007. 271 p. ISBN: 9781416924920pa. *JS*

Even though she has been overweight all her life, Ryan Burke has never been unpopular. In fact her popularity has increased since her ex-boyfriend, Noah, hit it big in the music business and wrote a song inspired by her. Sick of being asked about Noah, Ryan loses herself in her photography by taking a weekend course with her ex–best friend and next-door-neighbor Josh. As the two learn together, they grow close again. Ryan finds a new love as she learns to accept her figure by embracing life.

Body Image • Photography

Forde, Catherine

Fat Boy Swim. New York: Delacorte Press, 2004. 240 p. ISBN: 9780385732055; 9780440238911pa; (aud). *MJ*

Extremely overweight fourteen-year-old Jim Kelly faces severe bullying at school, but at home he finds confidence in his cooking skills. Keeping his skills a carefully guarded secret from everyone but his family, things change for Jim when the soccer coach, Joe, helps him to take control of his health by teaching him how to swim in exchange for Jim cooking for a school fund-raiser. Finding freedom in the pool and an attraction to intelligent girl Ellie, who has limited vision, helps Jim to embrace his talent, even as he learns long-held secrets about his biological parents.

Weight Control • Swimming • Bullies and Bullying • Prejudice • Cooking • Loneliness • Scotland

Frazer, Megan

Secrets of Truth and Beauty. New York: Disney/Hyperion, 2009. 352 p. ISBN: 9781423117117. *S*

Seventeen-year-old Dara Cohen, who won the title of Little Miss Maine at age seven, is now overweight. When her autobiographical English presentation includes commentary on society's obsession with thinness, Dara is sent to a counselor, and her enraged parents take her out of school. To escape her problems, Dara finds refuge with her estranged older sister, Rachel, who is a cheese artisan on Jezebel's Goat Farm, a Massachusetts commune that has served as a shelter for homeless lesbian teens. There Dara is able to discover herself with the help of the people she meets, including gay high school senior Owen, his younger brother Milo, and the farm's matriarch, Belinda, as she uncovers important elements of her family history.

Summer • Family Secrets • Body Image • Coming-of-Age

Going, K. L.

Fat Kid Rules the World. New York: G.P. Putnam's Sons, 2003. 187 p. ISBN: 9780399239908. Michael L. Printz Honor Book; YALSA Best Books; School Library Journal Best Books. *JS*

Three-hundred-pound Troy is unhappy, insecure, and unable to deal with life. Contemplating suicide by jumping under a subway train, he is stopped by drug-addicted punk rocker, Curt MacCrae, who has problems of his own. The two become friends, and Curt convinces Troy to play drums in his band. Troy finds acceptance and in turn helps Curt to deal with his own difficulties.

Musicians • Drug Abuse • Suicide • Obesity • Rock Music • Social Acceptance

Hogan, Mary

Pretty Face. New York: HarperTeen, 2008. 213 p. ISBN: 9780060841119; 9780060841133pa. *JS*

High school junior Hayley has always struggled with what she considers her unattractive, overweight body in her image-obsessed Southern California town. But things are especially hard now that her mother has lost weight and insists that the family eat lots of tofu. When her parents offer her the chance to spend ten weeks in Italy on a visit to her mother's college roommate and her family, Hayley jumps at the chance to escape the pressures of her life. In Italy Hayley discovers the beauty of the country and finds herself naturally slimming down a bit, and along the way she also gains some self-esteem as she comes to accept her body when she falls in love with and loses her virginity to an Italian boy, Enzo, who loves Haley for who she is on the inside.

Body Image • Self-Acceptance • Dating • Travel • Dieting

Johnson, Kathleen Jeffrie

The Parallel Universe of Liars. Brookfield, CT: Roaring Brook Press, 2002. 192 p. ISBN: 9780761317463; 9780440238522pa. YALSA Quick Picks. *S*

Overweight fifteen-year-old Robin begins to think everyone is a liar when she finds that her stepmother is sleeping with their gorgeous neighbor Frankie, whom she finds is also lying to his own girlfriend. With everyone around her obsessed with physical appearance, Robin finds that she is even unsure about herself and soon finds herself seduced by Frankie. Like her stepmother, she sneaks over to fool around with him. But when quirky boy Tri asks her out and she offends him, her best friend moves to Alabama, and she finds out that her brother and his wife are going to have a baby, Robin finds that these changes help her to confront the lies and deception and deal with the problems they have created.

Body Image • Large Persons • Sexual Ethics • Self-Perception • Coming-of-Age

Lowry, Brigid

Things You Either Hate or Love. New York: Holiday House, 2006. 179 p. ISBN: 9780823420049; 9780312363086pa. *J*

Fifteen-year-old Georgia Reeves does everything she can, including babysitting and working odd jobs, to earn the money she needs so she can fly to Melbourne to attend the concert of her favorite band, Natural Affinity. She hopes to attract her idol, Jacob, the band's lead singer. Through her struggles to live her dreams, Georgia also struggles with her weight and body image, and she tries to maintain a relationship with her single mom when secrets are revealed about her dead father. At one of her jobs, she falls for a cute clerk who enjoys her poetry, and she finds inner strength to stop living a life consumed by unattainable fantasy.

Body Image • Rock Music • Single Mothers • Romance • Coming-of-Age

Mackler, Carolyn

The Earth, My Butt, and Other Big, Round Things. Cambridge, MA: Candlewick Press, 2003. 246 p. ISBN: 9780763619589; 9780763620912pa. Michael L. Printz Honor Books; YALSA Best Books; Teens Top Ten. *J*

> Fifteen-year-old Virginia Shreves is blond, average, and fat in a family of dark, thin, above-average people, including her mother, adolescent psychologist Dr. Phyllis Shreves, who is obsessed with her daughter's weight. Hiding in baggy clothes, Virginia exists on the fringe of her private Manhattan high school. Her only potential boyfriend is Froggy Welsh, with whom she engages in groping sessions, even though he may just be using her. When her older brother, Byron, is suspended from Columbia University because he has committed date rape, she finds that her family is really not as perfect as they seem. She is gradually able to find the courage to stand up to her family and stand on her own two feet.
>
> *Family Problems • Weight Control • Misfits*

Paley, Sasha

Huge. New York: Simon & Schuster Books for Young Readers, 2007. 272 p. ISBN: 9781416935179; 9781416957959pa. *JS*

> Sent to a weight loss camp by her wealthy parents who are ashamed of their daughter's body because they own a chain of fitness centers, Will meets up-beat April when the two girls become roommates. April, who saved money for over a year so she could attend the camp, wants to change her life so she can become popular, while Will wants to gain weight so she can get back at her parents. As the girls go through the program and bond with each other, they change in many ways, especially when they both fall for the same guy and then take revenge on him when he humiliates them.
>
> *Friendship • Single Parent • Dieting • Revenge • Popularity • Camps • Self-Acceptance*

Potter, Ellen

Slob. New York, Philomel, 2009. 199 p. ISBN: 9780399247057. *MJ*

> Owen Birnbaum put on weight when he turned to food as a coping mechanism to find the comfort he needed when his life was overturned. Now the fattest kid in his school, Owen is teased by his classmates, tortured by his gym teacher, and concerned that the school psycho is out to get him. Also dealing with his sister who is coping with their life changes by joining a group called Girls Who Are Boys and changing her name to Jeremy, Owen loses himself by inventing fantastic devices. When the Oreos from Owen's lunch keep disappearing, he is sure he knows who the thief is and he invents a thief-catching device. Owen must realize that science will not always have all the answers to help him deal with the problems in his life.
>
> *Bullies and Bullying • Body Image • Family Problems*

Purtill, C. Leigh

All About Vee. New York: Razorbill, 2008. 310 p. ISBN: 9781595141804pa. *S*

When her father decides to marry his longtime girlfriend, eighteen-year-old Veronica "Vee" decides it is time to move to Los Angeles to pursue her passion for acting, just like her mother did years before. Unlike her small Arizona town where she was the star of all of her town's community theater productions, 217-pound Vee can't find a place in California and is forced to take a job at a coffee shop. As Vee falls in love and then discovers that her old friend is sabotaging her efforts to make it, she is forced to deal with the realities of love and loss so she can finally find the success she wants.

Large Persons • Friendship • Interpersonal Relations • Remarriage • Coming-of-Age

Rayburn, Tricia

The Melting of Maggie Bean. New York: Aladdin Paperbacks, 2007. 250 p. ISBN: 9781416933489. *M*

With the stress of her father being laid off, Maggie Bean has gained more than thirty pounds in the past year. Now she wants to be a member of her school synchronized swim team, the Water Wings, but her weight is an impediment to her looking good in the silver two-piece suit that is the team uniform. At her parents' insistence, Maggie begins to attend the meetings of the Pound Patrollers, and as she loses weight and masters the Water Wings complicated routines, she gains the confidence and self-esteem she needs to conquer all the obstacles in her life.

Sequel: *Maggie Bean Stays Afloat.* New York: Aladdin Mix, 2008. 316 p. ISBN: 9781416933472. *M*

Working at a day camp teaching swimming to young kids, Maggie Bean still struggles with her own body image. But as she starts a healthy-eating program for kids and finds a potential boyfriend, even with the stress caused by a fight she has with her best friend, Maggie is able to find confidence in herself and with her body.

Large Persons • Body Image • Weight Loss • Swimming • Coming-of-Age • Summer Camps • Friendship • Popularity

Shaw, Tucker

Flavor of the Week. New York: Hyperion, 2003. 224 p. ISBN: 9780786818907; 9780786856985pa. *J*

Overweight Cyril Bartholomew loves to cook and has a crush on beautiful Rose. When Cyril's best friend decides to win Rose for himself by passing off Cyril's cooking as his own, Cyril agrees, since this will be the only time he will be able to do something for her. When their ruse threatens to undermine Cyril's audition for the prestigious American Institute of Culinary Arts, Cyril must learn that in cooking as well as in affairs of the heart, the simple approach is best.

Large Persons • Cooking • Friendship • Love • Shyness

Supplee, Suzanne

Artichoke's Heart. New York: Dutton Juvenile, 2008. 288 p. ISBN: 9780525479024; 9780142414279pa. *J*

> When Rosemary Goode wore an all-green jacket to school in sixth grade, she was dubbed "the Artichoke." To cope with the humiliation, she turned to food. Years later, self-conscious Rosemary finds herself overweight. Feeling left out as she sees the pretty, popular girls prepare for dates at her mother's beauty salon and forced to endure her Aunt Mary's constant criticizing, Rosemary finally finds a friend in the fitness-obsessed new girl who helps her implement changes to lose the pounds. With her slimmed down body, Rosemary is befriended by the popular girls, and her crush starts showing interest in her, but when her single mother is diagnosed with cancer, Rosemary begins to look beyond herself to discover that everyone has their own vulnerabilities and flaws.

> *Weight Control • Beauty Shops • Dieting • Self-Esteem • Gossiping and Gossips • Popularity • Cancer • Football*

Vaught, Susan R.

Big Fat Manifesto. New York: Bloomsbury: Distributed to the trade by Holtzbrinck Publishers, 2008. 320 p. ISBN: 9781599902067. *S*

> Overweight high school senior Jamie Carcaterra is not willing to hide because of her weight. Writing a column called "Fat Girl Manifesto" for the school newspaper in the hope that it will help her to win a college journalism scholarship, Jamie recounts the trials endured by the overweight and stands up for the rights of fat people. Then her also-overweight boyfriend Burke decides to have controversial bariatric surgery, but despite the information this gives her for her column and the fear when he suffers some complications, Jamie finds herself out of sorts as Burke starts getting thin. She must deal with her own insecurities and doubts as she tries to come to terms with her body and the changes in her relationship with Burke.

> *Large Persons • Prejudice • Dieting • Self-Perception*

Whytock, Cherry

Angelica Cookson Potts Series. New York: Simon & Schuster Books for Young Readers

> Angelica Cookson deals with her crazy parents and the pressure she feels to slim down.

> *Weight Control • Dieting • Fashion Shows • Cooking • Friendship • England • Coming-of-Age • England • Vacations • Travel • Unrequited Love*

> *My Cup Runneth Over: The Life of Angelica Cookson Potts.* 2003. 163 p. ISBN: 9780689865466; 9780689865510pa. *MJ*

>> Fourteen-year-old full-figured Angelica "Angel" Cookson Potts dreams of becoming a chef one day, but this dream seems contrary to her desire to develop a lean figure. Spurred on by her former-model mother's pressure to slim down and with the hope of attracting her crush Adam, she tries to diet. When her attempts at dieting don't work

and Adam asks another girl to the school dance, Angel retreats into food. But when she buys a new supportive bra, she finds a boost of confidence. She decides to model in the school fashion show, where she stuns the crowd and discovers that the flaws she sees in herself only come from her distorted self-perception.

My Scrumptious Scottish Dumplings: The Life of Angelica Cookson Potts. 2004. 176 p. ISBN: 9780689865497; 9780689865527pa. *MJ*

After a vacation over Easter break to visit relatives in Scotland, Angel's father reconnects with his roots. Upon their return to England, he accuses Harrod's department store of selling substandard, unauthentic haggis. He is arrested, and the Cookson family is banned from shopping there. Angel gets the help of all of her friends, and even some of her enemies, to prove her father's claim and resolve the crisis.

My Saucy Stuffed Ravioli: The Life of Angelica Cookson Potts. 2006. 176 p. ISBN: 9780689865503. *MJ*

On a fabulous vacation in Italy, Angel is worried that her mother is being unfaithful, while at the same time she is watching her girlfriends' new romances blossoming as she misses the opportunity to develop her own relationship.

Yamanaka, Lois-Ann

Name Me Nobody. New York: Hyperion, 1999. ISBN: 9780786823949; 9780786814664pa. *MJ*

On Hawaii's Big Island, overweight fourteen-year-old Emi-Lou Kaya is an outsider. When two members of the Hilo High boy's volleyball team start paying attention to her and her longtime friend Yvonne develops a particularity close relationship with the catcher on her women's softball team, Emi-Lou feels like she is completely losing control. Even shedding a few pounds doesn't help solve her problems, and it is not until she comes to terms with her best friend's homosexuality and recognizes the ulterior motives of the boys that she is able to establish her own identity.

Friendship • Weight Loss • Coming-of-Age • Homosexuality

Chapter 14

Facing Illness and Disability

Adolescents are often required to face a wide range of physical challenges, sometimes including disabilities and illnesses. When teens are affected by these challenges, they must learn to cope with their changed circumstances and then incorporate any resulting lifestyle changes into their own sense of personal identity. In addition, they must also deal with the changed perceptions of others, including peers, who may lack understanding and acceptance of their problems. Finding the courage to keep a strong self-image and deal with the resulting difficulties of any physical issue is often a complicated endeavor for teens. The books listed in this chapter deal with the variety of physical challenges that some teens face. Working to incorporate a drastic change in one's body, such as the loss of a limb, a brain injury, or severe burns, into one's life is an uphill battle for some teens. For others, the challenge is to deal with disabilities such as cerebral palsy, autism, or Down syndrome. Another group of teens must work through the challenges of having illnesses such as diabetes or cancer.

Health and Wellness

Froese, Deborah

Out of the Fire. Toronto, Canada: Sumach Press, 2001. 282 p. ISBN: 9781894549097pa. YALSA Best Books. *JS*

> When sixteen-year-old Dayle Meryk becomes the girlfriend of popular Keith, she finds herself living two lives as she moves between life with her nerdy friends and a life with Keith's partying fast crowd. Finally alienating her old friends as she continually struggles with her grief over her grandmother's death, things turn disastrous when she is severely burned at a bonfire party where drinks are flowing. During her four months of painful physical and emotional recovery, Dayle must deal with her grief, learn who her true friends really are, and cope with her feelings of revenge for Keith's friend Pete, who was the one who caused the accident.
>
> *Burn Victims • Death*

Halpin, Brendan

Forever Changes. New York: Farrar, Straus & Giroux, 2008. 192 p. ISBN: 9780374324360. *S*

> Faced with the grim statistics of life expectancy for her disease, cystic fibrosis, eighteen-year-old Brianna Pelletier is uncertain about her future and wonders if she should even make plans for it despite her father's urging her to focus on college applications. Brianna has a future as a mathematician if she wants it, and with the help of friends and a calculus teacher who faces his own health concerns, Brianna learns to understand the potential of living life no matter how much time you have.

Cystic Fibrosis • High School • Father and Daughter

Hautman, Pete

Sweetblood. New York: Simon & Schuster Books for Young Readers, 2003. 192 p. ISBN: 9780689850486; 9780689873249pa. YALSA Best Books. *JS*

> Living a life consumed by her disease, sixteen-year-old diabetic Lucy Szabo spends a lot of time in a vampire chat room, where she calls herself Sweetblood. But when she submits a creative writing assignment proposing that vampire legends are based on the behavior of untreated diabetics, the adults in her life become concerned about her and insist that she see a therapist. Things don't get better, however, as Lucy starts to explore the Goth world outside of the computer and meets an older man, Wayne "Draco" Smith, who fancies himself a vampire. Getting farther away from her true friends, Lucy does not pay attention to her health, and her diabetes spirals out of control until one night at a Halloween party, she nearly dies. Facing her mortality, Lucy must learn to accept herself and become an individual despite her disease.

Diabetes • Chat Rooms • Goth Culture

Hershey, Mary

The One Where the Kid Nearly Jumps to His Death and Lands in California. New York: Razorbill, 2007. 288 p. ISBN: 9781595141507. *MJ*

> Thirteen-year-old amputee Alastair "Stump" Hudson, who lost his leg at the age of eight when he fell off a ski lift, finds himself spending the summer in California with his father and his father's new wife, Skyla, whom, he is surprised to learn, is a double amputee. Still angry with his dad over the events that caused his accident and his parents' subsequent divorce, Stump struggles to find a place in his rich stepmother's household that is filled with servants. Despite his stepmother's calm understanding, he remains intent on making his dad suffer. When Stump develops a crush on Skyla's niece, who is a teenage soap star, and starts training with a retired swim coach so he can enter a celebrity fund-raising triathlon to impress her, he begins to realize that things are not always what they seem, and he must deal with the grudge he has been holding against his father.

Amputees • Disabilities • Father and Son • Swimming • Blended Families • Divorce • Coming-of-Age

Katcher, Brian

Playing with Matches. New York: Delacorte Press, 2008. 272 p. ISBN: 9780385735445; 9780385735452pa. YALSA Best Books. *JS*

13

> Geeky high-school junior Leon Sanders has never had a girlfriend, but when he gets a partner for a class project and connects with disfigured burn victim Melody Hennon, after he shares a joke with her the pair begin to share details about their lives and form a friendship and then a romance. While Melody finds happiness because she feels beautiful for the first time, Leon worries about what others will think, and when gorgeous classmate Amy Green, who has until now always ignored him, starts paying him attention, he dumps Melody. Devastated by his actions, Melody manages to find the self-confidence and strength to go forward with her life. Leon realizes the emotional consequences of his actions and learns to do the right thing.

14

15

> *Burn Victims • Dating • Friendship • Loyalty*

16

Klam, Cheryl

The Pretty One. New York: Delacorte Press, 2008. 356 p. ISBN: 9780385733731pa. *JS*

17

> Sixteen-year-old Megan and her older sister Lucy are opposites. Lucy is the sexy, slim, and talented one who is majoring in drama at the Chesapeake School of the Arts in Baltimore that both girls attend. Megan is the big, unattractive techie nerd who majors in set design. Lucy has always seemed to love and support her sister, but when Megan overhears her making rude comments about her size, she runs from the building, only to be hit by an oncoming car. After months of recovery, the bandages come off, and Megan finds that plastic surgery has made her more beautiful than Lucy. While her new face brings many perks she has always longed for, Megan also finds that being pretty is not easy, and she no longer really knows who she is. She must work to figure out what is truly important in life.

18

19

> *Sisters • Plastic Surgery • Traffic Accidents • Sibling Rivalry*

20

Koertge, Ron

Stoner & Spaz. Cambridge, MA: Candlewick Press, 2002. 169 p. ISBN: 9780763616083; 9780763621506pa; (aud). YALSA Best Books; YALSA Quick Picks. *JS*

21

> Despite his overprotective grandmother's objections, sixteen-year-old Benjamin Bancroft, who has cerebral palsy, strikes up a friendship with tattooed, drug-addicted Colleen Minou when the two meet at the Rialto Theater during a screening of an old horror movie. As Colleen teaches Ben to embrace life and their friendship moves into a sexual relationship, both are able to find a new sense of self-acceptance, and Ben expands his love of film when he makes his own movie.

22

23

> *Cerebral Palsy • Drug Abuse • High School • Videos*

Mitchard, Jacquelyn

All We Know of Heaven: A Novel. New York: HarperTeen, 2008. 312 p. ISBN: 9780061345784; 9780061345807pa. *JS*

When sixteen-year-old Bridget Flannery and Maureen O'Malley are in a car crash, the rescuers mistakenly assume it was Maureen who died, and Bridget who was left in a coma. As weeks pass and the girl recovers, it is apparent that the girls were misidentified, and it was Maureen who survived. Leaving Bridget's family and boyfriend, Danny Carmody, to cope with their sudden grief, Maureen's family must now help her through her recovery and intense therapy. In addition to re-learning simple tasks such as walking and speaking, Maureen has to deal with the guilt she feels over the accident and the grief she feels for her friend. She also begins to explore the long-hidden feelings she has had for Danny when the pair develop a sexual relationship.

Traffic Accidents • Death • Grief • Brain Injury • Identity

Sheinmel, Courtney

Positively. New York: Simon & Schuster Books for Young Readers, 2009. 160 p. ISBN: 9781416971696; 9781442406223pa. *MJ*

When her mother dies of AIDS, thirteen-year-old Emmy starts to deal with her own HIV-positive status, since her mother unknowingly passed the virus on to her during pregnancy. Hoping to help her process her grief, her father and step-mother, who are expecting their first child, send Emmy away to a summer camp for HIV-positive girls. There Emmy begins to find the peace she needs as she gets to know other girls who are dealing with similar problems, even as she faces the realities of her condition when a friend must leave camp due to declining health.

AIDS • Death • Mothers • Summer Camps • Friendship • Blended Families

Trueman, Terry

7 Days at the Hot Corner. New York: Harper Tempest, 2007. 160 p. ISBN: 9780060574949. *S*

When high-school-senior Scott discovers his best friend, Travis, is gay, he is frightened when a bloody accident during their baseball batting practice leads him to believe that he might have been infected with AIDS. Waiting seven days for the results of the test, Scott must provide help to his friend, who has been kicked out by his parents. He must also come to grips with his fears for their safety and of what others may think of him after Travis gives an anonymous interview to the school paper.

Baseball • Gay Males • Friendship • Homosexuality • Prejudice • AIDS • Sports • Coming-of-Age

Trueman, Terry

Stuck in Neutral. New York: HarperCollins, 2000. 114 p. ISBN: 9780060285197; 9780064472135pa; (aud). Michael L. Printz Honor Book; YALSA Best Book; YALSA Quick Picks. *J*

Fourteen-year-old Shawn McDaniel has cerebral palsy, and although he can't interact with others or control his body, on the inside, he is a genius who remembers everything he hears. Finding a release for his trapped soul only during the seizures that move his body in ways he can't, Shawn must sit idly by, being cared for by his mother and older siblings, as he learns that his Pulitzer Prize–winning writer father, who left the family when Shawn was three, is coming to grips with the agonizing decision of whether he should kill Shawn to relieve his suffering.

Companion: *Cruise Control.* New York: Harper Tempest, 2004. 149 p. ISBN: 9780066239606; 9780064473774pa. *J*

Paul loves his younger brother Shawn, who has cerebral palsy, but he also feels guilty because he is a straight-A student who is active in a lot of sports, and these are two things that Shawn will never be able to do. Shouldering the responsibility for helping his mother and sister to care for Shawn, Paul hates his father, who abandoned the family years ago when he was unable to deal with the day-to-day problems of Shawn's condition. Taking out his anger by fighting with those around him, Paul must come to terms with his life and find healthy ways to channel his rage.

Disabilities • Cerebral Palsy • Brothers • Family Relationships • Basketball

Wolfson, Jill

Cold Hands, Warm Heart. New York: Henry Holt, 2009. 256 p. ISBN: 9780805082821. *J*

Waiting for a heart transplant to correct the heart condition that is slowly killing her, fifteen-year-old Dani meets fellow patients eight-year-old Wendy, who is waiting for a kidney, and seventeen-year-old Milo, who is waiting for a second liver transplant. When Dani and Wendy receive organs from the same donor, a fourteen-year-old gymnast named Amanda, Dani must deal with the emotions that come from getting another girl's heart as she finds herself falling in love with Milo. Revelations about how Amanda became the girls' savior are offered through the eyes of her older brother Tyler, who has discovered through Amanda's computer files her truly caring nature.

Brothers • Sisters • Death • Jewish Americans

Zimmer, Tracie Vaughn

Reaching for Sun. New York: Bloomsbury Children's Books: distributed to the trade by Holtzbrinck Publishers, 2007. 144 p. ISBN: 9781599900377. *MJ*

Seventh-grader Josie has cerebral palsy, and her disabilities have made her a social outcast. At home her mother is struggling to become a landscape designer and has little time for Josie. Her grandmother, who takes care of the farmhouse that they have owned for generations, is dealing with the land that is being sold so that large homes can be built. When a new neighbor, Jordan, moves in, he introduces Josie to scientific discovery, and with Gram, who loves plants and gardening, they conduct various experiments. But when Gram gets sick and Jordan leaves for camp, Josie struggles and skips her therapy sessions, an act that creates even more tension between her and her mother, which Josie must work through as she tries to discover who she is.

Cerebral Palsy • Grandmothers • Single Parent • Friendship • Intergenerational Relations • Novels in Verse • Coming-of-Age

Cancer

Buckingham, Dorothea N.

Staring Down the Dragon. Kailua, HI: Sydney Press, 2003. 207 p. ISBN: 9780972457736pa. YALSA Best Books. *J*

Returning to Kailua High after undergoing cancer treatments, Rell DeMello tries to readjust to life while dealing with the fact that her cancer may return.

Cancer • Death • Family Relationships

Hrdlitschka, Shelley

Sun Signs. Victoria, BC: Orca Book Publishers, 2005. 195 p. ISBN: 9781551433882; 9781551433387pa. *J*

Homebound while she fights cancer, fifteen-year-old Kayleigh Wyse attends online classes where she enlists the help of three classmates to join her as participants in a scientific study of astrology. She asks her group to send information about the accuracy of their horoscopes. As Kayleigh gathers more data, the project gets out of hand when it becomes apparent that her friends are hiding vital information. With their online environment hiding the truth, Kayleigh must examine the assumptions she has made as she tries to come to terms with fact that, like her friends, she has also used the digital world to hide her own illness.

Schools • Secrets • E-mail • Canada • Epistolary Novels

Koss, Amy Goldman

Side Effects. New Milford, CT: Roaring Brook Press, 2006. 144 p. ISBN: 9781596431676; 9780312602765pa. YALSA Best Books. *MJ*

When fourteen-year-old Isabella discovers enlarged glands in her neck and is diagnosed with stage-four Hodgkin's lymphoma, she faces the severe side effects, including nausea and hair loss that her chemotherapy treatments bring, as she also deals with her classmates' pity, gets closer to her best friend and her mother, and finds the humor to beat her disease.

Cancer • Best Friends • Friendship • Mother and Daughter • Family

McDaniel, Lurlene

A Rose for Melinda. New York: Bantam Books, 2002. 202 p. ISBN: 9780553570908pa. *JS*

Melinda, who has always wanted to be a ballerina, suddenly collapses one summer in a ballet class, and the doctors discover that she has leukemia. Facing this grim diagnosis, she is supported by her longtime friend Jess, who was forced to move to California with his mother when his parents divorced, and new friend Bailey. Both friends work hard to cheer her as she does everything in her power to overcome her dreadful disease.

Leukemia • Best Friends • E-mail • Diaries

Sonnenblick, Jordan

Drums, Girls, & Dangerous Pie. Sun Valley, ID: DayBue, 2004. 192 p. ISBN: 9780966894097; 9780439755207pa; (aud). YALSA Popular Paperbacks; Teens Top Ten. *MJ*

> When his five-year-old brother, Jeffrey, is diagnosed with leukemia, eighth-grader Steven is ignored as his mother focuses on caring for Jeffrey and his father can only complain about the mounting medical bills. Retreating to the basement where he can play his drums for hours, Steven stops doing his homework, avoids his friends, and tries to pursue unattainable Renee, despite the fact that his childhood friend Annette has a crush on him. When he realizes that his parents are just doing what they need to and they would do the same for him, Steven is able to find a way to move forward with his life despite the tragedy around him.

> *Brothers • Leukemia • Family Relationships • Family Problems • Music • Bands • Popularity • Interpersonal Relations • Coming-of-Age*

Turner, Ann

Hard Hit. New York: Scholastic, 2006. 167 p. ISBN: 9780439296809. *JS*

> When tenth-grader Mark Warren learns that his father has pancreatic cancer, his life falls apart. He struggles to maintain his relationships with his friends and girlfriend and keep his status as a star on the baseball team. Things become even worse when, despite his entreaties and promises to God, his father passes away. In the aftermath of this event, Mark must deal with the pain and grief of being left behind as he rebuilds his life.

> *Baseball • Death • Grief • Family Relationships • Novels in Verse*

Disability

Aronson, Sarah

Head Case. New Milford, CT: Roaring Brook Press, 2007. 173 p. ISBN: 9781596432147. YALSA Quick Picks. *S*

> When a drunk-driving accident leaves two people dead and Frank Marder paralyzed from the neck down, he must deal with the consequences, including people in the town who think he should be in jail for murder. Frank is angry and resentful upon his release from the hospital as he learns to deal with his new disability, which requires his mother to feed and care for him. He also has to learn sexual techniques for quadriplegics and how to drive a wheelchair. Ultimately Frank has to deal with his guilt as he makes the decision to address an all-school assembly to take responsibility for his actions.

> *Traffic Accidents • Drunk Driving • Guilt • Responsibility*

13

14

15

16

17

18

19

20

21

22

23

Brenna, Beverley

Wild Orchid. Calgary, Canada: Red Deer Press, 2006. 156 p. ISBN: 9780889953307pa. *S*

Terrified by the future but also excited by prospects such as having a boyfriend, eighteen-year-old Taylor, who has Asperger's syndrome, does not want to go with her mother to Prince Albert National Park for the summer. Taylor finds a job, and even though she faces many difficulties, such as not being able to look at people's faces, she makes her way through the summer and learns a lot about herself in the process.

Mother and Daughter • Asperger's Syndrome • Coming-of-Age

Brown, Teri

Read My Lips. New York: Simon Pulse, 2008. 256 p. ISBN: 9781416958680pa. *MJ*

Punk skater Serena Nelson has lived a pretty normal life even though she is oral deaf, meaning that although she has some hearing loss, she can speak and hear some things. But when she moves to a new town and the popular girls find out about her excellent ability to read lips, they convince Serena to use her ability to spy on other students to gather juicy gossip so she can enter their secret society. Serena just wants to fit in and date Miller, the school rebel, but soon things go too far. Serena must decide what price she is willing to pay for popularity.

Deaf Persons • High School • Popularity

Brugman, Alyssa

Finding Grace. New York: Delacorte Press, 2004. 228 p. ISBN: 9780385731164; 9780440238331pa. *S*

High school graduate Rachel is a perfectionist who thinks she knows most everything about the world—that is, until she meets Mr. Preston, a local attorney, who hires her to care for Grace, his friend who has brain damage. Rachel is completely clueless about how to care for Grace, but as she learns through some letters about Grace's interesting life before the accident, she finds her compassion growing, helping her to learn about a new world of experiences. Eventually she is forced to admit she does not know everything.

Brain Injury • Romance • Self-Discovery

Cheaney, J. B.

The Middle of Somewhere. New York: Alfred A. Knopf, 2007. 224 p. ISBN: 9780375837906; 9780440421658pa. *MJ*

Ronnie and her brother Gee, who suffers from attention-deficit/hyperactivity disorder, are sent on a road trip with the grandfather they hardly know after their mother has injured her knee and needs some peace and quite to recover. Joining their grandfather's search for locations for possible wind farms in Kansas, Ronnie is constantly trying to keep Gee out of trouble and keep her own outlook positive. When Gee disappears and their grandfather gets hurt, things reach a crisis point, but Ronnie ultimately learns about the depth of a family's love.

Attention-Deficit Disorder • Grandparents • Humor • Self-Discovery

Crowley, Suzanne

The Very Ordered Existence of Merilee Marvelous. New York: Greenwillow, 2007. 384 p. ISBN: 9780061231971; 9780061231995pa; (aud). *M*

> Thirteen-year-old Marilee has Asperger's syndrome; she needs her life to be in order and hates to be touched. One day, Biswick, a new boy with fetal alcohol syndrome, arrives in town with his poet father, and Marilee's ordered life suddenly becomes very disordered by the inquisitive and needy boy. With the help of family and friends, the pair are able to deal with Biswick's father's alcoholism and death and in the end find out how their uniqueness make them special.

> *Asperger's Syndrome • Belonging • Friendship*

Ferris, Jean

Of Sound Mind. New York: Farrar, Straus & Giroux, 2001. 215 p. ISBN: 9780374355807; 9780374455842pa. YALSA Best Books; YALSA Popular Paperbacks. *S*

> As the only hearing member of his family, high school senior Theo has shouldered a lot of responsibility for his family over the years. When his father has a stroke that incapacitates him, Theo finds himself shouldering an even greater burden as he must care for his dependent younger brother and his unstable mother. Theo meets and falls for Ivy, a spunky young entrepreneur who runs a small catering business and who, because of her deaf father, can also sign. Ivy helps Theo, and in the end, he is able to find a way to care for his family while still pursuing his own dreams.

> *Deaf Persons • Family Relationships • Father and Son*

Mass, Wendy

A Mango-Shaped Space: A Novel. New York: Little, Brown, 2003. 220 p. ISBN: 9780316523882; 9780316058254pa. *MJ*

> Thirteen-year-old Mia Winchell has synesthesia, a condition in which her visual cortex is activated when numbers, letters, words, or sounds cause a dizzying onslaught of colors. Keeping this condition secret until eighth grade when the color visions make math and foreign languages impossible, she goes to her parents and then a doctor for help. Learning that she is not alone, Mia begins to build a community of others with her condition. As she delves further into this world, she disrupts her relationships with her family and friends until extreme guilt over her beloved cat's illness and death as well as grief over her grandfather's passing help her to begin to rebuild the relationships she has neglected.

> *Friendship • Death • Guilt • Family Relationships • Secrets*

Rorby, Ginny

Hurt Go Happy. New York: Tom Doherty Associates, 2006. 267 p. ISBN: 9780765314420; 9780765353047pa. *J*

> Joey Willis, who has been deaf since her father beat her, lives an isolated existence because her mother won't allow her to learn American Sign Lan-

guage. When she meets her elderly neighbor, Dr. Charles Mansell, who works with a chimpanzee named Sukari, that uses sign language, the world opens up to her, and Joey finds the strength to conquer what is to come, especially after Charles dies and Joey must decide Sukari's future.

Deaf Persons • Mother and Daughter • Intergenerational Relations • Animal Rights

Rottman, S. L.

Head above Water. Atlanta, GA: Peachtree, 1999. 196 p. ISBN: 9781561451852; 9781561452385pa. YALSA Best Books; YALSA Popular Paperbacks. *JS*

For sixteen-year-old Skye, life is a struggle as she cares for Sunny, her older brother with Down syndrome while her divorced mother works two jobs. Working to maintain her grades, she hopes to compete in a swim competition and win a scholarship. When she begins dating popular Mike Banner, she succumbs to pressure from him for more attention and ditches her brother, covering up her behavior with a variety of lies. When Mike starts pressuring her to have sex and then rapes her, Skye must find the strength to build her own identity and think for herself.

Down Syndrome • Swimming • Developmentally Disabled • Sports

Stork, Francisco X.

Marcelo in the Real World. New York: Arthur A. Levine Books, 2009. 320 p. ISBN: 9780545054744; (aud). *S*

Seventeen-year-old Marcelo Sandoval has Asperger's syndrome, and his father Arturo has decided it is time for him get out of his comfort zone. Instead of letting him work the summer in the stables at the special school he attends, he forces Marcelo to take a summer job in the mailroom at his law firm. Thrown into the realities of the real world, Marcelo must learn to deal with duplicitous people who try to take advantage of not only him, but of other less fortunate people as well. Along the way, Marcelo makes important decisions about his future as he makes personal connections with the new friends he has made.

Christianity • Autism • Interpersonal Relations • Ethics • Work

Willis, Jeanne

Naked without a Hat. New York: Delacorte Press, 2004. 218 p. ISBN: 9780385731669. *S*

Unable to stand living with his mother anymore, nineteen-year-old Will Avery decides to live in a boarding house with roommates Rocko, an artist; James, who always has sex on his mind; and motherly Chrissy. When Will falls for Zara, an Irish Gypsy, and his mother finds out about their sexual relationship, she threatens to reveal to everyone that Will has Down syndrome and has had plastic surgery to cover it up, leaving Will to deal with these revelations as he establishes his life as an adult.

Down Syndrome • Developmentally Disabled • Family Secrets • Plastic Surgery • Prejudice • England

Chapter 15

Dealing with Dysfunction

Some teens' relationships are characterized by abuse, neglect, drug addiction, alcoholism, or other factors that make their lives dysfunctional, and many adolescents must deal with challenges that come with not having the love and security of a stable support system. The tasks required of teens to develop their own identity are made more difficult when they lack support. The books listed in this chapter deal with the challenges that teens confront when their lives are characterized by dysfunctional relationships. For example, some teens must deal with dysfunctional families. These family relationships are different from those that are dealt with in Part I of this book in that the families depicted here have stopped functioning and work outside the normal, healthy patterns of most family relationships. When families stop functioning because of mental illness, violence, or alcoholism and drug abuse, many teens are caught in the middle and must find ways to overcome the challenges. For some teens, the solution to getting away from family difficulties comes from an outside source when they are placed in foster care or gain assistance from government agencies or other supportive groups.

Dysfunctional Families

Auseon, Andrew

Funny Little Monkey. Orlando, FL: Harcourt, 2005. 298 p. ISBN: 9780152053345; 9780152054137pa. *JS*

Physically bullied by his 6'2"-tall fraternal twin, Kurt, fourteen-year-old Arty Moore, who is 4'2" due to a growth hormone deficiency, is angry. To get revenge, he teams up with a group of misfits to lead a prank that will find his brother accused of destroying the school mascot. Caught up in the scheme, Arty also finds a new sense of popularity when rich, beautiful, and smart Leslie shows an interest in him. When the prank goes too far and Leslie is revealed just to be out for the attention, Arty is forced to face up to things by confronting his brother and mending their relationship.

Twins • Violence • Anger • Misfits • Coming-of-Age

Barkley, Brad, and Heather Hepler

Jars of Glass: A Novel. New York: Dutton Children's Books, 2008. 208 p. ISBN: 9780525479116; 9780142414897pa. *J*

> With their mother committed to a mental institution, sisters fourteen-year-old Chloe and fifteen-year-old Shana are trying to cope. Chloe finds some relief in mementos of their mother, and Shana involves herself in the local Goth scene. With their father spiraling into alcoholism, which threatens the loss of the family business, and facing the potential of their adopted brother being taken away, it is up to the girls to work together to heal their family and themselves.

> *Family Problems* • *Mental Illness* • *Adoption* • *Goth Culture*

Beard, Philip

Dear Zoe: A Novel. New York: Viking, 2005. 198 p. ISBN: 9780670034017; 9780452287402pa; (aud). *S*

> Fifteen-year-old Tess DeNunzio feels disconnected from her life and family. Moving in with her drug-dealing father Nick allows her to escape from her mother, stepfather, and half-sister. Tess is consumed with guilt after her three-year-old sister, Zoe, is killed by a car when she was supposed to be watching her on September 11, 2001. In letters to Zoe, Tess chronicles her attempt at a fresh start. Having a romance and sex with pot-smoking bad-boy Jimmy and a summer job at a theme park are also great escapes, until another accident forces Tess to deal with her grief as she learns to understand the healing power of love.

> *Family* • *Death* • *Epistolary Novels* • *Coming-of-Age*

Booth, Coe

Kendra. New York: PUSH, 2008. 320 p. ISBN: 9780439925365. YALSA Best Books; YALSA Quick Picks. *JS*

> Abandoned by her mother who has been working toward a college degree, fifteen-year-old Kendra is once again disappointed when her mother finishes school and gets a one-bedroom apartment that cannot accommodate her. Still living with her grandmother who raised her, Kendra is looking for love and finds it with Nashawn. Overwhelmed by Nashawn's sexual pressures and agreeing to sexual acts that will leave her virginity intact, Kendra feels guilty and has no one to turn to. But a chance to finally live with her mom changes everything, and Kendra must come to understand herself and the other women in her life.

> *Mother and Daughter* • *Family Problems*

Brown, Susan Taylor

Hugging the Rock. Berkeley, CA: Tricycle Press, 2006. 170 p. ISBN: 9781582461809; 9781582462363pa. ALA Notable Children's Books. *JS*

> After watching her mother, who has bipolar disorder, pack up the car and leave without her, Rachel blames herself for the departure and ignores her schoolwork and friends. When her father steps in to become more involved and affectionate, he soon reveals the fact that her mother never wanted children, and it was he who wanted them so desperately that he convinced her to stay with him and raise their

baby. Together the two face the truth and grow closer as they create a new family unit.

Divorce • Mother-Deserted Children • Family Problems • Mental Illness • Novels in Verse

Buffie, Margaret

Out of Focus. Tonawanda, NY: Kids Can Press, 2006. 240 p. ISBN: 9781553379553; 9781553379560pa. *JS*

An amateur photographer, sixteen-year-old Bernie Dodd is struggling to keep her life and that of her two younger siblings together in the face of the broken promises and job losses of her alcoholic mother, Celia. Finding the deed to a rundown lodge in Ontario that her great-aunt Charlotte left to the family, Bernie threatens to call social services and have the kids taken away if they don't leave the horrible place where they now live and move there. In Ontario the family thrives as they work to make the house habitable. As Bernie develops her photography skills and discovers secrets about Charlotte's life, Bernie realizes she is quite similar to her mother and learns to bring her life back into focus and trust again.

Family Relationships • Family Problems • Photography • Alcoholism • Brothers • Sisters • Moving • Obsessive-Compulsive Disorder

Caletti, Deb

The Queen of Everything. New York: Simon Pulse, 2002. 384 p. ISBN: 9780743436847pa. *S*

Seventeen-year-old Jordan McKenzie lives a peaceful life with her divorced father on the San Juan Islands just off the coast of Washington State. Along with her best friend Melissa, who is very focused on popularity, Jordan works for a Christian couple who run a weight loss program. Things go terribly wrong, however, when Jordan's father falls in love and has an affair with a beautiful, wealthy, married woman, Gayle D'Angelo, and in a fit of jealousy kills her husband. With her life spiraling out of control, Jordan also has to deal with her grandfather's death and the loss of her virginity to a popular but cruel boy. With support from her friends, Jordan must work through her sadness and rebuild her own life.

Trust • Betrayal • Abandonment • Death

Carlson, Melody

Diary of a Teenage Girl: Maya Series. Sisters, OR: Multnomah

Maya moves in with her cousin's family and finds a new way of life as well as a new faith.

Christianity • Family Problems • Diary Novel

A Not-So-Simple Life. 2008. 256 p. ISBN: 9781601421173pa. *JS*

Maya does not miss the bad sides of her glamorous Hollywood life when her mother is sent to prison and her pop-star father is away on tour. She is sent to live with her cousins and explores and embraces their faith.

It's a Green Thing. 2009. 256 p. ISBN: 9781601421180pa. *JS*

> Things are starting to be normal for Maya as she makes a new life with her cousins and uncle.

Corrigan, Eireann

Splintering. New York: Scholastic, 2004. 192 p. ISBN: 9780439535977; 9780439489928pa. YALSA Best Books. *J*

> Fifteen-year-old Paulie and her older brother Jeremy must deal with the aftermath when a crazed drug addict, high on PCP and brandishing a machete, breaks into their older sister Mimi's apartment where they are holding a family gathering. Fundamentally changing their family's relationships, all the siblings go in different directions. Mimi, who has separated from her husband, returns home and becomes a couch potato, Paulie spends most nights with her boyfriend, and Jeremy is preoccupied with winning the heart of a scarred girl. Things look dim as the family starts to break apart. Soon they must confront their rage and misunderstandings as they heal from their trauma.

Family Relationships • Violence • Crime • Family Problems • Drug Abuse • Memory • Psychic Trauma • Novels in Verse

Curtis, Christopher Paul

Bucking the Sarge. New York: Wendy Lamb Books, 2004. 240 p. ISBN: 9780385323079; 9780440413318pa; (aud). School Library Journal Best Books; ALA Notable Children's Books; YALSA Best Books. *MJ*

> Fifteen-year-old Luther T. Farrell's mother, called Loser by some, has made herself rich by scams such as evicting poor families from slum housing and loan sharking. Luther hates his vicious mother, whom he calls "the Sarge" because she forced him to help with her "businesses." Luther has responsibility for running The Happy Neighbor Group Home for Men where he cares for the four men and drives them around with his forged license. All Luther wants is to live an honest life. At school Luther wants to win the science fair, even though his main rival is the girl he has loved since kindergarten and doing so will probably not get him the action he wants for the vintage condom in his wallet. Soon Luther is able to build his confidence and take revenge on the Sarge so he can build his own independent life.

Family Problems • African Americans • Group Homes

Ellis, Ann Dee

Everything Is Fine. New York: Little, Brown Books for Young Readers. 2009. 160 p. ISBN: 9780316013642; 9780316014434pa; (aud). *MJ*

> Since her baby sister died, Mazzy's mother has been severely depressed. When her sportscaster father leaves for a job, Mazzy is left alone to care for herself and her mother. While next-door neighbors try to help, things continue to deteriorate as Mazzy works to keep her situation hidden. Soon, however, things hit rock bottom, and Mazzy must accept the fact that things must change. Then her father finally steps in and takes charge.

Family Problems • Mothers • Mental Illness

Felin, M. Sindy

Touching Snow. New York: Atheneum Books for Young Readers, 2007. 240 p. ISBN: 9781416917953; YALSA Best Books. *MJ*

> Fourteen-year-old Karina and her family are Haitian immigrants. She feels isolated, especially at school where she is taunted. The conflicts between Karina and her stepfather grow more heated, and when he brutally beats her sister Enid, nearly killing her, the family is reported to social services. Facing the threat of deportation or the need to go on welfare, Karina takes the blame for Enid's injuries but along the way meets Rachel, whose parents work for social services. The two develop a friendship that gives Karina the courage to not be a victim anymore and to work to make a safe life for her family.

> *Child Abuse • Family Problems • Coming-of-Age*

Geerling, Marjetta

Fancy White Trash. New York: Viking, 2008. 257 p. ISBN: 9780670010820; YALSA Best Books. *J*

> Fifteen-year-old Abby Savage's mother is pregnant by much-younger husband Steve, who had also dated Abby's older sisters Kait and Shelby. Abby is determined not to commit the same mistakes when it comes to love. Unsure of the identity of the father of Kait's child, Abby suspects it might be her former crush, Jackson, who is the older brother of her best friend, Cody. She tries to distance herself from him. While supporting Cody, who is trying to admit he is gay, Abby uncovers family secrets and finds her own place among the women who surround her.

> *Family Problems • Dating • Homosexuality • Friendship • Single Mothers*

Giles, Gail

Playing in Traffic. Brookfield, CT: Roaring Brook Press, 2004. 176 p. ISBN: 9781596430051; 9781416909262pa. YALSA Quick Picks. *J*

> Matt Lathrop has always been an anonymous outcast at school and is shocked when Goth girl Skye Colby shows an interest in him. When Skye reveals that at home she has a sister with Down's syndrome and a father who abuses her, Matt moves to save her. But soon he is led to realize there are flaws in her story, and he questions her many demands and their secret meetings to have sex. When Skye's demands turn criminal and she threatens to harm his thirteen-year-old younger sister, Matt must stand up for himself and extricate himself from the bad relationship.

> *Family Problems • Brothers • Sisters • Stepfathers • Murder • Family Secrets • Dishonesty • Betrayal • Goth Culture*

Going, K. L.

King of the Screwups: A Novel. Boston: Houghton Mifflin Harcourt, 2009. 320 p. ISBN: 9780152062583. *S*

> Talented, straight athlete and high school senior Liam shares his mother's interest in fashion. Embracing his popularity, Liam parties and achieves

only average grades, disappointing his verbally abusive father, who kicks him out after he is caught in a delicate situation with a girl. Living with his gay cross-dressing uncle in his trailer, Liam is determined to live up to his father's expectations and makes changes like joining the audio-visual club. In the end, he has to discover who he is on his own and realize that he cannot please everyone.

Gay Males • Uncles • Personal Conduct • Fashion • Transvestites

Going, K. L.

Saint Iggy. Orlando, FL: Harcourt, 2006. 272 p. ISBN: 9780152057954; 9780152062484pa; (aud). YALSA Best Books; School Library Journal Best Books. *JS*

Advised by his principal to make a difference in the world, sixteen-year-old Iggy makes an effort to change his life while awaiting a hearing that will decide whether he should be expelled after an altercation with a teacher. Born addicted to crack, Iggy has no support from his drug-addicted mother and father, so for help, he turns to his former tutor, Mo, a pot-smoking college dropout who is a devotee of Eastern religions. Iggy finds some parental role models in Mo's parents even as his friendship with Mo creates problems.

Missing Persons • Drug Abuse • Family Problems

Hrdlitschka, Shelley

Kat's Fall. Custer, WA: Orca Book Publishers, 2004. 168 p. ISBN: 9781551433127pa. YALSA Quick Picks. *J*

With their mother in prison, charged with dropping his sister Kat from a balcony, and with a father who is disinterested, it has fallen upon fifteen-year-old Darcy Frasier to raise his now eleven-year-old sister, who is deaf and suffers from epileptic seizures. When the family learns that their mother is being released, Darcy, who believes his mother does not deserve another chance, struggles until he begins to remember the truth that he was the one who caused the accident. When he is accused of molesting his sister and a girl he babysits, he is finally able to come to terms with his mother as she and his teacher help to clear his name.

Mother-Separated Families • Disabilities • Guilt • Accidents • Canada

Jones, Carrie

Girl, Hero. Woodbury, MN: Flux, 2008. 307 p. ISBN: 9780738710518. *J*

After her beloved stepfather's death three years earlier, high school freshman Lily Faltin writes letters to John Wayne seeking advice, even though he has been dead for years. This helps her deal with her family problems, which include a possibly gay truck-driving father and a lonely mother who brings home her drunken, unemployed, abusive boyfriend, Mike O'Donnell. Empowered by Wayne's tough-talking movie personas, Lily learns to take charge of her life.

Family Problems • Divorce • Single Parent

Jones, Patrick

Stolen Car. New York: Walker, 2008. 288 p. ISBN: 9780802797001. *J*

> Danielle is certain that she can find the kind of love she deserves by breaking the pattern set for her by her waitress mother, who lives with an abusive drunken boyfriend. Thinking she has found the perfect boy in older, charismatic Reid, who sweet-talks her and gives her great gifts, Danielle disregards the concerns of her friends Ashley and Evan, who can see Reid is just using her. Danielle brushes them off and lies to them to be with Reid. Standing by their friend, Ashley and Evan support Danielle until she recognizes Reid's lies and discovers that he has been unfaithful, and then they help her get revenge on him.

> *Mother and Daughter • Family Problems • Friendship • Automobile Driving*

Koertge, Ron

Margaux with an X. Cambridge, MA: Candlewick Press, 2004. 165 p. ISBN: 9780763624019; 9780763626792pa. YALSA Best Books. *JS*

> Unsatisfied with her seemingly perfect life and lacking true connections with her best friend Sara and her remote parents, beautiful and popular Margaux Wilcox, who has a huge vocabulary and a sharp wit, is drawn to bookish outcast Danny Riley. As the pair bond, forming an unlikely friendship, they begin to share their childhood sorrows, and Margaux is able to confront painful secrets about her father's gambling, giving her the courage to escape from her parents and remake her identity into something very different from her formally shallow facade.

> *Sexual Abuse • Family Violence • Family Problems • Family Secrets • Popularity • Coming-of-Age*

Kogler, Jennifer Anne

Ruby Tuesday. New York: HarperCollins, 2005. 307 p. ISBN: 9780060739560; 9780060739584pa. *MJ*

> Thirteen-year-old Ruby Tuesday Sweet learns secrets about her quirky family when her father, Hollis, is arrested for the murder of her "Uncle" Larry. It is revealed that Hollis is a professional gambler and Larry was his bookie. When her cigar-smoking mother takes Ruby to her hard-drinking, gambling grandmother in Las Vegas, Ruby is able to have some adventures that help her build greater understanding not only of her parents but of herself as well.

> *Baseball • Family Secrets • Gambling • Musicians*

McCormick, Patricia

My Brother's Keeper. New York: Hyperion Books for Children, 2005. 192 p. ISBN: 9780786851737; 9780786851744pa. *MJ*

> Thirteen-year-old Toby Malone is doing everything he can to hold his family together after their father deserted them. His hairstylist mother struggles to support the family and has found a new relationship with a local busi-

nessman. While his older brother, Jake, who is a star baseball player, descends into addiction, Toby tries to care for his sensitive younger brother, Eli, who spends most of his time playing in the yard or hiding beneath a blanket. Finally things turn around for the family when Eli has an accident on his bicycle and is brought home by a policeman, and then another officer also returns Jake home after he has a minor drunk-driving accident.

Father-Deserted Families • *Divorce* • *Drug Abuse* • *Family Secrets* • *Baseball* • *Family Problems*

Orenstein, Denise Gosliner

The Secret Twin. New York: Katherine Tegen Books, 2007. 400 p. ISBN: 9780060785642. *MJ*

Thirteen-year-old Noah thinks of himself as only half a boy because when he was separated from his conjoined twin, he lived but his twin died. Now living with his grandmother, Mademoiselle, after his parents died in a car crash, he is taken care of by an overweight nurse named Grace while Mademoiselle is recovering from a facelift. Grace, whose brother died in a car accident, and Noah bond over the fact that they have both lost someone, and Grace fattens Noah up since he has been living on only the salads that his grandmother prefers. But when a sniper terrorizes the neighborhood, leaving tarot cards at the scenes, Noah believes that the culprit is his twin who has lived and is terrorizing him. He must face his grief so he can build his own individual identity.

Twins • *Secrets* • *Grandmothers* • *Self-Discovery*

Paul, Dominique

The Possibilities of Fireflies. New York: Simon & Schuster Books for Young Readers, 2006. 224 p. ISBN: 9781416913108; 9781416913115pa. *J*

Fifteen-year-old Ellie deals with her neglectful mother's brutal unpredictability, which surfaces after her parents separate, by hiding the problems from her friends and just trying to keep away from the controversy. Her older sister Gwen, however, deals with the change by rebelling with extreme partying and drug use. Trying to reconcile the wonderful memories she has of her mother with the reality of her new persona, Ellie turns to her new neighbor, Leo, for the parental figure she needs in her life, and she is able to find the happiness she has lost.

Mother and Daughter • *Sisters* • *Father-Deserted Families* • *Child Neglect* • *Hope* • *Coming-of-Age*

Plummer, Louise

Finding Daddy. New York: Delacorte Press, 2007. 165 p. ISBN: 9780385730921. YALSA Quick Picks. *J*

Fifteen-year-old Mira is determined to find the father she has only known through a few pictures and stories. After a little detective work, she is able to find a way to contact him. In the e-mails they exchange, she finds him to be a gracious and caring man. But when the family's dog is killed, someone breaks into their house, and her mother is terrified after they are attacked, Mira learns the truth about her psychopathic father, who is bent on getting revenge on her family.

Father and Daughter • *Stalking* • *Friendship* • *Love* • *Violence*

Strasser, Todd

Boot Camp. New York: Simon & Schuster Books for Young Readers, 2007. 256 p. ISBN: 9781416908487; 9781416959427pa. YALSA Quick Picks. *JS*

Abducted in the middle of the night and taken to Lake Harmony, a boot camp for teens with drug or violent behavior problems, fifteen-year-old Garrett knows he doesn't belong there. Finding that his parents have sent him there because they cannot tolerate his sexual relationship with his math teacher and have decided that the camp is the place to modify his behavior, Garrett lives through the physical and psychological abuse inflicted on the residents. Without anywhere else to turn for help, Garrett finally befriends two other students, and together they execute a plan to escape into Canada.

Family Problems • Juvenile Delinquency • Interpersonal Relations • Emotional Abuse

Strauss, Linda Leopold

Really, Truly, Everything's Fine. New York: Marshall Cavendish, 2004. 160 p. ISBN: 9780761451631. *MJ*

When eighth-grader Jill Rider's father is arrested for his involvement in a jewel theft ring, her life falls apart. Her parents' marriage dissolves, and Jill is left with her bitter mother, who throws herself into work to make up for the family's loss of income. Jill must shoulder the burden of caring for her younger brother Markie. At school Jill's plans to run for student government are in jeopardy when her classmates start treating her differently. Convinced by her best friend, Mary Kate, to stay in the race, Jill throws an unchaperoned party that ends in a disaster and finally gives her and her family the impetus to get the help they need to face the challenges of their situation.

Criminals • Fathers • Family Problems

Valentine, Jenny

Broken Soup. New York: HarperTeen, 2009. 224 p. ISBN: 9780060850715. *J*

Two years after her older brother Jack's death, fifteen-year-old Rowan finds herself alone and caring for her six-year-old sister, Stroma, when her parents divorce and her mother escapes into drug-induced sleeping spells. Trying also to deal with her own grief, Rowan stumbles across some new information when a boy named Harper gives her a photo negative that he mistakenly thought dropped out of her purse at a coffee shop. When the developed photo reveals a picture of Jack, Rowan is led to Bee, a girl who was romantically involved with her brother. When her mother attempts suicide, Rowan finds the support she needs with the new friendships she has developed with Bee and especially Harper, with whom she has fallen in love.

Grief in Families • Death • Brothers • Friendship • England

Wiess, Laura

Leftovers. New York: Pocket Books, 2008. 232 p. ISBN: 9781416546627pa. *JS*

Friends Ardith and Blair both suffer from abuse, ridicule, and abandonment at the hands of their families. Ardith, who lives with a low-class abusive family, and wealthy Blair, who has a father who keeps a girlfriend while her social-climbing mother uses her as a pawn to advance her career, meet in ninth grade and become friends. As the year progresses, the girls get involved in sex, drugs, and alcohol, and when they find they have had enough at home, they decide to take revenge on all the adults who have disappointed them.

Friendship • Rape • Family Problems • Revenge • Violence

Alcoholism of a Family Member

Bauer, Cat

Harley, Like a Person. Delray Beach, FL: Winslow Press, 2000. 248 p. ISBN: 9781890817480. YALSA Best Books; YALSA Quick Picks; YALSA Popular Paperbacks. *J*

Harley Columbia wishes she were adopted because of her alcoholic father and a mother who does nothing about it. When the discovery of her birth certificate reveals some discrepancies, her wish comes true, and Harley sets out in search of the high school boyfriend of her mother, who is her birth father. Hoping he will give her the refuge that her wild friends at school cannot, she sets out to meet him, only to discover that things hoped for may not turn out like you want them to, and it is important to deal with the life you have.

Sequel: *Harley's Ninth.* New York: Alfred A. Knopf, 2007. 208 p. ISBN: 9780375837364. *S*

Disowned by her mother, sixteen-year-old Harley is living with her birth father in New York City, where she is eagerly awaiting the opening of her first art exhibit. The day does not go as planned, however, when Harley discovers that she might be pregnant and fights with her boyfriend. Discovering a long-lost grandmother only adds to the confusion, as Harley must figure out how to deal with her life so she can continue to connect to her artistic passion.

Child Abuse • Fathers • Adoption • Artists • Family Problems • Pregnancy • Creativity • Sexuality

Brooks, Martha

Mistik Lake. New York: Farrar, Straus & Giroux, 2007. 206 p. ISBN: 9780374349851; (aud). USBBY Outstanding International Books; YALSA Best Books; Canadian Library Association Young Adult Canadian Book Award. *S*

Having watched her mother Sally sink into alcoholism until she finally leaves her husband and family to live in Iceland with another man, seventeen-year-old Odella is coping and trying to keep her family together. Then she hears of her mother's death. Returning with her family to her Aunt Gloria's cottage on Mistik Lake, where they have spent previous summers, Odella is comforted by her kind new boyfriend Jimmy, who shows her the unique aspects of her Icelandic heritage. Odella is finally able to forgive her mother and heal when Aunt Gloria, who has been keeping her homosexuality secret, brings her partner to meet the family and secrets about the car accident that happened on the lake many years ago, of which Sally was the only survivor, are revealed.

Mother and Daughter • *Single Parent* • *Lesbians* • *Family Problems* • *Grief*

Connelly, Neil O.

St. Michael's Scales. New York: Arthur A. Levine Books, 2002. 309 p. ISBN: 9780439194457; 9780439491716pa. *J*

Fifteen-year-old Keenan Flannery's twin brother, Michael, died just after their birth. Now Keenan believes he is responsible for that death and that his brother wants Keenan to kill himself on their sixteenth birthday—in just fourteen days. Then Keenan is asked by the coach to join the wrestling team to fill in for an injured player at Our Lady of Perpetual Help High School, and he joins as penance for his guilt. Despite dealing with the bullying and hazing by his teammates, Keennan connects with the team and especially a fellow wrestler, who is starving himself to get to the right weight. These experiences allow Keenan to face the truth and deal with his mother's mental illness that has her committed to a mental institution, his father's distance from his son brought on because he is unable to deal with his own guilt, and the fact that his older brother ran away years ago.

Mental Illness • *Family Problems* • *Grief* • *Wrestling* • *Belonging* • *Catholic Schools*

Connor, Leslie

Waiting for Normal. New York: Katherine Tegen Books, 2008. 290 p. ISBN: 9780060890889. YALSA Best Books; ALA Notable Children's Books; School Library Journal Best Books. *M*

Separated from her beloved stepfather and half-sisters, twelve-year-old Addie is forced to live with her mother in a small trailer by the railroad tracks. Despite the fact that her dyslexia makes it hard for her to read the music, Addie still loves participating in the school band. While her mother's erratic behavior results in Addie being severely neglected, she does find a friend in a nearby neighbor, Soula, who is undergoing chemotherapy. With patience and perseverance, Addie makes the best of a really bad situation and soon realizes that sometimes loving someone means having to let them go.

Mother and Daughter • *Stepfathers* • *Coping* • *Friendship*

Davis, Deborah

Not Like You. New York: Clarion Books, 2007. 268 p. ISBN: 9780618720934; 9780547076157pa. *JS*

Fifteen-year-old Kayla tries to believe that her move to New Mexico will be different than all the others. Forced to take charge in the face of her mother's abandonment, binge drinking, lack of money, and loser boyfriends, Kayla looks for acceptance through meaningless sex. For a time, things do look different, as Kayla starts a dog-walking business and makes friends with Remy, a twenty-four-year-old musician. But when her mother starts drink-

13
14
15
16
17
18
19
20
21
22
23

ing again and Remy leaves for Colorado, Kayla must deal with her hate and disappointment to free herself from making the same mistakes her mother does.

Moving • Single Parent • Mother and Daughter

Dean, Carolee

Comfort. Boston: Houghton Mifflin, 2002. 230 p. ISBN: 9780618138463; 9780618439126pa. *J*

Kenny Wilson's abusive mother has a dream of turning his alcoholic father, who is just getting out of prison, into a country music star. Forced to give up football and band, as well as a chance to compete with his poetry in the University Interscholastic League competition, Kenny slaves away at their twenty-four-hour family café. Surviving to break out of his dysfunctional family, Kenny secretly saves the money he needs to leave the small town of Comfort, Texas, and his words and poetry give him the ability to stand up to his mother.

Dysfunctional Families • Poetry • Work • Mothers

Dessen, Sarah

Lock and Key: A Novel. New York: Viking, 2008. 422 p. ISBN: 9780670010882; 9780142414729pa; (aud). *JS*

Abandoned previously by her father and older sister, Ruby suddenly finds herself alone when her alcoholic mother disappears. Discovered by social services, she is forced to move in with her older sister, whom she has not seen in ten years, and her wealthy husband. Ruby just doesn't fit in at her new private school. She won't depend on anybody, until she meets gorgeous next-door-neighbor Nate, who is dealing with his own problems, including an abusive father. In bonding with her family and learning to love Nate, Ruby soon learns how important it is to have other people in her life.

Dysfunctional Families • Child Abuse • Sisters • Romance

Deuker, Carl

Runner. Boston: Houghton Mifflin, 2005. 216 p. ISBN: 9780618542987; 9780618735051pa. YALSA Quick Picks. *JS*

When his alcoholic Gulf War veteran father can't keep a job, runner Chance Taylor worries about how they will pay the fees to keep their home, a dilapidated thirty-foot sailboat in Puget Sound. Chance's worries soon dissolve when a marina worker offers him a job to pick up and deliver packages. Even though he is sure the packages are part of some illegal scheme, Chance keeps on with the job until his friendship with smart student Melissa begins to grow, and he starts to worry again. Things soon come to a terrifying conclusion, and when Chance's father is able to save him, it allows him to see his struggling parent in a whole new light.

Running • Fathers • Poverty • Work

Friend, Natasha

Lush. New York: Scholastic Press, 2006. 192 p. ISBN: 9780439853460; 9780439853477pa. YALSA Quick Picks. *J*

Thirteen-year-old Samantha has a great father—when he is sober. But drunk, as he increasingly is, he is mean and abusive. Clinging to the hope that he'll change, Sam's mother denies the problem and hides it from the world, so it falls on Sam to protect her four-year-old brother. When she leaves a letter in a library book asking for advice and it is answered by a writer know only by initials, Sam is finally able to have a friend to open up to about her family problems, as well as fears about her developing body and her crush on an older boy. As the friendship progresses, Sam must face reality when her father hurts her brother. Accepting some hard truths, she finds that she has the courage to handle whatever comes her way.

Dysfunctional Families • Family Violence • Child Abuse • Family Secrets

Han, Jenny

Shug. New York: Simon & Schuster Books for Young Readers, 2006. 256 p. ISBN: 9781416909422; 9781416909439pa. *M*

Tall, gawky seventh-grader Annemarie "Shug" Wilcox feels alone as she starts the seventh grade. With bitter fighting at home between her alcoholic mother and her father, who is always away on business, and with her best girlfriend, Elaine, wrapped up with new boyfriend Hugh and vying for a spot with the popular crowd, Shug has nowhere to turn. When Mark, her neighbor and friend, begins acting distant to her and then asks another girl to the school dance, Shug's dreams of romance with him are shattered. Things look even worse when she is called upon to tutor her bad-boy nemesis, Jack, but she soon finds in him someone who can relate to all her problems. With his support, Shug is able to gain some much needed self-confidence.

Friendship • Sibling Rivalry • Family Problems • Teasing • Infatuation • Coming-of-Age

MacCready, Robin Merrow

Buried. New York: Dutton Books, 2006. 224 p. ISBN: 9780525477242; 9780142411414pa. YALSA Best Books. *S*

High school senior Claudine looks after her alcoholic mother in their mobile home, acting as the parent as she cares for her and cleans up after her. When her mother disappears once again, Claudine tells everyone she is in rehab and finds that she is relieved and worried at the same time. As time wears on, Claudine falls deeper into her obsessive-compulsive behaviors, and even the other supportive adults in her life cannot help her until she can face the truth about her mother and rebuild her own life.

Mental Illness • Single Parent • Mother-Deserted Children • Friendship • Coping

Pearson, Mary E.

A Room on Lorelei Street. New York: Henry Holt, 2005. 272 p. ISBN: 9780805076677; 9780312380199pa. YALSA Best Books. *S*

> Overcome with the stress of caring for her alcoholic mother while still attending school and working to support herself, seventeen-year-old Zoe finally moves into a small room in an old house. Despite the support of her new landlady, Opal, Zoe struggles in the adult world as her need for attention leads her into numerous sexual relationships and poor financial decisions. It is not until she cannot make enough to pay rent that she realizes how important her place on Lorelei Street is and that it is time to start a new life.
>
> *Family Problems • Family Relationships • Dysfunctional Families • Coming-of-Age*

Rottman, S. L.

Stetson. New York: Viking, 2002. 222 p. ISBN: 9780670035427; 9780142501948pa. YALSA Best Books. *S*

> Abandoned by his mother many years ago, seventeen-year-old Stetson lives with his alcoholic father, placing bets at school so he can buy food, since his father spends all his money at the bar. Dreaming that he can be the first person in his family to graduate high school, even though the stunts he pulls almost get him expelled, Stetson's life collapses when he arrives home to find that not only is his mother dead, but he has a fourteen-year-old sister, Kayla, who has come to live with them now that she has nowhere else to go. Soon the pair team up to protect each other from their father, forging a bond between them that helps Stetson deal with the loss of his mother. He learns that he can get help from others, including his friend Jason, who owns the salvage yard where Stetson works to try and turn a wrecked vehicle into his dream car.
>
> *Brothers • Sisters • Father • Dysfunctional Families • Abandonment • Bets*

Foster Care

Benedict, Helen

The Opposite of Love: A Novel. New York: Viking, 2007. 290 p. ISBN: 9780670061358. *S*
> Seventeen-year-old Madge and her boyfriend Krishna are the only two people of color in their small Pennsylvanian town, where prejudice runs rampant. Having never known her Jamaican dad and dealing with her ex-con and illegal British immigrant mother, Madge is supported by her aunt and her few friends. On a visit to her cousin in New York City, Madge meets Timmy, an abused, poverty-stricken Hispanic four year old. Vowing not to be indifferent to his plight, she takes him home so she can care for him as her own child. Losing interest in her friends and letting her grades slide, she wonders if she has done the right thing, but as Madge's love for Timmy grows, she must decide what is best for both of them.
>
> *Prejudice • Interracial Persons • Abandonment • Mother and Daughter*

De La Pena, Matt

Ball Don't Lie. New York: Delacorte Press, 2005. 280 p. ISBN: 9780385732321; 9780385734257pa. YALSA Best Books; YALSA Quick Picks; YALSA Popular Paperbacks. *S*

> Shuttled between foster homes and living life on the street for most of his life, seventeen-year-old Sticky has finally found a family among the serious basketball players at Lincoln Rec, a Los Angeles gym. Basketball is also his way out of his current life, as Sticky dreams of a college basketball scholarship and is supported by girlfriend Anh-thu. When one bad decision makes Sticky face dark memories, he must find power within himself to overcome his past and move into a new life.

> *Basketball • Child Abuse • Obsessive-Compulsive Disorder*

Frank, E. R.

America. New York: Atheneum Books for Young Readers, 2002. 256 p. ISBN: 9780689847295; 9780689857720pa. YALSA Best Books; YALSA Quick Picks; School Library Journal Best Books. *JS*

> America is a fifteen-year-old boy of mixed race who has been abandoned by his crack-addicted mother. He soon finds himself lost in the child-welfare system. Even though he found some stability with the elderly Mrs. Harper, he was constantly being shuffled between foster homes and institutions. When he returns to Mrs. Harper, her half-brother and caretaker, Browning, sexually abuses him. After a suicide attempt, America finds himself in a residential treatment center. Over the course of several years and with the help of a therapist, he is able to confront his past and find himself amid the chaos that is his life.

> *Emotional Problems • Mental Illness • Interracial Persons*

Frost, Helen

Keesha's House. New York: Frances Foster Books/Farrar, Straus & Giroux, 2003. 116 p. ISBN: 9780374340643; 9780374400125pa. YALSA Best Books; YALSA Popular Paperbacks; Michael L. Printz Honor Book. *JS*

> When Keesha finds a home with Joe, she is able to stay in school as well as escape her father's alcoholism and abuse. Along the way, she lets others know about the safe place where kids who have nowhere else to go can get help. In this way, she helps sixteen-year-old Stephie, who is pregnant by a boyfriend who does not know about the baby; Harris, who is homeless after his dad threw him out because he is gay; Carmen, who is fighting an addiction; and Dontay, who doesn't feel comfortable in his foster home where he was placed because his parents are in jail.

> *Family Problems • Interpersonal Relations • Homosexuality • Pregnancy • Street Life • Novels in Verse*

13

14

15

16

17

18

19

20

21

22

23

Giff, Patricia Reilly

Pictures of Hollis Woods. New York: Wendy Lamb Books, 2002. 166 p. ISBN: 9780385326551; 9780440415787pa; (aud). YALSA Best Books; ALA Notable Children's Books; Newbery Honor Books. *M*

> Twelve-year-old Hollis Woods has been in many foster homes since being abandoned as a baby, and every time she goes to a new home, she runs away—until she is placed with artist and retired teacher Josie Cahill. With Josie's help, Hollis is able to embrace her creativity and artistic talent. But Hollis's new life is threatened when Josie begins to show signs of dementia, forcing Hollis to skip school to care for her. When a social worker shows up, it is up to Hollis to find a way to save both of them.

> *Family • Orphans • Artists*

Hartinger, Brent

The Last Chance Texaco. New York: Harper Tempest, 2004. 228 p. ISBN: 9780060509125; 9780060509149pa; (aud). YALSA Quick Picks. *J*

> Ever since she lost her parents in a car accident, fifteen-year-old Lucy Pitt has been in a lot of trouble. Her last chance before being sent to a detention facility is Kindle Home, a foster home located in a run-down mansion in an upscale neighborhood. Lucy connects with the counselors and knows she has found the place she wants to stay. Lucy finds herself falling in love with a rich kid at school, but when someone starts setting cars in the neighborhood on fire, Lucy's new life is threatened.

> *Orphans • Group Homes*

Hernandez, Jo Ann Yolanda

The Throwaway Piece. Houston, TX: Pinata Books, 2006. 246 p. ISBN: 9781558853539pa. *JS*

> Jewel has spent her life taking care of her mom and protecting herself from her mother's many abusive boyfriends until her mother sends her into the foster care system just before her sixteenth birthday. Going through several homes, Jewel finally finds a place where she feels she belongs. At her new school, an English teacher sees past her tough girl exterior and realizes Jewel is very smart. The teacher convinces her that she can be a math tutor for her classmate. Through the process, Jewel is able to learn to love herself as she touches the lives of many around her. When her mother returns, she must decide between taking care of her or taking care of herself.

> *Self-Esteem • Hispanic Americans • Single Parent • Friendship • Dysfunctional Families • Racism • Rape • Coping • Coming-of-Age*

Jordan, Dream

Hot Girl. New York: St. Martin's Griffin, 2008. 214 p. ISBN: 9780312382841pa. YALSA Quick Picks. *J*

> With the help of her social worker and her new foster parents, Kate is trying to remake herself from her previous tough-girl demeanor that had her bouncing between juvenile facilities and foster homes. When her good friend Felicia goes away for the summer, Kate meets stylish Naleejah, who is being neglected by her parents. Finding someone who she thinks can help her win the heart of her crush,

things start to self-destruct as Naleejah is a bad influence on Kate. She must overcome Naleejah's influence to keep the family and stability she has finally found.

Friendship • African Americans

Koertge, Ronald

Strays. Cambridge, MA: Candlewick, 2007. 176 p. ISBN: 9780763627058; 9780763643775pa. YALSA Best Books; YALSA Quick Picks. *JS*

Working in his parents pet store, sixteen-year-old Ted O'Connor has always had a natural affinity for animals, and this bond has become especially strong after his parents are killed in a car accident. He finds himself in a new foster home, with his older roommate and talented mechanic, Astin, and another boy, C.W., who has been in numerous homes. With their support, Ted is finally able to find a place to belong as he learns how to express himself and to trust the people around him.

Orphans • Grief • Belonging • Coming-of-Age

Lowell, Pamela A.

Returnable Girl. New York: Marshall Cavendish, 2006. 229 p. ISBN: 9780761453178; 9780761455929pa. YALSA Quick Picks. *MJ*

After being abandoned by her drug-addict mother, thirteen-year-old Veronica "Ronnie" has been shuttled between many foster homes. Eventually, she finds a good home with Alison, who as a counselor is able to deal with Ronnie's lying, stealing, and violence—so much so that she wants to adopt her. But even with her newfound stability, Ronnie still has dreams of reuniting with her mother and has a hard time trusting anyone. At school, looking for the acceptance she craves, Ronnie abandons her needy friend, Cat, to the cruelty of the popular crowd when she reveals that Cat is having oral sex. In the end, Ronnie is able to learn that part of loving is forgiving, as she finds the courage to follow her own heart.

Drug Abuse • Friendship • Anger • Depression • Popularity • Love • Healing • Diary Novel • Coming-of-Age

Lundgren, Mary Beth

Love, Sara. New York: Henry Holt, 2001. 199 p. ISBN: 9780805067972. *JS*

High school junior Sara Reichert, who was sexually abused by her father and other men, finds herself living in a stable foster home with Carol and her two children. Dealing with the normal problems of growing up and school, Sara tries to overcome her past by writing about her feelings in her honors English class. Despite the fact that Sara has learned over the years not to trust anyone, she finally finds someone to trust in her best friend, Dulcie. When Dulcie begins a doomed relationship with boyfriend Jon, who comes from a wealthy family, and she gets pregnant, the friends enter into a suicide pact. It is only Carol's loving intervention that saves Sara from also being killed in the resulting accident.

Best Friends • Adoption • E-mail • Pregnancy • Sexual Abuse • Diary Novel

Monninger, Joseph

Baby. Asheville, NC: Front Street, 2007. 173 p. ISBN: 9781590785027. YALSA Best Books. *J*

> Fifteen-year-old Baby has been abandoned by her alcoholic mother once again. A home in New Hampshire is her last chance at a foster home before she ends up in a juvie home. Finding a place with an older couple, Mary and Fred Potter, who race sled dogs, Baby is able to find solace with the dogs as she learns to care for and race them. When a natural affection builds with one dog in particular, a pure white Alaskan husky named Laika, Baby is able to find peace and healing as she finally stops trying to return to her old life, despite enticements when her old boyfriend Bobby returns. She is able to make difficult decisions about herself and her place in the world.

> *Mother-Deserted Children • Alcoholism • Trust • Coming-of-Age*

Sweeney, Joyce

The Guardian. New York: Henry Holt, 2009. 177 p. ISBN: 9780805080193. *MJ*

> After the death of their foster father, Mike, thirteen-year-old Hunter LaSalle and his three foster sisters are left only with their greedy, abusive foster mother, Stephanie. Bullied at school and treated negatively by teachers, Hunter has nowhere to turn until his ex-con father, Gabriel Salvatore, swoops in and seemingly saves him after a confrontation with Stephanie. When Gabriel takes him away, Hunter realizes that he is still in a very dangerous situation and must figure out the best way to find safety in his unstable life.

> *Brothers • Sisters • Bullies and Bullying • Birthparents • Criminals • Kidnapping*

Tolan, Stephanie

Surviving the Applewhites. New York: HarperCollins, 2002. 216 p. ISBN: 9780066236025; 9780786272594pa; (aud). YALSA Best Books; ALA Notable Children's Books; ALA Newbery Honor Book; School Library Journal Best Books. *MJ*

> Thirteen-year-old bad-boy Jake Semple is sent to the Applewhite's home as a last chance to redeem himself. The Applewhites, who homeschool their children without any structure, are free-spirited artistic people. Among their clan is E.D., a daughter who finds that her normalcy often makes her feel invisible. Left mostly on his own, Jake builds a relationship with this eccentric family and is pulled into their family production of *The Sound of Music*, an event that E.D. expertly organizes and one that helps Jake finally to find a place where he belongs.

> *Family • Homeschooling • Country Life*

Woodson, Jacqueline

After Tupac and D Foster. New York: G.P. Putnam's Sons, 2008. 160 p. ISBN: 9780399246548; 9780142413999pa. Newbery Honor Books; YALSA Best Books; ALA Notable Children's Books. *MJ*

> In their African American neighborhood in Queens, a trio of girls becomes inseparable when foster child "D" wanders onto their block. The girls are surrounded by the music of Tupac Shakur and violence and are embroiled in legal troubles with

one of the girl's gay older brother, who is serving prison time after being framed for a hate crime. When D's mother returns and takes her away, the girls find they have learned lessons about the sustaining power of love and friendship as they each embrace their own purpose in life.

African Americans • Mother-Deserted Children • Friendship • Rap Music • Race Relations • Loss • Street Life • Coming-of-Age

13

14

15

16

17

18

19

20

21

22

23

Part III

Teen Life at the Extremes

In real life, many teens face extremely intense situations and events. Sometimes these situations are caused by immature choices or behavior, while other times, teens may find they have no control over what happens to them. Some teens who make poor choices may find themselves enmeshed in dangerous situations of crime or violence, or they may lapse into drug and alcohol abuse. Other teens may find themselves facing unexpected life-changing events such as discovering that they are pregnant, becoming suddenly homeless, or being forced to deal with racism. Because of emotional, biological, or chemical issues, many teens find themselves facing the challenges of a mental illness. Still others must face the loss of a loved one through death, or even the possibility of their own death. Often, without support from family and friends, teens face extreme life events on their own or must find ways to develop their own support systems to cope with the challenges confronting them. However, adolescents are very resilient, and despite being forced to face extreme situations, there is much hope and optimism that teens will be able to cope with any difficulties they face and grow into competent adults. This part lists books that deal with some extraordinary events that may affect teens.

Chapter 16

Dealing with Pregnancy

Teen pregnancy occurs in all segments of society. Adolescents who engage in sexual activity may find themselves accidently pregnant, or parenthood may look like a positive option for some teens who dream of the emotional closeness they would enjoy by having a baby. No matter what the circumstances or reasons, teenage mothers and fathers face many challenges. Providing economically and emotionally for their child, the difficulties with finishing school, being unable to participate in typical teen social activities, and dealing with the impact that a new baby has on one's relationships all put strains on the lives of teenagers dealing with pregnancy and raising a child. The books listed in this chapter deal with the pains and some of the joys that come into the lives of pregnant teens. For everyone involved, from the teenage mothers and fathers to their friends and family, there is a great range of physical changes and emotional realities that teens must grapple with as they take up the role of a parent.

General Pregnancy

Adams, Lenora

Baby Girl. New York: Simon Pulse, 2007. 240 p. ISBN: 9781416925125. YALSA Quick Picks. *JS*

Finding herself pregnant and abandoned by the drug-dealing older man she thought loved her, Sheree runs away from home. At a women's shelter Sheree writes a letter to her mom expressing all the things that have gone wrong in her life. A letter back from her mother convinces Sheree to return home, where things begin to improve, in part because Sheree's father, who never had anything to do with her, starts acting like a father. With the birth of her baby, Sheree finally realizes what true love is and determines to make a better life for him than what she had.

African Americans • Sexuality • Runaways • Coming-of-Age • Epistolary Novels

Baratz-Logsted, Lauren

Angel's Choice. New York: Simon & Schuster, 2006. 256 p. ISBN: 9781416925248. *S*

After a drunken one-night stand with Tim at a party, seventeen-year-old Angel Hansen finds herself pregnant. Facing rejection from family and friends and pressure from Tim to have an abortion, Angel must make the right choices for herself and the baby.

Sexuality • Abortion • Diary Novels • Coming-of-Age

Brooks, Martha

True Confessions of a Heartless Girl. New York: Farrar, Straus & Giroux, 2003. 192 p. ISBN: 9780374378066; 9780060594978pa. Canadian Library Association Young Adult Canadian Book Award; YALSA Best Books; School Library Journal Best Books. *S*

> Scared and pregnant seventeen-year-old Noreen steals money and a car from her boyfriend, Wesley, and ends up at the Molly Thorvaldson Café in a small Canadian town called Pembian Lake. There she is offered refuge by the café's owner, Lynda, who is trying to raise her young son, Seth, after escaping an abusive marriage. Noreen is staying in a bungalow owned by Del. Noreen sets a fire in the bungalow and destroys photographs of Del's dead brother. She nearly kills Seth's dog by giving it a chicken bone, then miscarries the baby. It begins to seem that things will never go right. But with the support of seventy-six-year-old Dolores, who is coping with her daughter's death, Noreen is able to confront her rage, and her new friends realize that help comes from the other people that are in your life.

> *Single Mothers • Canada • Interpersonal Relations*

Caseley, Judith

Losing Louisa. New York: Farrar, Straus & Giroux, 1999. 235 p. ISBN: 9780374346652. *JS*

> Sixteen-year-old Lacey Levine takes care of her family while her mother Leonora acts like a teenager, obsessing about her ex-husband and agonizing about her body and clothing. Working through her crush on David, who turned out to be a jerk, and then falling in love with sweet boy Rob makes things look good for Lacey. But when she accidently finds her smart cheerleader sister Rosie having sex in the basement and then later finds that Rosie is pregnant, she must find strength in her family as her mom, grandma, dad, and her dad's new wife work together to help Rosie decide if she should have an abortion or give the baby up for adoption.

> *Family Relationships • Sexuality • Abortion • Sisters*

Dessen, Sarah

Someone Like You. New York: Viking, 1998. 281 p. ISBN: 9780670877782; 9780142401774pa; (aud). YALSA Best Books; YALSA Quick Picks; School Library Journal Best Books. *JS*

> Attracted to dangerous boy Macon, sixteen-year-old Halley is drawn into a world of drugs, alcohol, and sex. Finding no comfort from her strained relationship with her domineering psychologist mother or from her grandma who is dying, Halley turns to longtime best friend Scarlett. Halley is shocked to find out that Scarlett has gotten pregnant by a boy who was killed in a car accident. Refusing to have an abortion, Scarlett and Halley bond until the night when the baby is born, and Halley must learn to confront her fear and make her own choices.

> *Romance • Friendship • Sexuality • Drug Use • Drinking • Death • Traffic Accidents*

Dowd, Siobhan

A Swift Pure Cry. Oxford; New York: David Fickling Books, 2007. 320 p. ISBN: 980385751087; 9780440422181pa. *J*

13

Fifteen-year-old Michelle "Shell" lives in Ireland with her parents. When her mom dies, things fall apart as her father devotes himself to religion and drinking, while the family lives in poverty with a little money he steals from their church. Finding comfort with her boyfriend, things turn even worse when he leaves for America and she finds herself pregnant. She keeps her condition a secret, and the baby is stillborn. When a dead baby is found, it comes out that Shell was pregnant, and the police think the infant is hers. Even worse, they think her pregnancy was caused by abuse from her father or their priest, and Shell must find courage to overcome the problems she faces.

14

15

Alcoholism • Family Secrets • Scandals • Sexuality • Child Abuse • Catholics

Feinberg, Anna

16

Borrowed Light. New York: Delacorte Press, 2000. 278 p. ISBN: 9780385327589; 9780440228769pa; (aud). YALSA Best Books. *JS*

17

Sixteen-year-old Callisto "Cally" finds that she is pregnant, and her surfer boyfriend, Tim, will take no responsibility. With a distracted "spiritualist" mother who is only interested in herbal medicine and séances, and a distant, often absent father, her only anchors are her little brother Jeremy and the connection she feels to the power of the moon and stars through her grandmother, a well-known astrophysicist who inspired her name based on one of Jupiter's moons. As Cally decides the path she should take, family secrets come to light, and when she finds additional support, she is able to find her own strength.

18

19

Family Problems • Brothers • Sisters • Abortion • Sexuality • Grandmothers • Australia

Hrdlitschka, Shelley

20

Dancing Naked: A Novel. Victoria, Canada: Orca Book Publishers, 2001. 249 p. ISBN: 9781551432106pa. YALSA Quick Picks. *S*

A few months after her seventeenth birthday, Kia realizes that she is pregnant. She must deal with her own fears and also the feelings of her parents and her friends from her church youth group as she decides whether to withstand the pressure put on her by her boyfriend to have an abortion or to give the baby up for adoption.

21

Sexuality • Adoption • Canada

22

Johnson, Varian

23

My Life as a Rhombus. Woodbury, MN: Flux, 2007. 304 p. ISBN: 9780738711607pa. *MJ*

Fourteen-year-old math wiz Rhonda Lee finds herself alone and pregnant after a nasty breakup with her rich, popular boyfriend, Christopher. Forced by her father into believing that abortion is the only option, Rhonda is now trying to put her life back together, get her grades up, and win back her overprotective father's trust. Focusing on getting a scholarship to Georgia Tech, Rhonda has sworn off boys and spends her time earning money by tutoring classmates. But when she begins tutoring popular Sarah Gamble in trigonometry and finds that Sarah is pregnant, Rhonda must face the heartbreak of her past decisions as she supports her new friend and tries to figure out the feelings she has for Sarah's brother, David.

Abortion • Tutors • Ambition • African Americans • Family Problems

McDonald, Janet

Spellbound. New York: Frances Foster Books, 2001. 138 p. ISBN: 9780786247844; 9780142501931pa. YALSA Best Books. *JS*

Despite growing up poor with an uneducated mother, sixteen-year-old Raven Jefferson had plans to attend college like her older sister Dell. When Raven has sex for the first time with a stranger and gets pregnant, her plans change dramatically. Now stuck at home caring for a baby, she must face the limited job market for a high school dropout and finds her only outlet is with her girlfriend Aisha, who is also a single mother. Raven decides she will not let her choices hold her back and soon finds that a spelling bee that provides a scholarship program may help her achieve her original dreams.

Companion: ***Chill Wind.*** New York: Frances Foster Books, Farrar, Straus & Giroux, 2002. 144 p. ISBN: 9780374399580; 9780374411831pa. Coretta Scott King Award. *S*

With her welfare running out and no help from her children's father, nineteen-year-old high school dropout Aisha refuses to enter the minimum wage workforce and procrastinates in making decisions about what to do with her future until she answers an ad from Bigmodels, Inc., where she is able to impress the company's president and find success in a way that helps her make peace with her family.

African Americans • Welfare • Single Mothers • Sexuality • Scholarships • Ambition • Success

McWilliams, Kelly

Doormat: A Novel. New York: Delacorte Press, 2004. 144 p. ISBN: 9780385731683; 9780440238751pa. *J*

When Jamie's gorgeous best friend, fourteen-year-old Melissa, thinks that she is pregnant, Jamie tries to help by buying a pregnancy test kit but is locked out when Melissa tries to conceal her condition and will not talk about what solutions she has for the situation. In the end, Jamie must learn to take charge of her life as she supports Melissa but at the same time, Melissa's friendship does not hold her back, as she gets the lead in the school play and finds a boyfriend of her own.

Best Friends • Boyfriends • Theater • Diaries • Friendship

Olsen, Sylvia

The Girl with a Baby. Winlaw, Canada: Sono Nis Press, 2003. 203 p. ISBN: 9781550391428pa. *MJ*

> Leaving the reservation because of resentment against their white father, fourteen-year-old Jane Williams and her family face prejudice for being Native American. With her mother dead, her father almost always gone, and her brothers dropping out of school, Jane finds support with her strong grandmother, Teh, and a friend at school. When Jane finds herself pregnant and abandoned by the baby's father, she wants to stay in school and raise her baby. With a good support system and a talent for acting, things begin to look up for Jane.

> *Native Americans • Grandmothers • Canada • Coming-of-Age*

Plummer, Louise

A Dance for Three. New York: Delacorte Press, 2000. 230 p. ISBN: 9780385325110; 9780440227144pa. YALSA Best Books. *J*

> Fifteen-year-old Hannah Ziebarth is pregnant and although she loves the baby's father, Milo, he has no love for her and refuses to accept his responsibility as the father. Despairing over being rejected, as well as dealing with the grief over her father's death and trying to support her mother's agoraphobia, Hannah is sent to a mental hospital. As she makes decisions regarding the baby's future with the support of those around her, Hannah works to come to terms with her life as she and her mother seek the strength to heal.

> *Mental Illness • Family Problems • Grief • Emotional Abuse • Mother and Daughter*

Sweeney, Joyce

Waiting for June. New York: Cavendish Children's Books, 2003. 144 p. ISBN: 9780761451389; 9780761453291pa. *S*

> Badly treated by her friends and alienated from her best friend Joshua and her single mother because of her pregnancy, high school senior Sophie refuses to tell anyone who the baby's father is. Since Sophie never knew the identity of her own father, she is sure this will not be a hindrance as she deals with going to college and raising the baby on her own. When Sophie starts having powerful dreams about whales, someone who knows the identity of the baby's father starts threatening her, and her mother reveals that her father was black, Sophie must figure out a way to come to terms with her past while finding a way to embrace the future she wants.

> *Family Secrets • Stalking • Friendship • Interracial Persons • Mother and Daughter • Single Mothers*

13

14

15

16

17

18

19

20

21

22

23

Teenage Fathers

Bechard, Margaret

Hanging on to Max. Brookfield, CT: Roaring Brook Press, 2002. 142 p. ISBN: 9780761315797; 9780689862687pa. YALSA Best Books; YALSA Quick Picks; School Library Journal Best Books. *S*

> Seventeen-year-old single teen parent Sam Pettigrew has taken on the responsibility of caring for his baby son Max after he refuses to let his girlfriend give him up for adoption. Living with his father, Sam is able to attend a high school with child care, but after graduation, college is out of the question since his father insists he go to work for a construction company. Sam has taken responsibility for his actions and is dealing with the tough consequences, but meeting fellow teen parent Claire helps Sam see his life in a new light and make important decisions about his future.

> *Single Fathers • High School • Infants*

Caletti, Deb

The Nature of Jade. New York: Simon & Schuster Books for Young Readers, 2007. 304 p. ISBN: 9781416910053; 9781416910060pa. *S*

> Despite being named for one of the strongest materials in the world, seventeen-year-old Jade is not very strong and suffers from debilitating panic attacks. Along with therapy and prescribed medication, Jade finds that working at a Seattle zoo taking care of the elephants also calms her. When she sees a cute boy named Sebastian on the elephant house webcam and later meets him, the two fall in love. But Sebastian's life is complicated. He is the single father of a fifteen-month-old son. Then Sebastian's ex-girlfriend shows up, and secrets of his past come to light. Jade fears that she will be unable to cope with the situation. Dealing with her parents' deteriorating marriage, including an absent father and a hovering mother, Jade finds herself drifting apart from her school friends as she bears her heavy load of advanced placement classes. Through all the stress, Jade must deal with all her life's complications and learn how to face them without fear.

> *Single Fathers • Grandmothers • Dysfunctional Families • Family Problems • Secrets • Volunteers • Panic Disorders*

Hornby, Nick

Slam. New York: G.P. Putnam's Sons, 2007. 370 p. ISBN: 9780399250484; 9781594483455pa; (aud). YALSA Best Books; School Library Journal Best Books. *J*

> Fifteen-year-old skateboarder Sam Jones finds out his girlfriend Alicia, whom he had broken up with a week earlier, is pregnant. He realizes he has made the same mistake his parents did when they found themselves in this situation at age sixteen. Having dealt with what it feels like to be an unwanted baby, Sam turns to his idol skateboarder Tony Hawk for support and he has imaginary conversations with the Hawk poster on his bedroom wall. Even though he knows his future has

changed, Sam finds ways to cope with the consequences of his decisions as he grows into an adult.

Skateboards and Skateboarding • Parenthood • Infants • Coming-of-Age • England

Horniman, Joanne

Mahalia. New York: Alfred A. Knopf, 2003. 184 p. ISBN: 9780375823251; 9780440237891pa. *S*

Abandoned by his girlfriend Emmy a few months after their daughter's birth, seventeen-year-old Matt is left alone to raise their baby, Mahalia. Having dropped out of school, Matt struggles to care for an infant while trying to get his life back without the help of his own mother. Moving into a rental house with a twenty-two-year-old music student for a roommate, Matt sometimes fails to cope with the complexities of caring for a baby, but soon, with the help of friends, he is able to realize that he can't do everything by himself and must find a way to do things better so he can be a good parent.

Companion: *Little Wing.* Crows Nest, Australia: Allen & Unwin, 2006. 172 p. ISBN: 9781741148572pa. *S*

When seventeen-year-old Emily becomes too overwhelmed with caring for her baby, Mahalia, she runs away, leaving the infant in her boyfriend Matt's care. Finding a home with her aunt, Emily struggles to deal with her decision to leave while at the same time dealing with severe postpartum depression as she alleviates the pain she feels by cutting herself. Even with the support of her caring aunt and concerned parents, it is not until Emily meets Martin and his son Pete that she is able to see what a parent-child relationship could really be like. Once again ready to care for her daughter, she must deal with the changes that have happened over the year she has taken to heal.

Single Fathers • Infants • Father and Daughter • Coming-of-Age • Teenage Mothers • Runaways • Self-Mutilation • Australia

Johnson, Angela

The First Part Last. New York: Simon & Schuster Books for Young Readers 2003. 144 p. ISBN: 9780689849220; 9780689849237pa; (aud). Coretta Scott King Award; Michael L. Printz Award; YALSA Best Books; YALSA Quick Picks; YALSA Popular Paperbacks; Teens Top Ten. *JS*

Despite the advice of the two families, sixteen-year-old Bobby decides to raise his baby, Feather, when his girlfriend Nia falls into an irreversible coma caused by seizures, which were complications of her pregnancy. Even though Bobby realizes his parents were right and he should have used birth control and that adoption could have meant freedom, he is still devoted to caring for his daughter. As Bobby deals with the pressures of caring for an infant, he puts his college plans on hold and struggles to balance school all while dealing with friends who don't understand his new commitments. Even as he tries to be a loving father, Bobby finds himself snapping under the pressure. When he paints a picture on a brick wall, he is arrested for vandalism, and soon he must find the courage to deal with his life and the choices he has made.

African Americans • Single Fathers • Father and Daughter • Coma Patients • Coming-of-Age

Martin, C. K. Kelly

I Know It's Over. New York: Random House, 2008. 256 p. ISBN: 9780375845666; 9780375845673pa. *S*

When sixteen-year-old Nick learns that his ex-girlfriend, Sasha, is pregnant, he reminisces about their time together from the moment they fell in love to the events that brought them to become parents. Also dealing with his divorced parents and a struggling gay best friend, Nick must learn to deal with the situations around him as he grows into an independent man.

Sexuality • Love • Pregnancy • Ex-Girlfriends • Interpersonal Relations • Emotional Problems • High School • Canada

Chapter 17

Living without a Home

Because of varying circumstances, some adolescents are forced to face life alone on the streets. Fleeing of their own volition from overwhelming problems or even finding themselves thrown out of their homes because of high levels of conflict within the family, there are many teens facing homelessness. Life on the streets is difficult. Teens in this situation face adverse circumstances and are called upon to use extreme measures to survive. Homeless teens face death, health problems, drugs, and violence on a daily basis. Endeavoring to survive, teens on the streets may turn to dangerous endeavors such as panhandling, theft, or even prostitution. Even with these struggles, some teens find help with social services agencies, and others find support with fellow homeless teens, creating their own family units. The books listed in this chapter deal with the variety of challenges that homeless teens face while living on the streets. No matter what the circumstances, from teens who run away to those who are abandoned by their families, there are teens who defy the odds and make their way alone.

Homelessness

Blank, Jessica

Almost Home. New York: Hyperion, 2007. 250 p. ISBN: 9781423106425; 9781423106432pa. YALSA Quick Picks. *JS*

Prostitution, violence, and drugs permeate the lives of seven homeless teens on the streets of Los Angeles. Having left home because of incest, abuse, boredom, or abandonment, the teens struggle to survive the dangerous realities around them as they bond together and strive for release.

Drug Abuse • Prostitution • Child Abuse • Family Problems

Booth, Coe

Tyrell. New York: PUSH, 2006. 320 p. ISBN: 9780439838795; 9780439838801pa. YALSA Best Books; YALSA Quick Picks. *JS*

Life in the Bronx is not easy for fifteen-year-old Tyrell, who does not want to end up in prison like his father. Living in a roach-infested shelter after his mother committed welfare fraud, Tyrell is struggling to keep his little brother safe and to prevent him from dropping out of school like he did. Struggling with his attraction to fellow shelter resident Jasmine, despite his long relationship with girlfriend Novisha, Tyrell works to put on a secret dance party to help him raise money so he can provide for his family without resorting to selling drugs.

Poverty • Family • Responsibility • Making Money

Brooks, Martha

Being With Henry. New York: Dorling Kindersley, 2000. 216 p. ISBN: 9780789425881. YALSA Best Books. *JS*

When her new marriage and pregnancy disrupts the close relationship Laker has with his mother, he acts out by drinking and avoiding home. Laker's bad behavior culminates in a violent attack on his stepfather, and Laker is kicked out of the house. After catching a bus out of town, Laker starts panhandling and meets 83-year-old widower Henry, who is learning to adjust to life after his wife's death. The two start an uneasy relationship when Henry asks Laker to stay with him in exchange for some yard work just to annoy his daughter. Soon the two become friends, and together they take a trip that allows them each to confront their past, and Laker learns the truth about his biological father.

Interpersonal Relations • Friendship • Canada • Coming-of-Age

Griffin, Paul

Ten Mile River. New York: Dial Books, 2008. 188 p. ISBN: 9780803732841. *MJ*

Fourteen-year-old Ray has survived foster care and juvenile detention with the help of his best friend, reckless fifteen-year-old Jose. Both are now hiding from parole officers at a burned-out old railway stationhouse in a wooded area of New York where they steal and do odd jobs to survive. The pair befriends a girl named Trini, and Ray falls for her. With the help of her hairdresser aunt, Trini encourages the boys to make an honest living. Ray struggles with what to do as he tries to stay loyal to Jose while finding the courage to make something of himself.

Runaways • Friendship • Street Life

Haworth-Attard, Barbara

Theories of Relativity. Toronto, Canada: Harper Trophy Canada, 2003. 200 p. ISBN: 9780805077902; 9780006392996pa. USBBY Outstanding International Books. *JS*

Finding refuge in a youth center, a bakery, and the library, sixteen-year-old Dylan Wallace faces life on the streets after his mother kicked him out to make room for a new boyfriend. Unable to find his long-lost grandfather, Dylan finds that his only recourse is to work for the pimp, Vulture, like sexually abused Jenna has been doing. But when Dylan is drugged and beaten when he tries to escape, he falls into a hallucinatory state where he encounters his idol Einstein. The scientist helps Dylan develop a new theory for himself. With his new resolve, he is able to take some small steps for himself. Now more open to the help concerned adults have been trying to give him, Dylan forges new ties and resolves his bitterness toward those who have failed him.

Family • Brothers • Street Life • Loneliness • Canada

Hopkins, Ellen

Tricks. New York: Margaret K. McElderry Books, 2009. 640 p. ISBN: 9781416950073. *S*

13

> Five struggling teens find themselves pulled into prostitution. Seth is gay and has been kicked out of his family's house, so without other options, he hooks up with a controlling man and follows him to Las Vegas. Also in Vegas, Cody, who is already lost in drugs and gambling, finds himself crushed when his stepfather dies, so he goes looking for love. In Boise, Idaho, Eden, a preacher's daughter, is banished to the Tears of Zion reform camp, when her parents catch her with her boyfriend; while there, unwilling sex is the only way she can gain the trust of the guards. In California, Whitney craves male attention and pretends to enjoy deviant sex, and Ginger realizes that as a child, her mother sold her so that strangers could rape her. As the teens struggle with their desperation and powerlessness, they cling to the glimmers of hope that life can get better.

14

15

16

> *Prostitution • Street Life • Family Problems • Emotional Problems • Coming-of-Age • Novels in Verse*

Hyde, Catherine Ryan

17

Becoming Chloe. New York: Alfred A. Knopf, distributed by Random House, 2006. 224 p. ISBN: 9780375832581; 9780375832604pa. *S*

> Near the abandoned building where they both live, seventeen-year-old Jordan rescues eighteen-year-old Chloe from a group of men who are raping her. The two homeless teens join together to face their dismal life on the streets. Driven to the streets to survive by being a prostitute because of an abusive homophobic father, gay Jordan soon becomes a fugitive after a violent incident. Hoping to help Chloe face the horrors of her own past, he decides they must leave New York and set out on a cross-country trip, during which he hopes they will find the beauty and decent people they both know must exist.

18

19

20

> *Gay Males • Friendship • Street Life • Dysfunctional Families • Travel • Automobiles • Prostitution • Child Abuse*

Koja, Kathe

21

The Blue Mirror. New York: Farrar, Straus & Giroux, 2004. 119 p. ISBN: 9780786269600; 9780142406939pa. YALSA Best Books. *S*

> Seventeen-year-old artist Maggy first sees beautiful dark-eyed homeless boy Cole outside the window of the local café where she spends hours drawing. When the two finally meet, Maggy falls in love, feeling that she has finally found someone to help her escape her alcoholic mother at home. Despite the advice of her friends, Maggy is drawn into Cole's destructive lifestyle, and it is not until she faces tragedy that she is forced to face the truth about Cole's dark side.

22

23

> *Artists • Runaways • Emotional Problems • Alcoholism • Mother and Daughter*

Leavitt, Martine

Heck, Superhero. Asheville, NC: Front Street, 2004. 144 p. ISBN: 9781886910942. ALA Notable Children's Books; YALSA Best Books. *MJ*

> When they are evicted from their apartment after his depressed waitress mother loses her job and then leaves him, thirteen-year-old Heck finds himself homeless. Retreating into his drawings of superheroes, Heck believes that all the good deeds he does will allow him to find his mother and make everything right. Surviving alone on the streets and afraid to ask the adults around him for help, Heck finally meets eighteen-year-old Marion Ewald, who lives in a fantasy world, and things start to change.

> *Mother and Son* • *Mental Illness* • *Abandonment* • *Art* • *Friendship*

Strasser, Todd

Can't Get There from Here. New York: Simon & Schuster Books for Young Readers, 2004. 208 p. ISBN: 9780689841699; 9780689841705pa. YALSA Best Books; YALSA Quick Picks. *JS*

> Thrown out by her abusive mother onto the streets of New York, Maybe creates a surrogate family with other homeless children, including HIV-positive 2Moro, club-hopping Jewel, and Tears, the youngest member of the group. Exposed not only to the harsh winter elements but to the violence, drugs, sex, and other dangers inherent in life on the street, the members of the group find their dismal circumstances preferable to what they left behind. Watching her friends die around her from things like alcohol poisoning, Maybe has no hope for the future until she meet Anthony, a kind librarian, who reunites Tears with her family and provides the possibility of safety for Maybe.

> *Street Life* • *Abandonment* • *Emotional Problems* • *Death*

Runaways

Amateau, Gigi

A Certain Strain of Peculiar. Somerville, MA: Candlewick Press, 2009. 272 p. ISBN: 9780763630096. *MJ*

> Unable to deal with the bullying she faces at school, thirteen-year-old Mary Harold steals her mother's trunk and runs away to Alabama to her grandmother's farm, the only place where she feels like she can be herself. She makes friends with the farm's manager Bud and his two daughters mean Delta and Dixie, who thinks she is a horse. Mary does farm chores, including caring for her own cow, and she adopts a fawn. Along the way, she is able to find the strength she needs as, with the help of her grandmother, she realizes that running from problems never solves them.

> *Grandmothers* • *Friendship* • *Bullies and Bullying* • *Interpersonal Relations*

Baskin, Nora Raleigh

All We Know of Love. Cambridge, MA: Candlewick Press, 2008. 201 p. ISBN: 9780763636234. *S*

> Fleeing an obsessive boyfriend, possible pregnancy, and her poor relationship with her best friend, sixteen-year-old Natalie runs away just like her mother did four years earlier. On her trip from Connecticut to Florida, Natalie dreams of finding her mother and asking her why she left. During the trip, she encounters a variety of people who help her come to terms with her life as she confronts her mother and learns lessons about the true nature of love.
>
> *Travel • Mother and Daughter • Emotional Problems*

De Palma, Toni

Under the Banyan Tree. New York: Holiday House, 2007. 185 p. ISBN: 9780823419654. *JS*

> After being abandoned by her mother, fifteen-year-old Irena runs away from her abusive father and finds herself alone in Key West. Finding a job at the Banyan Tree Motel changes her life. Connecting to the family that runs the motel, including the kindhearted siblings Carlotta and Antonio and the pregnant bookkeeper Lynette, Irena finds the love and acceptance she desires. All this is threatened when the financially strapped motel may be forced to close. The strangers, who have now become family, must draw together to save the business.
>
> *Work • Family • Homelessness*

Fletcher, Christine

Tallulah Falls. New York: Bloomsbury Children's Books, distributed to the trade by Holtzbrinck Publishers, 2006. 372 p. ISBN: 9781582346625pa. *S*

> After yet another fight with her mother and in a desperate attempt to fulfill a request from her twenty-something bipolar friend Maeve, junior Debbie Badowski colors her hair blonde, starts calling herself Tallulah, and leaves her home in Portland, Oregon, with a boy she has just recently met. Arriving in Tennessee, she is robbed and abandoned by the boy and finds herself broke and homeless. When she rescues a dog that was left to die she takes him to a veterinarian and she finds a home at Dr. Poteet's clinic. With a part-time job helping with the animals at the clinic and with the clinic's redneck staff, Tallulah finds the comfort, safety, and caring she has always wanted.
>
> *Mental Illness • Friendship • Veterinarians • Dogs • Self-Acceptance • Travel*

Harmon, Michael B.

Skate. New York: Knopf, distributed by Random House, 2006. 256 p. ISBN: 9780375875168. YALSA Quick Picks. *J*

> When his drug-addicted mother's negligence forces fifteen-year-old Ian and his little brother Sammy, who has fetal alcohol syndrome, into foster

care, the two run away to avoid being separated. Also fleeing an incident at school where Ian broke a coach's jaw, the two set out to find their father in a 160-mile hike from Spokane to Walla Walla. Surviving in the wilderness, escaping the harsh weather, and experiencing run-ins with the law, the two arrive to find that things don't always turn out as you plan.

Family Problems • Brothers • Skateboards and Skateboarding • Drug Abuse • Father-Deserted Families • Travel • Coming-of-Age

Hobbs, Valerie

Letting Go of Bobby James: Or How I Found My Self of Steam. New York: Farrar Straus Giroux/Frances Foster Books, 2004. 144 p. ISBN: 9780374343842. YALSA Quick Picks. *S*

After only thirteen weeks of marriage, sixteen-year-old Sally Jo "Jody" Walker finds herself alone in Florida with only $20 after her husband, Bobby James, hit her and then deserted her. She finds a job washing dishes at Thelma's Café and meets Marilyn, the diner's kind waitress; Effaline, a pregnant runaway teen who comes into the diner; and Dooley, a mentally disabled boy who mops the floors at the local movie theater. When Hurricane Emma hits and Jody helps Dooley deliver Effaline's baby in the women's room of the movie theater, Jody finds the friendship and courage she needs to stand up to her abusive husband when he returns.

Friendship • Abandonment • Homelessness • Coming-of-Age

James, Brian

Tomorrow, Maybe. New York: Push/Scholastic, 2003. 248 p. ISBN: 9780439490351pa. *J*

Having left her home two years earlier when her widowed father married an abusive woman, fifteen-year-old runaway Gretchen, nicknamed "Chan," is living on the streets of New York City, trying her best to survive. One night she and friend Jef encounter eleven-year-old Elizabeth, and while the others want her to leave, Chan becomes attached and takes her in. As they try to save money from their begging to leave town, Chan and Elizabeth find themselves betrayed and narrowly escape a trap that would have sent them into enslaved prostitution. Chan's betrayal is complete when Elizabeth steals their money. Without other options, she is forced to call her father for help.

Child Abuse • Street Life • Homelessness • Prostitution

Johnson, Angela

Bird. New York: Dial Books, 2004. 144 p. ISBN: 9780803728479; 9780142405444pa. YALSA Best Books; ALA Notable Children's Books. *MJ*

Leaving her home in Ohio, thirteen-year-old Bird sets out to find her stepfather, Cecil, in the hope that she can bring him home. Arriving in Alabama, Bird locates Ethan, whom she knows to be Cecil's nephew from family photographs, and hides out on his family's farm waiting for the time when Cecil will come. But when Ethan catches her dancing in the moonlight, the two teens become friends, and Bird learns that Ethan is recovering from a heart transplant; the organ he now has once belonged to the younger brother of Ethan's neighbor Jay. With the help of elderly neighbor Mrs. Pritchard, Bird, Ethan, and Jay all become friends, and together they find safety and love.

African Americans • Thieves • Best Friends • Intergenerational Relations • Grief • Death

Lowry, Brigid

Guitar Highway Rose. New York: Holiday House, 2003. 196 p. ISBN: 9780823417902; 9780312342968pa; (aud). *J*

Attracted by new student Asher's disregard for authority when he challenges the school's dress code, wearing dreadlocks and toting his guitar, fifteen-year-old good girl Rosie Moon finds the exciting life she has been seeking. When Asher is falsely accused of stealing from a teacher, the pair runs away together to escape their troubles with each of their parents. As the pair hitchhike up the coast of Australia, ignoring their terrified families, they learn a lot about each other, themselves, and their families.

Family Problems • Travel • Australia • Coming-of-Age

MacCullough, Carolyn

Stealing Henry. Brookfield, CT: Roaring Brook Press, 2005. 196 p. ISBN: 9781596430457. *S*

Savannah's mother, Alice, fled the boredom of a small town after getting pregnant and has never settled down. Things begin to look up for seventeen-year-old Savannah and her eight-year-old half-brother Henry, when her mom meets Jack and puts down some roots. Soon Savannah is unable to handle her stepfather's violent abuse any longer, so she hits him over the head with a frying pan, takes Henry, and leaves. The two travel from New Jersey to Maine to find a long-lost great aunt.

Family Problems • Stepfathers • Pregnancy

Phillips, Suzanne

Chloe Doe. New York: Little, Brown, 2007. 192 p. ISBN: 9780316014137; 9780316014144pa. *S*

Seventeen-year-old Chloe is a prostitute who is sent to the Madeline Parker Institute for Girls after she propositions an undercover police officer. At the institute, Chloe identifies her feelings of alienation and loss by taking on the name "Doe." With the help of intensive therapy, she is able to deal with her past, including her mother's neglect, the abuse of her stepfather, and the hurt and pain inflicted on her by her pimp Manny Marquez, as she moves toward a positive new path for her life.

Prostitution • Child Abuse • Family Problems • Psychotherapy

Rapp, Adam

33 Snowfish. Cambridge, MA: Candlewick Press, 2003. 179 p. ISBN: 9780763618742; 9780763629175pa. YALSA Best Books. *J*

Bobbie, who killed his parents, stole their car, and kidnapped his brother, is the eldest of three runaway kids who join forces to survive on the streets.

Fifteen-year-old Curl is Bobbie's girlfriend, who is also a prostitute and drug addict. Custis, who has recently escaped from his "owner," an abusive pedophile who produces pornography, is a racist who carries a loaded gun. The three cross the country trying to find a buyer for Bobbie's infant brother, so they can have a source of income. It is only when Bobbie and Curl die from exposure that Custis, along with the baby, is able to face his past and develop healthy relationships for the future.

Orphans • *Street Life* • *Homelessness* • *Prostitutes* • *Child Abuse* • *Kidnapping* • *Drug Abuse*

Rapp, Adam

Punkzilla. Westminster, MD: Candlewick Press, 2009. 256 p. ISBN: 9780763630317. *JS*

Fourteen-year-old Jamie "Punkzilla" has run away from his military school and is living on the streets or in a halfway house in Portland, Oregon, where he spends his days mugging people, stealing iPods and DVD players, and taking cheap drugs. When he discovers that his older brother, Peter, a gay playwright, is dying of cancer, Jamie starts hitchhiking his way from Oregon to Memphis. On the road, he is often exploited because of his androgynous features, including getting jumped in a roadside restroom. Along with the bad, he does meet some helpful people, including a female-to-male transsexual, and a girl with whom he loses his virginity. It is not until he arrives in Memphis that he is finally able to find the shelter and support that gives him options for the future.

Brothers • *Cancer* • *Travel* • *Gay Males* • *Thieves* • *Epistolary Novels* • *Coming-of-Age*

Smith, Sherri L.

Lucy the Giant. New York: Delacorte Press, 2002. 217 p. ISBN: 9780385729406; 9780440229278pa. YALSA Best Books. *J*

Abandoned by her mother when she was seven, extremely tall fifteen-year-old Lucy just tries to stay out of everyone's way, something that is especially important with her alcoholic father. After the stray dog she adopted dies, Lucy is unable to cope with her life. So she runs away and unexpectedly gets a job aboard a crabbing boat. Lying about her age, Lucy joins the crew as an adult woman named Barbara, but when her enemy, a disgruntled crabber, reveals her secret, Lucy must weather a storm at sea so she can return home to weather the storm there with the help of her supportive new friends.

Family Problems • *Alcoholism* • *Work* • *Coming-of-Age*

Van Draanen, Wendelin

Runaway. New York: Alfred A. Knopf, 2006. 256 p. ISBN: 9780375835223; 9780440421092pa. *M*

In a journal given to her by a teacher, twelve-year-old Holly Janquell recounts the pain and anger she feels after her mother overdoses and she is sent to stay in a succession of foster homes. Having run away from the abuse of her current foster family, Holly finds herself alone on the streets, hungry and cold, as she steadily makes her way to Los Angeles. Living what she sees as a gypsy lifestyle, she makes a home wherever she can, including libraries and schools. Help comes when she meets Sammie at the soup kitchen and he introduces her to a mother and her daughter.

Homelessness • Orphans • Mothers • Death • Drug Use • Psychic Trauma • Foster Care • Child Abuse • Diaries

Yansky, Brian

Wonders of the World. Woodbury, MN: Flux, 2007. 227 p. ISBN: 9780738710846. *S*

Remembering better times with his unreliable father who vanished years ago, seventeen-year-old Eric now faces the grim hardships of life on the street where he wants to protect a homeless girl, Catgirl, from the powerful Bluebeard. When Bluebeard offers them the chance to make money by appearing in pornographic movies, the possibility that this might get him off the streets and the chance to be with Catgirl is tempting. But another offer to act in a local theater production helps Eric find a use for the talent he loves, forcing him to choose between the two worlds as he tries to rescue Catgirl.

Street Life • Homelessness • Father and Son • Criminals

Yee, Lisa

Absolutely Maybe. New York: Scholastic, 2009. 288 p. ISBN: 9780439838443. *S*

When the man who is going to become her mother's seventh husband tries to rape her, Maybelline "Maybe," who is named for her mother's favorite mascara brand, joins her friend Ted and their buddy Hollywood when he moves to California to start film school. Hoping to find her biological father, her dreams are soon dashed when the trio runs out of money and hope. But she is able to craft a new identity that is different from the one of dyed hair, baggy T-shirts, and ragged sneakers that she had used to rebel against her mother.

Mother and Daughter • Alcoholism • Friendship • Interracial Friendships • Sex Crimes

---

Abandonment

Bowsher, Melodie

My Lost and Found Life. New York: Bloomsbury Children's Books, 2006. 320 p. ISBN: 9781582347363; 9781599901558pa. *S*

After her mom is accused of embezzling funds and disappears, seventeen-year-old Ashley finds herself homeless and abandoned by all her elite friends. Moving into a camper van behind her mother's ex-boyfriend's gas station, she finds work at a local coffeehouse despite her girlfriends' encouragement to become a stripper. When she meets an older fellow employee, Irishman Patrick, she sheds her pretentious and snobby attitudes.

Homelessness • Work • Mother and Daughter • Coming-of-Age

Fusco, Kimberly Newton

Tending to Grace. New York: Knopf, distributed by Random House, 2004. 176 p. ISBN: 9780375828621; 9780553494235pa. YALSA Best Books. *MJ*

> Fourteen-year-old Cornelia Thornhill is abandoned by her mother and lives with her elderly great aunt, Agatha, in a dirty backwoods cottage that doesn't even have a toilet. Cornelia hides her stuttering by hardly speaking, so everyone assumes she is not very smart. Cornelia finds her only comfort in the silence of her books. But as she works through her volatile relationship with Agatha and finds new friends, Cornelia is able to find strength.

> *Aunts • Eccentricities • Friendship • Emotional Problems • Stuttering*

Love, D. Anne

Picture Perfect. New York: Margaret K. McElderry Books, 2007. 304 p. ISBN: 9780689873904. *MJ*

> Fourteen-year-old Phoebe Trask and her family are abandoned when her mother, Beth, lands a job as a spokeswomen for the Bee Beautiful Cosmetics Company. Often left alone with her big brother, Zane, by their busy father, who is a judge, Phoebe feels even more lost since her best friend has recently moved. But when gorgeous Beverly Grace, a writer who has recently returned from Italy, moves in next door and develops a friendship with her father, Phoebe finds herself worrying about her parents' marriage in addition to her worries about her first dance and her first kiss. Things become even more worrisome when Zane gets in trouble with the law, their father is violently attacked, and their mother returns because she has been diagnosed with cancer. In the end, Phoebe learns about forgiveness as everyone reconciles their differences.

> *Mother-Separated Families • Father and Daughter • Cancer • Forgiveness*

Nolan, Han

Born Blue. San Diego, CA: Harcourt, 2001. 277 p. ISBN: 9780152019167; 9780152046972pa. YALSA Best Books; School Library Journal Best Books. *JS*

> Abandoned and forced to move constantly between increasingly bad foster homes and situations, the only thing Janie has to cling to is her singing. She finds herself connecting to Harmon, a fellow foster child, and her social worker Doris, who are both African American. Despite her own white skin, Janie renames herself Leshaya and becomes determined to follow in the footsteps of her idols, Aretha Franklin and Etta James. When she is finally able to join a blues band, there is no fame but rather drug use and an unwanted pregnancy after she has careless sex. Struggling to reach her dream despite the setbacks, Janie meets guitar player Paul, who teaches her music theory while helping her stay away from drugs. Soon Janie must face her problems alone and find a way to confront her heroin-addicted mother so that she can finally build her own identity.

> *Mother and Daughter • Foster Care • Music • African Americans*

Chapter 18

Facing Psychological Difficulties

Adolescents can face a variety of mental health issues, including psychological disorders, disabilities, and mental traumas. Whether it is their own mental health or the illness of friends or family, psychological problems create many difficulties in a teen's life. Although some mental illnesses have no known cause, many are linked to biological causes or to chemical imbalances in the brain, whereas others are a result of environmental or social causes. Whatever the source, psychological difficulties have long-term implications for teens and their ability to function in daily routines such as going to school, working, sleeping, or even eating. For each of these disorders, it is important to receive timely interventions from mental health care professionals. These professionals can assist those who are ill in developing important coping skills and thereby help prevent tragedies. The books listed in this chapter deal with the wide scope of mental health issues that teens must face in their own lives and in the lives of those around them, including anxiety disorders, schizophrenia, depression, and self-mutilation. Such illnesses prevent teens from fully experiencing the pleasures of life. Among the serious psychological disorders are the eating disorders that impact the lives of both teen boys and girls. Often linked to society's obsession with looks, eating disorders involve an intense fear of gaining weight and a distorted body image that can be so serious as to lead to premature death.

Mental Illness

Cameron, Peter

Someday This Pain Will Be Useful to You. New York: Farrar, Straus & Giroux, 2007. 229 p. ISBN: 9780374309893; 9780312428167pa; (aud). YALSA Best Books. S

Eighteen-year-old James Sveck's lifelong dream has been to purchase a nice house in a small Midwestern town where he can avoid the people he doesn't like. But until that happens, his life is very complicated. His older sister is involved in an affair with a married man, his mother's third husband is gambling away her money, and James is left to work a dull job in the Manhattan art gallery that his mother owns. At work James finds himself attracted to John, his mother's older assistant. Discovering John's profile on a gay dating site, James fills in one of his own that exactly matches John's, a ploy that succeeds in attracting him. When John finds out, he is angry at being manipulated and accuses James of sexual harassment. All these experiences culminate in panic attacks that have landed James in psychotherapy. There he is able to recall past experiences that help him to deal with the pain that comes from his difficulty to forge emotional bonds.

Anxiety • Alienation • Panic Disorders • Self-Perception • Psychotherapy • Homosexuality

Chappell, Crissa-Jean

Total Constant Order. New York: Katherine Tegen Books, 2007. 278 p. ISBN: 9780060886059. *MJ*

To gain control over her life, fourteen-year-old Frances engages in obsessive behaviors such as counting everything, washing her hands until they are raw, and brushing her teeth in multiples of threes. Since her parents' divorce and her move from Vermont to Miami, things have gotten worse, and even though her therapist has prescribed medications that have devastating side effects, nothings helps. Very isolated at school because most of the other students find her behavior strange, Frances is only able to make friends with Thayer, a brilliant classmate who is on medication for learning disabilities and attention-deficit disorder. Through this friendship and with the help of her therapist, Frances is finally able to find order and make some sense out of her life.

Obsessive-Compulsive Disorder • Emotional Problems • Parent and Child • Psychotherapy • Family Relationships

Deaver, Julie Reece

The Night I Disappeared. New York: Simon Pulse, 2002. 256 p. ISBN: 9780743439794pa. *S*

Moving to Chicago for the summer where her lawyer mother is defending a high-profile child abuse case, seventeen-year-old Jamie Tessman begins to experience severe panic attacks and realistic fantasies of her friend Webb, who is supposedly backpacking through Europe. When her slips with reality result in a bike accident and a trip to the emergency room, her problem is recognized, and Jamie is institutionalized. She makes friends in Morgan and Morgan's aunt, who becomes her psychiatrist. With their help, Jamie is able to confront the truth about Webb's existence and the terrifying trauma that caused her psychological problems.

Psychic Trauma • Panic Disorders

Frank, Hillary

I Can't Tell You. Boston: Houghton Mifflin, 2004. 196 p. ISBN: 9780618412020; 9780618494910pa. *S*

After a fight with his best friend and roommate, Sean, has him saying something very hurtful that he can't take back, Jake decides that it is safer to communicate with written messages and takes a vow of silence. Although they are unsure about this approach, his friends and his separated parents humor him as Jake tries to deal with his feelings through written words and find some understanding of who he is, while also trying to win the girl, Xandra.

College • Interpersonal Relations • Family Problems

Harrar, George

Not as Crazy as I Seem. Boston: Houghton Mifflin, 2003. 224 p. ISBN: 9780618263653; 9780618494804pa. *J*

Fifteen-year-old Devon, who has obsessive-compulsive disorder, must do everything in fours and protect himself from germs by not eating in the cafeteria and constantly washing his hands. His father detests his behavior, and the kids at his new private school make fun of him. Wanting to fit in and not make trouble, Devon is supported by his mother and his therapist, Dr. Wasserman. With burgeoning friendships with an African American girl named Tanya and troubled Ben, who vandalizes the school, Devon uses his inner strength to overcome his compulsions.

Obsessive-Compulsive Disorder • Death • Grandfathers • Vandalism

Hautman, Pete

Invisible. New York: Simon & Schuster Books for Young Readers, 2005. 149 p. ISBN: 9780689868009; 9780689869037pa. YALSA Best Books. *S*

Seventeen-year-old Douglas "Doug" MacArthur Hanson, a loner nerd, is focused on building his model railway town and its replica of the Golden Gate Bridge and talking with his best friend and neighbor Andy Morrow, a popular actor and football player. The reader can tell something isn't quite right, though, as Doug escapes to the sanctuary of his own mind, unwilling to face the trauma of something that has happened to Andy. At school Doug is violently bullied. He sees a psychiatrist but won't take his medications, and he is fixated on a girl, Melanie Haver, who he spies on to watch her undress. But things are crumbling, and soon he has to face the truth.

Psychic Trauma • Bullies and Bullying • Friendship • Social Isolation • Secrets

Price, Charlie

Lizard People. New Milford, CT: Roaring Brook Press, 2007. 192 p. ISBN: 9781596431904. *S*

Seventeen-year-old Ben Mander's estranged father spends his days in bars and cheap motels, leaving Ben alone to care for his mentally ill mother, who refuses to take her medication. When his mother is hospitalized, Ben meets Marco, who says his mother is also in the hospital, and the two begin a tentative friendship. But when Marco tells Ben that he can time travel to the year 4000 and has discovered a cure for mental illness, Ben becomes overwhelmed by his friend's strange tales and erratic nature, and starts to question his own sanity. Ben is forced to discover what is real and what is not as he remakes his life.

Schizophrenia • Family Problems • Mother and Son • Alcoholism

13

14

15

16

17

18

19

20

21

22

23

Sones, Sonya

Stop Pretending: What Happened When My Big Sister Went Crazy. New York: HarperCollins, 1999. 149 p. ISBN: 9780060283872; 9780064462181pa. YALSA Best Books; YALSA Quick Picks. *M*

> Thirteen-year-old Cookie's sister is hospitalized after she begins to hear voices in her head. When her parents' marriage starts unraveling and fearing her friends' reactions if they find out about her sister, Cookie distances herself. Alone, she must face her own fears that she, too, has a mental illness. When she falls in love with the new boy and is introduced to photography, Cookie finally finds the outlet she needs not only to heal herself but also to help her sister continue her life.

> *Brothers • Sisters • Photography • Family Problems • Novels in Verse*

Tashjian, Janet

Multiple Choice. New York: Holt, 1999. 186 p. ISBN: 9780805060867; 9780439174848pa. *MJ*

> Fourteen-year-old Monica Devon's obsessive-compulsive disorder makes her so worried about doing things perfectly that she can't make proper decisions. So she creates a game called "Multiple Choice" where randomly selected letters tell her how to act in any given situation. At first the game is liberating, but it soon alienates her friends. When she endangers a child she is babysitting, the adults in her life finally take notice, and Monica must learn to take charge of her behavior.

> *Obsessive-Compulsive Disorder • Friendship*

Trueman, Terry

Inside Out. New York: Harper Tempest, 2003. 117 p. ISBN: 9780066239620; 9780064473767pa. YALSA Best Books; YALSA Quick Picks. *S*

> Sixteen-year-old Zach is held hostage in a Spokane coffee shop by two teenage brothers who are desperate and worried about their single mother, who is out of work and has cancer. Impulsive and hearing voices in his head, Zach is without his antipsychotic medication that he has been waiting for his mother to bring and agrees to remain even after the other hostages are released. As the standoff progresses, the three troubled teens bond over their troubles and when a stray police bullet wounds one of them, they finally surrender, and Zach is released, only to meet with tragedy soon after.

> *Schizophrenia • Robbery • Suicide*

Vizzini, Ned

It's Kind of a Funny Story. New York: Miramax Books/Hyperion Books For Children, 2006. 448 p. ISBN: 9780786851966; 9780786851973pa. YALSA Best Books. *J*

> Fifteen-year-old Craig has worked very hard to get into a top Manhattan High School, but just when he thought he had arrived, he finds himself battling severe depression. Overwhelmed by suicidal thoughts, Craig puts himself into the psychiatric unit of a local hospital, where he meets other teens who are battling their own illnesses. In the hospital, Craig finds the support he needs to learn how to handle his life.

> *Depression • Psychiatric Hospitals • Drug Use • Artists • Friendship • Eating Disorders*

Depression

Colasanti, Susane

Waiting for You. New York: Viking Childrens Books, 2009. 336 p. ISBN: 9780670011308. *J*

> After a freshman year consumed with battling her anxiety disorder and depression, Marisa just wants to start the new year with a clean slate. She has had a crush on popular boy Derek for a long time, and things look great when he asks her out. Soon Marisa's obsessive negative thoughts get the better of her, and she suspects that Derek is having a relationship with his ex-girlfriend. With the mysterious advice-giving DJ, Dirty Dirk, and her chemistry partner, nerdy Nash, Marisa is able to find the advice she needs to cope with her life.

Mental Illness • Anxiety • Dating • Ex-Girlfriends • Family • Divorce

Colebank, Susan

Black Tuesday. New York: Dutton Children's Books, 2007. 264 p. ISBN: 9780525477662. *JS*

> Sixteen-year-old Jayne Tompkins is pressured by her newscaster mother to be the best. Watching out for her diabetic younger sister Ellie, whom their mother pays little attention to, complicates things. But Jayne is able to keep an ideal high school transcript that makes it likely she will be valedictorian while also being captain of the girls' varsity tennis team, making it likely she'll get admission to Harvard —that is, until she is driving speedily to tennis practice while talking on her cell phone to Ellie and runs a red light. The resulting accident leaves a six-year-old girl brain-dead, and when the family decides to take her off life support, Jayne falls into a deep depression. Her life begins spinning out of control as she starts getting tattoos and partying with her new bad-boy boyfriend. Falling deeper into her despair, her grades drop, and she distances herself from family and friends. Ordered to fulfill community service hours by the court, she is finally able to redefine her life and live with the mistakes she has made.

Mother and Daughter • Sisters • Traffic Accidents • Guilt • Community Service

Goobie, Beth

The Dream Where the Losers Go. Custer, WA: Orca Book Publishers, 2006. 204 p. ISBN: 9781551434551pa. *JS*

> Living in a mental facility after a suicide attempt, sixteen-year-old Skey escapes into her dreams of dark tunnels where she is safe. Released from the facility, Skey reconnects with her old friends, including boyfriend Jigger, who is controlling and often violent. Soon Skey begins to realize how much the gang controls her as she meets a wandering boy in her dream world. This boy is connected to a classmate who faces his own demons. Ultimately Skey is able to face the trauma that caused her breakdown and finds the courage to save herself and some of those around her.

Mental Illness • Suicide • Peer Pressure

Halpern, Julie

Get Well Soon. New York: Feiwel and Friends, 2007. 193 p. ISBN: 9780312367954; 9780312581480pa. YALSA Quick Picks. *JS*

Because of panic attacks, depressive episodes, and behavior problems, overweight high school junior Anna Bloom is sent to Lakeland Mental Hospital by her parents. She discusses her experiences there in letters to her friend Tracy. During her stay, Anna finds friendships and love as she works to build her confidence and repair her poor self-image by coming to an understanding of where she belongs in the world.

Mental Illness • Panic Disorders • Overweight • Friendship • Self-Perception • Epistolary Novels

Holmes, Sara

Letters from Rapunzel. New York: HarperCollins, 2006. 192 p. ISBN: 9780060780739. *M*

After her father is hospitalized for clinical depression, twelve-year-old Cadence "Rapunzel" Brogan finds a mysterious soul-baring letter addressed to a post office box number written in her father's handwriting, and she feels that she has discovered the key to unlocking the secrets to the complex problems in her life. As she writes to the unknown holder of the box, Cadence is able to come to terms with her father's illness and deal with the other stresses of growing up.

Mental Illness • Gifted Teenagers • Family Problems • Suicide • Letters • Epistolary Novels • Coming-of-Age

Jenkins, A. M.

Damage. New York: HarperCollins, 2001. 186 p. ISBN: 9780060290993; 9780064472555pa; YALSA Best Books. *S*

High school senior Austin Reid is depressed even though he is the star of the Parkersville Panthers football team and his girlfriend Heather is the prettiest girl in school. Hiding his depression from everyone and drifting through life where nothing, even sex, makes him feel alive, Austin soon finds himself considering suicide. But when he is able to deal with his feelings, Austin gains understanding into his mental state as he finds things that are worth living for.

Mental Illness • Death • Fathers • Football • Suicide

Marchetta, Melina

Saving Francesca. New York: Alfred A. Knopf, distributed by Random House, 2004. 256 p. ISBN: 9780375829826; 9780375829833pa; (aud). YALSA Best Books; YALSA Popular Paperbacks; School Library Journal Best Books. *JS*

High school junior Francesca is forced to transfer to newly coed St. Sebastian's school, where she starts to make new friends. When her mother, Mia, falls into a severe depression, Francesca begins to flounder without the support she needs at home. As the year moves on and she falls for Will, who can't choose between her and his current girlfriend, things spin out of control until her anger at her father and the way he is handling things bursts out. Francesca must figure out who she is and determine what is really important in life.

Mothers • Mental Illness • Sexism • Australia

Rapp, Adam

Under the Wolf, Under the Dog. Cambridge, MA: Candlewick Press, 2004. 304 p. ISBN: 9780763618186; 9780763633653pa. YALSA Best Books. *S*

Sixteen-year-old Steve Nugent has been hospitalized in a facility for troubled teens where he struggles to find his own place among his fellow patients, who are suicidal or have substance abuse problems. Trying to deal with the depression that has plagued him after the death of his mother from cancer and the discovery of his brother's suicide, Steve participates in counseling, falls for a girl who brushes him off, loses his virginity, and finds new friends, all while harboring the hope that he can curb his erratic behavior so he can move out of the facility.

Mental Illness • Psychiatric Hospitals • Family Problems • Drug Abuse • Suicide • Cancer • Mothers • Death

Schumacher, Julie

Black Box. New York: Delacorte Press, 2008. 176 p. ISBN: 9780385735421; (aud). YALSA Best Books; YALSA Quick Picks. *J*

When her older sister Dora is hospitalized for depression, high school freshman Elena tries to deal with the changes despite her parents' constant arguing and their treating Dora's condition as a shameful secret. Finding support in talking to her neighbor and bad boy Jimmy Zenk, who has gone through the same thing with his brother, Elena is able to hold things together until Dora returns a changed person. Now skipping school and lying to her parents, Dora pressures Elena into keeping her secrets. When the pressure of protecting her sister without betraying her becomes too much, Elena must realize she alone can't make Dora better.

Mental Health • Psychiatric Hospitals • Sisters • Family Problems • Interpersonal Relations • Guilt

Young, Janet

The Opposite of Music. New York: Atheneum Books for Young Readers, 2007. 352 p. ISBN: 9781416900405; 9781416958239pa. *J*

Fifteen-year-old Billy, his mom, and his sister, Linda, hope that someday they will be able to find a way to treat their father's depression. Trying just to cope as he becomes more withdrawn and traditional therapies fail to help, the entire family is negatively affected. Billy is forced to stay home with his father while his mother is at work, and so he withdraws from his own friends and stops writing songs. Linda is terrified and always crying. Things soon come to a head when Billy goes to a concert with his friends and leaves his father alone for thirty minutes with disastrous results, but somehow they are able to find strength as a family and find a way to help get their lives back into a new pattern of normal.

Father and Son • Family Problems • Suicide • Psychotherapy • Coping

13

14

15

16

17

18

19

20

21

22

23

Eating Disorders

Anderson, Laurie Halse

Wintergirls. New York: Viking, 2009. 288 p. ISBN: 9780670011100; (aud). *JS*

Lia and Cassie had been best friends forever, and they share much in common—including eating disorders. But at eighteen, the girls become estranged and when Cassie kills herself, Lia feels guilty that she did not answer the phone when Cassie called her the night of her death. In her grief, Lia's need to be thin intensifies, and her carefully controlled life spirals even more out of control as she deals with her parents, stepmother, friends, and younger stepsister. Nothing helps, and Lia's cutting habit and anorexia take over until her self-mutilation goes horribly wrong.

Suicide • Anorexia • Friendship • Self-Mutilation • Death

Antieau, Kim

Mercy, Unbound. New York: Simon Pulse, 2006. 165 p. ISBN: 9781416908937. *MJ*

Feeling a burden to save the world, fifteen-year-old Mercy believes she is growing wings and becoming an angel who can accomplish that goal. As an angel, Mercy knows she does not have to eat, so she cannot understand why her parents are forcing her into an eating disorders treatment center in New Mexico. Faced with her fellow patients, Mercy must deal with the consequences of her disorder and delusions.

Body Image • Mental Illness

Bell, Julia

Massive. New York: Simon Pulse, 2005. 272 p. ISBN: 9781416902072pa. *MJ*

Fourteen-year-old Carmen's mother Maria has an eating disorder, but when she insists that they must move to Birmingham, leaving Carmen's stepfather behind to be with her family, things become even worse. Maria draws Carmen, whom she calls Piggy, into her incessant dieting and exercising. Unable to withstand the pressure without her stepfather, Carmen succumbs and becomes bulimic. Trapped in her compulsive behavior and dealing with her mother's ill health, Carmen must learn whom she can trust.

Bulimia • Mother and Daughter

Eliot, Eve

Insatiable: the Compelling Story of Four Teens, Food and Its Power. Deerfield Beach, FL: Health Communications, 2001. 284 p. ISBN: 9781558748187pa. *JS*

Samantha, Hannah, Jessica, and Phoebe have learned to control their lives by controlling their eating. Binging, purging, or refusing to eat, the girls have their own complex problems, and they meet in group therapy, where they try to deal with them.

Psychotherapy • Body Image • Self-mutilation • Death

Friedman, Robin

Nothing. Woodbury, CT: Flux, 2008. 232 p. ISBN: 9780738713045pa. *S*

Seventeen-year-old Parker Rabinowitz has a seemingly perfect life. He is good-looking and rich, maintains perfect grades, and has just the right amount of extracurricular projects that are certain to get him into Princeton. But soon his sister Danielle, despite her jealousy of the attention he gets, notices that he is binging and purging to release some of the pressure he feels. When the lies he tells to cover up his habit and the eating disorder itself begin to control his life, his health is severely affected. Parker is admitted to the hospital to begin his recovery and is forced to deal with his family problems.

Bulimia • Family Problems • Jewish Men • Brothers • Sisters • Novels in Verse

Friend, Natasha

Perfect. Minneapolis, MN: Milkweed Editions, 2004. 172 p. ISBN: 9781571316523; 9781571316516pa. *J*

To deal with her grief over the death her father, thirteen-year-old Isabelle Lee turns to binging and purging. But when her little sister April discovers her secret, Isabelle is sent to therapy, where she is shocked to encounter popular Ashley Barnum, who is also bulimic. The two girls bond, and Ashley takes unpopular Isabelle into her world, introducing her to new ways to deal with food, including the use of laxatives. But with the help of therapy, Isabelle soon realizes that everyone has problems to deal with, and she is able to talk about her feelings as she ultimately finds new ways to deal with her grief.

Grief • Body Image • Bulimia • Friendship

Halverson, Deborah

Big Mouth. New York: Delacorte Press, 2008. 342 p. ISBN: 9780385733946. *JS*

Overweight fourteen-year-old Shermie Thuff works in his grandfather's ice-cream parlor and dreams of becoming a competitive eater, just like he has seen on TV on The Glutton Bowl. He is setting his sights on the Fourth of July hot-dog-eating contest to start his career. With the help of his friends, Shermie eats as much as he can and then throws up. When he finds that eighteen hot dogs is his limit, Shermie decides that losing weight is the answer, and with the help of his friend and wrestler, Gardo, he is able to drop the pounds on a drastic starvation diet. In the end, Shermie must face the fact that his behavior is covering up a serious eating disorder.

Weight Control • Friendship • Bullies and Bullying

Littman, Sarah Darer

Purge. New York: Scholastic Press, 2009. 234 p. ISBN: 9780545052351. *JS*

When high school junior Janie is admitted to a psychiatric hospital to be treated for her bulimia, she joins in group therapy with other patients, including others with an eating disorder, a boy who is gay, and a superficial jock. But when tragedy strikes, Janie must face her inner demons to work toward her recovery.

Bulimia • Psychiatric Hospitals • Friendship • Secrets

Porter, Tracey

A Dance of Sisters. New York: Joanna Cotler Books, 2002. 276 p. ISBN: 9780060281823; 9780064407519pa. *MJ*

> Enrolled in a rigorous ballet academy in Washington, D.C., and pressed on by her tyrannical teacher, thirteen-year-old Delia obsesses about dance to the exclusion of everything else in her life. Still struggling with her grief over her mother's death, Delia diets and exercises to be the best, while her older sister deals with it by exploring witchcraft, which gets her sent to boarding school by their work-obsessed father after she is expelled from her private day school. Things come crashing down for Delia when her teacher rejects her, leaving her with nothing, and she must remake her life with only the help of her older sister Pearl.

Ballet • Anorexia • Self-Esteem • Mothers • Death

Tokio, Marnelle

More Than You Can Chew. Plattsburgh, NY: Tundra Books, 2003. 234 p. ISBN: 9780887766398pa. *S*

> Institutionalized for an eight-month stay in Silver Lake Hospital for treatment of her anorexia, seventeen-year-old Marty is dealing with forced therapy sessions and an outgoing staff. She is also dealing with the life she left behind, including her alcoholic mother and a father who won't show up for family therapy. Even though she falls into a very dark place, therapy starts to open her eyes, and when a friendship develops with an eight-year-old fellow patient, Lily, Marty finds her compassionate side.

Alcoholism • Anorexia • Coming-of-Age

Vrettos, Adrienne Maria

Skin. New York: Margaret K. McElderry Books, 2006. 240 p. ISBN: 9781416906551; 9781416906568pa. YALSA Best Books; YALSA Quick Picks. *JS*

> With his parents constantly fighting and his sixteen-year-old sister Karen suffering from anorexia, fourteen-year-old Donnie has learned that it is easiest to stay invisible. An outcast even at school, Donnie suffers humiliation at the hands of his classmates and also deals with a crush on Amanda, his sister's best friend. When Donnie lies about his relationship with Amanda to impress his friends, it drives a wedge between them. Through it all Donnie watches as his sister lets her illness kill her and is then left to deal with the anger and betrayal he feels as he tries to deal with his own problems and embrace life.

Anorexia • Family Problems • Dysfunctional Families • Social Acceptance

Cutting

Hoban, Julia

Willow. New York: Dial Books, 2009. 336 p. ISBN: 9780803733565; 9780142416662pa. *JS*

Dealing with terrible guilt over the fact that her lack of experience as a driver caused a terrible accident and resulted in her parents' death, sixteen-year-old Willow Randall is now living with her older brother, David, and his wife. David doesn't want to talk about the accident, and Willow feels the other students at school are always gossiping about her. The only way Willow is able to release her anger is to secretly cut herself with razors. One day in the library, Willow meets Guy, a boy who wants to get to know her and understand her pain and grief.

Self-Mutilation • Death • Guilt • Grief • Brothers • Sisters

McCormick, Patricia

Cut. Asheville, NC: Front Street, 2000. 136 p. ISBN: 9781886910614; 9780439324595pa; (aud). YALSA Best Books; YALSA Quick Picks. *JS*

Callie cuts herself and has stopped talking in a desperate cry for help. She wants relief from the burden of caring for her asthmatic brother, which she must do because of her nonfunctioning mother and her escaping father. She is now one of a group of teens hospitalized at Sea Pines. Along with others, such as anorexic Becca and Tara, overeater Debbie, and Tiffany and Sydney who are addicted to tobacco, alcohol, and drugs, the teens in the hospital work in group therapy to try and heal. But it is not until Amanda, who is scarred from her own cutting behavior, arrives in the group, that Callie is able to face her own fear and guilt.

Mental Illness • Psychiatric Hospitals • Self-Mutilation • Family Problems • Emotional Problems

13

14

15

16

17

18

19

20

21

22

23

Chapter **19**

Dealing with Crime and Violence

Whether teens are involved in committing crimes, are victims of crimes, or are surrounded by violent acts, the lives of many adolescents are severely affected by crime and violence. Some types of violent crimes are more likely to be committed by adolescents, such as bullying, school shootings, and participation in gangs. Other crimes such as murder, rape, robbery, assault, arson, or fraud not only can be committed by juvenile offenders but can impact the lives of teens who are victims of these crimes. For another group of teens, their lives are surrounded by violence because of participation in gangs, through association with violent family members or friends, or because of their own inability to curb their anger. Whatever the type of crime or violent act, many teens' lives are fundamentally changed because of criminal behavior. The books listed in this section deal with not only the criminal and violent acts perpetuated by teens but also the changes that come into the lives of teens as they deal with crime and violence around them. From petty crimes such as theft to severe crimes such as drunk driving, murder, and rape, there are any number of acts that have an impact on teens' lives. Although some teens have problems dealing with their aggressive behavior, others find themselves involved in gangs, and for both groups there are often difficulties in finding a way out of their circumstances. Among the most significant crimes that teens face today is bullying. Whether emotional or physical, many teens must deal with bullying. This negative attention from their peers may cause the pain to become so severe that some feel their only answer is to return the violence with violent acts of their own.

General Crime and Violence

Deuker, Carl

High Heat. Boston: Houghton Mifflin, 2003. 277 p. ISBN: 9780618311170; 9780060572488pa. YALSA Popular Paperbacks. *JS*

When his father commits suicide after being arrested for money laundering, Shane Hunter's life is ripped apart. Their newly found poverty forces his family to live in public housing and attend public school. Arrested for stealing beer, Shane is sentenced to community service to repair a baseball diamond, where he meets a coach who encourages him to try out for the team. Returning to the sport he once loved and excelled at, Shane must face his old team from Shorelake High School. But when Shane's anger gets the better of him and one of his fast-balls puts star player Reese in the hospital, Shane must find a way to get his life back on track.

Family Problems • Suicide • Baseball • Community Service

Draper, Sharon M.

The Battle of Jericho. New York: Atheneum Books for Young Readers, 2003. 304 p. ISBN: 9780689842320; 9780689842337pa. Coretta Scott King Honor Book. *JS*

When sixteen-year-old Jericho and his cousin Josh are asked to pledge his school's exclusive service club, the Warriors of Distinction, he has conflicting emotions. Jericho is excited to wear their black silk jacket and go to great parties, but he is disappointed, especially when he has to give up his music competition to be at the initiation week. He decides to take the honor anyway. As the initiation rituals become increasingly intense and threaten students' lives and even Jericho's future as a musician, he is even more confused about his place in the club. When at the initiation ceremony, Dana, a girl who has sneaked in and demanded the right to pledge, is singled out and viciously abused, Jericho is afraid and appalled. Still wanting to be included, Jericho must live with the results of his actions as he faces his fears and decides if he has the courage to face the peer pressure and tell the truth.

Sequel: *November Blues.* New York: Atheneum Books for Young Readers, 2007. 320 p. ISBN: 9781416906988; 9781416906995pa. Coretta Scott King Honor Books. *JS*

After spending the night with her boyfriend Josh, November Nelson finds that she is pregnant, and things get even more complicated when Josh is killed because of some fraternity hazing. Unable to tell her mother and shatter their dreams of November going to college, she finds the support she needs from her girlfriends and from Josh's cousin Jericho, who is battling the guilt he feels over Josh's death. When Josh's parents hire a lawyer to get custody of their grandchild, November must stand up for herself and the baby as she tries to make a future for them both.

Sequel: *Just Another Hero.* New York: Atheneum Books for Young Readers, 2009. 288 p. ISBN: 9781416980643. *JS*

During their senior year, Arielle, Kofi, November, and Jericho are facing many problems. Arielle is being treated poorly by the wealthy, controlling man whom her mother has recently married. Kofi is dealing with a prescription drug addiction that is threatening his future. At school everything turns into a mystery when student property keeps disappearing and there are frequent fire alarms. But one day when the fire alarm sounds, Arielle, November, Jericho, and their friends think it is just another false alarm, until it becomes apparent that a student has entered the school with an automatic weapon and is intent on using it.

African Americans • Peer Pressure • Pregnancy • Death • Grief • Family • Drug Abuse • School Shootings

Flake, Sharon G.

Bang! New York: Jump at the Sun/Hyperion Books for Children, 2005. 304 p. ISBN: 9780786818440; 9780786849550pa; (aud). YALSA Best Books; YALSA Quick Picks. *S*

Mann's father has done everything he can to toughen up his son so he can survive life on the violence-ridden streets after Mann's six-year-old brother is killed in a shooting. As part of this strategy and influenced by African rituals where boys are sent to the wilderness to survive, he abandons thirteen-year-old Mann and his friend Kee-Lee at a distant campsite. But even after being forced into illegal and dangerous acts to return home, Mann's father kicks them out of the house to continue their quest to find out what path they will follow. When things end tragically, Mann must decide if events will force him to surrender to the violent gangs and their criminal activity on the street or if he can make something good come out of the suffering around him.

African Americans • Family Problems • Street Life • Coming-of-Age

Halverson, Deborah

Honk If You Hate Me. New York: Delacorte Press, 2007. 243 p. ISBN: 9780385733939. *JS*

Ten years after being blamed for starting the fire that destroyed a furniture plant that cost many people their jobs, sixteen-year-old Monalisa "Mona" Kent is constantly reminded of that night, even though she can't remember any of it. The anniversary of the fire when the media descend is the only time her father pays attention to her, and he revels in his hero status since he saved Mona and her best friend Glen the night of the fire. Mona plays along with him but still keeps a low profile and finds solace in collecting bumper stickers for their wisdom. But as her memory begins to return, Mona finds herself shouting her sticker slogans on the tops of tables in fast-food restaurants, and with this crazy act people become intrigued. Mona finds herself starting a trend of "poetry raiding" in the town, allowing for the real story about the fire to finally come to light.

Accidents • Friendship • Forgiveness • Guilt

Hrdlitschka, Shelley

Gotcha. Custer, WA: Orca Book Publishers, 2008. 259 p. ISBN: 9781551437378pa. *JS*

Spurred on by her need for money, Katie joins an underground game called Gotcha! where the person who collects the most beads from other players gets the more than $3,000 jackpot. Despite being banned by the school administration, the game goes on and continues to bring out the worst in people, as they betray friends and risk physical harm to avoid having their beads captured. Even Katie begins to question the intentions of her boyfriend Joel, wondering if his attentions are real or something he is using to manipulate the game. Things go horribly wrong when Katie, who as class treasurer is keeping the prize money in her bank account, lends it to her dad, who has a gambling addiction, and it is lost. Katie now must win the game at all costs, even though those costs may be too high.

Betrayal • Competition • Father-Separated Families • Mother and Daughter • Canada

Mahy, Margaret

24 Hours. New York: Margaret K. McElderry Books, 2000. 200 p. ISBN: 9780689838842; 9780689839030pa. *S*

Seventeen-year-old aspiring actor Ellis has a grand adventure when he and former schoolmate Jackie Cattle crash a posh party and befriend two beautiful sisters, Ursa and Leona. As they take the two girls home from the party, they become embroiled in a variety of dangerous escapades. This experience allows Ellis to learn to stand on his own two feet as the group works to save a baby from a suicidal maniac.

Suicide • Inner-City • Actors and Actresses • New Zealand

Myers, Walter Dean

Sunrise Over Fallujah. New York: Scholastic Press, 2008. 304 p. ISBN: 9781410410191; 9780439916257pa. School Library Journal Best Books. *S*

Embracing his need to stand up for his country after 9/11, Robin Perry joins the army. Assigned to a Civil Affairs unit, Robin does not think he will see much action, but when he arrives in Iraq, the horrors of war, including the violence, death, destruction, and fear, tear at Robin as he realizes that he has landed in the middle of a war he does not understand.

Depression • Coping • Ethics • Iraq • Military

Simmons, Michael

Vandal. New Milford, CT: Roaring Brook Press, 2006. 176 p. ISBN: 9781596430709; 9780312371470pa. *JS*

Sixteen-year-old Will has conflicted feelings about his delinquent older brother Jason, who, despite his remorseful attitude, always returns to his abusive and criminal behavior. When Jason returns from doing time in juvenile prison, Will tries everything he can to help Jason, even giving him a job as a roadie for the KISS tribute band for which Will plays lead guitar. Then when Jason causes a car accident that leaves their younger sister Olivia with crippling injuries, Will must accept that his brother may never reform.

Brothers • Musicians • Rock Music • Vandalism • Bullies and Bullying • Family Problems • Traffic Accidents

Trueman, Terry

No Right Turn. New York: Harper Tempest, 2006. 176 p. ISBN: 9780060574918; 9780060574932pa. *S*

Three years after finding his father after he had shot himself, sixteen-year-old Jordan is still unable to cope with life until his mother begins dating Don, a neighbor who owns a '76 Corvette Stingray. Falling in love with the car, Jordan finds some new energy in stealing it for joyriding. When the car catches the attention of cheerleader Becka, things get even better as he takes risks behind the wheel, but he soon finds himself busted for speeding. With reality hitting hard, Jordan must regain Don and Becka's trust as he finally works through his pain.

Suicide • Grief • Guilt

Wallens, Scott

Sevens Series. New York: Puffin Books

This series follows the struggles, fears, and pain in the lives of teens over a seven-week period.

Fires • Friendship • Drug Use • SAT

Shattered. 2002. 201 p. ISBN: 9780142300985pa. *JS*

Pete is bound to a wheelchair. Meena is being molested by a family friend and is withdrawing and pouring her pain into drinking and smoking. Danny is fighting against taking the drugs prescribed to him for his hyperactivity. Jeremy is struggling with his sexuality as feelings begin to surface when he encounters Josh. Jane is obsessed with good grades. These childhood friends are dealing with various problems while they are all having nightmares after a terrible incident that happened seven years earlier.

Exposed. 2002. 182 p. ISBN: 9780142300992pa. *JS*

Seventeen-year-old Jeremy, a popular athlete, realizes that he is gay despite his having a girlfriend. But when he is caught kissing a guy and is outed on the school's Web site, he must face ridicule from his parents and this classmates.

Pushed. 2002. 188 p. ISBN: 9780142301005pa. *JS*

Danny is a talented composer who does not understand why he needs to be on medication when the drugs dull his creativity and make him emotionally numb. The decision to stop taking his meds helps Danny feel more like himself, but after an incident with his history teacher, things begin to go wrong.

Meltdown. 2002. 187 p. ISBN: 9780142301012pa. *JS*

Jane is a stressed out, overachieving brain, but when she completely fails the SAT, she must face the pressure that has been placed on her to succeed.

Torn. 2002. 188 p. ISBN: 9780142301029pa. *JS*

Karyn doesn't want to be like her mom, who needs to be wanted and loved and so moves from man to man. With a good boyfriend like T.J., she thinks she is doing well, but things go wrong when she realizes that she really loves T.J.'s brother, Reed.

Betrayal. 2002. 188 p. ISBN: 9780142301043pa. *JS*

Reed has always looked out for his brother T.J. But when the coach at Boston College calls and offers Reed the starting quarterback position that T.J. thought was his, Reed must decide if he should betray his brother.

Redemption. 2002. 188 p. ISBN: 9780142301043pa. *JS*

> Peter has always felt he has received his punishment for an accident seven years earlier. But when his childhood friends, with whom he experienced the accident, come back into his life, they must face their past if Peter is able to find the forgiveness he seeks.

Woodson, Jacqueline

Hush. New York: Putnam, 2002. 181 p. ISBN: 9780399231148; 9780142500491pa; (aud). YALSA Best Books; School Library Journal Best Books. *JS*

> Forced to leave everything she knows when her father testifies that he saw two of his fellow white policemen shoot an unarmed black teenager and the family is placed in witness protection, Toswiah, who has changed her name to Evie, must deal with a new life. Watching as her father falls deeper into a depression that culminates in a suicide attempt, looking at her mother's efforts to find answers with religion, and standing by as her older sister tries to get into college early, Evie tries to establish her new identity without a past to build on.

African Americans • Moving • Police

Anger

Blobel, Brigitte

Red Rage. Toronto: Annick Press, 2007. 246 p. ISBN: 9781554511020; 9781554511013pa. *J*

> Fifteen-year-old Mara's life is consumed with an anger that often makes her lose control. Falling for sweet boy Tibor who doesn't care about her home life and finding a job at a preschool with the help of a teacher at school helps curb some of the rage. Mara sees Tibor with another girl, who Mara doesn't know is his sister, and is so consumed by a fit of anger, she beats the girl senseless. This experience causes her to finally face her problem and seek help.

Violence • Jealousy • Bullies and Bullying • Emotional Problems

Freymann-Weyr, Garret

After the Moment. Boston: Houghton Mifflin Harcourt, 2009. 336 p. ISBN: 9780618605729. *S*

> Upon the death of the father of his stepsister, seventeen-year-old Leigh Hunter moves to Washington, D.C., to support the family and meets an anorexic who cuts herself, Maia Morland, who eats meals with the family as part of her recovery. Leigh soon falls in love, but when Maia is filmed while being raped by three classmates while he is away, Leigh reacts with violence, beating up the students. He must then deal with the consequences of his own actions.

Dating • Rape • Violence • Romance • Emotional Problems

Jones, Patrick

Nailed. New York: Walker, distributed to the trade by Holtzbrinck Publishers, 2006. 224 p. ISBN: 9780802780775; 9780802796486pa. *JS*

Sixteen-year-old Bret Hendricks has never fit in at his school where conforming athletes are worshipped; he's an actor with green tinted hair in a ponytail. At home Bret finds little solace because he is the only artist in a blue-collar family and is always being compared to his hardworking older brother, a mechanic. Only truly at home onstage or making music with his band, Radio-Free Flint, Bret endures the taunts and teasing at school for a time, then he begins to buck the established order and stand up for himself. His argumentative tendencies and aggressive responses lead to school suspensions, loss of his driving privileges, and a potential lawsuit when he damages a classmate's car. But only when Bret sees his girlfriend, Kylee, making love with his bandmate Sean and he reacts with extreme violence, does Bret realize he abhors what he has become.

Athletes • Father and Son • Self-Perception • High School • Conformity • Sex Role

Krovatin, Christopher

Venomous. New York: Atheneum Books for Young Readers, 2008. 323 p. ISBN: 9781416924876. YALSA Quick Picks. *S*

High-school junior Locke Vinetti has no control when he gets angry. At times he feels seized by a venomous alter ego that forces him to assault other people. He feels estranged from the people around him because of his unpredictable nature until his new friend Randall invites him to a party, where he meets a wider circle of friends with whom he feels accepted. Drawn to Casey, an angry gay teen, and Renee, a girl he begins to fall in love with, Locke learns that he must lower his defenses and deal with his anger if he does not want to put those around him in danger.

Emotional Problems • Violence • Single Parent • Brothers • Interpersonal Relations

Lynch, Chris

Who the Man. New York: HarperCollins, 2003. 192 p. ISBN: 9780066239385; 9780064410984pa. *MJ*

Bigger than all the other kids in the school, thirteen-year-old Earl Pryor does not hesitate to solve any conflict that comes his way with physical violence. Earl's anger always seems to get the better of him, especially now with his classmates teasing him; his neighbor, sixteen-year-old Louisa, deflecting his advances, claiming she is to old for him; and the escalating problems at home with his parents' marriage. When his fighting gets him a week's suspension and he catches his tough-talking father, who taught him to never back down from a fight, with another woman, creating the final split for his parents, Earl learns that relationships are complicated.

Emotional Problems • Violence • Interpersonal Relations • Coming-of-Age

Neri, Greg

Chess Rumble. New York: Lee & Low Books, 2007. 62 p. ISBN: 9781584302797. ALA Notable Children's Books; YALSA Quick Picks. *MJ*

> Having engaged in numerous fist fights in his inner-city neighborhood, middle-schooler Marcus learns to fight in a different way when he meets Chess Master, CM, and takes his aggression to the chessboard, where he learns to love the game as well as how to contain his temper and take responsibility for his actions.

> *Bullies and Bullying • Emotional Problems • Family Problems • Chess*

Sanchez, Alex

Bait. New York: Simon & Schuster Books for Young Readers, 2009. 239 p. ISBN: 9781416937722. *JS*

> Landing in juvenile court on an assault charge after one too many fights, sixteen-year-old Diego MacMann is assigned to a sympathetic parole officer, Mr. Vidas. With his help, Diego is able to deal with the anger that has resulted in his cutting himself with a shark's tooth and with the fears that he might become like the man who molested him or that he might be gay.

> *Sexual Abuse • Self-Mutilation • Emotional Problems*

Bullies and Bullying

Adoff, Jaime

Names Will Never Hurt Me. New York: Dutton Children's Books, 2004. 192 p. ISBN: 9780786852147; 9781423104001pa. *JS*

> A film crew records the experiences of four high-school students at the one-year anniversary of a classmate's murder. Ryan, a football god; Kurt, an outcast; Floater, the principal's snitch; and Tisha, a biracial girl, have all faced bullies in their lives, and when the cameras are turned on them, their frustration and hurt come to the fore with explosive consequences.

> *High School • Emotional Problems • Films • Novels in Verse*

Anderson, M. T.

Burger Wuss. Cambridge, MA: Candlewick Press, 1999. 192 p. ISBN: 9780763606800; 9780763631789pa. *JS*

> After Turner steals his girlfriend, Anthony gets a job at O'Dermott's fast-food franchise where Turner works, where he is dubbed the "Burger Wuss" and is bullied and beaten by Turner. Vowing to get revenge with a plan that will humiliate both Turner and the O'Dermott's restaurant franchise, Anthony teams up with an animal rights fanatic and pits his fellow employees against those of rival Burger Queen. While dealing with his own drama, Anthony's best friend and his girlfriend are dealing with their own issues as they fall in love, have sex, and then

break up. But when Anthony's real chance for revenge arrives, he must realize that everyone makes his or her own decisions.

Work • Revenge • Romance • Breaking Up

Behrens, Andy

Beauty and the Bully. New York: Dutton Books, 2008. 250 p. ISBN: 9780525478980. *J*

Carly Garfield is the love of Duncan Boone's life, but she doesn't even know he exists—that is, until he slips during his band's practice session and is hit with a falling speaker, leaving him black and blue. At school Carly decides to take him on as her next do-gooder project to protect him from the bullies who she thinks must have beat him up. When the bruises fade, so does Carly's interest, and Duncan convinces Freddie, the new guy at school, to bully him in exchange for letting Freddie's sister play in his band. When his agreement turns his bandmates against him, Duncan must decide between friendship and love.

Friendship • Dating

Ellis, Ann Dee

This Is What I Did. New York: Little, Brown, 2007. 176 p. ISBN: 9780316013635; 9780316013628pa. YALSA Best Books. *MJ*

Filled with shame after having witnessed a violent altercation between his best friend Zyler, Zyler's abusive father, and a girl named Cami, eighth-grader Logan and his family move to a new neighborhood for a new start. But when his parents reveal his past, rumors start to fly. Logan is tormented by his friends both at school and in his Boy Scout troop. Finding solace in building sets for the school play, Logan begins to find new strength to heal from his trauma as he makes friends with palindrome-loving Laurel and builds a relationship with a sympathetic counselor.

Family Violence • Friendship • Camping

Flinn, Alex

Fade to Black. New York: Harper Tempest, 2005. 184 p. ISBN: 9780060568399; 9780060568429pa. *S*

After being attacked by a teenager with a baseball bat, Hispanic HIV-positive high school junior Alejandro "Alex" Crusan is hospitalized. Clinton Cole, who fears Alex and has tormented him before, swears that he is innocent of the crime. However Daria Bickell, a teen with Down syndrome who has witnessed some of Clinton's other attacks, saw him at the scene. While Alex knows that Clinton is innocent as well, when Daria's testimony begins showing holes, he must decide if he should just let him take the blame anyway.

Hate Crimes • HIV • Down Syndrome • Prejudice • Misfits • Racism

Foley, John

A Mighty Wall. Woodbury, MN: Flux, 2009. 240 p. ISBN: 9780738714486pa. *S*

As one of the smaller boys in school, seventeen-year-old high school junior Jordan "Jordo" escapes the school's bullies with the protection of his football player buddies, AJ and Casey, and by climbing at a local gym. But when AJ is killed in a climbing accident and the bullying escalates, Jordo escapes to the mountains to find himself and overcome his guilt.

Death • Coming-of-Age

Fullerton, Alma

In the Garage. Calgary: Red Deer Press, 2006. 181 p. ISBN: 9780889953710pa. *JS*

A victim of bullying because of the scar on her face, BJ has one friend in Alex. The two most popular girls in school pressure BJ to steal Alex's journal, where she learns that he is gay. When the journal is lost and his homosexuality becomes common knowledge, BJ must deal with the consequences.

Gay Males • Friendship • Popularity • Coming Out • Homophobia • Peer Pressure • Hate Crimes • Novels in Verse

Gardner, Graham

Inventing Elliot. New York: Dial Books, 2004. 181 p. ISBN: 9780803729643; 9780142403440pa; (aud). *MJ*

A victim of bullying in his old school, fourteen-year-old Elliot tries to remake himself at his new school. After passing a violent initiation requirement by the Guardians, the school's secret ruling gang, Elliot moves from victim to bully. Facing his father's severe depression and his mother's struggles to support them, Elliot begins to lose what friendships he has as he becomes more entrenched in the gang. Soon Elliot finds a new friend in one of the gang's victims, and, finally listening to his mother's advice, Elliot comes clean to the school principal.

Violence • Gangs • High School • Family Problems

George, Madeleine

Looks. New York: Viking, 2008. 240 p. ISBN: 9780670061679; 9780142414194pa. YALSA Best Books. *J*

Meghan Ball is overweight and tormented by the boys at her school. Aimee Zorn is an anorexic who pours her anger into writing poetry. When popular girl, Cara, shuns Meghan because of her weight and passes Aimee's poetry off as her own, the two girls join forces in the common cause to exact revenge on Cara.

Popularity • Family Problems • Dysfunctional Families • Revenge • Body Image • Overweight • Eating Disorders • Friendship

Gorman, Carol

Games: A Tale of Two Bullies. New York: HarperCollins, 2007. 288 p. ISBN: 9780060570279; 9780060570286pa. *MJ*

When book lover Mick Sullivan and music lover Boot Quin start fist fighting at school, the principal sentences them to play board games for several hours together in an effort to help them get along. But the fighting continues, and the boys dare each other to do serious challenges, including acts of vandalism and theft. As the boys deal with the repercussions of their acts, they begin to bond as they realize they are both dealing with problems at home.

Alcoholism • Child Abuse • Music • Peer Pressure • Dares • Competition

Griffin, Adele

Amandine. New York: Hyperion Books for Children, 2001. 220 p. ISBN: 9780786806188; 9780786814411pa. YALSA Best Books; YALSA Quick Picks. *MJ*

As the new girl at DeWolf High, fourteen-year-old Delia Blaine would like to be a member of the popular crowd. Instead, she is drawn into a friendship with dangerous artist Amandine. Repulsed by Amandine's gruesome drawings but at the same time drawn in by her magnetic personality, Delia soon finds that she needs to remove herself from the unhealthy, manipulative relationship. But when she does, Amandine exacts revenge and spreads vicious rumors about her family until Delia can find her own inner strength and stand up for herself.

Emotional Problems • Friendship • Revenge

Harmon, Michael B.

Brutal. New York: Alfred A. Knopf, 2009. 256 p. ISBN: 9780375840999; (aud). *J*

Sixteen-year-old Poe Holly is abandoned by her physician mother who is taking a sabbatical to give medical services to people in South America. Poe is forced to live with the father she hardly knows. Getting to know her misfit neighbor Velveeta, who is constantly picked on by the bullies at school, Poe decides to change the social order at their school that facilitates the bullying so she can bring an end to the reign of terror.

Bullies and Bullying • Moving • Mother-Separated Families

Hyde, Catherine Ryan

Diary of a Witness. New York: Alfred A. Knopf, 2009. 208 p. ISBN: 9780375856846. *JS*

Sticking together to present a united front, overweight Ernie Boyd and his lanky, acne-prone friend Will Manson endure constant bullying at school at the hands of five mean jocks. While Ernie has support at home with his mom and Uncle Max, Will is left alone with his alcoholic father and younger brother, Sam. To escape their pain, the boys enjoy fishing. One day their boat capsizes and Sam drowns, causing their father to be arrested for child endangerment. Will cannot face his guilt and attempts suicide, only to be saved at the last minute by Ernie, who recognized the danger. But at school the bullies hold no compassion and continue their harassment, until Will is unable to take any more and plans to end their torment by bringing a gun to school. He is, once again, helped by Ernie, who chooses to do the right thing.

Overweight • Guilt • Single Parent • Death • Diaries

Klass, David

Home of the Braves. New York: Farrar, Straus & Giroux, 2002. 312 p. ISBN: 9780374399634; 9780060531713pa. *J*

Senior Joe Brickman's dreams of being the star of his high school soccer team and getting a date with his neighbor and childhood friend Kristine are dashed when Antonio Silva, a Brazilian soccer star, transfers to Lawndale High School and not only takes Joe's starring role on the team but his potential girlfriend as well. When Antonio refuses to submit to the dominance of the school's football team and fights with one of its players, he injures him. Tension between the two teams heats up. Joe refuses to get involved, keeping silent when questioned even after bullies beat up his quiet friend Ed. But even metal detectors and security at the school can't change things. After Ed is beaten again and Joe fights with Kristine when she confronts him, he must find the strength to face the football team's ringleader to stop the violence.

Soccer • High School • Violence • Football

Koss, Amy Goldman

Poison Ivy. New Milford, CT: Roaring Brook Press, 2006. 176 p. ISBN: 9781596431188; 9780312384531pa. *MJ*

In a mock trial designed to help the students learn about government, middle school teacher Ms. Gold decides to give unpopular girl Ivy a chance to find justice against the bullies who harass her. With shy and insecure Daria as Ivy's lawyer, and a jury made up of people who really don't want to be considered Ivy's peers, the trial unfolds. Things get ugly as Ms. Gold realizes that she did not count on the power the popular girls hold.

Interpersonal Relations • Popularity • Peer Pressure

Kraft, Erik P.

Miracle Wimp. New York: Little, Brown, 2007. 256 p. ISBN: 9780316011655; 9780316011662pa. *J*

Sophomore Tom Mayo deals with the insecurities and self-doubt that come with growing up as he endures high school classes and copes with the bullying group called the Donkeys. When Larry, a special-education student whom Tom also teased, is killed in an accident, Tom realizes that his teasing makes him no different than the bullying Donkeys.

Friendship • High School • Cliques • Popularity

Love, D. Anne

Defying the Diva. New York: Simon & Schuster/McElderry, 2008. 272 p. ISBN: 9781416934813. *J*

> Freshman gossip columnist Haley Patterson gets in big trouble when she publishes an article in the school newspaper about a drunken party hosted by popular Camilla Quinn. Launching a campaign against Haley, Camilla turns Haley's friends against her and sends her e-mails suggesting she should commit suicide. Instead of telling anyone, Haley gets through it by looking forward to getting away from it all during a summer with her aunts. Remaking her life during the summer, Haley gets a job at a pool, where she is able to make new friends and find love with a handsome life-guard. With these experiences, she is able to find the courage to confront Camilla when another girl presses charges against her and Haley steps forward to testify.
>
> *Parties • Popularity • Self-Esteem*

Lyga, Barry

The Astonishing Adventures of Fanboy & Goth Girl. Boston: Houghton Mifflin, 2006. 320 p. ISBN: 9780618723928; 9780618916528pa. School Library Journal Best Books; YALSA Best Books. *J*

> Bullied at school, fifteen-year-old Fanboy is also struggling at home with his pregnant mother and controlling stepfather. Dealing with his frustra-tion and anger through his art, Fanboy spends hours creating his own graphic novel and sharing it with his friend Cal, who will only show him friendship outside of school. When he receives an instant message from Kyra, a rebel Goth chick, containing pictures that document the cruelty he endures, the two build an enigmatic friendship, and Kyra helps give Fanboy the confidence he needs to stand up to the bullies.
>
> *Goth Culture • Family Problems • Friendship • Artists*

MacLeod, J. E.

Waiting to Score. Lodi, NJ: WestSide Books, 2009. 200 p. ISBN: 9781934813010. *S*

> Fifteen-year-old hockey player Zack Chase's life has been made miserable by the team's captain, Mac. Zack won't stand for Mac's bullying, especially after he learns that Mac has been sexually harassing the girls at the school. Then Zack finds himself interested in Goth girl Jane. But when the team's alco-hol-fueled parties are discovered and tragedy strikes, Zack, his friends, and the adults in their lives must decide just how to take control of the situation.
>
> *Moving • High Schools • Hockey*

McNeal, Laura, and Tom

Crooked. New York: A. Knopf, 1999. 346 p. ISBN: 9780679893004; 9780440229469pa. YALSA Best Books. *J*

> Ninth-graders Clara Wilson and Amos McKenzie turn to each other for support when Clara's best friend ditches her and her parents separate,

while Amos is dealing with the death of his father and with a best friend who is obsessed with an intangible girl. Soon their support turns to love. When bullies Charles and Eddie Tripp make Clara and Amos their targets and they beat Amos, Amos acquires hero status at school. The pair are drawn even closer as they face down the intimidating bullies.

Family Problems • Death • Best Friends • Violence

McNeal, Laura, and Tom

Crushed. New York: Knopf, distributed by Random House, 2006. 308 p. ISBN: 9780375831058; 9780375831218pa. *J*

Having left their private school, Audrey Reed and her friends, Lea and C.C., who love cucumber sandwiches and Gilbert and Sullivan music, move to the public Jemison High School. At the new school, the popular girls harass Audrey. Confident, sophisticated Wickham Hill romances her, and he seems OK until she finds out that he does not want love but only her help to cheat in physics. When a slanderous gossip rag called The Yellow Paper surfaces, Audrey believes that shy, awkward Clyde Mumsford who has a crush on her, is the author because he has uncovered secrets about Wickham he has tried to tell her about. But when the truth comes out, Audrey must face reality as she learns who her friends really are.

Gossiping and Gossips • Family Problems • Secrets • Cancer • Friendship • Cheating • Dating

Page, Katherine Hall

Club Meds. New York: Simon Pulse, 2006. 176 p. ISBN: 9781416909033pa. *J*

Freshman Jack Sutton receives medication daily from the school nurse for his attention-deficit disorder. When drug addict Chuck Williams begins demanding that Jack hand over his medication, Jack, afraid that he will be beat up, complies until he and his other friends who must also take medications decide to take their revenge and teach Chuck a lesson.

Attention-Deficit Disorder • Friendship • Drug Abuse

Pascal, Francine

The Ruling Class. New York: Simon & Schuster, 2004. 176 p. ISBN: 9780689873324; 9780689873331pa. *JS*

Sixteen-year-old Twyla Gay doesn't fit in at her new school in a wealthy suburb of Dallas and becomes the target of vicious bullying. Dealing with the torment, Twyla considers just dropping out, but she does not want to follow the same path as her mother. When the bullying clique of girls, lead by gorgeous Jenette Sue, lures Twyla to a deserted mall where she is almost raped, Twyla decides, with the help of her only friend Deena, who has been deemed the school slut, that it is time to take revenge and take down the mean girls.

Cliques • Social Classes • Revenge

Philip, Gillian

Crossing the Line. New York: Bloomsbury, 2009. 288 p. ISBN: 9780747599937pa. *S*
Seventeen-year-old Nick is dealing with a lot of problems. His dad is an alcoholic, his radio-personality mother is always working, and his fourteen-year-old sister Allie is dealing with the death of her boyfriend, Aiden, by bringing him back to life as an imaginary friend. Aiden was killed in a school stabbing by Nick's one-time friend, Kev. It is up to him to distance himself from Kev and the other bullies to bring his life back together.

Alcoholism • Friendship • Violence • Death

Phillips, Suzanne

Burn. New York: Little, Brown, 2008. 288 p. ISBN: 9780316001656; 9780316001663pa. *J*
When high school freshman Cameron Grady is mistaken for a girl by a coach because of his short stature and long hair, he becomes a target for the school bullies, who taunt him with labels of "gay" and "fag." Without any friends for support, things come to a head when Cameron is assaulted in the locker room and nude photos of him are posted on the Internet. Overcome with anger, Cameron begins burning matches, as well as his skin, in the woods near his home. When he breaks psychologically and turns on the bullies' other target with fatal consequences, it is only with the help of his mother's boyfriend, a police officer, that Cameron is able to find help for his problems.

Psychic Trauma • Emotional Problems • Teasing • Violence

Pixley, Marcella Fleischman

Freak. New York: Farrar, Straus & Giroux, 2007. 144 p. ISBN: 9780374324537. *MJ*
Seventh-grader Miriam Fisher is an accomplished poet who reads the Oxford English Dictionary just for fun. Miriam has always been accompanied by her older sister, Deborah—that is, until Deborah becomes part of the popular crowd her freshman year and leaves her sister behind. When high school senior Artie Rosenberg comes to live with the Fishers while his parents are working in India, the relationship between the sisters is further strained as they both vie for his attentions and Deborah wins. To add to her stress, Miriam is also daily humiliated by bullying classmates, until one day she explodes and recrafts her identity by shaving her head, an act that gives her the courage to stand up to the bullies.

Misfits • Sisters • Interpersonal Relations

Plum-Ucci, Carol

What Happened to Lani Garver. San Diego, CA: Harcourt, 2002. 307 p. ISBN: 9780152168131; 9780152050887pa. YALSA Best Books. *JS*
Most of his classmates think androgynous new student Lani Garver is gay, but when popular cheerleader, sixteen-year-old Claire McKenzie, gets to know him, she finds that his wisdom and kindness make her think he is an

angel. Claire has her own problems: dark dreams that the leukemia she once survived is back, her eating disorder, and her alcoholic mother. Claire must face the peer pressure and homophobia directed at Lani by the popular crowd.

Peer Pressure • Gay Males • Homosexuality • Prejudice • Alcoholism • Eating Disorders • Coming-of-Age

Portman, Frank

King Dork. New York: Delacorte Press, 2006. 352 p. ISBN: 9780385732918; 9780385734509pa; (aud). YALSA Best Books. *S*

Sophomore Tom Henderson is often humiliated at school by his vice principal, who mocks him, and by his classmates, who give him horrible nicknames. Bored even with his AP classes, Tom finds an outlet in writing songs and creating names for an imaginary band with his best friend, Sam. When he finds his dead father's copy of *The Catcher in the Rye*, Tom discovers secret messages and begins a quest to decode them so he can uncover his father's past and solve the mystery behind his father's death.

Friendship • Music • Death

Prose, Francine

Bullyville. New York: HarperTeen, 2007. 272 p. ISBN: 9780060574970; 9780060574994pa. *JS*

When Bart Rangely awakes with the flu and his mother stays home from work to care for him on September 11, 2001, she is saved from the attacks that kill his father, who recently left the family for another woman. The media attention brought to his case earns him a scholarship to a prestigious school. Bart is immediately drawn into intense hazing, until he can't stand it anymore and keys the car of Tyro Bergen who has been leading the hazing. When he is caught and assigned to community service, Bart must come to terms with his life and deal with the bullies.

Grief • Death • Loss • Coming-of-Age • Community Service

Voight, Cynthia

Bad Girls Series. New York: Scholastic; New York: Atheneum Books for Young Readers

Michelle "Mikey" Elsinger and Margalo Epps, two girls who can't be bothered to act nice or docile and who find joy in acting out and manipulating people, form a friendship and deal with a lot of problems.

Athletes • Misfits • Robbery • Peer Pressure • Cliques

Bad Girls. 1996. 277 p. ISBN: 9780590601344; 9780590601351pa. *M*

Mikey is a loud, mean, and aggressive troublemaker. Margalo is calm and devious, preferring to use mind games and rumors to start trouble. When they meet in Mrs. Chemsky's fifth-grade class, these two bad girls form a tentative friendship that is cemented when Mikey refuses to let Margalo be punished alone for a sneaky prank she committed.

Bad, Badder, Baddest. 1997. 266 p. ISBN: 9780590601368; 9780439080965pa. *M*

Mikey's parents are getting a divorce, and she is trying to do anything she can to get them to stay together, including becoming a nice, dutiful daughter. But when that does not work, she decides to run away from home with Margalo, who, having been through two divorces, has much advice to offer. But even with all their plans, Mikey is unable to prevent the divorce, and things go truly bad when at school a new classmate, Gianette, captivates the school with her knowledge of witchcraft and then blackmails the girls as they work to uncover the truth about her background as a thief and con artist.

It's Not Easy Being Bad. 2000. 241 p. ISBN: 9780689824739; 9780689851155pa. *M*

Now in seventh-grade, Mikey and Margalo are finding that their bad behavior and lack of popularity make it hard to fit into the social structure of their middle school. They come up with a plan to be part of the "in" crowd, but when the plan fails miserably, the girls must decide if they should get revenge or figure out how they can become content just being who they are.

Bad Girls in Love. 2002. 233 p. ISBN: 9780689824715; 9780689866203pa. *M*

At fourteen, Mikey and Margalo find themselves falling in love. Mikey has a crush on Shawn Macavity, the cutest guy in their class—and everyone around knows it because she follows him around and begs him to take her to the school dance, despite his obvious disinterest. Margalo also has a crush, but she keeps hers a secret because she has fallen for a teacher, Mr. Schramm. While both girls must learn that the course of true love does not always run smooth, Mikey is also dealing with her mother's announcement that she is going to marry her rich older boyfriend.

Bad Girls, Bad Girls, Whatcha Gonna Do? 2006. 448 p. ISBN: 9780689824746. *M*

Mikey's tennis coach subtly pressures her to cheat, and she is subsequently thrown off the team. Margalo must uncover a thief who stole more than $200. Both girls still find time to come up with a plan to oust the bullies who are tormenting their friend Hadrian and help a girl whose boyfriend is pressuring her to have sex.

Williams-Garcia, Rita

Jumped. New York: Amistad/HarperTeen, 2009. 176 p. ISBN: 9780060760915. *JS*

Leticia wants to mind her own business, but when she learns that basketball player Dominique is planning to beat up artist Trina just because she bumped into her in the hallway, she has to decide if she should take her best friends Bea's advice and tell Trina what is about to happen or if she should just stand by and watch.

Violence • African Americans

Drunk Driving

Elkeles, Simone

Leaving Paradise. Woodbury, CT: Flux, 2007. 303 p. ISBN: 9780738710181pa. *S*

After his release from prison where he was sent after a drunk-driving accident that severely injured his classmate Maggie, seventeen-year-old Caleb lives with guilt. At the same time, Maggie, having spent a year healing, is returning to school feeling ugly and disconnected since she can no longer play tennis because of her injuries. Both are dealing with the consequences of the accident and are trying to fit in again, but they must deal with the harassment from their classmates and their changed relationships.

Traffic Accidents • Alcohol Use • Ex-Convicts • Guilt • Family Problems

Frank, E. R.

Wrecked. New York: Atheneum Books for Young Readers, 2005. 247 p. ISBN: 9780689873836; 9780689873843pa. YALSA Best Books. *J*

Anna is left with a lacerated eye and Ellen with a punctured lung and other serious injuries when they are involved in a drunk-driving accident that leaves the drunk driver, Cameron, who is her brother's girlfriend, dead. Facing the aftermath of the tragedy alone when her emotionally abusive father refuses to let her have therapy, Anna must repair her relationship with her brother, Jack, as she deals with her own guilt. With the help of eye movement desensitization and reprocessing therapy she finally receives, she learns to handle what life brings to her.

Traffic Accidents • Alcohol Use • Death • Grief • Guilt • Family Relationships • Family Problems

Johnson, Peter

What Happened. Asheville, NC: Front Street, 2007. 133 p. ISBN: 9781932425673. *JS*

Abandoned by their father and with their mother dead, Kyle and his younger brother find themselves in a quandary when, as passengers in a car driven by their friend Duane's wealthy father, they are involved in a hit-and-run accident and find themselves pressured to remain silent. The need to do what is right is clouded by their drunkenness that night and also by the fact that Kyle is in love with Duane's sister. Duane is frustrated and afraid the boys will find out that his father was once in love with their mother and hates their father. The boys must fend off Duane and his antagonistic father as they try to decide what is the right thing to do.

Brothers • Traffic Accidents • Alcohol Use • Father and Son • Deception • Ethics

Keizer, Garret

God of Beer. New York: HarperCollins, 2002. 242 p. ISBN: 9780060294564; 9780064472760pa; (aud). *S*

High school senior Kyle Nelson and his friends Quake, Diana, Condor, and David, decide to start the Beer Rebellion, a nonviolent social protest that they hope will lower the drinking age and raise acceptability of drinking. Then Condor gets drunk at a party and gets behind the wheel, killing Diana in the resulting accident, and David reacts by smashing beer bottles in the parking lot of a mini-mart, where he is subsequently arrested. When Quake follows David's example and smashes bottles at his trial, Kyle watches as the pair is assigned to community service and he works to understand how his own choices have affected the situation.

Traffic Accidents • Alcohol Use • Community Service

McDaniel, Lurlene

Hit and Run. New York: Delacorte Press, 2007. 180 p. ISBN: 9780385731614; 9780440238706pa. *S*

Lives are changed when Quinn, an athlete who is pushed by his father, hits bicyclist Analise while driving drunk and then hides the crime. Analise is now trapped in her own body and boyfriend Jeremy sits by hoping she will come back, while Laurie, who witnessed the accident, blackmails Quinn into dating her so she can be part of the popular crowd. As all four teens work through the consequences of the choices that were made, they must learn important lessons about love and life.

Traffic Accidents • Alcohol Use • Guilt • Popularity • Secrets

Theft

Burnham, Niki

Sticky Fingers. New York: Simon Pulse, 2005. 288 p. ISBN: 9780689876493pa. *S*

Jenna has been accepted to Harvard, and her life and goals are on track, but she is distracted by her boyfriend Scott's pressures to have sex. He thinks it is the perfect time. She does love him but is just not ready. While Scott appears to support her decision, in reality he plans to slip a drug into her drink one night and rape her. Jenna's best friend, Courtney's weight is dropping way too low as she is trying to deal with her own problems, including the fact that she is a shoplifter. Noticing that Courtney and Scott seem to spend a lot of time together without her, Jenna believes that there might be other problems when she overhears them having an argument. Little does she know that Courtney knows about the drugs and what Scott is planning to do with them.

Shoplifting • Peer Pressure • Date Rape

Graff, Lisa

The Life and Crimes of Bernetta Wallflower. New York: Laura Geringer Books, 2008. 250 p. ISBN: 9780060875923. *M*

When best friend Ashley steals school assignments from her older sister, sells them, and then frames twelve-year-old Bernetta Wallflower for the scheme, Bernetta loses her scholarship to her private school. When handsome Gabe proposes a plan for her to use her slight of hand skills, developed as she assisted her father with his magic show to run a cleaver con game, Bernetta sees a way to earn the tuition money she needs to return to school. But when it appears that Gabe has double-crossed her and the truth reveals Ashley was involved again, the two join forces to exact revenge, until their schemes are confessed and the aftermath is dealt with.

Cheating • Family • Friendship

Hoffmann, Kerry Cohen

The Good Girl. New York: Delacorte Press, 2008. 176 p. ISBN: 9780385736442. *J*

Fifteen-year-old Lindsey has always been a good girl, but when her older brother Mark dies in a car crash, her father's psychiatry practice closes because of a malpractice suit, and her mother leaves the family, Lindsey finds herself even more pressed into behaving so as not to cause any more trouble the way her younger sister does. At school, Lindsey gives in to what is expected of her when she gives up her dream to be in the school play because of the pressure of a mean-spirited classmate and agrees to take on the obligation of being the school ambassador, even though she knows the school's dean is pressuring her and a cute boy she really likes is encouraging her to do otherwise. Soon the pressure becomes too much, and Lindsey rebels and starts stealing money from her father and small items from stores. Soon her compulsions get worse. When school-wide locker thefts attract the attention of the police, Lindsey soon finds that she must deal with the consequences of her actions and find other outlets.

Emotional Problems • Shoplifting • Kleptomania

Lurie, April

The Latent Powers of Dylan Fontaine. New York: Delacorte Press, 2008. 211 p. ISBN: 9780385731256; 9780440238478pa. *JS*

Sixteen-year-old Dylan is angry and insecure, with a mother who left the family to live with her art teacher, an obstetrician father who is always working, an older brother who is constantly smoking marijuana, and his best friend Angie, who does not return his romantic feelings. When, thinking he sees his mother, he runs out of a store without paying and is accused of shoplifting, he lands in the police station. Angie decides to make him the subject of her summer-school movie project. With the experiences he has, Dylan is able to work through his problems, gaining the confidence and courage to take chances.

Family Problems • Brothers • Marijuana • Drug Use • Bands • Mother-Separated Families • Coming-of-Age

McDonald, Janet

Harlem Hustle. New York: Frances Foster Books, 2006. 192 p. ISBN: 9780374371845. *S*

Seventeen-year-old Eric "Hustle" Samson was put in prison for stealing and now finds himself out on probation, abandoned by his druggy parents and living with a friend in Harlem. Supported by best friend Manley "Ride" Freeman and potential girlfriend Jeannette Simpson, Hustle is now committed to changing his life by becoming the next great rap artist. But when Hustle runs up against the ruthless music producers who manipulate and threaten him to get his music for next to nothing, he must find his inner strength and courage to leave his past behind and achieve his dream.

African Americans • *Rap Music* • *Abandoned Teenagers* • *Grandmothers* • *Self-Esteem* • *Hip-Hop Culture*

Pollack, Jenny

Klepto. New York: Viking, 2006. 273 p. ISBN: 9780670060610; 9780142410721pa. *J*

Freshman Julie Prodsky is attending the famous High School of the Performing Arts where on her first day she meets Julie Braverman, who introduces her to the art of shoplifting. Julie Prodsky's conscience begins to trouble her, and while shoplifting, she is caught by a security officer who lets her off with a warning. She decides to go to a therapist to help her overcome her kleptomania. Her actions strain her relationship with Julie Braverman until they are able to reconcile when she learns that her friend was caught at another store and is also trying to change her ways.

Shoplifting • *Friendship* • *First Love* • *Kleptomania* • *Social Acceptance*

Scott, Elizabeth

Stealing Heaven. New York: HarperTeen, 2008. 307 p. ISBN: 9780061122804; 9780061122828pa. YALSA Best Books. *S*

Moving from town to town with her mother, eighteen-year-old Danielle "Dani" has been trained as a thief. While her mother attracts rich men to mine them for information about their next potential job, Dani has been left without friends, school, or even a place to call home. When they land in the small town of Haven, Dani begins to have second thoughts about their lifestyle as she befriends and falls for a man who happens to be a cop. Realizing it is her new friend's home they are targeting, Dani decides that she can no longer follow her mother's expectations, and she must craft a life for herself.

Mother and Daughter • *Thieves* • *Interpersonal Relations* • *Friendship*

Tracy, Kristen

Crimes of the Sarahs. New York: Simon Pulse, 2008. 354 p. ISBN: 9781416955191pa. *JS*

Four girls named Sarah embark on a summer filled with activities including outdoor walks, volunteer work, and committing petty crimes. Sarah Trestle is happily part of the group and is great at driving the getaway car. When things go wrong on one shoplifting excursion, she is worried that mean-girl Sarah Aberdeen will no longer accept her in the group. Sarah Trestle is ready to do anything to be able to stay, but soon she must decide if a life of crime is really the right thing.

Cliques • *Thieves* • *Crime* • *Peer Pressure* • *Shoplifting*

Volponi, Paul

Black and White. New York: Viking, 2005. 160 p. ISBN: 9780670060061; 9780142406922pa. YALSA Best Books; YALSA Quick Picks; YALSA Popular Paperbacks. *S*

> Finding fast-food jobs too demeaning, African American high school senior Marcus Brown and his white best friend Eddie Russo, turn to armed robbery, using a gun that belonged to Eddie's dead grandfather, to get a little extra money for clothes and school fees. When on their third robbery, they shoot and wound their target, Marcus and Eddie realize that they have put their basketball careers and their potential scholarships in jeopardy as they wait in anguish for the police to find and arrest them. When Marcus is identified and refuses to finger Eddie, he must face the consequences while Eddie, under pressure from his parents, abandons his friend.

> *Interracial Friendships* • *Best Friends* • *African American* • *Robbery* • *Race Relations* • *Basketball*

Whitney, Kim Ablon

See You Down the Road. New York: Alfred A. Knopf, 2004. 192 p. ISBN: 9780375824678; 9780440238096pa. YALSA Best Books. *JS*

> Sixteen-year-old Bridget and her family are Travelers, who move across the United States in trailers and make money through con jobs and stealing. Bridget starts to question a lifestyle that is filled with lies, just like her older sister who broke away years ago, and she longs to go to school and to defy tradition by choosing her own husband. Joining her brother, Patrick, the boy her parents plan for her to marry, and her uncle in a high-risk scam, she is finally able to make the difficult decisions about her future and separate her own desires from her family's expectations.

> *Thieves* • *Dishonesty* • *Sex Role*

Murder

Cassidy, Anne

Looking for JJ. Orlando, FL: Harcourt, 2007. 319 p. ISBN: 9780152061906; 9780152066383pa; (aud). YALSA Best Books. *S*

> Seventeen-year-old Alice Tully has found some peace in her life, even though she wonders if she even deserves to be safe and happy after changing her identity when she was released from prison for killing her childhood friend. The British tabloids are looking for Jennifer Jones, and soon the details of her childhood with an irresponsible and abusive mother, who moved from a failing modeling career to become a prostitute, come to light. Even now with a boyfriend to whom she loses her virginity, a job, a home with a kind woman, and plans for the future, Alice must deal with her past in the hope that she can finally find her own love and happiness.

> *Mother and Daughter* • *Single Parent* • *Child Abuse* • *Emotional Problems* • *Guilt*

Cormier, Robert

The Rag and Bone Shop. New York: Delacorte Press, 2001. 154 p. ISBN: 9780385729628; 9780440229711pa; (aud). YALSA Best Books. *MJ*

After his neighbor, seven-year-old Alicia Bartlett, is found murdered, seventh-grader Jason Dorrant, who was the last person to see her alive, becomes the prime suspect. With no physical evidence to link him to the crime, police interrogator Trent extracts a confession, but all the while he believes in Jason's innocence. When another confesses to the crime, Trent's reputation is damaged, and Jason must deal with the psychological trauma that has lead him to believe that he might be capable of murder.

Murder • Police • Ethics

Flinn, Alex

Nothing to Lose. New York: Harper Tempest, 2004. 288 p. ISBN: 9780060517502; 9780060517526pa. YALSA Best Books; YALSA Quick Picks. *S*

Seventeen-year-old Michael Daye ran away from home a year ago and has been working with a traveling carnival. Upon returning, he finds his mother, Lisa Monroe, on trial for the murder of her millionaire husband, who is Michael's abusive stepfather. The only person who knows the whole truth about the crime is Michael, and while the cops try to track him down for questioning, he is afraid to come forward. Even though he loves his mother, Michael's growing love for another carnival worker, Kirstie, and his desire to not relive the past, make the decision challenging, but soon he asks a lawyer to help him prepare to testify, and the secret he has been keeping is revealed.

Runaways • Stepfathers • Rich People • Family Violence • Anger • Secrets

Giles, Gail

Right Behind You: A Novel. New York: Little, Brown, 2007. 304 p. ISBN: 9780316166362; 9780316166379pa. YALSA Quick Picks. *J*

At age fourteen, Kip McFarland has spent four years in a juvenile detention facility after, in a jealous rage, he set a boy afire, killing him. After his release, Kip becomes Wade and tries to make a new life with his father and stepmother in Indiana. While things are normal for a while, they soon fall apart when he reveals his past while drunk. Forced to move, the family ends up in Texas, where Wade finds a friend in neighbor Sam, a girl who is dealing with her own problems.

Psychotherapy • Secrets • Social Acceptance

Giles, Gail

Shattering Glass. Brookfield, CT: Roaring Brook Press, 2002. 215 p. ISBN: 9780761315810; 9780689858000pa; (aud). YALSA Best Books; YALSA Quick Picks. *J*

Young Steward is a member of the popular group led by powerful Rob Haynes. When the group takes on the task of making the school nerd, Simon, popular with new clothes and diet and exercise, things move forward, and Simon gains confidence, eclipsing Rob in popularity. Using Simon to help him hack into the school's computers, Young benefits from the scheme. But when Simon learns a secret about Rob and spreads it around, Rob is furious. His group, including Young, beat Simon to death, leaving Young to deal with the consequences.

Popularity • Violence

Jones, Patrick

Cheated. New York: Walker, distributed to the trade by Macmillan, 2008. 196 p. ISBN: 9780802796998; 9780802798473pa. *J*

Friends Mick, Brody, and Aaron have all been abandoned by their fathers and are dealing with serious personal problems. In particular, fifteen-year-old Mick is filled with guilt since he was the one who instigated his father's leaving when he revealed that his father was cheating on his mother, even though his dad did not want him to tell. Feeling adrift in a sea of preppy classmates and football players, Mick escapes into his music and alcohol. Things go from bad to worse. Mick helps his friend cheat on a homework assignment and then cheats on his girlfriend. And when a night of drinking and poker with friends results in a homeless man being killed, Mick must face his choices when the attempt to cover up the crime and avoid punishment lands the friends in the custody of the police.

Dysfunctional Families • Guilt • Alcohol • Cheating • Homelessness • Friendship • Responsibility

Klass, David

Dark Angel. New York: Farrar, Straus & Giroux, 2005. 311 p. ISBN: 9780374399504; 9780060887001pa. YALSA Quick Picks. *S*

Despite their outward appearance as a perfect churchgoing family, seventeen-year-old Jeff Hastings's family has kept the secret of his older brother Troy's life sentence for premeditated murder a secret for five-and-a-half years. When Troy's sentence is suddenly reversed on a technicality and he returns home after being released, Jeff's life collapses as his girlfriend and his friends leave him alone. Things take a turn for the worse when one of Jeff's teammates disappears, and everyone assumes Troy is the guilty party. During the ensuing chaos, Jeff must work through his suspicions and anger toward his brother to find the courage he needs to uncover the truth behind all the events that have conspired to complicate his life.

Ex-Convicts • Prejudice • Family Secrets

Lester, Julius

When Dad Killed Mom. San Diego, CA: Silver Whistle, 2001. 183 p. ISBN: 9780152163051; 9780152046989pa. YALSA Quick Picks. *S*

When their psychologist father shoots their mother, Jenna and her brother Jeremy must deal with the aftermath. Jenna has always been closer to her father and Jeremy closer to their mother. Now the two must face their complex grief as Jeremy discovers their mother's diary, helping them to shed light on the circumstances that ultimately led to the shooting.

Dysfunctional Families • Family Problems • Artists • Brothers • Sisters • Family Violence • African Americans

Myers, Walter Dean

Monster. New York: HarperCollins, 1999. 281 p. ISBN: 9780060280772; 9780064407311pa; (aud). Coretta Scott King Honor Books; Michael L. Printz Award; YALSA Best Books; YALSA Quick Picks. *JS*

> In prison awaiting his trial for murder for the role he played as a lookout for a robbery that left the owner of a drugstore dead, sixteen-year-old Steve Harmon, who dreams of being a filmmaker, recounts the circumstances that led up to his incarceration, as if they were a movie screenplay. Wrestling with his conscience, Steve tries to retain his humanity as he works toward his acquittal and proof that he is not the monster the prosecutor made him out to be.
>
> *Prisons • Violence • Robbery • Films*

Nelson, Blake

Paranoid Park. New York: Penguin Group, 2006. 176 p. ISBN: 9780670061181; 9780142411568pa. YALSA Quick Picks. *JS*

> Looking for excitement, a sixteen-year-old skateboarder goes to a shady underground skate park and with a street kid jumps a train so they can go to the grocery to get beer. A railroad security officer catches them and goes after them with his club. When they fight back and hit him with a skateboard, they kill him. The young skateboarder does not reveal his problem to his divorcing parents and his cheerleader girlfriend, who just wants to lose her virginity. Over time it becomes even harder to consider confessing, until his neighbor Macy, who has grown very attractive over the years, listens to him and, realizing his pain, convinces him that if he can talk about it, he should write about it.
>
> *Skateboards and Skateboarding • Death • Ethics • Divorce • Coming-of-Age*

Rottman, S. L.

Shadow of a Doubt. Atlanta, GA: Peachtree, 2003. 172 p. ISBN: 9781561452910; 9781561453542pa. YALSA Popular Paperbacks. *J*

> Ernest "Shadow" Thompson has cultivated a disinterested persona by wearing all black and donning sunglasses ever since his older brother, Daniel, devastated him by suddenly disappearing seven years ago. Now fifteen, the same age Daniel was when he left, Shadow is facing the rigors of starting high school. When Daniel unexpectedly calls, announcing that he is in jail because he has been accused of murder, Shadow's life is torn apart as his parents focus on Daniel's needs, leaving him alone to try to uncover the truth and decide if he can give Daniel a second chance.
>
> *Brothers • Runaways • Family Problems • Friendship*

13
14
15
16
17
18
19
20
21
22
23

Volponi, Paul

Rucker Park Setup. New York: Viking, 2007. 149 p. ISBN: 9780670061303; 9780142412077pa. YALSA Quick Picks. *S*

Mackey's dream of competing in the legendary Rucker Park street basketball tournament is about to come true when he, along with his friend J.R., are picked to play on a team with the rap star J-Greene. On the court, J.R. is killed, and Stove, J.R.'s father and also a referee for the game, realizes that Mackey is not sharing all the information about the accident. Mackey must face the anger and guilt he feels.

Basketball • Friendship • African Americans

Watt, Alan

Diamond Dogs. New York: Grand Central, 2001. 256 p. ISBN: 9780446677844pa. *S*

While driving home after a night of drinking, high school football star Neil Garvin hits and kills classmate Ian Curtis. Disoriented, Neil stuffs the body in his trunk and then drives home and passes out. Finding the body gone the next day, Neil knows his abusive father, who is the local sheriff, has found it and covered up his crime. But as his father goes through the motions of trying to find the boy who has now been identified as missing, Neil finds himself getting close to Ian's family and especially his sister, so the pressure increases. When the FBI is brought in, he must finally deal with his fear and self-loathing and make the right choices.

Violence • Drinking

Weingarten, Lynn

Wherever Nina Lies. New York: Point, 2009. 316 p. ISBN: 9780545066310; 9780545066334pa. *JS*

When she finds a drawing made by her wild older sister Nina, who left two years ago, in a donation box at a thrift store, sixteen-year-old Ellie starts on a quest in the hope it will lead her to her Nina. With the help of her friend Amanda, she is able to track down the origin of the picture, and when she meets Sean, who understands how she feels since his brother died recently, the two set out on a cross-country journey following the clues she has uncovered. When she finds that Sean is not who he says he is and that he murdered his brother, who was Nina's boyfriend, and that he now plans to murder both her and Nina, Ellie must save herself.

Missing Persons • Sisters • Family Relationships • Travel

School Shootings

Garden, Nancy

Endgame. Orlando, FL: Harcourt, 2006. 287 p. ISBN: 9780152054168. School Library Journal Best Books. *J*

Suspended from his middle school for carrying a knife he used to fend off bullies, fifteen-year-old Gray Wilton is looking forward to a new start when his family moves from Massachusetts to Connecticut. But Greenford High has its own set of ruling jocks who begin to pick on Gray and his friend Ross Terrel. Forced to perform acts like oral sex, the hazing escalates into severe physical violence and culminates in the jocks killing Gray's dog. Ignored by teachers and administrators and forced to feel utterly worthless by his father, Gray takes the situation into his own hands.

Bullies and Bullying • *Revenge* • *Schools* • *Father and Son* • *Family Problems* • *Murder* • *Oral Sex*

Koertge, Ron

The Brimstone Journals. Cambridge, MA: Candlewick Press, 2001. 113 p. ISBN: 9780763613020; 9780763617424pa. YALSA Best Books; YALSA Quick Picks. *S*

Violent racist Boyd, who is neglected by his father, is encouraged by an adult to join a white supremacist group, and he builds an arsenal of guns and chemicals. With these actions fueling his anger, Boyd compiles a list of anyone who ever made him angry and becomes intent on starting a school shooting spree. When the existence of the list is revealed and Boyd warns his favorites to stay home one Tuesday, three classmates reveal his intentions to the local police, and his plan is brought to an end. Around him, fifteen senior classmates react as they deal with their own problems, including Tran, who feels trapped by the dreams his immigrant father has for him; Allison, who is being sexually abused by her stepfather; and Sheila, who is trying to decide if she is a lesbian.

Violence • *High School* • *Immigrants* • *Sexual Abuse* • *Lesbians* • *Diary Novel* • *Novels in Verse*

Myers, Walter Dean

Shooter. New York: Harper Tempest, 2004. 224 p. ISBN: 9780786269693; 9780064472906pa; (aud). YALSA Quick Picks. *S*

Senior Len Gray kills the school's star football player and then shoots himself after injuring six others. The community, including Len's best friend, seventeen-year-old Cameron, one of the few black students in the school, looks back, trying to uncover the bullying and harassment that were ignored by the adults in the school and that led to the tragic events.

Murder • *Suicide* • *Family Problems* • *Emotional Problems* • *Bullies and Bullying*

Strasser, Todd

Give a Boy a Gun. New York: Simon & Schuster Books for Young Readers, 2000. 146 p. ISBN: 9780689811128; 9780689848933pa. *JS*

Overweight, quiet Gary, and thin, defensive Brenden have put up with years of harassment and cruelty from the football players at their high school. With no adults stepping in to stop the bullying, Gary and Brenden take matters into their own hands as they arm themselves and storm the school dance. In the aftermath of their rampage, which leaves one of them dead and the other one severely injured, the community, including students, parents, and teachers, look back on the events that led up to the tragedy.

Violence • *Bullies and Bullying*

13

14

15

16

17

18

19

20

21

22

23

Watson, C. G.

Quad. New York: Razorbill, 2007. 296 p. ISBN: 9781595141385. YALSA Quick Picks. *JS*

Typical high school cliques dole out humiliation, violence, and gossip on their classmates. There are many who wish they could get back at the unfairness of all their behavior. When gunshots ring out at school and a girl is murdered, many figure that Stone, who was kicked off the football team for steroid use and was then videotaped trying to rape a girl, is the shooter. But when the truth of the shooter's identity is revealed, it shocks the entire student body.

Athletes • Misfits • Cliques • Popularity • Social Acceptance • Teasing • Cheating • Murder • Violence

Rape

Anderson, Laurie Halse

Speak. New York: Farrar, Strauss & Giroux, 1999. 197 p. ISBN: 9780374371524; 9780141310886pa; (aud). YALSA Best Books; YALSA Quick Picks; Michael L. Printz Honor; School Library Journal Best Books. *JS*

Melinda Sordion begins her freshman year of high school as a social outcast. Everyone, including her best friend, hates her, branding her a snitch since she was the one who called the police that broke up their end-of-the-summer party. Melinda is hiding the real reason behind her call, and now without support she is struggling to heal psychologically from the trauma that forced her to act in the way she did at the party.

High School • Friendship • Popularity • Psychic Trauma • Emotional Problems

Dessen, Sarah

Just Listen: A Novel. New York: Viking Children's Books, 2006. 384 p. ISBN: 9780670061051; 9780142410974pa. YALSA Best Books; Teens Top Ten. *JS*

Annabel Greene's life looks great from the outside, but inside everything is falling apart. Annabel is ostracized by her classmates, who think she was cheating with her friend's boyfriend. At the same time, she is dealing with her sister's eating disorder and trying to continue a career in modeling that no longer interests her. She is aggravated by her family's refusal to acknowledge their problems. During this chaos, she is drawn to notorious loner Owen, who exposes her to music she has never heard and coaches her to deal with her anger and confront the trauma in her life.

Social Isolation • Anorexia • Attempted Rape • Coming-of-Age

Draper, Sharon M.

Darkness before Dawn. New York: Atheneum Books for Young Readers, 2001. 233 p. ISBN: 9780689830808; 9780689851346pa. YALSA Quick Picks. *S*

Keisha Montgomery is beginning to heal after her ex-boyfriend Andy committed suicide and her good friend was killed in a car accident. When the handsome college-age son of the principal becomes the new track coach and shows in interest in her, Keisha is flattered and happy. But when he attempts to rape her after a dinner date, Keisha is left shaken and depressed. She wants to be able to move on and embrace the future that comes after graduation.

Suicide • Traffic Accidents • Death • Attempted Rape • African Americans

Johnson, Kathleen Jeffrie

Target. Brookfield, CT: Roaring Brook Press, 2003. 175 p. ISBN: 9780761319320; 9780440239109pa. YALSA Best Books. *S*

Raped by two men, sixteen-year-old Grady West is unable to cope with life. Living in fear that his friends will find out about the rape, Grady decides to move to a new school. There he meets outsiders Jess, Fred, and Pearl. Dealing with his feelings of guilt over not fighting back, as well as flashbacks to his childhood, Grady is able to find help with Fred, who is gay, and Jess, a closet poet. As he finds he has feelings for Pearl, who is dealing with problems of her own, Grady begins to heal. When the school newspaper's investigative reporter, Gwendolyn, tries to expose Grady's secret, he must learn to trust his new friends as he struggles to hang on to life and reform his beliefs about his identity and his sexuality.

Rape • Teenage Boys • Secrets • Healing • Anorexia • Homosexuality • Race Relations

Lynch, Chris

Inexcusable. New York: Atheneum Books for Young Readers, 2005. 176 p. ISBN: 9780689847899; 9781416939726pa. School Library Journal Best Books; YALSA Best Books. *S*

When he is accused of date-raping a girl, high school senior Keir Sarafian proclaims his innocence and attempts to defend his character. By rationalizing his past exploits where he crippled an opponent during a game and he and his football teammates engaged in violent hazing, drinking, drugs, and vandalism, Keir reveals himself as a frightening aggressor who needs to recognize himself for what he is.

Date Rape • Violence • Responsibility • Alcohol Use • Drug Use

Martin, C. K. Kelly

One Lonely Degree. New York: Random House Children' Books, 2009. 256 p. ISBN: 9780375851636. *JS*

Haunted by a bad experience at a party with gorgeous Adam Porter, Finn has kept the whole incident hidden from everyone but her best friend Audrey. When her father moves out and her mother withdraws from life, things start falling apart, especially when childhood friend Jersy comes back into town and he and Audrey start dating. Soon Finn finds herself attracted to Jersy, forcing her to come to terms with her past experiences and to figure out how she feels about friendship and love.

Best Friends • Dating • Romance

Martino, Alfred C.

Over the End Line. New York: Houghton Mifflin, 2009. 320 p. ISBN: 9780152061210. *J*

Jonny Fehey idolizes his best friend, popular soccer star Kyle Saint-Claire, and is content to be the sidekick until he scores the winning goal of the championship soccer game and things change. After the victory party, Jonny awakes to find himself disoriented with a hangover and with horrible memories that a classmate was raped at the party. In the aftermath, Jonny's friendship with Kyle is tested as he also deals with his anger at bad-boy teammate Erick, and works through his feelings for new girl Annalisa.

Soccer • Friendship • Jealousy • Popularity • Revenge

Reinhardt, Dana

Harmless. New York: Wendy Lamb Books, 2007. 240 p. ISBN: 9780385746991; 9780553494976pa; (aud). YALSA Quick Picks. *J*

Anna, Emma, and Mariah are friends and high school freshmen. When they say they are going to a movie but instead have a drunken party with Mariah's senior boyfriend and his friends, their parents discover that they were not at the movie. To cover up their indiscretion and avoid being grounded, the girls concoct a story that Emma was attacked and nearly raped by a stranger, only to be rescued by Anna and Mariah. When their parents pursue the case with the police and the community, the girls fall deeper into their lies until the truth is finally revealed.

Attempted Rape • Honesty • Interpersonal Relations • Police

Shaw, Susan

Safe. New York: Dutton Children's Books, 2007. 208 p. ISBN: 9780525478294. YALSA Quick Picks. *MJ*

Even though the perpetrator was caught and sent to prison, thirteen-year-old Tracy cannot recover from her fear after she is raped and left for dead by the older brother of one of her classmates. Even though she tries to convince her loyal friends, her loving father, and her therapist that she is OK, Tracy is nearly unable to leave the house and retreats into a solitary world. As she finds a passion for playing the piano and a solace in Eileen Spinelli poems, Tracy seeks to heal and find the sense of safety she has lost.

Psychic Trauma • Mother • Friendship • Family

Williams-Garcia, Rita

Every Time a Rainbow Dies. New York: HarperCollins, 2001. 166 p. ISBN: 9780688162450; 9780064473033pa. YALSA Best Books. *JS*

Sixteen-year-old Thulani witnesses a brutal rape that happens in the alley below the Brooklyn apartment where he lives with his self-absorbed older brother and sister-in-law and steps up to help the injured victim, Ysa. Trying to get to know her even though she turns him away, Thulani finds himself freed for the first time in three years from his grief over his mother's death after she returned home to Jamaica. With his persistence, Thulani and Ysa are able to share secrets as they both find healing and different paths into their futures.

Romance • Brothers • Secrets

Gangs

Coburn, Jake

Prep. New York: Dutton Books, 2003. 182 p. ISBN: 9780525471356; 9780142403075pa. YALSA Best Books. *JS*

At their Manhattan prep school, Nick finds out that the younger brother of his best friend and the girl he loves, Kris, is being threatened by a gang. To help out, Nick gets in touch with his friends from his days as a legendary graffiti artist but gets drawn into the gang circle he has been trying to avoid. Facing difficult memories of his past, including the knifing incident that nearly killed his friend Kodak, Nick tries to rise above the threat of violence that now surrounds him.

Prep Schools • Violence • Friendship • Brothers

Myers, Walter Dean

Autobiography of My Dead Brother. New York: Harper Tempest Amistad, 2005. 224 p. ISBN: 9780060582913; 9780060582937pa; YALSA Best Books. YALSA Popular Paperbacks. *JS*

Bonded as blood brothers since childhood, fifteen-year-old Jessie has always looked up to older friend Rise, as they worked together with their other friend and musician, C.J. in their social club called the Counts. When Rise starts pulling away and dealing drugs, Jessie tries to make sense of the changes in his friend as he uses his artistic talent to create a pictorial biography of Rise that helps him cope when tragedy strikes.

African Americans • Artists • Best Friends • Death • Coming-of-Age

Randle, Kristen D.

Breaking Rank. New York: Morrow Junior Books, 1999. 201 p. ISBN: 9780688162436. YALSA Best Books. *S*

Everyone thinks she is crazy and possibly in great danger when seventeen-year-old Casey Willardson decides to tutor Thomas Fairbairn, who has just transferred to the honors program, even though this goes against the rules of the outsider group called the Clan, of which he as a member. As the pair get to know each other, Casey is impressed by Thomas's love of learning, especially about the classical philosophers, and they both learn that labels can lead us to judge people negatively, especially because people are not always what they seem. As they fall deeply in love with each other, Thomas must deal not only with expulsion from the clan when he fails to treat Casey as a sex object and consummate their relationship, but also with the resulting violent clash between the Clan and the school jocks.

Tutors • Romance • Prejudice

Stork, Francisco X.

Behind the Eyes. New York: Dutton, 2006. 256 p. ISBN: 9780525477358. *JS*

On the gritty streets of El Paso, sixteen-year-old Hector's brother Filiberto is murdered in a gang war by the leaders of the Discipulos when they disagree about a girl. After he exacts his revenge, Hector is given a second chance to live his dream of going to college when a social worker gets him into the Furman juvenile detention center to protect him from the gang as he serves his time. At school, Hector makes friends with his roommate X-Lax and the school bully Sanson as he excels, even winning an award for an essay that honors his father. Soon Hector's past catches up with him when a Discipulos gang member shows up at Furman intent on murder, forcing Hector to once again find the help he needs to save himself.

Mexican Americans • Death • Violence • Prisons • Coming-of-Age

Strasser, Todd

If I Grow Up. New York: Simon & Schuster Books for Young Readers, 2009. 240 p. ISBN: 9781416925231. *S*

DeShawn has worked to do well in school and stay out of Douglass Disciples, the gang that rules his housing project. As he becomes a young adult, however, the lure of fast money draws DeShawn into the gang as the pressure of supporting his pregnant girlfriend and the rest of his family becomes too much. Despite the influence of his determined grandmother as well as a concerned policeman and a teacher who try to help him, DeShawn falls deeper into the gang until a murderous plot within the gang's ranks forces him to face the consequences of the lifestyle he has chosen.

Violence • Poverty • Inner City • African Americans • Street Life

Van Diepen, Allison

Snitch. New York: Simon Pulse, 2007. 297 p. ISBN: 9781416950301pa. YALSA Quick Picks. *J*

Julia DiVino and her best friend made a pact back in seventh grade never to get involved with a gang, a promise that they have kept despite being students at a high school where gangs are ever present. New student Eric arrives and immediately joins the Crips. Julia gets involved with the gang when she falls for Eric and then warns him of an impending attack by a rival gang. After she is badly beaten for being a snitch, her friends are afraid to be around her, and the Crips girls get revenge, meaning that Julia owes them a debt of honor that must be paid. Now involved in what she thought she could avoid, Julia enters a world of drugs, sex, and violence. In this new life, Julia sees a very dim future, especially when Eric shows his true colors and starts lying to her.

Friendship • Interpersonal Attraction • Revenge • Street Life

Zephaniah, Benjamin

Gangsta Rap. New York: Bloomsbury Children's Books, 2004. 200 p. ISBN: 9781582348865pa. Teens Top Ten. *J*

Fifteen-year-old Ray and his best friends Prem and Tyrone are passionate about hip-hop music and little else. The three are expelled from school and then jailed for getting into a fight. With the help of a former headmaster and Manga Man, an older Jamaican who owns a music shop, the trio gets into a progressive performing arts school and form a band, the Positive Negatives. When the boys find success and sign a record deal, they attract the attention of a rival band. Spurred on, the two groups have some violent battles, but soon come to regret their actions.

Rap Music • *Prison* • *School* • *Violence* • *England* • *Success*

13

14

15

16

17

18

19

20

21

22

23

Chapter 20

Surviving Abuse

Abuse comes in many forms, including physical, emotional, and sexual, and it is perpetrated on adolescents from a variety of sources, including parents, teachers, and friends. Abuse affects a teen's normal patterns of physical, emotional, spiritual, and sexual development. To protect themselves, teens develop a variety of coping mechanisms. For those who survive the pains inflicted on them by abuse, therapies and the development of supportive relationships can provide hope for the future as they resolve their traumatic memories. The books listed in this chapter deal with the painful realities of abuse. Teens who are sexually abused by parents, extended family members, or other adults such as teachers must deal with the negative consequences of the abuse. Other teens find their own ways to overcome the negative consequences of emotional or verbal abuse inflicted on them by family or others.

General Abuse

Chaltas, Thalia

Because I Am Furniture. New York: Viking Children's Books, 2009. 368 p. ISBN: 9780670062980. *J*

> With her mother standing by in complete denial, high school freshman Anke, unlike her older siblings, Darren and Yaicha, is the only one to escape her father's physical and sexual abuse. Feeling conflicting emotions of relief that her father has left her alone but jealousy for the attention her siblings get since their father hardly acknowledges her existence, Anke feels invisible and is unable to speak up. Despite her father's wishes to the contrary, she joins the volleyball team and on the court finds the ability to make herself heard and the courage to confront her father.

> *Sexual Abuse • Guilt • Family Problems • Novels in Verse*

Galante, Cecilia

Hershey Herself. New York: Aladdin Paperbacks, 2008. 330 p. ISBN: 9781416954637pa.
MJ

> After her mother's boyfriend beats up both her and her mother, eighth-grader Hershey and her family, including her baby sister Ella, move into a battered-women's shelter. Adjusting to her new home, Hershey finds strength in her friendship with a Colombian woman, Lupé, who teaches her to play the piano.

> *Moving • Mother and Daughter • Friendship*

Grover, Lorie Ann

Hold Me Tight. New York: Margaret K. McElderry Books, 2005. 336 p. ISBN: 9780689852480; 9781416967538pa. *M*

> When, during the Thanksgiving holiday, her father announces he is leaving, twelve-year-old Essie's mother, who is pregnant and unable to work, falls into a depression and struggles to care for Essie and her seven-year-old brother, Dale. Things get worse when a friend of Essie's is kidnapped, and Mr. Paul, a friend of the family, assaults Essie. Supported by those around them, the family struggles to remake their identity.

> *Sexual Abuse • Family Problems • Kidnapping • Schools • Abandonment • Novels in Verse*

Hernandez, David

Suckerpunch. New York: HarperTeen, 2008. 217 p. ISBN: 9780061173301. YALSA Best Books; YALSA Quick Picks. *S*

> Seventeen-year-old Marcus "Nub" Mendoza, who lost his finger in a rollerblading accident, is very quiet, just the opposite of his younger brother Enrique, who is an outgoing ladies' man. After being physically abused by their father, Enrique has dealt with his pain by turning to fighting and dating lots of girls. Marcus gets stoned. They are both shocked to find that their mother is considering letting their father come home. Because of this new revelation, the two, along with Enrique's girlfriend and one of Marcus's friends, who is dealing with his own parental problems, set out on a road trip to hunt down their father and get the vengeance they feel they deserve.

> *Child Abuse • Family Relationships • Hispanic Americans • Coming-of-Age*

Hopkins, Ellen

Identical. New York: Margaret K. McElderry Books, 2008. 565 p. ISBN: 9781416950059. (aud). YALSA Quick Picks; Teens Top Ten. *S*

> Sixteen year olds Kaeleigh and Raeanne are identical twins who have a seemingly perfect life, but reality holds dark secrets. Their alcoholic and drug-addicted father sexually abuses Kaeleigh and controls her entire life. While Kaeleigh binges and cuts herself to escape the pain, Raeanne reacts by seeking escape in sex and drugs. As Kaeleigh withdraws from her friends, including her best friend, Ian, who also loves her, the twins struggle to break through the secrets of their family life so they can face their own psychic injuries.

> *Family Problems • Emotional Problems • Sexual Abuse • Novels in Verse*

Hurwin, Davida Wills

Circle the Soul Softly. New York: Harper Collins, 2006. 169 p. ISBN: 9780060775056. *JS*

After her father dies from cancer, tenth-grader Kaitlyn "Katie" O'Connor finds herself in a new home and school in Los Angeles with a soon-to-be new stepfather. Looking forward to a new start, Katie soon finds it difficult to fit in with her new rich and often hostile classmates. Only feeling truly at home acting on the stage, Katie finds some relief when she gets into the school play, and it doesn't hurt that her fellow costar, David, is very cute. But when Katie becomes overwhelmed with the stresses of her mother's impending wedding and her challenging schoolwork, she begins to have vague nightmares. Finally, when she and David decide to have sex, Katie begins to realize her nightmares are repressed memories of the abuse she suffered from her father as a child. While her mother at first does not believe her stories, Katie is soon able to gain her support, as well as support from others around her, as she confronts her past.

Child Abuse • Incest • Memory • Blended Families

Jones, Patrick

Chasing Tail Lights. New York: Walker & Co., 2007. 304 p. ISBN: 9780802796288; 9780802797629pa. *S*

With her father dead, her oldest brother Robert imprisoned for life, and an alcoholic mother who looks the other way, seventeen-year-old Christy Mallory lives in constant fear of her brother Ryan's sexual abuse. Watching the cars go past from her vantage point at the top of a bridge, Christy wants nothing more than to follow them out of town, although she knows there is no money to provide her the typical escape routes, such as attending college. With little self-esteem to build on, Christy finds hope through a book her English teacher has recommended. When a suicide attempt gets Christy the therapy she needs, she is finally able, with the help of her three friends Anne, Glen, and Terrel, as well as her younger brother and ten-year-old niece, to find the support and courage to confront her abuser and come to terms with his betrayals.

Sexual Abuse • Drug Dealers • Family Problems • Brothers • Poverty • Emotional Problems • Incest • Rape • Coming-of-Age

Klass, David

You Don't Know Me. New York: Frances Foster Books, 2001. 262 p. ISBN: 9780374387068; 9780064473781pa. YALSA Best Books. *J*

Since he was left alone to be abused by his mother's fiancé who lives with them, fourteen-year-old John has escaped into his own head. After John has a disastrous date with beautiful Gloria, he acts out and verbally abuses his algebra teacher, resulting in a suspension that sends John home to face vicious beatings that almost kill him. However, it is this event that reveals the abuse and allows John to see that he is liked by his classmates and the girl of his dreams.

Child Abuse • Single Parents • Musicians

Knowles, Johanna

Lessons from a Dead Girl. Cambridge, MA: Candlewick Press, 2007. 215 p. ISBN: 9780763632793. YALSA Quick Picks. *J*

> In fifth grade popular and beautiful Leah Green initiates make-out sessions with plain, quiet Lanie that she insists are practice sessions, readying them for their future boyfriends. Although they thought they would be best friends forever, Lanie is uncomfortable with the experiences, and when their intimacy finally stops, Leah holds the secret of their liaisons over Lanie's head. It is not until a phone call reports that Leah's self-destructive behavior has finally lead to her death that sixteen-year-old Lanie begins to uncover the truth that lead Leah to behave in the way she did, while at the same time she has to deal with her own guilt as she tries to figure out what her experiences mean for her own sexuality.

Sexual Abuse • Death • Guilt • Fatal Traffic Accidents • Interpersonal Relations • Self-Discovery

Konigsburg, E. L.

Silent to the Bone. New York: Atheneum Books for Young Readers, 2000. 261 p. ISBN: 9780786231690; 9780689836022pa; (aud). YALSA Best Books; School Library Journal Best Books. *MJ*

> When baby Nikki is rushed to the hospital where she slips into a coma, the British nanny, Vivian, claims that it was her brother, thirteen-year-old Branwell "Bran" Zamborska, who dropped her on her head. Now in a juvenile behavioral center, Bran refuses to speak. Ashamed by the responses he had when he saw Vivian naked in the bathtub after she knowingly left the door open, Bran has been unable to tell his parents that Vivian is abusing the baby. It is not until his best friend, Connor Kane, creates a way to communicate with Bran through flashcards that the truth is uncovered.

Emotional Problems • Traffic Accidents • Remarriage • Brothers • Sisters • Blended Families

Lynch, Chris

Sins of the Fathers. New York: Harper Tempest, 2006. 240 p. ISBN: 9780060740375. *MJ*

> Thirteen-year-old Drew is worried that his friend Hector might be suffering sexual abuse after Hector retreats into a disturbing silence and starts taking large doses of aspirin after a new young priest with unconventional religious opinions arrives at their Catholic school. Standing by with their other friend Skitz, who may soon be expelled from school, the boys try to support each other as they realize that they must take personal responsibility to stand up to the things that are happening to them.

Friendship • Sex Crimes • Sexual Abuse • Catholic Schools

Moore, Peter

Caught in the Act. New York: Viking, 2005. 256 p. ISBN: 9780670059904. *J*

> Ethan Lederer is trying to hold his life together and not disappoint his parents despite the fact that he can't keep up with his sophomore honors classes. Meeting exotic Lydia, Ethan is entranced by the risks she takes, but when Lydia becomes manipulative and dangerous, even going so far as to threaten a teacher with sex-

ual harassment charges to get Ethan a good grade, he realizes the problem and tries to break things off.

Mental Illness • Dysfunctional Families • Family Relationships • Dishonesty

Oates, Joyce Carol

Freaky Green Eyes. New York: Harper Tempest, 2003. 341 p. ISBN: 9780066237596; 9780064473484pa. *J*

Fifteen-year-old Francesca "Franky" Pierson's father, Reid, a former football hero and popular sportscaster, is controlling and abusive. Escaping into her alter ego, Freaky Green Eyes, she is able to survive the violence and defend herself from being raped. One day her mother and her mother's male friend disappear. When they are discovered murdered, Franky must find the courage to uncover the truth and deal with the conflicting feelings she has about her parents.

Fathers • Missing Persons • Family Violence • Emotional Abuse • Coming-of-Age

Prose, Francine

Touch. New York: HarperTeen, 2009. 272 p. ISBN: 9780061375170. *J*

Maisie has been friends with Kevin, Chris, and Shakes since preschool, but after spending eighth grade in Wisconsin living with her mother, she returns for ninth grade with well-developed breasts, and the boys are awkward around her. Soon the three boys take advantage of her and explore her newly developed body in the back of the school bus. Rumors spread that Maisie lets guys touch her for money. When Maisie's stepmother finds out and sues the school board, Maisie wonders if things will ever work out with her friends, but the truth of the situation is hard to come by as Maisie must deal with the consequences of her actions.

Sexual Harassment • Family Problems • Best Friends

Scott, Elizabeth

Living Dead Girl. New York: Simon Pulse, 2008. 170 p. ISBN: 9781416960591; 9781416960607pa; (aud). YALSA Best Books; YALSA Quick Picks. *JS*

Abducted at age ten, Alice spends five years being sexually and emotionally abused by her captor Ray, believing that her family is in danger if she leaves and that there is no one who will help her. As her body matures, she knows that Ray will kill her when she can no longer satisfy him, and her suspicions are confirmed when Ray presses her to help him find a new victim and train her to his needs. In the process, she meets a needy teen boy and a police officer, and both want to help her.

Kidnapping • Sexual Abuse

Shaw, Susan

Black-Eyed Suzie. Honesdale, PA: Boyds Mills Press, 2002. 167 p. ISBN: 9781563977299; 9781590785331pa. *M*

> To protect herself from her mother's physical abuse, twelve-year-old Suzie retreats to a catatonic state, spending days crouched in a chair without eating, sleeping, or talking. When a concerned uncle gets her admitted to a mental hospital, it is there, with the help of her therapist, that Suzie is able to confront the trauma and find the courage to save her older sister.

Mental Illness • Child Abuse

Shaw, Susan

The Boy from the Basement. New York: Dutton Children's Books, 2004. 198 p. ISBN: 9780525472230; 9780142405468pa. YALSA Quick Picks. *MJ*

> After spending years imprisoned in his basement by his violent father, twelve-year-old Charlie escapes and is placed in a loving foster home. He finds it hard to feel safe in the outside world and still longs to be back with his parents. Charlie stays with his foster parents, and, with the help of a psychiatrist, he works through the trauma.

Child Abuse • Foster Care

Springer, Nancy

Somebody. New York: Holiday House, 2009. 117 p. ISBN: 9780823420995. *J*

> Overweight fifteen-year-old Sherica lives a secretive life, constantly moving around the country with her father and her older brother. In each new place, she is forced to remake herself with a new name and hairstyle. In her newest town, Sherica finds she is fed up with secrets and decides she is going to find out about her past. When she goes to the library so she can do research on the computers, she meets Mason, who helps her to discover that her father is lying and had kidnapped her and her brother. Armed with this new knowledge, Sherica tries to contact her mother, but as she tries to reclaim her identity, she must come to terms with what the future holds for every member of her family.

Kidnapping • Father and Daughter • Brothers • Sisters • Moving • Emotional Abuse

Tashjian, Janet

Fault Line. New York: Henry Holt, 2003. 248 p. ISBN: 9780805072006; 9780805080636pa; (aud). *S*

> Seventeen-year-old aspiring comic Becky meets fellow comic Kip Costello when they are performing at the same club. She thinks she has found the perfect boyfriend. Soon the two are inseparable, but when Kip's adoration for her becomes controlling and so violent that it lands her in the hospital, Becky must decide whether or not she can stay with him, while he works through his own issues with an abusive family.

Dating Violence • Boyfriends

Werlin, Nancy

The Rules of Survival. New York: Dial Books, 2006. 272 p. ISBN: 9780803730014; 9780142410714pa; (aud). YALSA Best Books; YALSA Quick Picks; School Library Journal Best Books. *S*

> Along with his older sister Callie, seventeen-year-old Matthew Walsh shelters their younger sister Emmy from the abuse of Nikki, their unpredictable, psychotic mother. With their distant father and apathetic aunt unwilling to help, Matthew sees some hope in their neighbor Murdoch, who, because of his own violent past, decides to get involved. With Murdoch's help, Matthew is able to push the adults around him to do the right thing so the children can survive.
>
> *Brothers • Sisters • Parent and Child • Dysfunctional Families • Child Abuse • Mental Illness • Single Mothers • Father-Separated Families • Emotional Problems*

Wiess, Laura

Such a Pretty Girl. New York: Pocket Books/MTV Books, 2007. 224 p. ISBN: 9781416521839pa. YALSA Best Books; YALSA Quick Picks. *J*

> Fifteen-year-old Meredith had hoped to finish high school in safety, with her father who abused her, as well as other boys and girls, locked away for nine years. But when he is released early for good behavior, her dreams are shattered. While Meredith is filled with fear, her mother is ecstatic about his return and plans to have another child with him. Despite the fact he is under strict orders not to be alone with his daughter, it becomes apparent that he has not changed. It is only with the support of her paraplegic friend, Andy, and the help of her grandmother who is working to get custody, that Meredith can take steps to ensure that neither she nor any other child will be hurt by her father again.
>
> *Father and Daughter • Sexual Abuse • Grandmothers • Disabilities • Neighbors • Friendship • Dysfunctional Families • Psychic Trauma*

Williams, Lori Aurelia

When Kambia Elaine Flew in from Neptune. New York: Simon & Schuster, 2000. 246 p. ISBN: 9780689824685; 9780689845932pa; (aud). YALSA Best Books. *M*

> Twelve-year-old Shayla Dubois is shocked when she finds that her fifteen-year-old sister, Pia, has run away after she has an argument with their mother over Pia's relationship with an older man. But as Shayla gets to know her new neighbor Kambia, who weaves strange magical stories that cover up the sexual abuse Kambia has been suffering, she realizes that sometimes people have to make wrong choices to find out what is right.
>
> *Child Abuse • Incest • African Americans*

Zarr, Sara

Sweethearts: A Novel. New York: Little, Brown, 2008. 217 p. ISBN: 9780316014557; 9780316014564pa; (aud). YALSA Best Books. *S*

> Seventeen-year-old Jenna's life has changed significantly from the time she was overweight and only had one friend, a boy named Cameron. Now popular and slim, her life is threatened when Cameron returns, even though she had believed him to be dead. Facing the past and dealing with the memories of incidents relating to Cameron's cruel and abusive father, Jenna must develop a whole new identity that integrates her past and her present.

> *Bullies and Bullying* • *Popularity* • *Coping* • *Memory* • *Child Abuse* • *Friendship* • *Weight Control* • *Coming-of-Age*

Abuse by a Teacher

Cummings, Priscilla

What Mr. Mattero Did. New York: Dutton Children's Books, 2005. 192 p. ISBN: 9780525476214; 9780142408568pa. *M*

> To get their class schedules changed, seventh-graders Jenna, Suzanne, and Claire make accusations of sexual abuse against their teacher, Mr. Mattero. Even though they are surprised when everyone believes Mr. Mattero is guilty and their lies force the teacher to leave the school, the girls decide to stand behind what they said. At home, Mr. Mattero's family, including his eighth-grade daughter Melody, suffers and begins to fall apart when the media gets involved and rumors escalate. Soon Suzanne and Claire begin to waver in their resolve, and the truth comes out.

> *Teacher-Student Relationships* • *Dishonesty* • *Sex Crimes*

Frank, E. R.

Friction: A Novel. New York: Atheneum Books for Young Readers, 2003. 197 p. ISBN: 9780689853845; 9780689853852pa; (aud). YALSA Best Books. *M*

> Twelve-year-old Alex enjoys attending the Forest Alternative School. Playing soccer, having the best coach, and attending classes with Tim, her best friend, make things perfect; that is, until new girl Stacy arrives. Telling tales that show sex in everything, even in the way classmate Simon feels about Alex, Stacy starts to make Alex second-guess Simon's motives, even though Alex does not believe anything Stacy says. Giving in to the peer pressure, Alex becomes confused and scared and can't open up about her feelings, even to her parents. But as things come to light, everyone realizes that Stacy is just acting out her own pain as Alex learns how to deal with the false accusations and define her personal boundaries.

> *Teacher-Student Relationships* • *Sexual Abuse* • *Family Secrets* • *Sexuality* • *Coming-of-Age*

Levchuk, Lisa

Everything Beautiful in the World. New York: Farrar, Straus & Giroux, 2008. 203 p. ISBN: 9780374322380. *S*

> Seventeen-year-old Edna's mother is diagnosed with cancer, leaving a fight they were having unresolved when she enters the hospital. Unable to go anywhere near her mother and with her father concentrating on his job and getting his wife well, Edna finds that she can do what she wants. This freedom leads to her having an affair with her art teacher, Mr. Howland. When Mr. Howland's marriage breaks up and his neediness scares her, Edna is finally able, with the help of a psychiatrist, to confront the emotions that led to her affair.

> *Teacher-Student Relationships • Mother-Separated Families • Cancer • Emotional Problems • Coming-of-Age*

Lyga, Barry

Boy Toy. Boston: Houghton Mifflin, 2007. 410 p. ISBN: 9780618723935; 9780547076348pa; YALSA Best Books. *S*

> Eighteen-year-old Josh Mendel suffers trauma from the time he endured sexual abuse at the hands of his seventh-grade teacher, Eve Sherman. Still dealing with the consequences, Josh has spent five years not speaking to his friend Rachel after he was sexually inappropriate with her and his own abuse was revealed, sending Eve to jail. Before graduation, Rachel reaches out to him, and Josh is able to come to terms with his past as he reveals all the details of his experience.

> *Teacher-Student Relationships • Sexuality • Sex Crimes • Child Abuse • Coping • Baseball • Psychotherapy*

Maclean, Christine Kole

How It's Done. Woodbury, MN: Flux, 2006. 332 p. ISBN: 9780738710297; 9780738711638pa. *S*

> Raised in a strict fundamentalist Christian household, eighteen-year-old Grace rebels against her strict father's rules when she attends a lecture with friend Liv at a local college and meets Michael, an older professor, who sweeps her off her feet. Fearing that she might be pregnant, she gets engaged to Michael, but when Liv betrays her and a new boy catches her interest, Grace must decide what is the right thing to do as she learns where she fits in the world.

> *Teacher-Student Relationships • Self-Discovery • Christianity • Coming-of-Age*

McDaniel, Lurlene

Prey. New York: Delacorte Press, 2008. 196 p. ISBN: 9780385734530. YALSA Quick Picks. *JS*

> Handsome freshman Ryan Piccoli is drawn to the companionship of his thirty-year-old history teacher, Lori Settles, and the two become sexually involved. When the relationship becomes more than either of them bargained

for, Ryan must work through the situation as he deals with the suspicions and jealousy of his longtime friend Honey.

Teacher-Student Relationships • Sexual Abuse • Sex Crimes • Emotional Problems

Nelson, R.A.

Teach Me. New York: Razorbill, 2005. 264 p. ISBN: 9781595140845; 9781595140852pa. *S*

Feeling out of place in her small Alabama town, high school senior Carolina "Nine" finds a kindred spirit in her English teacher, Mr. Mann, who shares her obsession with Emily Dickinson. But when Mr. Mann initiates a physical relationship that is consummated on her eighteenth birthday and then dumps her for another woman, Nine is obsessed with finding out what happened. Confiding in her best friend, Schuyler, Nine commits some childish acts of revenge, but in the end she must learn from her mistakes and come to terms with her despair.

Teacher-Student Relationships • Breaking Up • Revenge • Stalking

Oates, Joyce Carol

Sexy. New York: Harper Tempest, 2005. 263 p. ISBN: 9780060541491; 9780060541514pa. *S*

Shy sixteen-year-old Darren Flynn is uncertain about how to deal with the attention his good looks garner him from both men and women. But after an innocent encounter with his English teacher, Mr. Tracy, things become even more complicated as rumors begin to surface that Mr. Tracy is gay. When some of Darren's swimming teammates implicate the teacher as a child molester to get revenge when their friend Jimmy Kovaks gets kicked off the varsity team for plagiarizing, Darren refuses to participate. But as the school and police get involved, Mr. Tracy turns to Darren for help, and he must deal with his situation.

Athletes • Sexuality • Teacher-Student Relationships • Revenge

Abuse by a Boyfriend

Dessen, Sarah

Dreamland: A Novel. New York: Viking, 2000. 250 p. ISBN: 9780670891221; 9780142401750pa; (aud). YALSA Best Books. *JS*

Sixteen-year-old Caitlin's sister Cass has run away with her boyfriend. Caitlin's family is struggling with this ordeal. Making the cheerleading squad does little to garner the right kind of attention from her mother, and Caitlin's life begins to spiral out of control as she falls in love with dynamic Rogerson Briscoe. Drawn into his world of drugs and sex, Caitlin is dominated and physically abused by him. When things escalate out of control and he beats her in public, Caitlin realizes she has no self-respect and must find a way to rebuild her life and identity.

Dating Violence • Emotional Abuse • Mental Illness

Flinn, Alexandra

Breathing Underwater. New York: HarperCollins, 2001. 224 p. ISBN: 9780060291983. YALSA Best Books; YALSA Quick Picks. *J*

13

> High school sophomore Nick Andreas has everything. Finding the girl of his dreams in Caitlin, he thinks everything is perfect, but Nick has only had the example of his abusive father as a pattern of how to treat a lady, so he bullies and beats Caitlin. When his former friends turn against him and Caitlin takes out a restraining order, Nick must deal with his problems as he is forced to take anger management classes. Nick must overcome his past and realize the depths to which he has sunk as he learns important lessons about self-control.

14

15

Sequel: *Diva*. New York: Harper Tempest, 2006. 272 p. ISBN: 9780060568436; 9780060568467pa. *JS*

> Struggling to find herself after leaving an abusive relationship with boyfriend Nick, Caitlin McCourt is trying to come to terms with her body image as she explores her talent for singing opera by trying out for a spot at Miami High School for the Performing Arts. Dealing with a mother who wants to remain young and is having an affair with a married man, Caitlin finds friendship with a gay classmate, Sean, at school. After patching things up with Nick, who has reformed through therapy, Caitlin is accepted to a summer opera program in New York.

16

17

> *Dating Violence • Anger • Child Abuse • Father and Son • Self-Confidence • New Students • Blogs • Family Problems • Diaries*

18

Jones, Patrick

Things Change. New York: Walker, 2004. 216 p. ISBN: 9780802789013; 9780802777461pa. YALSA Quick Picks. *JS*

19

> Sixteen-year-old Johanna has always worked hard to please her controlling parents and is now a straight-A student with near perfect SAT scores, but she has never been a true success socially. So when handsome senior Paul, whom she has admired from afar, begins to notice her and they start dating, Johanna is ecstatic. As she and Paul become closer, he becomes increasingly possessive and insulting, and soon his aggressive attacks turn violent. With his promises to change, Johanna lets her heart win out over her head and takes him back, but the abuse continues, her grades drop, and she loses the trust of her parents and best friend because of her lies. In the end, Johanna must regain her dignity as she struggles to gain the courage to end the relationship.

20

21

> *Gifted Teenagers • Dating Violence • Emotional Problems • Mother and Daughter*

Stratton, Allan

23

Leslie's Journal. Buffalo, NY: Annick Press, 2000. 196 p. ISBN: 9781550376654; 9781550376647pa. *JS*

> Supported only by her friend Katie, high school sophomore Leslie pours out her pain into an English journal that her teacher promises he will never read. Unable to communicate with her mother and with her dad now living

with his girlfriend, Leslie becomes obsessed with her older boyfriend, Jason. After Jason gets drunk and rapes her, his behavior turns increasingly abusive, and while Leslie tries to leave him, he stalks and threatens her until she fears for her life. Her small hope of help is dashed when a new English teacher reads the journal and reports the abuse, but the school principal takes Jason's side, leaving Leslie to take matters into her own hands.

Date Rape • Dating Violence • Diaries

Wiess, Laura

How It Ends. New York: Pocket Books/MTV Books, 2009. 368 p. ISBN: 9781416546634pa. *JS*

Hanna has wanted to catch the eye of cool, guitar-playing Seth since sophomore year, but when she finally does, their hurtful, critical relationship is not what she expected. Trying to understand Seth's treatment of her, Hanna reaches out to Helen, her terminally ill neighbor. While fulfilling her school community service requirement, she is able to find wisdom as she listens to an audio book with Helen, and secrets about Helen's past are revealed.

Intergenerational Relations • Community Service

Chapter 21

Taking Drugs and Drinking Alcohol

Many teens often ignore the dangers of drug and alcohol use, causing them to develop serious substance abuse problems. Adolescents turn to drugs and alcohol for a variety of reasons, including making themselves feel happier or more confident, to serve as a numbing agent during or after stress, because they feel socially isolated or rejected, or they may want to be part of a group in which this behavior is the norm. When drug and alcohol use becomes so consuming that it overtakes one's life and interferes with normal social and emotional functioning, a teen must deal with the negative consequences of substance abuse. The books listed in this chapter deal with the issues that teens face when dependence on drugs or alcohol has an impact on their lives. Dealing with their own dependence, as well as abuse by friends or family, teens must navigate the behavioral and relationship problems that are associated with drug and alcohol use. For some groups of teens, such as athletes, there are other problems they must cope with, including the pressures to perform at peak levels, which lead them into the dangerous world of drugs.

Brooks, Kevin

Candy. New York: Scholastic, 2005. 368 p. ISBN: 9780439683272; 9780439683289pa. *JS*
Suburban teen Joe falls in love at first sight with Candy outside a London train station after a doctor's appointment. But something is not quite right, and Joe soon finds that Candy is a heroin addict with a terrifying pimp, Iggy, who supplies her with the drugs. Joe knows he has to get involved and try to get her off the streets, so he spends time with her and even nurses Candy through her withdrawal symptoms. His actions draw him into her world of danger and violence.

Drug Abuse • *First Love* • *Violence*

Coburn, Jake

LoveSick. New York: Dutton Children's Books, 2005. 240 p. ISBN: 9780525473831; 9789990835656pa. YALSA Best Books. *S*
Ted is an alcoholic who has been sober for ninety days after the court ordered him to attend Alcoholics Anonymous following the drunk-driving accident that wrecked his knee and forced him to lose his scholarship and his future plans. Erica

is a bulimic who lives on Park Avenue with a father who will do anything to try and cure her. With the help of friend Michael, Erica's father convinces Ted to spy on Erica's eating in exchange for another scholarship. Ted and Erica bond over their own addictions and soon fall in love. When Ted tells Erica the truth about his arrangement, their relationship is threatened.

College • Drunk Driving • Bulimia • Alcoholism • Addiction • Secrets • Drinking • Eating Disorders • Father and Daughter • Athletes • Coming-of-Age

Cohn, Rachel

You Know Where to Find Me. New York: Simon & Schuster Books for Young Readers, 2008. 204 p. ISBN: 9780689878596; 9780689878602pa. *JS*

Consumed by grief when her cousin Laura commits suicide with an overdose of prescription drugs, overweight high school senior Miles starts withdrawing from life and taking prescription pills. Miles struggles with her addiction as she searches for herself and tries to answer tough questions about life and death. When her absentee father shows up to look after her when her mother runs off with her boyfriend to London and she finds herself falling in love with one of her best male friends, Miles is finally able to make some sense of the world and figure out where she belongs.

Cousins • Shyness • Suicide • Drug Abuse • Family • Depression • Family • Self-Esteem

Coy, John

Crackback. New York: Scholastic Press, 2005. 208 p. ISBN: 9780439697330; 9780439697347pa. YALSA Quick Picks. *JS*

Things look great for sophomore football star Miles, who is obsessed with the game and believes that his team has a great chance of winning his junior-year season. But when his favorite coach resigns, Miles can't deal with the dictatorship the new coach creates. Even though Miles is struggling to deal with school and football and is also struggling at home with his angry father, he refuses the steroids his friend Zach tries to give him. Through his trials, Miles begins to learn that life is almost always complicated. He uncovers the secret that drives his father, and with the help of an interesting girl and the second-string football players, he realizes that there is more to life than the game he loves.

Football • Father and Son • Football • Steroids • Drug Use

Deuker, Carl

Gym Candy. Boston: Houghton Mifflin, 2007. 313 p. ISBN: 9780618777136; 9780547076317pa. *JS*

Feeling the pressure to live up to and surpass the pro career of his football player father, Mick Johnson is devastated when, during an important game, he is taken down just before he can make a goal. Mick turns to steroids when he realizes that weights, vitamins, and protein powder are not enough to give him the muscles he thinks he needs. The muscle-bulking effects of the drugs allow him to start breaking records, and his father is very proud, but the side effects of acne, paranoia, and depression lead to Mick's breakdown. When he tries to commit suicide, the truth comes out, and Mick is put in counseling. But even with this help, he is not sure he will ever be able to stay away from the drugs.

Drug Use • Football • Suicide • Father and Son

Harazin, S. A.

Blood Brothers. New York: Delacorte Press, 2007. 224 p. ISBN: 9780385733649. YALSA Quick Picks. *S*

When his popular, class valedictorian friend Joey ends up in the hospital on a respirator after he shows up high on drugs and is so violent that he must fight him off, seventeen-year-old Clay is uncertain what happened to make his friend behave in that way. Even while dealing with his own disjointed life, Clay watches over his sick friend during his work at the hospital as a medical technician, a job that he loves. Soon it is apparent that it is Clay who must uncover the identity of the person who gave his friend the PCP that resulted in his violent behavior.

Friendship • Drug Abuse • Coma Patients • Jealousy • Self-Esteem • Diary Novel

Hopkins, Ellen

Crank. New York: Simon Pulse, 2004. 537 p. ISBN: 9780689865190pa; (aud). YALSA Quick Picks. *S*

Sixteen-year-old Kristina has a comfortable home with a caring mother, but after a visit to her estranged, drug-addicted father, where she is introduced to methamphetamines by slick-talking Adam, Kristina finds herself morphing into her newly created, bolder alter ego, Bree. Bree succumbs to the attraction of the drugs, and upon returning home, she finds guys who help her to get high without shame. Soon she is fully addicted and has lost her top grades at school and all her stable friends, but when she starts selling drugs for the Mexican Mafia and a brutal date rape leaves her scarred and pregnant, she must figure out how to change her now-uncertain future.

Sequel: *Glass.* New York: Margaret K. McElderry Books, 2007. 688 p. ISBN: 9781416940906; 9781416940913pa; (aud). *S*

Having overcome her meth addiction, Kristina is trying to get her life back on track by caring for her baby and studying for her GED. When the monotony of life becomes too much and Kristina finds herself depressed about her post-baby figure, she succumbs to the allure of the drugs once again and finds herself in an abusive relationship with two men who are also addicted. With her life once again out of her control, her mother kicks her out and gains custody of the baby. Kristina must deal with the permanent hold drugs have on her life as she tries to find the courage to live with the life-altering choices she has made.

Drug Abuse • Pregnancy • Addiction • Rape • Novels in Verse

Hyde, Catherine Ryan

The Year of My Miraculous Reappearance. New York: Alfred A. Knopf, 2007. 240 p. ISBN: 9780375832574; 9780375832611pa. *JS*

When her grandparents decide to take over the care of her three-year-old brother with Down syndrome, Bill, thirteen-year-old Cynnie is devastated. Having cared for Bill since her alcoholic mother, who goes through a steady stream of boyfriends, could not, Cynnie now finds herself at a loss and turns to drinking to ease the pain, soon becoming an alcoholic herself. She convinces Snake, a neighborhood boy she has known since childhood and who is trying now to reestablish their friendship, to help her kidnap Bill with the hope that they can start a new life together. However, a drunk-driving accident that nearly kills them all lands Cynnie with a court order to attend Alcoholics Anonymous.

Alcoholism • Brothers • Sisters • Down Syndrome • Grandparents • Kidnapping • Family Problems • Drunk Driving • Emotional Problems • Coming-of-Age

Lipsyte, Robert

Raiders Night. New York: Harper Tempest, 2006. 240 p. ISBN: 9780060599461; 9780060599485pa. YALSA Popular Paperbacks. *S*

As co-captain of the Nermount Raiders high school football team, Matt Rydek is being recruited by various Division One schools, and his future looks assured. But the pressure to win has left Matt addicted to his regular shots of steroids, and he can't deal with his developmentally disabled brother or his father, who lives out his dreams vicariously through Matt. Things come to a head when Matt witnesses his co-captain, Ramp, brutally sexually assaulting another player, Chris, in a hazing ritual. Matt helps to cover up the incident at first, but when Chris faces Ramp with a gun, he soon realizes that he must listen to his conscience and cooperate with the investigation that is launched.

Football • Steroids • Athletes • Drug Use • Father and Son • Rape

Lynn, Tracy

Rx. New York: Simon Pulse, 2005. 272 p. ISBN: 9781416911555pa. *S*

Desperate to succeed and get into a great college, seventeen-year-old Thyme is stressed and convinced that she has attention-deficit/hyperactivity disorder. When her parents don't believe her, she steals a bottle of Ritalin from her friend, Will, and finds extraordinary focus and control when she takes the pills. Hanging on to her newfound ability, Thyme becomes an addict and lies, steals, and then becomes a dealer to support her habit. It is not until a fellow student overdoses that she finally realizes the danger she is in.

Drug Use • Suicide • SAT • College

McDonnell, Nick

Twelve. New York: Grove Press, 2002. 244 p. ISBN: 9780802117175; 9780802140128pa. YALSA Quick Picks. *S*

Even though he does not drink or do drugs himself, seventeen-year-old high school dropout "White Mike," who lives on Manhattan's Upper East Side, deals drugs to the rich kids in the city. In the week following Christmas vacation, "White Mike" encounters a lot of different people during his business dealings, including gorgeous Sara Ludlow; debutante Jessica, who trades sex for drugs; Nana and Charlie, who are found dead one night; and rival drug dealer Lionel. Events culminate at a rich kids' New Year's Eve bash, where everyone must face the consequences of their lives of excess.

Drug Dealers • Sexuality • Prep Schools • Coming-of-Age

Murray, Jaye

Bottled Up: A Novel. New York: Dial Books, 2003. 220 p. ISBN: 9780803728974; 9780142402405pa. YALSA Best Books. *S*

Sixteen-year-old troublemaker Phillip "Pip," who drinks and smokes, is given an ultimatum by his school principal: he can either be expelled and the principal will call home or he can start attending classes and get counseling. Terrified of what his violent, alcoholic father and drug-addicted mother would do, Pip agrees to therapy. While at first he has no intention of changing, the process allows Pip to see the destructive path he is on, as he must arrive at sessions clean and sober. He is also able to see his six-year-old brother Mikey not as the burden he thought he was, but as someone he needs to help.

Brothers • Drug Abuse • Alcoholism • Violence

Scott, Elizabeth

Love You Hate You Miss You. New York: HarperTeen, 2009. 288 p. ISBN: 9780061122835; 9780061122859pa. *JS*

Remaining isolated after she returns from her stay in an alcohol treatment center, sixteen-year-old Amy is still trying to punish herself for her part in the death of her best friend, Julia. Looking back on experiences she shared with Julia, including partying, shoplifting, taking drugs, and having sex, Amy tries to heal.

Death • Alcoholism • Best Friends • Friendship

Tharp, Tim

The Spectacular Now. New York: Alfred A. Knopf, 2008. 304 p. ISBN: 9780375851797 (aud). YALSA Best Books. *S*

Abandoned by his father and neglected by his mother, high school senior Sutter Kelly is a party boy who is only looking for his next drink. Unable to make a commitment to a girl, especially when they want attention and make demands on him, Sutter inexplicably finds himself falling for outcast Aimee, whom he started dating as a project to reform her social status. But even Aimee's love may not be enough to reform Sutter.

Dating • Father-Deserted Families • Alcoholism • Drug Abuse

Van Diepen, Allison

Street Pharm. New York: Simon Pulse, 2006. 304 p. ISBN: 9781416911548pa. YALSA Quick Picks. *S*

When his father is put in prison, seventeen-year-old Ty Johnson finds himself dealing drugs to protect his father's territory. A bright businessman, Ty has the self-discipline and brains to face down the competition that comes from out-of-town dealers, but when he meets twenty-one-year-old single mother Alyse in class at their local alterative high school, things start to change. With Alyse in his life, his current line of business does not look as promising as he envisioned, but it is not until a drive-by shooting in which he is injured and his work is revealed to both his mother and Alyse that Ty decides living under the constant threat of losing his life and losing the people he loves is not worth the risk.

African Americans • Single Mothers • Drug Dealers • Violence • Street Life

Chapter 22

Coping with Death

That many adolescents will have to deal with death is one of the fundamental realities of life. When coping with death, teens go through varied emotions including fear, guilt, confusion, and sadness. This emotional upheaval affects teens in various ways and can lead to anything from minor behavioral problems to more serious problems such as eating disorders. Working through grief is a gradual process, and teens can find solace in various ways by finding support with friends or participating in religious rituals. The books listed in this chapter deal with the ways that teens approach the realities of death and dying. Learning to go on living after a parent or friend dies because of an unforeseen accident or after a lingering illness, teens must come to accept the deep and conflicting emotions that they feel. Teens with a terminal illness must face the fact that, despite heroic medical efforts, they will be called upon to face their own death. Others who cope with severe pain may lose the will to live, and they may consider suicide as a solution. Others must face life when they are left behind because a family member or friend has chosen to take their own life.

Death and Dying

Bunting, Eve

Blackwater. New York: Joanna Cotler Books, 1999. 146 p. ISBN: 9780060278380; 9780064408905pa; (aud). YALSA Quick Picks. *MJ*

Thirteen-year-old Brodie is touted as a hero when he jumps in a river and tries to save two drowning teens, Pauline and Otis. In the end, he must be rescued himself, and the others die. But when Brodie gets a note, he realizes someone knows the truth—he was partially responsible for the incident. In fact, at the river, where they have dammed-up a protected swimming hole, he was teaching his cousin, Alex, how to swim, and he saw Pauline, a girl he liked, with an older boy, Otis, sunning on a rock. Swimming over, he pulled Pauline into the water and when Otis pulled back, the two fell in. Sedated after the accident, Alex told a different version of the story, and now things are out of hand. Caught in a web of deceit, with the help of his supportive parents and his friend Hannah, Brodie must overcome his fear and admit his responsibility in the accident.

Deception • Secrets • Guilt

Crane, E. M.

Skin Deep. New York: Delacorte Press, 2008. 273 p. ISBN: 9780385734790; 9780440240341pa. *JS*

Sixteen-year-old Andrea Anderson is a plain, average, insecure girl who does not have any friends and is bullied by her angry mother. Stunned by the events when her homeroom teacher commits suicide in the teachers' lounge, Andrea reevaluates her life and starts pet-sitting a Saint Bernard for her eccentric neighbor, Honora, an artist who is battling cancer. A friendship grows between the two, which helps Andrea learn to love life and have confidence in herself.

Suicide • Dogs • Friendship • Self-Discovery • Single Parent • Coming-of-Age

Cummings, Priscilla

Red Kayak. New York: Dutton Children's Books, 2004. 209 p. ISBN: 9780525473176; 9780142405734pa. YALSA Best Books. *MJ*

Despite the resentment of his family and friends toward developers and tourists who threaten the fish they use for income, fifteen-year-old Brady develops a friendship with the rich neighboring summer family, the DiAngelos, and their toddler, Ben. But when Brady's friends, J.T. and Digger, enact a prank on the neighbor by drilling holes in the bottom of his kayak, the boys are shocked when Ben drowns in the boat, despite Brady's best efforts to save him. Racked with fear and guilt, the boys are unable to tell the truth, but as the evidence comes to light, Brady must come to terms with his responsibility and deal with his reluctance to rat on his friends.

Friendship • Guilt • Secrets • Grief • Loyalty

Freymann-Weyr, Garret

When I Was Older. Boston, MA: Houghton Mifflin, 2000. 167 p. ISBN: 9780618055456; 9780142300930pa. *J*

Fifteen-year-old Sophie Merdinger wishes she could stop time to preserve the memory of her younger brother, Erhart, who died from leukemia. With her parents' marriage broken after an affair, Sophie is struggling to forgive her father and throws herself into schoolwork and swimming to deal with the pain. When her mother starts dating a history professor, Sophie finds herself attracted to his good-looking seventeen-year-old son Francis, even though she has made every effort to avoid relationships. He understands her pain, having lost his mother nine years earlier. As she opens herself up to loving Francis, Sophie finds herself changing.

Brothers • Swimming • Romance • Father and Daughter • Loss

Grover, Lorie Ann

Loose Threads. New York: Margaret K. McElderry Books, 2002. 296 p. ISBN: 9780689844195; 9781416955627pa. *M*

Living with her mother, her grandmother Margie, and her great-grandmother Eula, seventh-grader Kay is devastated when Margie is diagnosed with breast cancer. Trying to deal with the turmoil this causes in her life and her grief, Kay works hard to deal with the other concerns of growing up, including school, friends, and boys.

Cancer • Grandmothers • Novels in Verse

Jocelyn, Marthe

Would You. New York: Wendy Lamb Books, 2008. 165 p. ISBN: 9780375837036; 9780739380086 pa; (aud). USBBY Outstanding International Books. *J*

Natalie's sister Claire is hit by a car when she runs into the street after an emotional breakup with her boyfriend. Claire suffers massive head trauma that leaves her in a coma with a swollen body hooked to tubes and machines. For the next twelve days, Natalie must face the guilt she feels about being alive. She must also deal with her family as her mother uses tranquilizers to numb the pain and her father angrily searches for someone to blame.

Sisters • Coma Patients • Traffic Accidents • Grief • Family Relationships

Kephart, Beth

House of Dance. New York: HarperTeen, 2008. 272 p. ISBN: 9780061429286. *J*

Fifteen-year-old Rosie Keith finds herself alone and struggling to deal with the care of her terminally ill grandfather after her mother is caught up in a disastrous affair with her married boss. Sorting through her grandfather's belongings, Rosie discovers more about his fascinating life filled with travel, music, and dancing. Trying to recapture the power of those memories one last time, Rosie plans an elaborate party and begins taking ballroom dancing lessons at a quirky studio so she can dance the night away and honor the love her grandparents shared.

Grandfathers • Mother and Daughter • Single Parent • Music • Intergenerational Relations • Summer • Coming-of-Age

Lytton, Deborah

Jane in Bloom. New York: Dutton Children's Books, 2009. 224 p. ISBN: 9780525420781. *M*

On Jane's twelfth birthday, her sister—beautiful, smart, and popular Lizzie—is hospitalized for an eating disorder. After she comes home, things don't get any better, and she soon dies, leaving her family to deal with their guilt and anger. When her mother is unable to cope and escapes to her parents' house and her father goes on a business trip, Lizzie finds support with an understanding older woman who cares for her as she learns to accept her sister for what she was.

Sisters • Anorexia • Eating Disorders • Family Problems • Grief

MacCullough, Carolyn

Drawing the Ocean. New Milford, CT: Roaring Brook Press, 2006. 176 p. ISBN: 9781596430921. *JS*

Sixteen-year-old Sadie loves to draw and has done so since her twin, Ollie, was killed in a car accident four years earlier. With her past haunting her, Sadie and her family have moved to the East Coast. At her new school, Sadie just wants to be normal, and when she meets Lila, she is drawn into the popular crowd with its lifestyle of parties, drinking, and hot football players. When poetry-writing loner Frying Ryan, catches her attention, Sadie must decide what truly matters to her.

Twins • Brothers • Sisters • New Students • Friendship • Moving • Grief • Loss • Popularity

Mack, Tracy

Birdland. New York: Scholastic Press, 2003. 198 p. ISBN: 9780439535908; 9780439535915pa; (aud). YALSA Best Books. *MJ*

When diabetic Zeke, fourteen-year-old Joseph "Jed" Diamond's older brother, dies of insulin shock, their family is torn apart. As a memorial and to fulfill an English assignment, Jed, who has a speech impediment and finds a way to speak through a camera, and his friend Flyer, set out to make a video of all the places on Manhattan's Lower East Side that Zeke wrote about in his journals and poems. Discovering a homeless girl who holds the secret to why Zeke died, Jed tries to reach out to her. When tragedy strikes, it is his parents who help him save her life as they begin to recognize his needs and they all deal with their grief.

Videos • School Projects • Brothers • Stuttering

McCarthy, Maureen

Rose by Any Other Name. New York: Roaring Brook Press, 2008. 336 p. ISBN: 9781596433724. *S*

Nineteen-year-old Rose is certain that her trip to the Australian coast to visit her dying grandmother will provide lots of fodder for her column for *Sauce* magazine, especially when her mother decides to tag along. Having avoided family in the past, Rose is finally able to look back on her life, including her desire to study law like her father, how her life fell apart when her parents divorced, her affair with a much older man, and the collapse of her friendship with longtime friend Zoe. As the trip progresses, Rose is able to make some sense of her life as she reconciles her past and redeems her future.

Mother and Daughter • Grandmothers • Cancer • Divorce • Travel • Automobiles • Australia

McGhee, Alison

All Rivers Flow to the Sea. Cambridge, MA: Candlewick Press, 2005. 176 p. ISBN: 9780763625917; 9780763633721pa. YALSA Best Books. *S*

Seventeen-year-old Rose Latham survived a car accident that left her eighteen-year-old sister Ivy in a vegetative state. Rose must struggle with grief as she and her mother face the decision of whether to take Ivy off life support. Seeking experiences to help her feel again, including having sex with random boys, Rose is finally assisted by older neighbor William, who offers advice on their rides to visit her sister, and by childhood friend and potential boyfriend Tom Miller, and she is able to cope with her loss.

Traffic Accidents • Sisters • Friends • Love • Grief

McMullan, Margaret

Cashay. Boston: Houghton Mifflin Harcourt, 2009. 176 p. ISBN: 9780547076560. MJ

Filled with anger after her younger sister, Sashay, is accidently killed in a drug-related shooting, forcing her mother to relapse into her drug addiction, thirteen-year-old Cashay finds hope when Allison, a white stockbroker, becomes her mentor.

Grief • Sisters • Interracial Persons

Noel, Alyson

Saving Zoë. New York: St. Martin's Griffin, 2007. 230 p. ISBN: 9780312355104pa. *J*

When her sister's former boyfriend gives fifteen-year-old Echo the journal of her sister Zoë, who was murdered a year ago, she delves into Zoë's secret world of Internet social networking sites and date-rape drugs. Finding that her sister was not the girl Echo thought she was, she must deal with the truths that are now coming to light a year after the killer was caught. Dealing with her own grief as she struggles with overprotective parents and fellow students who ostracize her, Echo must learn how to embrace the memory of her sister while rebuilding her own life and that of her family.

Sisters • Internet Predators • Grief • Diaries • Murder • Date Rape

Pagliarulo, Antonio

A Different Kind of Heat. New York: Delacorte Press, 2006. 181 p. ISBN: 9780385732987pa. YALSA Quick Picks. *S*

After a cop kills her brother and she is involved in a riot at a violent protest against police brutality, seventeen-year-old Puerto Rican American Luz Cordero is sent to the St. Therese Home for Boys and Girls. While there, she is able to find the help she needs to come to terms with the rage she feels over her brother's death and to find better ways to deal with the problems she has with those in authority who try to help her.

Puerto Ricans • Brothers • Sisters • Friendship • Ethnicity • Anger • Coping

Qualey, Marsha

Just Like That. New York: Dial Books, 2005. 233 p. ISBN: 9780803728400; 9780142408308pa. YALSA Best Books. *S*

Out on a walk on a cold Minneapolis night, eighteen-year-old Hanna is the last one to see two teens before they die. Consumed with guilt because she believes she could have warned them of the danger they faced, Hanna draws away from her friends and family, pours her grief into her artwork, and revisits the site of the accident where she meets Will, who shares her guilt over the deaths. The two bond over the tragedy and soon become physically intimate. When Hanna learns that Will is only fourteen, she stops the romance. However, she can't stay away or stop the friendship that develops with his family as she works through her grief and learns to forgive herself and find new strength in life.

Artists • Accidents • Friendship • Dating • Grief • Guilt • Trust • Coming-of-Age

Runyon, Brent

Maybe. New York: Alfred A. Knopf, 2006. 208 p. ISBN: 9780375835438; 9780553495089pa. *JS*

His family is looking for a fresh start in a new town when his brother is killed during a car accident. Trying to find a place at his new school, sixteen-year-old Brian struggles to deal with typical teenage problems, like deciding whether he should break up with his annoying girlfriend, even though she offers him the chance to lose his virginity. When Brian joins a theater group and lands a part in a play, he has an emotional breakthrough that allows him to deal with his anger and come to terms with his brother's death.

Traffic Accidents • Anger • Sexuality • Grief • Moving

Sandell, Lisa Ann

A Map of the Known World. New York: Scholastic Press, 2009. 273 p. ISBN: 9780545069700. *MJ*

Still dealing with grief over the death of her older brother Nate in a car accident, fourteen-year-old Cora finds herself isolated and unable to talk about her brother, especially as her father begins drinking and her mother acts increasingly overprotective. When Cora gets to know Damian, Nate's best friend, despite the fact that her parents blame him for the accident because he survived, Cora is able to learn truths about Nate personality and his future plans that help her find some inner peace.

Family Problems • Art • Grief • Secrets • Friendship • Interpersonal Relations • Coming-of-Age

Smith, Cynthia Leitich

Rain Is Not My Indian Name. New York: HarperCollins, 2001. 135 p. ISBN: 9780688173975; (aud). *MJ*

Cassidy "Rain" Berghoff and Galen have been best friends forever, but on Rain's fourteenth birthday, their relationship turns to romance. Love quickly turns to despair when, the next morning, Rain finds out that Galen has been killed in an accident. Unable to cope, Rain cuts herself off from her family and friends. Six months later, Rain is still trying to get her life back together when politicians try to cut the funding for her Aunt Georgia's American Indian Youth Camp, where Rain, at the urging of her older brother, is attending. There she learns about her heritage while she rediscovers her love for photography.

Grief • Photography • Native Americans • Summer Camps

Smith, Jennifer E.

The Comeback Season. New York: Simon & Schuster Books for Young Readers, 2008. 246 p. ISBN: 9781416938477; 9781416996064pa. *J*

High school freshmen Ryan and Nick become friends from the moment they meet outside Wrigley Field and bond over a shared passion for the Chicago Cubs. Together the pair helps each other as Ryan deals with the grief that has overwhelmed her since her father's death in a boating accident five years earlier and Nick faces the fact that his chemotherapy may not cure his bone cancer. When Ryan bargains with fate that if the Cubs continue to lose, Nick will be alright, she believes it is her fault when the Cubs improve and Nick worsens.

Friendship • Cancer • Fathers • Baseball

Volponi, Paul

Rooftop. New York: Viking, 2006. 208 p. ISBN: 9780670060696; 9780142408445pa. YALSA Best Books; YALSA Quick Picks. *S*

After being enrolled in a day-school drug program by his parents, seventeen-year-old Clay is now drug-free and studying for his GED. His eighteen-year-old African American drug-dealer cousin, Addison, soon joins him in the program, but the pair's reunion is cut short when Addison is killed in a shootout by a white cop. Trying to be faithful to his cousin, Clay, who witnessed the incident, lies about the role that Addison played, and a political uproar led by activists ensues over the racially corrupt justice system. However, Clay is soon unable to deal with the pressure, and he seeks redemption as he helps Darrell, Addison's younger brother, deal with the killing.

Friendship • Race Relations • Drug Abuse • African Americans

Williams, Lori Aurelia

Broken China. New York: Simon & Schuster Books for Young Readers, 2005. 272 p. ISBN: 9780689868788; 9781416916185pa. YALSA Quick Picks. *S*

When her two-year-old daughter dies, fourteen-year-old China Cup Cameron embraces her adult status when she finds work checking coats at a strip club to pay for the lavish funeral she wants for her baby. Living with her wheelchair-bound Uncle Simon since her mother died years earlier, China endures severe harassment at the club to earn large tips, but along the way, she finds support from Trip, the baby's father, despite her best efforts to push him away.

African Americans • Mother and Daughter • Single Parent • Uncles

Woods, Brenda

Emako Blue. New York: G. P. Putnam's Sons, 2004. 124 p. ISBN: 9780399240065; 9780142404188pa. YALSA Quick Picks. *JS*

In Los Angeles, high school friends Monterey, Jamal, Eddie, and Emako, were planning to beat the odds and make something of themselves despite the difficulties they face. When Emako is shot in a drive-by shooting outside her home after her older brother is released from prison and the life of their friend, who was a talented singer, is taken, all the friends mourn her senseless loss as they try to find direction in their own lives.

African Americans • *Best Friends* • *Jealousy* • *Interpersonal Relations* • *Death* • *Loss* • *Grief*

Death of a Parent

Acampora, Paul

Defining Dulcie. New York: Dial Books, 2006. 168 p. ISBN: 9780803730465; 9780142411834pa. YALSA Popular Paperbacks. *JS*

Forced to move from Connecticut to California after her father's death, sixteen-year-old Dulcie cannot adjust and takes her father's old truck, just before it is sold, to return home. After humorous adventures, she arrives to live with her grandfather and begins assisting him as a janitor in the local high school where her father had worked. There she develops a strong friendship with another student janitor, Roxanne, and finds the support to heal and the security she needs.

Family • *Fathers* • *Moving* • *Grandfathers* • *Work*

Altebrando, Tara

The Pursuit of Happiness. New York: Pocket Books: MTV Books, 2006. 277 p. ISBN: 9781416513285. *JS*

Betsy's life doesn't seem to work out as planned after her mother dies from breast cancer. Her boyfriend dumps her, and she is stuck working at the Morrisville Historic Village dressed in Early American clothing and doing demonstrations for tourists. In the midst of it all, fellow employees, Goth girl Liza Henske and carpenter James, help her to learn that everyone is dealing with something, and it might just be possible to survive if you have friends.

Grief • *Mothers* • *Cancer* • *Friendship* • *Work* • *Goth Culture*

Bryant, Jennifer

Pieces of Georgia. New York: Knopf, distributed by Random House, 2006. 176 p. ISBN: 9780375832598. *MJ*

Thirteen-year-old Georgia McCoy, who is grieving her mother's death, has frequent stomachaches and has stopped participating in class, which requires her to go and see the school counselor. Urged by her counselor to write down her thoughts, things begin to change when a free membership to the Brandywine River Museum arrives. Finding in the museum a connection to the world of art that linked her to her mother and her own artistic talent, Georgia grows out of her shyness as she struggles to help her overachieving friend Tiffany, who is on the brink of collapse. As Georgia begins to accept her life, she comes to an understanding of why her father is also struggling.

Mothers • *Grief* • *Artists* • *Shyness* • *Best Friends* • *Diary Novel*

Clark, Catherine

The Alison Rules. New York: Harper Tempest, 2004. 272 p. ISBN: 9780060559809; 9780060559823pa. *MJ*

> To deal with the grief of her mother's death, Alison decides to live her life by a set of superstitious rules. Even though she is supported by her best friend Laurie, things start to fall apart when new student Patrick arrives and the rules just don't work any more. When a love triangle develops between the three, Alison's emotions explode and another tragic death forces her to finally deal with her grief.
>
> *Mothers • Friendship • Grief • Romance*

Cooley, Beth

Shelter. New York: Delacorte, 2006. 224 p. ISBN: 9780385733304. *J*

> After the sudden death of her father, fifteen-year-old Lucy finds that he left his family with large amounts of debt. With her mother and four-year-old brother, Lucy is forced to leave her affluent lifestyle and private school to live in a homeless shelter. While living with a lack of privacy and constant noise, Lucy struggles to find a way to help her family.
>
> *Grief • Aunts • Financial Crises • Family Problems • Family Secrets • Homelessness • Coming-of-Age*

Dessen, Sarah

The Truth about Forever. New York: Viking, 2004. 382 p. ISBN: 9780670036394; 9780142406250pa. Teens Top Ten. *JS*

> Having watched her father die from a heart attack on an early morning run, sixteen-year-old Macy Queen deals with the grief by throwing herself into a safe and predictable life. Enabled by safe, predictable boyfriend Jason and her mother, who is struggling with her own grief, Macy is just trying to survive until Jason puts their relationship on hold while he is away for the summer and Macy takes a job at the chaotic Wish Catering Company. Around forgetful Delia, neighbors Kristy and Monica, and motherless brothers Burt and Wes, Macy beings to feel alive again. As Macy finds herself attracted to and in love with Wes, she begins to break through her grief and heal by learning how to take risks and live spontaneously.
>
> *Fathers • Grief • Work • Romance*

Ehrenhaft, Daniel

The After Life: A Novel. New York: Razorbill, 2006. 272 p. ISBN: 9781595140807pa. YALSA Popular Paperbacks. *S*

> Nineteen-year-old Will, who has never met his dad, is shocked when he receives a party invitation from his stepsister. Finding that his dad, an extremely rich hippie, is dead, Will learns that to earn a $2 million inheritance, he must drive his dad's Volvo from Miami to New York in 48 hours. Because he can't drive, he is joined by his twin step-siblings, Kyle and Liz. The

13

14

15

16

17

18

19

20

21

23

three teens work out their feelings for their father and each other as family secrets are revealed on this drug-fueled, insane road trip.

Stepsisters • Travel • Automobiles • Drug Use • Coming-of-Age

Johnson, Maureen

The Key to the Golden Firebird. New York: HarperCollins, 2004. 304 p. ISBN: 9780060541385; 9780060541408pa. YALSA Best Books. *JS*

When their father suddenly dies from a heart attack, three sisters—all named after baseball players, Brooks, Palmer, and May—each deal with their grief in their own unique way. Star athlete Brooks quits softball and is drawn into a life filled with alcohol and sex when she starts hanging out with bad-boy Dave. Also an athlete, Palmer begins to have panic attacks and starts throwing herself more fully into her sports. Middle sister May tries to stay stable and hides her grief as she tries to unite the siblings and support their overworked mother. Clinging to the memories represented by their father's Pontiac Firebird, the girls find a way to unite and move into the future.

Father and Daughter • Grief • Automobile Driving • Alcoholism • Panic Disorders

Manning, Sarra

Let's Get Lost. New York: Dutton Books, 2006. 352 p. ISBN: 9780525476665; 9780142411858pa. *JS*

Sixteen-year-old Isabel takes advantage of her reputation as a bad girl as she insults her friends, takes revenge on her enemies, defies and steals from her father, bullies her brother, and drinks—all to stave off the pain and grief she feels over her mother's death. When she meets college student Smith at a party, she lies about her age, and the two begin a sexual relationship. When her lies catch up with her, Isabel must deal with the consequences as a near tragedy forces her to deal with the heart of her rage and grief.

Mothers • Sexuality • Popularity • Cliques • Emotional Problems • Guilt • Grief • England

Mass, Wendy

Jeremy Fink and the Meaning of Life. New York: Little, Brown, 2006. 289 p. ISBN: 9780316058292; 9780316058490pa. *M*

Just before he turns thirteen, Jeremy finds an elaborate box, a gift from his dead father, that has the words "The Meaning of Life" engraved on the top. Excited to discover what it contains, Jeremy is thwarted by the box's four locks, the keys to which are now missing. Because Jeremy is afraid of change, he enlists the help of his best friend Lizzy, who is a risk taker, to help him find the keys. Together they hunt in flea markets, office buildings, and museums to find the keys. Along the way, they also gain important insight into topics such as science and art, but also into important values such as friendship and family.

Father and Son • Summer • Friendship

Maynard, Joyce

The Usual Rules. New York: St. Martin's Press, 2003. 390 p. ISBN: 9780312242619; 9780312283698pa. YALSA Best Books. *MJ*

13

On the evening before September 11, thirteen-year-old Wendy argues with her mother, who works on the 87th floor of the twin towers. When her mother is killed, Wendy feels guilty that she didn't get a chance to apologize. Wendy's half-brother Louie and her bass-playing stepfather Josh are both left to grieve as well. Unable to deal with her own grief, let alone that of her family, when her father, Garrett, shows up from California, Wendy decides to go back there with him to escape. In California, she meets Garrett's cactus-growing girlfriend, Carolyn. She also meets the owner of a secondhand bookshop and his autistic son, an unwed seventeen-year-old mother who has kept her baby but can't manage him, and a skateboarder, Todd, who is on a quest to find his long-lost older brother. With the help of these new influences, Wendy is eventually able to share her pain and find appreciation for the insights and love others have to give.

14

15

16

Loss • Grief • Forgiveness • Coming-of-Age

McMahon, Jennifer

17

My Tiki Girl. New York: Dutton Books, 2008. 246 p. ISBN: 9780525479437. *J*

Guilty that she caused the fatal car accident that took her mother's life, Maggie, who was left lame by the accident, leaves her friends and is drawn into the fantasy world of outsider Dahlia "Tiki" and her mentally ill mother. Crafting the new identity of "LaSamba," Maggie falls in love with Dahlia, and as she faces prejudice, she finds a place in the music group that she and her friends create.

18

Traffic Accidents • Guilt • Disabilities • Infatuation • Lesbianism • Bands • Homosexuality • Coming-of-Age

19

Mills, Tricia

20

Heartbreak River. New York: Razorbill, 2009. 288 p. ISBN: 9781595142566pa. *JS*

Feeling responsible for the white-water rafting accident that killed her father, sixteen-year-old Alex is left behind to run her family's rafting business with her grandparents and cousin Mala after her mother goes to Florida to be with other relatives. Distancing herself from boyfriend Sean, whom she also blames for the accident, Alex is unable to get over her feelings for him. When she faces her fear of the water and nearly drowns in the same place her father had and then another employee dies, Alex gains insight into how the accident happened.

21

22

Fathers • Guilt • Grief • Romance

Monthei, Betty

23

Looking for Normal. New York: HarperCollins, 2005. 183 p. ISBN: 9780060725051. *M*

Twelve-year-old Annie is called out of class one day and learns that her father has shot and killed her mother and then killed himself. Moving in with their maternal grandparents, Annie and her younger brother, Ted, try to cope with their grief without any friends while dealing with their grandma's drinking and mental abuse, and their grandfather's emotional distance, as he spends all his time at the office. When their grandmother's abuse turns physical, she is sent away. The family is then able to deal with their problems and heal as their grandfather pulls things together.

Murder • Suicide • Grief • Family Violence • Family Problems

Oates, Joyce Carol

After the Wreck, I Picked Myself Up, Spread My Wings, and Flew Away. New York: Harper Tempest, 2006. 304 p. ISBN: 9780060735258; 9780060735272pa. *J*

Dealing with her own guilt and grief after a car crash that killed her mother but left her alive, fifteen-year-old Jenna moves to New Hampshire to live with her aunt and uncle. Unable to navigate the physical and emotional healing required after the accident, Jenna falls deeper into despair. Distancing herself from her dad and unable to accept any pity from anyone, Jenna hits rock bottom as she becomes friends with a drug-addicted girl, Trina. Jenna steals and overdoses on OxyContin and narrowly escapes being raped. Soon Jenna finds solace with Crow, a gorgeous biker, and she is able to confront her past.

Emotional Problems • Drug Abuse • Traffic Accidents • Family Relationship • Gangs • Guilt • Grief

Parkinson, Siobhan

Second Fiddle: Or How to Tell a Blackbird from a Sausage. New Milford, CT: Roaring Brook Press, 2007. 192 p. ISBN: 9781596431225. *M*

Dealing with her grief over her father's recent death, twelve-year-old Margaret "Mags" Rose Clarke hears beautiful music while exploring the woods near her new home and discovers Gillian playing the violin. As the girls become friends, Mags becomes Gillian's support as she hunts for her missing father, whom she needs to ask for money so she can get the plane ticket she needs to get to her audition at a prestigious music school, a process that helps Mags deal with her own loss.

Violinists • Divorce • Fathers • Friendship • Music

Powell, Randy

Tribute to Another Dead Rock Star. New York: Farrar, Straus & Giroux, 1999. 215 p. ISBN: 9780786221912; 9780374479688pa. YALSA Best Books. *J*

When his rock-star mother dies from an overdose, fifteen-year-old Gary Grennan must return to Seattle to speak at a concert honoring her. He is dreading the event that will force him to face his family, including his architect father Mitch, his stepmother Vickie, and his mentally disabled half-brother Louie. Vickie, a committed Christian, often clashes with Gary, who must decide what to do with his future because he is no longer able to live with his grandmother, who has remarried. His only choices are moving in with Mitch and Vickie or enrolling in a study-abroad program in Europe. After spending time with Louie, Gary is able to find some understanding about his mother and himself and come to terms with Vickie.

Mothers • Family Problems • Developmentally Disabled • Christianity

Rabb, Margo

Cures for Heartbreak. New York: Delacorte Press, 2007. 256 p. ISBN: 9780385734028; 9780385734035pa. *MJ*

> Ninth-grader Mia faces tragedy when, within the same year, her mother dies of cancer and her father is hospitalized after he has a heart attack. She copes with her grief by reading books about orphans and losing herself in sleep. Mia is left alone to deal with her relationship with her older sister and her father's new girlfriend, as well as to navigate the trials of school and disastrous experiences with falling in love. When her class starts learning about the Holocaust, Mia connects to her Jewish family history, and as she befriends Sasha, a young man who is a cancer survivor, Mia begins to embrace her life again.
>
> *Parent and Child • Grief • Family Relationships • Interpersonal Relations*

Rodrigues, Carmen

Not Anything. New York: Berkley Trade, 2008. 240 p. ISBN: 9780425219287. *J*

> After her mom dies, Susie Shannon does everything she can to keep herself together, especially without anyone to look to for support, since she has no boyfriend, her best friend is constantly missing, and her father is disconnected from his daughter. But then she meets Danny Diaz when her teacher asks her to tutor him, and Susie is in for a life-changing experience.
>
> *Grief • Friendship • Romance*

Ryan, Darlene

Five Minutes More. Custer, WA: Orca Book Publishers, 2009. 224 p. ISBN: 9781554690060. *J*

> D'Arcy is trying to cope with her grief after her father, unable to deal with his Lou Gehrig's disease, commits suicide by driving his car off a bridge. She withdraws from her friends and family, cuts classes at school, and begins to drink. Playing on the sympathies of her teachers and counselors, she gets away with her behavior, but when her math tutor, Seth, who has offered her comfort with his unquestioning presence, also tries to commit suicide, D'Arcy must decide if running away is the answer or if she has the courage to face the challenges of dealing with her grief.
>
> *Fathers • Tutors • Drinking • Suicide • Grief • Mother and Daughter*

Smith, Andrew

Ghost Medicine. New York: Feiwel and Friends, 2008. 368 p. ISBN: 9780312375577 (aud). YALSA Best Books. *JS*

> Escaping from the grief he feels over his mother's recent death, as well as his emotionally distant father, sixteen-year-old Troy spends the summer working with his friends, including Tom Buller, a farmhand; Gabe Benavidez, the son of the wealthy ranch owner; and Gabe's sister Luz, whom Troy loves. Also finding strength in a Native American philosophy with rituals that pay homage to the forces of nature, Troy wonders if he can make this

13
14
15
16
17
18
19
20
21

22

23

time last forever. When the sheriff's son tries to rape Luz, Troy must face reality and come to terms with his own identity.

Bullies and Bullying • Friendship • Grief • Father and Son • Coming-of-Age

Sones, Sonya

One of Those Hideous Books Where the Mother Dies. New York: Simon & Schuster Books for Young Readers, 2004. 272 p. ISBN: 9780689858208; 9781416907886pa. YALSA Best Books; YALSA Quick Picks; YALSA Popular Paperbacks. *J*

> After her mother's death, fifteen-year-old Ruby Miliken leaves Boston to live in Los Angeles with her father, Whip Logan, the famous movie actor she has never met. Angry at him for divorcing her mother before she was born and longing to be back with her best friend and boyfriend, Ruby is unimpressed by his mansion and luxurious lifestyle. As she struggles to adjust and overcome her grief, revelations help her to finally accept her father.

Actors and Actresses • Celebrities • Mothers • Father and Daughter • Grief • Moving • Interpersonal Relations • Homosexuality

Spollen, Anne

The Shape of Water. Woodbury, MN: Flux, 2008. 312 p. ISBN: 9780738711010. *J*

> By escaping into her imagination, where she interacts with a family of fishes and starts destructive fires in the marshes near her home, fifteen-year-old Magdalena tries to deal with the anxiety and loneliness she feels after her mother commits suicide. Supported by her father, who is working through his own grief, and her Aunt Hannah, who helps to keep the household running, Magdalena must finally face reality when her father remarries a widow whose son also tries to commit suicide.

Mothers • Grief • Fires • Suicide

Swanson, Julie A.

Going for the Record. Grand Rapids, MI: Eerdmans Books for Young Readers, 2004. 217 p. ISBN: 9780802852731. *S*

> High school senior Leah Weiczynkowski has made the regional Olympic Development Team and is a shoe-in for any of the best college soccer programs—that is, until her father is diagnosed with pancreatic cancer and is given three months to live. As she struggles to cope, Leah finds her life and her dreams for the future disrupted. Fortunately, she is supported by her tight-knit Catholic family, and when her father dies, Leah is able to realize that the real value of life is in relationships.

Soccer • Cancer • Grief • Catholics

Tolan, Stephanie S.

Listen! New York: HarperCollins, 2006. 208 p. ISBN: 9780786290239; 9780060579371pa. *M*

> Still mourning the loss of her mother and recovering from a car accident herself, twelve-year-old Charley expects a bleak summer because she is being neglected by her workaholic father, and her best friend is away attending tennis camp. She begins taking long walks in the woods to strengthen her injured leg, despite the

memories the place holds of her mother. There she meets a stray dog that she names Coyote. As her relationship with dog develops, she is able to work through her grief.

Dogs • Traffic Accidents • Grief

Facing One's Own Death

Crutcher, Chris

Deadline. New York: Greenwillow Books, 2007. 320 p. ISBN: 9780060850890; 9780060850913pa. YALSA Quick Picks. *JS*

Eighteen-year-old Ben Wolf has incurable leukemia, and he dives into life to live fully what little time he has left. Forgoing treatment and keeping his condition a secret from his family and friends, Ben wants a normal senior year at his Idaho high school. Being normal while embracing the remainder of his life involves ditching the cross-country team and joining his quarter-back brother, Cody, on the football team; hooking up with his gorgeous crush Dallas Suzuki; and petitioning to have a street in town named after Malcolm X. But Ben's illness takes its toll, and he must learn to live with it and deal with the consequences of keeping his condition a secret.

Terminal Illness • Football • Dysfunctional Families

Downham, Jenny

Before I Die. New York: David Fickling Books, 2007. 336 p. ISBN: 9780385751551; 9780385751834pa; (aud). Teens Top Ten. *JS*

Sixteen-year-old Tessa knows she doesn't have much time left to live because of the leukemia she was diagnosed with four years earlier. Making a list of ten things to do before she dies, including driving, sex, breaking the law, and getting her parents back together, Tessa dives into making the most of the life she has left. Love and sex with neighbor Adam fulfills one item on her list. She also works to help her friend Zoe, who is faced with having an abortion, and to teach her little brother Cal about courage and love. She helps her mother overcome her depression and her father let go of his possessiveness. As her illness progresses, Tessa learns a lot about her friends and family as she embraces what she really wants in the little time she has left.

Terminal Illness • Leukemia • Friendship • Sexuality • Abortion

Ehrenhaft, Daniel

Ten Things to Do before I Die. New York: Delacorte Press, 2004. 244 p. ISBN: 9780385730075; 9780385734066pa. YALSA Quick Picks. *JS*

Having always played it safe, sixteen-year-old Ted Burger is ready for a walk on the wild side. On the first day of spring break while they eat at a local diner, his friends, Mark and Nikki, make a list of ten things to do before he dies. Learning that a disgruntled employee has poisoned the food, Ted believes he only has twenty-four hours to complete the list. Jumping into his adventures that include experimenting with drugs and sex, confronting a bully, and partying with his favorite punk rock band, Ted learns to embrace life.

Virginity • Death • Coming-of-Age

McDaniel, Lurlene

Breathless. New York: Random House Children's Books, 2009. ISBN: 9780385734592. *JS*

Champion diver Travis Morrison is enjoying his summer vacation and looking forward to starting his junior year of high school until one day while hanging out with his friends, he dives off a cliff and injures his leg. In the hospital, Travis learns that he has bone cancer, and as he gets sicker, he finds his only comfort in the death-with-dignity and right-to-die groups he discovers. Clinging to a hope that his little sister Emily, his girlfriend Darla, and his best friend Cooper, who are all facing their own problems and challenges, will help him to find the dignity and peace he seeks in his final days, Travis deals with a year and a half of chemo treatments, amputation, and deteriorating health.

Suicide • Amputees • Romance • Cancer

Death of a Friend

Altebrando, Tara

What Happens Here. New York: MTV Books, 2008. 242 p. ISBN: 9781416541110. *MJ*

Separated from longtime best friend Lindsey when her family takes a European vacation, Chloe enjoys the trip immensely but at the same time regrets not only being unable to share the wonderful sights with her friend but the fight they had before she left. Dreams of a glorious reunion are shattered when she returns home to find Lindsey has been murdered. Coping with the news, Chloe must deal with her own grief by finding her own identity and reconciling her feelings for Danny, a boy she met in Europe, with her growing affection for Lindsey's brother, Noah.

Friendship • Grief • Summer • Murder

Green, John

Looking for Alaska. New York: Dutton Children's Books, 2005. 237 p. ISBN: 9780525475064; 9780142402511pa; (aud). Michael L. Printz Award; YALSA Best Books; YALSA Quick Picks; YALSA Popular Paperbacks; Teens Top Ten; School Library Journal Best Books. *S*

Sixteen-year-old Miles Halter leads a boring life until he moves from Florida to Alabama to attend boarding school. There he makes friends, including poor scholarship student Chip "the Colonel" and his friend Alaska, who take Miles on a walk on the wild side, teaching him to drink, smoke, and pull off elaborate pranks. But under her bravado, Alaska is hiding the unhappiness that eventually leads her to a drunk-driving accident that many believe was suicide. Mourning her death, the friends celebrate her memory by pulling one last massive prank.

Traffic Accidents • Suicide • Drunk Driving • Friendship • Interpersonal Relations • Loss • Boarding Schools

Henkes, Kevin

Olive's Ocean. New York: Greenwillow Books, 2003. 224 p. ISBN: 9780060535438; 9780060535452pa; (aud). YALSA Best Books; ALA Notable Children's Books; Newbery Honor Books. *M*

Just as she and her family are leaving to visit her grandmother, Godbee, at Cape Cod, twelve-year-old Martha Boyle is given a page from the journal of her shy classmate Olive Barstow, who died in a car crash a few weeks earlier. There she discovers that not only did Olive want to visit the ocean, she had also hoped that Martha would be her friend. Also finding that Olive shared her dream of wanting to become a writer, Martha begins to realize just how fragile life can be. She gains a new level of self-awareness when she nearly drowns and has other life-changing experiences.

Grandmothers • Family • Writing • Vacations • Summer Romance

Henson, Heather

Making the Run: A Novel. New York: Joanna Cotler Books, 2002. 227 p. ISBN: 9780060297961; 9780064473392pa. *S*

With two months before graduation, Lucinda "Lu" McClellan is just biding her time before she can escape her small town of Rainey, Kentucky. She spends her days drinking and smoking with her best friend Ginny and taking photographs of the scenes around her with her 35mm camera. Still grieving her mother's death many years earlier and living with a father who is emotionally distracted, Lu finds a new sense of safety when she becomes the lover of her older musician brother Danny's boyhood friend, Jay Shepard. But when Ginny dies in a fiery car crash on a winding road that local kids travel at high speeds, the event forces Lu, her father, and Jay out of their selfishness as they move toward more healthy attitudes and relationships.

Love • Father and Daughter • Coming-of-Age • Traffic Accidents • Friendship

Hyde, Catherine Ryan

The Day I Killed James. New York: Alfred A. Knopf, 2008. 217 p. ISBN: 9780375841583. *S*

Theresa has always known that her neighbor James is in love with her. But this doesn't stop her from asking him at a party to help her make her boyfriend, Randy, who is constantly breaking up with her, jealous so that she can get him back one more time. When the plan works, Theresa is happy but is later crushed when she finds that James left the party and drove off a cliff. Shouldering responsibility for the incident, Theresa is unable to cope. She runs away to live in a trailer park and takes on a new identity. Afraid that if she ever loves anyone again she will hurt them as she did James, Theresa is shocked when she finds herself helping a homeless young girl who has been abused.

Guilt • Boyfriends • Love • Child Abuse • Diaries

Lion, Melissa

Swollen. New York: Wendy Lamb Books, 2004. 192 p. ISBN: 9780385746427; 9780553494082pa. *S*

> High school student Samantha "Sam" Pallas engages in meaningless sex with strange boys as a way to endure her lonely, empty life that nothing, not even her gift for running, can fill. Living with her playboy father and his unintentionally pregnant girlfriend, she has little support when she finds that popular classmate Owen Killgore, who has used her for sex, has unexpectedly died, and rumors of suicide begin to surface. Sam begins a new relationship with a mature sophisticated new boy at school, Farouk. When Sam feels that she is falling in love but Farouk moves on to other conquests after the two have become intimate, Sam is able to realize that she can be strong and find a better, long-lasting relationship.

> *Coping • Self-Esteem • Suicide • Running*

Lion, Melissa

Upstream. New York: Wendy Lamb Books, 2005. 149 p. ISBN: 9780385746434; 9780375839542pa. *S*

> Martha "Marty" is grieving the death of her boyfriend, Steven, after he is killed in a camping accident. Supported by her mother and younger sister, Marty soon finds more help in twenty-eight-year-old Katherine, who has just arrived from California and purchased the movie theater where Marty works. As Marty and Katherine explore the Alaskan wilderness around them, the pair learn from each other, and Marty is able to come to terms with the truth about Steven's death as she realizes that she must move away from the land she loves to explore the world after she graduates.

> *Grief • Work • Boyfriends • Love*

McDaniel, Lurlene

Telling Christina Goodbye. New York: Bantam Books, 2002. 224 p. ISBN: 9780553570878pa (aud). *S*

> High-school senior Trisha has always worried about Tucker, the controlling boyfriend of her best friend, Christina. She looks forward to the day when Christina will go off to college and leave Tucker behind. When Tucker drives recklessly one night after a basketball game and causes an accident, killing Christina, injuring Trisha, and leaving Trisha's boyfriend Cody in a coma, Trisha must deal with her anger as well as the pain and grief she has over losing her friend as she tries to return to her normal life.

> *Traffic Accidents • Friendship • Boyfriends*

Taylor, Brooke

Undone. New York: Walker, distributed to the trade by Macmillan, 2008. 310 p. ISBN: 9780802797636. YALSA Quick Picks. *J*

> Fifteen-year-old high school sophomore Serena Moore admires her only friend, wild-girl Kori Kitzler, so much that she models her persona after her. When Kori is

killed in a car accident, Serena takes it on herself to fulfill her friend's five unrealized dreams. While on this quest, she uncovers a shocking family secret.

Loss • Friendship • Traffic Accidents • Family Secrets

Vande Velde, Vivian

Remembering Raquel. Orlando: Harcourt, 2007. 160 p. ISBN: 9780152059767; 9780152066987pa. YALSA Quick Picks. *MJ*

Fourteen-year-old Raquel is killed when she steps off the curb and is hit by an oncoming car. The people around her remember her life and speculate about her death. Her life was full of creative potential despite the pain she experienced after her mother's death from cancer. From the people who knew her well, including her father and an online gaming friend who knew her as Gylindrielle, to those who think they know what happened, such as popular girl Stacy, and even those who use her death to campaign for safer streets, each person reminisces to create the human connections they crave as they face their own mortality and regret for things not said.

High School • Popularity • Traffic Accidents • Friendship

Wing-Smith, Emily

The Way He Lived. Woodbury, MN: Flux, 2008. 222 p. ISBN: 9780738714042pa. *MJ*

After Joel Espen died of exposure and dehydration on a poorly planned Boy Scout camping trip, six teens, Tabbatha, Joel's older sister who suffered a breakdown after his death, and his friends, Adlen, Miles, Claire, Norah, and Lissa, look back on the effect that Joel had on their lives as they try to deal with their grief over his death.

Faith • Sexuality • Loss • Camping

Suicide

Adoff, Jaime

The Death of Jayson Porter. New York: Jump at the Sun/Hyperion Books for Children, 2008. 320 p. ISBN: 9781423106913. *JS*

Sixteen-year-old Jayson Porter is fighting just to stay alive as he deals with an abusive and neglectful alcoholic mother and a crack-addict father. Struggling to hold his life together and keep up at his wealthy prep school, he smokes dope with his friend Trax. When Trax is killed and things finally hit rock bottom, Jayson feels that his only hope is to end his life by jumping off a building. As he falls, he realizes that life is precious and there is always hope. When he survives with only a broken neck, Jayson must face his fears and the lies his parents have told him if he is to rebuild his life.

Depression • Death • Child Abuse • Poverty • Novels in Verse

Asher, Jay

Thirteen Reasons Why. New York: Razorbill, 2008. 304 p. ISBN: 9781595141712; 9781595141880pa. YALSA Best Books; YALSA Quick Picks. *JS*

Two weeks after classmate Hannah Baker commits suicide, Clay Jenson is one of thirteen people who receive seven audio tapes. On the tapes, Hannah tells the story about various acts, both callous and criminal—including an auto accident that caused a death and a rape—that led to her unhappiness and to her decision to commit suicide. Clay, who secretly admired Hannah, experiences her pain as he listens to her story and, as Hannah requested on the tapes, visits the various locations where the incidents happened, all the while learning about the consequences of seemingly small actions.

Death • Rape • High School • Guilt

Borris, Albert

Crash into Me. New York: Simon Pulse, 2009. 224 p. ISBN: 9781416974352. *S*

Sharing the intent to commit suicide, four teens who meet online join on a road trip planning to visit the graves of celebrities who committed suicide, then finishing the trip in Death Valley, where they will kill themselves as well. As the trip progresses, lonely Owen, brash Audrey, lesbian Jin-Ae, and alcoholic Frank find themselves connecting with each other as they share their dreams and secrets. Developing deep friendships and romantic relationships, the teens find that at their destination, they must decide if their lives are worth living.

Automobiles • Travel • Friendship

Ford, Michael Thomas

Suicide Notes. New York: HarperTeen, 2008. 304 p. ISBN: 9780060737559. *J*

After slitting his wrists, fifteen-year-old Jeff awakes to find himself in a hospital, where he avoids therapy and refuses to integrate with his fellow patients because he is sure that, unlike them, he is normal. Meeting suicidal Sadie, Jeff finds someone who feels the same about the program as he does, but things change when he meets Rankin and the two have sex. Jeff is finally able to come to terms with his own suicide attempt and to accept his homosexuality.

Mental Illness • Death • Identity • Homosexuality

Freymann-Weyr, Garret

Stay with Me. Boston: Houghton Mifflin 2006. 320 p. ISBN: 9780618605712; 9780618884049pa. YALSA Popular Paperbacks. *JS*

Just like her two much older half-sisters, Clare and Rebecca, sixteen-year-old Leila Abranel struggles with dyslexia and is having a hard time figuring out just where she belongs. When Rebecca commits suicide, Leila is determined to discover the reason. When her parents go to Poland to build a hospital, she goes to live with Clare, where she meets television writer Eamon, who is fifteen years older than Leila. He becomes her lover, and she learns to accept herself, her abilities, and the world around her.

Death • Family Relationships • Interpersonal Relations • Family Secrets • Blended Families • Romance

Glenn, Mel

Split Image: Story in Poems. New York: HarperCollins, 2000. 159 p. ISBN: 9780688162498; 9780060004811pa. YALSA Best Books. *JS*

Chinese immigrant Laura Li is uncertain about her identity despite her perfect and popular outward appearance. Inside Laura is hurting as she deals with her businessman father's constant absence, an abusive mother who wishes she were still in China, and having to care for a brother with a severe disability. Unable to come to terms with the conflicts she faces, Laura tries to decide if she should end her life.

Chinese Americans • Child Abuse • Brothers • Disabilities

Hegamin, Tonya

M+O4evr. Boston: Houghton Mifflin, 2008. 176 p. ISBN: 9780618495702. *JS*

Going by the nickname O, Opal does not appreciate being named after a white gemstone when she has dark skin. When her longtime biracial best friend Marianne goes wild using drugs and fooling around with boys, then finally commits suicide, O is devastated. O loved Marianne in a way that Marianne could never return, and to deal with her grief, O recalls a family legend about an escaping slave. In the story, the slave's lover protects her by sacrificing his own life so that she can magically escape the slave catchers by flying over a ravine. The ravine of the legend is the same one where Marianne died, and O finds great comfort in the story as she learns that love can heal all wounds.

Best Friends • Friendship • Death • Lesbians • Grief

Hemphill, Stephanie

Things Left Unsaid. New York: Hyperion Books for Children, 2004. 261 p. ISBN: 9780786818501; 9780786837458pa. *S*

Eleventh-grader Sarah Lewis has always been good and has led a predictable life until she embraces a new rebellious friend, Robin. Trying all the things Robin does, including lying, vandalism, and smoking, Sarah is devastated when Robin attempts suicide. Even though she tries to support Robin while she is in the hospital, things have changed, and Sarah must reforge her own identity.

Best Friends • Hope • Coming-of-Age • Novels in Verse

Hopkins, Ellen

Impulse. New York: Margaret K. McElderry Books, 2007. 672 p. ISBN: 9781416903567; 9781416903574pa; (aud). YALSA Quick Picks. S

After failed suicide attempts, three teens find themselves in a psychiatric hospital. Vanessa is a manic-depressive who cuts herself to escape the pain of her absent father, her bipolar mother, and of an abortion she had in secret. Tony, who was abused as a child and was sent to a juvenile detention center after killing his mother's child-molesting boyfriend, is facing confusion about his sexuality and also dealing with his past, when he had sex for money. Connor, the son of rich, controlling parents, tried to shoot himself after his affair with a female teacher ended. The trio finds support from each other as they struggle to recover. When on a wilderness camping trip with other patients and staff that marks the end of their treatment, the pressures of returning home become overwhelming, the friends are able to discover an unexpected appreciation for life.

Overachievers • Sex Roles • Sexuality • Psychiatric Hospitals • Camping • Death • Mental Illness • Abortion • Friendship • Novels in Verse

LaCour, Nina

Hold Still. New York: Penguin Group, 2009. 229 p. ISBN: 9780525421559. (aud). *JS*
Sixteen-year-old Caitlin is devastated after her best friend Ingrid commits suicide. Returning to school Caitlin finds little support, especially in her photography class—the one place she thought she could find safety with the teacher she felt appreciated both her and Ingrid's creativity. Unexpectedly finding Ingrid's journal hidden under her bed, Caitlin starts to understand her friend and her hidden secrets that led to her depression. With this understanding, Caitlin begins to heal as she makes friends with her lesbian classmate Dylan, falls in love with gorgeous boy Taylor, and rediscovers her passion for photography.

Grief • Friendship • Depression

Lynch, Chris

Freewill. New York: HarperCollins, 2001. 148 p. ISBN: 9780060281762; 9780064472029pa. Michael L. Printz Honor Book; YALSA Best Books. *JS*
Seventeen-year-old Will is used to being alone with his wood carving, but when he begins to make friends with Angela, a student in his woodworking class at his high school for disturbed teenagers, he begins to open up. When his carvings begin turning up as memorials next to the dead bodies of local teenagers who died under mysterious circumstances, Will falls under suspicion, and he must face the truth as he decides whether the solution to his loneliness is suicide.

Grandparents • Grief • Artists • Friendship

Mayfield, Sue

Drowning Anna. New York: Hyperion, 2002. 320 p. ISBN: 9780786808700; 9780786809578pa. *J*
Melanie Blackwood looks back to the time when her sixteen-year-old, talented, intelligent, hockey-playing friend, Anna Goldsmith, moved from London to their small Yorkshire town. Befriended by popular Hayler Parking, even though she took her position on the hockey team, Anna soon finds herself the victim of cruel bullying and psychological attacks. When Anna can no longer bear the bullying, she attempts suicide with an overdose and ends up in a coma, while Melanie and those around Anna, including her mother, realize how they failed to help the situation.

Coma Patients • Bullies and Bullying • Hockey • England

Miller, Mary Beth

Aimee: A Novel. New York: Dutton, 2002. 276 p. ISBN: 9780525468943; 9780142400258pa. YALSA Best Books. *S*

> Seventeen-year-old Zoe has just been acquitted for murder in assisting her best friend, Aimee, to commit suicide. Now in a new town, she is prevented from communicating with old friends, and so at the request of her court-appointed psychiatrist, she keeps a journal in which she works through the guilt, anger, and grief she feels as she complains about the adults in her life—including her parents, who want her to forget and move on.
>
> *Murder • Suicide • Death • Best Friends • Friendship • Guilt*

Summers, Courtney

Cracked Up to Be. New York: St. Martin's Griffin, 2009. 224 p. ISBN: 9780312383695. *S*

> Popular cheerleader Parker Fadley has had a seemingly perfect life, until one night at a wild party, she encounters the boyfriend of her best friend Jessica with another girl. When she reveals this, Jessica hooks up with an older party crasher to get her revenge. This event sends Parker's life into a downward spiral when she witnesses the guy raping Jessica but is too drunk to step in. Consumed by guilt when Jessica goes missing and is then found dead, Parker starts drinking heavily and then attempts suicide to try and atone for her misdeeds.
>
> *Guilt • Cheerleaders • Emotional Problems • Popularity • Interpersonal Relations*

Toten, Teresa

The Game. Markham, Canada: Red Deer College Press, 2001. 160 p. ISBN: 9780889952324pa. YALSA Best Books. *JS*

> Unable to deal with her abusive father's high standards, Danielle "Dani" Webster tries to commit suicide. She is sent to a clinic for troubled youth, where she finds kindred spirits in roommate Scratch, who mutilates herself, and Kevin, who also tried suicide after his Christian fundamentalist parents would not accept his homosexuality. Along with their therapist, the trio is able to assist Dani in confronting her past as she tries to mend relationships with her mother and younger sister.
>
> *Abused Children • Dysfunctional Families • Friendship • Canadian*

Vaught, Susan

Trigger. New York: Bloomsbury Children's Books, distributed to the trade by Holtzbrinck Publishers, 2006. 304 p. ISBN: 9781582349206; 9781599902302pa. YALSA Best Books. *S*

> Seventeen-year-old Jersey Hatch is returning home after a year in a treatment center for a brain injury that was a result of his failed suicide attempt, an event he now has no memory of. Struggling with the physical consequences of his action, Jersey has trouble thinking sequentially and controlling his inappropriate vocalizations. Additionally, he must deal with the

13

14

15

16

17

18

19

20

21

22

23

emotional costs. With his parents broken by his actions, he struggles to find his place, as he is now despised and bullied by his peers. With the support of Mama Rush and her granddaughter Leza, who seem to be the only two people who will be honest with him, Jersey is able to delve into his memories as he seeks to remember why he tried to commit suicide in the first place.

Brain Injury • Memory • Coming-of-Age

Chapter 23

Facing Racism

Adolescents who are members of ethnic groups often find themselves facing racism and discrimination. When teens encounter racism, they may find themselves in high-stress situations that can lead to severe anxiety or social withdrawal. Because many teens will face racism, it is important that youth are taught not only to interact with a wide variety of people but also to deal with discrimination. When teens learn to cope with this problem, it helps them strengthen their self-esteem and find power in their ethnic or racial identities. The books listed in this chapter focus on racial differences that lead to discrimination. From discrimination in sports to racism that leads to violent acts, teens work through many challenges as they deal with intolerance toward diversity.

Adoff, Jaime

Jimi and Me. New York: Jump at the Sun/Hyperion, 2005. 329 p. ISBN: 9780786852147; 9781423104001pa. YALSA Quick Picks. *MJ*

> Forced to move with his mother to a small town in Ohio after his record-producer father is shot, thirteen-year-old Keith must learn to face life in a small town, with a racist bully who picks on Keith's biracial heritage. He must also live with his panic attacks. Filled with pain and doubt, Keith loses himself in the music of Jimi Hendrix, a love he shared with his father. Keith finds support with the shy, beautiful blonde Veronica as he works to protect his family and understand the secret his father had kept from them.

> *Interracial Persons • Bullies • Grief • Panic Disorders • Novels in Verse*

Cooney, Caroline B.

Burning Up. New York: Delacorte Press, 1999. 230 p. ISBN: 9780385323185; 9780440226871pa. YALSA Quick Picks. *J*

> During a local history project, fifteen-year-old Macey encounters the story of a 1959 arson case that targeted an African American. She becomes aware of her affluent community's racial prejudice when she is unexpectedly caught in a fire that was deliberately set in a church. Later, when an African American teen is murdered, Macey and her boyfriend, Austin, are lead to uncover long-held secrets about the original fire as they confront their community's racism and begin to assess their own level of responsibility.

> *African Americans • Prejudice • Arson • Secrets • Violence*

Crutcher, Chris

Whale Talk. New York: Greenwillow Books, 2001. 224 p. ISBN: 9780688180195; 9780440229384pa; (aud). YALSA Best Books; YALSA Outstanding Books for the College Bound. *S*

Tao "T.J." Jones is a smart and likable biracial high school senior. Even though he has athletic ability, T.J. refuses to join a team until Mr. Simet, the English teacher and coach, offers him the opportunity to pick his own swim team if he will anchor the group. Seeing a chance to take on racist bully Mike Barbour who has been harassing disabled teen Chris Coughlin since he started wearing a letter jacket that belonged to his dead brother, T.J. takes Chris on the team so he can earn his own jacket. Chris is a natural in the water, and T.J. and his team of misfits take on the jocks' prejudice. Along the way, T.J. deals with his love for a biracial girl who is dealing with vicious racist attacks from her stepfather.

Prejudice • *Swimming* • *Interracial Persons* • *Adoption*

Fogelin, Adrian

Crossing Jordan. Atlanta, GA: Peachtree, 2000. 140 p. ISBN: 9781561452156; 9781561452811pa. YALSA Best Books. *M*

Bonding over their love of running and the novel *Jane Eyre,* twelve-year-old Cass finds a new friend in her African American neighbor Jemmie. But even as their friendship deepens with the support of Jemmie's gospel-singing grandmother, Cass must hide her friendship from her racist father. But it is not until Cass's baby sister gets heatstroke and Jemmie's mother is the one to help that the two families are able to build a friendship.

Neighbors • *Running* • *Interracial Friendships*

Foley, John

Hoops of Steel. Woodbury, MN: Flux, 2007. 234 p. ISBN: 9780738709819pa. *S*

Estranged from his parents after a night of domestic violence fueled by his father's alcoholism, high school senior Jackson O'Connell is taken in by a neighbor, Granny Dwyer. He loses himself in his honors English class and basketball. But when he is relegated to the second string on the varsity team, racial tensions erupt on the court. Even though he is challenged, he realizes he must deal with his past as he learns important lessons about being loyal and forgiving others.

Sequel: ***Running with the Wind.*** Woodbury, MN: Flux, 2007. 210 p. ISBN: 9780738710020pa. *S*

About to graduate from high school with no plans for the future, Jackson O'Connell finds himself alone when Granny Dwyer dies. Taking a summer job at the local boatyard, Jackson learns to sail, and from this experience and with the help of old Conrad, he learns where his talents lie and is able to begin to make plans for his future.

Basketball • *Alcoholism* • *Family Problems* • *Coming-of-Age*

Krech, Bob

Rebound. New York: Marshall Cavendish, 2006. 271 p. ISBN: 9780761453192; 9780761455431pa. YALSA Best Books. *JS*

13

> The standard in his neighborhood is that the Polish kids wrestle and the black kids play basketball. Polish kid Ray Wisniewski wants to break the mold and play basketball. Always getting cut when he tries out for his high school team, Ray finally makes the team when a new coach is hired. Even though his dream has come true, Ray must still face the racism around him as he tries to figure out how he feels about racial differences.

14

> *Basketball • Race Relations • Gangs • Prejudice • Discrimination • Sports*

15

Myers, Walter Dean

The Beast. New York: Scholastic, 2003. 170 p. ISBN: 9780439368414; 9780439368421pa. *S*

16

> High-school senior Anthony "Spoon" Witherspoon plans to marry his girlfriend, Gabi, when he returns from a year at Wallingford Academy in Connecticut. He hopes his year at Wallingford will give him the opportunity to get into an Ivy League college. While he was away dealing with the class and racial divides at his prep school, Gabi has been absorbed in the problems surrounding her dying mother, her blind grandfather, and a younger brother who has started running with a gang. To deal with this stress, she has become addicted to drugs. Returning for Christmas break, Spoon faces the new realities of how Gabi has changed and he must make decisions as to where he really fits into the world and whether his future will include Gabi or Chanelle, a rich classmate who likes him.

17

18

> *Prep Schools • Race Relations • Social Classes • Drug Abuse • African Americans*

19

Sitomer, Alan Lawrence

Hoopster Trilogy. Los Angeles, CA: Milk Mug; New York: Jump at the Sun/Hyperion Books for Children

20

> Writer Andre Anderson faces racism, while his sister Theresa tries to overcome the violence on the streets and friend Teddy tries to bring a killer to justice.

> *African Americans • Racism • Friendship • Success • Sibling Rivalry*

21

The Hoopster. 2002. 160 p. ISBN: 9780786854837; 9780972188203pa. *S*

Seventeen-year-old budding African American writer Andre Anderson plans to spend the summer playing basketball with his friends and working at a magazine. Assigned to write an article about race, Andre is reluctant at first, but after looking around, he begins to understand the racism that is everywhere and writes an outstanding piece. The article incites a group of racists, who assault him, and Andre experiences violent racism firsthand.

22

Hip-Hop High School. 2006. 368 p. ISBN: 9780786838318; 9781423106449pa. *S*

Andre's younger sister, Theresa "Tee-Ay" Anderson, tries hard to fit in as she works to graduate from high school and make her dreams of going to college a reality despite the challenges of being African American in an urban environment. Joining to study for the SAT with smart Devon Hampton,

23

who also wants to go to college, Tee-Ay finds the strength she needs to keep on track until things look dim for Devon when he is shot in a street fight just before he sends in his college applications.

Homeboyz. New York: Jump at the Sun/Hyperion Books for Children, 2007. 283 p. ISBN: 9781423100300; 9781423100317pa. YALSA Quick Picks. *S*

Seventeen-year-old computer hacker Teddy sets out for revenge after a gang kills his sister Tina in a drive-by shooting. Put into the juvenile justice system when he is charged with attempted homicide, Teddy escapes a prison sentence when he is given the opportunity to work in a mentoring program for at-risk youth and is paired with hardnosed parole officer Mariana and wild twelve-year-old Micah. As Micah and Teddy become friends, the pair support each other as they bring Tina's killer to justice.

Volponi, Paul

Response. New York: Viking Children's Books, 2009. 160 p. ISBN: 9780670062836. *S*

Seventeen-year-old Noah Jackson finds himself the center of attention when he is beaten with a baseball bat by three Italian American teens after he and his friends come into their neighborhood to sell a car. When the bat wielder, Charlie Scaturro, and his friends are prosecuted for their hate crime against Noah and two of them agree to confess to avoid a trial, things get out of hand. When the issue polarizes the white kids at Noah's mostly black school against him, and the racist family and friends of the teens stir up controversy, Noah is left to wonder if justice will ever be served.

Hate Crimes • Prejudice • Race Relations • African Americans

Appendix A

Awards

Unlike other genres, there are no specific awards for realistic problem novels. However, all the major awards often include works of realistic fiction. The following are excellent places to find titles that fall into this genre.

American Library Association Awards

Belpré Medal

The Belpré Medal is given to a Latino or Latina writer for an outstanding work of literature for children and youth that best portrays, affirms, and celebrates the Latino cultural experience.

http://www.ala.org/ala/mgrps/divs/alsc/awardsgrants/bookmedia/belpremedal/index.cfm

Coretta Scott King Award

The Coretta Scott King Award is given to African American authors for outstanding inspirational and educational works that promote understanding and appreciation of the culture of all peoples and their contribution to the realization of the American dream of a pluralistic society.

http://www.ala.org/ala/mgrps/rts/emiert/cskbookawards/index.cfm

Michael L. Printz Award

The Printz Award is given yearly to a book that exemplifies literary excellence in young adult literature. In addition, a varying number of Printz Honor Books are also chosen each year.

http://www.ala.org/ala/mgrps/divs/yalsa/booklistsawards/printzaward/Printz.cfm

Newbery Medal and Honor Books

The Newbery Medal honors the authors of the most distinguished contributions to American literature for children the previous year. A varying number of Newbery Honor Books is also chosen each year.

http://www.ala.org/ala/mgrps/divs/alsc/awardsgrants/bookmedia/newberymedal/newberymedal.cfm

Schneider Family Book Awards

The Schneider Family Book Awards honor books that embody an artistic expression of the disability experience for adolescent audiences.

http://www.ala.org/ala/awardsgrants/awardsrecords/schneideraward/schneiderfamily.cfm

YALSA Best Books

This list is created annually by a committee of the Young Adult Library Services Association that annotates the most significant young adult books of that year.

http://www.ala.org/ala/mgrps/divs/yalsa/booklistsawards/bestbooksya/bbyahome.cfm

YALSA Popular Paperbacks

This list is created annually by a committee of the Young Adult Library Services Association and is designed to encourage young adults to read for pleasure.

http://www.ala.org/ala/mgrps/divs/yalsa/booklistsawards/popularpaperback/popularpaperbacks.cfm

YALSA Quick Picks

This list is created annually by a committee of the Young Adult Library Services Association and gives book recommendations for reluctant young adult readers.

http://www.ala.org/ala/mgrps/divs/yalsa/booklistsawards/quickpicks/quickpicksreluctantyoungadult.cfm

YALSA Teens Top Ten

This is a teen choice award for which books are nominated and the winners chosen by teens.

http://www.ala.org/ala/mgrps/divs/yalsa/teenreading/teenstopten/teenstopten.cfm

International Awards

Canadian Library Association Young Adult Canadian Book Award

This award honors authors of outstanding English-language books published in Canada that appeal to young adults between the ages of thirteen and eighteen.

http://www.cla.ca/AM/Template.cfm?Section=Young_Adult_Canadian_Book_Award&Template=/CM/HTMLDisplay.cfm&ContentID=7969

Carnegie Medal

The Carnegie Medal honors the authors of outstanding books for children published in the United Kingdom.

http://www.carnegiegreenaway.org.uk/carnegie/

Children's Book Council of Australia Children's Book of the Year

This annual award recognizes outstanding books for children and young adults published in Australia.

http://cbca.org.au/awards.htm

New Zealand Library Association Esther Glen Award

This annual award is given to the most distinguished contribution to literature for children written by an author who is a citizen or resident of New Zealand.

http://www.lianza.org.nz/events/childrensbookawards/awards.html#esther

Additional Awards

Boston-Globe Horn Book Award

This award honors quality and creative excellence in children's books.
http://www.hbook.com/bghb/default.asp

National Book Award for Young People's Literature

This award is presented annually by the National Book Foundation to American authors.

http://www.nationalbook.org/index.html

Booklists

International Reading Association Choices Booklists

This booklist features favorite books that have recently been published and are chosen by thousands of children, young adults, teachers, and librarians around the United States.

http://www.reading.org/Resources/Booklists.aspx

New York Public Library Books for the Teen Age

This annual list identifies quality books and media for young adults in a variety of categories.

http://teenlink.nypl.org

School Library Journal Best Books

This list of books identifies the best books reviewed in *School Library Journal.*

http://www.schoollibraryjournal.com/

USBBY Outstanding International Books

This booklist features books selected by the United States Board on Books for Young People that represent the most outstanding international books from that year.

http://www.usbby.org/outstanding_international_books_list.htm

Appendix B

Additional Genre Resources

The following lists include resources that professionals may find helpful in their continuing study of the genre. It serves as an aid in readers' advisory as well as in collection development.

Books on Adolescent Development

Dacey, John S., Maureen Kenny, and Deborah Margolis. 2004. *Adolescent Development*, 3rd ed. Mason, OH: Thomson.

Dahl, Ronald E., and Linda Patia Spear, eds. 2004. *Adolescent Brain Development Vulnerabilities and Opportunities*. New York: New York Academy of Sciences.

Erikson, Erik. 1968. *Identity, Youth and Crisis*. New York: Norton.

Jackson, Sandy, and Luc Goossens, eds. 2006. *Handbook of Adolescent Development*. New York: Psychology Press.

Nakkula, Michael J., and Eric Toshalis. 2006. *Understanding Youth: Adolescent Development for Educators*. Cambridge, MA: Harvard Education Press.

Novak, Gary. 2004. *Child and Adolescent Development: A Behavioral Systems Approach*. Thousand Oaks, CA: Sage.

Books on Young Adult Literature

Barr, Catherine. 2009. *Best Books for High School Readers: Grades 9–12*. Westport, CT: Libraries Unlimited.

Barr, Catherine. 2009. *Best Books for Middle School and Junior High Readers: Grades 6–9*. Westport, CT: Libraries Unlimited.

Bilz, Rachelle Lasky. 2004. *Life Is Tough Guys: Growing Up and Young Adult Literature*. Lanham, MD: Scarecrow Press.

Brown, Joanne. 2002. *Declarations of Independence: Empowered Girls in Young Adult Literature, 1990–2001*. Lanham, MD: Scarecrow Press.

Carpan, Carolyn. 2004. *Rocked by Romance: A Guide to Teen Romance Fiction.* Westport, CT: Libraries Unlimited.

Egoff, Sheila A. 1981. *Thursday's Child: Trends and Patterns in Contemporary Children's Literature.* Chicago: American Library Association.

Hahn, Daniel, Leonie Flynn, and Susan Reuben. 2008. *The Ultimate Teen Book Guide.* New York: Walker.

Herald, Diana Tixier. 2010. *Teen Genreflecting.* Westport, CT: Libraries Unlimited.

Hogan, Walter. 2005. *Humor in Young Adult Literature: A Time to Laugh.* Lanham, MD: Scarecrow Press.

James, Kathryn. 2009. *Death, Gender and Sexuality in Contemporary Adolescent Literature.* New York: Routledge.

Meloni, Christine. 2009. *Teen Chick Lit: A Guide to Reading Interests.* Westport, CT: Libraries Unlimited.

Reynolds, Nancy Thalia. 2009. *Mixed Heritage in Young Adult Literature.* Lanham, MD: Scarecrow Press.

Sprague, Marsha M. 2007. *Discovering Their Voices: Engaging Adolescent Girls with Young Adult Literature.* Newark, DE: International Reading Association.

Stringer, Sharon A. 1997. *Conflict and Connection: The Psychology of Young Adult Literature.* Portsmouth, NH: Boynton/Cook.

Tatar, Maria. 2009. *Enchanted Hunters: The Power of Stories in Childhood.* New York: Norton.

Younger, Beth. 2009. *Learning Curves: Body Image and Female Sexuality in Young Adult Literature.* Lanham, MD: Scarecrow Press.

Zitlow, Connie S., ed. 2002. *Lost Masterworks of Young Adult Literature.* Lanham, MD: Scarecrow Press.

Journals

Booklist, published by the American Library Association: http://www.booklistonline.com

The Horn Book, published by The Horn Book: http://www.hbook.com

Publishers Weekly, published by Reed Elsevier: http://www.publishersweekly.com/

School Library Journal, published by Reed Elsevier: http://www.schoollibraryjournal.com/

Voice of Youth Advocates (VOYA), published by Scarecrow Press: http://www.voya.com/

Web Sites

The following Web sites are excellent resources for discovering young adult litera-ture. Each includes book reviews, information about upcoming publications, and other useful information.

- Goodreads: http://www.goodreads.com/
- Shelfari: http://www.shelfari.com/
- Teen Reads.com: http://www.teenreads.com
- Teens Read Too: http://www.teensreadtoo.com
- Teens Talk about Books: http://www.genrefluent.com/teensread.htm

Many authors now have blogs that readers can access on the Web. Some favorite blogs by authors of realistic fiction are the following:

- Meg Cabot: http://www.megcabot.com/diary/
- John Green: http://www.sparksflyup.com/weblog.php
- Laurie Halse Anderson: http://halseanderson.livejournal.com
- Maureen Johnson: http://maureenjohnson.blogspot.com/

Other bloggers have lots to say about young adult books, and they often include reviews and contests related to realistic fiction. Some favorites are the following:

- Reading Rants! Out of the Ordinary Teen Booklists: http://www.readingrants.org/
- Serene Hours: http://serenehours.blogspot.com
- The Story Siren: http://www.thestorysiren.com
- Young Adult Book Reviews: http://youngadultbookreviews.com

Author Index

Title Index

About the Author

RACHEL L. WADHAM is the education librarian in the Harold B. Lee Library at Brigham Young University (BYU). She received a B.S. in sociology and with a minor in music from BYU before earning a master's degree in information science from the University of North Texas. She also holds a second master's degree in education from Pennsylvania State University, with a dual emphasis in curriculum and children's literature. In addition to being a librarian, she also teaches children's and adolescent literature courses at BYU, is a professional literary critic, and has served on local book award committees. She also writes for professional journals and has published books on other genres of young adult literature. Rachel's other interests include music, needlecrafts, quilting, and traveling.